THE BOOK OF DISCIPLINE
OF
THE UNITED METHODIST CHURCH

THE
BOOK OF DISCIPLINE
OF THE
UNITED METHODIST
CHURCH
1980

19183

The United Methodist Publishing House
Nashville, Tennessee

"The Book Editor, the Secretary of the General Conference, the Publisher of The United Methodist Church, and the Committee on Correlation and Editorial Revision shall be charged with editing the Discipline. These editors, in the exercise of their judgment, shall have the authority to make changes in phraseology as may be necessary to harmonize legislation without changing its substance."

—Plan of Organization and Rules of Order of the General Conference, 1980

See Judicial Council Decision 96 which declares the Discipline to be a book of law.

The Book of Resolutions of the 1980 General Conference will be edited by the Standing General Commission on Communication and published separately.

Ronald P. Patterson
Book Editor of The United Methodist Church

J. B. Holt
Secretary of the General Conference

John E. Procter
Publisher of The United Methodist Church

The Committee on Correlation and Editorial Revision
C. Faith Richardson, Chairperson
Bishop L. Scott Allen
John K. Bergland
Ronald K. Johnson

Jean Kerr Crawford
Assistant Editor

ISBN 0-687-03705-0

PRINTED IN THE UNITED STATES OF AMERICA

EPISCOPAL GREETINGS

To all people and pastors of United Methodism:
  Grace is yours and peace from God our Father and the Lord
  Jesus Christ.

The Discipline is the book of law of The United Methodist
Church. It is the product of the many General Conferences of
historic religious bodies which now form The United Methodist
Church.

The Discipline as the instrument for setting forth the laws,
plan, polity, and process by which United Methodists govern
themselves remains constant. Each General Conference modifies, elaborates, clarifies, and adds its own contribution to the
Discipline. We do not see the Discipline as sacrosanct or infallible,
but we do consider it as a document suitable to our heritage. It
reflects our understanding of the Church and of what is expected
of its ministers and members as they seek to be effective witnesses
in the world as a part of the whole Body of Christ.

The Discipline sets forth the theological grounding of The
United Methodist Church in biblical faith, and affirms that we go
forward as "loyal heirs to all that [is] best in the Christian past."
The Discipline makes clear that The United Methodist Church is
an inclusive society without regard to ethnic origin, economic
condition, sex, or age of its constituents. It calls for the
amenability of bishops, district superintendents, ministers, and
lay members to the Church's faith and order. The Discipline
affirms connectionalism as a distinctive mark of United
Methodist ecclesiology, makes clear the global character of the
Church's mission, and declares interdependence with other
Christian bodies both in spirit and cooperation. The Discipline

affirms with John Wesley that solitary religion is invalid and that Christ lays claim upon the whole life of those who accept him as Lord and Savior.

We therefore commend this Discipline to all in our constituency and to friends beyond our bounds who would seek to understand what it means to be a United Methodist. Communication is essential for understanding what the Church is and does. We expect the Discipline to be found in libraries of local churches, colleges, universities, and seminaries, as well as in the homes of ministers and lay members of The United Methodist Church. We pray that it will exalt the meaning of faithful discipleship and inspire on the part of many a deeper desire to be more faithful to the Head of the Church, even Jesus Christ our Lord.

The Council of Bishops
Ralph T. Alton, President
Roy C. Nichols, President Designate
James K. Mathews, Secretary

CONTENTS

Note: The basic unit in the Book of Discipline is the paragraph (¶) rather than page, chapter, section, etc. The paragraphs are numbered consecutively within each chapter or section, but many numbers are skipped between parts, chapters, and sections in order to allow for future enactments and to fit with the following plan:

PART I
THE CONSTITUTION
¶¶ 1-66

PART II
DOCTRINE AND DOCTRINAL STATEMENTS AND THE GENERAL RULES
¶¶ 67-69

CONTENTS

PART III
SOCIAL PRINCIPLES
¶¶ 70-76

PART IV
ORGANIZATION AND ADMINISTRATION
¶¶ 101-2626

Chapter One

Chapter Two
THE LOCAL CHURCH

Chapter Three
THE DIACONAL MINISTRY

CONTENTS

Chapter Four
THE ORDAINED MINISTRY

Chapter Five
THE SUPERINTENDENCY

CONTENTS

Chapter Six
THE CONFERENCES

Chapter Seven
ADMINISTRATIVE ORDER

CONTENTS

UNITED METHODIST BISHOPS

*A List Compiled for
The Book of Discipline
by the Council of Bishops*

NAME	ELECTED	NAME	ELECTED
Thomas Coke	1784	Jacob J. Glossbrenner	1845
Francis Asbury	1784	William Hanby	1845
Richard Whatcoat	1800	William Capers	1846
Philip W. Otterbein	1800	Robert Paine	1846
Martin Boehm	1800	David Edwards	1849
Jacob Albright	1807	Henry B. Bascom	1850
William McKendree	1808	Levi Scott	1852
Christian Newcomer	1813	Matthew Simpson	1852
Enoch George	1816	Osman C. Baker	1852
Robert R. Roberts	1816	Edward R. Ames	1852
Andrew Zeller	1817	Lewis Davis	1853
Joseph Hoffman	1821	George F. Pierce	1854
Joshua Soule	1824	John Early	1854
Elijah Hedding	1824	Hubbard H.	
Henry Kumler, Sr.	1825	Kavanaugh	1854
John Emory	1832	Francis Burns	1858
James O. Andrew	1832	William W. Orwig	1859
Samuel Heistand	1833	Jacob Markwood	1861
William Brown	1833	Daniel Shuck	1861
Beverly Waugh	1836	John J. Esher	1863
Thomas A. Morris	1836	Davis W. Clark	1864
Jacob Erb	1837	Edward Thomson	1864
John Seybert	1839	Calvin Kingsley	1864
Henry Kumler, Jr.	1841	Jonathan Weaver	1865
John Coons	1841	William M. Wightman	1866
Joseph Long	1843	Enoch M. Marvin	1866
Edmund S. Janes	1844	David S. Doggett	1866
Leonidas L. Hamline	1844	Holland N. McTyeire	1866
John Russel	1845	John W. Roberts	1866

1

UNITED METHODIST BISHOPS

NAME	ELECTED	NAME	ELECTED
John Dickson	1869	James W. Hott	1889
John C. Keener	1870	Atticus G. Haygood	1890
Reuben Yeakel	1871	Oscar P. Fitzgerald	1890
Thomas Bowman	1872	Wesley M. Stanford	1891
William L. Harris	1872	Christian S. Haman	1891
Randolph S. Foster	1872	Sylvanus C. Breyfogel	1891
Isaac W. Wiley	1872	William Horn	1891
Stephen M. Merrill	1872	Job S. Mills	1893
Edward G. Andrews	1872	Charles C. McCabe	1896
Gilbert Haven	1872	Joseph C. Hartzell	1896
Jesse T. Peck	1872	Earl Cranston	1896
Rudolph Dubs	1875	Warren A. Candler	1898
Thomas Bowman	1875	Henry C. Morrison	1898
Milton Wright	1877	David H. Moore	1900
Nicholas Castle	1877	John W. Hamilton	1900
Henry W. Warren	1880	Edwin W. Parker	1900
Cyrus D. Foss	1880	Francis W. Warne	1900
John F. Hurst	1880	George M. Mathews	1902
Erastus O. Haven	1880	A. Coke Smith	1902
Ezekiel B. Kephart	1881	E. Embree Hoss	1902
Alpheus W. Wilson	1882	Henry B. Hartzler	1902
Linus Parker	1882	William F. Heil	1902
John C. Granbery	1882	Joseph F. Berry	1904
Robert K. Hargrove	1882	Henry Spellmeyer	1904
William X. Ninde	1884	William F. McDowell	1904
John M. Walden	1884	James W. Bashford	1904
Willard F. Mallalieu	1884	William Burt	1904
Charles H. Fowler	1884	Luther B. Wilson	1904
William Taylor	1884	Thomas B. Neely	1904
Daniel K. Flickinger	1885	Isaiah B. Scott	1904
William W. Duncan	1886	William F. Oldham	1904
Charles B. Galloway	1886	John E. Robinson	1904
Eugene R. Hendrix	1886	Merriman C. Harris	1904
Joseph S. Key	1886	William M. Weekley	1905
John H. Vincent	1888	William M. Bell	1905
James N. FitzGerald	1888	Thomas C. Carter	1905
Isaac W. Joyce	1888	John J. Tigert III	1906
John P. Newman	1888	Seth Ward	1906
Daniel A. Goodsell	1888	James Atkins	1906
James M. Thoburn	1888	Samuel P. Spreng	1907

UNITED METHODIST BISHOPS

NAME	ELECTED	NAME	ELECTED
William F. Anderson	1908	William H. Washinger	1917
John L. Nuelsen	1908	John M. Moore	1918
William A. Quayle	1908	William F. McMurry	1918
Charles W. Smith	1908	Urban V. W. Darlington	1918
Wilson S. Lewis	1908	Horace M. DuBose	1918
Edwin H. Hughes	1908	William N. Ainsworth	1918
Robert McIntyre	1908	James Cannon, Jr.	1918
Frank M. Bristol	1908	Matthew T. Maze	1918
Collins Denny	1910	Lauress J. Birney	1920
John C. Kilgo	1910	Frederick B. Fisher	1920
William B. Murrah	1910	Charles E. Locke	1920
Walter R. Lambuth	1910	Ernest L. Waldorf	1920
Richard G. Waterhouse	1910	Edgar Blake	1920
Edwin D. Mouzon	1910	Ernest G. Richardson	1920
James H. McCoy	1910	Charles W. Burns	1920
William H. Fouke	1910	H. Lester Smith	1920
Uriah F. Swengel	1910	George H. Bickley	1920
Homer C. Stuntz	1912	Frederick T. Keeney	1920
William O. Shepard	1912	Charles L. Mead	1920
Theodore S. Henderson	1912	Anton Bast	1920
Naphtali Luccock	1912	Robert E. Jones	1920
Francis J. McConnell	1912	Matthew W. Clair	1920
Frederick D. Leete	1912	Arthur R. Clippinger	1921
Richard J. Cooke	1912	William B. Beauchamp	1922
Wilbur P. Thirkield	1912	James E. Dickey	1922
John W. Robinson	1912	Samuel R. Hay	1922
William P. Eveland	1912	Hoyt M. Dobbs	1922
Henry H. Fout	1913	Hiram A. Boaz	1922
Cyrus J. Kephart	1913	John F. Dunlap	1922
Alfred T. Howard	1913	George A. Miller	1924
Gottlieb Heinmiller	1915	Titus Lowe	1924
Lawrence H. Seager	1915	George R. Grose	1924
Herbert Welch	1916	Brenton T. Badley	1924
Thomas Nicholson	1916	Wallace E. Brown	1924
Adna W. Leonard	1916	Arthur B. Statton	1925
Matthew S. Hughes	1916	John S. Stamm	1926
Charles B. Mitchell	1916	S. J. Umbreit	1926
Franklin E. E. Hamilton	1916	Raymond J. Wade	1928
Alexander P. Camphor	1916	James C. Baker	1928
Eben S. Johnson	1916	Edwin F. Lee	1928

3

UNITED METHODIST BISHOPS

NAME	ELECTED	NAME	ELECTED
Grant D. Batdorf	1929	W. Y. Chen	1941
Ira D. Warner	1929	George C. Lacy	1941
John W. Gowdy	1930	Fred L. Dennis	1941
Chih P'ing Wang	1930	Dionisio D. Alejandro	1944
Arthur J. Moore	1930	Fred P. Corson	1944
Paul B. Kern	1930	Walter E. Ledden	1944
Angie F. Smith	1930	Lewis O. Hartman	1944
George E. Epp	1930	Newell S. Booth	1944
Jashwant R. Chitambar	1930	Willis J. King	1944
Juan E. Gattinoni	1932	Robert N. Brooks	1944
J. Ralph Magee	1932	Edward W. Kelly	1944
Ralph S. Cushman	1932	W. Angie Smith	1944
Elmer W. Praetorius	1934	Paul E. Martin	1944
Charles H. Stauffacher	1934	Costen J. Harrell	1944
J. Waskom Pickett	1935	Paul N. Garber	1944
Roberto V. Elphick	1936	Charles W. Brashares	1944
Wilbur E. Hammaker	1936	Schuyler E. Garth	1944
Charles W. Flint	1936	Arthur F. Wesley	1944
G. Bromley Oxnam	1936	John A. Subhan	1945
Alexander P. Shaw	1936	J. Balmet Showers	1945
John M. Springer	1936	August T. Arvidson	1946
F. H. Otto Melle	1936	J. W. E. Sommer	1946
Ralph A. Ward	1937	J. W. E. Bowen	1948
Victor O. Weidler	1938	Lloyd C. Wicke	1948
Ivan Lee Holt	1938	John W. Lord	1948
William W. Peele	1938	Dana Dawson	1948
Clare Purcell	1938	Marvin A. Franklin	1948
Charles C. Selecman	1938	Roy H. Short	1948
John L. Decell	1938	Richard C. Raines	1948
William C. Martin	1938	Marshall R. Reed	1948
William T. Watkins	1938	H. Clifford Northcott	1948
James H. Straughn	1939	Hazen G. Werner	1948
John C. Broomfield	1939	Glenn R. Phillips	1948
William A. C. Hughes	1940	Gerald H. Kennedy	1948
Lorenzo H. King	1940	Donald H. Tippett	1948
Bruce R. Baxter	1940	Jose L. Valencia	1948
Shot K. Mondol	1940	Sante Uberto Barbieri	1949
Clement D. Rockey	1941	Raymond L. Archer	1950
Enrique C. Balloch	1941	David T. Gregory	1950
Z. T. Kaung	1941	Frederick B. Newell	1952

4

UNITED METHODIST BISHOPS

NAME	CONSECRATED	NAME	ELECTED
Edgar A. Love	1952	Edwin R. Garrison	1960
Matthew W. Clair, Jr.	1952	T. Otto Nall, Jr.	1960
John W. Branscomb	1952	Charles F. Golden	1960
H. Bascom Watts	1952	Noah W. Moore, Jr.	1960
D. Stanley Coors	1952	Marquis L. Harris	1960
Edwin E. Voigt	1952	James W. Henley	1960
F. Gerald Ensley	1952	Walter C. Gum	1960
A. Raymond Grant	1952	Paul Hardin, Jr.	1960
Julio M. Sabanes	1952	John O. Smith	1960
Friedrich Wunderlich	1953	Paul W. Milhouse	1960
Odd Hagen	1953	Pedro R. Zottele	1962
Ferdinand Sigg	1954	James S. Thomas	1964
Reuben H. Mueller	1954	W. McFerrin Stowe	1964
H. R. Heininger	1954	W. Kenneth Goodson	1964
L. L. Baughman	1954	Dwight E. Loder	1964
Prince A. Taylor, Jr.	1956	R. Marvin Stuart	1964
Eugene M. Frank	1956	Edward J. Pendergrass, Jr.	1964
Nolan B. Harmon	1956	Thomas M. Pryor	1964
Bachman G. Hodge	1956	H. Ellis Finger, Jr.	1964
Hobart B. Amstutz	1956	Earl G. Hunt, Jr.	1964
Ralph E. Dodge	1956	Francis E. Kearns	1964
Mangal Singh	1956	Lance Webb	1964
Gabriel Sundaram	1956	Escrivao A. Zunguze	1964
Paul E. V. Shannon	1957	Robert F. Lundy	1964
John G. Howard	1957	Harry P. Andreassen	1964
H. W. Kaebnick	1958	John W. Shungu	1964
W. Maynard Sparks	1958	A. J. Shaw	1965
Paul M. Herrick	1958	P. C. B. Balaram	1965
B. Foster Stockwell	1960	Stephen T. Nagbe	1965
Fred G. Holloway	1960	Franz W. Schäfer	1966
W. Vernon Middleton	1960	Benjamin I. Guansing	1967
W. Ralph Ward, Jr.	1960	L. Scott Allen	1967
James K. Mathews	1960	Paul A. Washburn	1968
O. Eugene Slater	1960	C. Ernst Sommer	1968
W. Kenneth Pope	1960	D. Frederick Wertz	1968
Paul V. Galloway	1960	Alsie H. Carleton	1968
Aubrey G. Walton	1960	Roy C. Nichols	1968
Kenneth W. Copeland	1960	Arthur J. Armstrong	1968
Everett W. Palmer	1960	William R. Cannon	1968
Ralph T. Alton	1960		

5

UNITED METHODIST BISHOPS

NAME	ELECTED
Abel T. Muzorewa	1968
Cornelio M. Ferrer	1968
Paul L. A. Granadosin	1968
Joseph R. Lance	1968
R. D. Joshi	1968
Eric A. Mitchell	1969
Federico J. Pagura	1969
Raimundo A. Valenzuela	1969
Armin E. Härtel	1970
Ole E. Borgen	1970
Finis A. Crutchfield, Jr.	1972
Joseph H. Yeakel	1972
Robert E. Goodrich, Jr.	1972
Carl J. Sanders	1972
Ernest T. Dixon, Jr.	1972
Don W. Holter	1972
Wayne K. Clymer	1972
Joel D. McDavid	1972
Edward G. Carroll	1972
Jesse R. DeWitt	1972
James M. Ault	1972
John B. Warman	1972
Mack B. Stokes	1972
Jack M. Tuell	1972
Melvin E. Wheatley, Jr.	1972
Edward L. Tullis	1972
Frank L. Robertson	1972
Wilbur Wong Yan Choy	1972
Robert M. Blackburn	1972
Emilio de Carvalho	1972
Fama Onema	1972
M. Elia Peter	1972
Bennie deQuency Warner	1973
J. Kenneth Shamblin	1976
Alonzo M. Bryan	1976
Kenneth W. Hicks	1976
James C. Lovern	1976
Leroy C. Hodapp	1976

NAME	ELECTED
Edsel A. Ammons	1976
C. Dale White	1976
Ngoy Kimba Wakadilo	1976
Almeida Penicela	1976
LaVerne D. Mercado	1976
Hermann L. Sticher	1977
Shantu Kumar A. Parmar	1979
William Talbot Handy, Jr.	1980
John Wesley Hardt	1980
Benjamin Ray Oliphint	1980
Louis Wesley Schowengerdt	1980
Melvin George Talbert	1980
Paul Andrews Duffey	1980
Edwin Charles Boulton	1980
John William Russell	1980
Fitz Herbert Skeete	1980
George Willis Bashore	1980
Roy Clyde Clark	1980
William Boyd Grove	1980
Emerson Stephen Colaw	1980
Marjorie Swank Matthews	1980
Carlton Printiss Minnick, Jr.	1980
Calvin Dale McConnell	1980

6

HISTORICAL STATEMENT

The Plan of Union proposed to bring together The Methodist Church and the Evangelical United Brethren Church, two churches that share a common historical and spiritual heritage. They hold the same fundamental doctrines of faith. Ecclesiastical organization is similar. They are Protestant churches, whose streams of spiritual life and thought come out of the Protestant Reformation of the sixteenth century.

Since their beginnings they had lived and worked side by side in friendly fellowship. Had it not been for the difference in language—the Methodist working among English-speaking people and the Evangelical and United Brethren working among those speaking German—they might, from the beginning, have been one church. Today the language barrier is gone and the uniting of forces for our common task and calling seems appropriate and timely. Brief historical sketches of the two churches, taken from their respective Disciplines, follow.

The Methodist Church

The Methodist Church is a church of Christ in which "the pure Word of God is preached, and the Sacraments duly administered." This church is a great Protestant body, though it did not come directly out of the Reformation but had its origin within the Church of England. Its founder was John Wesley, a clergyman of that church, as was his father before him. His mother, Susanna Wesley, was a woman of zeal, devotion, and strength of character who was perhaps the greatest single human influence in Wesley's life.

Nurtured in this devout home, educated at Oxford University, the young John Wesley, like a second Paul, sought in vain for religious satisfaction by the strict observance of the rules

7

of religion and the ordinances of the church. The turning point in his life came when, at a prayer meeting in Aldersgate Street, London, on May 24, 1738, he learned what Paul had discovered, that it is not by rules and laws, nor by our own efforts at self-perfection, but by faith in God's mercy as it comes to us in Christ, that man may enter upon life and peace.

The gospel which Wesley thus found for himself he began to proclaim to others, first to companions who sought his counsel, including his brother Charles, then in widening circles that took him throughout the British Isles. His message had a double emphasis, which has remained with Methodism to this day. First was the gospel of God's grace, offered to all men and equal to every human need. Second was the moral ideal which this gospel presents to men. The Bible, he declared, knows no salvation which is not salvation from sin. He called men to holiness of life, and this holiness, he insisted, is "social holiness," the love and service of their fellowmen. Methodism meant "Christianity in earnest." The General Rules, which are still found in the Discipline, are the directions which Wesley gave to his followers to enable them to test the sincerity of their purpose and to guide them in this life.

Wesley did not plan to found a new church. In his work he simply followed, like Paul, the clear call of God, first to preach the gospel to the needy who were not being reached by the Established Church and its clergy, second to take care of those who were won to the Christian life. Step by step he was led on until Methodism became a great and transforming movement in the life of England. He gathered his people in groups, in classes and societies. He appointed leaders. He found men who were ready to carry the gospel to the masses, speaking on the streets, in the open fields, and in private homes. These men were not ordained ministers but lay preachers, or "local preachers," as they were called. He appointed these men, assigned them to various fields of labor, and supervised their work. Once a year he called them together for a conference, just as Methodist preachers meet in their Annual Conference sessions today.

Wesley thus united in extraordinary fashion three notable activities, in all of which he excelled. One was evangelism; "The world is my parish," he declared. His preachers went to the people; they did not wait for the people to come to them, and he himself knew the highways and byways of England as did no other man of his day. The second was organization and administration, by which he conserved the fruits of this preaching and extended its influence. The third was his appreciation of education and his use of the printed page. He made the press a servant of the Church and was the father of the mass circulation of inexpensive books, pamphlets, and periodicals.

From England, Methodism spread to Ireland and then to America. In 1766 Philip Embury, a lay preacher from Ireland, began to preach in the city of New York. At about the same time Robert Strawbridge, another lay preacher from Ireland, settled in Frederick County, Maryland, and began the work there. In 1769 Wesley sent Richard Boardman and Joseph Pilmoor to America, and two years later Francis Asbury, who became the great leader of American Methodism.

Methodism was especially adapted to American life. These itinerant preachers served the people under conditions where a settled ministry was not feasible. They sought out the scattered homes, followed the tide of migration as it moved west, preached the gospel, organized societies, established "preaching places," and formed these into "circuits." Thus by the close of the American Revolution the Methodists numbered some fifteen thousand members and eighty preachers.

In the beginning Wesley had thought of his fellows not as constituting a church but simply as forming so many societies. The preachers were not ordained, and the members were supposed to receive the Sacraments in the Anglican Church. But the Anglican clergy in America were few and far between. The Revolution had severed America from England, and Methodism to all intents and purposes had become an independent church. Wesley responded to appeals for help from America by asking the Bishop of London to ordain some of his preachers. Failing in this, he himself ordained two men and set aside Dr. Thomas Coke, who was a presbyter of the Church of England, to be a superintendent, "to preside over the flock of Christ" in America. Coke was directed to ordain Francis Asbury as a second superintendent.

At the Christmas Conference, which met in Baltimore

December 24, 1784, some sixty preachers, with Dr. Coke and his companions, organized the Methodist Episcopal Church in America. Wesley had sent over *The Sunday Service,* a simplified form of the English Book of Common Prayer, with the Articles of Religion reduced in number. This book they adopted, adding to the articles one which recognized the independence of the new nation.

Our present Articles of Religion come from this book and unite us with the historic faith of Christendom. Our Ritual, too, though it has been modified, has this as its source. However, the forms for public worship taken from the Book of Common Prayer were not adapted to the freer religious life of American Methodism and never entered into common use. Instead, Methodism created a book of its own, its Discipline. This contains today the Articles of Religion, Wesley's General Rules, and a large section which deals with the ministry, the various church organizations, and the rules governing the life and work of the Church.

In the history of Methodism two notable divisions occurred. In 1828 a group of earnest and godly persons, largely moved by an insistence on lay representation, separated and became the Methodist Protestant Church. In 1844 there was another division, the cause being construed by some as the question of slavery, by others as a constitutional issue over the powers of the General Conference versus the episcopacy. After years of negotiation a Plan of Union was agreed upon; and on May 10, 1939, the Methodist Episcopal Church, the Methodist Episcopal Church, South, and the Methodist Protestant Church united to form The Methodist Church.

The Methodist Church believes today, as Methodism has from the first, that the only infallible proof of a true church of Christ is its ability to seek and to save the lost, to disseminate the Pentecostal spirit and life, to spread scriptural holiness, and to transform all peoples and nations through the gospel of Christ. The sole object of the rules, regulations, and usages of The Methodist Church is to aid the Church in fulfilling its divine commission. United Methodism thanks God for the new life and strength which have come with reunion, while realizing the new obligations which this brings. At the same time it rejoices in the fact that it is a part of the one Church of our Lord and shares in a common task. Its spirit is still expressed in Wesley's words: "I desire to have a league, offensive and defensive, with every soldier of Christ. We have not only one faith, one hope, one Lord, but are directly engaged in one warfare."

The Evangelical United Brethren Church

The Evangelical United Brethren Church had its roots in the spiritual quickening which emerged in the United States in the late eighteenth and early nineteenth centuries. This movement challenged not only religious indifference, but also the contemporary tendency to substitute "religion" for a vital and experiential relationship with God. In its present form the Evangelical United Brethren Church represents the union, consummated in 1946, of the Church of the United Brethren in Christ and the Evangelical Church.

I. CHURCH OF THE UNITED BRETHREN IN CHRIST

The eighteenth century witnessed the eruption of revolutionary ideas and programs in science, industry, and politics. In this agitated world there were marked evidences of religious revitalization. In the English-speaking world it was associated with, though not confined to, Wesleyanism; in the German-speaking world it was associated with pietism. In some places and in some persons, these two movements impinged upon each other.

Philip William Otterbein, an ordained minister of the German Reformed Church who served congregations in Pennsylvania and Maryland, and Martin Boehm, a Pennsylvanian of Mennonite parentage, were among those who sensed a call to preach the Good News of God's redeeming mercy and love as demonstrated in Jesus Christ, especially among neglected German-speaking settlers of the Middle Colonies. In obedience to this call, they invited men to accept salvation. To be saved, they held, meant both awareness, as real as any sensory awareness, of God's acceptance and personal commitment to Christ. Their labors were blessed, and thriving societies were established which were conceived not so much as alternatives or rivals to established churches as centers for renewal in those churches. This work expanded, and helpers were sought to devote themselves to this evangelistic effort. As persons responded, they were received as fellow laborers.

The gracious work of renewal and reformation spread through Pennsylvania, Maryland, and Virginia. Otterbein's leadership was increasingly acknowledged. In the larger "big meetings" and in more intimate circles, he emphasized the necessity to persuade men to accept the divine invitation to salvation and to lead a new kind of life. To share experiences in this ministry and to seek greater effectiveness in this mission, it was resolved that preachers' meetings be held. One such meeting was held in Baltimore, Maryland, in 1789; another in Paradise Township, York County, Pennsylvania, in 1791.

Beginning with the meeting, September 25, 1800, in Frederick County, Maryland, these ministers' meetings were held annually. They agreed each of them should have liberty as to the mode of baptism, each administering it according to his own conviction. They agreed that Otterbein and Boehm should be their leaders as superintendents or bishops. About this time the name United Brethren in Christ came into use. The work soon extended across the Appalachian Mountains into Ohio, and this prompted the decision to organize a Conference in Ohio in 1810.

Martin Boehm died in 1812; Philip William Otterbein was incapacitated by ill health. Accordingly, in 1813 Christian Newcomer was elected bishop to superintend the concerns of the growing church. Up to this time there was no book of Discipline, so it was determined that a General Conference should be called to provide such a book. The first General Conference of this church convened June 6, 1815, near Mt. Pleasant, Pennsylvania. After deliberation, the conference recommended a book of Discipline containing the doctrines and rules of the church with the exhortation that these together with the Word of God should be strictly observed and admonished the members that "God is a God of order, but where there is no order and no church discipline, the spirit of love and charity will be lost."

The book of Discipline, together with a Constitution which was adopted in 1841, provided regulations under which the Church of the United Brethren in Christ expanded in numbers and mission in the nineteenth and twentieth centuries. The Constitution, with several other factors, was the ground for a division in the denomination in 1889 as the majority, authorized by a referendum in the church, made changes in the Constitution.

II. THE EVANGELICAL CHURCH

Jacob Albright, an unordained Pennsylvania tilemaker-farmer, began preaching that religion was a personal, conscious, experiential relationship with God. About 1800, small groups of people living in three separated communities, impressed by Albright's ideas, covenanted themselves to seek God's grace which would enable them to live holily. Following his experience of salvation in 1791, Albright began to witness in the German language to God's saving grace. He and those associated with him agreed to measures of self-discipline and Christian witness. The number of those inclined to participate in this endeavor increased, and this in turn promoted the enlistment of helpers.

The transition from movement to ecclesiastical organization was marked by the first council of those acknowledging Albright as leader on November 3, 1803. Beginning in 1807, with a meeting at Kleinfeltersville, Lebanon County, Pennsylvania, the preachers gathered in annual meetings. In 1809 a book of Discipline was adopted and printed. In 1816, at the first General Conference of the body, the name, The Evangelical Association, was adopted. For the courageous ministry of this church, conversion was the central theme and purpose, a word which signified the gracious, conscious vitalization of the life of a man by an act of God.

During the nineteenth century the operations of this church enlarged in evangelism, education, and publications. In the latter part of the century differences arose in the Evangelical Association which in 1891 culminated in a division. A considerable number of ministers and laymen withdrew and took the name the United Evangelical Church, which held its first General Conference in 1894. Both churches continued their activities, side by side, both endeavoring to carry on the work of the Lord with zeal and devotion. Both churches grew in numbers and in missionary enterprise. By 1910 the growing conviction that the two churches should be reunited found articulate expression, and in 1922 the Evangelical Association and the United Evangelical Church were united under the name the Evangelical Church.

III. UNION IN 1946

Negotiations, beginning in 1933, were consummated in 1946 when the Church of the United Brethren in Christ and the Evangelical Church became the Evangelical United Brethren Church. This church sought to serve its Lord faithfully in the proclamation that salvation is available to any upon the free, personal acceptance of God's offer. Conversion, while personal, is not a private matter and finds its consummation in holy living and in serving as an instrument of God for the redemption of the whole world. In this task, it views itself as one fold, in the one flock, whose Shepherd is our Lord.

Black People and Their United Methodist Heritage

Prior to the organization of the Methodist Episcopal Church in 1784, black people were related to the Methodist societies. On November 29, 1758, John Wesley baptized his first Negro converts at Wandsworth, England. Mr. Wesley claimed that these were the first African Christians he had known.

These African Christians began immediately to "spread scriptural holiness" in the New World. They introduced Methodism in Antigua. By 1786, there were 1,569 Methodists in this country. Only two were white.

Black people embraced the Methodist faith in the United States very early. Two early Methodist societies in America were the John Street Society in New York City and the Log Meeting House in Frederick County, Maryland. Black members are included among the charter members. In the John Street Society, Beatty, a Negro servant of the Heck family, was a charter member. On Sam Creek in Frederick County, Maryland, Anne, a slave of the Schweitzer family, was a charter member. By 1786, there were 1,890 black members in the Methodist Episcopal Church.

Methodism won favor with the black people for two main reasons: (1) its evangelistic appeal; (2) the Church's attitude toward slavery. Later its social concern impressed black people.

14

The shortest list of early black Methodist evangelists must include Harry Hoosier, Henry Evans, and John Stewart. Harry Hoosier was a traveling companion of Francis Asbury. He accompanied him to preach to the colored people. In alluding to Harry Hoosier, Thomas Coke said: "I believe he is one of the best preachers in the world." A freeborn Negro of Virginia, Henry Evans possessed genius of organization. He organized the Fourth Street Church in Wilmington, Delaware. He is credited also with organizing the first inclusive church in Fayetteville, North Carolina. The Methodist historian Abe Stevens referred to him as the Father of the Methodist Episcopal Church, White and Black in that city. The first home missionary in the Methodist Episcopal Church was John Stewart. He was a freeborn mulatto from Virginia. He became a missionary to the Wyandotte Indians. The arduous labors of John Stewart led directly to the organization of the Home Missionary Society in the Methodist Episcopal Church.

From 1784 to 1864, the black people were included in the membership of the white churches. Black people persuaded the Church to organize them into their own churches. In 1794, the African Zoar Society was organized in Philadelphia. It was the first black society in the Methodist Episcopal Church.

In 1864, the General Conference authorized the organization of Mission Conferences among black people. The first black mission conference to be organized was the Delaware Conference on July 29, 1864. By 1900, nineteen conferences had been organized among the black people. These conferences had 1,705 ministers in full connection and 3,398 organized congregations with an aggregate church membership of 239,274.

Until 1920, these black conferences were supervised by white bishops. On May 19, 1920, Robert Elijah Jones was elected as the first black General Superintendent in the Methodist Episcopal Church. Previously, four black ministers had been elected as missionary bishops for Liberia. By 1975, nineteen other black elders had been consecrated.

On May 10, 1939, the Methodist Episcopal Church, South, the Methodist Protestant Church, and the Methodist Episcopal Church united into The Methodist Church. In order to perfect union, the Jurisdictional System was created. Five regional jurisdictions were created. In addition, the Central Jurisdiction was established to include all the black conferences.

The black conferences did not on the whole approve of the Central Jurisdiction. Most of the conferences opposed it for at least two reasons: (1) the Central Jurisdiction was written into the Constitution of the Church; and (2) it was a segregated unit.

The Central Jurisdiction continued as a segregated structural arrangement in the Constitution of The Methodist Church until 1968. In 1968, The Methodist Church and the Evangelical United Brethren Church united and became The United Methodist Church. The Constitution of the new Church did not provide for the Central Jurisdiction. Black conferences were transferred into the regional jurisdictions. By 1974, all black conferences had merged with the white conferences. United Methodism became inclusive on the associative level.

With the merger of The Methodist Church and the Evangelical United Brethren Church, some Blacks were added to the membership of The United Methodist Church from the former Evangelical United Brethren Church. Perhaps the earliest attempt of the former Evangelical Association in establishing a Negro Mission was in 1822. A Negro named Daniel Wilson opened his home in Orwigsburg, Pennsylvania to the Reverend John Seybert. This church had desultory contacts with American Negroes.

About two decades prior to union of the former Evangelical United Brethren Church and The Methodist Church, the former Evangelical United Brethren Church began to recognize the needs of changing communities in the cities where this denomination was located. Through its Board of National Missions in cooperation with some Annual Conferences, this Church began to minister to the religious needs of black people.

The United Methodist Church

The United Methodist Church brings together two streams of spiritual life with similar emphases which had their beginnings in the evangelistic concerns and passion of John Wesley, Francis Asbury, Philip William Otterbein, Jacob Albright, Martin Boehm, and others who labored with them. These men were dedicated to the task of preaching the gospel to their fellow countrymen.

Since they were men who were deeply moved by a common faith and zeal and held a like emphasis upon personal spiritual experience of salvation, it is no surprise to find instances of fraternity and cooperation among them. They often conferred with each other and sometimes traveled together on their preaching missions. In many communities they shared the same building, with the Methodist preachers conducting services in English at one hour and the Evangelical or United Brethren preachers conducting a German service at another hour. There are many references to the Asbury groups as "English Methodists" and the Otterbein-Boehm-Albright groups as "German Methodists" or "Dutch Methodists."

The firm conviction that Christian faith and experience ought to be expressed in holy living led these early leaders to adopt similar patterns of ecclesiastical organization and discipline to assist Christians in spiritual growth and Christian witness.

When Asbury was ordained and consecrated as bishop in 1784, Otterbein participated with the laying on of hands. When Otterbein ordained Christian Newcomer in 1813, he requested that a Methodist minister participate. William Ryland responded and joined Otterbein in the act of ordination.

There is evidence that Asbury conferred with Otterbein when he was working on the book of Discipline for the Methodists. When this Discipline was later translated into German, it became the basis for the Discipline of the *Evangelische Gemeinschaft* (later known as the Evangelical Church) and—to a lesser degree—the *Vereinigten Bruder* (later known as the United Brethren in Christ).

Over the years there have been many conversations concerning union. Bishop Newcomer's journal records such a conversation as early as April 1, 1803. In 1871 the Evangelical Association voted by a narrow margin of one to join the Methodists, but union was never consummated. During the years these conversations, under the instruction and authorization of the respective General Conferences, led to a plan and basis of union that united the Evangelical United Brethren Church and The Methodist Church into The United Methodist Church. This union embodies the history and traditions of the following churches which are Methodist in name or tradition:

The Methodist Episcopal Church

The Methodist Episcopal Church, South

The Methodist Protestant Church

The Methodist Church (merged into the Protestant Methodist Church in 1877)

United Brethren in Christ

The Evangelical Association

The United Evangelical Church

The Evangelical Church

The Methodist Church

The Evangelical United Brethren Church

Part I

THE CONSTITUTION

PREAMBLE

The Church is a community of all true believers under the Lordship of Christ. It is the redeemed and redeeming fellowship in which the Word of God is preached by persons divinely called, and the Sacraments are duly administered according to Christ's own appointment. Under the discipline of the Holy Spirit the Church seeks to provide for the maintenance of worship, the edification of believers, and the redemption of the world.

The Church of Jesus Christ exists in and for the world, and its very dividedness is a hindrance to its mission in that world.

The prayers and intentions of The Methodist Church and The Evangelical United Brethren Church have been and are for obedience to the will of our Lord that His people be one, in humility for the present brokenness of the Church and in gratitude that opportunities for reunion have been given. In harmony with these prayers and intentions these churches do now propose to unite, in the confident assurance that this act is an expression of the oneness of Christ's people.

Conversations concerning union between the two churches and their constituent members have taken place over a long period of years, and the churches have a long and impressive history of fellowship and cooperation.

Therefore, we, the Commissions on Church Union of The Methodist Church, and of The Evangelical United Brethren Church, holding that these churches are essentially one in origin, in belief, in spirit, and in purpose, and desiring that this essential unity be made actual in organization and administration in the

19

United States of America and throughout the world, do hereby propose and transmit to our respective General Conferences the following Plan of Union and recommend to the two churches its adoption by the processes which they respectively require.[1]

DIVISION ONE—GENERAL

¶ **1.** *Article I. Declaration of Union.*—The Evangelical United Brethren Church and The Methodist Church shall be united in one Church. The united Church, as thus constituted, is, and shall be, the ecclesiastical and legal successor of the two uniting churches.

¶ **2.** *Article II. Name.*—The name of the Church shall be The United Methodist Church. The name of the Church may be translated freely into languages other than English as the General Conference may determine.

¶ **3.** *Article III. Articles of Religion and the Confession of Faith.*—The Articles of Religion and the Confession of Faith shall be those currently held by The Methodist Church and The Evangelical United Brethren Church respectively.

¶ **4.** *Article IV. Inclusiveness of the Church.*—The United Methodist Church is a part of the Church Universal, which is one Body in Christ. Therefore all persons, without regard to race, color, national origin, or economic condition, shall be eligible to attend its worship services, to participate in its programs, and, when they take the appropriate vows, to be admitted into its membership in any local church in the connection. In The United Methodist Church no conference or other organizational unit of the Church shall be structured so as to exclude any member or any constituent body of the Church because of race, color, national origin, or economic condition.[2]

---

[1]The Constitution was adopted in Chicago, Illinois, on Nov. 11, 1966, by the General Conferences of The Evangelical United Brethren Church and The Methodist Church and thereafter by the requisite vote in the Annual Conferences of the two churches. The Plan of Union was made effective by the Uniting Conference in Dallas, Texas, on April 23, 1968.

[2]*See* Judicial Council Decisions 242, 246, 340, 351, 362, 377, 398, and Decisions 4 and 5, Interim Judicial Council.

¶ **5.** *Article V. Ecumenical Relations.*—As part of the Church Universal, The United Methodist Church believes that the Lord of the Church is calling Christians everywhere to strive toward unity; and therefore it will seek, and work for, unity at all levels of church life: through world relationships with other Methodist churches and united churches related to The Methodist Church or The Evangelical United Brethren Church, through councils of churches, and through plans of union with churches of Methodist or other denominational traditions.

¶ **6.** *Article VI. Title to Properties.*—Titles to properties in The Evangelical United Brethren Church and The Methodist Church shall, upon consummation of the union, automatically vest in The United Methodist Church. Nothing in the Plan of Union at any time after the union is to be construed so as to require any local church or any other property owner of the former The Evangelical United Brethren Church or the former The Methodist Church to alienate or in any way to change the title to property contained in its deed or deeds at the time of union, and lapse of time or usage shall not affect said title or control.

DIVISION TWO—ORGANIZATION

Section I. Conferences.

¶ **7.** *Article I.*—There shall be a General Conference for the entire Church with such powers, duties, and privileges as are hereinafter set forth.

¶ **8.** *Article II.*—There shall be Jurisdictional Conferences for the Church in the United States of America, with such powers, duties, and privileges as are hereinafter set forth;[3] *provided* that in The United Methodist Church there shall be no jurisdictional or central conference based on any ground other than geographical and regional division.

---

[3]*See* Judicial Council Decision 128.

¶ **9. *Article III.***—There shall be Central Conferences for the Church outside the United States of America and, if necessary, Provisional Central Conferences, all with such powers, duties, and privileges as are hereinafter set forth.

¶ **10. *Article IV.***—There shall be Annual Conferences as the fundamental bodies of the Church and, if necessary, Provisional Annual Conferences, with such powers, duties, and privileges as are hereinafter set forth.[4]

¶ **11. *Article V.***—There shall be a Charge Conference for each church or charge with such powers, duties, and privileges as are hereinafter set forth.

Section II. General Conference.

¶ **12. *Article I.***—1. The General Conference shall be composed of not less than 600 nor more than 1,000 delegates, one half of whom shall be ministers and one half lay members, to be elected by the Annual Conferences. The Missionary Conferences shall be considered as Annual Conferences for the purpose of this article.

2. Delegates shall be elected by the Annual Conferences except that delegates may be elected by other autonomous Methodist churches if and when the General Conference shall approve concordats with such other autonomous Methodist churches for the mutual election and seating of delegates in each other's highest legislative conferences.

3. In the case of The Methodist Church in Great Britain, mother church of Methodism, upon mutual approval of the concordat now pending, provision shall be made for the reciprocal election and seating of four delegates, two clergy and two lay.[5]

¶ **13. *Article II.***—The General Conference shall meet in the month of April or May once in four years at such time and in such place as shall be determined by the General Conference or by its duly authorized committees.

A special session of General Conference, possessing the

---

[4]*See* Judicial Council Decision 354.
[5]Amended 1968; *See* Judicial Council Decisions 333, 402.

authority and exercising all the powers of the General Conference, may be called by the Council of Bishops, or in such other manner as the General Conference may from time to time prescribe, to meet at such time and in such place as may be stated in the call. Such special session of the General Conference shall be composed of the delegates to the preceding General Conference or their lawful successors, except that when a particular Annual Conference or Missionary Conference shall prefer to have a new election it may do so.[6] The purpose of such special session shall be stated in the call, and only such business shall be transacted as is in harmony with the purpose stated in such call unless the General Conference by a two-thirds vote shall determine that other business may be transacted.[7]

¶ **14.** *Article III.*—The General Conference shall fix the ratio of representation in the General, Jurisdictional, and Central Conferences from the Annual Conferences, Missionary Conferences, and the Provisional Annual Conferences, computed on a two-factor basis: (1) the number of ministerial members of the Annual Conference and (2) the number of church members in the Annual Conference; *provided* that each Annual Conference, Missionary Conference, or Provisional Annual Conference, except for the Provisional Annual Conferences of a Central Conference or a Provisional Central Conference, shall be entitled to at least one ministerial and one lay delegate in the General Conference and also in the Jurisdictional or Central Conference.[8]

¶ **15.** *Article IV.*—The General Conference shall have full legislative power over all matters distinctively connectional, and in the exercise of this power shall have authority as follows:[9]

1. To define and fix the conditions, privileges, and duties of church membership which shall in every case be without reference to race or status.

2. To define and fix the powers and duties of elders,

---

[6]*See* Judicial Council Decisions 221, 226, 228, 238, 302.
[7]*See* Judicial Council Decision 227.
[8]*See* Judicial Council Decision 403.
[9]*See* Judicial Council Decisions 96, 232, 236, 318, 325.

deacons, supply preachers, local preachers, exhorters, and deaconesses.[10]

3. To define and fix the powers and duties of Annual Conferences, Provisional Annual Conferences, Missionary Conferences and Missions, and of Central Conferences, District Conferences, Charge Conferences, and Congregational Meetings.[11]

4. To provide for the organization, promotion, and administration of the work of the Church outside the United States of America.[12]

5. To define and fix the powers, duties, and privileges of the episcopacy, to adopt a plan for the support of the bishops, to provide a uniform rule for their retirement, and to provide for the discontinuance of a bishop because of inefficiency or unacceptability.[13]

6. To provide and revise the Hymnal and Ritual of the Church and to regulate all matters relating to the form and mode of worship, subject to the limitations of the first and second Restrictive Rules.

7. To provide a judicial system and a method of judicial procedure for the Church, except as herein otherwise prescribed.

8. To initiate and to direct all connectional enterprises of the Church and to provide boards for their promotion and administration.[14]

9. To determine and provide for raising and distributing funds necessary to carry on the work of the Church.[15]

10. To fix a uniform basis upon which bishops shall be elected by the Jurisdictional Conferences and to determine the number of bishops that may be elected by Central Conferences.

11. To select its presiding officers from the bishops, through a committee; *provided* that the bishops shall select from their own number the presiding officer of the opening session.[16]

12. To change the number and the boundaries of Jurisdic-

[10]*See* Judicial Council Decisions 58, 313.
[11]*See* Judicial Council Decision 411.
[12]*See* Judicial Council Decision 182.
[13]*See* Judicial Council Decisions 35, 114, 312, 365, 413.
[14]*See* Judicial Council Decisions 214, 364, 411.
[15]*See* Judicial Council Decision 30.
[16]*See* Judicial Council Decision 126.

tional Conferences upon the consent of a majority of the Annual Conferences in each Jurisdictional Conference involved.[17]

13. To establish such commissions for the general work of the Church as may be deemed advisable.

14. To secure the rights and privileges of membership in all agencies, programs, and institutions in The United Methodist Church regardless of race or status.[18]

15. To enact such other legislation as may be necessary, subject to the limitations and restrictions of the Constitution of the Church.[19]

Section III. Restrictive Rules.

¶ **16.** *Article I.*—The General Conference shall not revoke, alter, or change our Articles of Religion or establish any new standards or rules of doctrine contrary to our present existing and established standards of doctrine.[20]

Article II.—The General Conference shall not revoke, alter, or change our Confession of Faith.

¶ **17.** *Article III.*—The General Conference shall not change or alter any part or rule of our government so as to do away with episcopacy or destroy the plan of our itinerant general superintendency.

¶ **18.** *Article IV.*—The General Conference shall not do away with the privileges of our ministers of right to trial by a committee and of an appeal; neither shall it do away with the privileges of our members of right to trial before the church, or by a committee, and of an appeal.[21]

¶ **19.** *Article V.*—The General Conference shall not revoke or change the General Rules of Our United Societies.[22]

¶ **20.** *Article VI.*—The General Conference shall not appropriate the net income of the publishing houses, the book concerns, or the Chartered Fund to any purpose other than for

[17]*See* Judicial Council Decisions 55, 56, 215.
[18]*See* Decisions, 4, 5, Interim Judicial Council, Judicial Council Decisions 427, 433, 442, 451.
[19]*See* Judicial Council Decision 215.
[20]*See* Judicial Council Decisions 86, 142, 243, 358.
[21]*See* Judicial Council Decision 351.
[22]*See* Judicial Council Decision 358, 468.

the benefit of retired or disabled preachers, their spouses, widows, or widowers, and children or other beneficiaries of the ministerial pension systems.[23]

[¶ **21.** *Article VII.*]—(This article is deleted from the Constitution as of 1980, the termination of the first three quadrenniums following the union of The Evangelical United Brethren Church and The Methodist Church during which it was in effect.)[24]

Section IV. Jurisdictional Conferences.

¶ **22.** *Article I.*—The Jurisdictional Conferences shall be composed of as many representatives from the Annual Conferences and Missionary Conferences as shall be determined by a uniform basis established by the General Conference. The Missionary Conferences shall be considered as Annual Conferences for the purpose of this article.

¶ **23.** *Article II.*—All Jurisdictional Conferences shall have the same status and the same privileges of action within the limits fixed by the Constitution. The ratio of representation of the Annual Conferences and Missionary Conferences in the General Conference shall be the same for all Jurisdictional Conferences.

¶ **24.** *Article III.*—The General Conferences shall fix the basis of representation in the Jurisdictional Conferences; *provided* that the Jurisdictional Conferences shall be composed of an equal number of ministerial and lay delegates to be elected by the Annual Conferences, the Missionary Conferences, and the Provisional Annual Conferences.

¶ **25.** *Article IV.*—Each Jurisdictional Conference shall meet at the time determined by the Council of Bishops or its delegated committee, each Jurisdictional Conference convening on the same date as the others and at a place selected by the Jurisdictional Committee on Entertainment, appointed by its College of Bishops unless such a committee has been appointed by the preceding Jurisdictional Conference.

¶ **26.** *Article V.*—The Jurisdictional Conferences shall have

---

[23]*See* Judicial Council Decisions 322, 230.
[24]*See* Judicial Council Decisions 333, 356, 388, 408.

the following powers and duties and such others as may be conferred by the General Conferences:

1. To promote the evangelistic, educational, missionary, and benevolent interests of the Church and to provide for interests and institutions within their boundaries.[25]

2. To elect bishops and to cooperate in carrying out such plans for their support as may be determined by the General Conference.

3. To establish and constitute Jurisdictional Conference boards as auxiliary to the general boards of the Church as the need may appear and to choose their representatives on the general boards in such manner as the General Conference may determine.[26]

4. To determine the boundaries of their Annual Conferences; *provided* that there shall be no Annual Conference with a membership of fewer than fifty ministers in full connection, except by the consent of the General Conference; and *provided* further that this provision shall not apply to Annual Conferences of the former Evangelical United Brethren Church during the first three quadrenniums after union.[27]

5. To make rules and regulations for the administration of the work of the Church within the jurisdiction, subject to such powers as have been or shall be vested in the General Conference.

6. To appoint a Committee on Appeals to hear and determine the appeal of a traveling preacher of that jurisdiction from the decision of a trial committee.

Section V. Central Conferences.

¶ 27. *Article I.*—There shall be Central Conferences for the work of the Church outside the United States of America with such duties, powers, and privileges as are hereinafter set forth. The number and boundaries of the Central Conferences shall be determined by the Uniting Conference. Subsequently the General Conference shall have authority to change the number

---

[25]*See* Judicial Council Decision 67.
[26]*See* Judicial Council Decision 183.
[27]*See* Judicial Council Decision 447.

and boundaries of Central Conferences. The Central Conferences shall have the duties, powers, and privileges hereinafter set forth.

¶ **28.** *Article II.*—The Central Conferences shall be composed of as many delegates as shall be determined by a basis established by the General Conference. The delegates shall be ministerial and lay in equal numbers.

¶ **29.** *Article III.*—The Central Conferences shall meet within the year succeeding the meeting of the General Conference at such times and places as shall have been determined by the preceding respective Central Conferences or by commissions appointed by them or by the General Conference. The date and place of the first meeting succeeding the Uniting Conference shall be fixed by the bishops of the respective Central Conferences, or in such manner as shall be determined by the General Conference.

¶ **30.** *Article IV.*—The Central Conferences shall have the following powers and duties and such others as may be conferred by the General Conference:

1. To promote the evangelistic, educational, missionary, social-concern, and benevolent interests and institutions of the Church within their own boundaries.

2. To elect the bishops for the respective Central Conferences in number as may be determined from time to time, upon a basis fixed by the General Conference, and to cooperate in carrying out such plans for the support of their bishops as may be determined by the General Conference.[28]

3. To establish and constitute such Central Conference boards as may be required and to elect their administrative officers.[29]

4. To determine the boundaries of the Annual Conferences within their respective areas.

5. To make such rules and regulations for the administration of the work within their boundaries including such changes and adaptations of the General Discipline as the

---

[28]*See* Judicial Council Decision 370.
[29]*See* Judicial Council Decision 69.

conditions in the respective areas may require, subject to the powers that have been or shall be vested in the General Conference.[30]

6. To appoint a Judicial Court to determine legal questions arising on the rules, regulations, and such revised, adapted, or new sections of the Central Conference Discipline enacted by the Central Conference.

7. To appoint a Committee on Appeals to hear and determine the appeal of a traveling preacher of that Central Conference from the decision of a Committee on Trial.

Section VI. Episcopal Administration in Central Conferences.

¶ **31.** *Article I.*—The bishops of the Central Conferences shall be elected by their respective Central Conferences and inducted into office in the historic manner.

¶ **32.** *Article II.*—The bishops of the Central Conferences shall have membership in the Council of Bishops with vote.

¶ **33.** *Article III.*—The bishops of the Central Conferences shall preside in the sessions of their respective Central Conferences.

¶ **34.** *Article IV.*—The bishops of each Central Conference shall arrange the plan of episcopal visitation within their Central Conference.

¶ **35.** *Article V.*—The Council of Bishops may assign one of their number to visit each Central Conference. When so assigned, the bishop shall be recognized as the accredited representative of the general Church and when requested by a majority of the bishops resident in that conference may exercise therein the functions of the episcopacy.

Section VII. Annual Conferences.

¶ **36.** *Article I.*—The Annual Conference shall be composed of ministerial members as defined by the General Conference, together with a lay member elected by each charge, the conference president of United Methodist

---

[30]*See* Judicial Council Decision 142, 147, 313.

Women, the conference president of United Methodist Men, the conference lay leader, the president of the conference youth organization, and two young persons under twenty-five (25) years of age from each district to be selected in such manner as may be determined by the Annual Conference.[31] Each charge served by more than one minister shall be entitled to as many lay members as there are ministerial members. The lay members shall have been for the two years next preceding their election members of The United Methodist Church[32] and shall have been active participants in The United Methodist Church for at least four years next preceding their election.

If the lay membership should number less than the ministerial members of the Annual Conference, the Annual Conference shall, by its own formula, provide for the election of additional lay members to equalize lay and ministerial membership of the Annual Conference.[33]

¶ **37.** *Article II.*—The Annual Conference is the basic body in the Church and as such shall have reserved to it the right to vote on all constitutional amendments, on the election of ministerial and lay delegates to the General and the Jurisdictional or Central Conferences, on all matters relating to the character and conference relations of its ministerial members, and on the ordination of ministers and such other rights as have not been delegated to the General Conference under the Constitution, with the exception that the lay members may not vote on matters of ordination, character, and conference relations of ministers. It shall discharge such duties and exercise such powers as the General Conference under the Constitution may determine.[34]

¶ **38.** *Article III.*—The Annual Conference shall elect ministerial and lay delegates to the General Conference and to its Jurisdictional or Central Conference in the manner provided in this section, Articles IV and V. The persons first elected up to the number determined by the ratio for representation in the

---

[31]Amended 1968, 1970.
[32]Amended 1972.
[33]*See* Judicial Council Decisions 24, 113, 129, 349, 378, 479, and Decision 7, Interim Judicial Council.
[34]*See* Judicial Council Decisions 78, 79, 132, 405, 406, 415.

General Conference shall be representatives in that body. Additional delegates shall be elected to complete the number determined by the ratio for representation in the Jurisdictional or Central Conference, who, together with those first elected as above, shall be delegates in the Jurisdictional or Central Conference. The additional delegates to the Jurisdictional or Central Conference shall in the order of their election be the reserve delegates to the General Conference.[35] The Annual Conference shall also elect reserve ministerial and lay delegates to the Jurisdictional or Central Conference as it may deem desirable.

¶ **39.** *Article IV.*—The ministerial delegates to the General Conference and to the Jurisdictional or Central Conference shall be elected by the ministerial members in full connection with the Annual Conference or Provisional Annual Conference; *provided* that such delegates shall have been traveling preachers in the constituent churches forming this union or in The United Methodist Church for at least four years next preceding their election and are in full connection with the Annual Conference or Provisional Annual Conference electing them when elected and at the time of holding the General and Jurisdictional or Central Conferences.[36]

¶ **40.** *Article V.*—The lay delegates to the General and Jurisdictional or Central Conferences shall be elected by the lay members of the Annual Conference or Provisional Annual Conference without regard to age, *provided* such delegates[37] shall have been members of The United Methodist Church for at least two years next preceding their election, and shall have been active participants in The United Methodist Church for at least four years next preceding their election, and are members thereof within the Annual Conference electing them at the time of holding the General and Jurisdictional or Central Conferences.[38]

¶ **41.** *Article VI.*—For a period of twelve years following union, Annual Conferences shall not have their names or

---

[35]*See* Judicial Council Decision 352.
[36]*See* Judicial Council Decisions 1, 162, 308, 403, 473.
[37]Amended 1972.
[38]*See* Judicial Council Decisions 346, 354, 403.

boundaries changed without their consent; and during such
period Annual Conferences formerly of The Evangelical
United Brethren Church may in electing delegates to
General, Jurisdictional, or Central Conferences and their
superintendents of districts continue their time-honored
methods, the provisions of Division Two, Section VII, Arts.
IV and V; Division Two, Section VIII, Art. IV; and Division
Three, Art. IX, notwithstanding; but nothing herein shall be
construed as preventing the elimination of Annual Conferences based on race.

Section VIII. Boundaries.

¶ **42.** *Article I.*—The United Methodist Church shall
have Jurisdictional Conferences made up as follows:

Northeastern—Maine, New Hampshire, Vermont, Mas-
sachusetts, Rhode Island, New York, Connecticut, Pennsylvania, New Jersey, Maryland, West Virginia, Delaware, District
of Columbia, and Puerto Rico.

Southeastern—Virginia, North Carolina, South Carolina, Georgia, Florida, Alabama, Tennessee, Kentucky,
Mississippi.

North Central—Ohio, Indiana, Illinois, Michigan, Wis-
consin, Minnesota, Iowa, North Dakota, South Dakota.

South Central—Missouri, Arkansas, Louisiana, Nebraska,
Kansas, Oklahoma, Texas, New Mexico.

Western—Washington, Idaho, Oregon, California, Nevada,
Utah, Arizona, Montana, Wyoming, Colorado, Alaska and
Hawaii.

¶ **43.** *Article II.*—The work of the Church outside the
United States of America may be formed into Central Conferences, the number and boundaries of which shall be determined
by the Uniting Conference, the General Conference having
authority subsequently to make changes in the number and
boundaries.

¶ **44.** *Article III.*—Changes in the number, names, and
boundaries of the Jurisdictional Conferences may be effected by
the General Conference upon the consent of a majority of the

Annual Conferences of each of the Jurisdictional Conferences involved.[39]

¶ **45.** *Article IV.*—Changes in the number, names, and boundaries of the Annual Conferences may be effected by the Jurisdictional Conferences in the United States of America and by the Central Conferences outside the United States of America according to the provisions under the respective powers of the Jurisdictional and the Central Conferences.[40]

¶ **46.** *Article V. Transfer of Local Churches.*—1. A local church may be transferred from one Annual Conference to another in which it is geographically located upon approval by a two-thirds vote of those present and voting in each of the following:

  a) The Charge Conference
  b) The Congregational Meeting of the local church
  c) Each of the two Annual Conferences involved

The vote shall be certified by the secretaries of the specified conferences or meetings to the bishops having supervision of the Annual Conferences involved, and upon their announcement of the required majorities the transfer shall immediately be effective.

2. The vote on approval of transfer shall be taken by each Annual Conference at its first session after the matter is submitted to it.

3. Transfers under the provisions of this article shall not be governed or restricted by other provisions of this Constitution relating to changes of boundaries of conferences.

Section IX. District Conferences.

¶ **47.** *Article I.*—There may be organized in an Annual Conference, District Conferences composed of such persons and invested with such powers as the General Conference may determine.

---

[39]*See* Judicial Council Decisions 55, 56, 85, 215.
[40]*See* Judicial Council Decisions 28, 85, 217, and Decisions 1, 2, Interim Judicial Council.

Section X. Charge Conferences.

¶ 48. *Article I.*—There shall be organized in each charge a Charge Conference composed of such persons and invested with such powers as the General Conference shall provide.

¶ 49. *Article II. Election of Church Officers.*—Unless the General Conference shall order otherwise, the officers of the church or churches constituting a charge shall be elected by the Charge Conference or by the members of said church or churches at a meeting called for that purpose, as may be arranged by the Charge Conference, unless the election is otherwise required by local church charters or state or provincial laws.

DIVISION THREE—EPISCOPAL SUPERVISION

¶ 50. *Article I.*—There shall be a continuance of an episcopacy in The United Methodist Church of like plan, powers, privileges, and duties as now exist in The Methodist Church and in The Evangelical United Brethren Church in all those matters in which they agree and may be considered identical; and the differences between these historic episco-pacies are deemed to be reconciled and harmonized by and in this Plan of Union and Constitution of The United Methodist Church and actions taken pursuant thereto so that a unified superintendency and episcopacy is hereby created and established of, in, and by those who now are and shall be bishops of The United Methodist Church; and the said episcopacy shall further have such powers, privileges, and duties as are herein set forth.[41]

¶ 51. *Article II.*—The bishops shall be elected by the respective Jurisdictional and Central Conferences and conse-crated in the historic manner at such time and place as may be fixed by the General Conference for those elected by the jurisdictions and by each Central Conference for those elected by such Central Conference.[42]

----

[41]*See* Judicial Council Decisions 4, 114, 127, 363.
[42]*See* Judicial Council Decision 21.

¶ **52.** *Article III.*—There shall be a Council of Bishops composed of all the bishops of The United Methodist Church. The council shall meet at least once a year and plan for the general oversight and promotion of the temporal and spiritual interests of the entire Church and for carrying into effect the rules, regulations, and responsibilities prescribed and enjoined by the General Conference and in accord with the provisions set forth in this Plan of Union.[43]

¶ **53.** *Article IV.*—The bishops of each Jurisdictional and Central Conference shall constitute a College of Bishops and such College of Bishops shall arrange the plan of episcopal supervision of the Annual Conferences, Missionary Conferences, and Missions within their respective territories.

¶ **54.** *Article V.*—The bishops shall have residential and presidential supervision in the Jurisdictional Conferences in which they are elected or to which they are transferred. Bishops may be transferred from one jurisdiction to another jurisdiction for presidential and residential supervision under the following conditions: (1) The transfer of bishops may be on either of two bases: *(a)* a jurisdiction which receives a bishop by transfer from another jurisdiction may transfer to that jurisdiction or to a third jurisdiction one of its own bishops eligible for transfer, so that the number transferred in by each jurisdiction shall be balanced by the number transferred out, or *(b)* a jurisdiction may receive a bishop from another jurisdiction and not transfer out a member of its own College of Bishops. (2) No bishop shall be transferred unless that bishop shall have specifically consented. (3) No bishop shall be eligible for transfer unless the bishop shall have served one quadrennium in the jurisdiction which elected the bishop to the episcopacy. (4) All such transfers shall require the approval by a majority vote of the members, present and voting, of the Jurisdictional Conferences which are involved after consideration by the Committees on Episcopacy. After the above procedures have been followed, the transferring bishop shall become a member of the receiving College of Bishops and shall be subject to residential assignment by that Jurisdictional Conference.

---

[43]*See* Judicial Council Decision 424.

A bishop may be assigned by the Council of Bishops for presidential service or other temporary service in another jurisdiction than that which elected the bishop, provided request is made by a majority of the bishops in the jurisdiction of the proposed service.

In the case of an emergency in any jurisdiction or Central Conference through the death or disability of a bishop or other cause, the Council of Bishops may assign a bishop from another jurisdiction or Central Conference to the work of the said jurisdiction or Central Conference with the consent of a majority of the bishops of that jurisdiction or Central Conference.

¶ **55.** *Article VI.*—The bishops, both active and retired, of The Evangelical United Brethren Church and of The Methodist Church at the time union is consummated, shall be bishops of The United Methodist Church.

The bishops of The Methodist Church elected by the jurisdictions, the active bishops of The Evangelical United Brethren Church at the time of union, and bishops elected by the jurisdictions of The United Methodist Church shall have life tenure. Each bishop elected by a Central Conference of The Methodist Church shall have such tenure as the Central Conference electing him shall have determined.[44]

The Jurisdictional Conference shall elect a standing Committee on Episcopacy, to consist of one ministerial and one lay delegate from each Annual Conference, on nomination of the Annual Conference delegation. The committee shall review the work of the bishops, pass on their character and official administration, and report to the Jurisdictional Conference its findings for such action as the conference may deem appropriate within its constitutional warrant of power. The committee shall recommend the assignments of the bishops to their respective residences for final action by the Jurisdictional Conference.

¶ **56.** *Article VII.*—A bishop presiding over an Annual, Central, or Jurisdictional Conference shall decide all questions of law coming before the bishop in the regular business

---

[44]*See* Judicial Council Decisions 4, 303, 361.

of a session;[45] *provided* that such questions be presented in writing and that the decisions be recorded in the journal of the conference.

Such an episcopal decision shall not be authoritative except for the pending case until it shall have been passed upon by the Judicial Council. All decisions of law made by each bishop shall be reported in writing annually, with a syllabus of the same, to the Judicial Council, which shall affirm, modify, or reverse them.

¶ 57. *Article VIII.*—The bishops of the several Jurisdictional and Central Conferences shall preside in the sessions of their respective conferences.[46]

¶ 58. *Article IX.*—In each Annual Conference there shall be one or more district superintendents who shall assist the bishop in the administration of the Annual Conference and shall have such responsibilities and term of office as the General Conference may determine.[47]

¶ 59. *Article X.*—The bishops shall appoint, after consultation with the district superintendents, ministers to the charges; and they shall have such responsibilities and authorities as the General Conference shall prescribe.

DIVISION FOUR—THE JUDICIARY

¶ 60. *Article I.*—There shall be a Judicial Council. The General Conference shall determine the number and qualifications of its members, their terms of office, and the method of election and the filling of vacancies.

¶ 61. *Article II.*—The Judicial Council shall have authority:

1. To determine the constitutionality of any act of the General Conference upon an appeal of a majority of the Council of Bishops or one fifth of the members of the General Conference, and to determine the constitutionality of any act of a Jurisdictional or Central Conference upon an appeal of a

---

[45]*See* Judicial Council Decision 33.
[46]*See* Judicial Council Decision 395.
[47]*See* Judicial Council Decisions 368, 398.

majority of the bishops of that Jurisdictional or Central Conference or upon the appeal of one fifth of the members of that Jurisdictional or Central Conference.

2. To hear and determine any appeal from a bishop's decision on a question of law made in the Annual Conference when said appeal has been made by one fifth of that conference present and voting.

3. To pass upon decisions of law made by bishops in Annual Conferences.

4. To hear and determine the legality of any action taken therein by any General Conference board or Jurisdictional or Central Conference board or body, upon appeal by one third of the members thereof, or upon request of the Council of Bishops or a majority of the bishops of a Jurisdictional or a Central Conference.

5. To have such other duties and powers as may be conferred upon it by the General Conference.

6. To provide its own methods of organization and procedure.

¶ **62.** *Article III.*—All decisions of the Judicial Council shall be final. When the Judicial Council shall declare unconstitutional any act of the General Conference then in session, that decision shall be reported back to that General Conference immediately.

¶ **63.** *Article IV.*—The General Conference shall establish for the Church a judicial system which shall guarantee to our ministers a right to trial by a committee and an appeal and to our members a right to trial before the church, or by a committee, and an appeal.

DIVISION FIVE—AMENDMENTS

¶ **64.** *Article I.*—Amendments to the Constitution shall be made upon a two-thirds majority of the General Conference present and voting and a two-thirds affirmative vote of the aggregate number of members of the several Annual Conferences and Missionary Conferences present and voting, except in the case of the first, second, and seventh Restrictive Rules which shall require a three-fourths majority of all the members of the

Annual Conferences and Missionary Conferences present and voting. The vote, after being completed, shall be canvassed by the Council of Bishops, and the amendment voted upon shall become effective upon their announcement of its having received the required majority.[48]

¶ 65. *Article II.*—Amendments to the Constitution may originate in either the General Conference or the Annual Conferences.

¶ 66. *Article III.*—A Jurisdictional Conference may by a majority vote propose changes in the Constitution of the Church, and such proposed changes shall be submitted to the next General Conference. If the General Conference adopts the measure by a two-thirds vote, it shall be submitted to the Annual Conferences according to the provision for amendments.

---

[48]*See* Judicial Council Decisions 154, 243, 244, 349, 483.

Part II
DOCTRINE AND DOCTRINAL STATEMENTS AND THE GENERAL RULES[1]

¶ 67. SECTION 1—HISTORICAL BACKGROUND

The pioneers in the traditions that flowed together in The United Methodist Church—the Wesleys, Albright, Otterbein, Boehm—understood themselves as standing in the center stream of Christian spirituality and doctrine, loyal heirs to all that was best in the Christian past. As John Wesley had claimed, theirs was

> "the old religion, the religion of the Bible, the religion . . . of the whole church in the purest ages."

Their gospel was rooted in the biblical message of God's gracious response to man's deep need, in his self-giving love revealed in Jesus Christ. Their interest in dogma as such was minimal; thus they were able to insist on the integrity of Christian truth even while allowing for a decent latitude in its interpretation. This was the point to their familiar dictum: "As to all opinions *which do not strike at the root of Christianity,* we think and let think."

But, even as they were fully committed to the principles of

---

[1]It is the ruling of the Judicial Council that Sections I and III of this Part II "are legislative enactments and neither part of the Constitution nor under the Restrictive Rules" (*cf.* Judicial Council Decision 358; *see also* Decisions 41, 176).

40

religious toleration and doctrinal pluralism, they were equally confident that there is a "marrow" of Christian truth that can be identified and that must be conserved. This living core, as they believed, stands revealed in Scripture, illumined by tradition, vivified in personal experience, and confirmed by reason. They were very much aware, of course, that God's eternal Word never has been, nor can be, exhaustively expressed in any single form of words. They were also prepared, as a matter of course, to reaffirm the ancient creeds and confessions as valid summaries of Christian truth. But they were careful not to invest them with final authority or to set them apart as absolute standards for doctrinal truth and error.

In this same spirit, they also declined to adopt any of the classical forms of the "confessional principle"—the claim that the essence of Christian truth can, and ought to be, stated in precisely defined propositions, legally enforceable by ecclesiastical authority. Instead, they turned to a unique version of the ancient "conciliar principle," in which the collective wisdom of living Christian pastors, teachers and people was relied upon to guard and guide their ongoing communal life. Wesley's agency for this collegial process he called the *Conference,* and he was followed in this usage by both Albright and Otterbein. In its original aim and function, every United Methodist Conference, at whatever level, is both a consultative and legislative body, responsible for valid applications of church teaching and polity to theoretical and practical questions alike. The earliest agenda of Wesley's Conferences focused on three basic questions:

1. What to teach? (the substance of the gospel)
2. How to teach? (the proclamation of the gospel)
3. What to do? (the gospel in action)

Wesleyan Doctrinal Standards
The *Sermons* and the Notes

In addition to his own personal leadership and that of the Conference, Wesley provided his people with published sermons and a simplified biblical commentary for their doctrinal guidance. Over the span of fourteen years (beginning in 1746), he issued four volumes of forty-four *Sermons on Several Occasions,* in which he set forth the sum of his basic teaching on all the main themes of Christian doctrine, together with many of his own most distinctive theological opinions. In 1754 he prepared and published a volume of *Explanatory Notes Upon the New Testament* as a guide for Methodist biblical exegesis and doctrinal interpretation. In both the *Sermons* and the *Notes,* the primary doctrinal norm is Scripture, first and last, but always Scripture as interpreted by living tradition and vital faith. Indeed, his very first theological tract *(The Doctrine of Salvation, Faith and Good Works,* 1738) was a digest of the first five *Homilies* of the Church of England (1547).

It was inevitable that the paired rights of Methodist preachers to freedom in their pulpits and of the Methodist people to the hearing of sound doctrine from their preachers would stir occasional conflicts requiring adjudication. Accordingly, in 1763, Wesley produced a "Model Deed" for his chapels, which stipulated the authority of their lay trustees, under the overall direction of the conference:

> . . the major part of the Trustees of the said premises, for the time being, shall from time to time, and at all times forever thereafter, permit such persons as shall be appointed at the yearly Conference of the people called Methodists, in London, Bristol, or Leeds, and no others, to have and enjoy the said premises for the purposes aforesaid: Provided always, that the said persons preach no other doctrine than is contained in Mr. Wesley's *Notes Upon the New Testament,* and four volumes of *Sermons.*

The aim here was not to impose an inflexible system of doctrine or to inhibit responsible intellectual freedom, but rather to provide a broad and flexible framework of doctrine which would define the outside limits for public teaching in the societies in disputed cases. These standards were more flexible than any of the classical creeds or confessions or articles; they gave the Methodists a measure of protection from doctrinal eccentricity, and they gave Methodist laymen a new role in the assessment of doctrinal standards. This particular collegial formula for doctrinal guidance was unique in Christendom. It committed the Methodist people to the biblical revelation as primary without proposing a literal summary of that revelation in any single propositional form. It anchored Methodist theology to a stable core, but allowed it freedom of movement in the further unfoldings of history.

The Wesleyan Perspective in the *Sermons* and the *Notes*

Even a brief synopsis of the *Sermons on Several Occasions* underscores the integral logic of the Christian message, as Wesley understood it. *Faith* is everywhere the foundation of all else—faith understood as trust, faith as man's grateful acceptance of God's gracious gift of pardon ("justification"). The prime effect of faith is to transform the believer's consciousness from an inward dread of God's justice to a lively assurance of his merciful, healing love in Christ. This is the theme of the first five sermons (I-V). The first fruits of faith of this sort are "righteousness," "the marks of the new birth," and "the witness of the Spirit"; these become the topics for the second sermon cluster (VI-XV). "The righteousness of faith" generates its own distinctive life-style, which has been delineated best of all in Jesus' Sermon on the Mount. Wesley, therefore, proceeds to devote his largest single sermon bloc to an exposition of that Sermon—thirteen connected essays which amount to a broad-spectrum commentary on the ethical imperatives of grace (XVI-XXVIII). Here, he stresses the vital interplay between the freedom of the "Gospel" and the self-constraints of the moral "Law." Thus, in the following sermons, Wesley shows how a final polarization between these two may be avoided (XXIX-XXXIV). This brings him to the keystone-arch of his doctrinal "system": to "the fullness of faith"—which is what he meant by "Christian Perfection" (XXXV). After this, it was enough to add a concluding miscellany (XXXVI-XLIV) of practical advices on the personal and social implications of Christian faith in day-to-day Christian living (e.g., "the Use of Money," XLIV).

In the *Explanatory Notes* we may see Wesley's way of interpreting biblical language as conveying the mysteries and insights of revelation to the eyes of faith rather than merely literal propositions to philosophers and critics. Revelation is everywhere in Scripture and everywhere open to seeking minds, but always its summit and summation is Jesus Christ. Human understanding of biblical truth depends upon the Spirit's "inward testimony" in the hearts of faithful believers in the community of faith. Consequently, the primary aim of biblical interpretation is to guide the Christian seeker toward insights of his own, to assist him in his Christian witness, and to direct him in his mission of service to God and neighbor.

American Methodists and the Wesleyan "Standards"

From their beginnings, the Methodists in America understood themselves as the dutiful heirs of Wesley and the Wesleyan tradition. In 1773, they affirmed their allegiance to the principles of the "Model Deed" and ratified this again in 1784, when they stipulated that "The London Minutes," including the doctrinal minutes of the early Conferences and the Model Deed, were accepted as their own doctrinal guidelines. In this way they established a threefold agency—the *Conference*, the *Sermons*, and the *Notes*—as their guides in matters of doctrine.

The Articles of Religion

Wesley expected that the new American church would need a fundamental liturgy, and he undertook to provide this in his personal abridgment of the Book of Common Prayer (in its 1662 edition). This so-called "Sunday Service" included his revisions of the Thirty-Nine Articles of Religion (set as an appendix even as they also appeared in his own copy of the Book of Common Prayer). He reduced their number from thirty-nine to twenty-four and made slight textual revisions, chiefly by omission. In the earliest American *Disciplines* (beginning in 1788) these Articles (with an additional Article now numbered XXIII, asserting the autonomy of the new American nation) were also printed as an appendix. In 1792, without recorded authorization, they were moved forward to the front of the *Discipline*, where they have remained ever since. Then, when "The Sunday Service" failed to gain acceptance in the new church, the Articles survived in the

Discipline, where their prominence has seemed to suggest that they were more of a doctrinal "confession" than had ever been intended.

The original distinction between the intended functions of the Articles on the one hand, and of the *Sermons* and *Notes* on the other, may be inferred from the double reference to them in the First Restrictive Rule (adopted in 1808 and unchanged ever since). On the one hand, it forbids any further *alterations* of the Articles and, on the other, any further contrary *additions* "to our present existing, and established standards of doctrine" (i.e., the Minutes, *Sermons,* and *Notes*). At that time, the Wesleyan appeal to the fourfold norms of Scripture, tradition, experience, and reason was so widely understood that it was taken for granted.

The Fading Force of Doctrinal Discipline

In the climate of "The Second Great Awakening," the normative influence of European traditions was sharply diminished, especially on the opening frontier. Indeed, the great frontier revivals wrought a transformation in American Christianity generally. Critical reason as a criterion in theological reflection was applied unevenly at best. In the "free" churches especially, Christian doctrine focused more and more on "Christian experience," understood chiefly as "saving faith in Christ." Among the Methodists in particular there was a consistent stress on free will, infant baptism, and informal worship (and this led to protracted controversies with the Presbyterians, Baptists, and Episcopalians respectively). At the same time, Methodist concerns about formal standards of doctrine were correspondingly diminished. Indeed, it was the Wesleyan hymnody that served as the most important single means of communicating the doctrinal substance of the gospel and in its guardianship as well. By the end of the nineteenth century, and thereafter increasingly in the twentieth, Methodist theology had become decidedly eclectic, with less and less specific attention paid to its Wesleyan sources as such. Despite continued and quite variegated theological development, there has been no significant project in formal doctrinal re-formulation in Methodism since 1808.

Doctrinal Traditions in the Evangelical Church and the United Brethren Church

The unfolding of doctrinal concerns among the Albright Evangelicals and Otterbein's United Brethren in Christ has run a course roughly parallel to that of the Methodists—with such differences as there were springing largely from the different ecclesiastical heritage which they had brought from Germany and Holland, together with the mellowed Calvinism of the Heidelberg Catechism. In the German-speaking communities of America, Albright and Otterbein believed it more important to stress evangelism than theological speculation. Their constant and common stress was on "conversion," on "justification by faith confirmed by a sensible assurance thereof," on Christian nurture, on the priesthood of all true believers in a shared ministry of Christian witness and service, and on "entire sanctification" as the goal and crown of Christian life.

As with Wesley, their primary source and norm for Christian teaching was Scripture. Otterbein enjoined his followers "to be careful to preach no other doctrine than what is plainly laid down in the Bible." Each new member was asked "to confess that he received the Bible as the Word of God." Ordinands were required to affirm the plenary authority of Scripture "without reserve." Matched with these affirmations was the conviction that "converted" Christians are enabled by the Holy Spirit to read Scripture with a special "Christian consciousness," and this principle was prized as the supreme guide in biblical interpretation.

Jacob Albright was directed by the Conference of 1807 to prepare a list of Articles of Religion. Before he could attempt the task he died. George Miller then assumed the responsibility. He recommended to the Conference of 1809 the adoption of a German translation of the Methodist Articles of Religion, with the addition of a new one, "Of the Last Judgment." The recommendation was adopted. This suggests a conscious choice of the Methodist *Articles* as normative, since the added article was their only other borrowing—from the Augsburg Confession (Article XVII), on a theme strangely omitted in the Anglican Articles.

These Twenty-Six Articles were generally interpreted among the Albright Evangelicals in a typically non-dogmatic temper.

In 1816, the original Twenty-Six Articles were reduced to twenty-one by the excision of five of the most polemical ones in the earlier text: XI.—"Of Works of Supererogation," XIV.—"Of Purgatory," XIX.—"Of Both Kinds" (all aimed at Roman Catholics), XXI.—"Of the Marriage of Ministers" (aimed at both Roman Catholics and Anabaptists), and XXV.—"Of a Christian Man's Oath" (aimed originally at sixteenth century sectaries!). This act of deletion was a notable instance of a conciliar spirit in a time of bitter controversy.

In 1839, a few slight further changes were made in the text of 1816 and it was then stipulated that "the Articles of Faith . . . should be constitutionally unchangeable among us." In 1851, it was discovered that Article I had been altered without authorization, and this was promptly corrected. In the 1870's a proposal that the Articles be extensively revised touched off a flurry of debate, but the Conference of 1875 decisively rejected the proposal. In later action the Twenty-One Articles were reduced to nineteen in number by combining several of them, but without omitting any of their original content. These nineteen were brought intact into the Evangelical United Brethren union of 1946.

Among the United Brethren in Christ, a summary of normative teaching was formulated in 1813 by the disciples and colleagues of William Otterbein, Christian Newcomer, and Christopher Grosch. Its first three paragraphs follow the order of the Apostles' Creed. Paragraphs four and five affirm the primacy of Scripture and the universal proclamation of "the biblical doctrine . . . of man's fall in Adam and his deliverance through Jesus Christ." An added section commends "the ordinances of baptism and the remembrance of the Lord" and approves foot-washing as optional. In the first General Conference of the United Brethren in Christ (1815) a slight revision of this earlier statement was formally adopted as their official Confession of Faith. A further slight revision was adopted in 1841, with the stipulation that there should be no subsequent changes in the Confession:

No rule or ordinance shall at any time be passed to change or do away with the Confession of Faith as it now stands.

Even so, agitation for change continued, and in 1885 a Church Commission was appointed to:

prepare such a form of belief and such amended fundamental rules for the government of this church in the future as will, in their judgment, be best adapted to secure its growth and efficiency in the work of evangelizing the world.

The resulting proposal for a new Confession of Faith and Constitution was submitted to the general membership of the Church (the first such referendum on a Confession of Faith in its history) and was then placed before the General Conference of 1889. Both the general membership and the Conference approved it by preponderant majorities, and it was thereupon enacted by episcopal "Proclamation." However, this action was protested by a minority as a violation of the restrictive rule of 1841 and became a basic cause for a consequent schism (The United Brethren Church [Old Constitution]).

The Confession of Faith of 1889 was more comprehensive than any of its antecedents, with articles on depravity, justification, regeneration and adoption, sanctification, the Christian Sabbath, and "the future state." Its article on sanctification, though brief, is significant in its reflection of the doctrine of holiness of the Heidelberg Catechism. It was this Confession of 1889 that was brought by the United Brethren into the union of 1946.

The Evangelical United Brethren Confession of Faith

In that union, the Evangelical Articles and the United Brethren Confession were both printed in the *Discipline* of the new Evangelical United Brethren Church. A dozen years later, however, the General Conference of the united church authorized its Board of Bishops to prepare a new Confession of Faith. This was done after extensive consultation. A new Confession, with sixteen Articles, of a somewhat more modern character than any of its antecedents, was presented to the General Conference of 1962 and adopted without amendment. In it the influence of the Evangelical statement on "Entire Sanctification and Christian Perfection" is reflected as a distinctive emphasis. This Confession was declared to supplant both former Articles and Confession, and was brought over intact into the *Discipline* of The United Methodist Church (1968).

Doctrinal Standards in the
United Methodist Church *Discipline* (1968)

In the Plan of Union for The United Methodist Church, the Preface to the Methodist Articles of Religion and the Evangelical United Brethren Confession of Faith explains that both had been accepted as doctrinal standards for the new church. It was declared that "they are thus deemed congruent if not identical in their doctrinal perspectives, and not in conflict." Additionally, it was stipulated that although the language of the First Restrictive Rule has never been formally defined, Wesley's *Sermons* and *Notes* were specifically included in our present existing and established standards of doctrine by plain historical inference. This, however, raises the question as to the status and function of "doctrinal standards" in The United Methodist Church without supplying a clear answer. There are abundant references throughout the *Discipline* to "our standards of doctrine"—along with prohibitions against contrary teaching and provisions for disciplinary action against deviant public teaching—but there is no precise reference to the "standards" thus referred to. The *Discipline* seems to assume that for the determination of otherwise irreconcilable doctrinal disputes, the Annual and General Conferences are the appropriate courts of appeal, under the guidance of the first two Restrictive Rules (which is to say, the Articles and Confession, the *Sermons* and the *Notes*).

There are, however, at least two general principles with respect to the discipline of doctrine in The United Methodist Church on which there has been broad and basic agreement. In the first place, the Articles and the Confession are *not* to be regarded as positive, juridical norms for doctrine, demanding unqualified assent on pain of excommunication. They are and ought to remain as important landmarks in our complex heritage and ought rightly to be retained in the *Discipline*. The United Methodist Church would be much the poorer if they were simply relegated to the attic of history's discards. But, since they are not accorded any status of finality, either in content or rhetoric, there is no objection in principle to the continued development of still other doctrinal summaries and liturgical creeds that may gain acceptance and use in the church—without displacing those we already have. This principle of the historical interpretation of all doctrinal statements, past and present, is crucial. Such statements never have been and ought not to be legal tests for membership. We should interpret them, appreciatively, in their historic contexts, seeking always to appropriate the contributions of our Christian past even as we also stretch forward toward the Christian future.

By the same token, there is likewise general agreement that The United Methodist Church stands urgently in need of doctrinal reinvigoration for the sake of authentic renewal, fruitful evangelism, and the effective discharge of our ecumenical commitments. Seen in this light, the recovery and updating of our distinctive doctrinal heritage—"truly catholic, truly evangelical and truly reformed"—takes on a high priority. It calls for a concerted double movement: zealous repossession of our traditions and also vigorous promotion of theological dialogue and development within the denomination and in all our ecumenical endeavors. There are many effective agencies in the Church that must share in the joint endeavor to stimulate an active interest in doctrinal standards and doctrinal statements—educational institutions, boards and agencies at every level, ministers and lay persons in the Conferences, the Council of Bishops, etc. At all these levels there is a pressing need of renewed effort both to repossess our legacy from the churches we have been and to re-mint this for the church we aspire to be.

The General Rules and Christian Social Concerns

No motif in the Wesleyan tradition has been more constant or insistent than the linkage between Christian doctrine and

Christian ethics. Methodists have always been strictly enjoined never to divorce faith from good works. This is mirrored in the abundance of "rules" and "directions" for the various groups in the Societies and their leaders. The most famous of these directives was Wesley's original pamphlet, "The Nature, Design and General Rules of the United Societies" (1743). In 1784, a slight revision of this earlier text was adopted by the American Methodists and has appeared in all subsequent *Disciplines,* with further slight revisions.

The General Rules were originally designed as moral directives for members of a religious society quite self-consciously included within the sacramental life of the Church of England. Wesley's own statement of the purpose of a Methodist Society is described in the Rules as "a company . . . united in order to pray together, to receive the word of exhortation, and to watch over one another in love, that they may help each other to work out their salvation." The terms of membership in these societies were simple and personal (and deliberately quite different from the conditions of church membership): "a desire to flee from the wrath to come and to be saved from their sins." But Wesley insisted that evangelical faith should manifest itself in evangelical living, and he spelled this out in his three-part formula in the Rules. There it is thrice-repeated that, "It is expected of all who continue therein that *they shall continue* to evidence *their desire of salvation*" by:

1. Doing no harm, avoiding evil, especially that which is most generally practiced, such as . . . (then follows a listing of specific examples).
2. Doing good of every possible sort and, as far as possible to *all* men . . .
3. By attending upon all the ordinances of God. Such are . . .

Wesley's illustrative cases under each of these three rules serve to remind us of the endless task of the Christian conscience in the constant crises of passing from general principles to actual ethical decisions. They range over many problems of self-restraint and social control; they touch on many of the great issues of what was then current secular policy, and they stress the crucial importance of private prayer and corporate worship—always as the spiritual spring of ethical action. It was clearly Wesley's intention that these three basic principles—"doing no harm, doing good and using the means of grace"—should be accepted as constants and that the inventories of their applied cases might be updated *at any time,* in keeping with changing times and circumstance. That he did not intend them to be interpreted in any legalistic spirit is plain from his second sermon on the Sermon on the Mount (XXII) where he repeats the same three rules and then denounces any undue reliance on them as "only the outside of that religion for which (the true believer) insatiably longs." This true religion he then defines as "the knowledge of God in Christ Jesus," "the life which is hid with Christ in God," and "the righteousness that (the true believer) thirsts after." And as Augustine before him, Wesley concludes: "Nor ever can he (the true believer) rest till thus he rests in God."

Upon such evangelical premises, United Methodists have sought to conceive and exercise their responsibility for the moral and spiritual quality of secular society. Our historic oppositions to smuggling, or slavery, or alcohol, or child labor etc., were, in each instance, founded in a vivid sense of God's wrath against human injustice and wastage. Our struggles for human dignity and social reform have reflected a vision of God's demand for justice, even as they have also reflected a woeful ambivalence in our actual ethical behavior. Intention here, as elsewhere, has all too often surpassed performance. And yet, on one point we have been clear, in principle at least: there is no "personal gospel" worth the name that does not express itself in relevant and effective social concerns; there is no "social gospel" that can be regarded as authentically Christian that is not rooted in our daily prayer— *"Thy* Kingdom come, *Thy* will be done *on earth!"*

In 1908, the Methodist Episcopal Church promulgated a Social Creed and was followed in this by the Methodist Episcopal Church, South, in 1914, and by the Methodist Protestants in 1916. In 1913 the United Brethren adopted the same general document in the form that had been ratified by the then newly formed Federal Council of Churches. In 1946, the present

Evangelical United Brethren statement on Social Issues and Moral Standards was formulated for the E.U.B. *Discipline*. Every United Methodist Annual and General Conference has produced its quota of resolutions and pronouncements seeking to apply the Christian vision of righteousness to current social, economic and political issues. It is crucial, however, that Christians should not confuse the *roots* and *fruits* of faith. Moral zeal apart from man's grateful response to God's unfailing grace tends either toward self-righteous and joyless moralism or else toward some variant of the cult of human self-sufficiency.

The last paragraph of the General Rules—providing for the expulsion of delinquent members of the Methodist Societies— poses the agonizing problem of how discipline is to be administered in a community of compassion in extreme cases. Originally, of course, there was no thought in Wesley's mind of "excommunication" from the sacraments—he had no canonical warrant for *that*. And he always stressed the therapeutic tasks of the religious society, so that expulsion from the society was never for any single lapse in itself, but for persistent disloyalty after patient warnings and prolonged pastoral counsel. But the problem persists even now in the changed circumstances of The United Methodist Church, since our *Discipline* provides for both reprimands and expulsions, of both pastors and laity—always in cases of last resort. The history of church discipline cannot always provide valid answers for particular cases. It does, however, point to two interacting general principles: *accountability* to the community of the church is an inherent obligation on those who claim that community's *support*. Support without accountability promotes moral weakness; accountability without support is a form of cruelty. A church that rushes to punishment is deaf to God's mercy; but a church lacking the conviction and courage to act decisively loses its claim to moral authority. One either side, the balance is struck only as the church understands itself primarily as a community of the reconciled and reconciling in Christ—in whom God continues to "reconcile the world to himself."

Conclusion

Legacies affect their heirs in different ways. Some are content to ignore them and never know their loss. Others cling too closely to their past and so forfeit its full value to themselves and others. Still others are led to seek appropriate ways of receiving what has been bequeathed them and of sharing it gladly with others. It is some such combination of loyalty and freedom that bespeaks the true liberty of Christian men and women—our true confidence in Christ's Lordship over our pasts and our futures. This was the way of Wesley and Albright and Otterbein—and still may be the way of their sons and daughters in the faith.

¶ 68. SECTION 2—FOUNDATION DOCUMENTS

[A Bibliographical Preface: The Articles of Religion are here reprinted from Wesley's original text in *The Sunday Service of the Methodists* . . . (1784), collated against their first printing in *A Form of Discipline, For The Ministers, Preachers, and Members of The Methodist Episcopal Church in America* (1788), and the text of the *Discipline* of 1812 (when the first Restrictive Rule took effect). To these are added two Articles: "Of Sanctification" and "Of The Duty of Christians to The Civil Authority," which are legislative enactments and not integral parts of the Constitution (cf. Judicial Council Decisions 41, 176). The text of the Confession of Faith is identical with that of its original in *The Discipline of The Evangelical United Brethren Church* (1963).

John Wesley's "standard" *Sermons* have been frequently reprinted from Thomas Jackson's edition of his *Works* (1829-31), most recently by the Zondervan Press (Grand Rapids, 1958). An annotated edition by E. H. Sugden—*The Standard Sermons of John Wesley*—was first published in 1921 and most recently reprinted in 1961. The most recent edition of *The Explanatory Notes Upon the New Testament* is that of John Lawson (London: Epworth Press, 1955). A selection of Wesley's sermons and doctrinal essays is included in the volume *John Wesley,* in A LIBRARY OF PROTESTANT THOUGHT (New York: Oxford University Press, 1964). The General Rules are printed here in the text of 1812 (when the fifth Restrictive Rule took effect).]

54

THE ARTICLES OF RELIGION
OF THE METHODIST CHURCH
(1784)

Article I.—Of Faith in the Holy Trinity

There is but one living and true God, everlasting, without body or parts, of infinite power, wisdom, and goodness; the maker and preserver of all things, both visible and invisible. And in unity of this Godhead there are three persons, of one substance, power, and eternity—the Father, the Son, and the Holy Ghost.

Article II.—Of the Word, or Son of God, Who Was Made Very Man

The Son, who is the Word of the Father, the very and eternal God, of one substance with the Father, took man's nature in the womb of the blessed Virgin; so that two whole and perfect natures, that is to say, the Godhead and Manhood, were joined together in one person, never to be divided; whereof is one Christ, very God and very Man, who truly suffered, was crucified, dead, and buried, to reconcile his Father to us, and to be a sacrifice, not only for original guilt, but also for the actual sins of men.

Article III.—Of the Resurrection of Christ

Christ did truly rise again from the dead, and took again his body, with all things appertaining to the perfection of man's nature, wherewith he ascended into heaven, and there sitteth until he return to judge all men at the last day.

Article IV.—Of the Holy Ghost

The Holy Ghost, proceeding from the Father and the Son, is of one substance, majesty, and glory with the Father and the Son, very and eternal God.

55

Article V.—Of the Sufficiency of the Holy Scriptures for Salvation

The Holy Scripture containeth all things necessary to salvation; so that whatsoever is not read therein, nor may be proved thereby, is not to be required of any man that it should be believed as an article of faith, or be thought requisite or necessary to salvation. In the name of the Holy Scripture we do understand those canonical books of the Old and New Testament of whose authority was never any doubt in the Church. The names of the canonical books are:

Genesis, Exodus, Leviticus, Numbers, Deuteronomy, Joshua, Judges, Ruth, The First Book of Samuel, The Second Book of Samuel, The First Book of Kings, The Second Book of Kings, The First Book of Chronicles, The Second Book of Chronicles, The Book of Ezra, The Book of Nehemiah, The Book of Esther, The Book of Job, The Psalms, The Proverbs, Ecclesiastes or the Preacher, Cantica or Songs of Solomon, Four Prophets the Greater, Twelve Prophets the Less.

All the books of the New Testament, as they are commonly received, we do receive and account canonical.

Article VI.—Of the Old Testament

The Old Testament is not contrary to the New; for both in the Old and New Testament everlasting life is offered to mankind by Christ, who is the only Mediator between God and man, being both God and Man. Wherefore they are not to be heard who feign that the old fathers did look only for transitory promises. Although the law given from God by Moses as touching ceremonies and rites doth not bind Christians, nor ought the civil precepts thereof of necessity be received in any commonwealth; yet notwithstanding, no Christian whatsoever is free from the obedience of the commandments which are called moral.

Article VII.—Of Original or Birth Sin

Original sin standeth not in the following of Adam (as the Pelagians do vainly talk), but it is the corruption of the nature of every man, that naturally is engendered of the offspring of Adam, whereby man is very far gone from original righteousness, and of his own nature inclined to evil, and that continually.

Article VIII.—Of Free Will

The condition of man after the fall of Adam is such that he cannot turn and prepare himself, by his own natural strength and works, to faith, and calling upon God; wherefore we have no power to do good work, pleasant and acceptable to God, without the grace of God by Christ preventing us, that we may have a good will, and working with us, when we have that good will.

Article IX.—Of the Justification of Man

We are accounted righteous before God only for the merit of our Lord and Saviour Jesus Christ, by faith, and not for our own works or deservings. Wherefore, that we are justified by faith, only, is a most wholesome doctrine, and very full of comfort.

Article X.—Of Good Works

Although good works, which are the fruits of faith, and follow after justification, cannot put away our sins, and endure the severity of God's judgment; yet are they pleasing and acceptable to God in Christ, and spring out of a true and lively faith, insomuch that by them a lively faith may be as evidently known as a tree is discerned by its fruit.

Article XI.—Of Works of Supererogation

Voluntary works—besides, over and above God's commandments—which they call works of supererogation, cannot be taught without arrogancy and impiety. For by them men do declare that they do not only render unto God as much as they are bound to do, but that they do more for his sake than the bounden duty is required; whereas Christ saith plainly: When you have done all that is commanded you, say, We are unprofitable servants.

Article XII.—Of Sin After Justification

Not every sin willingly committed after justification is the sin against the Holy Ghost, and unpardonable. Wherefore, the grant of repentance is not to be denied to such as fall into sin after justification. After we have received the Holy Ghost, we may depart from grace given, and fall into sin, and, by the grace of God, rise again and amend our lives. And therefore they are to be condemned who say they can no more sin as long as they live here; or deny the place of forgiveness to such as truly repent.

Article XIII.—Of the Church

The visible Church of Christ is a congregation of faithful men in which the pure Word of God is preached, and the Sacraments duly administered according to Christ's ordinance, in all those things that of necessity are requisite to the same.

Article XIV.—Of Purgatory[2]

The Romish doctrine concerning purgatory, pardon, worshiping, and adoration, as well of images as of relics, and also invocation of saints, is a fond thing, vainly invented, and grounded upon no warrant of Scripture, but repugnant to the Word of God.

Article XV.—Of Speaking in the Congregation in Such a Tongue as the People Understand

It is a thing plainly repugnant to the Word of God, and the custom of the primitive Church, to have public prayer in the

---

[2]For the contemporary interpretation of this and similar articles (i.e., Articles XIV, XV, XVI, XVIII, XIX, XX and XXI), *cf. A Resolution of Intent* of the General Conference of 1970 (*Journal,* pp. 254-55) and *The Book of Resolutions* (1968, pp. 65-72).

church, or to minister the Sacraments, in a tongue not understood by the people.

Article XVI.—Of the Sacraments

Sacraments ordained of Christ are not only badges or tokens of Christian men's profession, but rather they are certain signs of grace, and God's good will toward us, by which he doth work invisibly in us, and doth not only quicken, but also strengthen and confirm, our faith in him.

There are two Sacraments ordained of Christ our Lord in the Gospel; that is to say, Baptism and the Supper of the Lord.

Those five commonly called sacraments, that is to say, confirmation, penance, orders, matrimony, and extreme unction, are not to be counted for Sacraments of the Gospel; being such as have partly grown out of the *corrupt* following of the apostles, and partly are states of life allowed in the Scriptures, but yet have not the like nature of Baptism and the Lord's Supper, because they have not any visible sign or ceremony ordained of God.

The Sacraments were not ordained of Christ to be gazed upon, or to be carried about; but that we should duly use them. And in such only as worthily receive the same, they have a wholesome effect or operation; but they that receive them unworthily, purchase to themselves condemnation, as St. Paul saith.

Article XVII.—Of Baptism

Baptism is not only a sign of profession and mark of difference whereby Christians are distinguished from others that are not baptized; but it is also a sign of regeneration or the new birth. The baptism of young children is to be retained in the church.[3]

---

[3]*See* Judicial Council Decision 142.

Article XVIII.—Of the Lord's Supper

The Supper of the Lord is not only a sign of the love that Christians ought to have among themselves one to another, but rather is a sacrament of our redemption by Christ's death; insomuch that, to such as rightly, worthily, and with faith receive the same, the bread which we break is a partaking of the body of Christ; and likewise the cup of blessing is a partaking of the blood of Christ.

Transubstantiation, or the change of the substance of bread and wine in the Supper of our Lord, cannot be proved by Holy Writ, but is repugnant to the plain words of Scripture, overthroweth the nature of a sacrament, and hath given occasion to many superstitions.

The body of Christ is given, taken, and eaten in the Supper, only after a heavenly and spiritual manner. And the mean whereby the body of Christ is received and eaten in the Supper is faith.

The Sacrament of the Lord's Supper was not by Christ's ordinance reserved, carried about, lifted up, or worshiped.

Article XIX.—Of Both Kinds

The cup of the Lord is not to be denied to the lay people; for both the parts of the Lord's Supper, by Christ's ordinance and commandment, ought to be administered to all Christians alike.

Article XX.—Of the One Oblation of Christ, Finished upon the Cross

The offering of Christ, once made, is that perfect redemption, propitiation, and satisfaction for all the sins of the whole world, both original and actual; and there is none other satisfaction for sin but that alone. Wherefore the sacrifice of masses, in the which it is commonly said that the priest doth offer Christ for the quick and the dead, to have remission of pain or guilt, is a blasphemous fable and dangerous deceit.

Article XXI.—Of the Marriage of Ministers

The ministers of Christ are not commanded by God's law either to vow the estate of single life, or to abstain from marriage; therefore it is lawful for them, as for all other Christians, to marry at their own discretion, as they shall judge the same to serve best to godliness.

Article XXII.—Of the Rites and Ceremonies of Churches

It is not necessary that rites and ceremonies should in all places be the same, or exactly alike; for they have been always different, and may be changed according to the diversity of countries, times, and men's manners, so that nothing be ordained against God's Word. Whosoever, through his private judgment, willingly and purposely doth openly break the rites and ceremonies of the church to which he belongs, which are not repugnant to the Word of God, and are ordained and approved by common authority, ought to be rebuked openly, that others may fear to do the like, as one that offendeth against the common order of the church, and woundeth the consciences of weak brethren.

Every particular church may ordain, change, or abolish rites and ceremonies, so that all things may be done to edification.

Article XXIII.—Of the Rulers of the United States of America

The President, the Congress, the general assemblies, the governors, and the councils of state, *as the delegates of the people,* are the rulers of the United States of America, according to the division of power made to them by the Constitution of the United States and by the constitutions of their respective states. And the said states are a sovereign and independent nation, and ought not to be subject to any foreign jurisdiction.

Article XXIV.—Of Christian Men's Goods

The riches and goods of Christians are not common as touching the right, title, and possession of the same, as some do falsely boast. Notwithstanding, every man ought, of such things as he possesseth, liberally to give alms to the poor, according to his ability.

Article XXV.—Of a Christian Man's Oath

As we confess that vain and rash swearing is forbidden Christian men by our Lord Jesus Christ and James his apostle, so we judge that the Christian religion doth not prohibit, but that a man may swear when the magistrate requireth, in a cause of faith and charity, so it be done according to the prophet's teaching, in justice, judgment, and truth.

The following Article from the Methodist Protestant *Discipline* is placed here by the Uniting Conference (1939). It was not one of the Articles of Religion voted upon by the three churches.

Of Sanctification

Sanctification is that renewal of our fallen nature by the Holy Ghost, received through faith in Jesus Christ, whose blood of atonement cleanseth from all sin; whereby we are not only delivered from the guilt of sin, but are washed from its pollution, saved from its power, and are enabled, through grace, to love God with all our hearts and to walk in his holy commandments blameless.

The following provision was adopted by the Uniting Conference. This statement seeks to interpret to our churches in foreign lands Article XXIII of the Articles of Religion. It is a legislative enactment but is not a part of the Constitution. (*See* Judicial Council Decisions 41, 176, and Decision 6, Interim Judicial Council.)

Of the Duty of Christians to the Civil Authority

It is the duty of all Christians, and especially of all Christian ministers, to observe and obey the laws and commands of the governing or supreme authority of the country of which they are citizens or subjects or in which they reside, and to use all laudable means to encourage and enjoin obedience to the powers that be.

THE CONFESSION OF FAITH
OF THE EVANGELICAL UNITED BRETHREN CHURCH

Article I.—God

We believe in the one true, holy and living God, Eternal Spirit, who is Creator, Sovereign and Preserver of all things visible and invisible. He is infinite in power, wisdom, justice, goodness and love, and rules with gracious regard for the well-being and salvation of men, to the glory of his name. We believe the one God reveals himself as the Trinity: Father, Son and Holy Spirit, distinct but inseparable, eternally one in essence and power.

Article II.—Jesus Christ

We believe in Jesus Christ, truly God and truly man, in whom the divine and human natures are perfectly and inseparably united. He is the eternal Word made flesh, the only begotten Son of the Father, born of the Virgin Mary by the power of the Holy Spirit. As ministering Servant he lived, suffered and died on the cross. He was buried, rose from the dead and ascended into heaven to be with the Father, from whence he shall return. He is eternal Savior and Mediator, who intercedes for us, and by him all men will be judged.

Article III.—The Holy Spirit

We believe in the Holy Spirit who proceeds from and is one in being with the Father and the Son. He convinces the world of sin, of righteousness and of judgment. He leads men through faithful response to the gospel into the fellowship of the Church. He comforts, sustains and empowers the faithful and guides them into all truth.

Article IV.—The Holy Bible

We believe the Holy Bible, Old and New Testaments, reveals the Word of God so far as it is necessary for our salvation. It is to be received through the Holy Spirit as the true rule and guide for faith and practice. Whatever is not revealed in or established by the Holy Scriptures is not to be made an article of faith nor is it to be taught as essential to salvation.

Article V.—The Church

We believe the Christian Church is the community of all true believers under the Lordship of Christ. We believe it is one, holy, apostolic and catholic. It is the redemptive fellowship in which the Word of God is preached by men divinely called, and the sacraments are duly administered according to Christ's own appointment. Under the discipline of the Holy Spirit the Church exists for the maintenance of worship, the edification of believers and the redemption of the world.

Article VI.—The Sacraments

We believe the sacraments, ordained by Christ, are symbols and pledges of the Christian's profession and of God's love toward us. They are means of grace by which God works invisibly in us, quickening, strengthening and confirming our faith in him. Two sacraments are ordained by Christ our Lord, namely Baptism and the Lord's Supper.

We believe Baptism signifies entrance into the household of faith, and is a symbol of repentance and inner cleansing from sin, a representation of the new birth in Christ Jesus and a mark of Christian discipleship.

We believe children are under the atonement of Christ and as heirs of the Kingdom of God are acceptable subjects for Christian baptism. Children of believing parents through baptism become the special responsibility of the Church. They should be nurtured and led to personal acceptance of Christ, and by profession of faith confirm their baptism.

We believe the Lord's Supper is a representation of our redemption, a memorial of the sufferings and death of Christ, and a token of love and union which Christians have with Christ and with one another. Those who rightly, worthily and in faith eat the broken bread and drink the blessed cup partake of the body and blood of Christ in a spiritual manner until he comes.

Article VII.—Sin and Free Will

We believe man is fallen from righteousness and, apart from the grace of our Lord Jesus Christ, is destitute of holiness and inclined to evil. Except a man be born again, he cannot see the Kingdom of God. In his own strength, without divine grace, man cannot do good works pleasing and acceptable to God. We believe, however, man influenced and empowered by the Holy Spirit is responsible in freedom to exercise his will for good.

Article VIII.—Reconciliation Through Christ

We believe God was in Christ reconciling the world to himself. The offering Christ freely made on the cross is the perfect and sufficient sacrifice for the sins of the whole world, redeeming man from all sin, so that no other satisfaction is required.

Article IX.—Justification and Regeneration

We believe we are never accounted righteous before God through our works or merit, but that penitent sinners are justified or accounted righteous before God only by faith in our Lord Jesus Christ.

We believe regeneration is the renewal of man in righteousness through Jesus Christ, by the power of the Holy Spirit, whereby we are made partakers of the divine nature and experience newness of life. By this new birth the believer becomes reconciled to God and is enabled to serve him with the will and the affections.

We believe, although we have experienced regeneration, it is possible to depart from grace and fall into sin; and we may even then, by the grace of God, be renewed in righteousness.

Article X.—Good Works

We believe good works are the necessary fruits of faith and follow regeneration but they do not have the virtue to remove our sins or to avert divine judgment. We believe good works, pleasing and acceptable to God in Christ, spring from a true and living faith, for through and by them faith is made evident.

Article XI.—Sanctification and Christian Perfection

We believe sanctification is the work of God's grace through the Word and the Spirit, by which those who have been born again are cleansed from sin in their thoughts, words and acts, and are enabled to live in accordance with God's will, and to strive for holiness without which no one will see the Lord.

Entire sanctification is a state of perfect love, righteousness and true holiness which every regenerate believer may obtain by being delivered from the power of sin, by loving God with all the heart, soul, mind and strength, and by loving one's neighbor as one's self. Through faith in Jesus Christ this gracious gift may be received in this life both gradually and instantaneously, and should be sought earnestly by every child of God.

We believe this experience does not deliver us from the infirmities, ignorance, and mistakes common to man, nor from the possibilities of further sin. The Christian must continue on guard against spiritual pride and seek to gain victory over every temptation to sin. He must respond wholly to the will of God so that sin will lose its power over him; and the world, the flesh, and the devil are put under his feet. Thus he rules over these enemies with watchfulness through the power of the Holy Spirit.

Article XII.—The Judgment and the Future State

We believe all men stand under the righteous judgment of Jesus Christ, both now and in the last day. We believe in the resurrection of the dead; the righteous to life eternal and the wicked to endless condemnation.

Article XIII.—Public Worship

We believe divine worship is the duty and privilege of man who, in the presence of God, bows in adoration, humility and dedication. We believe divine worship is essential to the life of the Church, and that the assembling of the people of God for such worship is necessary to Christian fellowship and spiritual growth.

We believe the order of public worship need not be the same in all places but may be modified by the Church according to circumstances and the needs of men. It should be in a language and form understood by the people, consistent with the Holy Scriptures to the edification of all, and in accordance with the order and *Discipline* of the Church.

Article XIV.—The Lord's Day

We believe the Lord's Day is divinely ordained for private and public worship, for rest from unnecessary work, and should be devoted to spiritual improvement, Christian fellowship and service. It is commemorative of our Lord's resurrection and is an emblem of our eternal rest. It is essential to the permanence and growth of the Christian Church, and important to the welfare of the civil community.

Article XV.—The Christian and Property

We believe God is the owner of all things and that the individual holding of property is lawful and is a sacred trust under God. Private property is to be used for the manifestation of Christian love and liberality, and to support the Church's mission in the world. All forms of property, whether private, corporate or public, are to be held in solemn trust and used responsibly for human good under the sovereignty of God.

Article XVI.—Civil Government

We believe civil government derives its just powers from the sovereign God. As Christians we recognize the governments under whose protection we reside and believe such governments should be based on, and be responsible for, the recognition of human rights under God. We believe war and bloodshed are contrary to the gospel and spirit of Christ. We believe it is the duty of Christian citizens to give moral strength and purpose to their respective governments through sober, righteous and godly living.

THE GENERAL RULES
OF THE METHODIST CHURCH

The Nature, Design, and General Rules of Our United Societies

In the latter end of the year 1739 eight or ten persons came to Mr. Wesley, in London, who appeared to be deeply convinced of sin, and earnestly groaning for redemption. They desired, as did two or three more the next day, that he would spend some time with them in prayer, and advise them how to flee from the wrath to come, which they saw continually hanging over their heads. That he might have more time for this great work, he appointed a day when they might all come together, which from thenceforward they did every week, namely, on Thursday in the evening. To these, and as many more as desired to join with them (for their number increased daily), he gave those advices from time to time which he judged most needful for them, and they always concluded their meeting with prayer suited to their several necessities.

This was the rise of the **United Society,** first in Europe, and then in America. Such a society is no other than *"a company of men having the* form *and seeking the* power *of godliness, united in order to pray together, to receive the word of exhortation, and to watch over one another in love, that they may help each other to work out their salvation."*

That it may the more easily be discerned whether they are indeed working out their own salvation, each society is divided into smaller companies, called **classes,** according to their respective places of abode. There are about twelve persons in a class, one of whom is styled the **leader.** It is his duty:

1. To see each person in his class once a week at least, in order: (1) to inquire how their souls prosper; (2) to advise, reprove, comfort or exhort, as occasion may require; (3) to receive what he is willing to give toward the relief of the preachers, church, and poor.

2. To meet the ministers and the stewards of the society once a week, in order: (1) to inform the minister of any that are sick, or of any that walk disorderly and will not be reproved; (2) to pay the stewards what he has received of his class in the week preceding.

There is only one condition previously required of those who desire admission into these societies: "a desire to flee from the wrath to come, and to be saved from their sins." But wherever this is really fixed in the soul it will be shown by its fruits.

It is therefore expected of all who continue therein that they should continue to evidence their desire of salvation,

First: By doing no harm, by avoiding evil of every kind, especially that which is most generally practiced, such as:

The taking of the name of God in vain.

The profaning the day of the Lord, either by doing ordinary work therein or by buying or selling.

Drunkenness: buying or selling spirituous liquors, or drinking them, unless in cases of extreme necessity.

The buying or selling of men, women, and children with an intention to enslave them.

Fighting, quarreling, brawling, brother going to law with brother; returning evil for evil, or railing for railing; the using many words in buying or selling.

The buying or selling goods that have not paid the duty.

The giving or taking things on usury—i.e., unlawful interest.

Uncharitable or unprofitable conversation; particularly speaking evil of magistrates or of ministers.

Doing to others as we would not they should do unto us.

Doing what we know is not for the glory of God, as:

69

The putting on of gold and costly apparel.
The taking such diversions as cannot be used in the name of the Lord Jesus.
The singing those songs, or reading those books, which do not tend to the knowledge or love of God.
Softness and needless self-indulgence.
Laying up treasure upon earth.
Borrowing without a probability of paying; or taking up goods without a probability of paying for them.

It is expected of all who continue in these societies that they should continue to evidence their desire of salvation.

Secondly: By doing good; by being in every kind merciful after their power; as they have opportunity, doing good of every possible sort, and, as far as possible, to all men:

To their bodies, of the ability which God giveth, by giving food to the hungry, by clothing the naked, by visiting or helping them that are sick or in prison.

To their souls, by instructing, reproving, or exhorting all we have any intercourse with; trampling under foot that enthusiastic doctrine that "we are not to do good unless *our hearts be free to it.*"

By doing good, especially to them that are of the household of faith or groaning so to be; employing them preferably to others; buying one of another, helping each other in business, and so much the more because the world will love its own and them only.

By all possible diligence and frugality, that the gospel be not blamed.

By running with patience the race which is set before them, denying themselves, and taking up their cross daily; submitting to bear the reproach of Christ, to be as the filth and offscouring of the world; and looking that men should say all manner of evil of them *falsely,* for the Lord's sake.

It is expected of all who desire to continue in these societies that they should continue to evidence their desire of salvation.

Thirdly: By attending upon all the ordinances of God; such are:

The public worship of God.
The ministry of the Word, either read or expounded.

The Supper of the Lord.
Family and private prayer.
Searching the Scriptures.
Fasting or abstinence.

These are the General Rules of our societies; all of which we are taught of God to observe, even in his written Word, which is the only rule, and the sufficient rule, both of our faith and practice. And all these we know his Spirit writes on truly awakened hearts. If there be any among us who observe them not, who habitually break any of them, let it be known unto them who watch over that soul as they who must give an account. We will admonish him of the error of his ways. We will bear with him for a season. But then, if he repent not, he hath no more place among us. We have delivered our own souls.

¶ 69. SECTION 3—OUR THEOLOGICAL TASK

The Gospel in a New Age

United Methodists, along with all other Christians, are a pilgrim people under the Lordship of Christ. Both our heritage in doctrine and our present theological task share common aims: the continuously renewed grasp of the gospel of God's love in Christ and its application in the ceaseless crises of human existence. Our forefathers in the faith reaffirmed the ancient Christian message, even as they applied it to their immediate circumstances. Their innovative efforts serve as an encouraging precedent for our attempts to relate the gospel to the needs and aspirations of our contemporary world. The purpose in Christian theologizing is to aid people who seek understanding of their faith, authentic worship and celebration, effective evangelical persuasion, openness to God's concern for the world's agonies and turmoil, infusion of that faith in life and work, and courageous ministries in support of justice and love.

We are called to proclaim and live out the eternal gospel in an age of catastrophic perils and soaring hopes. Humanity stands nearer the brink of irreversible disaster than ever before. Our reckless disregard of nature's fragile balances, our rush to overpopulation, pollution, the exhaustion of basic ecological support systems, the proliferation of nuclear weaponry go on unchecked. Inhumanity toward our fellow human creatures poses clear and present dangers, not only to mankind's well-being, but even to bare survival. At the same time, visions of a more fully human quality of life for all mankind haunt our imaginations and stir our aspirations as never before. Science and technology may threaten to engulf us, but they also hold the promise of triumph over many of the age-old barriers to human self-realization. Hopes for justice, peace, dignity, and community have never been higher. Demands that all persons be accorded a growing share in the goods and goodness of life have never been more insistent.

We who are caught up in this perplexing situation seek to understand our Christian faith and interpret it to others. Such a task calls for profound and urgent moral decisions. We do not possess infallible rules to follow, or reflex habits that suffice, or precedents for simple imitation. Whatever may be our differences of heritage or mindset, we are forced to re-examine our convictions and alter our attitudes toward our own future and the human future as well.

In this task of reappraising and applying the gospel according to the conciliar principle, we recognize the presence of theological pluralism. It is true that some would wish traditional doctrinal statements and standards recovered and enforced; others would demand that they be repealed; some would urge that they be perfected; others would insist that they be superseded. When doctrinal standards are understood as legal or juridical instruments, it is easy to suppose that a doctrinal statement of some sort could be drawn up that would be normative and enforceable for an entire Christian body. Many persons with quite different views on doctrine insist that our inherited statements (e.g., the Articles, Confession, *Sermons, Notes,* and General Rules) ought either to be reaffirmed and enforced or superseded by new propositions. The effort to substitute new creeds for old has a long history of partisanship and schism.

Our older traditions and our newer experiments in ecumenical theology provide a constructive alternative to this confessional tradition. This is fortunate because the theological spectrum in The United Methodist Church ranges over all the current mainstream options and a variety of special-interest theologies as well. This is no new thing. Our founders supported what Wesley called "catholic spirit," which also prevails in much contemporary ecumenical theology. But theological pluralism must not be confused with "theological indifferentism"—the notion that there are no essential doctrines and that differences in theology, when sincerely held, need no further discussion. Our newer historical consciousness allows us to retain the various landmarks of our several heritages, interpreting them in historical perspective. Similarly, our awareness of the transcendent mystery of divine truth allows us in good conscience to acknowledge the positive virtues of doctrinal pluralism even within the same community of believers, not merely because such an attitude is realistic.

The invitation to theological reflection is open to all—young and old, unlettered and learned, persons of all cultures, ethnic groups, and races. Rightly understood, our history of doctrinal diversity in The United Methodist Church has been a source of strength, producing fruitful tension when accompanied with a genuine concern for the vital unity of Christian truth and life. United Methodists can heartily endorse the classical ecumenical watchword: "In essentials, unity; in non-essentials, liberty; and, in all things, charity" (love that cares and understands).

United Methodists and the Christian Tradition

United Methodists never undertake the task of theologizing as a totally new venture. We share a common heritage with all other Christians everywhere and in all ages. There is a core of doctrine .which informs in greater or less degree our widely divergent interpretations. From our response in faith to the wondrous mystery of God's love in Jesus Christ as recorded in Scripture, all valid Christian doctrine is born. This is the touchstone by which all Christian teaching may be tested. This is the focus of catholic belief by which United Methodists identify themselves with all other Christian bodies.

With them we acknowledge belief in the triune God—Father,

Son, and Holy Spirit. We hold common faith in the mystery of salvation in and through Jesus Christ. We proclaim together that, in our willful alienation, God judges us, seeks us, pardons us, and receives us, only because he truly loves us. We therefore believe that the Holy Spirit prompts us to respond in faith and enables us to accept God's gift of reconciliation and justification. This sense of common Christian heritage is rich in our hymnody and liturgies: sound doctrine is often expressed with greater persuasive power in song than prose. Here we borrow, and gladly share our own historic and current contributions. And we also honor the intent and import of the historic creeds and confessions, even as we encourage new ventures in contemporary affirmation and formulation.

Our participation in this common Christian tradition has carried with it a typically practical attitude toward theological reflection. Generally, we have been more interested in relating doctrine to life than in speculative analysis. The ethical fruits of faith concern us more than systems of doctrine. But the freedom we foster in this regard has been a function of our larger sense of belonging to the whole People of God. We gratefully claim our place in this common Christian history.

The theological substance of this common heritage begins with the biblical witness to God's reality as Creator and to his gracious self-involvement in the dramas of history. We find no words adequate to describe the mystery of goodness that sustains our hopes or the mystery of evil which can plunge us into chaos and despair. In the created order, designed for harmony and human fulfillment, disruptions have fractured man's good intentions and have frustrated the intended course of human history. Estranged from God, men and women wound themselves and one another and wreak havoc throughout the natural order. Human hopes for achieving the good are thwarted so long as we seek to realize such ends apart from God. But in the midst of our condition of alienation, God's unfailing grace shows itself in his suffering love working for our redemption.

At the heart of the gospel of salvation is God's self-presentation in Jesus of Nazareth. Scripture focuses on the witness to Jesus' life and teachings, his death and resurrection, and his triumph within and over the agonies of history. Those who even now find in him their clue to God's redeeming love also find their hearts and wills transformed. In his life we see the power and wisdom of God, confirming his new covenant with his people in the revelation of the fullness of human possibilities.

Christian teaching from its beginning has known God's redemptive love in Jesus Christ as actualized by the activity of the Holy Spirit, both in personal experience and in the larger community of believers called the Body of Christ. "Life in the Spirit" means for individuals the life of prayer and inward searching, but it also involves them in the communal life of the church: in its corporate worship, service and mission. The church becomes the sacramental community when, by adoration, proclamation, and self-sacrifice, its members become conformed to Christ. Persons are initiated and incorporated into this community of faith by Baptism and Confirmation and accept their membership as confirmed by the Holy Spirit. By continuing celebration of the Lord's Supper, or Holy Communion, the church participates in the risen and present Body of Christ, being thereby nourished and strengthened for faithful discipleship. With churches of many traditions United Methodists affirm Baptism and the Lord's Supper as the *two* principal sacraments given by God to his people.

In these and many other ways we join our fellow Christians, affirming within "the communion of saints" our oneness in Christ. With them we gladly declare that the forgiveness of sins and life eternal are ours through the power of God's invincible love. In this love we live and move and have our being. In this love God made and sustains the good earth and all creation. In this love he creates in our hearts a desire for true community and arouses our impulses to engage in unselfish service. It is this love that puts us under moral obligation and increases our joy. It is this love that defines our chief aim in life: "to glorify God and to enjoy him forever."

Distinctive Emphases of United Methodists

Within this tradition of common Christian belief, each of the several Christian churches has developed particular traditions of its own. Just as these separate traditions ought never to be appealed to in defense of sectarianism, certainly they cannot be ignored, scorned, or lightly abandoned. One of our avowed ecumenical commitments is that our own distinctive emphases shall not simply disappear, but be gathered into the larger Christian unity, there to be made meaningful in a richer whole. But this requires a deliberate effort on our part to engage in critical self-understanding, as church, if we are to offer our best gifts to the common Christian treasury. Such self-knowledge is prerequisite to any and all productive ecumenical partnership. Thus when we speak of our distinctive doctrinal emphases, we ought to do so as Christians involved in dialogue with each other.

United Methodists have emphasized God's endowment of each person with dignity and moral responsibility. We do not overvalue human nature in and of itself but, with Christian humanists in all ages, we view humanity and its destiny as chief among God's purposes in earthly history. More than that, we see the splendor of full and true humanity in Jesus Christ, as God's personal revelation. In this divine-human synergism, or cooperation, there is real interaction. God's initiative cannot be fulfilled in man until decisive human response is activated.

One of the most familiar accents in traditional United Methodist teaching has been on the primacy of grace. By grace we mean God's loving action in human existence through the ever-present agency of the Holy Spirit. Grace, so understood, is the spiritual climate and environment surrounding all human life at all times and in all places. In Christian experience, it is self-conscious and personal. Out of our heritage we gratefully reaffirm belief in "prevenient grace," the divine love that anticipates all our conscious impulses and that persuades the heart toward faith. But grace signifies also God's accepting and pardoning love: the active cause of our justification, by which we are made new creatures in Christ. Even the wonder of God's acceptance and pardon does not end the working of God's grace. He continues to nurture the believers as they "grow in grace" and in Christian understanding. Finally, grace in its fullness crowns the Christian life with the perfection of love (sanctification).

Another United Methodist family trait has been an active stress on conversion and the new birth. Whatever our language or labels for it, we hold that a decisive change in the human heart can

76

and does occur under the promptings of grace and the guidance of the Holy Spirit. Such a change may be sudden, dramatic, gradual, cumulative. Always it is a new beginning in a process. Christian experience as personal transformation expresses itself in many different thought-forms and life-styles. All of these have a common feature: faith working by love.

Perhaps the most widely cherished doctrinal emphasis among United Methodists is that faith and good works belong together. Guided by the Spirit, our understanding swings between two poles. On the one side, faith is intensely personal ("Christ is *my* Savior"; "Christ for *us!*"). On the other side, as the General Rules remind us, this inward assurance, if genuine, is bound to show itself outwardly in good works. By joining heart and hand, United Methodists have stressed that personal salvation leads always to involvement in Christian mission in the world. Thus we assert that personal religion, evangelical witness, and Christian social action are reciprocal and mutually reinforcing.

Finally, the United Methodist view of faith and its fruits is linked with a distinctive emphasis on polity. In our understanding of the church, there has been a long-standing tension between our original image of small, voluntary "religious societies" organized for Christian fellowship and the worldwide church which has developed in the course of two centuries. These twin concepts of "religious society" and "institutional church" with their respective values and concerns have never been wholly reconciled. On the one hand, the basic premise of the small group is the principle of "subsidiarity" or voluntary association and local initiative. It is in the local communities and in small groups within them that the Holy Spirit nurtures meaningful experiences which then seek wider avenues of mission and outreach. On the other hand, United Methodists, believing themselves led by the same Spirit, have a long tradition of connectional administration which binds us together in seeing our task as a whole, in efficient planning, and in deploying our material and human resources. The church seeks to encourage optimum freedom for local initiative and action. Local churches are responsive to the connectional leadership of the whole Church, while the connectional leadership is accountable to representatives of

Annual Conferences and local congregations. Church structures are designed to support the local congregation and to provide effective channels for faith in action.

Doctrinal Guidelines in The United Methodist Church

Since "our present existing and established standards of doctrine" cited in the first two Restrictive Rules of the Constitution of The United Methodist Church are not to be construed literally and juridically, then by what methods can our doctrinal reflection and construction be most fruitful and fulfilling? The answer comes in terms of our free inquiry within the boundaries defined by four main sources and guidelines for Christian theology: Scripture, tradition, experience, reason. These four are interdependent; none can be defined unambiguously. They allow for, indeed they positively encourage, variety in United Methodist theologizing. Jointly, they have provided a broad and stable context for reflection and formulation. Interpreted with appropriate flexibility and self-discipline, they may instruct us as we carry forward our never-ending tasks of theologizing in The United Methodist Church.

Scripture

United Methodists share with all other Christians the conviction that Scripture is the primary source and guideline for doctrine. The Bible is the deposit of a unique testimony to God's self-disclosures: in the world's creation, redemption and final fulfillment; in Jesus Christ as the incarnation of God's Word; in the Holy Spirit's constant activity in the dramas of history. It is the primitive source of the memories, images, and hopes by which the Christian community came into existence and that still confirm and nourish its faith and understanding. Christian doctrine has been formed, consciously and unconsciously, from metaphors and themes the origins of which are biblical.

As we immerse ourselves in the biblical testimony, as we open our minds and hearts to the Word of God through the words of persons inspired by the Holy Spirit, faith is born and nourished, our understanding deepens and develops, and both the core of faith and the range of our theological opinions are expanded and enriched.

As the constitutive witness to God's self-revelation, Scripture is rightly read and understood within the believing community and its interpretation is informed by the traditions of that community. Scripture texts are rightly interpreted in the light of their place in the Bible as a whole, as this is illumined by scholarly inquiry and personal insight. The meaning of each text is best understood when its original intention and significance have been grasped. From this careful handling of Scripture, under the guidance of the Holy Spirit, believers may appropriately apply the truth to the circumstances of their own time and place.

Tradition

Christian interpretations of the biblical revelation have a complex history. In every age, Christian people have formulated and reformulated their understandings of what they have received in doctrines and liturgies that interact upon each other. All church traditions profess themselves bound to Scripture for their original insights and may rightly be judged by their essential faithfulness to its disclosures. An uncritical acceptance of tradition amounts to traditional-*ism*, deliverance from which requires an adequate understanding of history as a resource for acquiring new wisdom. Traditions are the residue of corporate experience of earlier Christian communities. A critical appreciation of them can enlarge our vision and enrich faith in God's provident love.

In contemporary Faith and Order discussions of "Tradition and Traditions," three dimensions have been delineated. First, there is tradition as a historical process, a function of historical development. In this process Christian memories, and their interpretation, aid in reinterpreting the Christian message and ethos from person to person, region to region, generation to generation. Second, there are the multiple traditions of the various churches understood as sociological phenomena: the specific historical differentiations within denominations or between them (as in their several polities, liturgies, and doctrinal statements). Tradition, in this sense, serves as a partial aid to

Christians, in their separate denominations, in identifying and understanding themselves and one another. In a third sense, however, "the Christian tradition" may be spoken of transcendentally: as the history of that environment of grace in and by which all Christians live, which is the continuance through time and space of God's self-giving love in Jesus Christ. It is in this transcendent *tradition* that Christians who have been isolated from one another by various barriers of schism, race, and rivalries may recognize one another as Christians together. Through their appreciation of these complex and dynamic traditions, modern Christians may bridge the chasms that have for so long divided the Body of Christ.

Experience

Experience is to the individual as tradition is to the Church as a whole: the personal appropriation of God's unmeasured mercy in life and interpersonal relations. There is a radical distinction between intellectual assent to the message of the Bible and doctrinal propositions set forth in creeds, and the personal experience of God's pardoning and healing love. Traditionally, personal faith and assurance have been described as "a sure trust and confidence of the mercy of God, through our Lord Jesus Christ, and a steadfast hope of all good things at God's hand." This new relationship of assurance is God's doing, his free gift through his Holy Spirit. This "new life in Christ" is what is meant by the phrase "Christian experience." Such experience opens faith's eyes to living truth in Scripture, informs and guides the Christian conscience in ethical decisions, and illumines the Christian understanding of God and creation.

Christian experience is not only deeply private and inward; it is also corporate and active. The Bible knows nothing of solitary religion. God's gift of liberating love must be shared if it is to survive. The range of reconciliation must continually be widened to embrace the world and all who are alienated and who suffer. "Christian experience" carries with it the imperative to engage in ministries of liberation and healing in the world.

This specialized usage of the term "experience" implies that any particular personal experiences of God's accepting love will affect one's total understanding of life and truth. This changed and changing understanding, in turn, will alter the believer's mindset and world-view. This applies equally to the empirical sciences, the arts, philosophy, and culture in general. All religious experience affects all human experience; all human experience affects our understanding of religious experience.

Reason

Christian doctrines which are developed from Scripture, tradition, and "experience" must be submitted to critical analysis so that they may commend themselves to thoughtful persons as valid. This means that they must avoid self-contradiction and take due account of scientific and empirical knowledge, and yet we recognize that revelation and "experience" may transcend the scope of reason. Since all truth is from God, efforts to discern the connections between revelation and reason, faith and science, grace and nature are useful endeavors in developing credible and communicable doctrine.

No claims are made for reason's autonomy or omnicompetence, but it does provide tests of cogency and credibility. When submitting doctrinal formulations to critical and objectively rational analysis, our proper intention is to enhance their clarity and verifiability.

These Guidelines in Interaction

These four norms for doctrinal formulations are not simply parallel and none can be subsumed by any other. There is a primacy that goes with Scripture, as the constitutive witness to biblical wellsprings of our faith. In practice, however, theological reflection may find its point of departure in tradition, "experience," or rational analysis. What matters most is that all four guidelines be brought to bear upon every doctrinal consideration. Insights arising from serious study of the Scriptures and tradition enrich contemporary experience of existence. Imaginative and critical thought enables us to understand better the Bible and our common Christian history.

Theological Frontiers and New Directions

In charting a course between doctrinal dogmatism on the one hand and doctrinal indifferentism on the other, The United Methodist Church expects all its members to accept the challenge of responsible theological reflection. The absence of a single official theological system does not imply approval of theological perspectives currently dominant in the church, nor disapproval of any serious exploration across new theological frontiers or the confronting of new issues, of which there are many. Indeed, it welcomes all serious theological opinions developed within the framework of our doctrinal heritage and guidelines, so long as they are not intolerant or exclusive toward other equally loyal opinions.

Theological reflections do change as Christians become aware of new issues and crises. The Church's role in this tenuous process is to provide a stable and sustaining environment in which theological conflict can be constructive and productive. Our heritage and guidelines support this position. United Methodism in doctrinal lockstep is unthinkable. Fortified with doctrinal guidelines, we have a frame of reference which protects us from sliding into confusion. "Our present existing and established standards of doctrine" are not rigid or juridical. Flexibly interpreted and applied, they properly honor and respect the integrity of serious and thoughtful persons.

Of crucial current importance is the surfacing of new theological emphases focusing on the great struggles for human liberation and fulfillment. Notable among them are black theology, female liberation theology, political and ethnic theologies, third-world theology, and theologies of human rights. In each case, they express the heart cries that dehumanization has produced. They are theologies born of conflict. They reflect the consequences of tragic victimization and deep natural yearnings for human fulfillment. More positively, they agree in their demands for human dignity, true liberty, and genuine community. Since these aspirations are inherent elements in God's original design for his highest creation, we cannot resent or deny the positive objectives these theologies espouse nor withhold support from their practical implementation. Indeed, The United

Methodist Church encourages such developments so long as they are congruent with the gospel and its contemporary application. However, no special-interest theology can be allowed to set itself in invidious judgment over against any or all of the others, or claim exemption from being critically assessed in the general theological forum.

The United Methodist Church also takes seriously other widely variant theological emphases of our time. Some of these may be short-lived, others may last. We witness recurring expressions of neofundamentalism, new pentecostalism, new forms of Christian naturalism and secularity. These, allied with experimental forms of ministry and community, may speak to us as we consider and evaluate them within the framework of our doctrinal heritage and guidelines. All claims to Christian truth deserve an open and fair hearing for their sifting and assessment. The viability of all doctrinal opinion demands that the processes of theological development must be kept open-ended, both on principle and in fact.

No single creed or doctrinal summary can adequately serve the needs and intentions of United Methodists in confessing their faith or in celebrating their Christian experience. We accept the historic creeds and confessions as cherished landmarks of Christian self-consciousness and affirmation, even as we favor serious and informed theological experimentation. We believe that theologizing can be filled with excitement, in the composition of affirmations and liturgical confessions using new forms and language, whether produced by individuals or groups. We encourage the writing of hymns and poems, productions in the visual and performing arts, and multimedia presentations that seek to capture and communicate authentic Christian truth, along with sermons, articles, and scholarly books proclaiming the faith with freshness and enthusiasm. Such a stance supports the principle of local initiative in the Church's theological task. But once again, all such productions, if they are to be taken seriously, should meet the two conditions: careful regard for our heritage and fourfold guidelines, and the double test of acceptability and edification in corporate worship and common life.

The United Methodist Church has firmly and repeatedly committed itself to the cause of Christian unity and the processes of dialogue and negotiation that lead toward that goal. The function of doctrinal standards in such dialogue is to encourage United Methodist representatives to be knowledgeable and faithful in their representations of our heritage and its meeting points with other Christian traditions. Even so, any objection to possible agreement must root in a clear conviction that something truly essential is in jeopardy, something belonging not only to our own heritage but to the Christian tradition at large.

At the same time, we recognize that the ecumenical process has expanded across the boundaries of Christian unity to include serious interfaith encounters and explorations between Christianity and other living religions of the world—including modern secular religions of humanism, communism, and utopian democracy. While we are increasingly aware of the larger whole of the Christian movement, without which we would never have had any meaningful existence, we must also be conscious that God has been and is now working among all people. There is a new sense in which we now must realize that we are given to one another on this fragile small planet, to work out with God the salvation, health, healing, and peace he intends for all his people. In these less familiar encounters, our aims are not to reduce doctrinal differences to some lowest common denominator of religious agreement, but to raise all such relationships to the highest possible level of human fellowship and understanding. To this end, a self-conscious and self-critical understanding of our own tradition, along with appreciative, accurate understandings of other traditions, is necessary.

Doctrinal statements are not the special province of any single body, board, or agency in The United Methodist Church, nor is there any single doctrinal statement to be repeated or cited by all official pronouncements. As all members and groups are responsible for clarifying the theological premises on which they operate, they are likewise under the same rule of reference: loyalty to our heritage and guidelines, relevance to current needs and opportunities.

Doctrine arises in the ongoing life of the Church—its worship, its crises of faith, its conflicts within, its challenges from the world which it seeks to serve. The processes of evangelism, nurture, and mission require a constant effort in translating authentic experience into rational thought, and rational thought into effective action. But the process works both ways: our efforts in Christian action and its consequences provide us with new dimensions of Christian experience and, therefore, with new data for theological reflection and doctrinal statement.

Conclusion

Serious concern for our "doctrine and doctrinal standards" should inform, evaluate, and strengthen all the forms of ministry by which we fulfill our calling. Occasionally, they have been considered impediments rather than motivations to new and creative ministries. Doctrine and doctrinal standards are never an end in themselves, nor even a resting place along the way. They must be a springboard from which we are propelled into creative living and our tasks as agents of reconciliation in the name of the loving God. Our shared tradition with all other Christians, as well as the distinctive United Methodist emphases, is the context in which we work. Our sources and guidelines of theology—Scripture, tradition, experience, and reason—mark out the broad boundaries of our endeavor.

As United Methodists see more clearly who we have been, as we understand more concretely what are the needs of the world, as we learn more effectively how to use our heritage and guidelines, we will become more and more able to fulfill our calling as a pilgrim people and discern who we may become. It is in this spirit that we seek to engage in the theological task with a confidence born of obedience, and we invite all our people to a continuing enterprise: to understand our faith in God's love, known in Jesus Christ, more and more profoundly and to give this love more and more effective witness in word, work, mission, and life.

Part III
SOCIAL PRINCIPLES

PREFACE

The United Methodist Church has a long history of concern for social justice. Its members have often taken forthright positions on controversial issues involving Christian principles. Early Methodists expressed their opposition to the slave trade, to smuggling, and to the cruel treatment of prisoners.

A social creed was adopted by the Methodist Episcopal Church (North) in 1908. Within the next decade similar statements were adopted by the Methodist Episcopal Church, South, and by the Methodist Protestant Church. The Evangelical United Brethren Church adopted a statement of social principles in 1946 at the time of the uniting of the United Brethren and The Evangelical Church. In 1972, four years after the uniting in 1968 of the Methodist Church and the Evangelical United Brethren Church, the General Conference of the United Methodist Church adopted a new statement of Social Principles, which was revised in 1976.

The Social Principles are a prayerful and thoughtful effort on the part of the General Conference to speak to the human issues in the contemporary world from a sound biblical and theological foundation as historically demonstrated in United Methodist traditions. They are intended to be instructive and persuasive in the best of the prophetic spirit. The Social Principles are a call to all members of The United Methodist Church to a prayerful, studied dialogue of faith and practice.

PREAMBLE

We, the people called United Methodists, affirm our faith in God our Father, in Jesus Christ our Savior, and in the Holy Spirit, our Guide and Guard.

We acknowledge our complete dependence upon God in birth, in life, in death, and in life eternal. Secure in God's love, we affirm the goodness of life and confess our many sins against God's will for us as we find it in Jesus Christ. We have not always been faithful stewards of all that has been committed to us by God the Creator. We have been reluctant followers of Jesus Christ in his mission to bring all persons into a community of love. Though called by the Holy Spirit to become new creatures in Christ, we have resisted the further call to become the people of God in our dealings with each other and the earth on which we live.

Grateful for God's forgiving love, in which we live and by which we are judged, and affirming our belief in the inestimable worth of each individual, we renew our commitment to become faithful witnesses to the gospel, not alone to the ends of earth, but also to the depths of our common life and work.

¶ 70.   I. THE NATURAL WORLD

All creation is the Lord's and we are responsible for the ways in which we use and abuse it. Water, air, soil, minerals, energy resources, plants, animal life, and space are to be valued and conserved because they are God's creation and not solely because they are useful to human beings. Therefore, we repent of our devastation of the physical and nonhuman world. Further, we recognize the responsibility of the Church toward life style and systematic changes in society that will promote a more ecologically just world and a better quality of life for all creation.

A) Water, Air, Soil, Minerals, Plants.—We support and encourage social policies designed to rejuvenate polluted water, air, and soil, as well as those that would prevent further desecration of these natural elements. We support measures which will halt the spread of deserts into formerly productive lands. We support regulations designed to protect plant life, including those that provide for reforestation and for conservation of grasslands. We urge policies that retard the indiscriminate use of chemicals, including pesticides, and encourage adequate research into their effects upon God's creation prior to utilization. We urge development of international agreements concerning equitable utilization of the ocean's resources for human benefit so long as the integrity of the seas is maintained. Moreover, we support policies on the part of governments and industries that conserve fossil and other fuels, and that eliminate methods of securing minerals that destroy plants, animals, and soil. We encourage creation of new sources for food and power, while maintaining the goodness of the earth.

B) Energy Resources Utilization.—We support and encourage social policies that are directed toward rational and restrained transformation of parts of the nonhuman world into energy for human usage, and which de-emphasize or eliminate energy-producing technologies that endanger the health, safety, and even existence of the present and future human and nonhuman creation. Further, we urge wholehearted support of the conservation of energy and responsible development of all energy resources, with special concern for the development of renewable energy sources, that the goodness of the earth may be affirmed.

C) Animal Life.—We support regulations that protect the life and health of animals, including those ensuring the humane treatment of pets and other domestic animals, and the painless slaughtering of meat animals, fish, and fowl. Furthermore, we encourage the preservation of animal species now threatened with extinction.

D) Space.—The moon, planets, stars, and the space between and among them are the creation of God and are due the respect we are called to give the earth. We support the extension of knowledge through space exploration, but only when that knowledge is used for the welfare of humanity.

¶ 71. II. THE NURTURING COMMUNITY

The community provides the potential for nurturing human beings into the fullness of their humanity. We believe we have a responsibility to innovate, sponsor, and evaluate new forms of community that will encourage development of the fullest potential in individuals. Primary for us is the gospel understanding that all persons are important—because they are human beings and not because they have merited significance. We therefore support social climates in which human communities are maintained and strengthened for the sake of every person.

A) The Family.—We believe the family to be the basic human community through which persons are nurtured and sustained in mutual love, responsibility, respect, and fidelity. We understand the family as encompassing a wider range of options than that of the two-generational unit of parents and children (the nuclear family), including the extended family, families with adopted children, single parents, couples without children. We affirm shared responsibility for parenting by men and women and encourage social, economic, and religious efforts to maintain and strengthen relationships within families in order that every member may be assisted toward complete personhood.

B) Other Christian Communities.—We further recognize the movement to find new patterns of Christian nurturing communities such as Koinonia Farms, certain monastic and other religious orders, and some types of corporate church life. We urge the Church to seek ways of understanding the needs and concerns of such Christian groups and to find ways of ministering to them and through them.

C) Marriage.—We affirm the sanctity of the marriage covenant which is expressed in love, mutual support, personal commitment, and shared fidelity between a man and a woman. We believe that God's blessing rests upon such marriage, whether or not there are children of the union. We reject social norms that assume different standards for women than for men in marriage.

D) Divorce.—Where marriage partners, even after thoughtful consideration and counsel, are estranged beyond reconciliation, we recognize divorce as regrettable but recognize the right of divorced persons to remarry. We express our deep concern for the care and nurture of the children of divorced and/or remarried persons. We encourage that either or both of the divorced parents be considered for custody of the minor children of the marriage. We encourage an active, accepting, and enabling commitment of the church and our society to minister to the members of divorced families.

E) Single Persons.—We affirm the integrity of single persons, and we reject all social practices that discriminate or social attitudes that are prejudicial against persons because they are unmarried.

F) Human Sexuality.—We recognize that sexuality is a good gift of God, and we believe persons may be fully human only when that gift is acknowledged and affirmed by themselves, the Church, and society. We call all persons to disciplines that lead to the fulfillment of themselves, others, and society in the stewardship of this gift. Medical, theological, and humanistic disciplines should combine in a determined effort to understand human sexuality more completely.

Although men and women are sexual beings whether or not they are married, sex between a man and a woman is only to be clearly affirmed in the marriage bond. Sex may become exploitative within as well as outside marriage. We reject all sexual expressions which damage or destroy the humanity God has given us as birthright, and we affirm only that sexual expression which enhances that same humanity, in the midst of diverse opinion as to what constitutes that enhancement.

We deplore all forms of the commercialization and exploitation of sex with their consequent cheapening and degradation of human personality. We call for stern enforcement of laws prohibiting the sexual exploitation or use of children by adults. We call for the establishment of adequate protective services, guidance, and counseling opportunities for children thus abused.

We recognize the continuing need for full and frank sex education opportunities for children, youth, and adults.

Homosexual persons no less than heterosexual persons are individuals of sacred worth, who need the ministry and guidance of the Church in their struggles for human fulfillment, as well as the spiritual and emotional care of a fellowship which enables reconciling relationships with God, with others, and with self. Further we insist that all persons are entitled to have their human and civil rights ensured, though we do not condone the practice of homosexuality and consider this practice incompatible with Christian teaching.

G) Abortion.—The beginning of life and the ending of life are the God-given boundaries of human existence. While individuals have always had some degree of control over when they would die, they now have the awesome power to determine when and even whether new individuals will be born. Our belief in the sanctity of unborn human life makes us reluctant to approve abortion. But we are equally bound to respect the sacredness of the life and well-being of the mother, for whom devastating damage may result from an unacceptable pregnancy. In continuity with past Christian teaching, we recognize tragic conflicts of life with life that may justify abortion. We call all Christians to a searching and prayerful inquiry into the sorts of conditions that may warrant abortion. We support the legal option of abortion under proper medical procedures. Nevertheless, governmental laws and regulations do not necessarily provide all the guidance required by the informed Christian conscience. Therefore, a decision concerning abortion should be made only after thoughtful and prayerful consideration by the parties involved, with medical, pastoral, and other appropriate counsel.

H) Death with Dignity.—We applaud medical science for efforts to prevent disease and illness and for advances in treatment that extend the meaningful life of human beings. At the same time, in the varying stages of death and life that advances in medical science have occasioned, we recognize the agonizing personal and moral decisions faced by the dying, their physicians, their families, and their friends. Therefore, we assert the right of every person to die in dignity, with loving personal care and without efforts to prolong terminal illnesses merely because the technology is available to do so.

¶ 72.   III. THE SOCIAL COMMUNITY

The rights and privileges a society bestows upon or withholds from those who comprise it indicate the relative esteem in which that society holds particular persons and groups of persons. We affirm all persons as equally valuable in the sight of God. We therefore work toward societies in which each person's value is recognized, maintained, and strengthened.

A) Rights of Racial and Ethnic Minorities.—Racism plagues and cripples our growth in Christ, inasmuch as it is antithetical to the gospel itself. Therefore, we reject racism in every form, and affirm the ultimate and temporal worth of all persons. We rejoice in the gifts which particular ethnic histories and cultures bring to our total life. We commend and encourage the self-awareness of all racial and ethnic minorities and oppressed people which leads them to demand their just and equal rights as members of society. We assert the obligation of society, and groups within the society, to implement compensatory programs that redress long-standing systematic social deprivation of racial and ethnic minorities. We further assert the right of members of racial and ethnic minorities to equal opportunities in employment and promotion; to education and training of the highest quality; to nondiscrimination in voting, in access to public accommodations, and in housing purchase or rental; and positions of leadership and power in all elements of our life together.

B) Rights of Religious Minorities.—Religious persecution has been common in the history of civilization. We urge politics and practices that ensure the right of every religious group to exercise its faith free from legal, political, or economic restrictions. In particular, we condemn anti-Semitism in both its overt and covert forms, and assert the right of all religions and their adherents to freedom from legal, economic, and social discrimination.

C) Rights of Children.—Once considered the property of their parents, children are now acknowledged to be full human beings in their own right, but beings to whom adults and society in general have special obligations. Thus, we support the development of school systems and innovative methods of education designed to assist every child toward full humanity. All children have the right to quality education, including a full sexual education appropriate to their stage of development that utilizes the best educational techniques and insights. Moreover, children have the rights to food, shelter, clothing, health care, and emotional well-being as do adults, and these rights we affirm as theirs regardless of actions or inactions of their parents or guardians. In particular, children must be protected from economic and sexual exploitation.

D) Rights of Youth and Young Adults.—Our society is characterized by a large population of youth and young adults who frequently find full participation in society difficult. Therefore, we urge development of policies that encourage inclusion of youth and young adults in decision-making processes and that eliminate discrimination and exploitation. Creative and appropriate employment opportunities should be legally and socially available for youth and young adults.

E) Rights of the Aging.—In a society that places primary emphasis upon youth, those growing old in years are frequently isolated from the mainstream of social existence. We support social policies that integrate the aging into the life of the total community, including sufficient incomes, increased and non-discriminatory employment opportunities, and adequate medical care and housing within existing communities. We urge social policies and programs that ensure to the aging the respect and dignity that is their right as senior members of the human community.

F) Rights of Women.—We affirm women and men to be equal in every aspect of their common life. We, therefore, urge that every effort be made to eliminate sex role stereotypes in activity and portrayal of family life and in all aspects of voluntary and compensatory participation in the church and society. We affirm the right of women to equal treatment in employment, responsibility, promotion, and compensation. We affirm the importance of women in decision-making positions at all levels of church life and urge such bodies to guarantee their presence through policies of employment and recruitment. We urge employers of persons in dual career families, both in the church and society, to apply proper consideration of both parties when relocation is considered.

G) Rights of Persons with Handicapping Conditions.—We recognize and affirm the full humanity and personhood of all individuals as members of the family of God. We affirm the responsibility of the church and society to be in ministry with all persons, including those persons with mental, physical and/or psychologically handicapping conditions whose disabilities or differences in appearance or behavior create a problem in mobility, communication, intellectual comprehension, or personal relationships, which interfere with their participation or that of their families in the life of the church and the community. We urge the church and society to receive the gifts of persons with handicapping conditions to enable them to be full participants in the community of faith. We call the church and society to be sensitive to, and advocate programs of rehabilitation, services, employment, education, appropriate housing and transportation.

H) Population.—Since growing populations will increasingly strain the world's supply of food, minerals, and water, and sharpen international tensions, the reduction of the rate of consumption of resources by the affluent and the reduction of current population growth rates have become imperative. People have the duty to consider the impact on the total society of their decisions regarding childbearing, and should have access to information and appropriate means to limit their fertility, including voluntary sterilization. We affirm that programs to achieve a stabilized population should be placed in a context of total economic and social development, including an equitable use and control of resources; improvement in the status of women in all cultures; a human level of economic security, health care, and literacy for all.

I) Alcohol and Other Drugs.—We affirm our long-standing support of abstinence from alcohol as a faithful witness to God's liberating and redeeming love for persons. We also recommend abstinence from the use of marijuana and any illegal drugs. As the use of alcohol or tobacco is a major factor in both disease and death, we support educational programs encouraging abstinence from such use.

Millions of living human beings are testimony to the beneficial consequences of therapeutic drug use, and millions of others are testimony to the detrimental consequences of drug misuse. We encourage wise policies relating to the availability of potentially beneficial or potentially damaging prescription and over-the-counter drugs; we urge that complete information about their use and misuse be readily available to both doctor and patient. We support the strict administration of laws regulating the sale and distribution of all opiates. We support regulations that protect society from users of drugs of any kind where it can be shown that a clear and present social danger exists. The drug dependent person is an individual of infinite human worth in need of treatment and rehabilitation, and misuse should be viewed as a symptom of underlying disorders for which remedies should be sought.

J) Medical Experimentation.—Physical and mental health has been greatly enhanced through discoveries by medical science. It is imperative, however, that governments and the medical profession carefully enforce the requirements of the prevailing medical research standard, maintaining rigid controls in testing new technologies and drugs utilizing human beings. The standard requires that those engaged in research shall use human beings as research subjects only after obtaining full, rational, and uncoerced consent.

K) Rural Life.—We support the right of persons and families to live and prosper as farmers, farm workers, merchants, professionals, and others outside of the cities and metropolitan centers. We believe our culture is impoverished and our people deprived of a meaningful way of life when rural and small-town living becomes difficult or impossible. We recognize that the improvement of this way of life may sometimes necessitate the use of some lands for nonagricultural purposes. We oppose the indiscriminate diversion of agricultural land for nonagricultural uses when nonagricultural land is available. Further, we encourage the preservation of appropriate lands for agriculture and open space uses through thoughtful land use programs. We support governmental and private programs designed to benefit the resident farmer rather than the factory farm, and programs that encourage industry to locate in nonurban areas.

L) Urban-Suburban Life.—Urban-suburban living has become a dominant style of life for more and more persons. For many it furnishes economic, educational, social, and cultural opportunities. For others, it has brought alienation, poverty, and depersonalization. We in the Church have an opportunity and responsibility to help shape the future of urban-suburban life. Massive programs of renewal and social planning are needed to bring a greater degree of humanization into urban-suburban life styles. Christians must judge all programs, including economic and community development, new towns, and urban renewal by the extent to which they protect and enhance human values, permit personal and political involvement, and make possible neighborhoods open to persons of all races, ages, and income levels. We affirm the efforts of all developers who place human values at the heart of their planning. We must help shape urban-suburban development so it provides for the human need to identify with and find meaning in smaller social communities. At the same time such smaller communities must be encouraged to assume responsibilities for the total urban-suburban community instead of isolating themselves from it.

¶ 73.　IV. THE ECONOMIC COMMUNITY

We claim all economic systems to be under the judgment of God no less than other facets of the created order. Therefore, we recognize the responsibility of governments to develop and implement sound fiscal and monetary policies that provide for the economic life of individuals and corporate entities, and that ensure full employment and adequate incomes with a minimum of inflation. We believe private and public economic enterprises are responsible for the social costs of doing business, such as unemployment and environmental pollution, and that they should be held accountable for these costs. We support measures that would reduce the concentration of wealth in the hands of a few. We further support efforts to revise tax structures and eliminate governmental support programs that now benefit the wealthy at the expense of other persons.

A) Property.—We believe private ownership of property is a trusteeship under God, both in those societies where it is encouraged and where it is discouraged, but is limited by the over-riding needs of society. We believe that Christian faith denies to any person or group of persons exclusive and arbitrary control of any other part of the created universe. Socially and culturally conditioned ownership of property is, therefore, to be considered a responsibility to God. We believe, therefore, governments have the responsibility, in the pursuit of justice and order under law, to provide procedures that protect the rights of the whole society, as well as those of private ownership.

B) Collective Bargaining.—We support the right of public and private (including farm, government, institutional, and domestic) employees and employers to organize for collective bargaining into unions and other groups of their own choosing. Further, we support the right of both parties to protection in so doing, and their responsibility to bargain in good faith within the framework of the public interest. In order that the rights of all members of the society may be maintained and promoted, we support innovative bargaining procedures that include representatives of the public interest in negotiation and settlement of labor-management contracts including some that may lead to forms of judicial resolution of issues.

C) Work and Leisure.—Every person has the right and responsibility to work for the benefit of himself or herself and the enhancement of human life and community and to receive adequate remuneration. We support social measures that ensure the physical and mental safety of workers, that provide for the equitable division of products and services and that encourage an increasing freedom in the way individuals may use their leisure time. We recognize the opportunity leisure provides for creative contributions to society and encourage methods that allow workers additional blocks of discretionary time. We support educational, cultural, and recreational outlets that enhance the use of such time. We believe that persons come before profits. We deplore the selfish spirit which often pervades our economic life. We support policies which encourage workplace democracy, cooperative and collective work arrangements. We support rights of workers to refuse to work in situations that endanger health and/or life, without jeopardy to their jobs. We support policies which would reverse the increasing concentration of business and industry into monopolies.

D) Consumption.—We support efforts to ensure truth in pricing, packaging, lending, and advertising. We assert that the consumers' primary responsibility is to provide themselves with needed goods and services of high quality at the lowest cost consistent with economic practices. They should exercise their economic power to encourage the manufacture of goods that are necessary and beneficial to humanity while avoiding the desecration of the environment in either production or consumption. Those who manufacture goods and offer services serve society best when they aid consumers in fulfilling these responsibilities. Consumers should evaluate their consumption of goods and services in the light of the need for enhanced quality of life rather than unlimited production of material goods. We call upon consumers to organize to achieve these goals.

E) Poverty.—In spite of general affluence in the industrialized nations, the majority of persons in the world live in poverty. In order to provide basic needs such as food, clothing, shelter, education, health care, and other necessities, ways must be found to more equitably share the resources of the world. Increasing technology and exploitative economic practices impoverish many persons and make poverty self-perpetuating. Therefore, we do not hold poor people morally responsible for their economic state. To begin to alleviate poverty, we support such policies as: adequate income maintenance, quality education, decent housing, job training, meaningful employment opportunities, adequate medical and hospital care, and humanization and radical revisions of welfare programs.

F) Migrant Workers.—Migratory and other farm workers, who have long been a special concern of the Church's ministry, are by the nature of their way of life excluded from many of the economic and social benefits enjoyed by other workers. We advocate their right to, and applaud their efforts toward, responsible self-organization and self-determination. We call upon governments and all employers to ensure for migratory workers the same economic, educational, and social benefits enjoyed by other citizens. We call upon our churches to seek to develop programs of service to such migrant people as come within their parish.

G) Gambling.—Gambling is a menace to society, deadly to the best interests of moral, social, economic, and spiritual life, and destructive of good government. As an act of faith and love, Christians should abstain from gambling, and should strive to minister to those victimized by the practice. Community standards and personal life styles should be such as would make unnecessary and undesirable the resort to commercial gambling, including public lotteries, as a recreation, as an escape, or as a means of producing public revenue or funds for support of charities or government.

¶ 74.   V. THE POLITICAL COMMUNITY

While our allegiance to God takes precedence over our allegiance to any state, we acknowledge the vital function of government as a principal vehicle for the ordering of society. Because we know ourselves to be responsible to God for social and political life, we declare the following relative to governments:

A) Basic Freedoms.—We hold governments responsible for the protection of the rights of the people to the freedoms of speech, religion, assembly, and communications media; to the right to privacy; and to the guarantee of the rights to adequate food, clothing, shelter, education, and health care. The use of detention and imprisonment for the harassment and elimination of political opponents or other dissidents violates fundamental human rights. Furthermore, the mistreatment or torture of persons by governments for any purpose violates Christian teaching and must be condemned and/or opposed by Christians and Churches wherever and whenever it occurs.

B) Political Responsibility.—The strength of a political system depends upon the full and willing participation of its citizens. We believe that the state should not attempt to control the Church, nor should the Church seek to dominate the state. "Separation of church and state" means no organic union of the two, but does permit interaction. The Church should continually exert a strong ethical influence upon the state, supporting policies and programs deemed to be just and compassionate and opposing policies and programs which are not.

C) Freedom of Information.—Citizens of every country should have access to all essential information regarding their government and its policies. National security must not be extended to justify or keep secret maladministration, or illegal and unconscionable activities directed against persons or groups by their own government or by other governments. We also strongly reject domestic surveillance and intimidation of political opponents by governments in power, and all other misuses of elective or appointive offices. We believe that such misuse constitutes moral grounds for removal from office.

D) Education.—We believe responsibility for education of the young rests with the family, the Church, and the government. In our society this function can best be fulfilled through public policies which ensure access for all persons to free public elementary and secondary schools and to post-secondary schools of their choice. Persons in our society should not be precluded by financial barriers from access to church-related and other independent institutions of higher education. We affirm the right of public and independent colleges and universities to exist, and we endorse public policies which ensure access and choice and which do not create unconstitutional entanglements between Church and state. The state should not use its authority to inculcate particular religious beliefs (including atheism) nor should it require prayer or worship in the public schools, but should leave students free to practice their own religious convictions.

E) Civil Obedience and Civil Disobedience.—Governments and laws should be servants of God and of human beings. Citizens have a duty to abide by laws duly adopted by orderly and just process of government. But governments, no less than individuals, are subject to the judgment of God. Therefore, we recognize the right of individuals to dissent when acting under the constraint of conscience and after exhausting all legal recourse, to disobey laws deemed to be unjust. Even then respect for law should be shown by refraining from violence and by accepting the costs of disobedience. We offer our prayers for those in rightful authority who serve the public and we support their efforts to afford justice and equal opportunity for all people. We assert the duty of churches to support everyone who suffers for cause of conscience, and urge governments seriously to consider restoration of rights to such persons while also maintaining respect for those who obey.

F) Crime and Rehabilitation.—To protect all citizens from those who would encroach upon personal and property rights, it is the duty of governments to establish police forces, courts, and facilities for rehabilitation of offenders. We support governmental measures designed to reduce and eliminate crime, consistent with respect for the basic freedom of persons. We reject all misuse of these necessary mechanisms, including their use for the purpose of persecuting or intimidating those whose race, appearance, life style, economic condition, or beliefs differ from those in authority, and we reject all careless, callous, or discriminatory enforcement of law. We further support measures designed to remove the social conditions that lead to crime, and we encourage continued positive interaction between law enforcement officials and members of the community at large. In the love of Christ who came to save those who are lost and vulnerable, we urge the creation of genuinely new systems of rehabilitation that will restore, preserve, and nurture the humanity of the imprisoned. For the same reason, we oppose capital punishment and urge its elimination from all criminal codes.

G) Military Service.—Though coercion, violence, and war are presently the ultimate sanctions in international relations, we reject them as incompatible with the gospel and spirit of Christ. We therefore urge the establishment of the rule of law in international affairs as a means of elimination of war, violence, and coercion in those affairs. We therefore reject national policies of enforced military service in peacetime as incompatible with the gospel. We acknowledge the agonizing tension created by the demand for military service by national governments. Thus, we support those individuals who conscientiously oppose all war, or any particular war, and who therefore refuse to serve in the armed forces or to cooperate with systems of military conscription. We also support those persons who conscientiously choose to serve in the armed forces or to accept alternate service. Pastors are called upon to be available for counseling with all youth who face conscription including those who conscientiously refuse to cooperate with a selective service system.

¶ 75.   VI. THE WORLD COMMUNITY

God's world is one world. The unity now being thrust upon us by technological revolution has far outrun our moral and spiritual capacity to achieve a stable world. The enforced unity of humanity, increasingly evident on all levels of life, presents the Church as well as all people with problems that will not wait for answer: injustice, war, exploitation, privilege, population, international ecological crisis, proliferation of arsenals of nuclear weapons, development of transnational business organizations that operate beyond the effective control of any governmental structure, and the increase of tyranny in all its forms. This generation must find viable answers to these and related questions if humanity is to continue on this earth. We commit ourselves, as a Church, to the achievement of a world community that is a fellowship of persons who honestly love one another. We pledge ourselves to seek the meaning of the gospel in all issues that divide people and threaten the growth of world community.

A) Nations and Cultures.—As individuals are affirmed by God in their diversity, so are nations and cultures. We recognize that no nation or culture is absolutely just and right in its treatment of its own people, nor is any nation totally without regard for the welfare of its citizens. The Church must regard nations as accountable for unjust treatment of their citizens and others living within their borders. While recognizing valid differences in culture and political philosophy, we stand for justice and peace in every nation.

B) National Power and Responsibility.—Some nations possess more military and economic power than do others. Upon the powerful rests responsibility to exercise their wealth and influence with restraint. We affirm the right and duty of the people of developing nations to determine their own destiny. We urge the major political powers to use their power to maximize the political, social, and economic self-determination of developing nations, rather than to further their own special interests. We applaud international efforts to develop a more just international economic order, in which the limited resources of the earth will be used to the maximum benefit of all nations and peoples. We urge Christians, in every society, to encourage the governments under which they live, and the economic entities within their societies, to aid and to work for the development of more just economic orders.

C) War and Peace.—We believe war is incompatible with the teachings and example of Christ. We therefore reject war as an instrument of national foreign policy and insist that the first moral duty of all nations is to resolve by peaceful means every dispute that arises between or among them; that human values must outweigh military claims as governments determine their priorities; that the militarization of society must be challenged and stopped; that the manufacture, sale, and deployment of armaments must be reduced and controlled; and that the production, possession, or use of nuclear weapons be condemned.

D) Justice and Law.—Persons and groups must feel secure in their life and right to live within a society if order is to be achieved and maintained by law. We denounce as immoral an ordering of life that perpetuates injustice. Nations, too, must feel secure in the world if world community is to become a fact.

Believing that international justice requires the participation of all peoples, we endorse the United Nations and its related bodies and the International Court of Justice as the best instruments now in existence to achieve a world of justice and law. We commend the efforts of all people in all countries who pursue world peace through law. We endorse international aid and cooperation on all matters of need and conflict. We urge acceptance for membership in the United Nations of all nations who wish such membership and who accept United Nations responsibility. We urge the United Nations to take a more aggressive role in the development of international arbitration of disputes and actual conflicts among nations by developing binding third-party arbitration. Bilateral or multilateral efforts outside of the United Nations should work in concert with, and not contrary to, its purposes. We reaffirm our historic concern for the world as our parish and seek for all persons and peoples full and equal membership in a truly world community.

¶ 76.   VII. OUR SOCIAL CREED

We believe in God, Creator of the world; and in Jesus Christ the Redeemer of creation. We believe in the Holy Spirit, through whom we acknowledge God's gifts, and we repent of our sin in misusing these gifts to idolatrous ends.

We affirm the natural world as God's handiwork and dedicate ourselves to its preservation, enhancement, and faithful use by humankind.

We joyfully receive, for ourselves and others, the blessings of community, sexuality, marriage, and the family.

We commit ourselves to the rights of men, women, children, youth, young adults, the aging, and those with handicapping conditions; to improvement of the quality of life; and to the rights and dignity of racial, ethnic, and religious minorities.

We believe in the right and duty of persons to work for the good of themselves and others, and in the protection of their welfare in so doing; in the rights to property as a trust from God, collective bargaining, and responsible consumption; and in the elimination of economic and social distress.

We dedicate ourselves to peace throughout the world and to the rule of justice and law among nations.

We believe in the present and final triumph of God's Word in human affairs, and gladly accept our commission to manifest the life of the gospel in the world. Amen.

(It is recommended that this statement of Social Principles be constantly available to United Methodist Christians and that it be emphasized regularly in every congregation. It is further recommended that our Social Creed be frequently used in Sunday worship.)

Part IV

ORGANIZATION AND ADMINISTRATION

Chapter One
THE MINISTRY OF ALL CHRISTIANS

Section I. The Heart of the Christian Ministry.

¶ **101.** In Christ the love of God came into this world in a unique way. He came not to be served but to serve (Mark 10:45) and to give his life in and for the world. Christ freely took the nature of a servant, carrying that servanthood to its utmost limits (Philippians 2:7). All Christian ministry is Christ's ministry of outreaching love. The Christian Church, as the Body of Christ, is that community whose members share both his mind and mission. The heart of Christian ministry is shown by a common life of gratitude and devotion, witness and service, celebration, and discipleship. All Christians are called to this ministry of servanthood in the world to the glory of God and for human fulfillment. The forms of this ministry are diverse in locale, in interest, and in denominational accent, yet also always catholic in spirit and outreach.

Section II. The Church as Covenant Community.

¶ **102.** From the beginning, God has dealt with the human family through covenants: with Adam and Eve, Noah, Abraham, Sarah and Hagar, Moses; with Deborah, Ruth, and Jeremiah and other prophets. In each covenant, God offered the chosen people the blessings of providence and commanded of them obedience to the divine will and way, that through them all the world should be blessed (Genesis 18:18; 22:18). In the new covenant in Christ, yet another community of hope was called out and gathered up, with the same promise and condition renewed that all who believe and obey shall be saved and made ministers of Christ's righteousness. John Wesley and our other spiritual forebears stressed this biblical theme of covenant-making and covenant-keeping as central in Christian experience.

¶ **103.** The biblical story is marred by disregarded covenants and disrupted moral order, by sin and rebellion, with the resulting tragedies of alienation, oppression, and disorder. In the gospel of the new covenant, God in Christ has provided a new basis for reconciliation—justification by faith and birth into a new life in the Spirit, which is marked by growth toward wholeness.

Section III.   The General Ministry.

¶ **104.** The Church as this community of the new covenant has participated in Christ's ministry of grace across the years and around the world. It stretches out to human needs wherever love and service may convey God's love and ours. The outreach of such ministries knows no limits. Beyond the diverse forms of ministry is this ultimate concern: that men and women may be renewed after the image of their creator (Colossians 3:10). This means that all Christians are called to minister wherever Christ would have them serve and witness in deeds and words that heal and free.

¶ **105.** This general ministry of all Christians in Christ's name and spirit is both a gift and a task. The gift is God's unmerited grace; the task is unstinting service. Entrance into the Church is acknowledged in Baptism and may include persons of all ages. In this Sacrament the Church claims God's promise, "the seal of the Spirit" (Ephesians 1:13). Baptism is followed by nurture and the consequent awareness by the baptized of the claim to ministry in Christ placed upon their lives by the Church. Such a ministry is ratified in confirmation, where the pledges of Baptism are accepted and renewed for life and mission. Entrance into and acceptance of ministry begin in a local church, but the impulse to minister always moves one beyond the congregation toward the whole human community. God's gifts are richly diverse for a variety of services; yet all have dignity and worth.

¶ **106.** The people of God are the Church made visible in the world. It is they who must convince the world of the reality of the gospel or leave it unconvinced. There can be no evasion or delegation of this responsibility; the Church is either faithful as a witnessing and serving community, or it loses its vitality and its impact on an unbelieving world.

Section IV. Representative Ministry.

¶ **107.** Within the people of God, there are those called to the representative ministry—ordained and diaconal. Such callings are evidenced by special gifts, graces, and promise of usefulness. God's call to representative ministry is inward as it comes to the individual and outward through the judgment and validation of the Church. When inner and outer call agree and are affirmed through election by an Annual Conference, the candidate may then be ordained or consecrated, according to such election, through symbolic acts which confer special roles of responsibility.

¶ **108.** *Diaconal Ministry.*—The diaconal ministers are called to specialized ministries of service, justice, and love within local congregations and in the wider world. Servant ministry must always involve a concern for justice as well as a love for persons. Diaconal ministers focus their service through a variety of ministries, such as, administration, education, evangelism, music, health ministries, and community development—to the local congregation and the wider community. Christ's service to humankind and the Church's responsibility for continuing that service in the world are both symbolized and enabled especially, but not exclusively, in diaconal ministry. Diaconal ministry exists to intensify and make more effective the self-understanding of the whole people of God as servants in Christ's name.

¶ **109.** *Ordained Ministry.*—The ordained ministers are called to specialized ministries of Word, Sacrament, and Order. Through these distinctive functions ordained ministers devote themselves wholly to the work of the Church and to the upbuilding of the general ministry. They do this through careful study of the Scripture and its faithful interpretation, through effective proclamation of the gospel and responsible administration of the Sacraments, through diligent pastoral leadership of their congregations for fruitful discipleship, and by following the guidance of the Holy Spirit in witnessing beyond the congregation in the local community and to the ends of the earth. The ordained ministry is defined by its intentionally representative character, by its passion for the hallowing of life, and by its concern to link all local ministries with the widest boundaries of the Christian community.

Section V. The Unity of Ministry in Christ.

¶ **110.** There is but one ministry in Christ, but there are diverse gifts and graces in the Body of Christ (Ephesians 4:4-16). The general and representative ministries in The United Methodist Church are complementary. Neither is subservient to the other. Both are summoned and sent by Christ to live and work together in mutual interdependence and to be guided by the Spirit into the truth that frees and the love that reconciles.

Chapter Two
THE LOCAL CHURCH

Section I. The Local Church and Pastoral Charge.

¶ 201. A local church is a community of true believers under the Lordship of Christ. It is the redemptive fellowship in which the Word of God is preached by persons divinely called, and the Sacraments are duly administered according to Christ's own appointment. Under the discipline of the Holy Spirit the Church exists for the maintenance of worship, the edification of believers, and the redemption of the world.

¶ 202. The Church of Jesus Christ exists in and for the world. It is primarily at the level of the local church that the Church encounters the world. The local church is a strategic base from which Christians move out to the structures of society. It is the function of the local church to minister to the needs of persons in the communities where the church is located, to provide appropriate training and nurture to all age groups, cultural groups, racial groups, ethnic groups, and groups with handicapping conditions as minimal expectations of an authentic church.

¶ 203. The local church is a connectional society of persons who have professed their faith in Christ, have been baptized, have assumed the vows of membership in The United Methodist Church, and are associated in fellowship as a local United Methodist church in order that they may hear the Word of God, receive the Sacraments, and carry forward the work which Christ has committed to his Church. Such a society of believers, being within The United Methodist Church and subject to its Discipline, is also an inherent part of the Church Universal, which is composed of all who accept Jesus Christ as Lord and Savior, and which in the Apostles' Creed we declare to be the holy catholic Church.

¶ 204. Each local church shall have a definite membership and evangelistic responsibility. It shall be responsible for ministering to all its members, wherever they live, and for persons who choose it as their church.

¶ 205. 1. A pastoral charge shall consist of one or more churches which are organized under, and subject to, the

Discipline of The United Methodist Church, with a Charge Conference, and to which a minister is or may be duly appointed or appointable as pastor in charge.[1]

2. A pastoral charge of two or more churches may be designated a **circuit** or a cooperative parish.

Section II. Cooperative Parish Ministries.

¶ **206.** 1. Local churches, with the guidance of the Holy Spirit, may enhance their witness to each other and to the world by showing forth the love of Jesus Christ through forms of mutual cooperation.

2. Annual Conferences shall consider a process of cooperative parish development through which **cooperative parish ministries** are initiated and developed. Parish development is an intentional plan of enabling congregations, church-related agencies, and pastors in a defined geographic area to develop a relationship of trust and mutuality which results in coordinated church programs and ministry, supported by appropriate organizational structures and policy. A superintendent or director of parish development may be appointed to work with the Cabinet(s) in the implementation of these ministries in a conference or an area.

3. Cooperative parish ministries may be expressed in forms such as the following: (1) Larger parish—a number of congregations working together using a parish-wide Administrative Board, Council on Ministries, and other committees and work groups as the parish may determine; providing representation on boards and committees from all churches; guided by a constitution or covenant; and served by a staff appointed to the parish and involving a director. (2) Multiple charge parish—a number of congregations or two or more charges maintaining clear charge identity on the organizational level and meeting parish-wide for Charge Conference; served by ministers appointed to charges and to the parish; and governed by a parish council. (3) Group ministry—a loosely organized group of two or more pastoral charges in which ordained ministers are appointed to charges. The ministers and/or lay council, representing all

---

[1]*See* Judicial Council Decisions 113, 319.

churches, may designate a coordinator. (4) Enlarged charge—two or more congregations of relatively equal size that work as a unit with the leadership of one pastor. There may be a charge Administrative Board, Council on Ministries, and necessary committees. (5) Extended or shared ministry—a larger membership church sharing ministry with a smaller membership church usually served by one pastor. (6) Cluster groups—a group of churches located in the same geographic area with a loosely knit organization which allows the participating congregations and pastoral charges to engage in cooperative programs in varying degree. A district may be divided into cluster groups for administrative purposes. (7) Probe staff—composed of ministers and other staff assigned to a geographic region to explore possibilities for cooperation and developing strategy for improved ministries to persons.

Section III. Churches in Transitional Communities.

¶ **207.** Since many of the communities in which the local church is located are experiencing transition, both in inner city urban areas and rural communities, special attention must be given to form of ministry required in such communities. The local church is required to respond to the changes which are occurring in its surrounding community and to organize its mission and ministry accordingly.

1. When the communities where the church is located experience transition especially identified as economic and or ethnic, the local church shall engage in deliberate analysis of the neighborhood change and alter its program to meet the needs and cultural patterns of the new residents. The local church shall make every effort to remain in the neighborhood and develop effective ministries to those who are newcomers, whether of a cultural, economic, or ethnic group different from the original or present members.

2. In communities in transition the local church shall be regarded as a principal base of mission from which structures of society shall be confronted, evangelization shall occur, and a principal witness to the changing community shall be realized.

111

Section IV. Church Membership.

¶ **208.** The United Methodist Church, a fellowship of believers, is a part of the Church Universal. Therefore all persons, without regard to race, color, national origin, or economic condition, shall be eligible to attend its worship services, to participate in its programs, and, when they take the appropriate vows, to be admitted into its membership in any local church in the connection.

¶ **209.** The membership of a local United Methodist church shall include all baptized persons who have come into membership by confession of faith or transfer and whose names have not been removed from the membership rolls by reason of death, transfer, withdrawal, or removal for cause. (*See* ¶¶ 230, 232, 236-243.)

¶ **210.** A member of any local United Methodist church is a member of the total United Methodist connection.

THE MEANING OF MEMBERSHIP

¶ **211.** When persons unite with a local United Methodist church, they profess their faith in God, the Father Almighty, maker of heaven and earth, and in Jesus Christ his only Son, and in the Holy Spirit. They covenant together with God and with the members of the local church to keep the vows which are a part of the order of confirmation and reception into the Church:

1. To confess Jesus Christ as Lord and Savior and pledge their allegiance to his kingdom,

2. To receive and profess the Christian faith as contained in the Scriptures of the Old and New Testaments,

3. To promise according to the grace given them to live a Christian life and always remain faithful members of Christ's holy Church,

4. And to be loyal to The United Methodist Church and uphold it by their prayers, their presence, their gifts, and their service.

¶ **212.** Faithful membership in the local church is essential for personal growth and for developing an increasing sensitivity to the will and grace of God. As members involve themselves in private and public prayer, worship, the Sacraments, study,

Christian action, systematic giving, and holy discipline, they grow in their appreciation of Christ, understanding of God at work in history and the natural order, and an understanding of themselves.

¶ **213.** Faithful participation in the corporate life of the congregation is an obligation of the Christian to fellow members of the Body of Christ. A member is bound in sacred covenant to shoulder the burdens, share the risks, and celebrate the joys of fellow members. A Christian is called to speak the truth in love, always ready to confront conflict in the spirit of forgiveness and reconciliation.

¶ **214.** A member of The United Methodist Church is to be a servant of Christ on mission in the local and worldwide community. This servanthood is performed in family life, daily work, recreation and social activities, responsible citizenship, the stewardship of property and accumulated resources, the issues of corporate life, and all attitudes toward other persons. Participation in disciplined groups is an expected part of personal mission involvement. Each member is called upon to be a witness for Christ in the world, a light and leaven in society, and a reconciler in a culture of conflict. Each member is to identify with the agony and suffering of the world and to radiate and exemplify the Christ of hope. The standards of attitude and conduct set forth in the Social Principles (Part III) shall be considered as an essential resource for guiding each member of the Church in being a servant of Christ on mission.

¶ **215.** Should any member give evidence of a lack of commitment to the faith, it shall be the responsibility of the local church, working through its Council on Ministries, to minister to that person to the end that that person may reaffirm faith and commitment to the Church and its ministry of loving service.

ADMISSION INTO THE CHURCH

¶ **216.** 1. All persons seeking to be saved from their sins and sincerely desiring to be Christian in faith and practice are proper candidates for full membership in The United Methodist Church. When such persons offer themselves for membership, it shall be the duty of the pastor, or of proper persons appointed by the pastor, to instruct them in the meaning of the Christian faith and the history, organization, and teaching of The United Methodist Church, using materials approved by The United Methodist Church to explain to them the baptismal and membership vows, and to lead them to commit themselves to Jesus Christ as Lord and Savior. When they shall have confessed their faith in Christ and have made known their desire to assume the obligations and become faithful members of The United Methodist Church, after the completion of a reasonable period of training, and after the Sacrament of Baptism has been administered to those who have not been previously baptized, the pastor shall bring them before the congregation, administer the vows, receive them into the fellowship of the Church, and duly enroll them as full members.

2. Membership training is a lifelong process and is carried on through all the activities which may have educational value. The instruction for which the pastor is specifically responsible is confirmation preparation and is a part of the fuller work of membership training. Confirmation preparation focuses attention upon the meaning of full membership and the need for church members to be in mission in all of life's relationships.

3. Preparation for the experience of confirmation shall be provided for all candidates for full membership, including adults, but youth who are completing the sixth grade shall normally be the youngest persons recruited for confirmation preparation and full membership. When younger persons, of their own volition, seek enrollment in confirmation preparation, such preparation shall be at the discretion of the pastor.

4. Persons in preparation for full membership make up the preparatory roll of the church. All baptized children shall be listed on the preparatory membership roll, and other persons who have declared their interest in church membership and have been enrolled in confirmation preparation may be listed as preparatory members. (*See also* ¶¶ 223, 232.2.)

¶ **217.** A duly authorized minister of The United Methodist Church while serving as chaplain of any organization, institution, or military unit, or as a campus pastor, or while otherwise present where a local church is not available, may receive a person into the membership of The United Methodist Church when such person shall have confessed faith in Christ and expressed a desire to assume the obligations and become a faithful member of the Church. After the vows of membership have been administered, such minister shall issue a statement of membership to the local church of the choice of the person concerned, and the pastor thereof on receiving such statement shall duly enroll that person as a member.

¶ **218.** When a person in military service or a member of the family of such person is received into the Church by a chaplain and has no local church to which the membership and records may be sent, the chaplain shall send the name, address, and related facts to the Division of Chaplains, Board of Higher Education and Ministry, which shall forward same to the Board of Discipleship for recording on the general roll of military service personnel and families. When a child of such a member is baptized by a chaplain, that record may be handled in the same manner. It is desirable that as soon as possible these persons be transferred to a local United Methodist church of their choice.

¶ **219.** Any candidate for church membership who for good reason is unable to appear before the congregation may, at the discretion of the pastor, be received elsewhere in accordance with the Ritual of The United Methodist Church. In any such case lay members should be present to represent the congregation. Names of such persons shall be placed on the church roll, and announcement of their reception shall be made to the congregation.

¶ **220.** A member in good standing in any Christian denomination who has been baptized and who desires to unite with The United Methodist Church may be received into membership by a proper certificate of transfer from that person's former church, or by a declaration of Christian faith, and upon affirming willingness to be loyal to The United Methodist Church. The pastor will report to the sending church the date of reception of such a member. It is recommended that instruction in the faith and work of the Church be provided for all such persons. Persons received from churches which do not issue certificates of transfer or letters of recommendation shall be listed as "Received from other denominations."

Children and the Church

¶ 221. Because the redeeming love of God, revealed in Jesus Christ, extends to all persons and because Jesus explicitly included the children in his kingdom, the pastor of each charge shall earnestly exhort all Christian parents or guardians to present their children to the Lord in Baptism at an early age. Before Baptism is administered, the pastor shall diligently instruct the parents or guardians regarding the meaning of this Sacrament and the vows which they assume. It is expected of parents or guardians who present their children for Baptism that they shall use all diligence in bringing them up in conformity to the Word of God and in the fellowship of the Church. It is desired that one or both parents or guardians shall be members of a Christian church or that sponsors who are members shall assume the baptismal vows. They shall be admonished of this obligation and be earnestly exhorted to faithfulness therein. At the time of Baptism they shall be informed that the Church, with its church school program, will aid them in the Christian nurture of their children.

¶ 222. The pastor of the church shall, at the time of administering the Sacrament of Baptism, furnish the parents or guardians of the child who is baptized with a **certificate of Baptism,** which shall also clearly state that the child is now enrolled as a preparatory member in The United Methodist Church. The pastor shall also admonish members of the congregation of their responsibility for the Christian nurture of the child. The pastor shall be responsible for seeing that the membership secretary adds the full name of the baptized child to the preparatory membership roll of the church. When the baptized child lives in a community not served by the pastor who administers the Sacrament of Baptism, the pastor is responsible for reporting the baptism to a pastor or district superintendent who serves in the area where the baptized child lives in order that the child's name might be properly entered on the preparatory membership roll. (*See* ¶ 223.)

¶ 223. The pastor shall keep and transmit to the succeeding pastor an accurate register of the names of all baptized children in

116

the charge, including both those who have been baptized there and those who have been baptized elsewhere. This register of baptized children, along with a list of other preparatory members (¶ 216.4), shall constitute the preparatory membership roll of the church. It shall give the full name of the child, the date of birth, the date and place of Baptism, and the names of the parents or guardians and their place of residence.

¶ 224. All baptized children under the care of a United Methodist church shall be retained as preparatory members in the church until this status is terminated by: confirmation and reception into full membership after a proper course of training both in the church school and in the pastor's class, transfer with their families to another United Methodist church, transfer with their families to a church of another Christian denomination, death, withdrawal, or transfer to the constituency roll of the church at the age of nineteen. The preparatory membership roll shall be corrected each year by adding and subtracting the names received and removed during the year, using the forms provided for this purpose.

¶ 225. It shall be the duty of the pastor, the parents or guardians, and the officers and teachers of the church school to provide training for the children of the church throughout their childhood that will lead to an understanding of the Christian faith, to an appreciation of the privileges and obligations of Church membership, and to a personal commitment to Jesus Christ as Lord and Savior. The pastor shall, at least annually, building on the preparation which boys and girls have received throughout their childhood, organize into classes for confirmation the youth who, preferably, are completing the sixth grade. This instruction shall be based on materials which the boys and girls have already used and on other resources produced by The United Methodist Church for the purpose of confirmation preparation. Wherever boys and girls so prepared shall give evidence of their own Christian faith and purpose and understanding of the privileges and obligations of Church membership, they may be received into full membership.

YOUTH

¶ **226.** Youth who are full members of the church have all rights and responsibilities of church membership. (*See* ¶ 264.2.) It is strongly recommended that each local church offer for senior high youth who are full members of the Church an advanced class of instruction in the meaning of the Christian life and Church membership. It is further recommended that this course, taught by the pastor, emphasize the doctrines of The United Methodist Church and the nature and mission of the Church, leading to continued growth in the knowledge, grace, and service of our Lord Jesus Christ.

AFFILIATE AND ASSOCIATE MEMBERSHIP

¶ **227.** A member of The United Methodist Church, residing for an extended period in a city or community at a distance from the member's home church, may on request be enrolled as an **affiliate member** of a United Methodist church located in the vicinity of the temporary residence. The home pastor shall be notified of this affiliate membership. Such membership shall entitle the person to the fellowship of that church, to its pastoral care and oversight, and to participation in its activities, including the holding of office, but that person shall be counted and reported only as a member of the home church. A member of another denomination may become an **associate member** under the same conditions.[2]

CARE OF MEMBERS

¶ **228.** The local church shall endeavor to enlist each member in activities for spiritual growth and in participation in the services and ministries of the Church and its organizations. It shall be the duty of the pastor and of the Council on Ministries by regular visitation, care, and spiritual oversight, to provide necessary activities and opportunities for spiritual growth through individual and family worship and individual and group

----

[2]*See* Judicial Council Decision 372.

study, and continually to aid the members to keep their vows to uphold the Church by attendance, prayers, gifts, and service. The Church has a moral and spiritual obligation to nurture its nonparticipating and indifferent members and to lead them into a full and active church relationship.

¶ **229.** The pastor in cooperation with the Council on Ministries may arrange the membership in groups—with a leader for each group—designed to involve the membership of the church in its ministry to the community. These groups shall be of such size, usually not larger than eight or ten families, as to be convenient and effective for service. Such groups may be especially helpful in evangelistic outreach by contacting newcomers and unreached persons, by visitation, by mobilizing neighbors to meet social issues in the community, by responding to personal and family crises, by holding prayer meetings in the homes, by distributing Christian literature, and by other means. Nonresident members should constitute a special group to be served by correspondence. The groups shall be formed and the leaders appointed by the Council on Ministries upon recommendation of the minister.

¶ **230.** While primary responsibility and initiative rests with each individual member faithfully to perform the vows of membership which have been solemnly assumed, if the member should be neglectful of that responsibility, these procedures shall be followed:

1. If a member residing in the community is negligent of the vows, or is regularly absent from the worship of the church without valid reason, the pastor and the membership secretary shall report that member's name to the Council on Ministries, which shall do all in its power to reenlist the member in the active fellowship of the Church. It shall visit the member and make clear that, while the member's name is on the roll of a particular local church, one is a member of The United Methodist Church as a whole, and that, since the member is not attending the church where enrolled, the member is requested to do one of four things: *(a)* renew the vows and become a regular worshiper in the church where the member's name is recorded, *(b)* request transfer to another United Methodist church where the member will be a regular worshiper, *(c)* arrange transfer to a particular church of

another denomination, or *(d)* request withdrawal. If the member does not comply with any of the available alternatives over a period of three years, the member's name may be removed. *(See* § 4.)

2. If a member whose address is known is residing outside the community and is not participating in the worship or activity of the church, the directives to encourage a transfer of membership shall be followed each year until that member joins another church or requests in writing that the name be removed from the membership roll; *provided,* however, that if after three years the council has not been able to relate that member to the church at the new place of residence, the name may be removed by the procedure of § 4 below.

3. If the address of a member is no longer known to the pastor, the membership secretary and the evangelism work area chairperson or the Commission on Evangelism shall make every effort to locate the member, including listing the name in the church bulletin, circularizing it throughout the parish, and reading it from the pulpit. If the member can be located, the directives of either § 1 or § 2 above shall be followed, but if after three years of such efforts the address is still unknown, the member's name may be removed from the membership roll by the procedure of § 4 below.

4. If the directives of §§ 1, 2, or 3 above have been followed for the specified number of years without success, the member's name may be removed from the membership roll by vote of the Charge Conference on recommendation of the pastor and the evangelism work area chairperson or the Commission on Evangelism, each name being considered individually; *provided* that the member's name shall have been entered in the minutes of the annual Charge Conference for three consecutive years preceding removal. On the roll there shall be entered after the name: "Removed by order of the Charge Conference"; and if the action is on the basis of § 3, there shall be added: "Reason: address unknown." The membership of the person shall thereby be terminated, and the record thereof shall be retained;[3] *provided* that upon request the member may be restored to membership by

---

[3] *See* Judicial Council Decision 207.

recommendation of the pastor; and *provided* further, that should a transfer of membership be requested, the pastor may restore the person's membership for this purpose and issue the certificate of transfer.

5. Recognizing that the Church has a continuing moral and spiritual obligation to nurture all persons, even those whose names have been removed from the membership roll, it is recommended that a roll of persons thus removed shall be maintained. It shall then become the responsibility of the Administrative Board to provide for the review of this roll at least once a year. (See *also* ¶ 235.) After the review has been made, it is recommended that the pastor and/or the Commission on Evangelism contact those whose names appear on this roll, either in person or by other means, in the most effective and practical manner. The names and addresses of those who have moved outside the local church's area should be sent to local churches in their new communities, that those churches may visit and minister to them.

¶ **231.** If a local church is discontinued, the district superintendent shall select another United Methodist church and transfer its members thereto, or to such other churches as the members may select.

MEMBERSHIP RECORDS AND REPORTS

¶ **232.** Each local church shall accurately maintain the following membership rolls:

1. **Full Membership Roll** (¶ 208).

2. **Preparatory Membership Roll** (¶ 216.4), containing the names and pertinent information of baptized children and youth of the church eighteen years of age and under who are not full members, and other persons who have been enrolled in confirmation preparation.

3. **Members Removed by Charge Conference Action** (¶ 230.4).

4. **Constituency Roll,** containing the names and addresses of such persons as are not members of the church concerned, including unbaptized children, dedicated children, church school members, preparatory members who have reached the age

of nineteen who have not been received into full membership, and other nonmembers for whom the local church has pastoral responsibility.

5. **Affiliate Membership Roll** (¶ 227).

6. **Associate Membership Roll** (¶ 227).

¶ **233.** The pastor shall report to each Charge Conference the names of persons received into the membership of the church or churches of the pastoral charge and the names of persons whose membership in the church or churches of the pastoral charge has been terminated since the last Charge Conference, indicating how each was received or how the membership was terminated. The Administrative Board shall appoint a committee to audit the membership rolls, submitting the report annually to the Charge Conference.

¶ **234.** The basic membership records in each local church shall consist of: a permanent church register and a card index or loose-leaf book.

1. The **permanent church register** shall be a bound volume of durable material prepared by The United Methodist Publishing House in the form approved by the Council on Finance and Administration. The names shall be recorded chronologically as each person is received into the fellowship of that church, and without reference to alphabetical order. The names shall be numbered in regular numerical order, and the number of each shall appear on the corresponding card or page in the card index or loose-leaf membership roll.

2. The **card index** or **loose-leaf membership record** shall be kept on a form approved by the Council on Finance and Administration. This record of membership shall be filed in alphabetical order and shall show the number appearing opposite each name on the permanent register. The pastor shall report annually to the Annual Conference the total membership of the charge as shown on the membership records.

¶ **235.** The **membership secretary** shall, under the direction of the pastor, keep accurate records of all membership rolls (*see* ¶ 232), shall be a member of the work area on evangelism (if it exists), and shall report regularly to the Administrative Board.

¶ **236.** Membership in a local church may be terminated by death, transfer, withdrawal, expulsion, or action of the Charge Conference. It shall be the duty of the pastor of the charge or of the membership secretary to keep an accurate record of all terminations of membership and to report to each Charge Conference the names of all persons whose membership has been terminated since the conference preceding, in each instance indicating the reason for such termination.

¶ **237.** If a member of a United Methodist church shall move to another community so far removed from the home church that the member cannot participate regularly in its worship and activity, this member shall be encouraged to transfer membership to a United Methodist church in the community of the newly established residence. As soon as the pastor is reliably informed of this change of residence, actual or contemplated, it shall be the pastor's duty and obligation to assist the member to become established in the fellowship of a church in the community of the future home and to send to a United Methodist pastor in such community, or to the district superintendent, or (if neither is known) to the Board of Discipleship, a letter of notification, giving the latest known address of the person or persons concerned and requesting local pastoral oversight.

¶ **238.** Lay persons in service outside the United States under the World Division of the General Board of Global Ministries and assigned to churches other than United Methodist may accept all the rights and privileges, including associate membership, offered them by a local church in their place of residence without impairing their relationship to their home local church.

¶ **239.** When a pastor discovers a member of The United Methodist Church residing in the community whose membership is in a church so far removed from the place of residence that the member cannot participate regularly in its worship and activity, it shall be the duty and obligation of the pastor to give pastoral oversight to such person and to encourage transfer of membership to a United Methodist church in the community where the member resides.

¶ **240.** When a pastor receives a request for a transfer of membership from the pastor of another United Methodist church, or a district superintendent, that pastor shall send the proper certificate directly to the pastor of the United Methodist church to which the member is transferring, or if there is no pastor, to the district superintendent. On receipt of such a **certificate of transfer,** the pastor or district superintendent shall enroll the name of the person so transferring after public reception in a regular service of worship, or if circumstances demand, public announcement in such a service. The pastor of the church issuing the certificate shall then be notified, whereupon said pastor shall remove the member from the roll.

Certificates of transfer shall be accompanied by two official forms. A "Notice of Transfer of Membership" is to be sent to the member by the pastor who transfers the membership. An "Acknowledgment of Transfer of Membership" is to be sent to the former pastor by the pastor who receives the transferred member.

In case the transfer is not made effective, the pastor shall return the certificate to the pastor of the sending church.

¶ **241.** A pastor upon receiving a request from a member to transfer to a church of another denomination, or upon receiving such request from a pastor or duly authorized official of another denomination, shall (with the approval of the member) issue a certificate of transfer and, upon receiving confirmation of said member's reception into another congregation, shall properly record the transfer of such person on the membership roll of the local church; and the membership shall thereby be terminated. For the transfer of a member of The United Methodist Church to a church of another denomination, an official "Transfer of Membership to Another Denomination" form shall be used.

¶ **242.** If a pastor is informed that a member has without notice united with a church of another denomination, the pastor shall make diligent inquiry and, if the report is confirmed, shall enter "Withdrawn" after the person's name on the membership roll and shall report the same to the next Charge Conference.

¶ **243.** If a member proposes to withdraw from The United Methodist Church, that member shall communicate the purpose in writing to the pastor of the local church in which membership is held. On receiving such notice of withdrawal, the pastor shall properly record the fact of withdrawal on the membership roll. If requested, the pastor shall give a statement of withdrawal to such member. Such person, upon written request, may be restored to membership on recommendation of the pastor.

Section V. Organization and Administration.

¶ 244. The local church shall be organized so that adequate provision is made for these basic responsibilities: (1) planning and implementing a program of nurture, outreach, and witness for persons and families within and without the congregation; (2) providing for effective pastoral and lay leadership; (3) providing for financial support, physical facilities, and the legal obligations of the church; and (4) insuring relationships of the local church organizations to appropriate district and Annual Conference structures and programs.

1. In every local church there shall be an administrative body to which the members, organizations, and agencies are amenable. It shall be amenable to and function as the executive agency of the Charge Conference. (See ¶ 248.)

2. In every local church there shall be a programatic body which shall consider, develop, and coordinate goals and program proposals for the church's mission.

¶ 245. The basic organizational plan for the local church shall include a Charge Conference, an Administrative Board, a Council on Ministries, a Committee on Pastor-Parish Relations, a Board of Trustees, a Committee on Finance, a Committee on Nominations and Personnel, and such other elected leaders, commissions, councils, committees, and task forces as the Charge Conference may determine.

1. Since a majority of United Methodist churches are of smaller membership (approximately 200 members or less) and may be limited as to numbers of leaders, program scope, missional resources, or by other circumstances, they may develop an organizational plan which combines the functions of several boards, councils, commissions, and committees in accordance with ¶¶ 245, 249.2.

a) The Administrative Board and the Council on Ministries may be combined in an **Administrative Council** provided adequate provision is made for the planning and implementing of the programs of nurture and outreach of the church and for the administration of its organizational and temporal life. The Administrative Council shall have all of the responsibilities of the Administrative Board (¶ 252 ff) and the Council on Ministries (¶ 256 ff). Its membership shall include the combined membership of the two bodies insofar as the offices listed in ¶¶ 253 and 257 exist within the local church.

b) The responsibilities of the work area chairpersons of education, higher education and campus ministry, worship, stewardship, and the membership care aspects of evangelism may be combined and assigned to a work area chairperson of nurture and membership care.

c) The responsibilities of the work area chairpersons of Christian unity and interreligious concerns, church and society, missions, religion and race, the health and welfare ministries representative, and the outreach function of evangelism may be combined and assigned to a work area chairperson of outreach.

d) The responsibilities and work of the coordinators of children's, youth, adult, and family ministries, may be combined and assigned to a coordinator of age-level and family ministries.

e) The function and responsibility of lay leader, lay member of the Annual Conference, and chairperson of the Administrative Council may be combined in some manner.

2. Churches of larger membership or with more leaders or more extensive program scope and missional resources, may establish commissions in one or more of the work areas (¶ 265), and/or councils in one or more of the age level and family ministries (¶ 264); and/or they may elect such other committees and task forces as may be advisable.

¶ 246. The Charge Conference, or Church Conference authorized by the district superintendent, shall elect upon nomination of the Committee on Nominations and Personnel (¶ 261.2) of each local church on the pastoral charge or by nomination from the floor and by vote of each such local church, at least the following leaders for the four basic responsibilities (¶ 244):

1. Chairperson of the Council on Ministries and chairperson of the Administrative Board or chairperson of the Administrative Council. (For election of recording secretary, *see* ¶ 250.3.)

2. The Committee on Nominations and Personnel (¶ 266.1) and the Committee on Pastor-Parish Relations and its chairperson (¶ 266.2).

3. A chairperson and additional members of the Committee on Finance (¶ 266.3); the financial secretary and the church treasurer(s) (if not paid employees of the local church); and the trustees as provided in ¶¶ 2520, 2522, unless otherwise required by state law.

4. The lay member(s) of the Annual Conference and lay leader(s).

5. Special attention shall be given to the inclusion of women, men, youth, young adults, persons with a handicapping condition, and racial and ethnic minority persons.

¶ **247.** The Charge Conference, or Church Conference authorized by the district superintendent, may elect, upon nomination of the Committee on Nominations and Personnel (¶ 266.1) of each local church on the pastoral charge or by nomination from the floor and by vote of each such church, such leaders and officers of the local church(es) as it may choose from among the following:

1. Chairpersons of work areas (Christian unity and interreligious concerns, church and society, education, evangelism, higher education and campus ministry, missions, religion and race, stewardship, worship), age-level coordinators (family, children, youth, adult), secretary of career planning and counseling (*see* ¶ 260.5*b*), superintendent of the church school, health and welfare ministries representative, coordinator of communications, district steward, church historian, and membership secretary.

2. Members at large of the Administrative Board as provided in ¶ 253.

3. Such other personnel and committees as it may choose or as may elsewhere be ordered by the Discipline.

4. Special attention shall be given to the inclusion of women, men, youth, young adults, persons with a handicapping condition, and racial and ethnic minority persons.

THE CHARGE CONFERENCE

¶ 248. *General Provisions.*—1. Within the pastoral charge the basic unit in the connectional system of The United Methodist Church is the **Charge Conference.** The Charge Conference shall therefore be organized from the church or churches in every pastoral charge as set forth in the Constitution (¶ 48). It shall meet annually for the purposes set forth in ¶ 249. It may meet at other times as indicated in § 6 below.

2. The membership of the Charge Conference shall be all members of the Administrative Board (or Administrative Boards, if more than one church is on the pastoral charge) named in ¶ 253 together with retired ministers who elect to hold their membership in said Charge Conference and any others as may be designated in the Discipline. (*See* ¶ 245.1a.)

3. The district superintendent shall fix the time of meetings of the Charge Conference. The Charge Conference shall determine the place of meeting.

4. The district superintendent shall preside at the meetings of the Charge Conference or may designate an elder to preside.

5. The members present at any duly announced meeting shall constitute a quorum.

6. Special sessions may be called by the district superintendent after consultation with the pastor of the charge or by the pastor with the written consent of the district superintendent. The purpose of such special session shall be stated in the call, and only such business shall be transacted as is in harmony with the purposes stated in such call. Any such special session may be convened as a Church Conference in accordance with ¶ 251.

7. Notice of the time and place of a regular or special session of the Charge Conference shall be given at least ten days in advance.

8. A Charge Conference shall be conducted in the language of the majority with adequate provision being made for translation.

9. A **Joint Charge Conference** for two or more pastoral charges may be held at the same time and place, as the district superintendent may determine.

¶ **249.** *Powers and Duties.*—1. The Charge Conference shall be the connecting link between the local church and the general Church and shall have general oversight of the Administrative Board(s). (*See* ¶ 245.1*a*.)

2. The Charge Conference, the district superintendent, and the pastor shall organize and administer the pastoral charge and churches according to the policies and plans herein set forth. When the membership size, program scope, mission resources, or other circumstances so require, the Charge Conference may, in consultation with and upon the approval of the district superintendent, modify the organizational plans (provided that the provisions of ¶ 244 are observed).

3. Its primary responsibility in the annual meeting shall be to receive reports, review and evaluate the total mission and ministry of the church, and adopt objectives and goals recommended by the Administrative Board which are in keeping with the objectives of The United Methodist Church (¶ 255.3).

4. The Charge Conference shall determine the number of members at large to serve on the Administrative Board in keeping with the following provisions: church of five hundred members or less may include at least four but not more than thirty-five members at large exclusive of ex officio and honorary members. In churches of more than five hundred members there may be elected additional members at large not to exceed the ratio of one for each thirty additional members. The members at large, if elected, shall include at least two young adults between the ages of nineteen and thirty-one and at least two youth nominated by the youth coordinator or Youth Council.

5. It shall examine and recommend to the district Committee on Ordained Ministry, faithfully adhering to the provisions of ¶ 404 (2), candidates for the ordained ministry who have been members in good standing of the local church for at least one year; whose gifts, graces, and call to the ministry clearly establish them as candidates; and who have met the educational requirements.

6. It shall examine and recommend, faithfully adhering to the provisions of ¶ 405, renewal of candidacy of candidates for the ordained ministry.

7. It shall examine and recommend to the responsible church agency any candidates for church-related vocations.

8. It shall affirm the good standing in the congregation of the persons seeking the diaconal minister relationship in the Annual Conference and transmit this information to the conference Board of Diaconal Ministry.

9. It shall recommend to the district or conference Committee on Lay Speaking for certification as lay speakers those persons who have met the standards set forth by the agency to which they are related and shall inquire annually into the gifts, labors, and usefulness of lay speakers (¶ 273).

10. It shall in consultation with the district superintendent set the salary and other remuneration of the pastor and other staff appointed by the bishop.[4]

11. As soon as practicable after the session of Annual Conference, each district superintendent or designated agent shall notify each local church in the district what amounts have been apportioned to it for World Service and conference benevolences. Following the Annual Conference, it shall be the responsibility of the pastor and the lay member of the Annual Conference and/or the church lay leader to present to a meeting of each Charge Conference a statement of the apportionments for World Service and conference benevolences, explaining the causes supported by each of these funds and their place in the total program of the Church. The district superintendent or designated agent shall also notify each Charge Conference of all other amounts properly apportioned to it. (*See* ¶ 932.)

12. It shall receive and act on the annual report from the pastor concerning all membership rolls (*See* ¶ 233.)

13. In those instances where there are two or more churches on a pastoral charge, the Charge Conference may provide for a charge-wide or parish Administrative Board, a charge-wide or parish Council on Ministries, a charge-wide or parish treasurer, and such other officers, commissions, committees, and task groups as necessary to carry on the work of the charge.

14. In those instances where there are two or more churches on a pastoral charge, the Charge Conference may elect a

---

[4]*See* Judicial Council Decisions 213, 252, 461.

charge-wide or parish Committee on Nominations and Personnel, a charge-wide or parish Pastor-Parish Relations Committee, a charge-wide or parish Committee on Finance, and a charge-wide or parish Board of Trustees in such instances where property is held in common by two or more churches of the charge. All churches of the charge shall be represented on such charge-wide or parish committees or boards. Charge-wide or parish organization shall be consistent with Disciplinary provisions for the local church.

15. In instances of multiple church charges, the Charge Conference shall provide for an equitable distribution of parsonage maintenance and upkeep expense or adequate housing allowance (if Annual Conference policy permits) among the several churches.

16. Such other duties and responsibilities as the General, Jurisdictional, or Annual Conference may duly commit to it.

¶ **250. 1.** The **lay leader** is the person elected by the Charge Conference for the following responsibilities:

a) membership in the Charge Conference, the Administrative Board, and the Council on Ministries where, along with the pastor, the lay leader shall serve as an interpreter of the actions and programs of the Annual Conference and the general Church;

b) continuing involvement in study and training opportunities to develop a growing understanding of the Church's reason for existence and the types of ministry that will most effectively fulfill the Church's mission;

c) assisting in the interpretation of the role of the local church in the community; and

d) alerting the Administrative Board and its Council on Ministries to the opportunities available for more effective ministry of the Church through its laity.

The lay leader shall be expected to take advantage of the training opportunities provided by the Annual Conference. In instances where more than one church is on a charge, the Charge Conference shall elect additional lay leaders so that there will be one lay leader for each church.

2. The **lay member(s)** of the Annual Conference and one or more alternates shall be elected annually or quadrennially as the Annual Conference directs. If the charge's lay representative to the Annual Conference shall cease to be a member of the charge

or shall for any reason fail to serve, an alternate member in the order of election shall serve in place.

Both the lay members and the alternates shall have been members in good standing of The United Methodist Church and of the local church from which they are elected for at least one year (*see* ¶ 36), except in a newly organized church, which shall have the privilege of representation at the Annual Conference session. No local pastor shall be eligible as a lay member or alternate.[5] United Methodist churches which become part of an ecumenical ministry of which The United Methodist Church is a sponsor shall not be deprived of their right of representation by a lay member in the Annual Conference. The lay member(s) of the Annual Conference along with the pastor shall serve as an interpreter of the actions of the Annual Conference session.

3. The **recording secretary** shall keep an accurate and permanent record of the proceedings and shall be the custodian of all records and reports, and with the presiding officer shall sign the minutes. A copy of the minutes shall be provided for the district superintendent. When there is only one local church on a charge, the secretary of the Administrative Board shall be the secretary of the Charge Conference. When there is more than one church on a charge, one of the secretaries of the Administrative Boards shall be elected to serve as secretary of the Charge Conference.

4. The Charge Conference may elect a **church historian,** who shall be responsible for preparing, where it does not exist, a history of the local church or churches from the time of organization; shall provide for preserving the same in permanent form; shall bring the history up to date at the close of each year; shall serve as a member of the Committee on Records and History; and shall provide for the preservation of all records and historical materials no longer in current use. There may be a local church Committee on Records and History to assist the church historian in fulfilling these responsibilities.

5. The Charge Conference may establish a limit to the consecutive terms of office for any or all of the elected or appointed officers of the local church except where otherwise

---

[5]*See* Judicial Council Decisions 170, 305, 328, 342, 469.

mandated. It is recommended that no officer serve more than three consecutive years in office.

6. The Charge Conference may make provision for the recognition of the faithful service of those members of the Administrative Board who have reached the age of seventy-two or who have become physically incapacitated by electing them honorary members. An honorary member shall be entitled to all the privileges of a member, except the right to vote.

¶ **251.** *The Church Conference.*—To encourage broader participation by members of the church, the Charge Conference may be convened as the **Church Conference,** extending the vote to all local church members present at such meetings. The Church Conference may be authorized by the district superintendent on written request of the pastor or the Administrative Board or 10 percent of the membership of the local church to the district superintendent, with a copy to the pastor, or at the discretion of the district superintendent. Additional regulations governing the call and conduct of the Charge Conference as set forth in ¶¶ 248-249 shall apply also to the Church Conference. A **joint Church Conference** for two or more churches may be held at the same time and place, as the district superintendent may determine. A Church Conference shall be conducted in the language of the majority with adequate provision being made for translation. (For Church Local Conference *see* ¶ 2521.)

THE ADMINISTRATIVE BOARD

¶ **252.** 1. *Purpose.*—The **Administrative Board** shall have general oversight of the administration and program of the local church. (*See* ¶ 245.1*a*.)

2. *Meetings.*—The Administrative Board shall meet at least quarterly. Special meetings may be ordered by the Administrative Board or called by the chairperson or the pastor.

3. *Quorum.*—The members present at any duly announced meeting shall constitute a quorum.

¶ **253.** *Membership.*—The membership of the Administrative Board shall consist of the following insofar as the offices and relationships exist within the local church:

The pastor and the associate pastor or pastors; diaconal ministers, deaconesses, and home missionaries appointed to serve therein; church and community workers under appointment by and certified by the National Division of the Board of Global Ministries, providing their memberships are in said local church, with an advisory relationship in all other churches to which they are assigned; the lay leader(s); the lay member(s) of the Annual Conference; chairperson of the trustees; the church administrator (business manager); the chairperson of the Committee on Finance; the chairperson of the Committee on Pastor-Parish Relations; the secretary of the Committee on Nominations and Personnel; the church treasurer(s); the financial secretary; the director or the associate of Christian education or the educational assistant; the director or the associate of evangelism; the director or the associate of music or the music assistant; the chairperson of the Council on Ministries; the work area chairpersons; the age-level and family coordinators; the superintendent of the church school; the health and welfare ministries representative; the coordinator of communications; the membership secretary; the president of United Methodist Women; the president of United Methodist Men; the president of the United Methodist Youth Council; members at large (¶ 247.2). The employed professional staff who are members of the Administrative Board shall not vote on matters pertaining to their employee relationship.

Members of the Administrative Board shall be persons of genuine Christian character who love the Church, are morally disciplined, are loyal to the ethical standards of The United Methodist Church set forth in the Social Principles, and are competent to administer its affairs. It shall include youth members chosen according to the same standards as adults. All shall be members of the local church, except where Central Conference legislation provides otherwise. The pastor shall be the administrative officer, and as such shall be an ex officio member of all conferences, boards, councils, commissions, committees, and task forces, unless restricted by the Discipline.[6]

¶ **254.** *Organization.*—The Administrative Board shall be organized annually by the election of a vice-chairperson and a

---

[6]*See* Judicial Council Decision 469.

recording secretary. These officers shall be lay persons elected by the members of the Administrative Board on the nomination of the Committee on Nominations and Personnel. Additional nominations may be made from the floor.

¶ 255. *Responsibilities.*—As the executive agency of the Charge Conference, the Administrative Board shall have general oversight of the administration and program of the local church (¶ 252). The pastor shall be the administrative officer. The Administrative Board shall initiate planning, establish objectives, adopt goals, authorize action, determine policy, receive reports, evaluate the church's ministries, and review the mission and ministry of the church.

1. The Administrative Board shall be responsible for administering the organization of the local church which shall include: the Council on Ministries (¶ 256), the Committee on Nominations and Personnel (¶ 266.1), the Committee on Pastor-Parish Relations (¶ 266.2), the Committee on Finance (¶ 266.3), and the trustees (¶ 2519). The Administrative Board may co-opt additional persons from time to time to assist the local church in fulfilling its mission.

2. The Administrative Board may adjust the local church's program year to correspond with the Annual Conference fiscal year. The Administrative Board shall determine the date when all elected personnel shall take office and establish their tenure except when the General Conference or the Annual Conference orders otherwise.

3. The Administrative Board shall:

a) Initiate planning, establish objectives, adopt goals and program plans for the ministries and the mission of the local church and evaluate their effectiveness. To fulfill this responsibility the board shall receive and act on recommendations from the Council on Ministries and other groups amenable to it. It shall submit an annual report to the Charge Conference.

b) Review the membership of the local church. To fulfill this responsibility the board shall receive reports from the pastor/membership secretary on membership changes, review practices of membership enlistment, training and care with the pastor and evangelism work area, and act on the goals and plans for membership growth recommended by the Council on Ministries.

c) Upon nomination by the Committee on Nominations and Personnel or from the floor, fill vacancies occurring among the lay officers listed in ¶ 247.1 between sessions of the Charge Conference.

d) Establish the budget on recommendation of the Committee on Finance.

e) Recommend to the Charge Conference the salary and other remuneration for the pastor(s) after receiving recommendations from the Committee on Pastor-Parish Relations.

f) Review the recommendation of the Pastor-Parish Relations Committee regarding the provision of adequate housing for the pastor, with attention to Annual Conference parsonage standards, and report the same to the Charge Conference for approval. It is the responsibility of the Administrative Board to provide for adequate housing for the pastor.

4. The Administrative Board shall ensure the promotion of all the benevolent causes authorized by the General, Jurisdictional, Annual, and District Conferences, and encourage the support of World Service, conference, and other benevolences. The board shall coordinate all financial promotion that takes place within the local church. It shall coordinate the promotion and interpretation of benevolences assigned to all local church persons or units, including the pastor (¶ 249.11), Committee on Finance (¶ 266.3), Council on Ministries (¶ 256), coordinator of communications (¶ 261.3), work area chairperson of missions (¶ 260.6), work area chairperson of education (¶ 260.3), and work area chairperson of stewardship (¶ 260.8). In the promotion of special days with offering (¶¶ 270-271) the Administrative Board shall assign responsibility to the local church program unit most closely related to the purpose of the offering.

5. It shall make proper and adequate provision for the financial needs of the church, including ministerial support (i.e., for the pastor or pastors, district superintendent, conference claimants, and bishops); approved items of local expense; World Service, conference, and other benevolences; other items apportioned to the church by the proper authorities; and all obligations assumed by the local church.

6. It shall discharge faithfully any and all duties and

responsibilities committed to it by the Charge Conference or by law of the Church.

7. It shall develop in the members of the congregation a concern for and responsibility in the establishment of new churches, new church schools, and other forms of ministry, and when specifically authorized by the district superintendent and the district Board of Church Location and Building (¶ 2514), it shall organize and sponsor new churches, church schools, and other forms of ministry needed in the community.

8. It shall foster understanding of the unity of the Church and shall initiate responsible participation in the ministries of the ecumenical community.

The Council on Ministries

¶ **256.** The local church **Council on Ministries** shall consider, develop, and coordinate goals and program proposals for the church's mission. It shall receive and, where possible, utilize resources for missions provided by the District, Annual, Jurisdictional, and General Conference Councils on Ministries, boards, and agencies, and shall coordinate these resources with the church's plan for ministries. The council shall be amenable to the Administrative Board, to which it shall submit its goals and program plans for revision and appropriate action. Upon adoption of the goals and program plans by the Administrative Board, the council shall implement and evaluate the goals and program plans which are assigned.

The Council on Ministries shall elect teachers, counselors, and officers for the church school except where these are subject to election by the Charge Conference. In local churches when size and organization permit, and where the educational program can be enhanced by division superintendents, the council may elect such person(s). Nominations for these positions shall be made by the work area chairperson of education upon the recommendation of the superintendent of the church school and after consultation with the pastor, the division superintendents, and such other groups or persons as the Council on Ministries may designate. It is recommended that the Committee on Nominations and Personnel be a resource in this process (¶ 265.1).

The Council on Ministries shall make recommendations to the Committee on Finance requesting the financial resources needed to undergird the ministries which it has developed, using local and connectional program suggestions, and which the council recommends to the Administrative Board.

The Council on Ministries, in consultation with the pastor, may make recommendations to the Pastor-Parish Relations Committee regarding the professional and other staff positions needed to carry out the program projected by the council.

Since local churches vary greatly in needs and size, the structure and organization required will differ. The Council on Ministries with its several elected representatives is the minimum structure for the development and administration of the local church program. The Council on Ministries, in order to implement the church's mission, may request expansion of the structure to include councils, commissions, task groups, committees, and other groups as needed. Where the committees, councils, task groups, commissions, etc., are not organized, the duties assigned to each become the responsibility of the Council on Ministries.

¶ **257.** The basic membership of the Council on Ministries shall include the following insofar as the offices and relationships exist within the local church: the pastor and other staff persons who are engaged in program work; the chairperson of the Administrative Board; the lay leader; the president of United Methodist Women; the president of United Methodist Men; the superintendent of the church school; the coordinators of age levels: children, youth, and adult; a coordinator of family ministry; the chairperson of each work area: Christian unity and interreligious concerns, church and society, education, evangelism, higher education and campus ministry, missions, religion and race, stewardship, and worship; the coordinator of communications; the local church health and welfare ministries representative; a lay member of Annual Conference; and two youth members (twelve through eighteen) and two young adult members (nineteen through thirty) of the congregation if not otherwise provided for.

The Charge Conference may elect to the Council on Ministries upon nomination of the Committee on Nominations and Personnel: a representative of United Methodist Youth

Ministry, coordinator of young adult ministries, and other persons on the basis of their competency in program planning.

The officers of the Council on Ministries shall be a chairperson, who shall be a lay person or a minister who is not a member of the local staff, a vice-chairperson, and a secretary. The chairperson shall be elected by the Charge Conference; the vice-chairperson and secretary shall be elected by the council from its own membership.

¶ **258.** *Age-Level and Family Coordinators.*—1. The Charge Conference shall elect annually a **coordinator of children's ministries,** a **coordinator of youth ministries,** a **coordinator of adult ministries,** and a **coordinator of family ministries.** Where young adult ministries would be enhanced, a **coordinator of young adult ministries** may be elected. Each of the coordinators shall, under the guidance of the minister or a representative from the employed professional staff and the chairperson of the Council on Ministries, study the needs of the age group and the goals of the congregation's ministry and coordinate the planning and implementation of a unified and comprehensive ministry with the age group. Each coordinator shall serve as liaison with organizations, persons, and resources in and beyond the local church which relate to the particular age level. The coordinator shall represent on the Council on Ministries the concerns of age-level organizations when they are not otherwise represented.

2. The **coordinator of family ministries** shall work with the age-level coordinators and the Council on Ministries to develop a family ministry for the local church, taking into consideration the suggestions of the general church agency and the Annual Conference agency responsible for family life. This coordinator shall keep the Council on Ministries aware of resources and activities to be used in planning family activities in the church and home, in the guidance of families in Christian living in the home, in the preparation of youth for marriage, and in helping families find opportunities for service in the community and the world.

¶ **259.** *Work Areas.*—Major concerns of the Church Universal and local church include Christian unity and interreligious concerns, church and society, education, evangelism, higher education and campus ministry, missions, religion and race, stewardship, and worship. Therefore the Charge Conference may elect annually the **chairperson of Christian unity and interreligious concerns,** the **chairperson of church and society,** the **chairperson of education,** the **chairperson of evangelism,** the **chairperson of higher education and campus ministry,** the **chairperson of missions,** the **chairperson of religion and race,** the **chairperson of stewardship,** and the **chairperson of worship.** Where desirable, the Charge Conference may combine coordinators' and work area chairpersons' assignments.

Each work area chairperson, with the guidance of the minister or a representative from the employed staff and the chairperson of the Council on Ministries, shall contact the program agencies, obtain guidance material, and study the implications for the work area in the total mission of the Church; shall interpret and recommend to the Council on Ministries ways of implementing the mission of the Church represented by the area; shall make specific recommendations of the work area for different age groups; shall serve as liaison within and beyond the local church. When an activity in the area of work is planned by the Council on Ministries to include two or more age levels, the chairperson of the work area may serve, when designated by the Council on Ministries, as chairperson of a group from the age levels to carry out the activity.

¶ **260.** 1. The work area **chairperson of Christian unity and interreligious concerns** shall encourage awareness and understanding of ecumenism at all levels (dialogue, councils, and unions). In keeping with standards and guidance materials supplied by the General Commission on Christian Unity and Interreligious Concerns and the Annual Conference commission (or comparble organization), the chairperson shall stimulate studies, plan programs, cooperate in specific ecumenical endeavors, and encourage conversation and fellowship with members of other Christian churches. It shall be the responsibility of the work area chairperson to interpret ecumenical structures and agencies, such as the Interdenominational Cooperation Fund, the World and National Councils of Churches, and the Consultation on Church Union to the local church.

2. The work area **chairperson of church and society** shall keep the Council on Ministries aware of the need for study and

action in the areas of peace and world order, human relations, political and economic affairs, and health and general welfare. In keeping with standards and guidance materials supplied by the Board of Church and Society and the Annual Conference Board of Church and Society (or comparable organization), the chairperson shall recommend to the Council on Ministries study/action projects in the field of social concerns. He/she shall cooperate with other commissions in surveying the needs of the local community and in recommendations for local social action projects.

3. The work area **chairperson of education** shall design and recommend to the Council on Ministries an organization of the educational program of the church in keeping with the standards and policies developed by the Board of Discipleship and shall keep the Council on Ministries aware of sound educational procedures. The chairperson shall nominate persons to the Council on Ministries for election as division superintendents (as needed), teachers, counselors, and officers of the church school.

The work area chairperson of education shall assure that persons of all ages are provided with opportunities to study the Bible and the Christian faith and life, and facilitate the use of resources which are based on curriculum plans which have been approved by the Board of Discipleship.

The work area chairperson of education shall assure that supervision is provided for week-day nursery and kindergarten programs where these are included as a part of the church's educational program. This supervision shall include selection, guidance, and training of leaders, resources, and budget.

The chairperson shall promote the local observance of Christian Education Sunday to emphasize the importance of Christian education and to receive an offering to strengthen Christian education in areas of greatest need. The offerings shall be sent to the treasurer of the conference, who shall distribute the funds in accordance with ¶ 271.3*e*.

4. The work area **chairperson of evangelism** shall keep the Council on Ministries aware of the aim and means of evangelism in the goals for the Church's ministry. In keeping with the standards and guidance material supplied by the General Board of Discipleship and the Annual Conference Board of Disciple-

ship (or comparable organization), he/she shall recommend activities and structure to respond to the evangelistic mission of the local church. He/she shall assist the age-group councils to respond to evangelistic opportunities in the community so that every person is included in the responsibility of a local church. In cooperation with the pastor and the Council on Ministries the chairperson shall develop and implement ministries for membership care including growth in the devotional life and distribution of *The Upper Room* and other devotional resources.

5.*a)* The work area **chairperson of higher education and campus ministry** shall keep the Council on Ministries aware of higher education concerns and provide locally for the promotion and support of the interest of higher education and campus ministry in accordance with the programs of the Annual Conference and the General Board of Higher Education and Ministry. This shall include plans for the ministry to students related to the local church, recruitment of students for United Methodist institutions, promoting the observance of United Methodist Student Day, and the receiving of an offering for the support of the United Methodist scholarships and for the United Methodist Student Loan Fund (¶ 271.3*h*).

b) The work area chairperson of higher education and campus ministry shall coordinate and guide, with the pastor and related interests of the local church, a program of interpretation and counseling which will assist persons in their career planning and occupational decisions related to the church.

c) The work area chairperson of higher education and campus ministry shall inform the appropriate church agencies and ministries of the names and addresses of young persons from the local church who attend school, receive training, join the military, or are in other situations which require their moving temporarily or permanently from the local church area.

6. The work area **chairperson of missions** shall keep the Council on Ministries aware of the purpose and needs of programs and institutions supported by the Church in the nation and around the world. In keeping with the standards and guidance material supplied by the Board of Global Ministries and the Annual Conference Board of Global Ministries (or comparable organization), the chairperson shall provide resources to be used in the

study program of the church. Through the council he/she shall cooperate with other commissions in surveying the needs of the local community and recommend to the Council on Ministries plans for local mission and service projects and for participation in enterprises related to the National Division or the Health and Welfare Ministries Division of the Board of Global Ministries in the geographic area of the local church. The chairperson shall recommend means of keeping the church informed of the qualifications and current needs for personnel to serve through the Church around the world. He/she shall develop a benevolence budget and submit it to the Council on Ministries for its recommendation to the Committee on Finance. The chairperson shall recommend Advance specials on behalf of the entire Church and in addition shall promote acceptance of Advance specials by individuals and groups.

7. The work area **chairperson of religion and race** shall keep the Council on Ministries and the congregation aware of the meaning of a racial and ethnic pluralistic United Methodist Church. In keeping with the standards and guidance material supplied by the Commission on Religion and Race and the Annual Conference Commission on Religion and Race (or comparable organization), he/she shall recommend to the Council on Ministries program opportunities for worship, fellowship, witness, study, nurture, and service with persons, groups, and congregations across racial and ethnic lines.

8. The work area **chairperson of stewardship** shall interpret the biblical and theological basis for stewardship consistent with the doctrines of The United Methodist Church and inform the church of the same through educational channels and study materials. The chairperson shall keep the Council on Ministries aware of the meaning of the stewardship of life, time, talent, and material possessions as evidences of the fruits of the Spirit. In keeping with the standards and guidance material supplied by the General and Annual Conference boards, he/she shall recommend to the Council on Ministries or the age-group councils, materials and methods for keeping the people involved in service and mission. In churches where the Commission on Stewardship is organized, the Council on Ministries shall elect representatives

of the Committee on Finance to serve on the commission. The chairperson of the work area on stewardship shall be a member of the Committee on Finance. (*See* ¶ 265.3.)

The chairperson of stewardship in cooperation with the Council on Ministries may organize a **Wills Task Force** which shall have the responsibility to (1) emphasize the need for adults of all ages to have wills and provide information on the preparation of wills by the members of the congregation, (2) stress the need for church members and constituents to make bequests and special gifts to United Methodist churches, institutions, agencies, and causes by means of wills, annuities, trusts, life insurance, memorials, and various types of property. The task force shall receive resources from the Board of Discipleship for program assistance and direction.

9. The work area **chairperson of worship** shall aid the congregation to become increasingly aware of the meaning, purpose, and practice of worship. In keeping with the standards and guidance material supplied by the Board of Discipleship, the chairperson shall recommend plans for the study by individuals and groups of the art of worship; shall cooperate with the pastor in planning and caring for worship, music, and the other arts, ushering, furnishings, appointments, and sacramental elements for congregational worship; shall recommend standards for the placement in the church of memorial gifts as aids to worship. To the end that music and other arts may contribute largely to the communication and celebration of the gospel, the work area chairperson shall promote adequate musical leadership in the church; cooperate with other educational enterprises of the church in teaching persons of all ages our heritage of song and the meaning of worship as it uses music and other arts both traditional and contemporary; encourage certification of music leaders as directors and ministers of music and music associates; encourage wider use and understanding of visual arts, dramatic arts, and architectural design as expressions of faith and means of proclamation of the gospel; seek guidance and resources from appropriate general agencies, commissions, or task groups.

¶ **261.** *Program Support Personnel.*—1. The Charge Conference may elect a **superintendent of the church school** who shall be responsible, under the guidance of the education work area chairperson or commission and the pastor or representative of the employed staff, for the supervision of the total program of education in the church. Responsibilities may include: *(a)* serving as the administrator of the church school; *(b)* recommending persons to the work area chairperson or Commission on Education for election by the Council on Ministries as teachers and leaders of the church school; *(c)* identifying the needs for various kinds of study opportunities and recommending plans for a study program in accordance with those needs; *(d)* serving as an educational consultant to persons responsible for the Christian education of children, the Christian education of youth, the Christian education of adults, and Christian education for marriage and family life; *(e)* developing and implementing programs to promote church school attendance and participation; and *(f)* evaluating the effectiveness of the study program of the church. When desirable, in churches with small membership, the Charge Conference may combine responsibilities of the superintendent of the church school and the chairperson of the work area on education.

2. The **health and welfare ministries representative,** if elected, shall assist the local church and its people to be involved in direct service to persons in need especially in the areas of child care, aging, health care, and handicapping conditions and shall help coordinate these ministries. The representative shall serve as the chairperson of the Committee on Health and Welfare Ministries, if it is organized, or may serve as a member of the work area commissions on missions and/or church and society.

The responsibilities of this representative shall be: *(a)* to act as liaison between the local church and the Annual Conference and general church Health and Welfare Ministries units and to make use of guidance materials and leadership training from these units; *(b)* to help the local church be knowledgeable about, supportive of, and make use of services provided through United Methodist–related health and welfare agencies in the Annual Conference or geographic area; *(c)* to promote within the local church the observance of the Golden Cross offering and other efforts to provide financial support for health and welfare ministries; *(d)* to work through the Council on Ministries and with other groups in the local church, particularly the work areas on missions and church and society, to locate human need in the church and community, to support existing programs or to initiate new programs, including local church direct service ministries, to meet those needs, and to advocate needed social change; *(e)* to encourage the local church to be aware of the needs of persons with handicapping conditions and mental retardation, especially the need for the local church to be structurally accessible.

3. The **coordinator of communications,** if elected, shall assist church members with communication tasks, which are a responsibility of all Christians, making available ideas, resources, and skills. The coordinator shall advise and assist work areas, committees and organizations of the local church with their communications. She or he shall help to accomplish effective communications throughout the congregation and make resources available, utilizing district, conference, and general church agencies. Major areas of responsibility are: *(a)* external communications, to the community; *(b)* internal communications, within the congregation; and *(c)* promotion of local, district, conference, and churchwide program and benevolences.

¶ **262.** *Program Agencies.*—The ministries of the local church are implemented through the encounter of persons with God's redeeming love for the world and with his action in the world. To achieve this ministry persons are involved in age-level or family groupings. Usually a variety of settings is essential. Some will be formed by the Council on Ministries. Others will emerge with the approval of the Council on Ministries. Another type is historical, expressing itself in organizational structures that are related to counterparts in Annual Conferences and the general Church. These are referred to as **program agencies** and are related to the Council on Ministries through its age-level and family coordinators, work area chairpersons, and councils or commissions of the Council on Ministries.

1. *The Church School.*—In each local church there shall be a **church school** for the purpose of accomplishing the church's educational ministry in accordance with ¶ 1308.

a) The church school provides a variety of settings and resources for all persons—children, youth, and adults—to explore the meanings of the Christian faith in all its dimensions, to discover and appropriate to themselves those meanings which are relevant for their lives and for society, and to assume personal responsibility for expressing those meanings in all their relationships. Through such experiences persons will be encouraged to commit themselves to Christ and to unite with the Christian community through membership in a local church. The Board of Discipleship, sets standards and provides guidance resources and plans for the organization, administration, grouping, and leadership of the church school (¶ 1309.1).

b) All the concerns of the church will be present in the church school's educational ministry: Christian unity and interreligious concerns, church and society, evangelism, higher education and campus ministry, missions, religion and race, stewardship, and worship. The curriculum of the church school will include the meanings and experiences of the Christian faith as found in the Bible, in history, and in human encounter with the natural world and contemporary society. The resources shall be based on curriculum plans approved by the Board of Discipleship (¶ 1323).

c) The church school shall be administratively related to the Commission on Education, if organized, or the unit responsible for Christian education. The superintendent of the church school, who is the administrator of the church school, shall be responsible for relating the church school to the total ministry of the church through the Commission on Education, if organized, and the Council on Ministries.

d) Church school settings include the Sunday church school and all other ongoing and short-term classes and learning groups for persons of all ages. The church school may be organized with three divisions if desired: children's divisions for persons from birth through the sixth grade; youth division for persons from the seventh grade through the twelfth grade; and adult division for persons beyond the twelfth grade. Division superintendents, teachers, counselors, church school secretary, curriculum resources secretary, librarian, and such other officers as needed to administer and operate the church school shall be nominated by the work area chairperson on education upon the recommendation of the superintendent of the church school in consultation with the minister or representative of the employed staff and elected by the Council on Ministries.

e) The chairperson of the work area on education may suggest to the Council on Ministries of the local church to recommend to the Administrative Board that the Fourth Sunday's church school offerings be set aside for World Service.

f) Mission education shall be a part of the church school education for children. The chairperson of the work area on education and the children's division superintendent (if elected) or the coordinator of children's ministries shall interpret the Children's Fund for Christian Mission (to be referred to as the United Methodist Children's Fund for Christian Mission) as a means of mission education for children. This fund is established in accordance with ¶¶ 1306.5 and 1308.7.

2. *Youth Ministry.*—The term "youth ministry" is an inclusive title, encompassing all the concerns of the church and all activities by, with, and for youth. The youth ministry of The United Methodist Church shall include all persons from approximately twelve through eighteen years of age (generally persons in the seventh grade through the twelfth grade, taking into account the grouping of youth in the public schools), who are currently or potentially associated with the church or any of its activities.

Youth who are full members of the church have all rights and responsibilities of church membership except voting on matters prohibited by state law. (*See* ¶ 226.) The coordinator of youth ministries and the Youth Council, when organized, shall be responsible for recommending to the Council on Ministries activities, program emphases, and settings for youth. The local church may designate one of its settings as the United Methodist Youth Fellowship. The coordinator and council shall use available resources and means to inform youth concerning the Youth Service Fund and shall cultivate its support; *provided* that prior to this cultivation or as a part of it, the youth shall have been challenged to assume their financial responsibilities in connection with the total program and budget of the local church.

challenged to assume their financial responsibilities in connection with the total program and budget of the local church.

3. *Young Adult Ministry.*—The ministry of the local church shall include and be extended to persons out of high school (approximately nineteen through thirty years of age). Such ministry shall seek to meet the needs of young adults and bring them to a knowledge of Jesus Christ. Such ministry shall be the responsibility of the Council on Ministries, working through its adult coordinator or young adult coordinator, if elected, or the Adult/Young Adult Council, if organized. A cooperative approach to young adult ministries with other churches, denominations, community organizations and groups shall be encouraged as a valid outreach ministry of the local United Methodist church.

4. *Older Adult Ministry.*—The ministry of the local church shall include and be extended to persons sixty-five years of age and older. Such ministry shall seek to meet the needs of older adults and bring them into the fellowship, ministry, and service of the local congregation. Such ministry shall be the responsibility of the Council on Ministries, working through its adult coordinator or older adult coordinator, if elected, or the Adult/Older Adult Council, if organized. A cooperative approach to older adult ministries with other churches, denominations, community organizations, and groups shall be encouraged as a valid outreach ministry of the local United Methodist church.

5. *United Methodist Women.*—In every local church there shall be an organized unit of **United Methodist Women.** The following is the authorized constitution:

Article 1. Name.—The name of this organization shall be United Methodist Women.

Article 2. Relationships.—The unit of United Methodist Women in the local church is directly related to the district and conference organizations of United Methodist Women and to the Women's Division of the Board of Global Ministries of The United Methodist Church.

Article 3. Purpose.—The organized unit of United Methodist Women shall be a community of women whose purpose is to know God and to experience freedom as whole persons through Jesus Christ; to develop a creative, supportive fellowship; and to expand concepts of mission through participation in the global ministries of the church.

Article 4. Membership.—Membership shall be open to any woman who indicates her desire to belong and to participate in the global mission of the church through United Methodist Women. The pastor(s) shall be an ex officio member of the local unit and of its executive committee.

Article 5. Officers and Committees.—The local unit shall elect a president, a vice-president, a secretary, a treasurer, and a Committee on Nominations. Additional officers and committees shall be elected or appointed as needed, in accordance with the plans of the Women's Division as set forth in the bylaws for the local unit of United Methodist Women.

Article 6. Funds.—*a)* The organized unit of United Methodist Women shall secure funds for the fulfillment of its purpose.

b) All funds, from whatever source secured by the unit of United Methodist Women, belong to the organization and shall be disbursed only in accordance with its constitution and by its order.

c) The total budget secured and administered by the organized unit in the local church shall include (1) pledges and other money for the programs and responsibilities of the Women's Division to be directed through regular channels of finance of United Methodist Women; and (2) funds to be used in mission locally, which shall include amounts for administration and membership development.

d) The organized unit in the local church shall make an annual pledge to the total budget of the district or conference organization of United Methodist Women.

e) All undesignated funds channeled to the Women's Division shall be appropriated by the division.

Article 7. Meetings.—The organized unit in the local church shall hold such meetings for implementing the purpose and transacting its business as the unit itself shall decide.

Article 8. Relationship in the Local Church.—The organized unit of United Methodist Women shall encourage all women to participate in the total life and work of the church and shall support them in assuming positions of responsibility and leadership.

Article 9. Amendments.—Proposed amendments to this constitution may be sent to the recording secretary of the Women's Division of the Board of Global Ministries before the last annual meeting of the division in the quadrennium.

Note: For a description of the Women's Division of the Board of Global Ministries and its subsidiary organizations see ¶¶ 1547-1555.

6. *United Methodist Men.*—Each church or charge shall be encouraged to have a fellowship of **United Methodist Men** chartered through the Board of Discipleship to provide another channel for involving men in the total ministry of the church.

a) Resources for organization and implementation of the ministry of men at the local church, district, conference, and jurisdictional levels shall be provided by the Board of Discipleship.

b) United Methodist Men shall be a creative supportive fellowship of men who seek to know Jesus Christ, to grow spiritually, and to seek daily his will. Its primary purpose is to declare the centrality of Christ in the lives of men and in all their relationships. The major concerns are:

(1) To encourage knowledge of and support for the total mission of The United Methodist Church.

(2) To engage in evangelism by sharing the fullness of the gospel in its personal and social dimensions.

(3) To clarify and speak to the identity and role of the man in contemporary society.

(4) To seek commitment to discipleship.

(5) To study and become familiar with The United Methodist Church, its organization, doctrines, and belief.

(6) To cooperate with all units of United Methodist Men in obtaining these objectives through district, conference, and church-wide goals.

c) Persons seeking membership in a local United Methodist Men's fellowship shall subscribe to the major concerns listed in §*b* above and to these personal objectives:

(1) To engage daily in Bible study and prayer.

(2) To bear witness to Christ's way in daily work and in all personal contacts through words and actions.

(3) To engage in some definite Christian service.

d) Fellowships of United Methodist Men may be formed in clusters and in other groupings of local chuches as needed.

e) The duly appointed pastor(s) of the church shall be ex officio member(s) of its fellowship and its executive committee.

¶ 263. *Age-Level and Family Councils.*—Where the size of the church and the extent of the program indicate the need, the work of the Council on Ministries may be facilitated by one or more **age-level councils** and/or a **family council,** or such other means as fit the needs of the congregation. The age-level councils shall work under the leadership of the age-level coordinators to expedite the work of the Council on Ministries in adapting the program to the age level.

The membership of these councils, except for ex officio members, shall be elected by the Council on Ministries and may include the following:

1. *Children's Council.*—Representative teachers and leaders of children's activities of the church (including its activities in music and the other arts), representative parents, and representatives of work areas (Christian unity and interreligious concerns, church and society, education, evangelism, higher education and campus ministry, missions, religion and race, stewardship, and worship) related to the church's ministry with children. The council may also include the director of the weekday nursery school or day care center (if such is provided), when the nursery school or day care center is sponsored by the local church.

2. *Youth Council.*—Representatives of adult leaders and counselors of youth, representative parents, representatives of work areas (Christian unity and interreligious concerns, church and society, education, evangelism, higher education and campus ministry, missions, religion and race, stewardship, and worship) related to the church's ministry with youth, representatives of the church's activities in music and the other arts, a youth and an adult from each youth-serving organization sponsored by the church, and in a number that is at least one youth for each adult on the council.

3. *Adult Council.*—Representatives of adult study/action groups, fellowship groups, administrative groups, and service organizations such as United Methodist Women, United Methodist Men, and young adult ministry; and representatives of work

areas (Christian unity and interreligious concerns, church and society, education, evangelism, higher education and campus ministry, missions, religion and race, stewardship, and worship) related to the church's ministry with adults. Where the young adult ministries would be enhanced, a **Young Adult Council** may be organized. Where the older adult ministries would be enhanced, an **Older Adult Council** may be organized.

4. *Family Council.*—When the size of the church and the extent of the program indicate the need, the Council on Ministries may designate a group including representatives of the age-group councils and work areas to work with the coordinator in planning program suggestions to be submitted to the Council on Ministries.

The minister or a member of the professional staff of the church appointed by the minister shall be an ex officio member of each council. Additional members, such as representatives of community agencies, may be elected to each council on the basis of their interest and competency.

The coordinators shall serve as the chairpersons of their respective councils except that the Council on Ministries may authorize the Youth Council to elect its own chairperson.

¶ **264.** *Work Area Commissions.*—When the size of the church and the extent of the program indicate the need, the Council on Ministries may choose to establish one or more work area commissions (Christian unity and interreligious concerns, church and society, education, evangelism, higher education and campus ministry, missions, religion and race, stewardship, and worship). Where a commission is established, it shall work under the leadership of the work area chairperson and shall assume the responsibilities herein assigned to that chairperson. The representative of the work area serving on each age-level council shall be a member of the commission. At least two youths shall be included in the membership of all commissions. The Council on Ministries may elect other persons to the commission because of unusual interest and competency in the area. The pastor or a representative of the employed professional staff appointed by the pastor shall serve as an ex officio member of each commission.

¶ **265. Task groups** may be formed by the Council on Ministries, its councils or commissions, for the purpose of accomplishing specific and particular goals of the Church's mission to the world. These groups shall be oriented to immediate tasks. They shall prepare for their mission by the study of the Scriptures' mandates in the light of the community's immediate needs. They shall meet regularly for study and for planning their strategy in mission. They shall be disciplined to individual and corporate action and shall be amenable to the Council on Ministries and report to it.

ADMINISTRATIVE COMMITTEES

¶ **266.** 1. There shall be elected annually by the Charge Conference in each local church a **Committee on Nominations and Personnel** composed of not more than nine persons, excluding the pastor, who shall be chairperson. The committee shall nominate to the Charge Conference or Church Conference in its annual session such officers and members of the Administrative Board and Charge Conference and committees as the law of the Church requires or as the conference may determine as necessary to its work; *provided* that to secure experience and stability the membership shall be divided into three classes, one of which shall be elected each year for a three-year term; *provided* further, that to begin the process of rotation on the first year one class be elected for one year, one class for two years, and one for three years; *provided* further, that each year the new class of members to serve on the Committee on Nominations and Personnel, and vacancies as they occur, shall be elected from nominees from the floor. At least one youth and one young adult, elected by the Charge Conference or Church Conference, shall serve as members of the Committee on Nominations and Personnel. Churches are encouraged to establish a policy that retiring members of the Committee on Nominations and Personnel not succeed themselves.

The Committee on Nominations and Personnel shall serve throughout the year to guide the Administrative Board on personnel matters (other than employed staff) so as to coordinate the leadership and service needs with personnel of the congregation, working in relationship to the Council on Ministries and the committees of the Administrative Board in both its nominations and personnel guidance.

In the nomination process, care shall be given that each board, committee, council, and work area, as well as the total nominated personnel shall, insofar as possible, be representative of the age level, sexual, cultural, racial/ethnic membership, as well as economic, social, and theological orientation of the congregation.

2. There shall be a **Committee on Pastor-Parish Relations (Staff-Parish Relations)** of not fewer than five nor more than nine lay persons representative of the total charge, including one young adult and a lay member of the Annual Conference; one senior high youth may be included. No staff member or immediate family member of a pastor or staff member may serve on the committee. If a person ineligible to serve on the committee is elected as a lay member to Annual Conference and there is no other elected lay member to the Annual Conference available to serve, the vacancy will be filled upon election by the Charge Conference following the nomination of the Committee on Nominations and Personnel.

a) The members, including the chairperson, shall be elected by the Charge Conference upon nomination by the Committee on Nominations and Personnel. In order to secure experience and stability, the membership shall be divided into three classes, one of which shall be elected each year for a three-year term. Where there is more than one church on a charge, the committee shall include at least one representative from each congregation.

b) In those charges where there is a multiple staff, full or part time, the committee shall relate to the entire staff, clergy and lay, providing to all staff members direct personal and professional access to the Pastor-Parish Relations Committee as well as to the pastor, the district superintendent, and the bishop. In such cases the committee may be known as the Staff-Parish Relations Committee.

c) In those charges where there is more than one church, the committee shall include at least one representative from each local church. The Charge Conference may appoint a local church pastoral advisory committee for those churches which desire such a committee, the chairperson of which shall be the church's representative on the charge committee.

d) The Pastor-Parish Relations Committees of charges which are in cooperative parish ministries shall meet together to consider the professional leadership needs of the cooperative parish ministry as a whole.

e) The committee shall meet at least quarterly. It shall meet additionally at the request of the bishop, the district superintendent, the pastor, any member of the professional staff, or the chairperson of the committee. The committee shall meet only with the knowledge of the pastor and/or the district superintendent. It may meet with the district superintendent without the pastor being present; however, when the pastor is not present, the pastor, or any member of the staff under consideration, shall be informed prior to such a meeting and immediately thereafter be brought into consultation either by the committee or by the district superintendent. In the event that only one congregation on a charge containing more than one church has concerns which it wishes to share, its member(s) in the committee may meet separately with the pastor or any member of the professional staff or the district superintendent, but only with the knowledge of the pastor and/or district superintendent. The committee may meet in closed session upon recommendation of the pastor, or any other person accountable to the committee, or the chairperson of the committee, or the district superintendent.

f) The duties of the committee shall include the following:

(1) To confer and counsel with the pastor and staff in making an effective ministry by being available for counsel, keeping the pastor and staff advised concerning conditions within the congregation as they affect relations between the pastor/staff and the people, and continually interpreting to the people the nature and function of the ministry.

(2) To counsel with the pastor and staff on matters pertaining to their relationship with the congregation, including priorities to be given in the use of their time and skill in relation to the goals and objectives set for the congregation's mission and the demands upon the ministry.

(3) To evaluate annually the effectiveness of the pastor and staff. It is recommended that materials provided by the conference Board of Ordained Ministry and the conference Board of Diaconal Ministry and other appropriate agencies be utilized in this process.

(4) To consult on matters pertaining to pulpit supply, proposals for salary, travel expense, vacation, health and life insurance, pension, continuing education, housing (which may be a church owned parsonage or housing allowance in lieu of parsonage if in compliance with the policy of the annual conference), and other practical matters affecting the work and families of the pastor and staff, and to make annual recommendations regarding such matters to the Administrative Board, reporting budget items to the Committee on Finance. The committee may arrange with the Administrative Board for the necessary time and financial assistance for the attendance of the pastor and/or staff at such continuing education events as may serve their professional and spiritual growth. The parsonage is to be mutually respected by the pastor's family as the property of the church and by the church as the private home of the pastor's family. The chairperson of the Pastor-Parish Relations Committee, the chairperson of trustees, and pastor shall make an annual review of the church owned parsonage to assure proper maintenance.

(5) To enlist, interview, evaluate, review, and recommend annually to the Charge Conference women and men of all races and ethnic origin for candidacy for ministry. The committee shall provide to the Charge Conference a list of ministerial students from the charge and shall maintain contact with these students, supplying the Charge Conference with a progress report on each student.

(6) To interpret preparation for ministry and the Ministerial Education Fund to the congregation.

(7) To confer with the pastor and/or other appointed members of the staff if it should become evident that the best interests of the charge and pastor(s) will be served by a change of pastor(s). The committee shall cooperate with the pastor(s), the district superintendent, and the bishop in securing clergy leadership. Its relationship to the district superintendent and the bishop shall be advisory only.

(8) To recommend to the Administrative Board, after consultation with the pastor and the Council on Ministries, the professional and other staff positions needed to carry out the work of the church or charge. After consultation with the pastor,

the committee shall recommend persons for employment in the staff positions created by the board which are not subject to episcopal appointment. In making recommendations of persons for professional staff positions, consideration shall be given to the training qualifications and certification standards set forth by the general church agency to which such positions are related. The committee shall further recommend to the Administrative Board a provision for adequate health, life, and pension benefits for all lay employees.

(9) To recommend to the Charge Conference, when the size of the employed staff of the charge makes it desirable, the establishment of a Personnel Committee. This committee shall be composed of such members of the Pastor-Parish Relations Committee as it may designate and such additional members as the Charge Conference may determine.

3. There shall be a **Committee on Finance,** elected annually by the Charge Conference upon nomination by the Committee on Nominations and Personnel, composed of the chairperson; the pastor(s); a lay member of the Annual Conference; the chairperson of the Administrative Board; the chairperson of the Council on Ministries; a representative of the trustees to be selected by the trustees; the chairperson of the work area on stewardship; the lay leader; the financial secretary; the treasurer; the church business administrator; and other members to be added as the Charge Conference may determine. It is recommended that the chairperson of the Committee on Finance shall be a member of the Council on Ministries. The financial secretary, treasurer, and church business administrator, if paid employees, shall be members without vote.

Inasmuch as giving is clearly an integral part of Christian life, a program should be developed within every local church to carry on education in the field of stewardship of possessions to the end that there may be growth in standard of giving, with an emphasis on concepts of proportionate giving and tithing. This program should be auxiliary to the stewardship program in the area of stewardship in the Board of Discipleship (¶ 260.6).

All financial askings to be included in the annual budget of the local church shall be submitted to the Committee on Finance. The Committee on Finance shall compile annually a complete budget for the local church and submit it to the Administrative Board for review and adoption. The Committee on Finance shall be charged with responsibility for developing and implementing plans which will raise sufficient income to meet the budget adopted by the Administrative Board. It shall administer the funds received according to instructions from the Administrative Board.

The committee shall carry out the Administrative Board's directions in guiding the treasurer(s) and financial secretary.

a) The committee shall designate at least two persons (preferably not of the same family) to count the offering, giving a record of funds received to both the financial secretary and church treasurer. Funds received shall be deposited promptly in accordance with procedures established by the Committee on Finance. The financial secretary shall keep records of the contributions and payments.

b) The **church treasurer(s)** shall disburse all money contributed to causes represented in the local church budget, and such other funds and contributions as the Administrative Board may determine. The treasurer(s) shall remit each month to the conference treasurer all World Service and conference benevolence funds then on hand. Contributions to benevolence shall not be used for any cause other than that to which they have been given. The church treasurer shall make regular and detailed reports on funds received and expended to the Committee on Finance and the Administrative Board.[7]

c) The committee shall make provision for an annual audit of the records of the financial officers of the local church and all its organizations and shall report to the Charge Conference.

d) The committee shall recommend to the Administrative Board proper depositories for the church's funds. Funds received shall be deposited promptly in the name of the local church.

e) Contributions designated for specific causes and objects shall be promptly forwarded according to the intent of the donor and shall not be used for any other purpose.

---

[7]*See* Judicial Council Decisions 63, 320.

f) After the budget of the local church has been approved, additional appropriations or changes in the budget must be approved by the Administrative Board.

g) The committee shall prepare annually a report to the Administrative Board of all designated funds which are separate from the current expense budget.

4. The Administrative Board may appoint such other committees as it deems advisable, including: Committee on Communications, Committee on Estate Planning, Committee on Records and History, and Committee on Health and Welfare.

Section VI. The Method of Organizing a New Local Church.

¶ 267. 1. A new local church or **mission** shall be established only with the consent of the bishop in charge and his Cabinet and with due consideration of the conference Board of Global Ministries' programs of home missions and church extension (if any; *see* ¶ 720). The bishop shall designate the district within whose bounds the church shall be organized. The district superintendent of that district shall be the agent in charge of the project and shall recommend to the district Board of Church Location and Building (¶ 2514) the site for the proposed new congregation. If there is a city or district missionary organization, that body shall also be asked to approve this site (¶ 1530.4).

2. The district superintendent shall call the persons interested in the proposed church to meet at an appointed time and place, or may by written authorization designate any pastor in the district to call such a meeting.

3. The district superintendent or the pastor to whom authority is designated shall preside and shall appoint a secretary to keep a record of the meeting. Following a period of worship, opportunity shall be given those in attendance to present themselves for membership by proper certificates of transfer. Pastors issuing such certificates to a church not yet organized shall describe therein the proposed new church to which it is issued, as, for instance, "the proposed new church on Boston Avenue."

4. Persons desiring to become members on profession of their faith in Christ shall also be given opportunity to present themselves for membership. When the presiding pastor is

satisfied as to the genuineness of their faith and purpose, they shall be received into the membership of the Church.

5. A list shall be made of all the persons received into the membership of the proposed church, by transfer and on profession. Those persons shall be members of the **Constituting Church Conference,** and each shall be entitled to vote.

6. The Constituting Church Conference shall then be called to order, and it shall proceed to choose the members at large of the church on nomination of a committee on nominations. Such committee shall be appointed by the presiding pastor or elected on nomination from the floor, as the conference may determine. In either case the presiding pastor shall be chairperson. When the members at large have been chosen in proper number, the presiding pastor shall declare the church properly constituted.

7. The presiding pastor shall then adjourn the Constituting Church Conference and call to order the Charge Conference of the pastoral charge. The membership of the Charge Conference shall be those newly elected and any others entitled to membership. The Charge Conference shall then elect such officers of the church as the Discipline requires, including trustees of church property, and shall set up commissions and committees as provided in the Discipline. When such officers have been duly elected and the proper commissions and committees constituted, the church is duly organized, and from this point its work shall proceed as described in the Discipline; *provided* that when a newly organized church is attached to a circuit, the Charge Conference shall not be held until such time as representatives from all the churches of the charge can be properly assembled for that purpose.

8. The Charge Conference may take action at its discretion, authorizing and directing the newly elected trustees to incorporate the newly organized church in accordance with local laws and the provisions of the Discipline.

Section VII. Transfer of a Local Church.

¶ 268. A local church may be transferred from one Annual Conference to another in which it is geographically located by a two-thirds vote of those present and voting in each of the following: (1) the Charge Conference, (2) a congregational meeting of the local church, and (3) each of the two Annual Conferences involved. Upon announcement of the required majorities by the bishop or bishops involved, the transfer shall immediately be effective. The votes required may originate in the local church or either of the Annual Conferences involved and shall be effective regardless of the order in which taken. In each case a two-thirds vote of those present and voting shall remain effective unless and until rescinded prior to the completion of the transfer by a vote of a majority of those present and voting.

Section VIII. Protection of Rights of Congregations.

¶ 269. Nothing in the Plan and Basis of Union at any time after the union is to be construed so as to require any local church of the former Church of the United Brethren in Christ, or of the former The Evangelical Church, or of the former The Evangelical United Brethren Church, or of the former The Methodist Church to alienate or in any way to change the title to property contained in its deed or deeds at the time of union; and lapse of time or usage shall not affect said title or control.

Section IX. Special Sundays.

¶ 270. The special Sundays in the United Methodist Church are intended to be illustrative of the nature and calling of the Church and are celebrated annually. The special Sundays are placed on the calendar in the context of the Christian year, which is designed to make clear the calling of the Church as the people of God, and to give persons the opportunity of contributing offerings to special programs.

Four special churchwide Sundays provide for churchwide offerings to do deeds expressive of our commitment: Human Relations Day, One Great Hour of Sharing, United Methodist Student Day, and World Communion Sunday. Three special Sundays without offering: Heritage Sunday, Laity Sunday, and World Order Sunday. One churchwide Sunday, Christian Education Sunday, and one Annual Conference Sunday, Golden Cross Sunday, provide opportunities for Annual Conference offerings.

General Provisions
Regarding Churchwide Special Sundays

¶ 271. The special Sundays approved by General Conference shall be the only Sundays of churchwide emphasis. The program calendar of the denomination shall include only the special Sundays approved by General Conference, special Sundays approved by ecumenical agencies to which The United Methodist Church is officially related, and the days and seasons of the Christian year.

1. *Special Sundays with Offering.*—The purpose of the churchwide offerings shall be determined by General Conference upon recommendation of the General Council on Finance and Administration, after consultation with the Council of Bishops and the General Council on Ministries. The purpose of these funds shall remain constant for the quadrennium and shall be promoted by the General Commission on Communication.

Each offering shall be promptly remitted by the local church treasurer to the Annual Conference treasurer, who shall transmit the funds to the General Council on Finance and Administration within thirty (30) days of receipt in the office of the Annual Conference treasurer.

2. *Special Sundays without Offering.*—The program functions assigned to the general agencies are carried out by the respective agencies through normal programmatic channels. Special Sundays are not needed for these program functions to be implemented.

The two special Sundays without offering are to be administered as follows:

a) Heritage Sunday—Commission on Archives and History

b) Laity Sunday—The Board of Discipleship

c) Any general agency of the Church which desires to recommend a theme for a given year for either of these two Sundays may do so one year prior to the observance for which the recommendation is made. This recommendation is to be made to the administering agency, and the decision of the annual theme of these Sundays shall be made by the voting members of the administering agency.

d) The Sundays without offering shall be approved by the General Conference upon recommendation of the General Council on Ministries, after consultation with the Council of Bishops.

3. *Churchwide Special Sundays.*—The churchwide special Sundays are as follows:

a) Human Relations Day shall be observed on the last Sunday of the Season of Epiphany with an offering goal recommended by the General Council on Finance and Administration. Epiphany is the season of manifesting God's light to the world. Human Relations Day calls the Church to recognize the right of all God's children in realizing their potential as human beings in relationship with each other. The purpose of the day is to further the development of better human relations through funding programs determined by the General Conference upon recommendation of the General Council on Finance and Administration after consultation with the General Council on Ministries.

For the 1981-84 quadrennium an annual goal of $750,000 shall be established; the offering receipts will be allocated and administered as follows:

(1) *Community Developers Program:* Fifty percent (administered by the National Division, General Board of Global Ministries).

(2) *United Methodist Voluntary Services Program:* Forty-five percent (administered by the National Division, General Board of Global Ministries).

(3) *Police-Community Relations Program:* Five percent (administered by the General Board of Church and Society).

Net receipts of the Human Relations Day Offering shall be distributed on ratio to the administering agencies.

b) One Great Houring of Sharing shall be observed on the fourth Sunday of Lent. Lent is the season of repentance, self-examination, and awareness of the hurts of the peoples of the world. One Great Hour of Sharing calls the Church to share the goodness of life with those who hurt. All local churches shall be fully informed and encouraged to receive a freewill offering in behalf of the relief program. The observance shall be under the general supervision of the General Commission on Communication. Insofar as possible, the planning and promotion of the One

Great Hour of Sharing shall be done cooperatively with other denominations through the National Council of Churches, it being understood, however, that receipts shall be administered by The United Methodist Church. Net receipts from the offering, after payment of the expenses of promotion, shall be remitted by the treasurer of the General Council on Finance and Administration to the United Methodist Committee on Relief Division of the General Board of Global Ministries, to be administered by that committee.

c) Heritage Sunday shall be observed on the Sunday following April 23, the date of birth of The United Methodist Church. It falls during Eastertide, the season in which we remember the Resurrection and triumph of our Lord. Heritage Sunday calls the Church to remember the past by committing itself to the continuing call of God.

d) Laity Sunday shall be observed on the second Sunday in October. Laity Sunday calls the Church to celebrate the ministry of all Christians, including lay men, lay women, and youth, as their lives are empowered for ministry by the Holy Spirit.

e) Christian Education Sunday shall be observed on a date determined by the Annual Conference. It calls the Church as the people of God to be open to growth and learning as disciples of Jesus Christ. If the Annual Conference so directs, an offering may be received for the work of Christian education within the Annual Conference. Local church treasurers shall remit the receipts of the offering to the Annual Conference treasurer, and receipts will be acknowledged in accordance with the procedure of the Annual Conference. Local churches shall report the amount of the offering in the manner indicated in the Local Church Report to the Annual Conference.

f) World Communion Sunday shall be observed the first Sunday of October. World Communion Sunday calls the Church to be the catholic inclusive Church. In connection with World Communion Sunday there shall be a churchwide appeal conducted by the General Commission on Communication in accord with the following directives: Each local church shall be requested to remit as provided in ¶ 915.6 all the communion offering received on World Communion Sunday and such portion of the communion offering received at other observances of the Sacrament of the Lord's Supper as the local church may designate.

The net receipts, after payment of promotional costs, shall be divided as follows: Fifty percent for Crusade Scholarships, to be administered by the Crusade Scholarship Committee; 35 percent for the Ethnic Minority Scholarship Program, and 15 percent for the Ethnic Minority In-Service Training Program; the last two to be administered by the General Board of Higher Education and Ministry.

g) *World Order Sunday* has been an ecumenical observance of the churches since the founding of the United Nations. This celebration in the churches is observed worldwide as United Nations Day. We affirm World Order Sunday as the symbol of our continuing witness of and support for the work of the United Nations. Because the United Nations works toward the purpose of peace and justice for the world's peoples, it is appropriate that World Order Sunday be observed on the Sunday or preceding October 24. It reminds the Church of its task and of the wholeness of the gospel which includes structures in the secular realm. It also suggests specific actions to the Church as it moves in that direction.

h) *United Methodist Student Day* shall be observed on the Sunday after Thanksgiving. United Methodist Student Day calls the Church to support students as they prepare for life in uniting faith with knowledge. The United Methodist Student Day offering, taken annually on the Sunday after Thanksgiving, shall be received for the support of The United Methodist Scholarships and The United Methodist Student Loan Fund. There shall be an annual goal of $2,000,000. Net receipts from the offering, after payment of the expenses of promotion, shall be remitted by the treasurer of the General Council on Finance and Administration to the General Board of Higher Education and Ministry, to be administered by that board.

Annual Conference Special Sundays

¶ **272.** 1. *Golden Cross Sunday* shall be observed annually on the first Sunday in May. If the Annual Conference so directs, an offering may be received for the work of health and welfare ministries in the Annual Conference. Local church treasurers shall remit the receipts of the offering to the Annual Conference treasurer, and receipts will be acknowledged in accordance with the procedure of the Annual Conference. Local churches shall report the amount of the offering in the manner indicated on the Local Church Report to the Annual Conference.

2. Annual Conferences may determine other special Sundays with or without offering. Special Sundays with offering shall be approved by the Annual Conference upon recommendation of the Annual Conference Council on Ministries in consultation with Annual Conference Council on Finance and Administration. Special Sundays without offering shall be approved by the Annual Conference upon recommendation of the Annual Conference Council on Ministries.

Section IX. Lay Speaking.

¶ **273.** 1. A **lay speaker** is a member of a local church who is ready and desirous to serve the Church and who is well informed on the Scriptures and the doctrine, heritage, organization, and life of The United Methodist Church and who has received specific training to develop skills in witnessing to the Christian faith through spoken communication. An applicant must be active in the support of his/her local church.

2. Lay speakers are to serve the church in any way in which the witness of the spoken word inspires the laity to deeper commitment to Christ and more effective churchmanship, including the interpretation or explanation of the Scriptures, doctrine, organization, and life of the Church.

3. Through continued study and training, a lay speaker should prepare to undertake one or more of the following functions, giving primary attention to service within the local church.

a) To take initiative in giving assistance and support to the program emphases of the Church and to assist in giving vital leadership to the total work of the Church.

b) To assist in the conduct of worship services and to lead meetings for prayer, study, and discussion when requested by the pastor.

c) To conduct services of worship, present sermons and addresses, and lead meetings for study and training in settings other than those in the local church in which the lay speaker holds membership, when recommended or requested by a pastor or district superintendent.

¶ 274. *Certification of Lay Speakers.*—1. A candidate may be certified as a lay speaker by the district or conference Committee on Lay Speaking (or other responsible group as the district or conference may determine) after the candidate has:

a) Completed a training course for lay speakers, which may be one recommended by the Board of Discipleship or an alternate approved by the appropriate committee.

b) Made application in writing to the appropriate committee and has been recommended by the pastor and the Administrative Board or the Charge Conference of the local church in which he or she holds membership.

c) Appeared before the appropriate committee for a review of his or her application and a consideration of the responsibilities of a lay speaker.

2. It is recommended that a consecration service be held in the district for persons certified as lay speakers.

¶ 275. *Renewal of Certification of Lay Speakers.*—1. The certification of a lay speaker shall be reviewed for renewal by the district or conference Committee on Lay Speaking (or other responsible group as the district or conference may determine), after the lay speaker has:

a) Requested in writing the renewal of certification.

b) Submitted an annual report to his or her Charge Conference and the appropriate committee, giving evidence of the satisfactory performance of activities related to the office of lay speaker.

c) Been recommended by the pastor and the Administrative Board or Charge Conference.

d) Completed at least once in every three years an advanced course for lay speakers, which may be one recommended by the Board of Discipleship or an alternate approved by the appropriate committee.

Chapter Three
THE DIACONAL MINISTRY

Section I. Relation to the Ministry of All Christians.

¶ **301.** The New Testament witness to Jesus Christ makes clear that the primary form of his ministry, in God's name, was that of service (diakonia) in the world. Very early in its history the Church came to understand that all of its members were commissioned, in baptism, to ministries of love, justice, and service, within local congregations and the larger communities in which they lived; all who follow Jesus have a share in the ministry of Jesus, who came not to be served, but to serve. There is thus a general ministry of all baptized Christians (¶¶ 104-106).

The Church also affirms that particular persons are called and set apart for representative ministries of leadership within the body, to help the whole of the membership of the Church be engaged in and fulfill its ministry of service (¶ 108). The purpose of such leadership is the equipping of the general ministry of the Church, to the end that the whole Church may be built up as the Body of Christ for the work of ministry. This set-apart ministry is not a substitute for the diaconal responsibility of all members of the general ministry. Rather, it exists to intensify and make more effective the self-understanding of the whole People of God as servants in Christ's name.

Section II. The Nature of Diaconal Ministry.

¶ **302.** The words *deacon, deaconess, diaconate,* and *diaconal* all spring from a common Greek root—*diakonia,* or "service." Very early in its history the Church instituted an order of ordained ministers to personify or focus the servanthood to which all Christians are called. These people were named deacons.

Those who are called to this representative ministry of service in the Church and world may be set apart to the office of diaconal minister. This ministry exemplifies the servanthood every Christian is called to live in both Church and world. Participating with the elder in the leadership of worship, working in a serving-profession in the Church, and serving the needs of the poor, the sick, or oppressed, the diaconal minister embodies the unity of the congregation's worship with its life in the world.

Section III.   Entrance into Diaconal Ministry.

¶ **303.** The diaconal ministry is recognized by The United Methodist Church as a called-out and set-apart ministry. Therefore, it is appropriate that those persons who present themselves as candidates for diaconal ministry be examined regarding the authenticity of their call by God to this office. Accordingly, let those who consider recommending such persons for candidacy as diaconal ministers in The United Methodist Church prayerfully and earnestly ask themselves these historic questions, as applied to the nature of diaconal ministry:

1. Do they know God as a pardoning God? Do they desire nothing but God? Are they holy in all manner of conversation?

2. Have they gifts, as well as graces, for the work of diaconal ministry? Have they the love of God abiding in them? Do they show forth that love in service to others? Have they an abiding sense of the urgency for justice in the world?

3. Have they fruit? Are others edified by their service?

As long as these signs are visible in them, we believe they are called of God to serve. These we receive as sufficient proof that they are moved by the Holy Spirit.[1]

¶ **304.** *Candidacy for Diaconal Ministry.*—Candidates for the diaconal ministry of The United Methodist Church, upon hearing and heeding the call to serve, shall take the first formal step toward the ministry by qualifying as candidates for the diaconal ministry. Candidates thus are under the care and supervision of the conference Board of Diaconal Ministry. (Where appropriate, candidates may also be related to a district committee on diaconal ministry.) A certificate of candidacy may be issued by the conference Board of Diaconal Ministry after candidates have met the following conditions.

---

[1] These questions were first asked by John Wesley at the third conference of Methodist preachers in 1746. They have been retained ever since, in substantially the same words, as the standards by which prospective Methodist ministers have been judged. Here they have been edited for the office of diaconal minister.

1. Each candidate must have agreed for the sake of the mission of Jesus Christ in the world and the most effective witness to the Christian gospel, and in consideration of his/her influence as a minister, to make a complete dedication of himself/herself to the highest ideals of the Christian life as set forth in ¶¶ 67-76 and to this end agreed to exercise responsible self-control by personal habits conducive to the bodily health, mental and emotional maturity, social responsibility, and growth in grace and the knowledge and love of God.

2. Each candidate must have been a member in good standing of a local United Methodist congregation for at least one year immediately preceding the application for candidacy. The recommendation for candidacy must then come from the Charge Conference of that congregation.

3. Each candidate must have been graduated from an accredited high school or its equivalent.

4. Each candidate must have met with the Pastor-Parish (Staff-Parish) Relations Committee and the pastor of his/her local congregation for consultation after submitting a written request and statement; the committee shall use the questions in ¶ 303 as a guide in examination of the candidate and shall make its recommendation to the Charge Conference.

5. Each candidate must have secured the recommendation of the Charge Conference in the following way: A Charge Conference for the purpose of recommending a candidate for diaconal ministry must be preceded by at least two public announcements. The authorized presiding elder shall counsel with those present regarding the ability and qualifications of the applicant and make plain the importance of such recommendation to the diaconal ministry; to be valid, such a recommendation must be voted by written ballot by two thirds of the members of the Charge Conference present at this meeting.

6. Each candidate must have applied to the conference Board of Diaconal Ministry in writing.

7. Each candidate must have appeared before the conference Board of Diaconal Ministry; made himself or herself available for any psychological and aptitude tests it may require; completed the studies exploring the spiritual, professional, academic, and personal potentialities of the candidate, as

recommended by the Division of Diaconal Ministry; and provided and supplied such other information as it may require for determining his/her gifts, graces, and fruits.

¶ **305.** *Continuation of Candidacy.*—The progress of candidates must be reviewed and candidacy renewed annually. On recommendation of the Charge Conference, continuing evidence of the candidate's gifts, graces, and fruits, and satisfactory progress in the required studies, candidacy shall be renewed by the conference Board of Diaconal Ministry.

1. A candidate who is preparing to become a diaconal minister and is enrolled in a school, college, university, or school of theology listed by the University Senate or approved by a regional or state accrediting agency shall present annually to the conference Board of Diaconal Ministry a statement of academic progress from the school the person is attending. This statement shall take the place of any formal examination, providing academic progress and character are satisfactory.

2. A candidate who is already certified in a professional career shall complete the foundational studies for diaconal ministers.

3. When candidacy has lapsed, it may be reinstated by action of the conference Board of Diaconal Ministry only when the candidate has completed satisfactorily the current candidacy requirements.

¶ **306.** *Completion of Candidacy.*—A person shall be eligible for consecration as a diaconal minister in the Annual Conference by vote of the Annual Conference on recommendation of its Board of Diaconal Ministry after meeting the following qualifications:

1. Each candidate must have been in candidacy for diaconal ministry for at least one year.

2. Each candidate must have been employed for a minimum of one year in a position approved by the board consistent with ¶ 310.1.

3. Each candidate must have met the following educational requirements:

a) Must have received a bachelor's degree from a college or university listed by the University Senate or approved by a regional or state accrediting agency or competency equivalence as approved by the General Board of Higher Education and Ministry.

b) Must have: (1) received a graduate theological or equivalent master's degree from a graduate school listed by the University Senate or approved by a regional or state accrediting agency; or (2) received competency equivalence to the graduate, theological, or professional degree as approved by the General Board of Higher Education and Ministry; or (3) completed the academic requirements for professional certification; or (4) been commissioned by the General Board of Global Ministries for service either in the United States or in other countries.

c) Must have completed the basic studies of the Christian faith—Bible, theology, church history (including United Methodist history), mission of the Church in the world, United Methodist doctrine and polity—either through a graduate degree program or through the Foundational Course of Study for Diaconal Ministers.

4. Each candidate must present a satisfactory certificate of good health by a physician on the prescribed form. Handicapping conditions are not to be construed as unfavorable health factors when such a person is capable of meeting the professional standards and is physically able to render effective service in the office of diaconal minister. The conference may require psychological tests to provide additional information on the candidate's fitness for the diaconal ministry.

5. Each candidate must have responded to a written or oral doctrinal examination administered by the conference Board of Diaconal Ministry. The candidate's reflections and the board's response should be informed by the insights and guidelines for the personal interview and examination of candidates for the office of diaconal minister:

a) Describe your personal experience of God and the understanding of God you derive from biblical, theological, and historical sources.

b) What is the Christian understanding of humanity, and the human need for divine grace?

c) How do you interpret the statement "Jesus Christ is Lord"?

d) What is your conception of the activity of the Holy Spirit in personal faith, in the community of believers, and in responsible living in the world?

e) The United Methodist Church holds that scripture, tradition, experience, and reason are sources and norms for belief and practice, but that the Bible is primary among them. What is your understanding of this theological position of the Church?

f) What are the marks of the Christian life? What is your understanding of the Christian life as set forth in the Articles of Religion, the statement of Our Theological Task, and the Social Principles in the Book of Discipline of The United Methodist Church?

g) Describe the nature and mission of the Church. What are its primary tasks today?

h) What is your understanding of (1) the Kingdom of God, (2) the Resurrection, (3) eternal life?

i) How do you perceive yourself, your gifts, your motives, your role, and your commitment as a diaconal minister?

j) What is the meaning and significance of diakonia?

k) What is the meaning of consecration and ordination, especially in the context of the general ministry of the Church?

l) What is your understanding of the organization, structure, and function of The United Methodist Church?

m) What is your understanding of the relationship of the diaconal minister to the Annual Conference and The United Methodist Church?

6. Each candidate must have had a personal interview with the conference Board of Diaconal Ministry to complete his/her candidacy.

Section IV.   Relationship to the Annual Conference.

¶ **307.** *Consecration.*—The diaconal minister's relationship to the Annual Conference of The United Methodist Church shall be conferred by the act of consecration. Consecration to the office of diaconal minister shall be at the Annual Conference. The Service for Consecration and the Service for Ordination may be incorporated into one service. The bishop and secretary of the

Annual Conference shall provide credentials to the diaconal minister upon consecration.

¶ **308.** *General Provisions.*—Diaconal ministers shall be amenable to the Annual Conference in the performance of their duties as diaconal ministers.

¶ **309.** *Rights of Diaconal Ministers.*—1. The diaconal minister shall be seated in the Annual Conference where church membership is held and given the privilege of the floor; shall be eligible to serve as a lay person on boards, commissions, or committees of the Annual Conference and hold office on the same; shall be eligible for election as a lay delegate to the General or Jurisdictional Conference.

2. The diaconal minister may become a member of the Annual Conference as a lay person when elected as a lay member of the Annual Conference, or as part of the Annual Conference lay equalization plan in accordance with ¶ 36.[2]

¶ **310.** *Service Appointment of Diaconal Ministers.*—1. Diaconal ministers may serve:

a) Within a local congregation or larger parish,

b) Through church-related agencies, or

c) Through other ministries which extend the witness and service of Christ's love and justice in the world.

2. Diaconal ministers serve in a nonitinerating ministry. A district superintendent or bishop may initiate or recommend an appointment, but they have no responsibility to do so.

3. The service appointment of the diaconal minister shall be:

a) Initiated by the individual diaconal minister or agency seeking his/her service;

b) Clarified by a written statement of intentionality of diakonia in order to establish a clear distinction between the work to which all Christians are called and the work for which diaconal ministers are appropriately prepared and authorized;

c) Recommended by the conference Board of Diaconal Ministry;

d) Reviewed by the Cabinet and approved by the bishop of the Annual Conference.

---

[2]*See* Judicial Council Decisions 391, 464.

¶ **311.** *Service of Diaconal Ministers.*—Service must be in a local congregation or larger parish, an agency of The United Methodist Church, an ecumenical church-related assignment, or a ministry which extends the witness and service of Christ's love and justice in the world. Service shall mean that the person's entire vocational time is devoted to the work of ministry in the field of labor in which he or she is approved by the bishop.

¶ **312.** *Credentials and Records.*—The diaconal ministers' credentials and records shall be maintained by the conference Board of Diaconal Ministry in the conference to which they relate. The diaconal ministers' credentials and records shall be transferred from one Annual Conference to another on recommendation of the conference Boards of Diaconal Ministry and the approval of the Annual Conferences involved.

¶ **313.** *Change in Conference Relationship.*—Diaconal ministers seeking a change in conference relationship shall make written request to their conference Board of Diaconal Ministry stating the reasons for the requested change in status. In addition, the Board of Diaconal Ministry may request personal interviews with diaconal ministers requesting the change in status. The conference Board of Diaconal Ministry will be in consultation with the Cabinet.

1. *Leaves of Absence.*—Each leave granted by the Annual Conference shall be recorded in the conference journal. When a diaconal minister requests a leave between sessions of the Annual Conference, the executive committee of the conference Board of Diaconal Ministry, in consultation with the diaconal minister, the district superintendent, and the employing agency, may recommend the leave of absence for approval by the bishop for the remainder of the conference year. Any such leave granted between sessions of the Annual Conference, with the effective date of such leave, shall be entered in the conference journal of the next regular session of the conference.

a) Disability Leave.—When diaconal ministers are forced to give up their ministry because of their physical or emotional disability, upon recommendation of the conference Board of Diaconal Ministry and by a majority vote of the members of the Annual Conference, they may be granted annual disability leave without losing their relationship to the Annual Conference. When diaconal ministers on disability leave recover sufficiently to resume their ministry, they may return to an active relationship to the Annual Conference through the process described for a service appointment (¶ 310).

b) Maternity/Paternity Leave.—Maternity/paternity leave up to one fourth of a year will be available to any diaconal minister who so requests it at the birth or adoption of a child. During the leave, the diaconal minister's Annual Conference relations shall remain unchanged, and the insurance claims will remain in force. Persons desiring maternity/paternity leave should file their request with the personnel committee of the employing agency and the conference Board of Diaconal Ministry prior to its beginning.

c) Study/Sabbatical Leave.—Diaconal ministers shall be encouraged to continue their education throughout their careers, including pursuit of carefully developed personal programs of study augmented periodically by involvement in organized educational activities. A study leave of up to one year negotiated by a diaconal minister and his/her employing agency shall not affect the relationship to the Annual Conference. The diaconal minister's continuing education program should allow for leaves of absence for study at least one week each year and at least one month during one year of each quadrennium. Such leaves shall not be considered as part of the diaconal minister's vacation and should be planned in consultation with his/her employing agency. Diaconal ministers shall be asked by the district superintendent in the Charge Conference to outline their programs of continuing education for the year.

d) Personal Leave.—When a diaconal minister is temporarily unable or unwilling to perform the work of his/her ministry, a personal leave of absence may be granted upon recommendation of the conference Board of Diaconal Ministry. This relation shall be approved annually and shall not be granted for more than three consecutive years.

2. *Retired Relationship.*—Retired diaconal ministers are those who at their own request or by action of the members of the Annual Conference, on recommendation of the conference Board of Diaconal Ministry, have been placed in the retired relationship.

a) By a two-thirds vote of those present and voting, the

Annual Conference may place diaconal ministers in the retired relation with or without their consent and irrespective of their age if such relation is recommended by the conference Board of Diaconal Ministry. The conference Board of Diaconal Ministry shall provide guidance and counseling to the retiring member.

b) Every diaconal minister whose seventieth birthday is on or before July 1 shall automatically be retired from the active relationship at the conference session closest to that date.

c) Retired diaconal ministers shall be listed annually in the journal of the Annual Conference in which their retired relationship is held.

3. *Termination of Conference Relationship.—a) Voluntary Termination.*—A diaconal minister who desires to withdraw from the Annual Conference may, after consultation with the conference Board of Diaconal Ministry, deposit his/her credentials with the bishop between sessions of the Annual Conference. When this action is taken between sessions of the Annual Conference, it shall be reported by the conference Board of Diaconal Ministry for confirmation by the Annual Conference at its next regular session.

b) Involuntary Termination.—A diaconal minister's relationship to the Annual Conference may be terminated by a two-thirds vote of the members of the Annual Conference on recommendation of the conference Board of Diaconal Ministry. Termination may be recommended, in consultation with the diaconal minister in question, on the basis of incompetence in professional function, indifference to the work of the ministry, or personal conduct which is deemed seriously to impair usefulness as a diaconal minister (Chapter Nine, Section II).

4. *Reinstatement.*—A diaconal minister's relationship to the Annual Conference may be reinstated by a two-thirds vote of the members of the Annual Conference on recommendation of the conference Board of Diaconal Ministry.

Section V. Relationships to the Charge Conference.

¶ **314.** 1. A person appointed as a diaconal minister to a local congregation or larger parish shall be a voting member of the Charge Conference of that local church or one of the local churches comprising the larger parish, and be related to the

Annual Conference in which that local congregation or larger parish is located.

2. A person appointed as a diaconal minister in a church-related agency within his/her Annual Conference shall relate to a local church and be a voting member of its Charge Conference in the community where he/she resides.

3. A person appointed as a diaconal minister in a church-related agency outside his/her Annual Conference shall relate to a local church and be a voting member of its Charge Conference in the community where he/she resides or shall have this relationship with a local church within his/her home Annual Conference, in which case he/she shall have an affiliate membership in the Charge Conference of a local church in the community in which he/she resides.

4. A person appointed as a diaconal minister in a ministry which extends the witness and service of Christ's love and justice in the world other than a church-related agency shall relate to a local church and be a voting member of its Charge Conference, after consultation with the pastor, in the community where he/she resides.

Section VI. Relationship to the Employing Agency.

¶ **315.** The employing agency in which a diaconal minister is serving shall provide:

1. Adequate salary, pension benefits, and health care insurance, all based on the recommendations of the Annual Conference.

2. Social Security benefits as required by Federal legislation.

3. Support for continuing education.

Chapter Four

THE ORDAINED MINISTRY

Section I.   Relation of Ordained Ministers to the Ministry of All Christians.

¶ **401.** Ministry in the Christian church is derived from the ministry of Christ, the ministry of the Father through the Incarnate Son by the Holy Spirit. It is a ministry bestowed upon and required of the entire Church. All Christians are called to ministry, and theirs is a ministry of the people of God within the community of faith and in the world. Members of The United Methodist Church receive this gift of ministry in company with all Christians and sincerely hope to continue and extend it in the world for which Christ lived, died, and lives again. The United Methodist Church believes that Baptism, confirmation, and responsible membership in the Church are visible signs of acceptance of this ministry. (*See* Chapter I on the Ministry of All Christians, ¶¶ 101-110.)

¶ **402.** There are persons within the ministry of the baptized who are called of God and set apart by the Church for the specialized ministry of Word, Sacrament, and Order (¶¶ 429-435).

Section II.   Entrance Procedures into Ordained Ministry.

STANDARDS FOR ORDAINED MINISTRY

¶ **403.** *Wesley's Questions for the Examiners.*—In order that The United Methodist Church may be assured that those persons who present themselves as candidates for ministry are truly called of God to this office, let those who consider recommending such persons for candidacy as ordained ministers in The United Methodist Church prayerfully and earnestly ask themselves these questions:

1. Do they know God as a pardoning God? Have they the

love of God abiding in them? Do they desire nothing but God? Are they holy in all manner of conversation?

2. Have they gifts, as well as grace, for the work? Have they a clear, sound understanding; a right judgment in the things of God; a just conception of salvation by faith? Do they speak justly, readily, clearly?

3. Have they fruit? Have any been truly convinced of sin and converted to God, and are believers edified by their preaching?

As long as these marks concur in them, we believe they are called of God to preach. These we receive as sufficient proof that they are moved by the Holy Spirit.[1]

CANDIDACY FOR ORDAINED MINISTRY

¶ **404.** *Candidacy for Ordained Ministry.*—Upon one's hearing and heeding the call to ordained ministry, the first formal step toward ordination and annual conference membership shall be to qualify as a candidate. In interpreting one's sense of call, The United Methodist Church provides a vocational guide called "The Christian as Minister." This should be read in consultation with one's pastor or another United Methodist minister.

Prerequisites for candidacy studies and procedures are *(a)* to have been a member of the local recommending United Methodist congregation for one year immediately preceding application, and *(b)* to have been graduated from an accredited high school or received a certificate of equivalency.

The steps to becoming a certified candidate for ordained ministry are (1) to consult with the pastor and Pastor-Parish Relations Committee after formulating a written statement reflecting one's call to ordained ministry and requesting recommendation for candidacy. To pursue candidacy, this committee must recommend the applicant to the Charge Conference. The committee shall interview the inquiring candidate, reflecting his/her statement and Wesley's historic question in ¶ 403; (2) to be recommended by the Charge Conference, in accordance the following method: a meeting for

---

[1]These questions were first asked by John Wesley at the third conference of Methodist preachers in 1746. They have been retained ever since, in substantially the same words, as the standards by which prospective Methodist preachers have been judged.

the purpose of recommending a candidate for the ministry must be preceded by at least two public announcements and must be held in the presence of the bishop, district superintendent, or an authorized elder, who shall counsel with those present regarding the ability and qualifications of the applicant and make plain the importance of such recommendation to the ordained ministry; to be valid such a recommendation must be voted by written ballot by two thirds of the members of the Charge Conference present at this meeting; (3) to apply to the district superintendent in writing for admission to candidacy studies as defined by the Division of Ordained Ministry; (4) to be assigned as a declared candidate to a supervising pastor by the district committee, and to complete appropriate candidacy studies after proper registration through the Annual Conference Candidacy Registrar and the Division of Ordained Ministry; (5) to appear before the district Committee on Ordained Ministry for such examination; make themselves available for any psychological and aptitude tests it may require; complete the studies exploring the spiritual, professional, academic, and personal potentialities of the candidate, as recommended by the Division of Ordained Ministry; provide and supply evidence of understanding the expectations and obligations of the itinerant system; provide and supply such other information as it may require for determining their gifts, graces, fruits, and demonstration of call; (6) to agree for the sake of the mission of Jesus Christ in the world and the most effective witness to the Christian gospel, and in consideration of their influence as ministers, to make a complete dedication of themselves to the highest ideals of the Christian life as set forth in ¶¶ 67-76 and to this end agree to exercise responsible self-control by personal habits conducive to bodily health, mental and emotional maturity, social responsibility, and growth in grace and the knowledge and love of God.[2]

---

[2] In adopting the statements in ¶¶ 404.6 and 414.7c (2) on the moral and social responsibility of ministers, the General Conference seeks to elevate the standards by calling for a more thoroughgoing moral commitment by the candidate and for a more careful and thorough examination of candidates by district committees and boards of the ministry.

The legislation in no way implies that the use of tobacco is a morally indifferent question. In the light of the developing evidence against the use of

¶ **405.** *Continuation of Candidacy.*—The progress of candidates must be reviewed and candidacy renewed annually. Candidacy may be renewed by the district Committee on Ordained Ministry (¶ 757) on recommendation of the Charge Conference and on evidence that the candidate's gifts, graces, and fruits continue to be satisfactory and that the candidate is making satisfactory progress in the required studies.

1. A candidate preparing to become a probationary member who is enrolled as a pretheological or theological student in a school, college, university, or school of theology listed by the University Senate or approved by a regional or state accrediting agency shall present annually to the district Committee on Ordained Ministry a statement of academic progress from the

---

tobacco, the burden of proof would be upon all users to show that their use of it is consistent with the highest ideals of the Christian life. Similarly, regarding beverage alcohol, the burden of proof would be upon users to show that their action is consistent with the ideals of excellence of mind, purity of body, and responsible social behavior.

Therefore, the changes here do not relax the traditional view concerning the use of tobacco and beverage alcohol by ministers in The United Methodist Church. Rather they call for higher standards of self-discipline and habit formation in all personal and social relationships. They call for dimensions of moral commitment that go far beyond any specific practices which might be listed. *See* Judicial Council Decision 318.

The General Conference, in response to expressions throughout the church regarding homosexuality and ordination, reaffirms the present language of the Discipline regarding the character and commitment of persons seeking ordination, and affirms its high standards.

For more than 200 years candidates for ordination have been asked Wesley's Questions, including ". . . Have they a clear, sound understanding; right judgment in the things of God; a just conception of salvation by faith? . . ." (¶ 403).

All candidates agree to make a complete dedication of themselves to the highest ideals of the Christian life, and to this end agree "to exercise responsible self-control, by personal habits conducive to bodily health, mental and emotional maturity, social responsibility, and growth in grace and the knowledge and love of God" (¶ 404).

The character and commitment of candidates for the ministry is described or examined in six places in the Book of Discipline. (¶ 403, 404.6, 414.7, 422, 425, and 431.) These say in part: "Only those shall be elected to full membership who are of unquestionable moral character and genuine piety, sound in the fundamental doctrines of Christianity and faithful in the discharge of their duties" (¶ 422).

The statement on ordination (¶ 431) states: *"It is expected that persons to be ordained shall:*

6. Be willing to make a complete dedication of themselves to the highest ideals of the

school the person is attending. This statement shall take the place of any formal examination, providing academic progress and character are satisfactory.

2. A candidate who is not a student as defined in ¶ 405.1 shall complete the studies for the license for the local pastor after being accepted as a candidate and shall continue preparation through the five-year course of study under the Division of Ordained Ministry. The course must be completed within eight years after the issuance of the license for the local pastor, except as provided in ¶ 408.2. An Annual Conference Board of Ordained Ministry may require one year in candidacy before application for licensing as a local pastor.

Christian life and agree to exercise responsible self-control in their personal habits.
    7. Be persons in whom the community can place trust and confidence."
    There are eight crucial steps in the examination of candidates. They are:
    (1) The self-examination of the individual seeking ordination as he or she responds to God's call in personal commitment to Christ and his church.
    (2) The decision of the Pastor-Parish Relations Committee which makes the first recommendation to the charge conference when a member seeks to become a ministerial candidate.
    (3) The decision of the charge conference which must recommend the candidate.
    (4) The decision of the district committee on the ministry which must recommend the candidate to the Conference Board of Ordained Ministry and, where applicable, the decision of the District Conference.
    (5) The decision of the Board of Ordained Ministry which must recommend deacon's ordination and probationary membership.
    (6) The decision of the ministerial members of the Annual Conference who must elect candidates to deacon's ordination and probationary membership.
    (7) The recommendation of the Board of Ordained Ministry for elder's ordination and full membership.
    (8) The election to elder's ordination and full membership by the ministerial members of the annual conference.
    All pastors are accountable as to character and effectiveness to the annual conference throughout their entire ministry.
    The General Conference has made it clear in the "Doctrine and Doctrinal Statements . . .," (Part II of the Discipline) that Scripture, tradition, experience, and reason are our guidelines. "United Methodists share with all other Christians the conviction that Scripture is the primary source and guideline for doctrine."
    In the Social Principles, the General Conference has said that "we do not condone the practice of homosexuality and consider this practice incompatible with Christian teaching." Furthermore, the Principles state that "we affirm the sanctity of the marriage covenant which is expressed in love, mutual support, personal commitment, and shared fidelity between a man and a woman. We believe that God's blessing rests upon such marriage, whether or not there are children of the union. We reject social norms that assume different standards for

3. When candidacy has lapsed, it may be reinstated at the discretion of the district Committee on Ordained Ministry only when the candidate has completed satisfactorily the current candidacy studies.[3]

¶ **406.** *Requirements for the License.*—In order for candidates for the ordained ministry to have the authority to perform the duties of the pastor as described in ¶ 438.2, they shall obtain a license as a local pastor in addition to the completion of the candidacy program for ordained ministry (¶ 404). All persons not ordained as deacons or elders who preach and conduct divine worship and perform the duties of a pastor under pastoral appointment shall have a license as a local pastor.

1. Persons applying for the license shall have completed the conditions for candidacy for ordained ministry in ¶ 404.

2. Persons who have completed one half of their seminary work in addition to requirements for candidacy may be granted a local pastor's license.

3. Persons applying for the license who have not completed at least one half of their seminary work shall complete the studies for the license as a local pastor as prescribed and supervised by the Division of Ordained Ministry.

4. Upon satisfactory completion of the requirements, the license shall be granted to persons by the district Committee on Ordained Ministry when they receive a pastoral appointment.

---

women than for men in marriage." Also, "we affirm the integrity of single persons and we reject all social practices that discriminate, or social attitudes that are prejudicial against persons because they are unmarried."

The General Conference affirms the wisdom of our heritage expressed in the Disciplinary provisions relating to the character and commitment of ordained ministers. The United Methodist Church has moved away from prohibitions of specific acts, for such prohibitions can be endless. We affirm our trust in the covenant community and the process by which we ordain ministers.

In our covenant we are called to trust one another as we recommend, examine, and elect candidates for the ordained ministry and conference membership. *See* Judicial Council Decision 480.

[3]*See* Judicial Council Decision 412.

5. Persons licensed as local pastors shall continue in the course of study, in college, or in seminary, as outlined in ¶ 405.

6. Each Local Pastor shall appear before the Board of Ordained Ministry prior to serving a full-time appointment. This provision becomes effective immediately following the 1980 General Conference.

¶ **407.** *Authority of a Licensed Person.*—The license as a local pastor is given only for the purpose of the practice of ministry while one is in preparation for conference membership and ordination. After the requirements of ¶ 406 are met, the district Committee on Ordained Ministry shall certify the completion of the prescribed studies to the candidates and the district superintendent and they shall be listed in the journal as eligible to be appointed as local pastors. Award of the license shall not be made until an appointment to a pastoral charge is made in accordance with ¶ 436. Authority granted by the license extends only within the appointment, under specific supervision of a counseling elder and subject to annual renewal by the district committee.

Local Pastor

¶ **408.** *Requirements for a Local Pastor.*—1. A **local pastor** is a person certified by the district Committee on Ordained Ministry for recommendation to the Board of Ordained Ministry to be approved by ministerial members in full connection and to be authorized to perform all the duties of a pastor (¶ 438.2) including the Sacraments of Baptism and Holy Communion as well as the service of marriage (where state laws allow), burial, confirmation, and membership reception, while assigned to a particular charge under the specific supervision of a counseling elder subject to annual renewal. Such authorization must be recertified by the bishop when assignments change between sessions of the Annual Conference.[4]

2. A local pastor may qualify for probationary membership and follow the specified procedure into full ministerial membership in the Annual Conference. A local pastor may qualify for

---

[4]*See* Judicial Council Decision 112.

associate membership. On completion of educational requirements, a local pastor may elect to remain in local relationship. A
local pastor shall complete the educational requirements within
eight years unless a family situation or other circumstance
preclude the local pastor's opportunity to meet said requirements. The local pastor may be granted an annual extension
beyond eight years on the educational requirements upon a
three-fourths vote of the district Committee on Ordained
Ministry, recommendation by the conference Board of Ordained
Ministry, and the vote of the ministerial members in full
connection. (*See* ¶ 409.5.)[5]
The registrar of the conference Board of Ordained Ministry
shall notify the Division of Ordained Ministry of such extensions.
These provisions shall be applied appropriately to ¶ 409.

3. A local pastor upon completing each year of educational
and other qualifications and upon recommendation of the Board
of Ordained Ministry shall be approved each year by the vote of
the ministerial members in full connection of the Annual
Conference.

4. Local pastors other than students defined in ¶ 409.4 who
are appointed to serve under a district superintendent shall
procure from the pastor or district superintendent a letter of
transfer of church membership and shall present it to the Charge
Conference of the charge to which they are appointed at its next
regular session. Their church membership shall be in the charge
to which they are appointed and they shall be members of the
Charge Conference subject to the annual authorization of the
Annual Conference.

5. Local pastors who are serving as student pastors while
attending a college, university, or school of theology listed by the
University Senate may retain their membership in their home
church and Charge Conference, but in the discharge of their
ministerial functions they shall be amenable to the district
superintendent under whom they serve.

6. Persons licensed as local pastors desiring to continue in
this classification must have their character, fitness, training, and

------

[5]*See* Judicial Council Decisions 436, 439.

187

effectiveness approved annually by the vote of the district Committee on Ordained Ministry and by the ministerial members in full connection in the Annual Conference after reference to and recommendation by its Board of Ordained Ministry.

7. Upon recommendation of the Board of Ordained Ministry, the ministerial members in full connection may vote approval annually for students of other denominations enrolled in a school of theology listed by the University Senate to serve as local pastors for the ensuing year under the direction of the district superintendent; *provided* that they shall indicate to the satisfaction of the Board of Ordained Ministry their agreement to support and maintain the doctrine and polity of The United Methodist Church while under appointment.

8. Local pastors shall be amenable to the Annual Conference in the performance of their pastoral duties. Local pastors in charge of a pastoral appointment shall attend the sessions of the Annual Conference.

9. The Board of Ordained Ministry shall require a satisfactory certificate of good health on a prescribed form from a physician approved by that board if the local pastor is to be a participant in the Comprehensive Protection Plan. The conference may require psychological and/or psychiatric tests and evaluations to provide additional information to qualify for such coverage.

The Board of Ordained Ministry shall certify to the conference Board of Pensions that a local pastor has satisfactorily met the requirements of good health as prescribed.

¶ **409.** *Categories of Local Pastor.*—In recommending to the Annual Conference those who have met the requirements to serve as local pastors for the ensuing year, the Board of Ordained Ministry shall classify them in three categories with educational and other requirements as hereinafter specified. All local pastors shall meet the educational requirements of their category. Any person who fails to meet these requirements shall not be appointed by a district superintendent. The categories shall be defined as follows:

1. *Those Eligible to be Appointed as Full-time Local Pastors.*— Full-time local pastors are lay persons (*see* ¶ 701.1) (*a*) who meet the provisions for the license as a local pastor (¶ 406); (*b*) who, unless they have completed the course of study, have met the

educational requirements by completing in the preceding year a full year's work in the ministerial course of study under the Division of Ordained Ministry in a school for courses of study (¶ 1629.2); *provided,* however, that in a case of emergency or unusual circumstances, on approval by the board, they may be authorized to pursue the course for the current year by correspondence; and *provided,* further, that for candidates beginning the course after the Uniting Conference not more than one year may be taken by correspondence; *(c)* who devote their entire time to the church in the charge to which they are appointed and its outreach in ministry and mission to the community; and *(d)* whose cash support per annum from all church sources is a sum equivalent to not less than the minimum salary established by the Annual Conference for full-time local pastors.

2. *Those Eligible to be Appointed as Part-time Local Pastors.*— Part-time local pastors are lay persons *(a)* who meet the provisions of ¶ 408; *(b)* who have completed in the preceding year a minimum of one half a year's work in the course of study, *provided* that the entire five-year course shall be completed in a maximum of ten years from the time of first enrollment; *(c)* who do not devote their entire time to the charge to which they are appointed; and *(d)* who do not receive in cash support per annum from all church sources a sum equivalent to the minimum salary established by the Annual Conference for full-time local pastors. A person who has met the qualifications for approval as local pastor may request to be classified as eligible to be appointed as a part-time local pastor for the ensuing year.

3. A person who has fulfilled all of the qualifications to become an associate member except the requirement of full-time services, and whose secular work, family situation, or other circumstances preclude his/her opportunity to meet said requirement, may be granted yearly extensions upon three-fourths vote of the district committee, recommendation of the Board of Ordained Ministry, and the vote of the ministerial members in full connection.

4. *Those Eligible to be Appointed as Student Local Pastors.*— These shall be enrolled as pretheological or theological students under the definitions and requirements of the Discipline and

shall be making appropriate progress as determined by the Board of Ordained Ministry.

5. None of the provisions in this legislation shall be interpreted to change or limit authorizations to local pastors ordained as deacon and elder prior to 1976 or enrolled in the appropriate studies prior to January 1, 1977.[6]

¶ **410.** *Exiting, Reinstatement, and Retirement of Local Pastors.*— 1. *Discontinuance of Local Pastor.*—Whenever a local pastor is no longer approved for appointment by the Annual Conference as required in ¶ 408, or whenever any local pastor severs relationship with The United Methodist Church, license and credentials shall be surrendered to the district superintendent for deposit with the secretary of the conference. This does not apply to persons who were licensed to preach prior to 1950. After consultation with the pastor, the former local pastor shall designate the local church in which membership shall be held. The Board of Ordained Ministry shall file with the resident bishop a permanent record of the circumstances relating to the discontinuance of local pastor status as required in ¶ 722.3*d*.

2. *Withdrawal Under Complaints and Charges.*—When a local pastor is accused of an offense under ¶ 2621 and desires to withdraw from the Church, the procedures described in ¶ 2626.2 shall apply.

3. *Trial of Local Pastor.*—When a local pastor is accused of an offense under ¶ 2621, the procedures described in ¶¶ 2623-2624 shall apply.

4. *Reinstatement of Local Pastor Status.*—Local pastors whose approved status has been discontinued from an Annual Conference of The United Methodist Church or one of its legal predecessors may be reinstated by the Annual Conference which previously approved them, or its legal successor, or the Annual Conference of which the major portion of their former conference is a part, only upon recommendation by the district Committee on Ordained Ministry, the Board of Ordained Ministry, and the Cabinet. When approved by the ministerial members in full connection as provided in ¶ 408.1, their license and credentials shall be restored, and they shall be eligible for

---

[6]*See* Judicial Council Decisions 436, 439.

appointment as pastors of a charge. They shall complete ministerial studies and meet requirements as provided in ¶ 408.3.

Whenever persons whose approval as local pastors has been discontinued by an Annual Conference are being considered for appointment or temporary employment in another Annual Conference, the Board of Ordained Ministry where these persons are being considered shall obtain from the Board of Ordained Ministry of the conference where approval has been discontinued certification of their qualifications and information about the circumstances relating to the termination of their approval as local pastors. Before such persons shall be appointed, they shall be recommended by the board and approved by the Annual Conference. A district superintendent may arrange for them to serve temporarily when the board and the Cabinet agree and when the board certifies that they are enrolled for those studies which they have not completed previously.

5. *Retirement of Local Pastor.*—On recommendation of the Board of Ordained Ministry and by vote of the ministerial members in full connection a local pastor who has served not less than four years as a local pastor (formerly an approved supply pastor or a lay pastor) and who will have attained age sixty-five on or before July 1 in the year in which the session of the conference is held may be recognized as a retired local pastor and so listed in answer to the business of the Annual Conference question: "Who are recognized as retired local pastors?"

¶ **411.** *Counseling Elders.*—Counseling elders are clergy members in full connection in an Annual Conference recommended by the Board of Ordained Ministry and assigned by the Cabinet to provide supervision and counsel for local pastors in fulfilling the requirements for associate and probationary membership. Such assignments should be done after consultation with the local pastor involved. The counseling elder shall work specifically in supervision and counsel regarding preaching and teaching the Scriptures, celebration of the Sacraments and other services of worship, ordering the life of the congregation for nurture and care, and all other aspects of the practice of ministry. Counseling elders shall work under the direction of and in consultation with the district superintendent and shall make regular reports of their activities to the district superintendent and the district Committee on Ordained Ministry. The Cabinet may consider appointing one counseling elder to supervise several local pastors, making adequate provision in both salary and available time for the counseling elder involved.

Section III.   Admission and Continuance.

¶ **412.** *General Provisions.*—1. The Annual Conference is the basic body of The United Methodist Church. The ministerial membership of an Annual Conference shall consist of members in full connection (¶ 422), probationary members (¶ 413), associate members (¶ 419), and local pastors under full-time appointment to a pastoral charge (¶ 409.1). All ministers are amenable to the Annual Conference in the performance of their duties in the positions to which they are appointed.[7]

2. Both men and women are included in all provisions of the Discipline which refer to the ministry.[8]

ADMISSION AND CONTINUANCE ON
PROBATIONARY MEMBERSHIP

¶ **413.** *Eligibility and Rights of Probationary Membership.*—Probationary members are on trial in preparation for membership in full connection with the Annual Conference. They are on probation as to character, preaching, and effectiveness as pastors. The Annual Conference has jurisdiction over probationary members. Annually the Board of Ordained Ministry shall review and evaluate their relationship and make recommendation to the ministerial members in full connection regarding their continuance. Probationary members may request discontinuance of this relationship or may be discontinued by the Annual Conference, upon recommendation of the Board of Ordained Ministry (¶ 448.1), without reflection upon their character.

1. Probationary members are eligible for ordination as deacons but may not be ordained elders until they qualify for membership in full connection in the Annual Conference.

2. Probationary members shall have the right to vote in the

---

[7]*See* Judicial Council Decisions 327, 371.
[8]*See* Judicial Council Decisions 317, 155.

Annual Conference on all matters except the following: *(a)* constitutional amendments; *(b)* election of delegates to the General and Jurisdictional or Central Conferences; *(c)* all matters of ordination, character, and conference relations of ministers.

3. Probationary members may serve on any board, commission, or committee of the Annual Conference except the Board of Ordained Ministry. They shall not be eligible for election as delegates to the General or Jurisdictional Conferences.

4. Probationary members shall be amenable to the Annual Conference in the performance of their ministry and shall be granted the same security of appointment as associate members and members in full connection as long as they are probationary members.

¶ **414.** *Qualifications for Election to Probationary Membership.*— Candidates may be elected to probationary membership by vote of the ministerial members in full connection on recommendation of its Board of Ordained Ministry after meeting the following conditions:

1. Each candidate must have been certified as a candidate for ministry for at least one year.

2. Each must have met the educational requirements (¶¶ 415, 416).

3. Each candidate must have been recommended in writing on the basis of a three-fourths majority vote of the district Committee on Ordained Ministry.

4. Each must present a satisfactory certificate of good health on the prescribed form from a physician approved by the board. The conference may require psychological and/or psychiatric tests and evaluations to provide additional information on the candidate's fitness for the ministry.

5. Each must file with the board, in duplicate on the prescribed form, a satisfactory written, concise autobiographical statement concerning age, health, family, Christian experience, call to the ministry, educational record, formative Christian experiences, and plans for service in the Church.

6. Each must present at least one written sermon on a biblical passage specified by the Board of Ordained Ministry.

7. Each must have been examined in written form covering

the areas indicated and approved by the Board of Ordained Ministry with respect to the following questions:

a) Theology and Vocation—(1) Describe your personal basic beliefs and experience as a Christian.

(2) How do you conceive your vocation as a minister? Are you presently convinced that the ordained ministry is the best way to fulfill your response to God? Explain.

(3) How do you understand the theological tasks of a United Methodist minister, with special reference to Part II of the Book of Discipline?

(4) What is your understanding of the Kingdom of God and the nature and mission of the church today?

b) The Practice of Ministry—(1) Describe and evaluate your personal gifts for ministry. What would be your areas of strength and areas in which you need to be strengthened?

(2) Are you willing to relate yourself to all persons without regard to race, color, national origin, or social status?

(3) Will you regard all pastoral conversations of a confessional nature as a trust between the person concerned and God?

c) The Christian Life—(1) What is your understanding of the Christian life as set forth in the Articles of Religion, the statement of Our Theological Task, and the Social Principles in the Discipline?

(2) For the sake of the mission of Jesus Christ in the world and the most effective witness to the Christian gospel, and in consideration of your influence as a minister, are you willing to make a complete dedication of yourself to the highest ideals of the Christian life; and to this end will you agree to exercise responsible self-control by personal habits conducive to bodily health, mental and emotional maturity, social responsibility, and growth in grace and the knowledge and love of God?

(3) What do you anticipate to be the risks and sacrifices entailed in serving in the United Methodist ministry?

(4) Indicate in some detail how your close personal relationships affect your ministry.

(5) Mismanagement of personal finances may detract from your effectiveness as a minister. Are you presently in debt so as to interfere with your work, or have you obligations to others which will make it difficult for you to live on the salary you may receive?

¶ **415.** *Educational Requirements.*—A candidate for probationary membership must (1) have been graduated with a Bachelor of Arts in liberal education or equivalent degree in a college or university listed by the University Senate or competency equivalence as certified by the University Senate, and (2) have completed at least one half of the work required for a Master of Divinity or equivalent first professional degree in a school of theology listed by the University Senate except under the special conditions of ¶ 417.

¶ **416.** *Special Conditions: Exceptional Promise.*—Under special conditions an Annual Conference may, by a three-fourths majority vote of the ministerial members in full connection, present and voting, admit to probationary membership a candidate who exhibits exceptional promise for the ministry in the following cases:

1. If the candidate is a graduate with a Bachelor of Arts in liberal education from a college not listed by the University Senate or competency equivalence as certified by the Division of Ordained Ministry, who has completed one half of the work required for the Master of Divinity or equivalent first professional degree in a school of theology listed by the University Senate.

2. If the candidate has *(a)* reached thirty-five years of age; *(b)* served as an associate member for a minimum of two years under full-time appointment; *(c)* completed a Bachelor of Arts or its equivalent degree in a college or university listed by the University Senate or competency equivalence as certified by the University Senate; *(d)* completed two years of advanced study prescribed by the Division of Ordained Ministry beyond the five-year ministerial course of study required for admission to associate membership, in cooperation with the United Methodist theological schools; and *(e)* been recommended by a three-fourths vote of the Cabinet and a three-fourths vote of the Board of Ordained Ministry, written statements of such recommendations having been read to the conference before the vote is taken, setting forth the particular ways the candidate's ministry is exceptional and the special reasons this person should be received into probationary membership.

¶ **417.** *Continuation in Probationary Membership.*—To be continued as probationary members, candidates shall make regular progress in their ministerial studies. In case of failure or delay, the Board of Ordained Ministry shall investigate the circumstances and judge whether to extend the time within the following limits: (1) for completing the theological course for the Master of Divinity or equivalent first professional degree, a total of eight years; (2) for completing the advanced studies in the ministerial course of study, a total of four years. In a case clearly recognized as exceptional the board, by a three-fourths vote, may recommend an extension beyond these limits, which may be approved by a three-fourths vote of the ministerial members in full connection, present and voting; *provided,* however, that no candidates shall be continued on probation beyond the eighth regular conference session following their admission to probationary membership.

¶ **418.** *General Provisions.*—1. An Annual Conference may designate a Master of Divinity or equivalent first professional degree from a school of theology listed by the University Senate as the minimum educational requirement for probationary membership.

2. The Board of Ordained Ministry shall require a transcript of credits from each applicant before recognizing any of the applicant's educational claims. In case of doubt, the board may submit a transcript to the Division of Ordained Ministry for evaluation.

3. In accordance with ¶ 723.3*a*, the Board of Ordained Ministry may seek from a school of theology information about the personal and professional qualities of an applicant for probationary membership or of a probationary member; *provided,* however, that the applicant or member consent to the provision of such information.

4. Whenever probationary members find it necessary to discontinue their theological education, the Board of Ordained Ministry shall review their relation to the Annual Conference. If they desire to continue in the ministry, they shall receive credit in the course of study for their theological work as the Division of Ordained Ministry shall determine.

5. Probationary members who are regularly appointed to a pastoral charge are subject to the provisions of the Discipline in the performance of their pastoral duties. The district superin-

tendent under whom they are appointed shall provide guidance through the Board of Ordained Ministry and the educational institution in performance of work.

6. Probationary members in appointments beyond the local church shall relate themselves to the district superintendent in the area where their work is done. The district superintendent shall give them supervision and report annually to their Board of Ordained Ministry.

7. Probationary members received under the provisions of ¶ 416.2 who are pursuing advanced studies in the course of study shall do so in a school for courses of study.

8. The educational standards and other requirements for admission and ordination shall be set by the Central and Provisional Central Conferences for the Annual and Provisional Annual Conferences within their territories, and outside such territories by the Annual or Provisional Annual Conference itself.[9]

ADMISSION AND CONTINUANCE AS AN ASSOCIATE MEMBER

¶ **419.** *Eligibility and Rights of Associate Members.*—Associate members of an Annual Conference are in the itinerant ministry of the Church and are available on a continuing basis for appointment by the bishop. They offer themselves without reserve to be appointed and to serve as their superiors in office shall direct. They shall be amenable to the Annual Conference in the performance of their ministry and shall be granted the same security of appointment as probationary members and members in full connection.

1. *Pastors from Other Denominations.*—On recommendation of the Board of Ordained Ministry the ministerial members in full connection may approve annually ministers in good standing in other Christian denominations to serve as pastors in charge while retaining their denomination affiliation; such ministers may be granted voice and vote in the Annual Conference on all matters except the following: *(a)* constitutional amendments; *(b)* election of delegates to the General or Jurisdictional or Central Confer-

---

[9]*See* Judicial Council Decision 187.

ences; *(c)* all matters of ordination, character, and conference relations of ministers; *provided* that they shall agree to the satisfaction of the Board of Ordained Ministry to support and maintain the doctrine and polity of The United Methodist Church while under appointment. Their ordination credentials shall be examined by the Board of Ordained Ministry and upon its recommendation may be recognized as valid in The United Methodist Church while they are under appointment.

2. *Ministers Serving in Ecumenical Ministry.*—Ministerial members of other denominations in good standing with their denominations who serve in an ecumenical ministry in which a United Methodist church is involved, or who serve in an administrative position in an ecumenical program where The United Methodist Church is a sponsor, shall not thereby be required to surrender their rights and privileges as ministerial members of their denominations, and they shall, when the Board of Ordained Ministry certifies that their credentials are at least equal to those of associate members, be accorded all the duties and privileges of associate members of the Annual Conference of The United Methodist Church, except security of appointment.

3. Associate members are eligible for ordination as deacons but may not be ordained elders unless they qualify through probationary membership for membership in full connection in the Annual Conference (¶ 424).

4. Associate members shall have the right to vote in the Annual Conference on all matters except the following: *(a)* constitutional amendments; *(b)* election of delegates to the General and Jurisdictional or Central Conferences; *(c)* all matters of ordination, character, and conference relations of ministers.

5. Associate members may serve on any board, commission, or committee of an Annual Conference except the Board of Ordained Ministry. They shall not be eligible for election as delegates to the General or Jurisdictional or Central Conferences.

6. Ordained ministers of Methodist or United Churches in other countries serving as missionaries certified by the General Board of Global Ministries within the bounds of the Annual Conference are associate members of the conference, without prejudice to their relationship to their churches of origin.

7. Associate members, except these named in §6, shall be subject to the provisions governing sabbatical leave, leave of absence, location, retirement, minimum salary, and pension.

¶ **420.** *Requirements for Election as Associate Members.*—Candidates may be elected to associate membership by vote of the ministerial members in full connection, upon recommendation of the Board of Ordained Ministry, when they have met the following conditions. They shall have (1) reached age thirty-five; (2) served four years as full-time local pastors; (3) completed the five-year ministerial course of study in addition to the studies for license as a local pastor, no more than one year of which may be taken by correspondence; (4) completed a minimum of sixty semester hours toward the Bachelor of Arts or an equivalent degree in a college or university listed by the University Senate or competency equivalence; (5) been recommended by the district Committee on Ordained Ministry and the Board of Ordained Ministry; (6) declared their willingness to accept continuing full-time appointment; (7) satisfied the board regarding their physical, mental, and emotional health (the Annual Conference may require psychological tests to provide additional information on the candidate's fitness for the ministry); and (8) prepared at least one written sermon on a biblical passage specified by the Board of Ordained Ministry and given satisfactory answers in a written doctrinal examination administered by the Board of Ordained Ministry. (Consideration shall be given to the questions listed in ¶ 425.)[10]

¶ **421.** *Progression into Full Membership.*—Associate members who exhibit exceptional promise for the ministry may qualify for probationary membership in the Annual Conference under special conditions as set forth in ¶ 416.2 upon receiving a three-fourths majority vote of the ministerial members of the conference in full connection, present and voting.

ADMISSION AND CONTINUANCE OF FULL
MEMBERSHIP IN THE ANNUAL CONFERENCE

¶ **422.** *Members in Full Connection.*—Members in full connection with an Annual Conference by virtue of their election and

---

[10]*See* Judicial Council Decision 343.

ordination are bound in special covenant with all the ordained ministers of the Annual Conference. In the keeping of this covenant they perform the ministerial duties and maintain the ministerial standards established by those in the covenant. They offer themselves without reserve to be appointed and to serve, after consultation, as the appointive authority may determine. They live with their fellow ordained ministers in mutual trust and concern and seek with them the sanctification of the fellowship. Only those shall be elected to full membership who are of unquestionable moral character and genuine piety, sound in the fundamental doctrines of Christianity and faithful in the discharge of their duties.[11]

¶ **423.** *Rights of Full Members.*—Members in full connection shall have the right to vote on all matters in the Annual Conference except in the election of lay delegates to the General and Jurisdictional or Central Conferences (¶ 701.1*a*) and shall have sole responsibility for all matters of ordination, character, and conference relations of ordained ministers. They shall be eligible to hold office in the Annual Conference and to be elected delegates to the General and Jurisdictional or Central Conferences under the provision of the Constitution (¶ 39, Art. IV). Every effective member in full connection who is in good standing shall receive an annual appointment by the bishop.[12]

1. Growth in competence and effectiveness through continuing education is expected of conference members. These are professional responsibilities which ministerial members are expected to fulfill and which represent a fundamental part of their accountability and a primary basis of their guaranteed appointment. These shall include:

a) Continuing availability for appointment.

b) Having pastoral effectiveness evaluated annually by Pastor-Parish Relations Committees and district superintendents trained in the process of evaluation to determine the gifts, graces, health, and readiness for ministry (¶¶ 723.2*j* and 518.2).

c) Annual participation in continuing education programs. The Board of Ordained Ministry (¶ 731.2*i*) shall set minimal

---

[11]*See* Judicial Council Decision 406.
[12]*See* Judicial Council Decisions 462, 473.

standards and specific guidelines for continuing education programs for members of their conference, and insure their availability.

¶ **424.** *Requirements for Admission.*—Candidates who have been probationary members for at least two years may be admitted into membership in full connection in an Annual Conference by vote of the ministerial members in full connection, on recommendation of the Board of Ordained Ministry,[13] after they have qualified as follows. They shall have (1) served full time under episcopal appointment under supervision personally assumed or delegated by the district superintendent satisfactorily to the Board of Ordained Ministry for at least two full Annual Conference years following the completion of the educational requirements specified in (3) below.[14] Those probationary members under appointment January 1981 shall not be subject to the provisions of this paragraph unless the Annual Conference otherwise provides; (2) been previously elected as probationary members and ordained deacons; (3) met educational requirements in one of the following ways: *(a)* graduation with a Master of Divinity or equivalent degree from a school of theology listed by the University Senate; *(b)* graduation with a Bachelor of Arts or equivalent degree from a college or university listed by the University Senate or competency equivalence as certified by the Division of Ordained Ministry and completion of two years of advanced study beyond the requirements for probationary membership (¶¶ 414-416) under the supervision of the Division of Ordained Ministry in an approved course of study school; *(c)* educational requirements in every case should include a minimum of two semester or quarter hours in each of the fields of United Methodist history, doctrine, and polity; *provided* that a candidate may meet the requirements by undertaking a special course of study and/or examination in these fields provided and administered by the Division of Ordained Ministry *(see* ¶ 1629.2); (4) satisfied the board regarding physical, mental, and emotional health; (5) prepared at least one written sermon on a biblical passage specified by the Board of Ordained Ministry; (6)

---

[13]*See* Judicial Council Decisions 157, 344.
[14]*See* Judicial Council Decision 440.

201

responded to a written or oral doctrinal examination administered by the Board of Ordained Ministry. The candidate should
demonstrate the ability to communicate clearly in both oral and
written form. The candidate's reflections and the board's
response should be informed by the insights and guidelines of
Part II of the Discipline. The following questions are guidelines
for the preparation of the examination:

a) Describe your personal experience of God and the
understanding of God you derive from biblical, theological, and
historical sources.

b) What is the Christian understanding of humanity, and the
human need for divine grace?

c) How do you interpret the statement "Jesus Christ is
Lord"?

d) What is your conception of the activity of the Holy Spirit
in personal faith, in the community of believers, and in
responsible living in the world?

e) The United Methodist Church holds that Scripture,
tradition, experience, and reason are sources and norms for
belief and practice, but that the Bible is primary among them.
What is your understanding of this theological position of the
Church?

f) How do you understand the following traditional evangelical doctrines: (1) repentance, (2) justification, (3) regeneration,
(4) sanctification? What are the marks of the Christian life?

g) What is the meaning and significance of the Sacraments?

h) Describe the nature and mission of the Church. What are
its primary tasks today?

i) What is your understanding of (1) the Kingdom of God,
(2) the Resurrection, (3) eternal life?

j) How do you perceive yourself, your gifts, your motives,
your role, and your commitment as an ordained minister?

k) What is the meaning of ordination, especially in the
context of the general ministry of the Church?

¶ **425.** *Historic Examination for Admission into Full Connection
and Associate Membership.*—The bishop as chief pastor shall engage
those seeking to be admitted in serious self-searching and prayer
to prepare them for their examination before the conference. At
the time of the examination the bishop shall also explain to the

conference the historic nature of the following questions and seek to interpret their spirit and intent. The questions are these and any others which may be thought necessary:

1. Have you faith in Christ?

2. Are you going on to perfection?

3. Do you expect to be made perfect in love in this life?

4. Are you earnestly striving after it?

5. Are you resolved to devote yourself wholly to God and his work?

6. Do you know the General Rules of our Church?

7. Will you keep them?

8. Have you studied the doctrines of The United Methodist Church?

9. After full examination do you believe that our doctrines are in harmony with the Holy Scriptures?

10. Will you preach and maintain them?

11. Have you studied our form of Church discipline and polity?

12. Do you approve our Church government and polity?

13. Will you support and maintain them?

14. Will you diligently instruct the children in every place?

15. Will you visit from house to house?

16. Will you recommend fasting or abstinence, both by precept and example?

17. Are you determined to employ all your time in the work of God?

18. Are you in debt so as to embarrass you in your work?

19. Will you observe the following directions?

a) Be diligent. Never be unemployed. Never be triflingly employed. Never trifle away time; neither spend any more time at any one place than is strictly necessary.

b) Be punctual. Do everything exactly at the time. And do not mend our rules, but keep them; not for wrath, but for conscience' sake.[15]

---

[15]These are the questions which every Methodist preacher from the beginning has been required to answer upon becoming a full member of an Annual Conference. These questions were formulated by John Wesley and have been little changed throughout the years.

¶ **426.** *General Provisions for Annual Conference Membership.*—
1. A full member of an Annual Conference shall be eligible for
ordination as elder by a bishop and such other elders as the
ordaining bishop may determine.

2. Under conditions regarded as exceptional, candidates
who were admitted to probationary membership by a three-
fourths vote (¶ 416), upon recommendation by the Board of
Ordained Ministry when they have completed advanced studies
specified by and under the direction of the Division of Ordained
Ministry and have met all the other requirements, may be
received into full membership by a three-fourths vote of the
ministerial members in full connection, present and voting.

¶ **427.** *Evaluation.*—Evaluation is a continuous process
which must take place in a spirit of understanding, acceptance,
and with a genuine desire to embody and carry forth more
effectively Christ's ministry in the world lest we create defensive-
ness and discouragement in the Church or the person being
evaluated. Pastoral effectiveness shall be evaluated annually
(¶ 266.2*d* (3)) by the Pastor-Parish Relations Committee and
district superintendent by criteria and processes developed by the
Board of Ordained Ministry and the Cabinet. The Board of
Ordained Ministry and/or the Cabinet shall conduct an annual
training program for Pastor-Parish Relations Committee members to enable them to evaluate the gifts, graces, family needs,
health, and readiness for ministry of the pastor (¶¶ 723.2 and
518.2).

TRANSFERS FROM OTHER DENOMINATIONS

¶ **428.** Ministers coming from other Christian churches,
provided they present suitable credentials of good standing
through the Board of Ordained Ministry,[16] give assurance of
their faith, Christian experience, and other qualifications, give
evidence of their agreement with United Methodist doctrine,
discipline, and polity, present a satisfactory certificate of good
health on the prescribed form from a physician approved by the
Board of Ordained Ministry, and meet the educational require-

---

[16]*See* Judicial Council Decisions 16, 361.

ments, may be received into the ordained ministry of The United Methodist Church in the following manner:

1. Between conference sessions, the Board of Ordained Ministry may receive them as pastors in charge while retaining their denominational affiliation pending the recognition of their orders. The bishop may make ad interim recognition of valid ordination after consultation with the Cabinet and executive committee of the Board of Ordained Ministry pending recognition by the vote of the ministerial members in full connection. In every case, prior examination shall be made of the ordained minister's understanding of United Methodist history, doctrine, and polity.

2. The district Committee on Ordained Ministry may receive as local pastors ministers from other denominations without orders, pending the recognition of their credentials. On recommendation of the Board of Ordained Ministry, the Annual Conference, by vote of the ministerial members in full connection, may recognize their ordination and receive them into probationary membership or associate membership in the conference.[17]

3. The Annual Conference, on recommendation of the Board of Ordained Ministry, may also receive in equal standing persons who are on probation in the ministry of another Methodist church, using, however, special care that before they are admitted to membership in full connection, they shall meet all the educational and other requirements.

4. The Board of Ordained Ministry of an Annual Conference is required to ascertain from a minister seeking admission into its membership on credentials from another denomination whether or not membership in the effective relation was previously held in an Annual Conference of The United Methodist Church or one of its legal predecessors, and if so when and under what circumstances the minister's connection with such Annual Conferences was severed.

5. Ministers seeking admission into an Annual Conference on credentials from another denomination who have previously withdrawn from membership in the effective relation in an Annual Conference of The United Methodist Church or one of

---

[17]*See* Judicial Council Decision 444.

its legal predecessors shall not be admitted or readmitted without the consent of the Annual Conference from which they withdrew or its legal successor, or the Annual Conference of which the major portion of their former conference is a part, such consent to be granted upon recommendation of its Board of Ordained Ministry.

6. Whenever the orders of a minister are recognized according to the foregoing provisions, that minister shall be furnished with a certificate signed by the bishop.

7. When the orders of a minister of another church shall have been duly recognized, the certificate of ordination by said church shall be returned to the minister with the following inscription written plainly across its face:

Accredited by the _____ *Annual Conference of The United Methodist Church, this* _____ *day of* _____ *, 19_____ , as the basis of new credentials.*

_____ , *President*

_____ , *Secretary*

8. With the consent of the resident bishop, who shall consult with the executive committee of the Board of Ordained Ministry, ordained ministers from other Methodist denominations may be received by transfer, if they meet United Methodist educational requirements, without going through the process required for ministers coming from other denominations. Similarly, ministers of The United Methodist Church may be transferred by a bishop to other Methodist churches with the consent of the proper authorities in said churches.

Section IV. Ordination.

¶ **429.** *Ordination and the Apostolic Ministry.*—1. The whole Church receives and accepts the call of God to embody and carry forth Christ's ministry in the world. Ordination originates in God's will and purpose for the Church. There are persons within the Church community whose gifts, graces, and promise of future usefulness are observable to the community, who respond to God's call and offer themselves in leadership as ordained ministers.

2. The pattern for this response to the call is provided in the development of the early Church. The apostles led in prayer and preaching, organized the Christian community to extend Christ's ministry of love and reconciliation, and provided for guardianship and transmission of the gospel, as entrusted to the early Church, to later generations. Their ministry, though distinct, was never separate from the ministry of the whole people of God.

¶ **430.** *The Purpose of Ordination.*—1. Ordination for such ministry is a gift from God to the Church. In ordination, the Church affirms and continues the apostolic ministry which it authorizes and authenticates through persons empowered by the Holy Spirit. As such, those who are ordained are committed to becoming conscious representatives of the whole gospel and are responsible for the transmission of that gospel to the end that all the world may be saved. Their ordination is fulfilled in the ministry of Word, Sacrament, and Order.

2. Ordained persons are authorized to preach and teach the Word of God, administer the Sacraments of Baptism and the Lord's Supper, equip the laity for ministry, exercise pastoral oversight, and administer the Discipline of the Church.

3. The efficacy of the mission of the Church is dependent on the viable interaction of the general ministry and the ordained ministry of the Church. Without creative use of the diverse gifts of the entire Body of Christ, the ministry of the Church is not effective. Without responsible leadership, there is no focus and definition of such ministry.

¶ **431.** *Qualifications for Ordination.*—Acceptance of the call to ordained ministry, together with the acknowledgment and authentication of such call by the Church, grants to the person ordained authority to serve the Church through sacramental and functional leadership. In this, the ordained person becomes representative of the entire ministry of Christ in the Church and of the ministry required of the entire Church to the world. Though no singular manifestation of God's call can be structured or required by the Church, the consciousness of such a call is crucial, and it must be submitted to the Church for authentication. It is expected that persons to be ordained shall:

1. Have personal faith in Christ and be committed to him as Savior and Lord.

2. Nurture and cultivate spiritual disciplines and patterns of holiness.

3. Be aware of a call by God to give themselves completely to their ministry, accepting God's call to be his servant.

4. Be committed to and engage in leading the ministry of the whole Church in loving service to humankind.

5. Be able to give evidence of the possession of gifts, graces, and promise of future usefulness.

6. Be willing to make a complete dedication of themselves to the highest ideals of the Christian life and agree to exercise responsible self-control in their personal habits.

7. Be persons in whom the community can place trust and confidence.

8. Be competent in the disciplines of Scripture, theology, church history, and church polity, and in the understanding and practice of the art of communication and human relations.

9. Be accountable to The United Methodist Church, accept its Discipline and authority, abide by the demands of the special relationship of its ordained ministers, and be faithful to their vows as ordained ministers of the Church of God.

¶ **432.** *The Act of Ordination.*—Ordination is a public act of the Church which indicates acceptance by an individual of God's call to the upbuilding of the Church through the ministry of Word, Sacrament, and Order and acknowledgment and authentication of this call by the Christian community through prayers and the laying on of hands.

It is a rite of the Church following New Testament usage as appears in the words of Paul to Timothy: "I remind you to rekindle the gift of God that is within you through the laying on of my hands" (II Timothy 1:6).

United Methodist tradition has entrusted persons in the ordained ministry with the responsibility for maintaining standards: for education and training and for examination and granting credentials to those who seek ordination. By the authorization of the ministerial members of the Annual Conference, candidates are elected into the Annual Conference and are ordained by the bishop.

Ordination, thus, is that act by which the Church symbolizes a shared relationship between those ordained for sacramental and functional leadership and the Church community from which the person being ordained has come. The community is initiated by God, is given meaning and direction by Christ, and is sustained by the Holy Spirit. This relationship is a gift which comes through the grace of God in assurance of the ministry of Christ throughout the world.

¶ **433.** *Classification of Ordination.*—The ordained ministry of The United Methodist Church consists of elders and deacons. No designations are to be applied so as to deprive any person of any right or privilege permanently granted by either The Methodist Church or The Evangelical United Brethren Church.[18]

1. Elders are ministers who have completed their formal preparation for the ministry of Word, Sacrament, and Order; have been elected itinerant members in full connection with an Annual Conference; and have been ordained elders in accordance with the Order and Discipline of The United Methodist Church.

2. Deacons are ministers who have progressed sufficiently in their preparation for the ministry to be received by an Annual Conference as either probationary members or associate members and who have been ordained deacons in accordance with the Order and Discipline of The United Methodist Church.

¶ **434.** *The Order of Deacon.*—A deacon is a minister who has been received by an Annual Conference either as a probationary member or as an associate member and has been ordained deacon. Deacons have authority to conduct divine worship, to preach the Word, to perform the marriage ceremony where the laws of the state or province permit, and to bury the dead. When invited to do so by an elder, they may assist in the administration of the Sacraments. When serving as regularly appointed pastors of charges, they shall be granted authority to administer the Sacraments on the charges to which they are appointed. Persons of the following classes are eligible for the order of deacon:

1. Local pastors who have been received into associate membership after having met the requirements of ¶ 420.

---

[18]*See* Judicial Council Decision 337.

2. Theological students who have been received into probationary membership after having met the requirements of ¶ 414.

3. A deacon shall be ordained by a bishop, employing the Order of Service for the Ordination of Deacons.

¶ **435.** *The Order of Elder.*—An elder is a minister who has met the requirements of ¶ 424 and therefore has full authority for the ministry of Word, Sacrament, and Order; who has been received as a minister in full connection with an Annual Conference; and who has been ordained elder.

Ministers of the following classes are eligible for the order of elder:

1. Deacons who have been probationary members of an Annual Conference, are graduates of theological schools listed by the University Senate, and have been elected to membership in full connection with an Annual Conference after having met the requirements of ¶¶ 424-426.

2. Deacons who have been probationary members of an Annual Conference for at least two years since being received from associate membership and who have been elected to membership in full connection with an Annual Conference after having met the requirements of ¶ 421.

3. An elder shall be ordained by a bishop, employing the Order of Service for the Ordination of Elders. The bishops shall be assisted by other elders in the laying on of hands.

4. The bishop and the secretary of the Annual Conference shall provide credentials to all members in full connection, certifying their ministerial standing and their ordination as elders.

Section V.   Appointments to Various Ministries.

¶ **436.** *General Provisions.*—All ministerial members who are in good standing in an Annual Conference shall receive annually appointment by the bishop unless they are granted a sabbatical leave, a disability leave, or are on leave of absence or retired.[19]

In addition to the ministers, persons who have been granted a license as local pastors and who have been approved by vote of the ministerial members in full connection may be appointed as

---

[19]*See* Judicial Council Decisions 380, 462.

pastors in charge under certain conditions which are specified in
¶¶ 408-409.

¶ **437.** *The Itinerant System.*—The itinerant system is the
accepted method of The United Methodist Church by which
ordained ministers are appointed by the bishop to fields of labor.
All ordained ministers shall accept and abide by these appointments. Persons appointed to multiple-staff ministries, either
in a single parish or in a cluster or larger parish, must have personal and professional access to the bishop and Cabinet, the
Pastor-Parish Relations Committee, as well as to the pastor in
charge. The nature of the appointment process is specified in
¶¶ 527-531.

1. Full-time service shall be the norm for ministry in the
Annual Conference. Full-time service shall mean that the
person's entire vocational time is devoted to the work of ministry
in the field of labor to which one is appointed by the bishop.

2. Less than full-time service may be rendered by a
ministerial member under the conditions stipulated in this
paragraph. Less than full-time service shall mean that a specified
amount of time less than full time agreed upon by the bishop and
the Cabinet, the ordained minister, and the Annual Conference
Board of Ordained Ministry is devoted to the work of ministry in
the field of labor to which the person is appointed by the bishop.
At his or her own initiative, a ministerial member may request and
may be appointed by the bishop to less than full-time service
without loss of essential rights or membership in the Annual
Conference, provided that the following conditions are met.

a) The minister seeking less than full-time service should
present a written request to the bishop and the chairperson of the
Board of Ordained Ministry at least six months prior to the
Annual Conference session at which the appointment is made.
This requirement is waived for 1980 Annual Conference sessions
only.

b) Following appropriate consultation, as established in
¶¶ 439 and 527-531, and upon joint recommendation of the
Cabinet and the Board of Ordained Ministry, the less than
full-time category shall be confirmed by a two-thirds vote of the
ministerial members of the Annual Conference.

c) Reappointment to less than full-time service shall be requested by the ordained minister and approved annually by the bishop and Cabinet and shall not be granted for more than a total of eight years except by a three-fourths vote of the ministerial members in full connection of the Annual Conference.

d) Ordained ministers who receive appointment at less than full-time service remain within the itineracy and as such remain available, upon consultation with the bishop and Cabinet, for appointment to full-time service. A written request to return to full-time appointment shall be made to the bishop and Cabinet at least six months prior to the Annual Conference session at which the appointment is to be made.

e) The bishop may make ad interim appointments at less than full-time service upon request of the minister following consultation as specified in ¶¶ 527-531 and upon recommendation of the Cabinet and executive committee of the conference Board of Ordained Ministry, the same to be acted upon by the next regular session of the Annual Conference. This provision shall be effective for 1980 Annual Conferences.

¶ **438.** *Appointment to a Pastoral Charge.*—1. A pastor is an ordained or licensed person approved by vote of the ministerial members in full connection (¶¶ 408-409), appointed by the bishop to be in charge of a station, circuit, larger parish, or on the staff of one such appointment.

2. *Duties of a Pastor.*—Pastors are responsible for ministering to the needs of the whole community as well as to the needs of the people of their charge, equipping them to fulfill their ministry to each other and to the world to which they are sent as servants under the lordship of Christ. Among the pastor's duties are the following:

a) To preach the Word, read and teach the Scriptures, and engage the people in study and witness.

b) To administer the Sacraments of Baptism and the Lord's Supper and all the other means of grace.

c) To give diligent pastoral leadership in ordering the life of the congregation for nurture and care.

(1) To instruct candidates for membership and receive them into the Church.

(2) To participate in denominational and conference programs and training opportunities.

(3) To give oversight to the total educational program of the church and encourage the distribution and use of United Methodist literature in each local church.

(4) To perform the marriage ceremony after due counsel with the parties involved. The decision to perform the ceremony shall be the right and responsibility of the pastor. Qualifications for performing marriage shall be in accordance with the laws of the state and The United Methodist Church.

(5) To counsel those who are under threat of marriage breakdown and explore every possibility for reconciliation.

(6) To counsel bereaved families and conduct appropriate memorial services.

(7) To visit in the homes of the church and community, especially among the sick, aged, and others in need.

(8) To counsel with members of the church and community as to the alternatives to military service.

d) To participate in the life and work of the community and in ecumenical concerns and to lead the congregation to become so involved.

e) To search out from among the membership and constituency men and women for pastoral ministry and other church-related occupation: to help them interpret the meaning of the call of God, to advise and assist when they commit themselves thereto, to counsel with them concerning the course of their preparation, and to keep a careful record of such decisions.

f) To assure that the organizational concerns of the congregations are adequately provided for.

(1) To administer the provisions of the Discipline and supervise the working program of the local church.

(2) To preside over the Charge Conference at the request of the district superintendent.

(3) To give an account of their pastoral ministries to the Charge and Annual Conferences according to the prescribed forms. The care of all church records and local church financial obligations shall be included.

3. *Support for Ministers Appointed to a Pastoral Charge.*—As-

sumption of the obligations of the itinerant ministry required upon admission to the traveling connection places upon the Church a counterobligation to provide adequate support for the entire ministry of the Church (¶ 930). The Church shall provide and the minister is entitled to receive not less than the equitable salary established by the Annual Conference for ministerial members according to provisions of ¶ 935.3.

a) Support for Ministers Appointed to Pastoral Charges Who Render Full-Time Service.—Each pastor of an Annual Conference who is in good standing and who is appointed to full-time service under the provision of ¶ 437.1 shall have a claim upon the conference Equitable Salary Fund and a right to receive not less than minimum salary established by the Annual Conference for persons in full-time service.

b) Support for Ministers Appointed to Pastoral Charges Who Render Less than Full-Time Service.—Each pastor who is in good standing and who is appointed by the bishop to less than full-time service under the provisions of ¶ 437.2 shall have a claim upon the conference Equitable Salary Fund in one-quarter increments according to the guidelines established by the Annual Conference Commission on Equitable Salaries.

¶ **439.** *Appointments Beyond the Local United Methodist Church.*— Conference members may be appointed to serve in ministries beyond the local church which extend the witness and service of Christ's love and justice. Conference members in these ministries remain within the itineracy and shall be accountable to the Annual Conference. They shall be given the same moral and spiritual support by it as are persons in appointments to pastoral charges.[20]

The institution or agency desiring to employ a conference member shall, when feasible, through its appropriate official, consult the member's bishop and secure approval before completing any agreement to employ the member. If the institution or agency is located in another area, the bishop of that area shall also be consulted.

A conference member in an appointment beyond the local church must be willing upon consultation to receive an appointment in a pastoral charge. Such consultation shall give

---

[20]*See* Judicial Council Decisions 321, 325, 466.

due regard to the individual's special training, experience, and skills. When initiated by a conference member, a request for appointment to a pastoral charge shall be made in writing to the bishop and the Cabinet. Such a request should be made at least six months prior to Annual Conference.

1. *Categories of Appointment.*—In order to establish a clear distinction between the work to which all Christians are called and the tasks for which ordained ministers are appropriately prepared and authorized, the following categories are established for appointments within the itineracy of The United Methodist Church.

a) Appointments within the connectional structures of United Methodism: district superintendents, staff members of conference councils, boards, and agencies, treasurers, bishops' assistants, superintendents or directors of parish development, staff of general boards and agencies, missionaries, faculty and administrators of United Methodist schools of theology and other educational institutions, campus ministers, and staff members of ecumenical agencies.[21]

b) Appointments to extension ministries of persons under endorsement by the Division of Chaplains and Related Ministries, such as: chaplaincy in the armed forces, Veterans Administration, industry, correctional health care fields, and other related ministries which the bishop and conference Board of Ordained Ministry may designate.[22]

c) Conference members in service under the World Division of the General Board of Global Ministries may be appointed to the ministries listed in *(a)* and *(b)* above. They may be assigned to service either in Annual Conferences or Central Conferences, or with affiliated autonomous churches, independent churches, churches resulting from the union of Methodist Churches and other communions, or in other denominational or ecumenical bodies. They may accept such rights and privileges, including affiliate membership, as may be offered them by overseas Annual Conferences or by other churches to which they are assigned, without impairing their relationship to their home Annual Conference.

[21]*See* Judicial Council Decisions 166, 167.
[22]*See* Judicial Council Decisions 321, 325, 329.

d) Conference members may receive appointments beyond the ministries usually extended through the local church and other institutions listed above in *(a)* and *(b)*,[23] when considered by the bishop and Board of Ordained Ministry to be a true extension of the Christian ministry of the church or an outreach ministry in keeping with the goals of the Annual Conference and one in which ordination to Word, Sacrament, and Order is useful or necessary. These ministries shall be initiated in missional response to the needs of persons in special circumstances and unique situations and shall reflect the commitment of the clergy to intentional fulfillment of their ordination vows to Word, Sacrament, and Order. These appointments may involve clergy with expertise from other vocations. Conference members in such appointments retain conference membership, and the Annual Conference may choose to extend financial support and benefits for its clergy by vote of the Annual Conference.

Those seeking such an appointment in this category shall submit to the bishop, the district superintendent, and the Board of Ordained Ministry a written statement of their intentional fulfillment of their ordination vows to be minister of Word, Sacrament, and Order not later than ninety (90) days before Annual Conference. In addition, a statement to the bishop shall be required from the institution in which the ministry is to be performed assuring freedom in the fulfillment of ordination vows.

On recommendation of the Cabinet and the Board of Ordained Ministry, such positions are to be confirmed by a two-thirds vote of the ministerial members of the Annual Conference.

The bishop may make ad interim appointments in this category after consultation with the Cabinet and executive committee of the Board of Ordained Ministry, the position to be formally acted upon by the next session of the Annual Conference.

e) Ordained ministers who are probationary or full members may be appointed by the bishop to attend any school, college, or theological seminary listed by the University Senate.

2. *Relation to the Annual Conference.—a) Accountability to the Annual Conference.*—Conference members under appointment

---

[23]*See* Judicial Council Decision 380.

beyond the local church are amenable to the Annual Conference of which they are members and insofar as possible should maintain close working relationship with and effective participation in the work of their Annual Conference, assuming whatever responsibilities they are qualified and requested to assume.

They shall submit annually to the bishop, the district superintendent, and the Board of Ordained Ministry a written report prepared in consultation with their immediate supervisor of their performance of the ministerial office. The report will use the official report developed for the Church by the General Council on Finance and Administration for use in the Annual Conference. This report shall serve as the basis for the evaluation of these clergy in light of the missional needs of the Church and the fulfillment of their ordination to be minister of Word, Sacrament, and Order. A written summary of the evaluation shall be prepared and sent to the minister under appointment by the bishop and the Cabinet. Ministers serving in appointments outside the conference in which they hold membership shall furnish a copy of their report also to the bishop of the area in which they reside and work. It is recommended that at the initiative of the superintendent, a personal interview with the district superintendent in the district in which they are serving be held.

b) Responsibility to the Annual Conference.—The bishop, representatives of the Cabinet, and the Committee on Chaplains and Related Ministries of the Board of Ordained Ministry shall provide an opportunity to meet annually with ordained ministers appointed beyond the local church who carry on their ministry within the bounds of Annual Conference, both of that Annual Conference and those who hold membership elsewhere. The bishop shall convene the meeting which is to be planned by the Cabinet and the Board of Ordained Ministry. The purpose of this meeting is to gain understanding of one another's role and function in ministry, to report to other ministers appointed beyond the local church and to discuss with them matters concerning the overall approach to ministry in the episcopal area, to interpret the role and function of extension ministries to the larger church through the offices of the bishop and his/her representatives, to nurture the development of various ministries as significant in assisting the mission of the Church, and to discuss specific programs and services which the bishop and his/her representatives may initiate in which the various ministers serving in appointments beyond the local church may be qualified as consultants and supervisors.

3. *Relation to the Local Church.*—*a*) Conference members appointed beyond the local church shall establish membership in a Charge Conference in their home Annual Conference in consultation with the pastor in charge and with approval of the district superintendent and the bishop. They shall submit to their home Charge Conference an annual report of pastoral duties and the fulfillment of their ordination through their special appointment, including ministerial activities in the charge where they have an affiliate membership relation and in other units of the Church at large, as well as continuing education work completed and anticipated. This report may be the one submitted to the bishop and Cabinet (¶ 439.2*a*).

All conference members, including those in extension ministries, shall be available and on call to administer the Sacraments of Baptism and the Lord's Supper as required by the Discipline (¶ 438.2*b*) and requested by the district superintendent of the district in which the appointment is held.

b) *Affiliate Relation to a Local Church.*—Ordained ministers under appointment beyond the local church and serving outside of the geographical bounds of their home Annual Conference shall be affiliate members without vote of a Charge Conference either within the district where they carry out the primary work of their appointment or within the district where they reside. The selection of the Charge Conference shall be made after consultation between the minister, district superintendent, and the pastor of the local United Methodist Church.

These ministers under appointment beyond the local church and serving outside the geographical boundaries of their home Annual Conference shall submit to the Charge Conference of which they are affiliate members a copy of the report submitted to their home Charge Conference and/or an oral report concerning their ministry and the fulfillment of their ordination. The district superintendent shall be responsible for the notification to these ministers concerning the time and place of the Charge Conference.

4. *Affiliate Relation to Annual Conference.*—Ordained clergy appointed beyond the local church outside the boundary of their Annual Conference may, at their own request, apply for affiliate membership in the Annual Conference in which their appointment is located. By a two-thirds vote of the executive session, such clergy may be received with rights and privileges, including service on conference boards, agencies, task forces, and committees, with voice but without vote. Voting membership shall be retained in the appointee's home Annual Conference for the duration of affiliate member relationship. Nomination to general church boards and agencies and election as delegates to General and Jurisdictional Conferences shall originate in the appointee's home Annual Conference. Such persons may serve on the board, agency, task force, or committee of only one Annual Conference at any one time.

5. *General Provisions.*—*a*) Persons in these appointments may be encouraged by the Cabinet to request the transfer of their conference membership to the Annual Conference in which they perform ministry.

b) Special appointments shall not be made to a position unrelated to an adequate accountability structure.

c) For information regarding pensions, the conference will continue to list the source of annuity claim for each of its clergy.

d) All conference secretaries shall submit to the editors of the General Minutes a list of such appointments beyond the local church made in their Annual Conferences, and there shall be published in the General Minutes a list of ministers in the Church serving in the major categories under these appointments.

e) Conference members appointed beyond the local church shall attend the Annual Conference in which membership is held.

¶ **440.** *Special Provisions.*—1. Pastors shall first obtain the written consent of the district superintendent before engaging for an evangelist any person who is not a conference-approved evangelist, a regular member of an Annual Conference, a local pastor, or a certified lay speaker in good standing in The United Methodist Church.

219

2. No pastor shall discontinue services in a local church between sessions of the Annual Conference without the consent of the Charge Conference and the district superintendent.

3. No pastor shall arbitrarily organize a pastoral charge. (*See* ¶ 267 for the method of organizing a local church.)

4. Ministers of The United Methodist Church are charged to maintain all confidences inviolate, including confessional confidences.

Section VI. Continuing Education for Full and Associate Members.

¶ **441.** *Continuing Education: Educational Leave.*—1. Ministers shall be encouraged to continue their education throughout their careers, including carefully developed personal programs of study augmented periodically by involvement in organized educational activities.

2. An ordained minister may request an educational leave of up to six months while continuing to hold a pastoral appointment. An Annual Conference may make such educational leaves available to its ordained ministers who have held full-time appointments for at least five years. Financial arrangements shall be negotiated by the pastor, district superintendent, and Pastor-Parish Relations Committee in consultation.

In most cases the ministers' continuing education program should allow for leaves of absence for study at least one week each year and at least one month during one year of each quadrennium. Such leaves shall not be considered as part of the ministers' vacation and shall be planned in consultation with their charges or other agencies to which they are appointed as well as the bishop, district superintendent, and Annual Conference Continuing Education Committee.

3. Pastors shall be asked by the district superintendent in the Charge Conference to outline their programs of continuing education for the year. The district superintendent shall also ask the local church to describe its provision for time and financial support for the pastor's program of continuing education.

¶ **442.** *Sabbatical Leave.*—A sabbatical leave should be allowed for a program of study or travel, approved by the conference Board of Ordained Ministry. Ministers who have been serving in a full-time appointment for six consecutive years from the time of their reception into full membership or for eight consecutive years from the time of their reception into associate membership may be granted a sabbatical leave for up to one year. Whenever possible, the salary level of the last appointment served before the leave should be maintained in the appointment made at the termination of the leave. The appointment to sabbatical leave is to be made by the bishop holding the conference upon the vote of the Annual Conference after recommendation by the Board of Ordained Ministry. Ministers shall submit a written request for a sabbatical leave, including plans for study or travel, to the Board of Ordained Ministry, with copies to the bishop and district superintendent, ordinarily six months before the opening session of the Annual Conference. To be eligible for an additional sabbatical leave ministers shall have served six consecutive years under full-time appointment following the previous sabbatical leave.[24]

Section VII. Changes of Conference Relationship for Full, Probationary, and Associate Members.

¶ **443.** Ministers seeking a change in conference relationship shall make written request to their Board of Ordained Ministry stating the reasons for the requested change of relationship. In addition, the Board of Ordained Ministry may request personal interviews with the minister requesting the change in relationship, except where personal appearance results in undue hardship.

¶ **444.** *Leave of Absence.*—1. This relationship is granted to ministers who are probationary, associate, and full members because of impaired health or for other equally sufficient reason when a minister is temporarily unwilling or unable to perform the full work of his/her appointment. This relationship may be initiated by the minister or the Cabinet, through the Board of Ordained Ministry, and granted or renewed by the vote of the ministerial members in full connection upon the board's recommendation. Between sessions of the Annual Conference this relation may be granted or terminated with the approval of

---

[24]*See* Judicial Council Decision 473.

the bishop, district superintendents, and executive committee of the Annual Conference Board of Ordained Ministry. This interim action shall be subject to the approval of the Annual Conference at its next session. This relation shall be approved annually upon written request of the ministerial member at least ninety days prior to Annual Conference and shall not be granted for more than five years in succession except by a two-thirds vote of the ministerial members in full connection. This leave shall be counted as a part of the eight-year limit for probationary members unless the Board of Ordained Ministry recommends otherwise. After consultation with the pastor, ministers on leave of absence shall designate the Charge Conference in which they shall hold membership. The exercise of their ministry shall be limited to the Charge Conference in which their membership is held and under the supervision of the pastor in charge, to whom they shall report all marriages performed, Baptisms administered, and funerals conducted, and shall be held amenable for their conduct and the continuation of their ordination rights to the Annual Conference. Should they reside outside the bounds of the Annual Conference, they shall forward to it annually a report similar to that required of a retired minister, and, in case of failure to do so, the Annual Conference may locate them without their consent. They shall have no claim on the conference funds except by vote of the ministerial members in full connection. They shall be eligible for membership on conference committees, commissions, or boards, except the Board of Ordained Ministry. They shall not receive pension credit and shall not be eligible to receive pension payments while in this relation.

2. When a member requests an end to the leave of absence, the Board of Ordained Ministry shall review the circumstances surrounding the granting of the relationship for the purpose of determining whether those circumstances have been alleviated.

3. Ministerial members who do not request an extension of the leave of absence or do not indicate willingness to return to the itinerant ministry at the end of the five-year period may be terminated.[25]

¶ **445.** *Maternity/Paternity Leave.*—Maternity/paternity leave

---

[25]*See* Judicial Council Decisions 450, 459, 473.

not to exceed one fourth of a year will be available to any probationary member, associate member, or minister in full connection who so requests it at the birth or adoption of a child.

1. During the leave, the minister's Annual Conference relations will remain unchanged, and the insurance plans will remain in force.

2. A maternity/paternity leave of up to one quarter of a year will be considered as an uninterrupted appointment for pension credit purposes.

3. The minister's salary will be maintained for no less than the first month of the leave.

4. During the leave time pastoral responsibility for the church or churches involved will be handled through consultation with the Pastor-Parish Relations Committee of the local church(es) and the district superintendent.

5. Persons desiring maternity/paternity leave should file their request with the Pastor-Parish Relations Committee after consulting with the district superintendent at least ninety days prior to its beginning to allow adequate pastoral care for the churches involved to be developed.

6. Special arrangements shall be made for district superintendents, bishops, and those under special appointment.

¶ **446.** *Disability Leave.*—1. When ministers who are associate members, probationary members, or members in full connection in an Annual Conference are forced to give up their ministerial work because of their physical or emotional disability, upon joint recommendations of the Board of Ordained Ministry and the conference Board of Pensions and by a majority vote of the ministerial members of the Annual Conference in full connection who are present and voting, they may be granted annual disability leave without losing their relationship to the Annual Conference; *provided,* however, that such leave may be granted or renewed only after a thorough investigation of the case and examination of medical evidence in accordance with §3 and §4 below. Each disability leave granted by the Annual Conference shall be recorded in the conference minutes.

2. When ministers are forced to give up their ministerial work between sessions of the Annual Conference on account of physical or emotional disability, with the approval of a majority of

the district superintendents, after consultation with the executive committee of the Board of Ordained Ministry and the executive committee of the conference Board of Pensions, a disability leave may be granted by the bishop for the remainder of the conference year; *provided,* however, that such leave may be granted only after examination of medical evidence in accordance with §3 or §4 below. Any such leave granted between sessions of the Annual Conference, with the effective date of such leave, shall be entered in the minutes of the next regular session of the conference.

3. Prior to January 1, 1982, ministers who are currently participating members of the Ministers Reserve Pension Fund at the time a disability occurs may be granted a disability leave only after medical evidence shall have been secured and reviewed by the General Board of Pensions in accordance with the regulations of the Ministers Reserve Pension Fund pertaining to disability benefits.

Prior to January 1, 1982, ministers who are not currently participating members of the Ministers Reserve Pension Fund at the time a disability occurs may be granted a disability leave only after a medical report shall have been submitted to the Joint Committee on Disability (¶ 732) by a medical doctor who has been approved by the joint committee. Such report shall be made on a form approved by the General Board of Pensions.

4. On and after January 1, 1982, ministers who are participants in the Comprehensive Protection Plan may be granted a disability leave only after medical evidence shall have been secured and reviewed in accordance with the provisions of that plan.

5. When ministers on disability leave recover sufficiently to resume ministerial work, with their consent they may receive an appointment from a bishop between sessions of the Annual Conference, thereby terminating the disability leave. Such appointment shall be reported immediately by the Cabinet to the Annual Conference Board of Pensions and to the General Board of Pensions. Such termination of leave, together with the effective date, shall also be recorded in the minutes of the Annual Conference at its next regular session.[26]

¶ **447.** *Retirement.*—Retired ministers are those who have been placed in the retired relation either at their own request or

---

[26] *See* Judicial Council Decision 473.

by action of the ministerial members in full connection upon recommendation of the Board of Ordained Ministry.[27] (*See* ¶¶ 1706-1709 for pension information.) Requests for retirement shall be stated in writing to the bishop, Cabinet, and Board of the Ordained Ministry at least ninety days prior to the conference session at which retirement is to be effective. The Board of Ordained Ministry shall provide guidance and counsel to the retiring member and family as they begin a new relationship in the local church. (*See* ¶¶ 1706-1709 for pension information.)

1. *Mandatory Retirement.*—Every ministerial member of an Annual Conference who will have attained age seventy on or before July 1 in the year which the conference is held shall automatically be retired.[28]

2. *Voluntary Retirement.*—*a) With Twenty Years of Service.*— Any members of the Annual Conference who have completed twenty years or more of service under appointment as ministers or as local pastors with pension credit prior to the opening date of the session of the conference may request the Annual Conference to place them in the retired relation with the privilege of receiving their pensions for the number of approved years served in the Annual Conference or conferences and such other benefits as the final Annual Conference may provide, payment to begin the first of any month after the session of the Annual Conference which occurs in the year in which the minister attains age sixty-two on or before July 1. If pension begins prior to the age at which retirement under ¶ 447.2c could have occurred, then the provisions of ¶ 1706.4i shall apply.

b) With Thirty-seven Years of Service or at Age Sixty-two.—At their own request and by vote of the ministerial members in full connection, any ministerial members who will have attained age sixty-two on or before July 1 or will have completed thirty-seven years of service under appointment in the year in which the session of the Annual Conference is held may be placed in the retired relation with an annuity claim for an actuarially reduced pension, payment to begin the first of the month after the session of the Annual Conference (*see* ¶ 1706.4i.)[29]

---

[27] *See* Judicial Council Decisions 87, 88.
[28] *See* Judicial Council Decisions 7, 165.
[29] *See* Judicial Council Decision 428.

c) With Forty Years of Service or at Age Sixty-five.—At their own request and by vote of the ministerial members in full connection, any ministerial members who will have attained age sixty-five on or before July 1 in the year in which the session of the conference is held or will have completed forty years of service under appointment as a minister, or as a local pastor with pension credit, as of the conference session may be placed in the retired relation with the privilege of making an annuity claim.[30]

d) The Annual Conference, at its discretion, upon joint recommendation of the Board of Ordained Ministry and the conference Board of Pensions, may designate any time within the ensuing conference year as the effective date of retirement of a minister who is placed in the retired relation under the provisions of §2*b* or §2*c* above.

3. *Involuntary retirement.*—By a two-thirds vote of those present and voting, the ministerial members of the Annual Conference in full connection may place any ministerial members in the retired relation with or without their consent and irrespective of their age if such relation is recommended by the Board of Ordained Ministry and the Cabinet.

4. *Pre-retirement Counseling.*—The Board of Ordained Ministry in cooperation with the Board of Pensions shall offer to all ministerial members anticipating retirement, pre-consultation at least five years prior to the date of anticipated retirement (¶ 723.2*j*). The purpose of the consultation will be to assist the clergy and spouses to plan and to prepare for the psychological and financial adjustments of retirement, as well as providing guidance and counsel for their return to a new relationship in the local church.

5. *Charge Conference Membership.*—*a)* All retired ministers who are not appointed as pastors of a charge, after consultation with the pastor, shall have a seat in the Charge Conference and all the privileges of membership in the church where they elect to hold such membership except as set forth in the Discipline. They shall report to the Charge Conference and to the pastor all marriages performed, Baptisms administered, and other pastoral functions. If they reside outside the bounds of the conference,

---

[30] *See* Judicial Council Decision 379.

they shall forward annually to the conference a report of their Christian and ministerial conduct, together with an account of the circumstances of their families, signed by the district superintendent or the pastor of the charge within the bounds of which they reside. Without this report the conference, after having given thirty days' notice, may locate them without their consent.

6. *Appointment of Retired Ministers.*—A retired minister shall be eligible to receive an appointment when requested by the bishop and Cabinet but not the same appointment from which he/she has been retired. A retired minister appointed to a pastoral charge shall have neither a claim upon minimum salary nor further pension credit.

7. *Return to Effective Relationship.*—A ministerial member who has retired under the provisions of ¶ 447.2 may at his/her own request be made an effective member upon recommendation of the Board of Ordained Ministry, the bishop, and Cabinet, and by majority vote of the ministerial members of the Annual Conference and thereby eligible for appointment so long as he/she remains in the effective relation or until ¶ 447.1 applies. Each minister requesting return to effective relationship after voluntary retirement must meet the following conditions: (1) Presentation of their certificate of retirement. (2) A satisfactory certificate of good health on the prescribed form from a physician approved by the Board of Ordained Ministry. However, any pension being received through the General Board of Pensions shall be discontinued upon their return to the effective relationship. The pension shall be reinstated upon subsequent retirement.

Section VIII. Termination of Conference Membership.

¶ **448.** *Voluntary Termination.*—1. *By Discontinuance from Probationary Membership.*—Probationary members may request discontinuance of this relationship or may be discontinued by the Annual Conference, upon recommendation of the Board of Ordained Ministry, without reflection upon their character. When this relationship is discontinued, they shall no longer be permitted to exercise ministerial functions and shall surrender their credentials to the district superintendent for deposit with the secretary of the conference, and their membership trans-

ferred by the district superintendent to the local church which
they designate after consultation with the pastor. The Board of
Ordained Ministry shall file with the resident bishop a permanent
record of the circumstances relating to discontinuance as a
probationary member as required in ¶ 723.3*d*. If after discontinuance, probationary members are classified and approved as local
pastors in accordance with the provision of ¶ 409 and under the
conditions outlined in ¶ 408, they may be permitted to retain
their credentials of ordination.

2. *By Honorable Location.*—*a)* An Annual Conference may
grant associate members or members in full connection
certificates of honorable location at their own request; *provided*
that it shall first have examined their character at the conference
session when the request is made and found them in good
standing; and *provided* further, that this relation shall be granted
only to one who intends to discontinue service in the itinerant
ministry. The Board of Ordained Ministry shall provide guidance
and counsel to the locating member and family as they return to a
new relationship in the local church.[31]

b) Location shall be certified by the presiding bishop.
Ministers located according to the provisions of this paragraph
shall not continue to hold membership in the Annual Conference. After consultation with the pastor, located ministers shall
designate the local church in which they shall hold membership.
As ministerial members of the Charge Conference, they shall be
permitted to exercise ministerial functions under supervision of
the pastor in charge. When approved by the executive committee
of the Board of Ordained Ministry, a person on honorable
location may be appointed ad interim by the bishop as a local
pastor. Otherwise the exercise of their ministry shall be limited to
the Charge Conference in which their membership is held. They
shall report to the Charge Conference and the pastor all
marriages performed, Baptisms administered, and funerals
conducted; and shall be held amenable for their conduct and the
continuation of their ordination rights to the Annual Conference
within which the Charge Conference membership is held. The

---

[31] *See* Judicial Council Decision 366.

provisions of this paragraph shall not apply to persons granted involuntary location prior to the General Conference of 1976. The names of located members after the annual passage of their character shall be printed in the journal.

3. *By Withdrawal to Unite with Another Denomination.*—When ministers in good standing withdraw to unite with another denomination or to terminate their membership in the denomination, their credentials should be surrendered to the conference, and if they shall desire it and the conference authorize it, the credentials may be returned with the following inscription written plainly across their face:

A. B. has this day been honorably dismissed by the _____ Annual Conference from the ministry of The United Methodist Church.

Dated: _____

_____, *President*

_____, *Secretary*

4. *By Surrender of the Ministerial Office.*—Associate members or members in full connection of an Annual Conference in good standing who desire to surrender their ministerial office and withdraw from the conference may be allowed to do so by the Annual Conference at its session. The minister's credentials shall be surrendered to the district superintendent for deposit with the secretary of the conference, and his/her membership may be transferred to a church which he/she designates, after consultation with the pastor, as the local church in which he/she will hold membership.

5. *By Withdrawal under Complaints or Charges.*—When ministerial members are accused of an offense under ¶ 2621 and desire to withdraw from the membership of the Annual Conference, it may permit them to withdraw under the provisions of ¶ 2626.2. The ministers' credentials shall be surrendered to the district superintendent for deposit with the secretary of the conference, and their membership may be transferred to a local church which they designate, after consultation with the pastor.

6. *By Withdrawal between Conferences.*—In the event that

withdrawal by surrender of the ministerial office, to unite with another denomination, or under complaints or charges, should occur in the interval between sessions of an Annual Conference, the member shall deposit with the bishop or district superintendent a letter of withdrawal from the ministry and his/her credentials. This action shall be reported by the Board of Ordained Ministry for confirmation by the Annual Conference at its next session.

¶ **449.** *Involuntary Termination.*—1. *General Provisions.*—Ordination and membership in an Annual Conference in The United Methodist Church is a sacred trust. The qualifications and duties of associate members, probationary members, and full members are set forth in the Book of Discipline of The United Methodist Church, and we believe they flow from the gospel as taught by Jesus the Christ and proclaimed by his Apostles. Whenever an ordained minister in any of the above categories violates this trust, the membership of his/her ministerial office shall be subject to review.

This review shall have as its purpose the reconciliation and restoration of the minister and the strengthening of the Church. If the remedial process is unfruitful, discontinuance or termination may follow.

a) Supervision.—In the course of the ordinary fulfillment of the superintending role, the bishop or district superintendent may receive complaints about the performance or character of a minister and the strengthening of the Church. The supervisory response, in cooperation with the Pastor-Parish Relations Committee for pastors, the district Committee on Superintendency for district superintendents, or appropriate personnel committee, shall be directed toward a reconciliation between all parties and the ordained minister. If the supervisory activity does not achieve the desired results the matter may be referred to the Joint Review Committee.

b) Formal Complaints.—A formal complaint must be based on any one or more of the offenses listed in ¶ 2621 and shall be submitted in written form and signed. No complaint shall be considered for any alleged offense which shall not have been committed within two years immediately preceding the filing of the complaint. The complainant shall be informed of the process and its purpose. Formal complaints may be initiated by the bishop, a district superintendent, the Cabinet, a ministerial member of the Annual Conference, a local church Pastor-Parish Relations Committee, or a personnel committee for appointment beyond the local church. If it is the judgment of the bishop that the complaint is of sufficient gravity, the bishop may temporarily suspend the ministerial member from ministerial duties until the matter is resolved. Formal complaints shall be lodged with the bishop, a district superintendent, and the chairperson of the Annual Conference Board of Ordained Ministry, who shall forward the complaint to the Joint Review within ten days of receipt for screening and evaluation.

c) Joint Review Committee.—In each Annual Conference there shall be a Joint Review Committee composed of an equal number of district superintendents appointed by the bishop and Board of Ordained Ministry members nominated by the chairperson and elected by the board.

This committee shall receive all referrals from the cabinet and all formal complaints and seek resolution of them. The work of this committee shall be informal and confidential and shall guarantee all persons related to the complaint the right to share their view. No witnesses will be called and no counsel shall be present. Should the ordained minister under complaint desire it, a clergyperson chosen by the minister may accompany him/her at meetings of the committee. If the desired results are not achieved, the Joint Review Committee may refer the matter and any written formal complaints to the Board of Ordained Ministry with any recommendations.

d) Disposition of Complaints.—When a formal complaint has been reported, the Board of Ordained Ministry shall develop a response based on the report of the Joint Review Committee and the needs of the church and the minister. The board may recommend remedial action, discontinuance, or termination, or it may dismiss the complaint. The board's recommendation will be shared with the minister, the bishop, the Cabinet, and the complainant.

e) Remedial Action.—In cooperation with the Cabinet and in consultation with the minister, the Board of Ordained Ministry may choose or recommend one or more of the following options

for a program of remedial action, subject to regular oversight by
the board and annual review:

(1) Program of continuing education (¶ 441)

(2) Leave of absence (¶ 444)

(3) Early retirement (¶ 447.2)

(4) Sabbatical leave (¶ 442)

(5) Honorable location (¶ 448.1)

(6) Surrender of ministerial office (¶ 448.4)

(7) Personal counseling or therapy

(8) Program of career evaluation

(9) Peer support and supervision

(10) Private reprimand: A letter signed by the chairperson
of the Board of Ordained Ministry and the minister's district
superintendent, addressed to the minister with a file copy in the
permanent file of the Board of Ordained Ministry stating the
appropriateness of the complaint, the specific remedial action
required, and the conditions under which the letter shall be
withdrawn from the file and destroyed.

f) Recommendation to Terminate Membership.—When a formal
complaint has been received and the Board of Ordained Ministry
recommends the discontinuance of a probationary member, or
the termination of an associate member or member in full
connection, the board shall prepare and sign the proper charges
and specifications. Copies shall be immediately sent to the
minister, the bishop, and the district superintendent of the
minister. The board, within seven days of the formal charges
being received by the minister, shall be responsible for informing
him/her of his/her right to elect trial as provided in ¶ 449.3 or
withdrawal under complaints and charges as provided in ¶ 448.5
as an alternative to this action.

If a person chooses trial, the Board of Ordained Ministry
shall prepare a written statement of charges which shall be
submitted to the Committee on Investigation.

2. *By Action of the Annual Conference: Administrative Location.*—*a)* An Annual Conference shall grant members certificates
of administrative location when, in the judgment of the Annual
Conference, members have demonstrated an inability effectively
and competently to perform the duties of full-time itinerant

ministry; provided that the Annual Conference shall have first examined their character and found them in good standing.

b) At least ninety (90) days before the opening of the next Annual Conference, the Cabinet wishing to initiate this procedure shall notify the members of the Board of Ordained Ministry, in writing, of its intention to do so. The Board of Ordained Ministry, or the executive committee, shall then, in consultation with the Cabinet and the member, establish a date no later than sixty (60) days before the opening of Annual Conference for a joint hearing at which the member, three district superintendents, one of whom shall be the member's district superintendent, and a committee of the Board of Ordained Ministry will be present. The chairperson of the Board of Ordained Ministry will preside, and will give full opportunity for all to be heard. Since this is an administrative hearing, and not a trial, proceedings will be informal and counsel will not be allowed.[32]

c) After the hearing, the Board of Ordained Ministry will review the committee's recommendation and make its own recommendation and notify the member and the Cabinet within one week. The board's recommendation shall take one of the following three forms:

(1) A recommendation to the Annual Conference to grant administrative location.

(2) Initiation of a remedial program with the member designed to overcome deficiencies, said program to last for one year. At the close of that year, on a date at least sixty (60) days preceding the opening of Annual Conference, another hearing as outlined in §2*b* would be held, unless such hearing be jointly waived in writing by the member, the Cabinet, and Board of Ordained Ministry or its executive committee, in which case the entire matter would be considered dismissed. After this hearing, the Board of Ordained Ministry would have to decide on option (1) or (3).

(3) A finding that the allegations of incompetence are not sustained.

d) The provisions of §2*b* above apply to administrative

---

[32]*See* Judicial Council Decision 384.

location, except that a person on administrative location may not
be given and interim appointments by the bishop.

3. *By Trial.*—If a bishop or ministerial member of an Annual
Conference chooses trial, the procedures are provided for in
¶ 2624.

Section IX.   Readmission to Conference Relationship.

¶ 450. *Readmission to Probationary Membership.*—Ministers
who have been discontinued as probationary members under the
provisions of ¶ 448.1 from an Annual Conference of The United
Methodist Church or one of its legal predecessors may be
readmitted by the Annual Conference in which they held
previously such membership and from which they requested
discontinuance or were discontinued or its legal successor or the
Annual Conference of which the major portion of their former
conference is a part upon their request and recommendation by
the district Committee on Ordained Ministry, the Board of
Ordained Ministry, and the Cabinet after review of their
qualifications as required in ¶ 414 and the circumstances relating
to their discontinuance. When reinstated by vote of the
ministerial members in full connection, their probationary
membership in the conference and their credentials shall be
restored, and they shall be authorized to perform those
ministerial functions for which they are qualified. They shall
resume ministerial studies as required by ¶¶ 415, 416.

¶ 451. *Readmission after Honorable or Administrative Location.*—Ministers requesting readmission after honorable or
administrative location must meet the following conditions:

1. Presentation of their certificate of location.

2. A satisfactory report and recommendation by the Charge
Conference and pastor of the local church in which their
membership is held.

3. A satisfactory certificate of good health on the prescribed
form from a physician approved by the Board of Ordained
Ministry. The Board of Ordained Ministry should require
psychological evaluation.

4. Recommendation by the district Committee on Ordained
Ministry, the Board of Ordained Ministry, and the Cabinet, after

review of their qualifications and the circumstances relating to their location. When reinstated by vote of the ministerial members in full connection, their membership in the conference shall be restored, and they shall be authorized to perform all ministerial functions.

¶ **452.** *Readmission after Surrender of the Ministerial Office.*— Ministers who have surrendered the ministerial office under the provisions of ¶ 448.4 to an Annual Conference of The United Methodist Church or one of its legal predecessors may be readmitted by the Annual Conference in which they held previously such membership and to which they surrendered the ministerial office or its legal successor or the Annual Conference of which the major portion of the former conference is a part upon their request and recommendation by the district Committee on Ordained Ministry, the Board of Ordained Ministry, and the Cabinet after review of their qualifications and the circumstances relating to the surrender of their ministerial office. When reinstated by vote of the ministerial members in full connection, their membership in the conference and their credentials shall be restored, and they shall be authorized to perform all ministerial functions.

¶ **453.** *Readmission after Termination by Action of the Annual Conference.*—Persons who have been terminated by an Annual Conference of The United Methodist Church or one of its legal predecessors may seek full membership in the Annual Conference in which they previously held membership and from which they were terminated or its legal successor or the Annual Conference of which the major portion of their former conference is a part upon recommendation of the Cabinet and completion of all requirements for full membership, including all requirements for election to candidacy and probationary membership. The provisions of this paragraph shall apply to all persons terminated or involuntarily located prior to General Conference of 1976.

Chapter Five

THE SUPERINTENDENCY

Section I. Nature of Superintendency.

¶ **501.** *Task.*—The task of superintending in The United Methodist Church resides in the office of bishop and extends to the district superintendent, with each possessing distinct responsibilities. From apostolic times, certain ordained persons have been entrusted with the particular tasks of superintending. Those who superintend carry primary responsibility for ordering the life of the Church. It is their task to enable the gathered Church to worship and to evangelize faithfully.

It is also their task to facilitate the initiation of structures and strategies for the equipping of Christian people for service in the Church and in the world in the name of Jesus Christ and to help extend the service in mission. It is their task, as well, to see that all matters, temporal and spiritual, are administered in a manner which acknowledges the ways and the insights of the world critically and with understanding while remaining cognizant of and faithful to the mandate of the Church. The formal leadership in The United Methodist Church, located in these superintending offices, is an integral part of the system of an itinerant ministry.

¶ **502.** *Guidelines for Superintending in this Age.*—The demands of this age on the leadership of bishops and district superintendents in The United Methodist Church can be seen in mode, pace, and skill:

1. *Mode.*—Leaders need to be able to read consensus and integrate it into a living tradition, to be open to the prophetic word, to be skilled in team-building, and to be effective in negotiation. The style of leadership should rise out of nurtured and cultivated spiritual disciplines and patterns of holiness, for the Spirit is given to the community and its members to the extent that they participate.

2. *Pace.*—Beyond formal systems of accountability, leaders need to open themselves to forms of accountability that they cultivate for themselves through a support group. Such a group can listen, can help, and can clarify, as well as participate with

the leader, as he/she thinks through time demands and constraints in the process of sorting out of priorities. Appropriate time must be taken for reflection, study, developing friendships, and self-renewal.

3. *Skill.*—Among the skills needed by leaders are spiritual discipline, theological reflection, building the unique community of the Church and of the larger community as well. Reading the signs of the times, analyzing, designing strategy, assessing needs, organizing a wide range of resources, and evaluating programs and personnel are yet other skills crucial for leaders.

Section II. Offices of Bishop and District Superintendent.

¶ 503. The offices of **bishop** and **district superintendent** exist in The United Methodist Church as particular ministries for which persons are elected or selected from the group of elders who are ordained to be ministers of Word, Sacrament, and Order and thereby participate in the ministry of Christ, in sharing a royal priesthood which has apostolic roots (I Peter 2:9; John 21:15-17; Acts 20:28; I Peter 5:2-3; I Timothy 3:1-7).

¶ 504. Bishops and superintendents share in the full ministry as ordained elders. The Body of Christ is one; yet many members with differing functions are all joined together in the one body. (I Corinthians 12:28).

Section III. Election, Assignment, and Termination of Bishops.

¶ 505. *Bishops in Jurisdictions.*—1. Each jurisdiction having 500,000 church members or less shall be entitled to six bishops, and each jurisdiction having more than 500,000 church members shall be entitled to one additional bishop for each additional 500,000 church members or major fraction thereof; *provided,* however, that in those jurisdictions where this requirement would result in there being an average of more than 55,000 square miles per episcopal area, such jurisdiction shall be entitled to six bishops for the first 400,000 church members or less, and for each additional 400,000 church members or two thirds thereof shall be entitled to one additional bishop; and *provided* further, that the General Conference may authorize any Jurisdictional Conference to elect one or more bishops beyond the quota herein specified in order to provide episcopal supervision for mission fields outside the territory of a Jurisdictional Conference. The provisions of this paragraph shall be effective immediately following the 1980 General Conference.[1]

¶ **506.** *Election.*—1. *Nomination.*—An Annual Conference, in the session immediately prior to the next regular session of the Jurisdictional Conference, may name one or more nominees for episcopal election. Balloting at Jurisdictional Conferences shall not be limited to nominees of Annual Conferences nor shall any Jurisdictional Conference delegate be bound to vote for any specific nominee. Each Jurisdictional Conference shall develop appropriate procedures for furnishing information about nominees from Annual Conferences. This shall be done at least two weeks prior to the first day of the Jurisdictional Conference. Similar procedures shall be developed for persons nominated by ballot who receive ten votes, or 5 percent of the valid votes cast, and the information shall be made available to the delegates at the site of the conference.

2. *Process.*—*a)* Jurisdictional Conference delegates, in electing bishops, shall give due consideration to the inclusiveness of The United Methodist Church with respect to sex, race, and national origin. In addition, consideration shall be given to the nature of superintendency as described in ¶¶ 501-502.

b) The Jurisdictional and Central Conferences are authorized to fix the percentage votes necessary to elect a bishop. It is recommended that at least 60 percent of those present and voting be necessary to elect.

c) Consecration of bishops may take place at the session of the conference at which election occurs or at a place and time designated by the conference. The consecration service may include bishops from other Jurisdictional and Central Conferences and representatives from other Christian communions.

¶ **507.** *Assignment Process.*—1. *Jurisdictional Committee on Episcopacy.*—The Jurisdictional Committee on Episcopacy, after consultation with the College of Bishops, shall recommend the boundaries of the episcopal areas and the assignment of the bishops to their respective residences for final action by the Jurisdictional Conference; it shall not reach any conclusion

---

[1] *See* Judicial Council Decision 84.

concerning residential assignments until all elections of bishops for that session are completed and all bishops have been consulted. A bishop shall not be recommended for assignment to the same residence for more than eight consecutive years. For strategic missional reasons only, a Jurisdictional Committee on Episcopacy on a two-thirds vote may recommend one additional four-year term in the same area.

The effective date of assignment for all bishops is September 1, following the Jurisdictional Conference.

A newly elected bishop shall be assigned to administer an area other than that within which his/her membership was most recently held, unless by a two-thirds vote the Jurisdictional Committee shall recommend that this restriction be ignored and by majority vote the Jurisdictional Conference shall concur.[2]

2. *Central Conferences.*—In the case of death, expiration of a term of service, or any disability of a bishop of a Central Conference, the Council of Bishops may assign one of its members to provide the episcopal supervision for the conference.[3]

3. *Special Assignments.*—The Council of Bishops may, with consent of the bishop and the concurrence of the Jurisdictional or Central Conference Committee on Episcopacy, assign one of its members for one year to some specific churchwide responsibility deemed of sufficient importance to the welfare of the total Church. In this event a bishop shall be released from the presidential responsibilities within the episcopal area for that term. Another bishop or bishops, active or retired, and not necessarily from the same Jurisdictional or Central Conference, shall be named by the Council of Bishops on recommendation of the College of Bishops of the jurisdiction involved to assume presidential responsibilities during the interim. This assignment may be renewed for a second year by a two-thirds vote of the Council of Bishops and majority vote of the Jurisdictional or Central Committee on Episcopacy and the consent of the bishop and the College of Bishops involved. The bishop so assigned shall continue to receive regular salary and support.

¶ **508.** *Termination of Office.*—An elder who is serving as a

[2]*See* Judicial Council Decisions 48, 57, 416.
[3]*See* Judicial Council Decision 248.

bishop up to the time of retirement shall have the status of a retired bishop; this provision includes all bishops of Central Conferences.[4]

1. *Mandatory Retirement.*—A bishop shall be retired on August 31 next following the regular session of the Jurisdictional Conference if the bishop's sixty-sixth birthday has been reached on or before July 1 of the year in which the Jurisdictional Conference is held. This shall be effective with the Jurisdictional Conferences of 1980.[5]

2. *Voluntary Retirement.*—*a)* Bishops who have completed twenty years or more of service under full-time appointment as elder, including at least one quadrennium as bishop, may request the Jurisdictional or Central Conference to place them in the retired relation with the privilege of receiving their pension as determined by the General Council on Finance and Administration. Payment of the pension will begin the first month after the sixty-fifth birthday.

Any bishop who seeks a voluntary retired status shall notify the president of the Council of Bishops at least six months prior to the General Conference.

b) A bishop may seek voluntary retirement for health reasons and shall be so retired by the Jurisdictional or Central Conference Committee on Episcopacy upon recommendation by the involved College of Bishops and upon presentation of satisfactory medical evidence. Such bishops shall receive their pensions as provided by the General Council on Finance and Administration in consultation with the Jurisdictional or Central Conference Committee on Episcopacy.

Pension and housing allowance as approved by the General Conference shall be payable on the first day of the following month after the close of the Jurisdictional or Central Conference.

If, however, the retired bishop accepts any one of the following assignments of churchwide responsibility, the General Council on Finance and Administration, after consultation with the Council of Bishops, shall set a level of compensation not to exceed 75 percent of the salary of an active bishop: (1) assignment

---

[4]*See* Judicial Council Decisions 361, 407.
[5]*See* Judicial Council Decision 413.

of a special nature with direct relationship and accountability to the Council of Bishops, or (2) assignment to a general agency or United Methodist Church–related institution of higher education. Only the difference between the compensation as established and the continuing pension shall be paid from the Episcopal Fund.

If a bishop is assigned to a general agency or United Methodist Church–related institution of higher education, that agency or United Methodist Church–related institution of higher education shall participate by payment of 50 percent of the difference between the compensation herein established and the pension of the bishop. The general agency or United Methodist Church–related institution of higher education shall further assume all responsibility for the bishop's operational and travel expenses related to the assignment.

Compensation for any special assignment shall cease after the bishop has reached the mandatory age of retirement for all ministers (¶ 447.1) or completes the assignment, whichever comes first. No assignment to a jurisdiction, Central Conference, Annual Conference, or non–United Methodist agency shall qualify for additional compensation from the Episcopal Fund under the provisions of this paragraph. The status of a retired bishop on special assignment shall, for purposes of housing and other benefits, be that of a retired bishop.

3. *Involuntary Retirement.*—*a)* A bishop may be placed in the retired relation regardless of age by a two-thirds vote of the Jurisdictional or Central Conference Committee on Episcopacy if, after not less than a thirty day notice in writing is given to the affected bishop and hearing held, such relationship is found by said committee to be in the best interests of the bishop and/or the Church. Appeal from this action may be made to the Judicial Council with the notice provisions being applicable as set forth in ¶ 2625.2.

b) A bishop, for health reasons, may be retired between sessions of the Jurisdictional or Central Conference by a two-thirds vote of the Jurisdictional or Central Conference Committee on Episcopacy upon the recommendation of one third of the membership of the involved College of Bishops. The affected bishop, upon request, shall be entitled to a review of his/her health condition by a professional diagnostic team prior to action by the involved College of Bishops. Notification of action to retire shall be given by the chairperson and secretary of the Jurisdictional or Central Conference Committee on Episcopacy to the secretary of the Council of Bishops and the treasurer of the Episcopal Fund. Upon such retirement, the bishop shall receive a pension as determined by the General Council on Finance and Administration. *See also* §2*b* above.

4. *Resignation.*—A bishop may voluntarily resign from the episcopacy at any time. The consecration papers of a bishop in good standing so resigning shall be properly inscribed by the secretary of the Council of Bishops and returned. He/she shall be furnished with a certificate of resignation which shall entitle him/her to membership as a traveling elder in the Annual Conference (or its successor) in which membership was last held. Notification of this action shall be given by the secretary of the Council of Bishops to the chairperson and secretary of the Jurisdictional or Central Conference Committee on Episcopacy. When the resigned bishop or surviving spouse and dependent children become conference claimants, the Episcopal Fund shall pay a pension as determined by the General Council on Finance and Administration.

¶ **509.** *Status of Retired Bishops.*—A retired bishop is a bishop of the Church in every respect and continues to function as a member of the Council of Bishops in accordance with the Constitution and other provisions of the Discipline.

1. Retired bishops shall not preside over any Annual Conference, Provisional Annual Conference, or Mission or make appointments or preside at the Jurisdictional or Central Conference, but may take the chair temporarily in any conference if requested to do so by the bishop presiding. They may participate in the Council of Bishops and its committees but without vote. When a retired bishop is appointed by the Council of Bishops to a vacant episcopal area or parts of an area under the provisions of ¶ 509.1, that bishop may function as a bishop in the effective relationship.[6]

---

[6]*See* Judicial Council Decision 248.

2. A retired bishop may be considered a member of an Annual Conference, without vote, for purposes of appointment to a local charge within the said conference.

3. A bishop retired under ¶¶ 508.1, 2 above may be appointed by the Council of Bishops upon recommendation of the involved College of Bishops to presidential responsibility for temporary service in an area in the case of death, resignation, disability, or procedure involving a resident bishop (¶ 2624.2). This appointment shall not continue beyond the next Jurisdictional or Central Conference.

4. Each Central Conference shall determine the rules for retirement of its bishops, *provided* that the age of retirement shall not exceed that fixed for bishops in the jurisdictions. In the event that retirement allowances are paid from the Episcopal Fund, these rules shall be subject to the approval of the General Conference.[7]

5. A bishop of a Central Conference who served as bishop up to the time of mandatory age retirement prior to the time of Union in 1968 shall be entitled to the following status and emoluments, prospectively and from the time of adoption of this provision: (1) has the right to use the title "bishop"; (2) has the right to attend sessions of the Council of Bishops; (3) has the right to have expenses paid for attendance at sessions of the Council of Bishops; (4) has the right to be seated among the bishops and retired bishops on the platform of the General Conference; (5) has the right to have expenses paid for attendance at sessions of the General Conference.

The foregoing provisions are separable and if the Judicial Council should hold one or more to be ineffective or invalid that shall not affect the others.

¶ **510.** *Leaves.*—1. *Renewal Leave.*—It is expected that every bishop in the active relationship shall take up to three consecutive months' leave from his/her normal episcopal responsibilities, for purposes of reflection, study, and self-renewal, once during each quadrennium. The College of Bishops, in consultation with the appropriate Jurisdictional or Central Conference Committee on Episcopacy, shall coordinate details pertaining to such leaves.

[7]*See* Judicial Council Decisions 199, 407

2. *Sabbatical Leave.*—A bishop who has served for at least two quadrenniums may be granted a sabbatical leave of not more than one year for a justifiable reason other than health if the request is made and if the involved College of Bishops, the Committee on Episcopacy of that jurisdiction or Central Conference, and the Council of Bishops or its executive committee approve. In this event the bishop shall, for the period for which the leave is granted, be released from the presidential responsibilities within the episcopal area; and another bishop or bishops, active or retired and not necessarily from the same jurisdiction or Central Conference, shall be designated by the Council of Bishops, on recommendation of the College of Bishops of the jurisdiction or Central Conference involved, to assume the presidential duties during the interim. The bishop shall continue to receive housing allowance and one-half salary for the period of the leave.

3. *Sick Leave.*—Bishops who by reason of impaired health are temporarily unable to perform full work may be released by the Jurisdictional or Central Conference Committee on Episcopacy from the obligation to travel through the connection at large. They may choose a place of residence, and the Council of Bishops shall be at liberty to assign them to such work as they may be able to perform. They shall receive support as provided by the Episcopal Fund.

¶ **511.** *Bishops in Central Conferences.*—The Central Conferences shall elect bishops, in the number determined by the General Conference, whose episcopal supervision shall be within the territory included in the Central Conference by which they have been elected, subject to such other conditions as the General Conference shall prescribe; *provided,* however, that a bishop elected by a Central Conference may exercise episcopal supervision in another Central Conference or a Jurisdictional Conference when so requested by such other Central Conference or Jurisdictional Conference.

1. Bishops elected by a Central Conference shall be constituted by election in a Central Conference and consecrated by the laying on of hands of three bishops or at least one bishop and two elders.

2. Bishops elected by a Central Conference shall have the

same authority as that exercised by bishops elected by or administering in a Jurisdictional Conference.

3. Bishops elected by a Central Conference shall have the same status, rights, and duties as a bishop elected by or functioning in a Jurisdictional Conference. A bishop elected by a Central Conference shall have membership in the Council of Bishops and shall have the privilege of full participation with vote. Attendance at the annual meetings of the Council of Bishops by bishops elected by Central Conferences shall be left to the option of the bishops in each Central Conference.

4. In a Central Conference where term episcopacy prevails, bishops whose term of office expires prior to the time of compulsory retirement because of age and who are not reelected by the Central Conference shall be returned to membership as traveling elders in the Annual Conference (or its successor) of which they ceased to be a member when elected bishop. Their term of office shall expire at the close of the Central Conference at which their successor is elected, and they shall therefore be entitled to participate as a bishop in the consecration of the successor. The credentials of office as bishop shall be submitted to the secretary of the Central Conference, who shall make thereon the notation that the bishop has honorably completed the term of service for which elected and has ceased to be a bishop of The United Methodist Church.[8]

Section IV. Specific Responsibilities of Bishops.

¶ **512.** *Leadership.—Spiritual and Temporal.*—1. To lead and oversee the spiritual and temporal affairs of The United Methodist Church, which confesses Jesus Christ as Lord and Savior, and particularly to lead the Church in its mission of witness and service in the world.

2. To travel through the connection at large as the Council of Bishops (¶ 524) to implement strategy for the concerns of the Church.

3. To provide liaison in ecumenical activities and relationships.

---

[8]*See* Judicial Council Decisions 61, 236, 370.

4. To organize such Missions as shall have been authorized by the General Conference.

5. To promote and support the evangelistic witness of the whole Church.

6. To discharge such other duties as the Discipline may direct.

¶ **513.** *Presidential Duties.*—1. To preside in the General, Jurisdictional, Central, and Annual Conferences.[9]

2. To form the districts after consultation with the district superintendents and after the number of the same has been determined by vote of the Annual Conference.[10]

3. To appoint the district superintendents annually (¶¶ 515-516).

4. To consecrate bishops, to ordain elders and deacons, to consecrate diaconal ministers, to commission deaconesses and home missionaries, and to see that the names of the persons commissioned and consecrated are entered on the journals of the conference and that proper credentials are furnished to these persons.

¶ **514.** *Working with Ministers.*—1. To make and fix the appointments in the Annual Conferences, Provisional Annual Conferences, and Missions as the Discipline may direct (¶¶ 527-531).

2. To divide or to unite a circuit(s), station(s), or mission(s) as judged necessary for missional strategy and then to make appropriate appointments.

3. To read the appointments of deaconesses, diaconal ministers, lay persons in service under the World Division of the General Board of Global Ministries, and home missionaries.

4. To fix the Charge Conference membership of all ordained ministers appointed to ministries other than the local church in keeping with ¶ 439.

5. To transfer, upon the request of the receiving bishop, ministerial member(s) of one Annual Conference to another, *provided* said member(s) agrees to said transfer; and to send immediately to the secretaries of both conferences involved, to

---

[9]*See* Judicial Council Decision 395.
[10]*See* Judicial Council Decision 422.

the conference Boards of Ordained Ministry, and to the clearing house of the General Board of Pensions written notices of the transfer of members and of their standing in the course of study if they are undergraduates.[11]

Section V. Selection, Assignment, and Term of District Superintendents.

¶ **515.** *Selection and Assignment.*—Inasmuch as the district superintendency is an extension of the general superintendency, the bishop shall appoint elders to serve as district superintendents. Prior to each appointment, the bishop shall consult with the Cabinet and the Committee on District Superintendency of the district to which the new superintendent will be assigned. Such consultation shall be for the purpose of determining leadership needs of the Annual Conference and the district (¶¶ 501-502). Due consideration shall be given to the inclusiveness of The United Methodist Church with respect to sex, race, and national origin.

¶ **516.** *Limitations on Years of Service.*—An elder may not be appointed a district superintendent for more than six years in any consecutive nine years. No elder shall serve as district superintendent more than twelve years. In addition, consideration shall be given to the nature of superintendency as described in ¶¶ 501-502.[12]

Section VI. Specific Responsibilities of District Superintendents.

¶ **517.** The district superintendent shall oversee the total ministry of the pastors and the churches in the communities of the district in its mission of witness and service in the world: (1) by giving pastoral support and supervision to the clergy of the district; (2) by encouraging their personal, spiritual, and professional growth; (3) by enabling programs throughout the district that may assist local churches to build and extend their ministry and mission with their people and to the community; (4) by working in cooperation with appropriate district and Annual Conference agencies to explore experimental and cooperative

---

[11] *See* Judicial Council Decisions 114, 254.
[12] *See* Judicial Council Decision 368.

ministry among the churches of the district; (5) by assisting the bishop in the administration of the Annual Conference; (6) by participating in the conference council on ministries and the district council on ministries where it exists. In the fulfillment of this ministry, the superintendent shall consult regularly with the Committee on District Superintendency. While carrying out all duties and responsibilities as may be indicated in various paragraphs of the Discipline, the district superintendent shall be especially conscious of responsibility in the following areas of concern.[13]

¶ **518.** *Supervision.*—1. To work with pastors, Pastor-Parish Relations Committees, and Charge Conferences in formulating statements of purpose for congregations in fulfilling their mission and in clarifying the pastors' priorities in accomplishing these purposes.

2. To establish a clearly understood process of supervision for clergy of the district, including observation of all aspects of ministry, direct evaluation, and feedback to the clergy involved.

3. To meet with Pastor-Parish Relations Committees when conditions require, in accordance with ¶ 529.

4. To make specific provision for the supervision of probationary members and local pastors appointed within the district and for building clusters for supervision with the assistance of counseling elders in the district.

¶ **519.** *Personnel.*—1. To work with pastors, Pastor-Parish Relations Committees, and congregations in interpreting the meaning of ministry and in identifying and enlisting candidates of the highest quality for ordained ministry, with special concern for the inclusiveness of the Church with respect to sex, race, and national origin.

2. To consult and plan with the district committee and conference Board of Ordained Ministry in order to make a thorough analysis of the needs of the district for clergy, implementing this planning with a positive and conscious effort to fill these needs.

3. To be the executive for the district Committee on Ordained Ministry, enabling a meaningful and appropriate

---

[13]*See* Judicial Council Decision 398.

examination of candidates into ordained ministry; to issue and renew licenses to preach when authorized (¶ 406); to keep careful records of all such candidates; to maintain regular communication with all candidates in order to advise and encourage them in spiritual and academic preparation for their ministry.

4. To develop adequate salary support for all clergy, including provision for housing, utilities, travel, and continuing education.

5. To require annually of each clergy person a report of his/her program of continuing education and to encourage congregations to give time and financial support for such programs.

6. To work with the bishop and Cabinet in the process of appointment and assignment for ordained ministers who hold Charge Conference relationship in the district and the Annual Conference.

¶ **520.** *Pastoral.*—1. To give pastoral support and care to the clergy and their families by traveling through the district, preaching, visiting, and maintaining the connectional order of the Discipline.

2. To counsel with clergy concerning their pastoral responsibilities and other matters affecting their ministry and personal life.

3. To encourage the building of peer groups among the clergy for mutual support and discipline; to build systems of mutual support for clergy families.

¶ **521.** *Administration.*—1. To schedule and preside, or authorize an elder to preside, in each annual Charge Conference or Church Conference within the district (¶¶ 248, 251).

2. To cooperate with the district Board of Church Location and Building and local church Boards of Trustees or building committees in arranging acquisitions, sales, transfers, and mortgages of property; and to ensure that all charters, deeds, and other legal documents conform to the Discipline and to the laws, usages, and forms of the county, state, territory, or country within which such property is situated.

3. To promote current and deferred financial support in local churches for district, conference, and denominational causes.

4. To see that the provisions of the Discipline are observed and to interpret and decide all questions of church law and discipline raised by the churches in the district, subject to an appeal to the president of the Annual Conference.

5. To maintain in the district office and transfer to one's successor a complete set of records pertaining to:

a) All abandoned church properties and cemeteries within the bounds of the district;

b) All church properties being permissively used by other religious organizations, with the names of the local trustees thereof;

c) All known endowments, annuities, trust funds, investments, and unpaid legacies belonging to any pastoral charge or organization connected therewith in the district and an accounting of their management;

d) Membership of persons from churches which have been closed.

6. To transfer members of a discontinued church to another United Methodist church of their choice or to such other churches as members may elect.

7. To recommend to the bishop for approval, after consultation with the churches involved, any realignment of pastoral charge lines and report them to the Annual Conference.

8. Prior to consenting to the proposed action to sell or transfer any United Methodist Church property to insure that an investigation be made and a plan of action be developed for the future missional needs of the community by The United Methodist Church.

¶ **522.** *Program.*—1. To administer the programs of the Church within the bounds of the district in cooperation with pastors and congregations, working with and through the district Council on Ministries where it exists while serving as its executive officer.

2. To serve as a member of the Annual Conference Council on Ministries and to work cooperatively with the conference council and its staff in all program concerns of the Church.

3. To appraise the needs and mission opportunities of the churches within the district and be available to them for counsel.

4. To establish long-range planning with an ecumenically responsive perspective and to initiate new forms of ministry.

5. To participate with the Cabinet in submitting to the Annual Conference a report reflecting the state of the conference, with recommendations for greater effectiveness.

Section VII. Corporate Expressions of Superintendency.

¶ **523.** The offices of bishop and district superintendent are linked with each other in ways described elsewhere (¶ 503). The interdependence of the offices calls for a collegial style of leadership. However, both the office of bishop and that of district superintendent are embedded in their own corporate contexts.

¶ **524.** *Council of Bishops.*—1. Bishops, although elected by Jurisdictional or Central Conferences, are elected general superintendents of the whole Church. As all ordained ministers are first elected into membership of an Annual Conference and subsequently appointed to pastoral charges, so bishops become through their election members first of the Council of Bishops before they are subsequently assigned to areas of service.

2. The Council of Bishops is thus the corporate expression of episcopal leadership in the Church and through the Church into the world. The Church expects the Council of Bishops to speak to the Church and from the Church to the world.

3. In order to exercise meaningful corporate leadership, the Council of Bishops is to meet at stated intervals. The Council of Bishops is charged with the oversight of the spiritual and temporal affairs of the whole Church, to be executed in regularized consultation and cooperation with other councils and service agencies of the Church.

¶ **525.** *Conference of Methodist Bishops.*—There shall be a Conference of Methodist Bishops, composed of all the bishops elected by the Jurisdictional and Central Conferences and one bishop or chief executive officer from each affiliated autonomous or United Church, which shall meet in each quadrennium immediately prior to the General Conference on call of the Council of Bishops. The travel and other necessary expense of bishops of affiliated autonomous or United Churches related to the meeting of the Conference of Methodist Bishops shall be paid on the same basis as that of bishops of The United Methodist Church.

¶ **526.** *Cabinet.*—1. District superintendents, although appointed to districts, are also to be given conference-wide responsibilities. As all ordained ministers are first elected into membership of an Annual Conference and subsequently appointed to pastoral charges, so district superintendents become through their selection members first of a Cabinet before they are subsequently appointed to service in districts.

2. The Cabinet under the leadership of the bishop is thus the corporate expression of superintending leadership in and through the Annual Conference. It is expected to speak to the conference and for the conference to the spiritual and temporal issues that exist within the region encompassed by the conference.

3. The Cabinet is thus also the body in which the individual district superintendents are held accountable for their work, both for conference and district responsibilities.

4. In order to exercise meaningful corporate leadership, the Cabinet is to meet at stated intervals. The Cabinet is charged with the oversight of the spiritual and temporal affairs of a conference, to be executed in regularized consultation and cooperation with other councils and service agencies of the conference.

Section VIII.   Appointment-Making.

¶ **527.** *Responsibility.*—1. Pastors and clergy in extension ministries shall be appointed by a bishop, who is empowered to make and fix all appointments in the episcopal area within which the Annual Conference is a part. Appointments are to be made with consideration of gifts, graces of those appointed, to the needs, characteristics, and opportunities of congregations and institutions, and to program and missional strategy of conferences and without regard to race, ethnic origin, sex, or color, consistent with the commitment to an open itinerary. Through appointment-making, the connectional nature of the United Methodist system is made visible.

2. To make visible the connectional nature of the United Methodist system and to relate appointment making to the

missional needs of the whole church, itineracy across conference lines shall be encouraged. The Jurisdictional Conference may authorize a Jurisdictional Committee on Ordained Ministry to support this policy in cooperation with bishops, Cabinets, and Boards of Ordained Ministry. Part of the jurisdictional committee responsibility should be to make a study of anticipated ministerial supply and demand in the conferences of the jurisdiction during the last quarter of each calendar year and provide this information to bishops, Cabinets, and Boards of Ordained Ministry by January 15. A part of this responsibility should be an annual study of the supply, demand, and mobility of ethnic clergy, clergy couples, and clergywomen within and across jurisdictions. The provisions of this paragraph shall be effective immediately following the 1980 General Conference.

¶ **528.** *Definition of Consultation.*—Consultation means conferring with the pastor and Pastor-Parish Relations Committee, taking into consideration the criteria of ¶ 530, a performance evaluation, needs of the appointment under consideration, and mission of the church. Consultation is not merely notification. Consultation is not committee selection or call of a pastor. Consultation is both a continuing process and a more intense involvement during the period of change in appointment.[14]

1. *Consultation in Appointment-Making.*—The process of consultation shall be mandatory in every Annual Conference.

2. The Council of Bishops shall inquire annually of their colleagues about the implementation of the process of consultation in appointment-making in their respective areas.

¶ **529.** *Process.*—1. The process for a change in appointment may be initiated by a pastor, a Pastor-Parish Relations Committee, a district superintendent, or a bishop.

2. The bishop and the Cabinet shall consider all requests for change of appointment in light of the criteria developed for each charge and the gifts and graces, professional experience, and family needs of the pastor.

3. When a change in appointment has been determined, the district superintendent should meet together or separately with

---

[14] *See* Judicial Council Decision 101.

the pastor and the Pastor-Parish Relations Committee where the pastor is serving, for the purpose of sharing the basis for the change and the process used in making the new appointment.

4. All appointments shall receive consideration by the bishop and the district superintendent(s) and the Cabinet as a whole until a tentative decision is made.

5. The process used in making the new appointment shall include:

a) The district superintendent shall confer with the pastor about a specific possible appointment (charge) and its congruence with gifts, graces, professional experience and expectations, and the family needs of the pastor identified in consultation with the pastor.

b) The district superintendent shall confer with the receiving Pastor-Parish Relations Committee about specific possible new pastor and her/his congruence with the criteria developed in consultation with the charge.

c) When appointments are being made to less than full-time ministry, the district superintendent shall consult with the minister to be appointed and the Pastor-Parish Relations Committee regarding proportional time, salary, and pension credit.

d) If during this consultative process it is determined by the bishop and Cabinet that this decision should not be carried out, the process is to be repeated until the bishop basing his/her decision on the information and advice derived from consultation, makes and fixes the appointment. A similar process of consultation shall be available to persons in extension ministries.

6. The announcement of that decision shall be made to all parties directly involved in the consultative process; that is, the appointment Cabinet, the pastor, and the Pastor-Parish Relations Committee, before a public announcement is made.

¶ **530.** *Criteria.*—Appointments shall take into account the unique needs of a charge in a particular setting and also the gifts and graces of a particular pastor. To assist bishops, Cabinets, pastors, and congregations to achieve an effective match of charges and pastors, criteria must be developed and analyzed in each instance and then shared with pastors and congregations.

1. *Congregations.*—The district superintendent and the Pastor-Parish Relations Committee of all churches shall develop criteria consistent with the needs, characteristics, and opportunities for mission of the charge. These shall be annually reviewed, updated, and filed with the district superintendent.

a) The general situation in which a congregation finds itself in a particular setting: size, financial condition, quality of lay leadership, history.

b) The convictional stance of the congregation: theology; prejudices, if any; spiritual life.

c) The ministry of the congregation among its people for the sake of the community: service programs, basis for adding new members, reasons for losing members, mission to community and world, forms of witness.

2. *Pastors.*—The district superintendent and the pastor shall identify the pastor's gifts, graces, and professional experience and expectations, and also the needs and concerns of the pastor's spouse and family:

a) Spiritual and personal sensibility: personal faith, call and commitment to ordained ministry, work through the institutional Church, integration of vocation with personal and family well-being, life-style.

b) Academic and career background: nature of theological stance, experience in continuing education, professional experience, record of performance, age.

c) Skills and abilities: in church administration, leadership development, worship and liturgy, preaching and evangelism, teaching and nurturing, counseling and group work, ability in self-evaluation.

d) Family situation: health and educational needs of the family, and the spouse's career.

¶ **531.** *Frequency.*—While the bishop shall report all pastoral appointments as they exist to each regular session of an Annual Conference, appointments to charges may be made at any time deemed advisable by the bishop and Cabinet.

Chapter Six
THE CONFERENCES

The United Methodist Church is a connectional structure maintained through its chain of conferences.

Section I. The General Conference.

¶ **601.** *Composition.*—The membership of the **General Conference** shall consist of an equal number of ministerial and lay delegates elected by the Annual Conferences as provided in the Discipline. The number of delegates to which an Annual Conference is entitled shall be computed on a two-factor basis: the number of ministerial members of the Annual Conference and the number of church members in the Annual Conference, as follows:[1]

1. One ministerial delegate for every 140 ministerial members of the Annual Conference and one additional ministerial delegate for each major fraction thereof,[2] and

2. One ministerial delegate for the first 44,000 church members of the Annual Conference and one ministerial delegate for each additional 44,000 church members and an additional ministerial delegate for each major fraction of 44,000 church members, and

3. A number of lay delegates equal to the total number of ministerial delegates authorized as above.

Delegates to the General Conference shall be elected at the session of the Annual Conference held in the calendar year preceding the session of the General Conference.

This formula is designed to comply with the Constitution, Division Two, Section II, Article I (¶ 12), which defines the minimum and maximum number of delegates to a General Conference. Should the computations provided in this paragraph result in a figure below the prescribed minimum or above the prescribed maximum for delegates, the secretary of the General Conference shall be authorized to remedy the situation by adjusting up or down the fractions necessary to entitle an Annual Conference to elect additional delegates, any such

[1]*See* Judicial Council Decision 333.
[2]*See* Judicial Council Decision 327.

adjustment to be the same for the factors of ministerial members and church members. In case of any such adjustments, the secretary of the General Conference shall notify the secretaries of the several Annual Conferences as promptly as possible. The term "ministerial members" as used above shall refer to both active and retired members of the Annual Conference. Every Annual Conference shall be entitled to at least one ministerial and one lay delegate. The secretaries of the several Annual Conferences shall furnish certificates of election to the delegates severally and shall send a certificate of such election to the secretary of the General Conference immediately after the adjournment of the said Annual Conferences.

¶ **602.** *Presiding Officers.*—The bishops shall be the presiding officers at the General Conference.

¶ **603.** *Election of Secretary-Designate.*—The Council of Bishops shall present a nomination from the ministry or lay membership of The United Methodist Church for secretary-designate. Other nominations shall be permitted from the floor. The election, if there be two or more nominees, shall be by ballot.

¶ **604.** The secretary-designate shall assume the responsibilities of the office of secretary as soon after the adjournment of the General Conference as all work in connection with the session, including the preparation, printing, and mailing of the journal, has been completed. The exact date of the transfer of responsibility to the secretary-designate shall be determined by the Commission on the General Conference, but shall not be later than twelve months after the adjournment of the General Conference. The secretary shall initiate procedures to inform delegates from outside the United States concerning both the operation of the General Conference and materials it will consider.

¶ **605.** *Rules of Order.*—The Plan of Organization and Rules of Order of the General Conference shall be the Plan of Organization and Rules of Order as published in the journal of the preceding General Conference until they have been altered or modified by the action of the General Conference.

¶ **606.** *Quorum.*—When the General Conference is in session, it shall require the presence of a majority of the whole number of delegates to the General Conference to constitute a quorum for the transaction of business; but a smaller number may take a recess or adjourn from day to day in order to secure a quorum, and at the final session may approve the journal, order the record of the roll call, and adjourn sine die.

¶ **607.** *Petitions to General Conference.*—Any organization, minister, or lay member of The United Methodist Church may petition the General Conference in the following manner:

1. Two copies of the petition must be sent to the petitions secretary.

2. Each petition must address only one paragraph of the Discipline or one issue.

3. Each petition must be signed by the person submitting it, accompanied by appropriate identification, such as address, local church, or United Methodist board or agency relationship.

4. Petitions must be postmarked by a national postal service no later than sixty days prior to the opening session of the General Conference.

5. If petitions are transmitted by a means other than a national postal service, they must be in the hands of the petitions secretary no later than forty-five days prior to the opening session of the General Conference.

Exceptions to the time limitations shall be granted for petitions originating from an Annual Conference session held within forty-five days prior to the opening session of the General Conference, and for other petitions at the discretion of the Committee on Reference.

¶ **608.** *Voting by Orders.*—The ministerial and lay members shall deliberate as one body and have equal rights. They shall vote as one body, but a separate vote shall be taken on any question when requested by one third of either order of delegates present and voting. In all cases of separate voting it shall require the concurrence of a majority of each order to adopt a proposed measure. However, in the case of changes in the Constitution, a vote of two thirds of the General Conference, as provided in the Constitution, shall be required.

¶ **609.** All legislation of the General Conference of The United Methodist Church shall become effective January 1 following the session of the General Conference at which it is enacted unless otherwise specified (¶ 638.22).

¶ **610.** *Speaking for the Church.*—1. No person, no paper, no organization, has the authority to speak officially for The United Methodist Church, this right having been reserved exclusively to the General Conference under the Constitution. Any written public policy statement issued by a general church agency shall clearly identify either at the beginning or at the end that the statement represents the position of that general agency and not necessarily the position of The United Methodist Church.[3]

2. *a)* Resolutions and positions adopted by the General Conference of The United Methodist Church are valid until they are specifically rescinded, amended, or superseded by action of subsequent sessions of the General Conference. All valid resolutions and positions of the General Conference of The United Methodist Church beginning with those adopted by the 1968 Uniting Conference shall be indexed in each edition of the Book of Resolutions.

b) The General Council on Ministries and the program boards and agencies shall review all valid resolutions and recommend to the General Conference the removal of time-dated material.

c) The Standing General Commission on Communication shall have responsibility for the editing of the Book of Resolutions. The book shall contain only those resolutions and/or study documents which the most recent General Conference approved and authorized for printing in the Book of Resolutions.

3. Any individual member called to testify before a legislative body to represent The United Methodist Church shall be allowed to do so only by reading, without elaboration, the resolutions and positions adopted by the General Conference of The United Methodist Church.

Section II. The Jurisdictional Conference.

¶ **611.** 1. There shall be an **Interjurisdictional Committee on Episcopacy** elected by the General Conference consisting of the persons nominated by their Annual Conference delegations to serve on the several Jurisdictional Committees on Episcopacy.

---

[3]*See* Judicial Council Decision 458.

The committee shall meet not later than the fifth day of the conference session and at the time and place set for their convening by the president of the Council of Bishops and shall elect from their number a chairperson, vice-chairperson, and secretary. The function of this joint committee shall be to discuss the possibility of transfers of bishops across jurisdictional lines at the forthcoming Jurisdictional Conferences for residential and presidential responsibilities in the ensuing quadrennium. It shall elect an executive committee consisting of the officers named above and two ministers and two lay persons from the nominees to each jurisdictional committee, elected by that committee to conduct consultations with bishops and others interested in possible episcopal transfers. The executive committee shall be responsible to the interjurisdictional committee.

2. No bishop shall be transferred across jurisdictional lines unless that bishop has consented to such transfer and has served at least one quadrennium in or under assignment by the jurisdiction in which the bishop was elected and unless a concurrent transfer is effected into the jurisdiction from which the bishop is transferring or unless the Jurisdictional Conference which is receiving that bishop has voted to waive this right. Such a transfer shall not be concluded until the Committee on Episcopacy of each jurisdiction involved has approved the plan insofar as it affects its own jurisdiction, by majority vote of those present and voting, and the Jurisdictional Conferences, meeting concurrently, have also approved.

¶ **612.** All Jurisdictional Conferences shall have the same status and the same privileges of action within the limits fixed by the Constitution.

¶ **613.** The membership of each Jurisdictional Conference shall consist of an equal number of ministerial and lay delegates elected by the Annual Conferences as provided in the Discipline. The number of delegates to which an Annual Conference is entitled shall be computed on a two-factor basis: the number of ministerial members of the Annual Conference and the number of church members in the Annual Conference, as follows:

1. One ministerial delegate for every seventy ministerial members of the Annual Conference and one additional ministerial delegate for each major fraction thereof, and

2. One ministerial delegate for the first 22,000 church members of the Annual Conference and one ministerial delegate for each additional 22,000 church members and an additional ministerial delegate for each major fraction of 22,000 church members, and

3. A number of lay delegates equal to the total number of ministerial delegates authorized as above; *provided* that no Annual Conference shall be denied the privilege of four delegates, two lay and two ministerial.

¶ **614.** The ministerial and lay delegates and reserves to the Jurisdictional Conferences shall be elected by ballot in accordance with the provisions of the Constitution.

¶ **615.** The ministers and lay delegates shall deliberate in one body.

¶ **616.** Each Jurisdictional Conference shall meet within the period prescribed by the Constitution at such time and place as shall have been determined by the preceding Jurisdictional Conference or by its properly constituted committee.

¶ **617.** The Jurisdictional Conference shall adopt its own procedure, rules, and plan of organization. It shall take a majority of the whole number of delegates elected to make a quorum for the transaction of business; however, a smaller number may take a recess or adjourn from day to day, and at the final session may approve the journal, order the record of the roll call, and adjourn sine die.

¶ **618.** The Jurisdictional Conference shall provide for the expenses of its sessions.

¶ **619.** 1. The Jurisdictional Conference may order a special session in such manner as it shall determine.

2. The College of Bishops of a jurisdiction by a two-thirds vote shall have authority to call a special session of the Jurisdictional Conference when necessary; *provided,* however, that if an episcopal area is left vacant by reason of death, retirement, or other cause within twenty-four months of the close of the preceding Jurisdictional Conference, the College of Bishops may by majority vote convene within three months, after giving not less than thirty days' notice, a special session of the Jurisdictional Conference for the purpose of electing and consecrating a bishop and of considering any other matters

specified in the call; and *provided* further, that in such case the standing Committee on Episcopacy may recommend to the conference reassignment of one or more of the previously elected bishops.

3. The delegates to a special session of the Jurisdictional Conference shall be the delegates last elected by each Annual Conference.

4. A called session of the Jurisdictional Conference cannot transact any other business than that indicated in the call.

¶ **620.** The Jurisdictional Conference shall be presided over by the bishops of the jurisdiction or a bishop of another jurisdiction or of a Central Conference. In case no bishop of the jurisdiction is present, the conference may elect a president from the ministerial delegates.

¶ **621.** Bishops elected by or administering in a Jurisdictional Conference shall be amenable for their conduct to their Jurisdictional Conference. Any bishop shall have the right of appeal to the Judicial Council.

¶ **622.** *Jurisdictional Committee on Episcopacy.*—1. There shall be a **Jurisdictional Committee on Episcopacy** elected by the Jurisdictional Conference as a standing committee consisting of one ministerial and one lay delegate from each Annual Conference on nomination of the Annual Conference delegations.

The committee shall be convened by the president of the College of Bishops at the close of the Jurisdictional Conference to which the delegates have been elected. It shall serve through the succeeding Jurisdictional Conference.

The committee shall elect from its members a chairperson, a vice-chairperson, and a secretary. It shall meet at least biennially.

Should there be a vacancy in an Annual Conference's elected representation on the Jurisdictional Committee on Episcopacy, the Jurisdictional Committee on Episcopacy shall declare that a vacancy exists and the Annual Conference delegation shall nominate another person. That person may begin to serve on the committee as a nominee until the Jurisdictional Conference can elect.

For purposes of transition, the members of the Jurisdictional Committee on Episcopacy elected at the Jurisdictional Conference of 1980 shall constitute the Jurisdictional Committee to serve through the Jurisdictional Conference of 1984.

2. The Jurisdictional Conference shall provide funding for the expenses of the Jurisdictional Committee on Episcopacy.

3. The Jurisdictional Committee on Episcopacy shall:

a) Review the work of the bishops, pass on their character and official administration, and report to the Jurisdictional Conference its findings for such action as the conference may deem appropriate within its constitutional warrant of power.

b) Recommend boundaries of the episcopal areas and the assignments of the bishops.

c) Be available to the Council/College of Bishops for consultation on matters of mutual concern.

d) Determine the number of effective bishops eligible for assignment.

e) Receive and act upon requests for possible voluntary and involuntary retirement of bishops.

f) Receive reports from the conference Committees on Episcopacy with respect to the needs for episcopal leadership and how best they can be fulfilled.

g) Establish a consultation process with each bishop regarding his/her episcopal assignment.

h) Prepare a report of its decisions, activities, and recommendations to be transmitted to its successor through the office of the secretary of the Jurisdictional Conference. The report shall be made available to delegates of the Jurisdictional Conference prior to the Jurisdictional Conference.

¶ **623.** The Jurisdictional Conference shall have powers and duties as described in the Constitution. It shall also have such other powers and duties as may be conferred by the General Conference, and in exercise thereof it shall act in all respects in harmony with the policy of The United Methodist Church with respect to elimination of discrimination based upon race.

¶ **624.** In all elections in a Jurisdictional Conference which are based on the number of church members within that jurisdiction, the number counted shall include lay members, ministerial members, and bishops assigned to that jurisdiction.

¶ **625.** The Jurisdictional Conference shall have authority to examine and acknowledge the journals of the Annual Conferences within its bounds and shall make such rules for the drawing up of the journals as may seem necessary.

¶ **626.** 1. The Jurisdictional Conference shall keep an official journal of its proceedings, duly signed by the secretary and president or secretary of the College of Bishops, to be sent for examination to the ensuing General Conference. This paragraph is effective May 1, 1980.

2. For the sake of convenience and uniformity the journal, when printed, should conform in page size and format to the General Conference journal, and the printing should be done at the expense of the jurisdiction by The United Methodist Publishing House.

JURISDICTIONAL AGENCIES

¶ **627.** The Jurisdictional Conference shall have the authority to appoint or elect such agencies as the General Conference may direct or as it deems necessary for its work. Insofar as possible the membership on councils, boards, and agencies of the Jurisdictional Conference shall include one-third clergy, one-third laywomen, and one-third laymen in keeping with the policies for general church agencies, except for the Board of Ordained Ministry and the Jurisdictional Committee on the Episcopacy. Special attention shall be given to the inclusion of clergywomen, youth, young adults, persons with a handicapping condition, and racial and ethnic minority persons.

¶ **628.** In each jurisdiction of The United Methodist Church there may be a **Jurisdictional Council on Ministries** organized as the jurisdiction shall determine and with the authority to coordinate the ministries of the general agencies within the jurisdiction.

¶ **629.** In each jurisdiction there may be jurisdictional program agencies related to the general program agencies organized as the Jurisdictional Conference shall determine.

¶ **630.** 1. There may be a **Jurisdictional Commission on Archives and History,** auxiliary to the general commission, to be composed of the chairperson of each Annual Conference Commission on Archives and History or the historian of each Annual Conference, the president of the Jurisdictional Historical

Society, and at least five members at large to be elected by the jurisdictional commission, or composed in a way the Jurisdictional Conference determines.

2. The jurisdictional commission may organize and promote a Jurisdictional Historical Society.

¶ **631.** In each jurisdiction there shall be a **Jurisdictional Association of Deaconesses/Home Missionaries** as described in the bylaws of the Committee on Diaconal Ministry.

¶ **632.** *Jurisdictional Youth Ministry Organization Convocation.*—There shall be a **Jurisdictional Youth Ministry Organization Convocation** to be held every other year in each jurisdiction (alternating years with the National Youth Ministry Organization Convocation ¶ 1401.3). Among the membership of the convocation for the purpose of the election of steering committee members, there shall be four voting representatives from each conference: the conference coordinator of youth ministries or designate; the conference Council on Youth Ministry chairperson or designate; two youth at large, to be elected as shall be determined by the conference Council on Youth Ministry. It is recommended that at least two members from each Annual Conference be racial/ethnic minority persons. Other persons may be added by jurisdictions according to their respective operational guidelines provided that the above categories are cared for and the recommended 50/50 racial/ethnic representation is observed. The expenses of the Jurisdictional Youth Ministry Organization Convocation shall be borne by the participating Annual Conference or the jurisdiction.

A responsibility of the Jurisdictional Youth Ministry Organization Convocations shall be to elect youth members to the National Youth Ministry Organization Steering Committee (*see* ¶ 1402.2). It is strongly recommended that two youth shall be elected from each jurisdiction, insofar as possible at least one of whom shall be a racial/ethnic minority person. Youth shall be seventeen years of age entering into the eleventh grade or younger; if not in school their age shall be sixteen or under at the time of their selection. Nominations shall come from Annual Conference Councils on Youth Ministry. The nominating process followed by the conference Councils on Youth Ministry shall include the solicitation of nominations from local churches, subdistricts, and districts. As far as possible members of the National Youth Ministry Organization Steering Committee from each jurisdiction shall be from five different Annual Conferences in that jurisdiction.

In addition to enabling the election of its two steering committee youth members, the following are suggested responsibilities for the Jurisdictional Youth Ministry Organization Convocation:

1. To initiate and support jurisdictional events (camps, conferences, workshops, etc.).

2. To recommend priorities, concerns, and/or policies to the National Youth Ministry Organization Steering Committee.

3. To promote the establishment and awareness of racial/ ethnic minority needs, concerns, issues, etc., through caucuses, camps, consultations, etc.

4. To promote the spiritual growth of participants in the Jurisdictional Youth Ministry Organization Convocation.

5. To promote an evangelistic outreach to and through youth.

6. To provide training and supportive experiences for conference youth personnel.

7. To enable communication between general and conference levels of youth ministry.

8. To nominate the jurisdictional youth member to the General Council on Ministries (¶ 1007.1(3)) in the years that Jurisdictional Conference meets.

¶ **633.** There may be jurisdictional Committees on the Ordained Ministry, auxiliary to the Division of Ordained Ministry. Where a Jurisdictional Board of Higher Education and Ministry exists, this committee may be part of that structure.

¶ **634. Constitution of United Methodist Women in the Jurisdiction.**—*Article 1. Name.*—In each jurisdiction there shall be a jurisdictional organization named United Methodist Women, auxiliary to the Women's Division of the Board of Global Ministries.

Article 2. Authority.—Each jurisdictional organization of United Methodist Women shall have authority to promote its work in accordance with the program and policies of the Women's Division of the Board of Global Ministries.

Article 3. Membership.—The jurisdictional organization of United Methodist Women shall be composed of the members of the Core Planning Group; six delegates from each conference organization, all of whom shall be conference officers; members of the Women's Division living within the jurisdiction; a representative of the jurisdictional Association of Deaconesses/Home Missionaries; and all the bishops of the jurisdiction.

Article 4. Meetings and Elections.—*a)* There shall be a meeting of the jurisdictional organization of United Methodist Women during the last year of the quadrennium. At that time the women nominees to the Board of Global Ministries shall be elected according to the Discipline (¶¶ 729.6*d*, 1554), and the president and any other officers shall also be elected.

b) There may be other meetings as needed.

Article 5. Amendments.—Proposed amendments to the constitution shall be sent to the recording secretary of the Women's Division prior to the last annual meeting of the division in the quadrennium.

¶ **635.** *Committee on United Methodist Men.*—In each jurisdiction there may be a **Committee on United Methodist Men,** auxiliary to the General Board of Discipleship.

Each jurisdictional Committee on United Methodist Men shall have authority to promote its work in accordance with the policies and programs of the board.

The conference presidents within the jurisdiction (or their representatives) shall elect the jurisdictional president during the last year of the quadrennium, who, by virtue of his election, shall be a member of the General Board of Discipleship (*see* ¶ 1304.1).

There may be meetings, retreats, and cooperative training events held by the jurisdiction United Methodist Men.

Section III. The Central Conference.

¶ **636.** *Authorization.*—1. In territory outside the United States, Annual Conferences, Provisional Annual Conferences, Missionary Conferences, Mission Conferences, and Missions in such numbers as the General Conference by a two-thirds vote shall determine may be organized by the General Conference into Central Conferences or Provisional Central Conferences, with such duties, privileges, and powers as are hereinafter set forth and as the General Conference by a two-thirds vote shall prescribe.[4]

2. There shall be such Central Conferences as have been authorized or shall be hereafter authorized by the General Conference; *provided* that a Central Conference shall have a total of at least thirty ministerial and thirty lay delegates on the basis of representation as set forth in this section, except as the General Conference may fix a different number. A Central Conference in existence at the time of union may be continued with a lesser number of delegates for reasons deemed sufficient by the Uniting Conference.

¶ **637.** *Organization.*—1. The **Central Conference** shall be composed of ministerial and lay members in equal numbers, the ministerial members elected by the ministerial members of the Annual Conference and the lay members by the lay members thereof. Their qualifications and the manner of election shall be determined by the Central Conference itself, subject only to constitutional requirements. Each Annual Conference and Provisional Annual Conference shall be entitled to at least two ministerial and two lay delegates, and no other selection of delegates shall be authorized which would provide for more than one ministerial delegate for every six ministerial members of an Annual Conference, except that a majority of the number fixed by a Central Conference as the ratio of representation shall entitle an Annual Conference to an additional ministerial delegate and to an additional lay delegate. Each Missionary Conference and Mission is authorized to elect and send one of its members to the Central Conference concerned as its representative, said representative to be accorded the privilege of sitting with the committees of the Central Conference with the right to speak in the committees and in the regular sessions of the Central Conference but without the right to vote. Representatives of Missionary Conferences or Missions shall have the same claim for payment of expenses as is allowed to members of the Central Conference.[5]

---

[4]*See* Judicial Council Decision 470.
[5]*See* Judicial Council Decision 371.

2. The first meeting of a Central Conference shall be called by the bishop or bishops in charge at such time and place as they may elect, to which members of the Annual Conferences, Provisional Annual Conferences, Missionary Conferences, and Missions concerned shall be elected on the basis of representation as provided herein. The time and place of future meetings shall be determined by the Central Conference or its executive committee.

3. Each Central Conference shall meet within the year succeeding the session of the General Conference at such time and place as the Central Conference itself or its bishops may determine, with the right to hold such adjourned sessions as it may determine. The sessions of said conference shall be presided over by the bishops. In case no bishop is present, the conference shall elect a temporary president from among its own members. The bishops resident in a Central Conference or a majority of them, with the concurrence of the executive committee or other authorized committee, shall have the authority to call an extra session of the Central Conference to be held at the time and place designated by them.[6]

4. The Council of Bishops may assign one or more of its number to visit any Central Conference or Provisional Central Conference. When so assigned, the bishop shall be an accredited representative of the general Church, and when requested by a majority of the bishops resident in that conference may exercise therein the functions of the episcopacy.

5. The presiding officer of the Central Conference shall decide questions of order, subject to an appeal to the Central Conference, and shall decide questions of law, subject to an appeal to the Judicial Council, but questions relating to the interpretation of the rules and regulations made by the Central Conference for the governing of its own session shall be decided by the Central Conference.[7]

6. Each Central Conference within the bounds of which the Board of Global Ministries has work shall maintain a cooperative and consultative relationship with the said board through a duly constituted executive committee, executive board, or council of

[6]*See* Judicial Council Decision 371.
[7]*See* Judicial Council Decisions 375, 376, 381.

cooperation; but the legal distinction between the Board of Global Ministries and the organized Church on the field shall always be kept clear.

7. The journal of the proceedings of a Central Conference, duly signed by the president and secretary, shall be sent for examination to the General Conference.

8. A Provisional Central Conference may become a Central Conference upon the fulfillment of the necessary requirements and upon the authorization of the General Conference.

9. In the case of a Central Conference the rule of proportionate representation shall be applied by each Annual Conference, and in the case of the delegates to the Central Conference of Central and Southern Europe the rule shall be applied to delegates coming from the two Annual Conferences of Switzerland, and the membership of the other Annual Conferences shall not figure in the computation.

¶ **638.** *Powers.*—1. To a Central Conference shall be committed for supervision and promotion, in harmony with the Discipline and interdenominational contractual agreements, the missionary, educational, evangelistic, industrial, publishing, medical, and other connectional interests of the Annual Conferences, Provisional Annual Conferences, Missionary Conferences, and Missions within its territory and such other matters as may be referred to it by said bodies or by order of the General Conference; and it shall provide suitable organizations for such work and elect the necessary officers for the same.

2. A Central Conference, when authorized by a specific enabling act of the General Conference, may elect one or more bishops from among the traveling elders of The United Methodist Church. The number of bishops to be elected by each Central Conference shall be determined from time to time by the General Conference.

3. When a Central Conference shall have been authorized to elect bishops, such elections shall be conducted under the same general procedure as prevails in the Jurisdictional Conferences for the election of bishops. A Central Conference shall have power to fix the tenure of bishops elected by the said Central Conference.[8]

---

[8]*See* Judicial Council Decisions 311, 430.

4. A Central Conference shall participate in the General Episcopal Fund on payment of its apportionment on the same percentage basis as that fixed for Annual Conferences in Jurisdictional Conferences. When the total estimated support, including salaries and all allowances for the bishops elected by it, and the estimated receipts on apportionment have been determined by a Central Conference, a statement of these amounts in itemized form shall be submitted to the General Council on Finance and Administration. This council, after consideration of the relative cost of living in various Central Conferences, shall determine the amount to be paid from the General Episcopal Fund in meeting the budget, after which the treasurer of the General Episcopal Fund shall pay the amount established to the bishop concerned, or as the Central Conference may determine.

5. A minister who has served a term or part of a term as a bishop in a Central Conference where term episcopacy has prevailed shall upon retirement from the effective relation in the ministry be paid an allowance from the General Episcopal Fund in such sum as the General Council on Finance and Administration shall determine for the years during which the minister served as a bishop.[9]

6. A Central Conference, in consultation with the bishops of that Central Conference, shall fix the episcopal areas and residences and make assignments to them of the bishops who are to reside in that Central Conference. The bishops of a Central Conference shall arrange the plan of episcopal visitation within its bounds.

7. The secretary of a Central Conference in which one or more bishops have been chosen shall report to the secretary of the General Conference the names of the bishop or bishops and the residences to which they have been assigned by the Central Conference.

8. A Central Conference shall have authority to elect and support general officers in all departments of the work of the Church within the boundaries of the Central Conference but may not determine the number of bishops.

---

[9]*See* Judicial Council Decision 394.

9. A Central Conference shall have power to make such changes and adaptations as the peculiar conditions on the fields concerned require regarding the local church, ministry, special advices, worship, and temporal economy within its territory, including the authorizing of associate members to participate in the offices of the local church under such rules as it may see fit; *provided* that no action shall be taken which is contrary to the Constitution and the General Rules of The United Methodist Church. Subject to this restriction, a Central Conference may delegate to an Annual Conference within its boundaries the power to make one or the other of the changes and adaptations referred to in this paragraph, upon the request of such Annual Conference.[10]

10. A Central Conference shall have the authority to change the provisions for the ordination of ministers in such way that the ordination of an elder may follow immediately upon ordination as a deacon; *provided* that other conditions are fully met.

11. A Central Conference shall fix the boundaries of the Annual Conferences, Provisional Annual Conferences, Missionary Conferences, and Missions within its bounds, proposals for changes first having been submitted to the Annual Conferences concerned as prescribed in the Discipline of The United Methodist Church; *provided*, however, that the number of Annual Conferences which may be organized within the bounds of a Central Conference shall first have been determined by the General Conference. No Annual Conference shall be organized with fewer than thirty-five ministerial members except as provided by an enabling act for the quadrennium, which shall not reduce the number below twenty-five. Nor shall an Annual Conference be continued with fewer than twenty-five ministerial members except as provided by an enabling act for the quadrennium.

12. A Central Conference may advise its Annual Conferences and Provisional Annual Conferences to set standards of character and other qualifications for admission of lay members.

13. A Central Conference shall have power to make changes and adaptations in procedure pertaining to the Annual, District,

---

[10]*See* Judicial Council Decision 313.

and Charge Conferences within its territory and to add to the business of the Annual Conference supplementary questions considered desirable or necessary to meet its own needs.

14. A Central Conference shall have authority to examine and acknowledge the journals of the Annual Conferences, Provisional Annual Conferences, Missionary Conferences, and Missions located within its bounds and to make rules for the drawing up of the journals as may seem necessary.

15. A Central Conference may have a standing **Committee on Women's Work.** This committee should preferably be composed of the women delegates and such other persons as the Central Conference may elect. The duty of this committee shall be to study the relation of women to the Church and to devise ways and means of developing this portion of the church membership to the end that it may assume its rightful responsibilities in the extension of the kingdom. The committee shall make recommendations to the Central Conference regarding women's organizations within its areas. A Central Conference organization may become a member of the World Federation of Methodist Women and may elect a representative to the World Federation of Methodist Women within the provisions of the Federation.

16. A Central Conference may organize a women's unit, after consultation with the Committee on Women's Work, in connection with any Annual Conference or Provisional Annual Conference within its bounds and provide a constitution and bylaws for it.

17. A Central Conference shall have authority to adopt rules of procedure governing the investigation and trial of its ministers, including bishops, and lay members of the Church and to provide the necessary means and methods of implementing the said rules; *provided,* however, that the ministers shall not be deprived of the right of trial by a ministerial committee, and lay members of the Church of the right of trial by a duly constituted committee of lay members; and *provided* also, that the rights of appeal shall be adequately safeguarded.[11]

---

[11]*See* Judicial Council Decision 310.

18. A Central Conference is authorized to prepare and translate simplified or adapted forms of such parts of the Ritual as it may deem necessary, such changes to require the approval of the resident bishop or bishops of the Central Conference.

19. A Central Conference shall have the power to conform the detailed rules, rites, and ceremonies for the solemnization of marriage to the statute laws of the country or countries within its jurisdiction.

20. Subject to the approval of the bishops resident therein, a Central Conference shall have the power to prescribe courses of study, including those in the vernaculars, for its ministry, both foreign and indigenous, including local preachers, lay speakers, Bible women, deaconesses, teachers both male and female, and all other workers whatsoever, ordained or lay. It shall also make rules and regulations for examination in these courses.

21. A Central Conference shall have authority to edit and publish a Central Conference Discipline which shall contain, in addition to the Constitution of the Church, such sections from the general Discipline of The United Methodist Church as may be pertinent to the entire Church and also such revised, adapted, or new sections as shall have been enacted by the Central Conference concerned under the powers given by the General Conference.

22. In a Central Conference or Provisional Central Conference using a language other than English, legislation passed by a General Conference shall not take effect until twelve months after the close of that General Conference in order to afford the necessary time to make adaptations and to publish a translation of the legislation which has been enacted, the translation to be approved by the resident bishop or bishops of the Central Conference. This provision, however, shall not exclude the election of delegates to the General Conference by Annual Conferences within the territory of Central Conferences or Provisional Central Conferences.

23. A Central Conference is authorized to interpret Article XXIII of the Articles of Religion *(page 61)* so as to recognize the governments of the country or countries within its territory.

24. A Central Conference shall have power to authorize the congregations in a certain state or country to form special

organizations in order to receive the acknowledgment of the state or country according to the laws of that state or country. These organizations shall be empowered to represent the interests of the Church to the authorities of the state or country according to the rules and principles of The United Methodist Church, and they shall be required to give regular reports of their activities to their respective Annual Conferences.

25. A Central Conference may, with the consent of the bishops resident in that conference, enter into agreements with churches or missions of other denominations for the division of territory or of responsibility for Christian work within the territory of the Central Conference.

26. A Central Conference shall have the right to negotiate with other Protestant bodies looking toward the possibility of church union; *provided* that any proposals for church union shall be submitted to the General Conference for approval before consummation.[12]

27. A Central Conference, where the laws of the land permit, shall have the power to organize and incorporate one or more executive committees, executive boards, or councils of cooperation, with such membership and such powers as may have been granted by the Central Conference for the purpose of representing it in its property and legal interests and for transacting any necessary business that may arise in the interval between the sessions of the Central Conference or that may be committed to said boards or committees by the Central Conference.

28. A Central Conference, through a duly incorporated property-holding body or bodies, shall have authority to purchase, own, hold, or transfer property for and on behalf of The United Methodist Church and of all the unincorporated organizations of The United Methodist Church within the territory of that Central Conference or on behalf of other organizations of The United Methodist Church which have entrusted their property to that Central Conference.

29. A Central Conference shall have authority to make the necessary rules and regulations for the holding and management

---

[12]*See* Judicial Council Decision 350.

of such properties; *provided,* however, that *(a)* all procedure shall be subject to the laws of the country or countries concerned, *(b)* no transfer of property shall be made from one Annual Conference to another without the consent of the conference holding title to such property, and *(c)* the status of properties held by local trustees or other holding bodies shall be recognized.

30. A Central Conference shall not, directly or indirectly through its incorporated property-holding body or bodies, alienate property or proceeds of property without due consideration of its trusteeship for local churches, Annual Conferences, the Board of Global Ministries and other organizations, local or general, of the Church.

31. A Central Conference or any of its incorporated organizations shall not involve the Board of Global Ministries or any organization of the Church in any financial obligation without the official approval of said board or organization. All invested funds, fiduciary trusts, or property belonging to an Annual Conference, a Provisional Annual Conference, a Missionary Conference, or a Mission, or any of its institutions, acquired by bequest, donation, or otherwise and designated for a specific use, shall be applied to the purpose for which they were designated. They shall not be diverted to any other purpose except by the consent of the conference or mission involved, and with the approval of the Central Conference concerned, and civil court action when necessary. The same rule shall apply to similar funds or properties acquired by a Central Conference for specific objects. In cases involving the diversion of trust funds and properties within the territory of a Central Conference, the Central Conference concerned shall determine the disposition of the interests involved, subject to an appeal to the Judicial Court of the Central Conference.

32. When former Central Conferences of The United Methodist Church become or have become autonomous churches, or entered into church unions, retired bishops therein shall continue to have membership in the Council of Bishops if the retired bishops involved so desire.

33. A Central Conference which adapts and edits the Discipline as provided in ¶ 638.21 shall establish a Judicial Court which, in addition to other duties which the Central Conference

may assign to it, shall hear and determine the legality of any action of the Central Conference taken under the adapted portions of the Discipline or of a decision of law by the presiding bishop of the Central Conference pertaining to the adapted portions of the Discipline upon appeal by the presiding bishop or by one fifth of the members of the Central Conference. Further, the Judicial Court shall hear and determine the legality of any action of an Annual Conference taken under the adapted portions of the Discipline or of a decision of law by the presiding bishop of the Annual Conference pertaining to the adapted portion of the Discipline upon appeal of the presiding bishop or of such percentage of the members of the Annual Conference as may be determined by the Central Conference concerned.

Section IV. Provisional Central Conferences.

¶ **639.** Annual Conferences, Provisional Annual Conferences, Missionary Conferences, and Missions outside the United States which are not included in Central Conferences or in the territory of affiliated autonomous churches, and which because of geographical, language, political, or other considerations have common interests that can best be served thereby, may be organized into **Provisional Central Conferences** as provided in ¶ 638.1.

¶ **640.** The organization of Provisional Central Conferences shall conform to the regulations prescribed for Central Conferences insofar as they are considered applicable by the bishop in charge.

¶ **641.** The General Conference may grant to a Provisional Central Conference any of the powers of a Central Conference except that of electing bishops.[13]

¶ **642.** In the interval between General Conferences, the Board of Global Ministries, upon the recommendation of the bishops in charge and after consultation with the Annual Conferences, Provisional Annual Conferences, Missionary Conferences, and Missions concerned, may make changes in the boundaries of a Provisional Central Conference and may grant to a Provisional Central Conference or to any of its component parts

---

[13]*See* Judicial Council Decision 403.

any of the powers of a Central Conference except that of electing bishops. All changes in boundaries and all grants of powers authorized by the Board of Global Ministries shall be reported to the ensuing session of the General Conference and shall expire at the close of that session unless renewed by the General Conference.

¶ 643. An Annual Conference or a Provisional Annual Conference in the field of a Provisional Central Conference shall have the power to set standards of character and other qualifications for admission of its lay members.

¶ 644. To Annual Conferences, Provisional Annual Conferences, Missionary Conferences, and Missions which are outside the United States and are not included in Central Conferences or Provisional Central Conferences, the General Conference may grant any of the powers of Central Conferences except that of electing bishops; and in the interval between General Conferences, the Board of Global Ministries may grant such powers when requested to do so by the bishop in charge and by the Annual Conference, Provisional Annual Conference, Missionary Conference, or Mission concerned.

¶ 645. The General Conference shall make provision for the episcopal supervision of work in the territory outside the United States which is not now included in Central Conferences.

¶ 646. The Council of Bishops may provide, if and when necessary, for episcopal visitation of mission fields not included in Central or Provisional Central Conferences.

Section V. Autonomous Churches, Affiliated Autonomous Churches, Affiliated United Churches, and Concordat Relationships.

¶ 647. *Autonomous Churches.*—1. A self-governing Methodist church in whose establishment The United Methodist Church or one of its constituent members (The Evangelical United Brethren Church and The Methodist Church) has assisted, but which has not established the covenant relationship of an affiliated autonomous church shall be known as an **autonomous Methodist church.**

2. When the requirements of such a Methodist church for its ministry are comparable to those of The United Methodist

Church, ministers may be transferred between its properly constituted ministerial bodies and the Annual and Provisional Annual Conferences of The United Methodist Church, with the approval and consent of the appointive authorities involved.

3. The Council of Bishops may assign one or more of its members for episcopal visitation to the autonomous Methodist churches.

4. If desired by the autonomous Methodist church, the Council of Bishops, in consultation with the General Board of Global Ministries, shall work out plans of cooperation with that church. The General Board of Global Ministries shall serve as the agent of The United Methodist Church for a continuing dialogue looking to the establishment of mission priorities with special reference to matters of personnel and finance.

5. An autonomous Methodist church may enter into a concordat agreement with The United Methodist Church under the provisions of ¶ 651.

¶ **648.** *Affiliated Autonomous Churches.*—A self-governing church in whose establishment The United Methodist Church or one of its constituent members (The Evangelical United Brethren Church and The Methodist Church) has assisted, and which, by mutual agreement has entered into a covenant of relationship with The United Methodist Church, shall be known as an **affiliated autonomous Methodist church.**

Such a covenant shall include the following provisions:

1. Certificates of church membership given by ministers in one church shall be accepted by ministers in the other church.

2. Ministers may be transferred between Annual and Provisional Annual Conferences of The United Methodist Church and of affiliated autonomous Methodist churches, and their ordination(s) recognized as valid, with the approval and consent of the bishops or other appointive authorities involved.

3. Each affiliated autonomous Methodist church shall be entitled to two delegates, one clergy and one lay person, to the General Conference of The United Methodist Church in accordance with ¶ 2401.2. They shall be entitled to all the rights and privileges of delegates, including membership on committees, except the right to vote. Such a church having more than seventy thousand full members shall be entitled to one additional

delegate. At least one of the three delegates shall be a woman. The bishop or president of the affiliated autonomous Methodist churches may be invited by the Council of Bishops to the General Conference.

4. A program of mutual visitation may be arranged by the Council of Bishops in cooperation with the equivalent leadership of the affiliated autonomous church. The Council of Bishops may assign one or more of its members for visitation to such churches.

5. Other provisions shall be as mutually agreed upon by the two churches.

6. The Council of Bishops, in consultation with the General Board of Global Ministries, shall work out plans of cooperation with that church. The Board of Global Ministries shall serve as the agent of The United Methodist Church for a continuing dialogue looking to the establishment of mission priorities with special reference to matters of personnel and finance.

BECOMING AN AFFILIATED AUTONOMOUS METHODIST OR UNITED CHURCH

¶ **649.** When conferences outside the United States which are parts of The United Methodist Church desire to become an affiliated autonomous Methodist or affiliated United Church, approval shall first be secured from the Central Conference involved and this decision be ratified by the Annual Conferences within the Central Conference by two-thirds majority of the aggregate votes cast by the Annual Conferences.

1. The conference shall prepare an historical record with reasons why autonomy is requested and shall consult with the Commission on Central Conference Affairs (¶ 2301) on proceedings for autonomy.

2. The Commission on Central Conference Affairs and the conferences involved shall mutually agree on the confession of faith and the constitution of the new church. These shall be prepared with care and shall be approved by the conferences.

3. Preparation of its Discipline is the responsibility of the conference(s) desiring autonomy.

4. Upon recommendation of the Commission on Central Conference Affairs, when all disciplinary requirements for affiliated autonomous relationship have been met, the General

Conference through an enabling act shall approve of and grant permission for the conference(s) involved to become an affiliated autonomous Methodist or United church.

5. Then the Central Conference involved shall meet, declare the present relationship between The United Methodist Church and the conference(s) involved dissolved, and reorganize as an affiliated autonomous Methodist or affiliated United Church in accordance with the enabling act granted by the General Conference. The Commission on Central Conference Affairs shall assist in this process, and when the plans are consummated, report to the Council of Bishops. The proclamation of affiliated autonomous status shall then be signed by the president of the Council of Bishops and the Secretary of the General Conference.

6. A plan of cooperation shall be developed in accordance with ¶ 648.6 above.

¶ **650.** *Affiliated United Churches.*—An affiliated United Church shall have the same relationship and privileges as affiliated autonomous Methodist churches in accordance with ¶¶ 648-649 above.

¶ **651.** *Concordat Agreements.*—1. There may be concordats with other autonomous Methodist churches in accordance with ¶ 12.2 and for The Methodist Church of Great Britain, in accordance with ¶ 12.3.

2. The purposes of such concordats are:

a) to manifest the common Methodist heritage,

b) to affirm the equal status of the two churches and express mutual acceptance and respect,

c) to create opportunities for closer fellowship between the two churches especially on the leadership level.

3. With the exception of The Methodist Church of Great Britain, such concordats may be established by the following procedure:

a) The autonomous Methodist church shall, through its major decision-making body, request a concordat relationship with The United Methodist Church through the Council of Bishops and the executive committee of the Commission on Central Conference Affairs. Concordats may also be initiated by The United Methodist Church acting through the Council of Bishops and the executive committee of the Commission on

Central Conference Affairs. This commission shall, in cooperation with the autonomous Methodist church in question, ascertain
that all disciplinary conditions are met and then prepare the
necessary enabling legislation for adoption by the General
Conference.

b) When such concordat agreement has been approved by
the General Conference, the executive committee of the
Commission on Central Conference Affairs shall prepare a
statement of the concordat agreement, to be signed by the
president of the Council of Bishops and the secretary of the
General Conference and two representatives of the autonomous
Methodist church with whom the concordat agreement is made.

4. Such concordat agreement shall entitle the two churches
to the following rights and privileges:

a) The two churches shall each elect two delegates, one
clergy and one lay, to be seated in each other's General
Conference or equivalent bodies, with all rights and privileges
except the right to vote. Agreements in existing concordats shall
be honored.

b) The host church shall make provisions for full hospitality,
including room and board, for the delegates of the other
concordat church. Travel and other expenses shall be the
responsibility of the visiting church.

c) A program of mutual visitation may be arranged by the
Council of Bishops in cooperation with the equivalent leadership
of the other concordat church. The Council of Bishops may
assign one or more of its members for episcopal visitation to
concordat churches.

d) Ministers may be transferred between the two churches in
accordance with ¶¶ 428.8 and 648.2 above.

BECOMING PART OF THE UNITED METHODIST CHURCH

¶ **652.** 1. An autonomous Methodist church or affiliated
autonomous Methodist church outside the United States may
become a part of The United Methodist Church, when all of the
following requirements are fulfilled:

a) Said church shall accept and approve the Constitution,
Articles of Faith, Discipline, and polity of The United Methodist
Church.

b) Said church shall apply for membership in a Central Conference. Such application shall be approved by that Central Conference and by the General Conference.

c) Said church shall declare its own constitution and church order null and void.

d) The Commission on Central Conference Affairs shall advise and assist said church in this process, and prepare the necessary enabling act for approval by the General Conference.

e) The General Conference shall approve legislation authorizing the necessary adjustments in the organization of the Central Conference involved.

f) The Commission on Central Conference Affairs shall assist said church in the process of becoming a part of The United Methodist Church, determine when all requirements are met, and report to the General Conference.

2. Other churches outside the United States may become a part of The United Methodist Church by following the same procedure.

This paragraph shall be effective immediately following the 1980 General Conference.

Section VI. Provisional Annual Conferences.

¶ 653. A **Provisional Annual Conference** is a conference which, because of its limited membership, does not qualify for Annual Conference status.

¶ 654. Any Missionary Conference or Mission established under the provisions of the Discipline may be constituted as a Provisional Annual Conference by the General Conference in consultation with the Central Conference, Provisional Central Conference, or Jurisdictional Conference within which the Missionary Conference or mission is located; *provided* that

1. no Provisional Annual Conference shall be organized with fewer than ten ministerial members, or be continued with fewer than six ministerial members;

2. the total financial support from the General Board of Global Ministries, including the Advance, shall not exceed an appropriate percentage as determined in consultation with the division to which the conference relates;

3. the membership and contributions of the conference

have shown a reasonable increase during the previous quadrennium and give evidence of an aggressive program for continued progress in both areas.

¶ **655.** *Organization.*—A Provisional Annual Conference shall be organized in the same manner and have the same powers and functions as an Annual Conference, subject to the approval of the presiding bishop; and its members shall share pro rata in the proceeds of The United Methodist Publishing House with members of the Annual Conferences, with the following exceptions:

1. The bishop having episcopal supervision of a Provisional Annual Conference in a foreign or a home mission field may appoint a representative as **superintendent,** to whom may be committed specific responsibility for the representation of the Board of Global Ministries in its relation to the indigenous church and also in cooperation with other recognized evangelical missions. Such duties shall be exercised so as not to interfere with the work of the district superintendent. This superintendent may also be a district superintendent; *provided* the superintendent is a member of the said conference. The superintendent shall be responsible directly to the bishop appointed to administer the work in that episcopal area, and shall make adequate reports of the work and needs of the field to the bishop and to the secretaries of the Board of Global Ministries immediately concerned.

2. A Provisional Annual Conference shall meet annually at the time appointed by the bishop. If there is no bishop present, the superintendent shall preside. In the absence of both, the presidency shall be determined as in an Annual Conference (¶ 702.5). The conference or a committee thereof shall select the place for holding the conference.

3. In a Provisional Annual Conference receiving major funding from the General Board of Global Ministries, the assigned staff of the appropriate division shall provide consultation and guidance in setting up the annual budget and Advance projects within the conference and in the promotion of new mission projects. The conference, in making requests for appropriations for support, including grants and loans for building projects, shall submit to the General Board of Global Ministries a statement of the proposed annual budget and

proposed financial plan for new mission and building plans. Items involving increased appropriations from the General Board of Global Ministries, or increased askings from the Advance, shall be subject to modifications by the General Board of Global Ministries.

4. A Provisional Annual Conference shall elect one minister and one lay person as delegates with full voting and other rights to the General Conference and to the Jurisdictional Conference. Delegates to Central Conferences shall be elected in accordance with ¶ 637.1.

¶ 656. In a Provisional Annual Conference in the United States, Puerto Rico, or the Virgin Islands, there shall be a conference Board of Global Ministries constituted as in an Annual Conference and having the same duties and powers.

Section VII. The Missionary Conference.

¶ 657. *Definition.*—A conference is a **Missionary Conference** because of its particular mission opportunities, its limited membership and resources, its unique leadership requirements and ministerial needs. The General Board of Global Ministries shall provide administrative guidance and major financial assistance including attention to the distinctive property matters.

¶ 658. *Organization.*—A Missionary Conference shall be organized in the same manner and with the same rights and powers as an Annual Conference (¶¶ 701-703), but with the following exceptions:

1. The College of Bishops shall provide episcopal supervision for any Missionary Conference(s) within its jurisdictional boundaries as are organized. The bishop thus placed in charge and having episcopal supervision within the respective episcopal area in cooperation with the General Board of Global Ministries shall appoint a conference superintendent and/or district superintendents. Such appointment(s) shall comply with limitations on years of service as found in ¶ 516.[14]

2. The General Board of Global Ministries shall give close supervision and guidance in setting up the administrative and promotional budgets and Advance projects within the confer-

---

[14]*See* Judicial Council Decision 448.

ence and in the promotion of new mission projects. The conference, in making requests for appropriations for support and grants and loans for building projects, shall submit to the General Board of Global Ministries a statement of the proposed annual promotional and administrative budget and the proposed financial plan for new mission and building projects. New work and building projects involving increased appropriations from the General Board of Global Ministries shall first have the approval of the General Board of Global Ministries. (*See also* ¶ 1529.18.)

3. Missionary Conferences shall elect ministerial and lay delegates to General and Jurisdictional Conference on the same basis as Annual Conferences as provided in ¶¶ 601 and 613.

4. *a) Membership.*—A Missionary Conference shall determine by majority vote whether it will establish the right of full ministerial membership.

b) A minister in full connection with an Annual Conference who is appointed to a Missionary Conference which has previously voted to include full membership under §4*a* may choose either to request the bishop of the Missionary Conference to seek the transfer of her or his membership into full membership with the Missionary Conference or retain her or his membership in a home conference and be considered in an affiliated relationship to the Missionary Conference. Affiliated relationship shall entitle the minister to the fellowship of the conference, to full participation in its activities, including holding office and representing the Missionary Conference in General and Jurisdictional Conferences. An affiliate member of a Missionary Conference shall not vote in his or her Annual Conference while retaining the affiliate relationship to a Missionary Conference. Such affiliate relationship to a Missionary Conference shall be only for the duration of the minister's appointment to the conference.

An affiliate member elected to a General or Jurisdictional Conference from a Missionary Conference shall not be eligible to be elected to such position from the conference where his or her membership is held.

c) A Missionary Conference may elect into full ministerial membership those persons desiring full membership in accordance with ¶ 659.

d) A pastor under full-time appointment in a Missionary Conference upon consultation with and the approval of the bishop and conference or district superintendent/Cabinet, may waive his or her claim upon the conference minimum salary. This waiver is to be reviewed annually and is to be effective until the time of subsequent appointment.

5. A Missionary Conference may include in its membership representation of such mission agencies within its boundaries as it deems advisable; provided, however, such representation shall not exceed a number equal to one third of the total membership of the Missionary Conference and that such representatives shall be members of The United Methodist Church in accordance with constitutional requirements.

6. *Clergy Couples.*—In a Missionary Conference, either or both pastors may at the time of their appointment on their own initiative waive their claim or any portion thereof on the Missionary Conference minimum salary upon consultation with the bishop and the conference superintendent or Cabinet. This waiver shall be reviewed annually and shall be effective until the time of subsequent appointment. Persons serving under such waiver may still be considered to be in full-time service under the supervision of the conference or district superintendent when so approved by the bishop, the conference superintendent, or the Cabinet and the executive committee of the Board of Ordained Ministry.

7. In order to provide traditional and experimental ministries, the bishop of the Missionary Conference may appoint an effective elder to other than full-time pastoral appointment combined with secular employment. This will in no way affect the conference relationship. Pension and other benefits shall be provided in consultation with the parties involved and with the approval of the Missionary Conference.

¶ **659.** Only the General Conference can create a Missionary Conference or change a Missionary Conference to a Provisional Annual Conference or an Annual Conference. A petition to the General Conference for change in status from a Missionary Conference shall set forth details of the history and status of the conference and shall be accompanied by a report and recommendation of the Board of Global Ministries.

¶ **660.** Missionary Conferences shall have the same rights as those given to Central Conferences in ¶ 640.9-.10 to make such changes and adaptations regarding the ministry and ordination of ministers as the effective use of indigenous leadership in the Missionary Conference may require; *provided* that no action shall be taken which is contrary to the Constitution and the General Rules of The United Methodist Church.

Section VIII. Missions.

¶ **661.** A Mission shall meet annually at the time and place appointed by the bishop in charge, who shall preside. In the absence of the bishop the superintendent of the Mission shall preside. The presiding officer shall bring forward the regular business of the meeting and arrange the work.

¶ **662.** *Administration of a Mission.*—1. Administration of a Mission in the United States, Puerto Rico, and the Virgin Islands shall be in the National Division until requirements have been met for the organization of a Provisional or an Annual Conference.

2. A Mission shall be composed of all regularly appointed missionaries, both lay and clerical, mission traveling preachers, and other lay members. The number of lay members and the method of their appointment shall be determined by the mission.[15]

3. The bishop assigned to a Mission, in cooperation with the associate general secretary of the appropriate division of the General Board of Global Ministries, may appoint a superintendent or as many superintendents of the Mission as may be wise and for whom support has been provided. The bishop shall determine the groups or charges over which the respective superintendents shall have supervision.

4. A bishop or, in the absence of a bishop, one of the superintendents chosen by ballot by the Mission, shall preside at the annual meeting. This meeting shall exercise, in a general way, the functions of a District Conference. It shall have the power to certify candidates for the ministry, to pass on the character of preachers not members of an Annual Conference, to receive on trial mission traveling preachers, and to recommend to an

[15]*See* Judicial Council Decision 341.

Annual Conference proper persons for deacon's orders. The bishop shall, at the annual meeting, assign the missionaries and mission traveling preachers to the several charges for the ensuing year; *provided* that no missionary shall be transferred to or from a Mission without previous consultation with the National Division of the General Board of Global Ministries.

5. Examination of local pastors and traveling preachers shall be held by the mission and certified to an Annual Conference. The Mission also shall make recommendations to reception on trial in an Annual Conference.

Section IX. The Annual Conference.

¶ **701.** *Composition and Character.*—1. The ministerial membership of an Annual Conference (¶ 412) shall consist of members in full connection (¶ 422), probationary members (¶ 413), associate members (¶ 419), and local pastors under full-time appointment to a pastoral charge (¶ 408.1).[16] (*See also* ¶ 36.)

a) Members in full connection shall have the right to vote on all matters in the Annual Conference except in the election of lay delegates to the General and Jurisdictional Conferences and shall have sole responsibility for all matters of ordination, character, and conference relations of ministers.

b) Probationary members shall have the right to vote in the Annual Conference on all matters except constitutional amendments, election of delegates to the General and Jurisdictional or Central Conferences, and matters of ordination, character, and conference relations of ministers.

c) Associate members shall have the right to vote in the Annual Conference on all matters except constitutional amendments, election of delegates to the General and Jurisdictional or Central Conferences, and matters of ordination, character, and conference relations of ministers.

d) Local pastors under full time appointment to a pastoral charge shall have the right to vote in the Annual Conference on all matters except constitutional amendments, election of delegates to the General and Jurisdictional or Central Confer-

---

[16]*See* Judicial Council Decisions 371, 477.

ences, and matters of ordination, character, and conference relations of ministers.

2. The following shall be seated in the Annual Conference and shall be given the privilege of the floor without vote: part-time and student local pastors; lay missionaries regularly appointed by the Board of Global Ministries in fields outside the United States; and diaconal ministers serving within the bounds of the Annual Conference. By authorization of a Central Conference national diaconal ministers may be given the same privileges.

3. The lay member or alternate, whoever was last seated in the Annual Conference, shall be seated in a special session of the Annual Conference when convened; *provided* that no local charge shall be deprived of its lay member due to death, serious illness, or cessation of membership. Under such circumstances another lay member may be elected by the Charge Conference.[17] (*See* ¶ 36.)

4. The lay members of the Annual Conference shall participate in all deliberations and vote upon all measures except on the granting or validation of license, ordination, reception into full conference membership, or any question concerning the character and official conduct of ministers. Lay members shall serve on all committees except those on ministerial relations and for the trial of ministers.

5. When at any time a lay member is excused by the Annual Conference from further attendance during the session, the alternate lay member may be seated instead. The lay member, or the alternate, shall be the lay member of the Annual Conference, and it shall be the duty of the lay member to report on actions of the Annual Conference.

6. It is the duty of every member and all probationers and local pastors of the Annual Conference to attend its sessions and furnish such reports in such form as the Discipline may require. Any such person unable to attend shall report by letter to the conference secretary, setting forth the reason for the absence. Should any minister in active service be absent from the session of the Annual Conference without a satisfactory reason for the absence, the matter shall be referred by the conference secretary to the Board of Ordained Ministry.

---

[17]*See* Judicial Council Decision 319.

¶ **702.** *Organization.*—1. Annual Conferences may become severally bodies corporate, whenever practicable, under the law of the countries, states, and territories within whose bounds they are located.[18]

· 2. The bishops shall appoint the times for holding the Annual Conferences.

3. The Annual Conference or a committee thereof shall select the place for holding the conference, but should it become necessary for any reason to change the place of meeting, a majority of the district superintendents, with the consent of the bishop in charge, may change the place.

4. A special session of the Annual Conference may be held at such time and in such place as shall have been determined by the Annual Conference after consultation with the bishop, or by the bishop, with the concurrence of three fourths of the district superintendents. A special session of the Annual Conference shall have only such powers as are stated in the call.[19]

5. The bishop assigned shall preside over the Annual Conference or, in case of inability, arrange for another bishop to preside. In the absence of a bishop the conference shall by ballot, without nomination or debate, elect a president pro tempore from among the traveling elders. The president thus elected shall discharge all the duties of a bishop except ordination.[20]

6. The Annual Conference at the first session following the General Conference or Jurisdictional or Central Conferences (or, if it may desire, at the last session preceding the General, Jurisdictional, or Central Conferences) shall elect a secretary and statistician to serve for the succeeding quadrennium. In the case of a vacancy in either office in the interim of the sessions, the bishop, after consultation with the district superintendents, shall appoint a person to act until the next session of the Annual Conference. (See ¶ 715 for election of the treasurer.)

7. The Annual Conference may designate a person who is a member in good standing of one of the local churches and who is a member of the bar of the state as **chancellor.** The chancellor, who shall be nominated by the bishop and elected by the Annual

---

[18]*See* Judicial Council Decision 108.
[19]*See* Judicial Council Decision 397.
[20]*See* Judicial Council Decisions 367, 373.

Conference, shall serve as legal advisor to the bishop and to the Annual Conference.

8. *a)* The **conference lay leader** is the elected leader of conference laity. The lay leader will have responsibility for fostering awareness of the role of the laity in achieving the mission of the Church, and enabling and supporting lay participation in the planning and decision-making processes of the Annual Conference, district, and local church in cooperation with the bishop, district superintendents, and pastors. The lay leader is a member of the Annual Conference, the conference Council on Ministries, and the executive committee, if any, of the conference Council on Ministries, and may be designated by virtue of office to membership on any conference agency by the Annual Conference.

b) The conference lay leader shall relate to the organized lay groups in the conference such as United Methodist Men, United Methodist Women, and United Methodist Youth, and support their work and help them coordinate their activities. The conference lay leader shall also have the general responsibility in (1) developing the advocacy role for laity in the life of the Church, (2) increasing the participation of laity in the sessions and structure of the Annual Conference, and (3) encouraging lay persons in the general ministry of the Church.

c) The conference lay leader shall be elected by the Annual Conference as the Annual Conference may determine. The method of nomination and term of office shall be determined by the Annual Conference.

¶ **703.** *Powers and Duties.*—1. The Annual Conference for its own government may adopt rules and regulations not in conflict with the Discipline of The United Methodist Church; *provided* that in exercise of its powers each Annual Conference shall act in all respects in harmony with the policy of The United Methodist Church with respect to elimination of discrimination on the basis of race.[21]

2. An Annual Conference cannot financially obligate The United Methodist Church or an organizational unit thereof except the Annual Conference itself.

---

[21]*See* Judicial Council Decisions 43, 74, 141, 318, 323, 367, 373, 418, 432, 435, 476.

3. The Annual Conference may admit into membership only those who have met all the Disciplinary requirements for membership and only in the manner prescribed in the Discipline.[22]

4. The Annual Conference shall have power to make inquiry into the moral and official conduct of its ministerial members. Subject only to the provisions of ¶¶ 2620-2626, the Annual Conference shall have power to hear complaints against its ministerial members and may try, reprove, suspend, deprive of ministerial office and credentials, expel, or acquit any against whom charges may have been preferred. The Annual Conference shall have power to locate a ministerial member for unacceptability or inefficiency.

5. The status of a ministerial member and of a probationer and the manner and conditions of a transfer of a ministerial member from one Annual Conference to another are governed by the section on the ordained ministry (Chapter Four).

6. Transfers of traveling preachers are conditioned on the passing of their character by the conference to which they are amenable. The official announcement that a preacher is transferred changes the preacher's membership so that all rights and responsibilities in the conference to which that preacher goes begin from the date of transfer. Such member of an Annual Conference shall not vote twice on the same constitutional question, nor be counted twice in the same year in the basis for election of delegates, nor vote twice in the same year for delegates to the General, Jurisdictional, or Central Conferences.

7. Whenever ministerial members, whether on trial or in full connection, are transferred to another Annual Conference, either in connection with a transfer of the pastoral charge to which they are appointed or by reason of the dissolution or merger of the Annual Conference, they shall have the same rights and obligations as the other members of the conference to which they are transferred.

8. The Annual Conference shall have power to make inquiry into the financial status of the local churches, and where there is a deficit in finances, it may require the pastor and the lay member

---

[22]*See* Judicial Council Decision 440.

to appear before the appropriate committee and make explanation.

9. The Annual Conference shall have the power to make inquiry into the membership status of the local churches, and where no members have been received on confession of faith during the year, it may require the pastor and the lay member to appear before the appropriate agency and make explanation.

10. The Annual Conference shall give recognition to any new churches that have been organized during the year and shall, through the presiding bishop and the secretary, send to each new church a **certificate of organization,** which the district superintendent shall, on behalf of the conference, present to the new church in an appropriate ceremony.

11. The Annual Conference shall secure, during the course of its annual session, the answers to the questions for conducting Annual Conference sessions, and the secretary to the Annual Conference shall include the answers to these questions in the conference record and in the report to the Council on Finance and Administration.

¶ **704.** *Business of the Conference.*—1. The session shall open with a period of devotion, followed by a call of the roll, including the roll of the local pastors and diaconal ministers.

2. The Annual Conference, to expedite the transaction of its business, may adopt an agenda as a basis of its procedure. Such agenda shall be prepared by the bishop, the district superintendents, and such others as the conference may name, and shall be submitted to the conference for adoption.

3. Members for all standing committees, boards, and commissions of the Annual Conference shall be selected in such manner as the Annual Conference may determine or as the Discipline may specifically require.

For the purpose of adjusting tenure a certain number of members may be elected or appointed for particular terms. Members shall hold office until their successors are elected. For the Annual Conference agencies provided for by the Discipline see ¶ 706.1 and for the agencies established by the Annual Conference itself see ¶ 706.2.

4. The business of the Annual Conference shall include the receiving and acting upon reports from the district superinten-

dents, the officers, the standing and special committees, the boards, commissions, and societies and also the making of such inquiries as the Council of Bishops shall recommend by the provision of a supplemental guide.[23]

5. The Annual Conference shall make inquiry into the moral and official conduct of its ministers. In response to the inquiry whether all ministerial members of the conference are blameless in their life and official administration, the district superintendent may answer for all the preachers in the district in one answer, or the Board of Ordained Ministry may make inquiry of each district superintendent about each minister in the district and make one report to the bishop and the conference in open session; *provided* that the conference or the bishop may order an executive session of the ministerial members to consider questions relating to matters of ordination, character, and conference relationships.[24]

6. At the conclusion of the examination of the standing of the ministers in the conference or at such later times as the bishop may designate, the presiding bishop may call to the bar of the conference the class to be admitted into full connection and receive them into conference membership after asking the questions to be found in ¶ 425. This examination of the ministers and the passing of their characters may be the business of one session.

¶ **705.** *Records and Archives.*—1. The Annual Conference shall keep an exact record of its proceedings according to the forms provided by the General, Jurisdictional, and Central Conferences. If there are no archives of the Annual Conference, the secretary shall keep the bound copy or copies to be handed on to the succeeding secretary. The conference shall send to its Jurisdictional Conference or Central Conference copies of the minutes of the quadrennium for examination.

2. Each Annual Conference shall send to the Council on Finance and Administration two printed copies of its annual journal and one printed copy to the Council on Ministries.[25]

---

[23]*See* Judicial Council Decision 367.
[24]*See* Judicial Council Decisions 42, 406.
[25]*See* Judicial Council Decision 481.

3. The Annual Conference journal shall include the following divisions, preferably in the following order:

a) Officers of Annual Conference
b) Boards, commissions, committees; rolls of conference members
c) Daily proceedings
d) Disciplinary questions
e) Appointments
f) Reports as ordered by the Annual Conference
g) Memoirs as ordered by the Annual Conference
h) Roll of dead—deceased ministerial members
i) Historical
j) Miscellaneous
k) Pastoral record (including the records of accepted local pastors in such manner as the conference may determine)
l) Statistics
m) Index

4. An Annual Conference in the United States and Puerto Rico shall include in its journal a list of the deaconesses and missionaries, ministerial and lay, active and retired, who have gone from the conference into mission service.

5. The Annual Conference journal shall include a listing of the consecrated diaconal ministers and their service records.

6. The secretary of each Annual Conference shall keep a service record of every ministerial member of the Annual Conference together with the date of marriage and the birth dates of the member, spouse, and children.

7. All records of secretaries, statisticians, and treasurers shall be kept according to the forms prepared by the Council on Finance and Administration so that all statistical and financial items shall be handled alike in all conferences and that uniformity of reporting shall be established as a churchwide policy.

¶ 706. The Annual Conference shall provide for the connectional relationship between the general boards and commissions and the conference, district, and local church.

1. The Annual Conference shall structure itself for effective mission in any mode deemed appropriate. In each Annual Conference, there may be conference program boards related to the general program boards organized as the Annual Conference shall determine. The Annual Conference shall provide for the connectional relationship between the general program boards and the conference, districts, and local churches, and shall specifically assign the program responsibilities related to the objectives and scope of the general program boards to agencies of the Annual Conference.[26]

2. The Annual Conference may appoint additional committees for the purpose of promoting the work of The United Methodist Church within the bounds of the said Annual Conference and may prescribe their membership and their powers and duties.

3. Each Annual Conference may make its agencies of such size as its work may require; *provided* that consideration shall be given to the inclusion of lay and clergy persons from small membership churches. Full-time local pastors serving charges are eligible for election or appointment to such agencies, except those dealing with qualifications, orders, and status of ministers and local pastors.

4. Insofar as possible, the membership on councils, boards, and agencies of the Annual Conference shall include one-third clergy, one-third laywomen, and one-third laymen, except for the Board of Ordained Ministry. Special attention shall be given to the inclusion of clergywomen, youth, young adults, persons with a handicapping condition, and racial and ethnic minority persons in keeping with policies for general church agencies.

5. Members of general agencies (¶ 801) shall serve as ex officio members of the corresponding Annual Conference agency (*see* ¶ 810.4).

---

[26]*See* Judicial Council Decisions 411, 417, 418.

THE CONFERENCE COUNCIL ON FINANCE AND ADMINISTRATION

¶ **707.** In each Annual Conference there shall be a **conference Council on Finance and Administration,** hereinafter called the council.

¶ **708.** The council's purpose, membership, organization, and relationships shall be as follows:

1. *Purpose.*—The purpose of the council shall be to develop, maintain, and administer a comprehensive and coordinated plan of fiscal and administrative policies, procedures, and management services for the Annual Conference.

2. *Membership.*—*a)* Each Annual Conference shall elect, at its session next succeeding the General Conference, a conference Council on Finance and Administration, composed of not less than five nor more than twenty-one members; in every case there shall be at least one lay person more than ministerial included on the council.[27] Persons shall be nominated for membership in a manner determined by the conference. Insofar as possible there shall be one-third laymen, one-third laywomen, and one-third clergy. It is recommended that in the nomination and election of members and in the filling of vacancies attention be given to appropriate representation of youth and minority persons. The term of office shall begin with the adjournment of the Annual Conference session at which they are elected and shall be for a period of four years and until their successors are elected. No member or employee of any conference agency and no employee, trustee, or director of any agency or institution participating in the funds of any conference budget shall be eligible for voting membership on the council.[28] Any vacancy shall be filled by action of the council until the next conference session, at which time the Annual Conference shall fill the vacancy.

b) The following shall be ex officio members of the council in addition to the number set by the Annual Conference under ¶ 708.2*a*: (1) the conference treasurer/director of administrative services, without vote; (2) any members of the General Council on Finance and Administration who reside within the bounds of the conference, with vote, unless voting membership is in conflict

[27]*See* Judicial Council Decision 441.
[28]*See* Judicial Council Decision 10.

with another provision of the Book of Discipline, in which case their membership shall be without vote; (3) a district superintendent chosen by the Cabinet, without vote; and (4) the director of the conference Council on Ministries or another representative of that council, without vote.

3. *Officers.*—The council shall elect from its voting membership a president, a vice-president, a secretary, and such other officers as it may deem necessary. The conference treasurer (¶ 715) shall be the treasurer of the council. The treasurer shall not be eligible for voting membership on the council and shall not be eligible for election to any of those offices which are to be filled by voting members of the council.

4. *Organization.*—*a)* The council may establish committees and task forces and define their duties and authority as it deems necessary for fulfilling its purpose and responsibilities.

b) The Annual Conference may enact bylaws governing meetings, quorum, and other matters of procedure for the council, or it may authorize the council to enact such bylaws; in any event such by-laws shall not be in conflict with the Book of Discipline.

c) If deemed necessary for the fulfillment of its functions, and if so authorized by the Annual Conference, the council may be incorporated.

5. *Amenability.*—The council shall be amenable and report directly to the Annual Conference.

6. *Relationships.*—*a)* The council and the Annual Conference Council on Ministries shall cooperate in the development of conference benevolences budget recommendations for conference program agencies (¶ 710.3).

b) In the interest of developing and implementing coordinated Annual Conference policies in the areas of fiscal management and administrative services, it shall serve in a liaison role among conference agencies with responsibilities in these areas. The council shall be authorized to convene representatives of Annual Conference administrative and ministerial support agencies for the purpose of consulting on matters of mutual concern, such as the coordination of fiscal management, fund-raising activities, and administrative services in the Annual Conference.

¶ **709.** *Responsibilities.*—The council shall have authority and responsibility to perform the following functions:

1. To recommend to the Annual Conference for its action and determination budgets of anticipated income and proposed expenditures for all funds which provide for Annual Conference ministerial support, Annual Conference administrative expenses and Annual Conference benevolence and program causes (¶ 710).

2. To receive, consider, report, and make recommendations to the Annual Conference regarding the following, prior to final decision by the Annual Conference: *(a)* any proposal to raise capital funds for any purpose; *(b)* funding considerations related to any proposal which may come before the conference; *(c)* any requests to conduct a special conference-wide financial appeal, whether by special collections, campaigns or otherwise, in the local churches of the conference.

3. To recommend to the Annual Conference for its action and decision, the methods or formulas by which apportionments to churches, charges, or districts for duly authorized general, jurisdictional, conference, and district funds shall be determined (¶ 711).

4. To cooperate with the Committee on Communication in providing district superintendents, pastors, and appropriate officers of the local churches and charge conferences with interpretive aids which will assist in gaining understanding and support of the conference budget and other approved conference causes.

5. To develop policies governing the investment of conference funds (except for pension funds as provided in ¶ 1708), whether in debt or equity, short-term or long-term instruments, with the aim of maximizing funds available for mission in a manner consistent with the preservation of capital and with the Social Principles of the Church. A statement of such policies shall be printed in the conference journal at least once in each quadrennium.

6. To recommend to the Annual Conference for its action and decision procedures for dealing responsibly with situations in which budgeted funds, as approved by the Annual Conference, are inadequate to meet emerging missional needs or unforeseen circumstances.

7. To review at least quarterly and to account to the Annual Conference for the disbursement of funds in accordance with budgets approved by the conference.

8. To recommend to the Annual Conference for its action and determination the conditions under which it may borrow funds for current expense purposes and the maximum amount of such borrowing.

9. To have authority and supervision over the treasurer/director of administrative services (¶¶ 715-716); to establish policies governing the treasurer/director's work.

10. To work in cooperation with other Annual Conference agencies for the design and implementation of a plan by which the Annual Conference may designate the conference treasury as a central treasury for funds designated for any or all conference agencies participating in conference funds.

11. To establish uniform and equitable policies and practices in the employment and compensation of personnel, in consultation and cooperation with other conference agencies which employ staff, unless the Annual Conference has designated another agency to carry this responsibility.

12. To cooperate with the General Council on Finance and Administration and with the General Board of Discipleship in promoting and standardizing the financial recording and reporting system in the local churches of the conference.

13. In cooperation with the General Council on Finance and Administration, related Annual Conference agencies and institutions, and local churches, to make recommendations to the Annual Conference regarding the development, promotion, and review of a broad general program of insurance protection and risk management, except for employee benefit programs.

14. To perform such other administrative and fiscal functions and services as the Annual Conference may assign.

¶ 710. *Budgets.*—The council shall recommend to the Annual Conference for its action and determination budgets of anticipated income and proposed expenditures for all funds to be apportioned to the churches, charges, or districts. Prior to each regular session of the Annual Conference the council shall make a diligent and detailed study of the needs of all the conference agencies and causes asking to be included in the budget of any conference fund. The chairperson of each conference agency, or other duly authorized representative, shall have opportunity to represent the claims of that agency before the council.

1. *Ministerial Support Budgets.*—*a)* It shall be the duty of the council, unless otherwise provided, to estimate the total amount necessary to furnish a sufficient and equitable support for the district superintendents of the conference, including salary and suitable provision for dwelling to the Annual Conference, for its action and determination, the amount to be set for the salary and for each of the other allowances specified above, for each of the several district superintendents.[29]

b) The council shall report to the Annual Conference at each session the percentage approved by the General Conference as the basis for the Episcopal Fund apportionment to the Annual Conference and shall include in its recommended ministerial support budget the amount determined by the treasurer of the General Council on Finance and Administration as necessary to meet this apportionment.

c) After consultation with the conference Board of Pensions, the council shall report to the Annual Conference the amounts computed by that agency as necessary to meet the needs for pensions and benefit programs of the conference. Such amounts need not be derived solely from apportionments.

d) It shall recommend to the Annual Conference an amount determined in consultation with the Commission on Equitable Salaries to be used for compliance with the approved schedule of equitable salaries for pastors (¶ 934).

e) It shall recommend to the Annual Conference estimates of the amounts needed for any other programs of ministerial support the conference may adopt, such as a Sustentation Fund (¶ 935) or provision for the moving expenses of pastors.

2. *Administration Budget.*—*a)* The council shall recommend to the Annual Conference estimates of the amounts needed for administrative expenses of the conference, including its own expenses and those of the conference treasurer's office. It shall consult with the conference agencies and officers to be included in the administrative budget regarding the estimated budgets of

---

[29]*See* Judicial Council Decision 44.

their expenses and base its conference administration budget recommendations on information thus received.

b) It shall include in its estimates recommendations regarding the conference's share of an area expense fund, if any, and apportionments for administration properly made by the Jurisdictional Conference and the General Conference (¶ 916.2).

3. *World Service and Conference Benevolences Budget.—a)* In preparing the conference benevolences budget the council, working together with the conference Council on Ministries as provided in ¶ 710.3*b*, shall make diligent effort to secure full information regarding all conference benevolence and service causes that none may be neglected, jeopardized, or excluded. Basing its judgment of needs upon the information secured, the council shall recommend to the Annual Conference for its action and determination the total amount to be apportioned for the conference benevolences budget. It shall also recommend the amount or the percentage of the total of the conference benevolences budget which shall be allocated to each cause included in the said budget, such recommendations to reflect agreement with the conference Council on Ministries on program agency allocations as specified below.[30]

b) In studying the requests of conference program agencies for allocations from the conference benevolences budget, the council and the Annual Conference Council on Ministries shall work together to establish and follow a procedure which shall preserve the following principles:

(1) It is the responsibility of the conference Council on Finance and Administration to establish the total amount to be recommended to the Annual Conference as the conference benevolences budget and, within that amount, the total sum to be recommended for distribution among the conference program agencies. It is likewise the responsibility of the council to study the budget requests for any agencies or causes to be included in the conference benevolences budget other than the conference program agencies, including the requests of the conference Council on Ministries, and to give the chairpersons or other authorized representatives of such agencies and causes opportunity to represent their claims before the council.

---

[30]*See* Judical Council Decision 400.

(2) It is the responsibility of the conference Council on Ministries to study the budget requests of the conference program agencies and to recommend to the conference Council on Finance and Administration amounts to be allocated from the conference benevolences budget to each such agency, within the total established by the conference Council on Finance and Administration.

(3) Before the conference benevolences budget recommendations are presented to the Annual Conference, the chairperson or other authorized representative of any conference program agency which requests it shall have the opportunity to represent the claims of that agency before the conference Council on Finance and Administration.

(4) It is the responsibility of the conference Council on Finance and Administration to present the conference benevolences budget recommendations to the Annual Conference. The recommended allocations to conference program agencies should reflect agreement between the council and the conference Council on Ministries.

c) The term **conference benevolences** shall include those conference allocations and expenditures directly associated with the program, mission, and benevolent causes of Annual Conference program agencies and institutions. **Annual Conference program agencies and institutions** shall be defined as those agencies with responsibilities parallel to those of the program-related general agencies (¶ 803) represented by voting membership on the conference Council on Ministries and institutions whose work is within the field of responsibility of one or more of those agencies. Administrative expenses which are directly related to the program, mission, and benevolent causes of conference program agencies, including the expenses of the conference Council on Ministries, may also be included in the conference benevolences budget. The term "conference benevolences" shall not include allocations and expenditures for other conference agencies and officers whose work is primarily administrative. It shall likewise not include Annual Conference ministerial support funds as set forth in ¶¶ 930-938, allocations and expenditures of conference agencies responsible for administering ministerial support funds, or apportionments made to the Annual Conference by the General or Jurisdictional Conferences.

d) The council, on receiving from the treasurer of the General Council on Finance and Administration a statement of the amount apportioned that Annual Conference for World Service, shall combine the total World Service apportionment, without reduction for the quadrennium, and the approved conference benevolences budget (¶ 710.3*a*). The sum of these two amounts shall be known as World Service and Conference Benevolences. The World Service and Conference Benevolences budget thus established shall include a statement of the percentage for World Service and the percentage for conference benevolences.[31] (*See also* ¶ 711.)

4. *Other Apportioned Causes.*—The council shall include in its budget recommendations all other amounts properly apportioned to the Annual Conference for the support of duly authorized general or other connectional funds. The budget recommendations shall likewise include any other amounts to be apportioned to the districts, charges, or churches by the Annual Conference for conference or district causes of any kind.

5. *Special Appeals.*—*a)* No Annual Conference agency or interest, including any related agency or institution such as a school, college, university, hospital, home, housing project, or other service institution, shall make a special conference-wide appeal to the local churches for funds without the approval of the Annual Conference upon recommendation of the council except in case of an extreme emergency when such approval may be given by a two-thirds vote of the district superintendents and of the council, acting jointly. Neither shall special conference-wide appeals to local churches for funds be made by such boards, interests, agencies, or institutions which are not related to the Annual Conference in which the appeal is to be made, unless approval for such an appeal is granted by the Annual Conference upon recommendation of the council. The Annual Conference approvals specified in this paragraph shall not be required for special churchwide financial appeals which have been approved under the provisions of ¶ 910.4, for solicitations which have been

---

[31]*See* Judicial Council Decision 348.

approved under the provisions of ¶ 911.3, or for any other general fund promotion or appeal authorized by the General Conference or approved and conducted under other provisions of the Book of Discipline.

b) When application is made to the council for the privilege of a special conference-wide financial appeal, whether by special collections, campaigns, or otherwise, the council shall investigate the application and its possible relation to other obligations of the conference, and in the light of the facts make recommendations to the conference for its action and determination. If application for privilege of a special appeal is made directly to the conference, the application shall be referred to the council before final action is taken.

c) The council may include in its budget recommendations to the Annual Conference amounts to be considered as goals for special appeals or other nonapportioned causes.

6. The council shall make its budget recommendations to the Annual Conference on a form prepared by the Committee on Official Forms and Records and approved by the General Council on Finance and Administration; when the budget has been approved by the Annual Conference, a copy shall be sent to the General Council on Finance and Administration.

¶ 711. *Apportionments.*—The council shall recommend to the Annual Conference for its action and determination the methods or formulas by which the approved budgeted amounts for ministerial support, administration, World Service and Conference Benevolences and other apportioned causes (¶¶ 711.1-.4) shall be apportioned to the districts, churches, or charges of the conference.

1. The council, on receiving from the General Council on Finance and Administration a statement of the amount apportioned to the Annual Conference for the several general funds authorized by the General Conference, shall apportion the same to the several districts, charges, or churches by whatever method the conference may direct, but without reduction.

2. The council shall recommend to the Annual Conference for its action and determination whether the apportionments referred to in this paragraph shall be made by the council to the districts only or to the churches or charges of the conference. If

the apportionments are made to the districts only, then the distribution to the churches or charges of each district shall be made as provided in ¶ 711.3. The conference may order that the entire distribution to all the churches or charges of the conference be made by the district superintendents.

3. Should the Annual Conference make the apportionments to the districts only, the distribution to the churches or charges of each district shall be made by its district Board of Stewards, composed of the district superintendent as chairperson and the district stewards elected by the several Charge Conferences (¶ 247). In that case the board, meeting on call of the district superintendent as soon as practicable after the adjournment of the Annual Conference, shall make the distribution to the churches or charges of the district, using such methods as it may determine, unless the Annual Conference shall have determined the method of distribution to the churches or charges.

4. The World Service and Conference Benevolences apportionment to the churches or charges of the conference, whether made by the conference directly, by the district Board of Stewards as provided in ¶ 711.3, or by the district superintendents, shall not be combined wih any other General, Jurisdictional, or Annual Conference apportionment made to the churches or charges of the conference.

¶ **712.** The council shall be responsible for designating a depository or depositories for conference funds.

¶ **713.** The council shall have the following authority and responsibility with respect to the auditing of the financial records of the conference and its agencies:

1. To have the accounts of the conference treasurer for the preceding fiscal year audited by a certified public accountant within 120 days after the close of the conference fiscal year, and to receive, review, and report such audit to the Annual Conference.[32]

2. To require and review at least annually audited reports, in such detail as it may direct, from all conference agencies and from all agencies, institutions, and organizations receiving any financial support from conference funds or from any authorized conference-wide appeal.

---

[32]*See* Judicial Council Decision 334.

¶ **714.** The council shall have the following authority and responsibility with respect to the bonding of conference and conference agency officers and staff whose responsibilities include the custody or handling of conference funds or other negotiable assets:

1. The council shall provide for the fidelity bonding of the conference treasurer and other staff under its authority and supervision in amounts it judges to be adequate.

2. In the case of those agencies, institutions, and organizations for which the conference treasurer does not serve as treasurer, the council shall have authority to require fidelity bonding of their treasurers in such amounts as it deems adequate and to withhold payment of the allocation of any such agency, institution, or organization until evidence of the required bonding has been submitted.

3. The council may provide, or require any conference agency to provide, directors' and officers' liability insurance in amounts it judges to be adequate.

4. The council shall require compliance with the policies established as provided by this paragraph and shall report annually to the Annual Conference on such compliance.

¶ **715.** *Conference Treasurer.*—1. Each Annual Conference, on nomination of its Council on Finance and Administration, shall at the first session of the conference after the quadrennial session of the General Conference, or at such other times as a vacancy exists, elect a **conference treasurer.**[33] The treasurer shall serve for the quadrennium or until a successor shall be elected and qualify. If a vacancy should occur during the quadrennium, the council shall fill the vacancy until the next session of the Annual Conference. After consultation with the bishop in charge, the council may remove the treasurer from office for cause and fill the vacancy until the next session of the conference. The treasurer shall be directly amenable to the council. The treasurer may sit with the council and its committees at all sessions and have the privilege of voice but not vote.

2. The conference treasurer shall receive and disburse, in accordance with the actions of the Annual Conference and the

---

[33]*See* Judicial Council Decision 185.

provisions of the Book of Discipline, remittances from local church treasurers for all duly authorized general, jurisdictional, Annual Conference, and district causes.[34]

a) Local church treasurers shall remit monthly to the conference treasurer all amounts contributed in each local church for (1) the World Service and Conference Benevolences fund; (2) all other funds authorized by the General Conference and apportioned to the Annual Conferences by the General Council on Finance and Administration; (3) all other jurisdictional, Annual Conference, and district funds or causes apportioned in accordance with ¶ 711, unless otherwise directed by the Annual Conference; (4) special Sunday offerings (¶ 271.1); (5) special appeals (¶¶ 710.5, 910.1); (6) Advance special gifts (¶ 913); (7) World Service special gifts (¶ 912); and (8) all other general, jurisdictional, Annual Conference, and district funds not otherwise directed.

b) The treasurer shall each month divide the total amount received from local churches for World Service and Conference Benevolences, setting aside the proper amount for World Service and the proper amount for conference benevolences, according to the ratio of each established by the Annual Conference in the total World Service and Conference Benevolences budget (¶ 710.3*c*). The treasurer shall, from the share received for conference benevolences, credit monthly the accounts of the several agencies or causes included in the conference benevolences budget or make monthly remittances to the treasurers of such agencies or causes according to the rightful share and proportion of each (¶ 710.3*a*) or according to a payment schedule approved by the conference Council on Finance and Administration which shall provide that the total allocated to each agency or cause during the year shall be equal to the rightful share and proportion of each. The treasurer shall remit each month to the treasurer of the General Council on Finance and Administration the total share received during the month for World Service. When the share so designated for World Service during a year exceeds the amount apportioned to the Annual Conference, the entire share contributed for World Service shall be remitted in

---

[34]*See* Judicial Council Decision 456.

regular order to the treasurer of the General Council on Finance and Administration before the end of the fiscal year.[35]

c) The treasurer shall, as far as practicable, remit monthly to the several district superintendents the amount due each of them (¶ 710.1*a*).

d) The treasurer shall likewise credit or remit each month all funds received and payable for other jurisdictional, Annual Conference, and district causes in accordance with budgets adopted by the Annual Conference.

e) The conference treasurer shall remit each month to the treasurer of the General Council on Finance and Administration the amounts received during the month for the General Administration Fund, the Episcopal Fund, the Interdenominational Cooperation Fund, the Black College Fund, the Temporary General Aid Fund, the Ministerial Education Fund, the Missional Priority Fund, World Service special gifts, Advance special gifts, general church special Sunday offerings (¶ 271.1) special churchwide appeals (¶ 910.4), and all other general causes not otherwise directed.

3. The conference treasurer may serve as treasurer for any or all agencies served by a conference central treasury (¶ 709.10). The treasurer shall enter the proper credits to each at the end of each month's business. Disbursements from funds allocated to any conference agency shall be made only on proper order from the agency.[36]

4. The treasurer shall prepare at regular intervals such financial statements and reports as may be required for the bishop in charge, the district superintendents, the Annual Conference, the council, the agencies served by the conference central treasury and its officers, and the treasurer of the General Council on Finance and Administration.

a) The treasurer shall make each month a full report of all general funds handled to the treasurer of the General Council on Finance and Administration and to the presiding bishop of the conference.

---

[35]*See* Judicial Council Decisions 306, 332, 400.
[36]*See* Judicial Council Decision 400.

b) The treasurer shall prepare annually a report of all receipts, disbursements, and balances of all funds under his or her direction, which report shall be printed in the conference journal. The reports shall be made on forms authorized by the General Council on Finance and Administration (¶ 906.12), so that all financial items going outside the local church shall be handled alike in all districts and conferences, and uniformity of financial reporting shall be established as a churchwide policy.

5. The treasurer may be authorized by the council to invest funds in accordance with policies and procedures established by the council (¶ 709.5). A listing of securities held shall be printed annually in the conference journal.

6. The treasurer shall provide counsel and guidance to local church business administrators, treasurers, financial secretaries, and Committees on Finance in the development of standardized financial recording and reporting systems (¶ 709.12).

7. The treasurer shall perform such other staff services as the council may require in the fulfillment of its functions and responsibilities.

¶ **716.** An Annual Conference may authorize its Council on Finance and Administration to assign to its conference treasurer the additional title and responsibilities of a **director of administrative services,** to have responsibility in one or more of the following areas: office management; payroll and personnel services; the provision of administrative services for Annual Conference officers and agencies; property management with respect to property owned by the Annual Conference or any of its agencies; and such other responsibilities of an administrative nature as the council, by mutual agreement with other Annual Conference officers and agencies, may assign. The council shall have authority and supervision over the director and shall, after consultation with those Annual Conference officers and agencies for whom the director might be expected to perform services, define his or her specific responsibilities.

ANNUAL CONFERENCE COUNCIL ON MINISTRIES

¶ **717.** In each Annual Conference of The United Methodist Church there shall be a **conference Council on Ministries;**

provided that such council or any component thereof may be organized on an area basis.

1. *Purpose.*—The purpose of the Annual Conference Council on Ministries shall be *(a)* to receive program recommendations from the local churches, the district agencies, the Annual Conference agencies, and the Jurisdictional and General Councils on Ministries; *(b)* to develop these recommendations into a coordinate program to be recommended to the Annual Conference for consideration, amendment, and adoption as the Annual Conference program; and *(c)* to provide implementation for and administration of the coordinated program as adopted by the conference.

2. *Membership.*—The membership of the Annual Conference Council on Ministries shall consist of the presiding bishop; the district superintendents; representatives of conference agencies as determined by the conference; the conference secretary; the area or conference superintendent or director of parish development; two representatives of the conference youth organization; two representatives of the conference United Methodist Women, one of whom shall be the president; two representatives of the conference United Methodist Men, one of whom shall be the president; two young adults; the conference lay leader; one lay person from each district; chairpersons of age-level and family departments; and such additional members as the Annual Conference may determine.

The following shall be members of the council without vote: salaried and volunteer Annual Conference staff, the conference treasurer, and one or more members of the Council on Finance and Administration.

The person or persons serving as members of the General Council on Ministries shall be member(s) of the Annual Conference Council on Ministries as full voting member(s).

3. *Officers.*—The officers of the council shall be a chairperson, a vice-chairperson, a secretary, and such other officers as the council shall determine. They shall be elected by the council.

4. *Executive Committee.*—There may be an **executive committee**, which also may serve as the Personnel Committee of the Conference Council on Ministries, consisting of the officers, the bishop, at least one district superintendent chosen by the Cabinet,

the director of the council, the elected representative of the General Council on Ministries, and other members as the council may determine. Approximately one half of the members of the executive committee shall be lay persons.

5. *Committees, Task Forces, and Consultations.*—The council may appoint a Committee on Communication, a Committee on Planning and Research, and a Committee on Leadership Development. It may appoint such other committees, task forces, and consultations as may be deemed essential to effective discharging of its responsibilities.

a) Committee on Communication.—In each Annual Conference Council on Ministries, chosen by it and amenable to it, there may be a **Committee on Communication.** It may assist the council in the performance of the responsibilities listed in ¶¶ 717.10*g-i, m, n* and may perform such other functions as are assigned to it by the council. A full-time conference or area staff person may be employed as **director of communications** to assist the committee in carrying out its functions. In the absence of a full-time staff person, responsibilities in communication shall be assigned as a part of the work of a member of the conference staff.

b) Committee on Planning and Research.—It should not be deemed necessary for all members of this committee to be members of the conference council. Due consideration should be given to the inclusion in the membership of the committee persons with expertise in planning and research. Its function shall be:

(1) To engage in planning and research on behalf of the council in the continuing ministry of The United Methodist Church within the conference.

(2) To serve as an advisory group in planning and research for the Annual Conference and its agencies.

(3) To serve as the clearinghouse for all planning and research projects under the sponsorship of the Annual Conference and its agencies.

(4) To relate to and cooperate with the planning and research projects of the General Council on Ministries.

c) Committee on Publishing House Liaison.—There may be organized in each Annual Conference a **Committee on Publishing House Liaison.** The committee shall consist of three members nominated and elected by the Annual Conference. The committee shall have lay and clergy members. Members of the General Board of Publication shall be members ex officio. The committee chairperson shall be a member of the conference Council on Ministries. The committee shall provide liaison contact with The United Methodist Publishing House to relate the work of the house to the work of the conference.

6. *Age-Level and Family Councils.*—The council may establish children, young adult, adult, and family ministry councils as it deems necessary to the performance of its duties. (*See* ¶ 732 concerning the establishment of a Council on Youth Ministry.)

7. *a) Director.*—The council shall elect, upon nomination by the Cabinet, in consultation with the Personnel Committee of the council or its equivalent, an executive officer to be known as the **conference council director.** The director shall be in a consultative relationship to the conference Cabinet on matters relating to coordination, implementation, and administration of the conference program, and other matters as the Cabinet and director may determine. The director shall not be present during the Cabinet discussions on matters related to the making of appointments.

b) Responsibilities.—The responsibilities of the conference council director shall be but are not limited to the following:

(1) To serve as the executive officer of the Annual Conference Council on Ministries.

(2) To be a communication link between the Annual Conference program agencies and the Jurisdictional (where they exist) and General Conference program agencies.

(3) To facilitate communication among the Annual Conference program agencies and the local churches.

(4) To serve as a resource person for district programs and the Annual Conference Council on Ministries agencies in their planning, implementation, and evaluation process.

(5) To supervise the Annual Conference Council on Ministries staff members.

(6) To serve on other Annual Conference agencies as determined by the Annual Conference, and/or by the conference Council on Ministries.

(7) To serve as a consultant to the conference Committee on Nominations.

8. *Staff.*—All Annual Conference council staff may be employed by, directed by, and amenable to the Annual Conference Council on Ministries. Insofar as possible, employees of the conference shall include women and minorities, lay and clergy, at every level. Ordained ministers on the staff are subject to being appointed by the presiding bishop.

9. *Relationships.*—The council shall have the following relationships, including the amenabilities indicated:

a) All Annual Conference program agencies shall cooperate with and be amenable, between sessions of the Annual Conference, to the Council on Ministries of the Annual Conference in matters relating to the development, implementation, and administration of the program.[37]

b) All Annual Conference agencies shall submit the elements of program which are to be promoted in, supported by, or implemented by the local churches of the conference to the council for consideration, coordinating, and calendaring prior to presentation to the local churches. The council may request district or Annual Conference agencies to implement a program for the entire conference.

c) The council staff shall be responsible, in cooperation with the district superintendents, for the implementation of the conference program.

d) The council may develop and carry out a program of conference Advance special giving, as prescribed in ¶ 1007.5.

10. *Responsibilities.*—The responsibilities of the Annual Conference Council on Ministries are:

a) To study the mission of the Annual Conference and the local churches of the conference and to determine program emphases which will assist the conference and the local churches to perform their mission.

b) To describe, coordinate, and organize opportunities to serve within the mission.

c) To receive program recommendations from the local churches, the district and Annual Conference agencies, and the

---

[37]*See* Judicial Council Decision 400.

Jurisdictional and General Councils on Ministries; to evaluate these recommendations; and to formulate a coordinated conference program to be presented to the Annual Conference for consideration.

d) To provide for implementation and administration of the program adopted by the conference.

e) To provide program resources and assistance in program planning and implementation for local churches.

f) To provide staff personnel for implementing and administering the conference program.

g) To promote principles of good communication within the conference; to provide two-way channels of communications among Annual Conference agencies, district Councils on Ministries, and local churches; to lead the conference in making creative use of communications and opportunities offered by modern mass media, including conference and general church periodicals and resources; and to offer counsel in public relations and conduct public relations activities for the conference.

h) To provide communications training opportunities for leaders in the Annual Conferences and the local churches.

i) To interpret the programs of the general Church and the Annual Conference to the local churches and to promote all general and conference benevolent causes in cooperation with the Standing General Commission on Communication.

j) To give leadership in research and planning for the conference and to cooperate with other research and planning agencies.

k) To cooperate in ecumenical projects and events which have been approved by the conference.

l) To study and coordinate the budget askings of the conference agencies as they relate to the conference program and to make recommendations regarding the same to the conference Council on Finance and Administration.

m) To interpret the conference program to the local churches with a view toward gaining the financial support needed in order to implement that program.

n) To provide for relationships with the media within the conference, including newspapers, radio and television; take initiative in television programming at the conference level and give counsel to districts and local churches concerning television, utilizing the resources of the General Commission on Communication; provide for the use of videotape or videodisc within the conference; perform public relations functions for the conference and assist in the public relations of agencies and institutions of the conference.

o) To provide guidance and training for district leaders and groups to support their various tasks with local churches and in their district and/or Annual Conference responsibilities.

p) To inform the general program agencies of the names of those Annual Conference agencies that provide for program responsibilities related to the objectives and scope of the general program agencies.

¶ **718.** 1. There may be a **conference Advance program,** established and carried out in the same spirit of partnership as the general Advance program.

2. A conference Advance special gift is one made to a conference Advance special project within bounds of the Annual Conference or episcopal area authorized by an Annual Conference upon recommendation by the conference Board of Global Ministries or its equivalent structure and consistent with the goals of the Advance. The funds as received shall be administered by the conference Board of Global Ministries or such structure as designated by the conference.

3. An Annual Conference may undertake a conference-wide campaign for a lump sum to be applied to its missionary and church extension. The funds so received shall be designated as conference Advance specials and shall be administered by the conference Board of Global Ministries or equivalent structure. Local churches shall report their contributions as conference Advance specials.

4. With the approval of the Annual Conference, a district within the conference may authorize and promote Advance specials for church extension and missionary needs within the district, such funds to be administered by a district missionary society organized for that purpose or by a similar body set up by the district. Such special funds secured and administered on a district level shall be reported by each local church to the Annual Conference as conference Advance specials.

5. Local churches shall report their contributions to general Advance specials and conference Advance specials to the charge conference and in the manner indicated on the Annual Conference report form.

OTHER CONFERENCE AGENCIES

¶ 719. 1. The Annual Conference shall provide for the connectional relationship between the General Board of Church and Society and the conference, district, and local church, and shall provide for church and society functions related to the objectives and scope of work of the General Board of Church and Society, as set forth in ¶¶ 1205-1206.

2. The Annual Conference shall determine the necessity for a **conference Board of Church and Society** to include as an ex officio member the mission coordinator for Christian social involvement of the conference United Methodist Women. Should the conference determine not to create such a board, it shall be the responsibility of the Annual Conference Council on Ministries to provide for the connectional relationship between the general board and conference, district, and local church organizations.

3. The conference board, in cooperation with the general board and the Annual Conference Council on Ministries, shall develop and promote programs on Christian social concerns within the bounds of the conference. To this end it may divide its membership into three committees of approximately equal size, patterned after the divisions of the general board. They shall have responsibility to cooperate with one another to advance the concerns of their respective divisions.

4. The board shall estimate annually the amount necessary for support of its work and shall report this amount according to the procedure of the Annual Conference. The work of the board may be considered a benevolence interest of the Church within the conference.

5. The Annual Conference may employ a person or persons to further its purposes. Two or more Annual Conferences may cooperate in developing their programs and in employing one or more persons.

¶ **720.** *Conference Board of Discipleship.*—The Annual Conference shall provide for the connectional relationship between the General Board of Discipleship and the conference, district, and local church, and shall provide for discipleship functions related to the objectives and scope of work of the General Board of Discipleship, as set forth in ¶¶ 1301 ff.

1. *General Responsibilities.*—*a)* To lead and assist the congregations and districts in the conference in their efforts to win persons as disciples of Jesus Christ, to build up the Christian community, and to celebrate and communicate the redeeming and reconciling love of God as revealed in Jesus Christ to persons of every age, ethnic background, and social condition.

b) To foster and promote such ministries as Christian education, camping and outdoor activities, evangelism, stewardship, worship, lay development, devotional life, age-level and family life ministries, leadership education, United Methodist Men, and such other areas of work as the Annual Conference may determine.

c) To provide guidance and training for related district leaders and agencies and for local church administrative boards, officers, and committees, Councils on Ministries, age-level and family councils, work area chairpersons of evangelism, stewardship, worship, and education, and work area commissions and task groups.

d) To develop a unified and comprehensive program for leadership training to serve all age groups in the home, Church, and community.

e) To provide continued training for pastors in effective ministry with children, child and faith development of children, and interpretation of curriculum resources.

f) To enable and strengthen the ministry with and to youth at all levels of the Church.

g) To determine the necessary directors, coordinators, or designated leaders for discipleship responsibilities at the Annual Conference level, including the maintenance of linkage with the General Board of Discipleship and related district committees within the Annual Conference.

2. *Responsibilities in the Area of Education.*—*a)* To develop and promote a conference program of Christian education that gives

children, youth, young adults, and adults a knowledge of and experience in the Christian faith as motivation for Christian service in the Church, the community, and the world. This may include guidance and training for district leaders responsible for Christian education and for local church chairpersons of the work area and commissions on education, superintendents of the church school, church school division superintendents, church school teachers, and other leaders in the educational ministry of local churches.

b) To develop and maintain an organized system for communicating and working with persons responsible for Christian education programs in local churches, districts, jurisdictions, and the General Board of Discipleship.

c) To encourage the observance of the first Sunday of Christian Education Week, or some other day designated by the Annual Conference, in each local church as Christian Education Sunday for the purpose of emphasizing the importance of Christian education and for receiving an offering for the work of Christian education. (*See* ¶ 271.3*e*.)

d) To develop and recommend to the Annual Conference plans for the acquisition of or disposition of conference camps and/or retreat properties in accordance with standards of camping developed by the General Board of Discipleship (¶ 1309.5).

e) To promote church school extension, the program of Christian education, and the use of church school resources approved by the General Board of Discipleship.

f) To assist local congregations in initiating programs of teacher recruitment, development, training, and retraining in biblical, theological, and ethical thinking, as well as in the procedures and methods of Christian education.

g) To cooperate in the promotion of knowledge about the support for all schools, colleges, universities, and seminaries related to the conference, the campus Christian movement, and the campus ministry of the conference, region, or area through the establishment and support of such programs as may be approved by the Annual Conference in harmony with the policies and procedures of the General Board of Higher Education and Ministry.

3. *Responsibilities in the Area of Evangelism.—a)* To plan and promote an effective program of comprehensive evangelism throughout the conference.

b) To create an understanding of, interest in, and commitment to evangelism throughout the conference.

c) To provide for the training of ministers and lay persons in evangelism, the distribution of promotional literature, and the encouragement and enlistment of local church participation in a year-round program of evangelism.

d) To give guidance to the groups responsible for the work of evangelism in the districts and to the work area chairperson of evangelism in the local church.

e) To give particular emphasis to the promotion of programs of evangelism in order that all persons living in a community where there is a local United Methodist church, and who are without a church affiliation or who make no profession of faith, will be included within the nurturing and caring responsibility of that local church.

f) To recommend annually, in consultation with the Board of Ordained Ministry, to the conference and to the bishop in charge the appointment of certain effective members of the conference as conference-approved evangelists, provided that such persons shall meet the standards set for approved evangelists by the General Board of Discipleship, the conference Board of Discipleship, or its equivalent, and the conference Board of Ordained Ministry.

4. *Responsibilities in the Area of Worship.—a)* To be responsible for the concerns of worship within the Annual Conference.

b) To foster the use of the best resources for worship at conference meetings and in all the churches of the conference, promote the use of the Book of Worship and the hymnal in all the churches of the conference, foster creative and regular individual and family worship throughout the conference, plan and promote seminars and demonstrations on forms of worship and the use of music and other arts.

c) To provide exhibits at the conference sessions, cooperate with the Fellowship of United Methodists in Worship, Music, and Other Arts, the General Board of Discipleship, and the conference Council on Ministries in promoting seminars and training events in the area of worship, including music and other arts.

5. *Responsibilities in the Area of Stewardship.*—*a)* To plan and promote an effective program of stewardship throughout the conference.

b) To interpret the biblical and theological basis for stewardship.

c) To promote giving consistent with a Christian life style.

d) To develop funding concepts within Annual Conference, district, and local church consistent with sound stewardship principles and the doctrine of The United Methodist Church.

e) To design and schedule training events, to distribute promotional material, and to enlist local church participation in a year-round program of stewardship.

f) To give guidance to the work area of stewardship in the districts and to the work area chairperson of stewardship and the Committee on Finance in the local church.

g) To develop a program that will create concern on the part of every local church for the ecological and environmental problems that confront the world and to motivate them to accept responsibility for aiding in the solution of such problems.

6. *Responsibilities in the Area of Devotional Life.*—*a)* To promote the development of the devotional life throughout the conference.

b) To conduct seminars and training events in the areas of private and corporate prayer.

c) To encourage and assist with the distribution and use of devotional resources as provided by The Upper Room and the General Board of Discipleship.

7. *Responsibilities in the Area of Lay Life and Work.*—*a)* To develop and promote programs to cultivate an adequate understanding of the theological and biblical basis for lay life and work among the members of the churches of the Annual Conference; to give special emphasis to programs and services which will enable laity to serve more effectively as leaders in both Church and community.

b) To provide support and direction for such lay programs as United Methodist Men, lay speaking, the observance of Laity Day, and the work of lay leaders on the local and district levels.

c) To provide support, training, and guidance for district coordinators, leaders, and groups for age-level and family ministries and for local church coordinators of age-level and family ministries.

d) To give support and direction to the conference and district program for local church officer development, coordinating and developing training experiences that will enable persons to serve more effectively as members of local church Councils on Ministries, Administrative Boards, and of the committees, commissions, and task forces related to these groups.

8. There may be in every Annual Conference a **conference Board of the Laity,** auxiliary to the General Board of Discipleship. It shall cooperate with the Annual Conference Council of Ministries.

a) The purpose of the conference Board of the Laity shall be:

(1) To foster an awareness of the role of the laity in achieving the mission of the church and to enable and support lay participation in the planning and decision-making processes of the Annual Conference, district, and local church in cooperation with the bishop, district superintendents, and pastors.

(2) To develop and promote stewardship of time, talent, and possessions within the Annual Conference in cooperation with the conference Council on Ministries.

b) The following membership of the board is recommended: the conference lay leader, the presidents and two representatives elected by each of the conference organizations of United Methodist Men, United Methodist Women, United Methodist Young Adults, and the conference Council on Youth Ministries, and in addition, the district lay leaders, two men, two women, and two youth elected by the Annual Conference upon nomination of the conference Nominating Committee, a district superintendent designated by the Cabinet, the director of the conference Council on Ministries, and the presiding bishop.

c) The officers of the board may be a president, who may be the conference lay leader, a vice-president, and such other officers as the board shall deem necessary.

d) The board shall relate to the organized lay groups in the conference such as United Methodist Men, United Methodist

Women, United Methodist Young Adults, and United Methodist Youth, and shall support their work and help them coordinate the activities of the organized laity of the conference.

¶ **721.** 1. The Annual Conference shall organize a Board of Global Ministries or an equivalent structure which shall provide for global ministries responsibilities related to the objectives and scope of work of the General Board of Global Ministries as set forth in ¶ 1502.

2. The **conference Board of Global Ministries** or equivalent structure shall be composed of those persons as determined by the Annual Conference and shall fulfill those responsibilities as assigned.

3. The conference Board of Global Ministries shall name the necessary liaison persons to work with various divisions of the General Board of Global Ministries.

4. The Annual Conference and the General Board of Global Ministries shall cooperate in carrying out the policies and promoting all phases of the work as related to the scope of the board as set forth in ¶ 1502.

a) Responsibilities.—(1) To designate the necessary committees, sections, or commissions and individual secretaries, coordinators, or other leaders for global ministries responsibilities at the Annual Conference level.

(2) To interpret to the Annual Conference the programs, plans, and policies of the General Board of Global Ministries and to plan and promote emphases on global ministries.

(3) To undergird with education, communication, and cultivation the total program of the General Board of Global Ministries.

(4) To plan and promote various kinds of meetings and experiences throughout the conference for the purpose of developing a spirit of mission and participation in global ministries for training, education, and leadership development of mission leaders and persons in the field of human services, health and welfare ministries.

(5) To cooperate with the General Board of Global Ministries in its program outside the United States.

(6) To identify with all who are alienated and dispossessed and to assist them in achieving their full human development—

body, mind, and spirit, including encouraging and implementing affirmative action programs.

(7) To engage in direct ministries to human need, both emergency and continuing institutional and noninstitutional, however caused.

(8) To cooperate with the conference organization of United Methodist Women and help equip all women for full participation in the mission of the Church.

(9) To cultivate, through the channels of the Church other than United Methodist Women, the Advance special gifts for national and overseas ministries administered by the National, World, and United Methodist Committee on Relief Divisions.

(10) To encourage, maintain, and strengthen the relationships between the Annual Conference and agencies related to the appropriate divisions of the General Board of Global Ministries and provide a channel through which these agencies shall report to the Annual Conference.

(11) To develop and implement church financial support of conference mission projects and programs, health and welfare ministries, with particular emphasis on benevolent care and Golden Cross, education and social service ministries, and Crusade Scholarships.

(12) To enable, encourage, and support the development of congregations, cooperative parishes, community centers, education and human services, and health and welfare ministries so that they may be units of mission in urban and rural areas, and partners with others in the worldwide mission of the Christian church.

(13) To encourage, and support specialized urban and town and country ministries enabling comprehensive mission related to broad metropolitan and rural issues, services ministering to the needs of persons, and supportive programs strengthening the local church.

(14) To assist districts and local churches in exploring and developing new methods and direct service ministries as changing conditions and societal forms demand.

(15) To cooperate with Church and secular leaders at all levels in strategic planning, developing programs, and advocating legislation which impacts community and national issues.

(16) To envision and engage in imaginative new forms of mission appropriate to changing needs and to share the results of experimentation.

(17) To develop strategies in response to critical community issues, with special attention to the needs of ethnic and language minorities, persons with handicapping conditions, people in transitional relationships, and those living under repressive systems.

(18) To support United Methodist Committee on Relief's refugee resettlement ministry by encouraging an Annual Conference Refugee Resettlement Committee capable of encouraging, advising, and assisting churches sponsoring the resettlement of refugees.

(19) To assist the program of Church and Community Ministry in setting goals, developing programs, providing funding, and evaluating the ministries.

(20) To cooperate with the General Board of Global Ministries in the recruitment of missionary personnel, and to cooperate with the appropriate conference units in the promotion and recruitment of persons for health and welfare service careers and other church-related occupations.

(21) To relate to Goodwill Industries.

(22) To review and certify applications to the General Board of Global Ministries for loans, donations, and grants; to administer such funds for their designated purposes in accordance with the established guidelines, and to participate with the General Board of Global Ministries in planning and evaluation processes related to these funds.

(23) To cultivate gifts for those special Sunday offerings which are administered through the General Board of Global Ministries.

(24) To work with the health and welfare agencies related to the Annual Conference to improve the quality and extent of services rendered.

(25) To review and make recommendations to the Annual Conference with regard to the establishment of new agencies and the expansion or change in existing agencies. Sponsors of any new hospital, home for the aging, child care service, housing project, or other health and welfare ministry which uses the

United Methodist name or property, or looks to any unit of the church for financial support shall first submit drafts of its charter, constitution, and bylaws; demonstration of need; and its plan of development, financing, and service to the Annual Conference unit responsible for health and welfare ministries or other appropriate church unit. This includes any new ecumenical ventures or an existing facility or service desiring to alter its major purpose or function, add a new facility, or make a major expansion on its present facilities. The Annual Conference unit may request the Health and Welfare Ministries Division of the General Board of Global Ministries to assist in reviewing these plans. The plan of development, financing, and service shall then be submitted to the Annual Conference to which it is related for approval before finalizing and proceeding with the project. If a specific project must proceed before the Annual Conference is to meet, the institution may receive approval for the Annual Conference unit responsible for health and welfare ministries or other designated unit, provided that the Annual Conference has delegated such authority to that unit.

(26) To provide for appropriate mutual representation between the Annual Conference unit responsible for health and welfare ministries and each health and welfare agency and institution related to the Annual Conference.

(27) To participate in, support, and implement the Certification Council program in relationship to health and welfare agencies within the boundaries of the Annual Conference.

(28) To assist the Annual Conference in development of health and welfare services to meet local needs.

(29) To work with the National Association of Health and Welfare Ministries of The United Methodist Church in leadership development programs and the promotion of United Methodist related health and welfare ministries.

(30) To help lift Christian, financial, and professional standards in all United Methodist–related health and welfare ministries in the Annual Conference.

(31) To aid in planning and developing a religious ministry in United Methodist–related hospitals and homes, and wherever practical, in state and non–United Methodist–related hospitals and homes where there is a need.

(32) To serve in an advisory capacity to the nominating processes of the Annual Conference in the selection of trustees for health and welfare agencies related to the Annual Conference.

(33) To provide the channel through which health and welfare agencies report to the Annual Conference.

(34) To promote an annual Golden Cross offering or other means of giving to be received in every local church on a day or days designated by the Annual Conference in support of the health and welfare ministries within the Annual Conference, and to provide financial support to care for the sick, older persons, children and youth, and persons with handicapping conditions; with special emphasis given to aiding those ministries which provide direct financial assistance to persons unable to pay.

5. The Annual Conference shall either establish a **Committee on Parish and Community Development** or assign this responsibility to an existing agency in the Annual Conference that will fulfill these responsibilities as related to the objectives and scope of the National Division, Board of Global Ministries (¶ 1529). The committee shall initiate and develop programs with: Agencies related to the National Division, Church and Community Ministry, Congregational Development, Town and Country Ministries, Urban Ministries, and other concerns as desired. The committee may form subcommittees for these areas. The committee shall be accountable to the conference Board of Global Ministries, or to such other agencies as the conference may determine. The chairperson of the committee and the chairperson of the subcommittees shall be members of the conference Board of Global Ministries or such body to which the committee shall be amenable.

a) The committee shall include persons involved in significant types of parish and community ministries, the area or conference superintendent or director of parish development, representatives of related church agencies and groups, and at-large community representatives.

b) The general responsibilities of the committee shall include research, evaluation, planning and strategy development, policy formulation, program implementation, local and national liaison related to parish and community development, and such other functions as the conference or agency to which the committee is accountable may determine.

c) Responsibilities of the subcommittee on agencies related to National Division may include developing a relationship to all such agencies within the Annual Conference; consulting with them in cooperative planning and strategy for the implementation of national mission concerns relative to needs in the area of social welfare as implemented through the ministries of community centers, residences, health care agencies, schools and other educational agencies; and working with funding sources to provide the support needed for effective service in such agencies.

d) In Annual Conferences where church and community workers are assigned through the National Division of the General Board of Global Ministries, responsibilities of the subcommittee on Church and Community Ministry shall include reviewing and evaluating projects; serving as liaison between projects and the National Division; and securing consultative and financial support for workers.

e) Responsibilities of the subcommittee on Congregational Development shall include encouraging and supporting the development of new and established congregations; conducting research studies and community surveys that plan for and assist with developing innovative strategies for mission; and reviewing, evaluating, and making recommendations for loans, donations, and grants from the National Division.

f) Responsibilities of the subcommittee on Town and Country Ministries shall include mission development and ministry in rural and town areas with under 50,000 population fulfilling the functions outlined in ¶ 721.5*h*.

g) Responsibilities of the subcommittee on Urban Ministries shall include mission development and ministry for metropolitan communities with over 50,000 population, fulfilling the functions outlined in ¶ 721.5*h*.

h) Responsibilities of the subcommittees on Town and Country Ministries and Urban Ministries shall include the following: consulting with the bishop, Cabinet, area or conference superintendent/director of parish development and the boards and agencies of the conference in the development of policies for Cooperative Parish Ministries, securing of funding for staff, and in initiating and strengthening these ministries; developing of a comprehensive related missional strategy for the mission of the Annual Conference, the districts, and the local churches, and, report this plan to the Annual Conference for consideration, with the understanding that the plan may relate to a regional mission organization for purposes of larger geographical coordination; initiating and/or assisting with programs to deal with needs such as: local church/community outreach organization and development; ministries with specialized constituencies and sectors of community life, agricultural and industrial production and other issue oriented ministries; the development and strengthening of regional and/or national networks and/or association; ethnic and language minorities; churches in transitional communities; small membership churches; the impact of oppressive systems on town and country and urban people and their communities; and to fulfill other functions as related to the objectives and scope of work of the National Division, Board of Global Ministries as set forth in ¶ 1529.

6. There may be in each Annual Conference a Committee on Deaconess and Home Missionary Service.

a) The membership of the committee shall be elected by the Annual Conference upon nomination by its nominating committee and in consultation with the conference Board of Global Ministries. If possible, at least one fourth of its members shall be deaconesses and home missionaries.

b) The responsibilities of the committee shall be:

(1) to interpret the work of deaconesses and home missionaries in and to the Annual Conference;

(2) to assist local churches and other agencies of the Annual Conference in mission education and in recruitment of persons for service in mission;

(3) to facilitate the involvement of deaconesses and home missionaries in the work of the Annual Conference;

(4) to cooperate with the Annual Conference Board of Diaconal Ministry in relation to persons who are both diaconal ministers and deaconesses or home missionaries;

(5) to provide for suitable recognition of retiring deaconesses and home missionaries at the Annual Conference sessions;

(6) to maintain continuing relationships with retired deaconesses and home missionaries living within the bounds of the Annual Conference;

(7) to keep a record of all persons in the Annual Conference who have been commissioned to the office of deaconess or the office of home missionary;

(8) to report annually to the Annual Conference for publication in the conference journal a roster of all persons within the bounds of the Annual Conference who are commissioned as deaconesses and home missionaries and of their appointments.

¶ **722.** 1. The Annual Conference shall provide for the connectional relationship between the General Board of Higher Education and Ministry and the conference, district, and local church and shall provide for higher education and ministry functions related to the objectives and scope of work of the General Board of Higher Education and Ministry as set forth in ¶ 1603.

2. There shall be a **conference Board of Higher Education and Campus Ministry.** The number of members shall be determined by the Annual Conference.

3. There may be an area or Annual Conference **coordinator of higher education and campus ministry** who shall be an ex officio member with vote of the conference Council on Ministries.

4. The Annual Conference chairperson of higher education and campus ministry shall be a member of the Annual Conference Council on Ministries.

5. The specific responsibilities of an Annual Conference Board of Higher Education and Campus Ministry include:

a) General Responsibilities.—(1) To provide the connectional relationship between the Division of Higher Education of the General Board of Higher Education and Ministry and conference, district, and local church organizations.

(2) To provide counsel, guidance, and assistance to institutions in their relationships with the state.

(3) To interact with public education as it reflects on the wholeness of persons and the meaning of life.

(4) To guard property and endowments entrusted to the institutions and to maintain and enforce trust and reversionary

clauses in accordance with the provisions of the Division of Higher Education under ¶ 1615.3c.

b) Planning/Fiscal Responsibilities.—(1) To evaluate higher education and professional campus ministries with concern for the quality of their performance and the integrity of their mission.

(2) To present to the Council on Ministries and then to the Council on Finance and Administration of the Annual Conference the financial needs for adequate support of the schools, colleges, universities, seminaries, campus Christian movements, Wesley Foundations,[38] and other campus ministries related to the conference for allocation of apportionments to the churches within the conference.

(3) To determine the distribution of the funds received from undesignated gifts, returns from special days, and receipts from missionary offerings in the church school.

(4) To work with the Annual Conference Council on Ministries to promote special days and funds: Black College Fund; Hispanic, Asian, Native Americans Fund; Ministerial Education Fund, United Methodist Student Day; Ministry Sunday; World Communion Sunday; Human Relations Day; and other funds and special days ordered by the General Conference.

(5) To maintain adequate fiduciary and legal relationships with institutions and campus ministries and to assist Annual Conferences and other judicatories in their responsibilities in these matters.

(6) To confer at once in the event of any institutional change of status with appropriate representatives of the General Board of Higher Education and Ministry to determine what resources and aid the board may be able to provide and to permit the Division of Higher Education to carry out its responsibilities under ¶ 1615.3. This is only in the event any educational institution, Wesley Foundation, or other campus ministry moves to sever or modify its connection with the Church or violate the rules adopted by the division in accordance with ¶ 1615.3.

(7) To hold the Wesley Foundation Board of Directors responsible for the direction and administration of the founda-

---

[38]*See* Judicial Council Decision 191.

tion in accordance with the policies and standards established by the conference committee or committees and the General Board of Higher Education and Ministry.[39] The foundation shall be related functionally and cooperatively through its Board of Directors to the United Methodist local church or churches in the immediate vicinity of the college or university. If or when incorporated, the Board of Directors may hold property according to the laws of The United Methodist Church and the state in which the foundation is located. Members of the Wesley Foundation Board of Directors shall be elected by the Annual Conference or Conferences on nomination of the conference Board of Higher Education and Campus Ministry.

(8) To provide that two or more Annual Conferences may, on recommendation of their Board of Higher Education and Campus Ministry, join in constituting an area or regional Committee or Commission on Higher Education and Campus Ministry, the membership, scope, and functions of which shall be determined by the cooperating conferences, in consultation with their bishop or bishops, and shall include representatives of the conference Board of Higher Education and Campus Ministry, with appropriate representation of ethnic minorities.

¶ 723. 1. Each Annual Conference at the first session following the General Conference shall elect for a term of four years a **Board of Ordained Ministry** consisting of not fewer than six ministers in full connection, and where possible at least one shall be a woman. The board membership should seek to reflect the racial and ethnic character of the conference. Where there is a Board of Higher Education and Ministry, there shall be a Division of Ordained Ministry.[40]

a) This board shall be directly responsible to the Annual Conference, notwithstanding its organizational relationship within any other program or administrative unit of the Annual Conference. At least two thirds of the members shall be graduates of seminaries listed by the University Senate. Members shall be nominated by the presiding bishop, after consultation with the chairperson of the board, the executive committee, or a

---

[39]*See* Judicial Council Decision 175.
[40]*See* Judicial Council Decision 415.

committee elected by the board of the previous quadrennium, and with the Cabinet.

b) It is recommended that each district be represented by a member of the board. The board may invite at least one member of the Cabinet to serve as a member of the board, if the Cabinet is not already represented in its membership. Vacancies shall be filled by the bishop after consultation with the chairperson or a committee of the board.

c) The board shall organize by electing from its membership a chairperson, a registrar, and such other officers as it may deem necessary. The board shall designate its executive committee.

d) The board shall meet at least once prior to its meeting at the time of the Annual Conference session and may set a deadline prior to Annual Conference for transacting its business.

e) The board shall select from its own membership an official representative to serve on each district Committee on Ordained Ministry, preferably from within said district.

2. The duties of the Annual Conference Board of Ordained Ministry shall be:

a) To study and interpret ministerial needs and resources of the Annual Conference, with due regard to the inclusive Church, in consultation with the Cabinet and the Division of Ordained Ministry. It shall, with the assistance of the local church Committee on Pastor-Parish Relations, conference agencies, and every minister of the conference, enlist women and men of all races and ethnic origins for the ministry and guide those persons in the process of education, training, and ordination, recommending colleges and schools of theology listed by the University Senate.

b) To receive annual reports on the progress made by each ministerial student enrolled in a theological school and to record credit for work satisfactorily completed.

c) To guide the ministerial candidate who is not enrolled in a theological school and who is pursuing the course of study as adopted by the Division of Ordained Ministry.

d) To examine all applicants as to their fitness for the ministry and make full inquiry as to the fitness of the candidate for: (1) annual election as local pastor; (2) election to associate membership; (3) election to probationary membership; (4) election to full conference membership.

e) To provide all candidates for ministry a written statement on the Disciplinary and Annual Conference requirements for the local pastor, associate, probationary, and full membership.

f) To interview and report recommendation concerning: (1) students, not yet elders in full connection, to be appointed to attend school and assigned to a Charge Conference; (2) candidates for ordination as deacons; (3) candidates for ordination as elders.[41]

g) To interview applicants and make recommendation concerning: (1) changes from the effective relation to a leave of absence or retirement; (2) return to the effective relation from other relations; (3) honorable location; (4) readmission of located persons and persons discontinued from probationary membership; (5) sabbatical leave; (6) disability leave; (7) appointment as a student; (8) termination; (9) changes to or from less than full-time ministry.

The board shall keep a record of these changes and the reason behind them.

h) To ensure confidentiality in relation to the interview and reporting process. The personal data and private information provided through the examinations of and by the Board of Ordained Ministry will not be available for distribution and publication. There are occasions when the Board of Ordained Ministry would not report privileged information, which in the judgment of the board, if revealed in the executive session would be an undue invasion of privacy without adding measurably to the conference's information about the person's qualifications for ministry.[42]

i) To be in consultation with the bishop, through the chairperson or the executive committee, at the bishop's initiative prior to making any transfer into the Annual Conference.

j) To provide support services for the ordained minister's career development, including personal and career counseling, continuing education, assistance in preparation for retirement,

---

[41]*See* Judicial Council Decision 405.
[42]*See* Judicial Council Decision 406.

and all matters pertaining to ministerial morale. In providing such support, the board in cooperation with the Cabinet shall give training and guidance to each local Pastor-Parish Relations Committee regarding its work and role.

k) To provide a means of evaluation and to study matters pertaining to the character and effectiveness of ministers in the Annual Conference (¶ 704.5). The board shall also interpret the high ethical standards of the ministry set forth in the Discipline.

l) To recommend to the full members of the Annual Conference for validation special ministries for which members seek appointment. The appointment to such ministries is the prerogative of the bishop and the Cabinet.

m) To administer the portion of the Ministerial Education Fund for use by the Annual Conference in its programs of enlistment, basic professional educational aid, continuing education, and professional growth of ordained ministers.

n) To cooperate with the Division of Ordained Ministry and assist in: (1) the interpretation of current legislation concerning ordained ministry; (2) the interpretation and promotion of the Ministerial Education Fund; (3) the promotion and observance of Ministry Sunday; (4) the supplying of a record of all information, recommendations, and action on each ministerial candidate after each session of the Annual Conference.

o) To promote in the Annual Conference and/or Jurisdictional Conference a system of financial aid to ministerial students. A conference transferring a person with less than three years of active service into another conference may require reimbursement either from the person or from the receiving conference for outstanding obligations for theological education financed through conference funds.

p) To work in cooperation with the Board of Diaconal Ministry, meeting together at least annually, to enhance the total ministry of the Church, recognizing that both diaconal ministry and ordained ministry are components of the professional ministry of the Church.

3. The board shall name a **registrar**.

a) The registrar shall keep full personnel records for all ministerial candidates, under the care of the board, including essential biographical data, transcripts of academic credit, instruments of evaluation, and, where it applies, psychological and medical test records, sermons, theological statements, and other pertinent data.

b) Pertinent information and recommendations concerning each candidate shall be certified to the Annual Conference in duplicate; one copy of this record shall be kept by the registrar and one copy shall be mailed after each conference session to the Division of Ordained Ministry.

c) The registrar shall keep a record of the standing of the students in the course of study and report to the conference when required. This record shall include the credits allowed students for work done in accredited schools of theology, in approved course of study schools or the course of study correspondence.

d) The registrar shall file in the bishop's office for permanent record a copy of circumstances involving the discontinuance of probationary membership or termination of the local pastor status.

e) All files owned by the Board of Ordained Ministry shall be maintained under the guidelines provided by the Division of Ordained Ministry.

¶ **724.** 1. Each Annual Conference at the first session following General Conference shall elect for a term of four years a **Board of Diaconal Ministry,** consisting of not fewer than nine persons, of whom at least one third shall be in diaconal ministry careers, preferably diaconal ministers. (*See* ¶¶ 301-315.)

a) The board shall be directly responsible to the Annual Conference, notwithstanding its organizational relationship with any other program or administrative unit of the Annual Conference.

b) The board shall be nominated by the presiding bishop after consultation with the chairperson of the board of the previous quadrennium or with a committee of the board, and with the Cabinet.

c) The board shall organize by electing from its membership a chairperson, a secretary, a registrar, other officers as may be necessary, and may name committees as needed.

d) Where there is a Board of Higher Education and Ministry the Board of Diaconal Ministry may function as the Division of Diaconal Ministry.

2. The board shall work in cooperation with the conference Board of Ordained Ministry, or, if necessary, the executive committee, meeting together, at least annually to enhance the total ministry of the Church, recognizing that both diaconal ministry and ordained ministry are components of the representative ministry of the Church.

3. The duties of the conference Board of Diaconal Ministry for the office of diaconal minister shall be:

a) To study diaconal ministry needs and resources of the Annual Conference with due regard to the inclusive Church.

b) To interpret diaconal ministry in the Annual Conference.

c) To enlist women and men of all races and ethnic origins for diaconal ministry, in cooperation with conference agencies, district superintendents, and all ministers of the conference.

d) To guide persons in the process of education, training, and consecration for diaconal ministry, recommending colleges, universities, and schools of theology listed by the University Senate.

e) To provide counsel and resources to the local church for its examination and recommendation of persons for candidacy as diaconal ministers (¶ 303).

f) To examine all applicants as to their fitness for diaconal ministry, and to make recommendations concerning their candidacy for diaconal ministry (¶¶ 304-305).

g) To guide and counsel candidates for diaconal ministry throughout their candidacy.

h) To maintain accurate records of work satisfactorily completed by candidates engaged in academic preparation for diaconal ministry, based on reports received from the appropriate bodies.

i) To ensure confidentiality in the interview and reporting process. Personal data and private information will not be available for distribution and publication without proper authorization.

j) To work with the presiding bishop to provide for an appropriate service of consecration during the session of Annual Conference. The services for consecration and ordination may be incorporated into one service.

k) To be responsible for the evaluation of the character and effectiveness of diaconal ministers in the Annual Conference and to make one report to the bishop and the Conference in open session annually.

l) To examine candidates who have completed their candidacy for diaconal ministry and to make recommendations to the Annual Conference concerning their consecration as diaconal ministers and their relationship to the Annual Conference (¶ 306).

m) To interview diaconal ministers requesting changes in their Annual Conference relationship and make recommendations for Annual Conference action concerning disability leave, maternity/paternity leave, study/sabbatical leave, personal leave, retirement, termination and reinstatement. The board shall keep a record of these changes and the reasons for them.

n) To recommend for Annual Conference action the transfer to another Annual Conference of the credentials and records of diaconal ministers whose service appointments so require. The receiving Annual Conference shall initiate the action for transfer.

o) To report annually to the Annual Conference for reading by the bishop and for publication in the conference journal the names of all persons consecrated to the office of diaconal minister and their places of service.

p) To insure that the significance of consecration into and retirement from diaconal ministry is appropriately recognized by the Annual Conference.

q) To work with the Annual Conference and the employing agency to assure responsible conditions of employment for the diaconal minister, to provide a supportive atmosphere that will empower his or her ministry, and to see that entrance into employment and departure from employment are open and fair to all persons involved.

r) To work with the Annual Conference and the employing agency to assure for the diaconal minister a pension plan, an insurance program, an adequate salary base, and other employee benefits commensurate with the diaconal minister's training, ability, and experience.

s) To provide support services for the diaconal minister's career development, including personal and career counseling, continuing education, assistance in preparation for retirement, and all matters pertaining to morale.

t) To work with the bishop and district superintendents in matters of mutual concern for the personal and professional support for diaconal ministers.

u) To cooperate with the Board of Ordained Ministry when the Ministerial Education Fund is used by the Annual Conference in its program of continuing education for diaconal ministers. (*See* ¶ 920.1.)

4. The duties of the conference Board of Diaconal Ministry for certification shall be:

a) To determine whether applicants meet the standards of the General Board of Higher Education and Ministry for certification in education, evangelism, music, and others that may be assigned.

b) To recommend to the Annual Conference for certification those who have met the standards for education, evangelism, music, and others that may be assigned; and to report the action of the Annual Conference to the General Board of Higher Education and Ministry.

c) To keep a record of all persons in the Annual Conference who have been certified in professional careers.

d) To renew or discontinue certification based on an annual review and evaluation of all persons who have been certified in professional careers.

e) To report annually to the Annual Conference for publication in the conference journal a roster of all persons certified in professional careers and the careers in which they are certified.

f) To work with the Annual Conference and the employing agency to assure responsible conditions of employment for the certified person, to provide a supportive atmosphere that will empower his or her service, and to see that entrance into employment and departure from employment are open and fair to all persons involved.

5. The duties of the conference Board of Diaconal Ministry for deaconesses and home missionaries shall be:

a) To keep a record of all persons in the Annual Conference who have been commissioned to the office of deaconess or the office of home missionary.

b) To report annually to the Annual Conference for publication in the conference journal a roster of all persons commissioned as deaconess and home missionary.

6. The board shall cooperate with the Division of Diaconal Ministry and assist in the study, interpretation, promotion, and support of diaconal ministry; the maintenance of standards and processes for consecration and certification; and the interpretation and promotion of the Ministerial Education Fund.

¶ **725.** *Conference Committee on Episcopacy.*—1. There shall be a **conference Committee on Episcopacy** elected quadrennially by the Annual Conference at the session following the General Conference and consisting of three laywomen, three laymen, three clergy persons, and three additional persons to make possible the representation of racial and ethnic minorities, youth, and young adults, and three additional persons appointed by the bishop, provided that at least five of the fifteen persons are clergy. The provisions of this paragraph shall be effective as of May 1, 1980.

Two or more conferences under the presidency of a single bishop may decide to have one Committee on Episcopacy, in which case each Annual Conference shall be represented as stated in the preceding paragraph and shall each elect its own representatives.

The lay and clergy members of the Jurisdictional Committee on Episcopacy shall be ex officio members with vote.

2. The committee shall meet at least annually. It shall be convened by the bishop and shall elect a chairperson, a vice-chairperson, and a secretary. The bishop and/or chairperson are authorized to call additional meetings when desired.

3. The functions of the conference Committee on Episcopacy shall be:

a) To support the bishop of the area in the oversight of the spiritual and temporal affairs of the Church, with special reference to the area where the bishop has presidential responsibility.

b) To be available to the bishop for counsel.

c) To assist in the determination of the episcopal needs of the area and to make recommendations to appropriate bodies.

d) To keep the bishop advised concerning conditions within the area as they affect relationships between the bishop and the people of the conference agencies.

e) To interpret to the people of the area and to conference agencies the nature and function of the episcopal office.

f) To engage in annual consultation and appraisal of the work of the bishop in the episcopal area including concern for the inclusiveness of the Church and its ministry with respect to sex, race, and national origin, and understanding and implementation of the consultation process in appointment-making.

g) To report needs for episcopal leadership to the Jurisdictional Committee on Episcopacy through the duly elected conference members of that committee.

4. The conference Council on Finance and Administration shall make provision in its budget for the expenses of this committee.

¶ **726.** *Conference Board of Pensions.*—1. *Authorization.*—There shall be organized in each Annual Conference a conference board, auxiliary to the General Board of Pensions, to be known as the **conference Board of Pensions,** hereinafter called the board, which shall have charge of the interests and work of providing for and contributing to the support, relief, assistance, and pensioning of ministers and their families, other church workers, and lay employees of The United Methodist Church, its institutions, organizations, and agencies within the Annual Conference, except as otherwise provided for by the general board.

2. *Membership.*—*a)* The board shall be composed of not less than twelve members not indebted to pension and benefit funds, plans, and programs, or receiving pensions therefrom; one-third laywomen, one-third laymen, and one-third clergy, elected for a term of eight years and arranged in classes as determined by the Annual Conference; in addition thereto, any ministerial member of the conference or lay member of a church within the conference who is a member of the General Board of Pensions. A vacancy in the membership of the board may be filled by the board for the remainder of the conference year in which the vacancy occurs, subject to the same qualifications before

provided, and at its next session the conference shall fill the vacancy for the remainder of the unexpired term.

b) The members shall assume their duties at the adjournment of the conference session at which they were elected.

3. *Organization.*—The board shall organize by electing a chairperson, vice-chairperson, secretary, and treasurer, who shall serve during the ensuing quadrennium or until their successors shall have been elected and qualified. These officers shall constitute an **executive committee;** *provided,* however, that three members may be added thereto by the board. The duty of the executive committee shall be to administer the work of the board during the conference year in the interim between regular or special meetings of the board. The office of secretary may be combined with that of treasurer. The treasurer may be a person who is not a member of the board, in which case the person shall be an ex officio member of the executive committee, without vote. Calls for special meetings of the board shall be issued by the secretary on request of the chairperson, or the vice-chairperson when the chairperson is unable to act.

4. *Proportional Payment.*—The board shall compare the records of the amounts paid by each pastoral charge for the support of pastors and for pension and benefit programs, computing the proportional distribution thereof and keeping a permanent record of defaults of the ministers of the conference who have failed to observe the following provisions pertaining to proportional payment, and shall render annually to each minister who is in default a statement of the amounts in default for that and preceding years.[43]

a) When the apportionment to the pastoral charges for the pension and benefit program of the Annual Conference has been determined; payments made thereon by each pastoral charge shall be exactly proportionate to payments made on the salary or salaries of the minister or ministers serving it.

b) The treasurer of the pastoral charge shall be primarily responsible for the application of proportional payment; but in the event of the treasurer's failure to apply it, the pastor shall adjust cash salary and payment according to the proper ratio, as

---

[43]*See* Judicial Council Decisions 50, 390, 401, 471.

provided above, before the pastor enters the respective amounts in the statistical report to the Annual Conference.

c) The conference statistical tables shall provide separate columns for reporting the amount apportioned to each pastoral charge for pension and benefit purposes and the amount paid thereon.

d) On retirement, the amount that a pastor is in default shall be subject to deduction from the pastor's pension, in accordance with rules and regulations of the specific program or programs under which the pension is provided.

e) If a retired minister, while serving as a supply pastor, fails to observe the provisions of this paragraph pertaining to proportional payment in any conference year, the amount of such default shall be deducted from the minister's pension the ensuing conference year.

f) It shall not be permissible for a pastor to receive a bonus or other supplementary compensation tending to defeat proportional payment. The board may recommend to the conference that the pastor's pension credit be disallowed for the year during which such bonus or supplementary compensation was so received.

5. *Reports to the Annual Conference and the General Board.—* *a)* The board shall report to the Annual Conference and to the General Board of Pensions the names, addresses, and years of service approved for pension credit of the annuitants of the conference, the names of those who have died during the year, and the names of dependent children of deceased ministerial members of the conference, and shall show separately the amount paid to each beneficiary by the conference from the annuity and necessitous funds.

b) The board shall report to the General Board of Pensions immediately following the session of the conference, on forms provided for that purpose by the general board, and shall report also the names and addresses of ministers who are members of funds, plans, or programs administered by the general board.

¶ **727.** 1. In each Annual Conference there shall be a **conference Commission on Archives and History.** The commission shall be elected by the Annual Conference upon the nomination of its nominating committee. The number of members of the commission and their terms of office shall be as the conference may determine. It shall be the duty of the commission to cooperate with and report, when requested, to the General and Jurisdictional Commissions on Archives and History; to preserve the records of the Annual Conference; to collect and preserve data relating to the organization and history of the conference; to maintain a firesafe historical and archival depository and to see that all current items which obviously will have value for future history are preserved therein; to provide for the ownership of real property and to receive gifts and bequests; to assist the bishop or the conference* program committee in planning for the historical hour at Annual Conference sessions; and to encourage and assist the local churches in preserving their records and compiling their histories.

2. The commission may organize a **conference Historical Society** and encourage individuals to become members of it for the purpose of promoting interest in the study and preservation of the history of the conference and its antecedents. The officers of the conference Commission on Archives and History may be the officers of the conference Historical Society. Individuals may become members of the Historical Society by paying dues as the society may direct, and in return they shall receive official publications and publicity materials issued by the commission and the society.

3. Each Annual Conference may have a historian to undertake specific duties as may be designated by the commission.

4. In those conferences having ethnic congregations, the Commission on Archives and History shall develop and keep records of the historical heritage of these congregations and their previous conferences.

¶ **728.** 1. Each Annual Conference shall create a **conference Commission or Committee on Christian Unity and Interreligious Concerns** to work with the Standing General Commission on Christian Unity and Interreligious Concerns. The agency will report each year to the conference in such manner as the conference may direct.

2. It is recommended that this organization be composed of two persons from each district (complying with ¶ 706.4), one of whom shall be district coordinator for ecumenical concerns, a member of the district staff of the Council on Ministries, and a liaison person with local church work areas on Christian unity and interreligious concerns in the district. Other members may be added to provide expertise and useful interchange with other agencies, as the conference directs. Any member of the Standing General Commission on Christian Unity and Interreligious Concerns, the Governing Board of the National Council of Churches of Christ in the U.S.A., or those who have been official United Methodist delegates to the most recent World Council of Churches Assembly or the plenary meeting of the Consultation on Church Union who reside within the conference bounds shall be ex officio members.

3. The commission or committee shall organize in order to carry out its work effectively. The chairperson shall be a member of the Annual Conference Council on Ministries and shall be an ex officio member of the conference representation to state councils or conferences of churches.

4. The duties of the commission or committee shall be to act in cooperation with the Annual Conference Council on Ministries, in coordination with the duties of the Standing General Commission on Christian Unity and Interreligious Concerns, as outlined in ¶¶ 2001-2006, and as it may recommend, and to take initiative in ecumenical and interreligious concerns as follows:

a) To interpret, advocate, and work for the unity of the Christian Church in every aspect of the life of the conference and its churches, and to encourage dialogue and cooperation with persons of other living faiths.

b) To recommend to the conference the goals, objectives, and strategies and to assist the conference, in cooperation with the bishop and the Cabinet, in the development of ecumenical relationships and planning for mission with other judicatories, particularly in the establishment of new churches, yoked congregations, and in the process of local church union efforts.

c) To stimulate participation in and evaluation of mission programs ecumenically planned and implemented, such as experimental parishes, ecumenical parish clusters, ecumenical task forces, and united ministries in higher education, and in other issue-oriented tasks.

d) To stimulate conference, district, and congregational participation in councils, conferences, or associations of churches, in coalition task forces, and in interreligious groups through ecumenical educational or shared time programs, jointly approved curriculum resources, interreligious study programs, or ecumenical community action projects such as institutional ministries and media communications and various other modes of interchurch cooperation.

e) To nominate, in cooperation with the conference Nominating Committee, for conference election the delegates to state councils or conferences or churches and to select representatives' district, area, and regional ecumenical task groups and workshops; and to be the body to which such delegates are accountable through the receiving of and action on their reports and recommendations.

f) To promote and interpret the work of national and world ecumenical bodies such as the National and World Council of Churches and the Consultation on Church Union, and to provide leadership for specific ecumenical experiences of worship and reflections, such as the Week of Prayer for Christian Unity, Pentecost Sunday, World Communion Sunday, Reformation Sunday, and other appropriate occasions.

g) To cooperate in and provide leadership for specific ecumenical experiences in worship and celebration, such as the Week of Prayer for Christian Unity, Pentecost Sunday, World Communion Sunday, Reformation Sunday, and other appropriate occasions.

h) To stimulate understanding and conversations with all Christian bodies, to encourage continuing dialogue with Jewish and other living faith communities, and to encourage an openness of mind toward an understanding of other major world religions.

i) To fulfill other functions assigned by the Annual Conference and to respond to such requests as may be made by its leadership.

¶ 729. 1. There shall be in each Annual Conference a **conference Commission on Religion and Race,** following the general guidelines and structure of the Standing General Commission on Religion and Race as outlined in ¶¶ 2101-2106 where applicable.

2. Insofar as possible, the Annual Conference commission should follow the principle of membership as found in the Standing General Commission on Religion and Race. Each Annual Conference should determine the number of the total membership, with a minimum of twelve. It is strongly urged that the Annual Conference commission be constituted so that the majority of the membership be represented by racial and ethnic minorities, proportionately reflecting the racial and ethnic minority constituency of the conference. Steps should also be taken to ensure adequate representation of both youth/young adults and women. Where a district has elected a **district director of religion and race,** that person shall serve on the conference Commission on Religion and Race with vote. These persons will be elected by the usual procedure of the conference and they shall serve as members of the Council on Ministries of their respective districts in order to act as liaison between the district and the conference. The commission shall create as many committees and task forces as it deems necessary in order to implement its responsibilities. Members of the Standing General Commission on Religion and Race shall be ex officio members of the conference Commission on Religion and Race with vote.

3. The Annual Conference commission will assume responsibility for such matters as:

a) Providing resources for the local church work area on religion and race.

b) Examining ethnic minority representation on all of the conference boards, agencies, commissions, and committees, as well as the governing boards of related institutions. After such an examination, appropriate recommendations for total inclusiveness should be made to the Annual Conference.

c) Working with Annual Conference boards and agencies as they seek to develop programs and policies of racial inclusiveness.

d) Providing a channel of assistance to racial and ethnic

minority groups as they seek to develop programs of empowerment and ministry to their communities.

e) Consulting with the Board of Ordained Ministry and the Cabinet to determine what provisions are made for the recruitment and itinerancy of racial and ethnic minority ministers.

f) Consulting with local churches which are seeking to establish multiracial fellowships and encouraging and supporting local churches in maintaining a Christian ministry in racially changing neighborhoods.

g) Coordinating the conference support and cooperation with various movements for racial and social justice in consultation with the conference Board of Church and Society, as appropriate.

h) Providing opportunities for multiracial and interethnic dialogue and meetings throughout the conference.

i) Providing programs of sensitization and education at every level of the conference, on the nature and meaning of racism—attitudinal, behavioral, and institutional.

j) Coordinating in consultation with the Standing General Commission on Christian Unity and Interreligious Concerns the conference programs of cooperation with black and other racial and ethnic minority denominations, especially those of the Methodist family.

k) Evaluating the priorities of the Annual Conference in light of the needs in the area of race relations. The commission shall develop recommendations to present to the appropriate agencies and report directly to the Annual Conference session. These recommendations shall lift up the need to deal with the pressing issue of racism, racial and ethnic minority group empowerment, and reconciliation among the races.

l) Evaluating the effects of merger and making appropriate recommendations to the Annual Conference session.

m) Reviewing the Annual Conference practices of employment, of Annual Conference program, business and administration, and office personnel, and reporting and recommending to the Annual Conference steps to be taken to actualize racial and ethnic minority inclusiveness; reviewing the Annual Conference–related institutions such as colleges, hospitals, homes for the aged, child-care agencies, etc., concerning their practices of racial and ethnic minority inclusiveness in clientele and employment and reporting to Annual Conference session.

4. The Annual Conference Commission on Religion and Race shall develop an adequate budget for its operation as a commission for inclusion in the Annual Conference budget.

¶ **730.** There shall be in each Annual Conference, including the Central Conferences, a **conference Commission on the Status and Role of Women.**

1. The responsibility of this commission shall be in harmony with the responsibility of the standing general commission (*see* ¶¶ 2202-2203) with the following objectives established as guidelines for adaptation to the needs of the respective Annual Conferences:

a) To be informed about the status and role of all women in the total life of the conference. Data shall be gathered which relate to all structural levels of the conference, including the local church. Such information will be regularly updated and disseminated.

b) To initiate cooperation with United Methodist Women at the Annual Conference level, and other levels as appropriate, in order to achieve full participation of women in the decision-making structures.

c) To develop ways to inform and sensitize the leadership within the conference at all levels on issues that affect women, which shall be projected into and through all districts within the conference by the commission.

d) To focus on major priorities of issues related to women and to enlist the support of the bishop, Cabinet, and conference staff in policies, plans, and practices related to those priorities.

e) To advise the general commission about the progress and effectiveness of efforts to achieve full participation of women in the life of the Church.

f) To participate in connectional programs and plans initiated or recommended by the general commission; and to utilize the resources available from the general commission as needed.

2. The basic membership of the conference commission shall be nominated and elected by established procedures of the

respective Annual Conferences. Each Annual Conference shall determine the number and composition of the total membership which shall consist of not fewer than twelve nor more than thirty-six. All must be members of The United Methodist Church. Special consultants without vote may be used as resource persons. Among the basic members of the commission shall be representatives from each district. There shall be at least six members at large. The addition of the at-large membership shall ensure that the total membership shall maintain the one-third laywomen, one-third laymen, one-third clergy balance. The majority of the commission shall be women, including both clergy and lay. In an Annual Conference where there is not a sufficient number of clergywomen to meet the required balance, additional laywomen shall be elected beyond the one-third proportion to bring the total membership to a majority of women.

Selection of commission members shall ensure adequate representation of racial and ethnic minorities, youth, young adults, and persons over sixty-five, and persons of varying life styles.

At least one member shall be named by the conference United Methodist Women.

3. The chairperson of the commission shall be a woman.

4. The commission shall propose a budget and submit it for inclusion in the budget of the Annual Conference, according to procedures for funding of all boards, commissions, and agencies of the Annual Conference.

¶ **731. United Methodist Women.**—*Constitution of United Methodist Women in the Conference.—Article 1. Name.*—In each Annual Conference there shall be a conference organization named United Methodist Women, auxiliary to the jurisdictional organization of United Methodist Women and to the Women's Division of the Board of Global Ministries.

Article 2. Function.—The function of the conference organization of United Methodist Women shall be to work with the district organizations and the local units of United Methodist Women in developing programs to meet the needs and interests of women and the concerns and responsibilities of the global Church; to encourage and support spiritual growth, missionary outreach, and Christian social action; and to promote the plans and responsibilities of the Women's Division.

Article 3. Authority.—Each conference organization of United Methodist Women shall have authority to promote its work in accordance with the plans, responsibilities, and policies of the Women's Division of the Board of Global Ministries.

Article 4. Membership.—The conference organization of United Methodist Women shall be composed of all members of local units within the bounds of the conference. The resident bishop shall be a member of the conference organization of United Methodist Women and of its executive committee.

Article 5. Officers and Committees.—The conference organization shall elect a president, a vice-president, a secretary, a treasurer, and a Committee on Nominations. Additional officers and committees shall be elected or appointed in accordance with the plans of the Women's Division as set forth in the bylaws of the conference organizations of United Methodist Women.

Article 6. Meetings and Elections.—*a)* There shall be an annual meeting of the conference organization of United Methodist Women, at which time there shall be presented a program designed to meet the needs of the women of the conference in harmony with the Purpose and the plans and responsibilities of the Women's Division of the Board of Global Ministries. Officers and the Committee on Nominations shall be elected, the necessary business transacted, and pledges made for the ensuing year.

b) The voting body of the annual meeting of the conference organization shall be composed of representatives from units in local churches as determined by the conference organization; such district officers as the conference organization may determine; the conference officers and chairpersons of committees; members of the Women's Division and officers of the jurisdictional organization residing within the bounds of the conference.

c) At the annual meeting of the conference organization prior to the quadrennial meeting of the jurisdictional organization, six conference officers shall be elected according to provisions in ¶ 634.3 for membership in the jurisdictional organization.

d) At the annual meeting of the conference organization prior to the quadrennial meeting of the jurisdictional organization, the conference organization shall nominate three women for membership on the Board of Global Ministries, the names to be sent to the jurisdiction organizational according to ¶ 634.4.

Article 7. Relationships.—a) The president of the conference organization of United Methodist Women is a member of the Annual Conference, as set forth in ¶ 36.

b) Designated officers shall represent the conference organization on the various agencies, councils, commissions, and committees of the conference as the constitutions and bylaws of such agencies provide.

c) The conference organization shall encourage women to participate in the total life and work of the Church, and shall support them in assuming positions of responsibility and leadership.

*Article 8. Amendments.—*Proposed amendments to this constitution may be sent to the recording secretary of the Women's Division prior to the last annual meeting of the division in the quadrennium.

¶ **732.** 1. In each Annual Conference there shall be a **conference Council on Youth Ministry** composed of both youth and adults. Its purpose shall be to strengthen the youth ministry in the local churches and districts of the Annual Conference. For administrative purposes the council shall be related to the Annual Conference Council on Ministries. (*See* ¶¶ 1401-1404 for the United Methodist National Youth Ministry Organization.)

2. *Membership.—*No more than one third of the membership of the council shall be adults. It is recommended that the council be composed of 50 percent racial and ethnic minority members. (It is suggested that members at large may be added toward achieving 50/50 ethnic-minority/white membership in a manner to be determined by the conference Council on Youth Ministry.) Where ethnic or language conferences overlap nonethnic conferences, provision shall be made for the inclusion of members of the ethnic or language conferences and vice-versa.

3. *Responsibilities.—a)* To initiate and support plans and activities and projects that are of particular interest to youth.

b) To be an advocate for the free expression of the convictions of youth on issues vital to them.

c) To support and facilitate, where deemed needed, the formation of youth caucuses.

d) To cooperate with the boards and agencies of the Annual Conference, receiving recommendations from and making recommendations to the same.

e) To recommend to the Annual Conference Committee on Nominations qualified youth for membership on boards and agencies.

f) To elect Annual Conference representatives to the Jurisdictional Youth Ministry Organization Convocation and the National Youth Ministry Organization Convocation in keeping with the provisions of ¶¶ 632 and 1401.2.

g) To receive and set the policy and criteria for its portion of the Youth Service Fund (¶ 1404). No more than one third shall be used for administrative purposes; at least one third shall be used for projects within the geographic bounds of the Annual Conference; and at least one third shall be used for projects outside the geographic bounds of the Annual Conference.

h) To establish the policy for Youth Service Fund education and be responsible for its promotion throughout the Annual Conference, in cooperation with the United Methodist Youth Ministry Organization.

i) To establish a Project Review Committee as an advisory committee with regard to the use of the Youth Service Fund receipts for projects. It is recommended that the committee be composed of at least 50 percent racial and ethnic minority group persons.

j) To participate with the appropriate conference agencies in the nomination of the conference coordinator of youth ministry, who shall serve as its advisor.

¶ **733.** There shall be a **Joint Committee on Disability** in each Annual Conference. It shall be composed of a minimum of two representatives each from the Board of Ordained Ministry and the conference Board of Pensions, who may be elected by those boards at the beginning of each quadrennium and at other times when vacancies occur, and a district superintendent appointed from time to time by the bishop to represent the Cabinet. Unless and until other members are elected, the chairperson and registrar of the Board of Ordained Ministry and the chairperson and secretary of the conference Board of Pensions, or others designated by them, shall be authorized to represent their respective boards. The committee shall organize at the beginning of each quadrennium by the election of a chairperson and a secretary. The duties of the Joint Committee on Disability shall be:

a) To study the problems of disability in the Annual Conference.

b) To provide for a continuing personal ministry to any disabled ministers of the conference and to aid them in maintaining fellowship with the members of the conference.

c) To determine what medical doctor or doctors it will approve for medical examinations and reports regarding disabled ministers and what medical doctor or doctors it will recommend to the General Board of Pensions for that purpose.

d) To make recommendations to the Board of Ordained Ministry, the conference Board of Pensions, and the Cabinet on matters related to disability, including steps for its prevention, disability leave, benefits, and programs of rehabilitation.

e) To cooperate with and give assistance to the General Board of Pensions in its administration of disability benefits through the Ministers Reserve Pension Fund or the Comprehensive Protection Plan.

Section X. The District Conference.

¶ **734. A District Conference** shall be held if directed by the Annual Conference of which it is a part and may be held upon the call of the district superintendent, which call shall specify the time and place.

¶ **735.** 1. A District Conference shall be composed of members as determined and specified by the Annual Conference.

2. The District Conference may choose its own order of business. The secretary duly elected shall keep an accurate record of the proceedings and submit it to the Annual Conference for examination.

3. The District Conference shall issue certificates of candidacy for the ordained ministry on recommendation of the district

Committee on Ordained Ministry and shall consider for approval the reports of this committee.

4. The District Conference may incorporate a **District Union,** under the laws of the state in which it is located, to hold and administer district real and personal property, receive and administer church extension and mission funds for use within the district, and exercise such other powers and duties as may be set forth in its charter or articles of incorporation as authorized by the Annual Conference having jurisdiction over said district. All such District Unions chartered or incorporated by districts of the churches which joined and united in adopting the Constitution of The United Methodist Church are declared to be disciplinary agencies of The United Methodist Church as though originally created and authorized by that Constitution, and may act for or as a District Conference when convened for that purpose by the district superintendent, who shall be its executive secretary, or by its president or other executive officer.

¶ 736. 1. The **district lay leader** is the elected leader of the district laity. The lay leader shall have responsibility for fostering awareness of the role of the laity in achieving the mission of the Church, and supporting and enabling lay participation in the planning and decision-making processes of the district and the local churches in cooperation with the district superintendent and pastors. The lay leader is a member of the District Conference and shall be a member of the district Council on Ministries and its executive committee.

2. There may be an associate district lay leader within a district. The associate district lay leader shall be elected as determined by the Annual Conference. The method of nomination and term of office shall be determined by the Annual Conference.

3. The district lay leader shall relate to the organized lay groups in the district such as United Methodist Women, United Methodist Men, and United Methodist Youth and support their work and help them coordinate their activities.

4. The district lay leader may designate persons to serve as proxy in any of the above groups except the District Conference, district Council on Ministries, and the Council on Ministries executive committee.

5. The district lay leader shall be elected as determined by the Annual Conference. The method of nomination and term of office shall be determined by the Annual Conference.

¶ **737.** Each district of an Annual Conference may organize a **district Council on Ministries.**

1. *Purpose.*—The purpose of the district Council on Ministries shall be to assist local churches to minister more effectively; to serve as a channel of communication between the local churches, the Annual Conference Council on Ministries, and the general agencies of the Church; to initiate programs for the district; and to help the Annual Conference Council on Ministries in the performance of its functions.

2. *Membership.*—Each Annual Conference may determine the membership and the method of election of its district Councils on Ministries. The membership structure need not be identical in each district. It may include the following: district coordinators of age-level and family ministries; the district director/president of United Methodist Men; representatives of program agencies (i.e., district directors of evangelism, education, religion and race, district missionary secretaries, work area chairpersons on stewardship) and representatives of clusters of local churches. It is recommended that a member of the Annual Conference Council on Ministries staff be included as a resource person in each district Council on Ministries. Membership shall be chosen, insofar as possible, to include one-third clergy, one-third laywomen, and one-third laymen (with special attention to the inclusion of clergywomen, youth, young adults, persons with handicapping conditions, and racial and ethnic minority persons) in keeping with policies for general church agencies. The Annual Conference may ask the District Conferences (¶ 734) to elect the membership of the district Council on Ministries.

3. *Officers.*—The officers of the district Council on Ministries shall be the chairperson, who shall be elected from the membership of the council, and such other officers as the Annual Conference or the district deems necessary.

4. *Staff.*—The district superintendent shall be the chief executive staff officer.

5. *Responsibilities.*—The responsibilities of the district Council on Ministries may be determined by the Annual Conference or

the district Council on Ministries. The following functions may be incorporated into its work:

a) To study the needs of the local churches in the district and help them establish and provide more effective ministry in and through the churches.

b) To keep local churches informed on the work of the whole Church and challenge each church to full participation.

c) To encourage local churches to engage in creative, innovative approaches to ministry.

d) To serve as a two-way channel of communication between the local churches and the Annual Conference and to assist local churches in communication with each other.

e) To study the needs of the district and establish priorities for district action.

f) To develop experimental types of ministry within the district and especially in urban districts to facilitate structures as provided in ¶¶ 1530.5 and 720.5*f* and *g*.

g) To provide leadership training events for local church leaders.

h) To relate the Annual Conference Council on Ministries and its staff to local church needs.

i) To make program and other recommendations to the Annual Conference Council on Ministries.

j) To assist in the implementation of the program of the Annual Conference.

k) To cooperate in ecumenical programs and events on the district level.

l) To plan and conduct inspirational events.

m) To elect the lay representative(s) from the district to membership on the Annual Conference Council on Ministries when requested by the Annual Conference Council on Ministries.

The district Councils on Ministries in an Annual Conference shall cooperate with the Annual Conference Council on Ministries so that a harmonious and holistic approach to the total ministry of the conference may be achieved. In order to coordinate the calendar and program plans of each district with the Annual Conference, the Annual Conference Council on Ministries may require the district councils to submit their program plans for approval.

The district Council on Ministries may appoint a **district coordinator of communications** to work in cooperation with the district and conference Councils on Ministries and with the conference Committee on Communication, if organized. The district Council on Ministries may create a district Committee on Communication to assist the council in carrying out district communication functions.

6. *Finances.*—Each Annual Conference shall determine the method by which its district Councils on Ministries shall be financed. It is recommended that an amount for the general operating expense of the district Councils on Ministries be included in the Annual Conference budget. As a general rule, major program expenditures for any district should be made through the budget of the Annual Conference Council on Ministries or the appropriate Annual Conference program board.

¶ **738.** The district superintendent, after consultation with the conference board, may appoint a **district director of church and society.** Also, if desirable, a district may create a Committee on Church and Society of laypersons and ministers, to work with the district superintendent to further the purposes of the conference board. The coordinator of the area of Christian social involvement of the district United Methodist Women shall be an ex officio member.

¶ **739.** There shall be a **district Committee on Ordained Ministry.**

1. It shall be composed of a representative from the Board of Ordained Ministry, named by the board after consultation with the district superintendent, and who may be named chairperson; the district superintendent, who may serve as the executive secretary; and at least five other ministers in full connection in the district, nominated annually by the district superintendent in consultation with the chairperson or executive committee of the Board of Ordained Ministry and approved by the Annual Conference. Interim vacancies may be filled by the district superintendent.

2. The district Committee on Ordained Ministry shall elect its officers at the first meeting following the Annual Conference session when the members are elected.

3. The committee shall maintain a list of all persons who have declared their candidacy for ministry and are pursuing candidacy studies under a supervising pastor. A duplicate list shall be forwarded to the Annual Conference registrar for candidacy; such list being made current at least prior to each session of the Annual Conference.

4. The committee shall offer counsel to candidates regarding pretheological studies.

5. The committee shall supervise all matters dealing with candidacy for ministry and with the license for local pastor.

6. The vote of the committee on all matters of candidacy shall be by individual written ballot, with a three-fourths majority vote of the committee present required for certification or approval or recommendation.

7. The committee shall recommend to the Board of Ordained Ministry those persons who qualify for associate and probationary membership, for continuance as local pastors, and for restoration of credentials. All persons shall have been current members of The United Methodist Church for at least one year immediately preceding certification, shall have been recommended by their Charge Conference, and shall, in the judgment of the committee, show evidence that their gifts, graces, and usefulness warrant such recommendation.

8. The committee shall examine all persons who apply in writing for certification or renewal of certificate. Where there is evidence that their gifts, graces, and usefulness warrant and that they are qualified under ¶¶ 404-406, and on recommendation of their Charge Conference, or the conference Board of Ordained Ministry, the committee shall issue or renew their certificate.

9. The committee shall assist the conference Board of Ordained Ministry in providing support services for all clergy under appointment within the district.

¶ **740.** *Committee on District Superintendency.*—There shall be a **Committee on District Superintendency.**

1. *Membership.*—This committee shall be composed of two laywomen, two laymen, two clergy, and two at-large members selected to make possible the representation of racial and ethnic minorities, youth, and young adults, and two additional persons

appointed by the district superintendent; *provided* that at least three of the ten persons are clergy.

2. *Selection.*—The members shall be selected in such manner as may be determined by the District Conference or, where there is no District Conference, by the Annual Conference. The district committee shall be authorized to co-opt members as advisory members who have expertise in areas of special need. The bishop of the area, or his/her authorized representative, shall be an ex officio member of said committee.

3. *Meeting.*—The district committee shall meet at least annually and upon call of the district superintendent and/or the chairperson of the committee. The committee shall elect a chairperson, vice-chairperson, and secretary.

4. *Responsibilities.*—The responsibilities of the Committee on District Superintendency shall be:

a) To support the district superintendent of the district in the oversight of the spiritual and temporal affairs of the Church, with special reference to the district where the superintendent has responsibilities.

b) To be available for counsel.

c) To assist in the determination of the leadership needs of the district and how they can be fulfilled best.

d) To keep the district superintendent advised concerning conditions within the district as they affect relations between the district superintendent, the people, and the district agencies.

e) To establish a clearly understood process for observing the district superintendent's ministry with direct evaluation and feedback; with special concern for the inclusiveness of the Church and its ministry with respect to sex, race, and national origin, and implementation of the consultative process in appointment-making.

f) To interpret to the people of the district and to the district boards and agencies the nature and function of the district superintendency.

5. *Consultation.*—The district committee and the district superintendent shall engage in an annual consultation and appraisal of the work of the district superintendent in the district and shall serve in an advisory relationship with the bishop of the area.

¶ **741. United Methodist Women.**—*Constitution of United Methodist Women in the District.*—*Article 1. Name.*—In each district there shall be a district organization named United Methodist Women, auxiliary to the conference organization of United Methodist Women and the Women's Division of the Board of Global Ministries.

Article 2. Responsibilities.—The responsibilities of the district organization of United Methodist Women shall be to work with local units in developing programs to meet the needs and interests of women and the concerns and responsibilities of the global Church; to encourage and support spiritual growth, missionary outreach, and Christian social action; and to promote the plans and responsibilities of the Women's Division and the conference organization of United Methodist Women.

Article 3. Authority.—Each district organization of United Methodist Women shall have authority to promote its work in accordance with the plans, responsibilities, and policies of the conference organization and the Women's Division of the Board of Global Ministries.

Article 4. Membership.—All members of organized units of United Methodist Women in the local churches of the district shall be considered members of the district organization. The district superintendent shall be a member of the district organization of United Methodist Women and of its executive committee.

Article 5. Officers and Committees.—The district organization shall elect a president, a vice-president, a secretary, a treasurer, and a Committee on Nominations. Additional officers and committees shall be elected or appointed in accordance with the plans of the Women's Division as set forth in the bylaws for the district organization of United Methodist Women.

Article 6. Meetings and Elections.—There shall be an annual meeting of the district organization of United Methodist Women, at which time there shall be presented a program designed to meet the needs of the women of the district in harmony with the Purpose and the plans and the responsibilities of the conference organization and the Women's Division of the Board of Global Ministries. Officers and the Committee on Nominations shall be elected, the necessary business transacted, and pledges made for the ensuing year.

Article 7. Relationships.—*a)* Designated officers shall represent the district organization of United Methodist Women on the various boards, councils, commissions, and committees of the district as the constitution and bylaws of such agencies provide.

b) The district president shall be the only district representative with vote on the conference executive committee.

c) The district organization shall encourage women to participate in the total life and work of the Church, and shall support them in assuming positions of responsibility and leadership.

Article 8. Amendments.—Proposed amendments to this constitution may be sent to the recording secretary of the Women's Division of the Board of Global Ministries prior to the last annual meeting of the division in the quadrennium.

Chapter Seven

ADMINISTRATIVE ORDER

Section I. General Provisions.

¶ 801. *General Agencies.*—The general agencies of The United Methodist Church are the regularly established councils, boards, commissions, or committees which have been constituted by the General Conference. Not included are such commissions or committees as are created by the General Conference to fulfill a special function within the ensuing quadrennium, ecumenical groups on which The United Methodist Church is represented, or committees related to the quadrennial sessions of the General Conference.[1]

¶ 802. *Amenability and Accountability.*—All the general agencies of The United Methodist Church that have been constituted by the General Conference are amenable to the General Conference, except as otherwise provided. Between sessions of the General Conference, the following general agencies are accountable to the General Council on Ministries: the General Board of Church and Society, the General Board of Discipleship, the General Board of Global Ministries, the General Board of Higher Education and Ministry, the Standing General Commission on Communication in matters pertaining to its program responsibilities, the Standing General Commission on Christian Unity and Interreligious Concerns, the Standing General Commission on Religion and Race, and the Standing General Commission on the Status and Role of Women.[2]

Evaluation of general agencies by the General Council on Ministries shall be part of the accountability relationship (¶ 1006.13). The evaluation process and its results shall be reported to each General Conference with recommendation for continuance or discontinuance of program as appropriate.

Local church groups, district, and Annual Conference organizations may receive an explanation of the evaluation process by requesting it from the General Council on Ministries.

---

[1]*See* Judicial Council Decision 139.
[2]*See* Judicial Council Decision 429.

364

Questions and concerns about programs, projects, or decisions of a particular agency may be addressed to that agency, with copies to the General Council on Ministries. Agencies shall acknowledge receipt of requests for information within thirty days and provide information as soon thereafter as it is available.

¶ **803.** *Definitions, Structures, and Titles.*—1. *General Council.*— An organization created by the General Conference to perform defined responsibilities of review and oversight on behalf of the General Conference in relation to the other general agencies and to perform other assigned functions shall be designated as a general council. General councils are amenable and accountable to the General Conference and report to it. These councils are the General Council on Finance and Administration and the General Council on Ministries. (Note: The Council of Bishops and Judicial Council are authorized by the Constitution and not created by the General Conference.)

2. *General Board.*—A continuing body of the Church created by the General Conference to carry out assigned functions of program, administration, and/or service shall be designated as a general board. Each general board, so far as possible, shall adopt the following levels in agency organization:

a) *Division*—an organizational unit within a general board along functional lines for the purpose of accomplishing a part of the total work of the general board.

b) *Section*—a functional subunit of a division.

c) *Office*—a support service unit within a general board.

3. a) *General Commission.*—An organization created by the General Conference for the fulfillment of a specific function for a limited period of time shall be designated as a general commission.

b) *Standing General Commission.*—A commission created by the General Conference for the fulfillment of a specific function for an indefinite period of time shall be designated as a standing general commission.

4. *Study Committee.*—An organization created by the General Conference for a limited period of time for the purpose of making a study ordered by the General Conference shall be designated as a study committee of the General Conference.

5. *Program-related General Agencies.*—The general boards and commissions which have program and/or advocacy functions shall be designated as program-related general agencies. These agencies are amenable to the General Conference and between sessions of the General Conference are accountable to the General Council on Ministries: the General Board of Church and Society, the General Board of Discipleship, the General Board of Global Ministries, the General Board of Higher Education and Ministry, the Standing General Commission on Religion and Race, and the Standing General Commission on the Status and Role of Women.

6. *Administrative General Agencies.*—The general boards and commissions which have primarily administrative and service functions shall be designated as administrative general agencies. These agencies are the General Board of Pensions, the General Board of Publication, the Standing General Commission on Archives and History, the Standing General Commission on Christian Unity and Interreligious Concerns, and the Standing General Commission on Communication, which also carries program-related responsibilities for which it is accountable to the General Council on Ministries.

7. Each general agency, unless otherwise provided, shall adopt the following executive staff titles:

a) General Secretary—the chief staff officer of a general agency. Each general agency is entitled to only one general secretary, who is its chief administrative officer.

b) Associate General Secretary—the associate staff officer of a general agency or the chief staff officer of a division of a general agency.

c) Assistant General Secretary—the assistant staff officer of a general agency or the chief staff officer of a section or office of a general agency.

8. *Missional Priority.*—A missional priority is a response to a critical need in God's world which calls for The United Methodist Church's massive and sustained effort through primary attention and ordering or reordering of program and budget at every level of the Church, as adopted by the General Conference or in accord with ¶ 1006.1. This need is evidenced by research or other

supporting data, and the required response is beyond the capacity of any single general agency or Annual Conference.

9. *Special Program.*—A special program is a quadrennial emphasis approved by the General Conference and assigned to a general agency, designed in response to a distinct opportunity or need in God's world which is evidenced by research or other supporting data, and proposes achievable goals within the quadrennium.

10. *Program.*—A program is an ongoing or special activity designed and implemented to fulfill a basic Disciplinary responsibility of a general agency accountable to the General Council on Ministries.

11. *Association or Fellowship.*—Organizations not created by nor officially related to the General Conference, and intended to provide professional relationships conducive to sharing professional techniques and information for groups within the denomination, shall be designated as associations or fellowships.

¶ 804. All the general agencies of the Church, including councils, boards, commissions, and committees constituted by the General Conference, shall account for receipts and expenditures of funds in a format designed by the General Council on Finance and Administration. A quadrennial report of such accounting shall be included in the report of General Council on Finance and Administration made to the General Conference. An annual report shall also be made available by the respective agency upon request.

Such reports shall be made available upon the request of Annual Conferences and local church administrative boards. The reports shall include a listing of organizations, individuals, coalitions, consultants, programs, and entities not formally part of the church, and the amount (expended annually) of monetary and in-kind contributions. The listing shall include but not be limited to office space, printing, staff assistance, purchases, travel expense, and other forms of financial assistance that have been granted to such entities.

¶ 805. *General Agency Membership.*—The following provisions shall govern the nomination and election of the voting membership of those general agencies to which the Jurisdictional Conferences elect members:

1. *Nominations by Annual Conferences.*—*a)* Each Annual and Missionary Conference, upon recommendation from a committee composed of the bishop and the General and Jurisdictional Conference delegation, and having allowed opportunity for nominations from the floor, shall elect persons to be submitted to a jurisdictional pool from which the Jurisdictional Nominating Committee shall select persons for election to the following general agencies: General Council on Ministries; General Board of Church and Society; General Board of Discipleship; General Board of Global Ministries; General Board of Higher Education and Ministry; General Board of Pensions; General Board of Publication; Standing General Commission on Christian Unity and Interreligious Concerns; the Standing General Commission on Communication; Standing General Commission on the Status and Role of Women; and Standing General Commission on Religion and Race.

b) Each Annual and Missionary Conference shall nominate at least fifteen persons to the jurisdictional pool, including, where available, at least one and not more than five persons in each of the following seven categories: (1) clergy (including at least one woman), (2) laywomen, (3) laymen, (4) racial and ethnic minority persons (at least one from each ethnic minority—Asian American, Black American, Hispanic American, Native American), (5) youth, (6) young adults, and (7) persons with a handicapping condition. No nominee shall be listed in more than one of these seven categories. Where possible, at least one clergy, one laywoman, and one layman nominated to the pool shall have been delegates to the previous General Conference (¶ 1007.1*a*).

c) All nominees shall list one to three preferences for agency membership. Names of all persons nominated by the Annual and Missionary Conferences but not elected by the jurisdiction shall be forwarded to the general agencies to be in a pool from which additional members may be selected (¶¶ 805.2*c*, 3*b*).

2. *General Program Board Membership.*—*a) Basic Membership.*—Each jurisdiction shall elect one person from each Annual and Missionary Conference to each program board. The jurisdiction membership on each program board shall incorporate one-third clergy (at least one of whom shall be a woman), one-third laymen, and one-third laywomen (with the exception of

¶ 1512.2), and shall ensure adequate representation of youth and young adults. The episcopal members shall not be counted in the computation of the clergy membership. In order to ensure adequate representation of racial and ethnic minority persons (Asian Americans, Black Americans, Hispanic Americans, Native Americans), it is recommended that at least 25 percent of a jurisdiction's membership on each general program board be racial and ethnic minority persons. Special attention shall be given to the inclusion of persons with a handicapping condition.[3]

b) Episcopal Membership.—The episcopal membership of not less than five nor more than ten members shall be nominated by the Council of Bishops and elected by the General Conference (*see* exception, ¶ 1512.6). At least one of the episcopal members of each general program board shall be a Central Conference bishop.

c) Additional Membership.—Additional members shall be elected by each general program board in order to bring into the board special knowledge or background and to perfect the representation of racial and ethnic minority persons, youth, young adults, persons with a handicapping condition, and distribution by geographic area. There shall be not less than five nor more than twelve additional members of each general program board. Such additional membership shall maintain the one-third laymen, one-third laywomen, and one-third clergy balance.[4]

3. *Other General Agencies.*—*a)* Each Jurisdictional Conference shall elect members from the jurisdictional pool nominated by the Annual and Missionary Conferences (¶ 805.1) in accordance with the specific membership provisions of those agencies as set forth in the Book of Discipline: General Council on Ministries (¶ 1007), General Board of Pensions, (¶ 1702.1*a*), General Board of Publication (¶ 1802), Standing General Commission on Christian Unity and Interreligious Concerns (¶ 2006), Standing General Commission on Communication (¶ 1107), Standing General Commission on the Status and Role of Women (¶ 2204), and the Standing General Commission on Religion and Race (¶ 2103).

---

[3]*See* Judicial Council Decisions 451, 467.
[4]*See* Judicial Council Decisions 377, 446.

b) Episcopal and additional or at-large members, if any, of the general agencies listed in ¶ 805.3*a* shall be nominated and elected by the procedures specified in the paragraphs listed in ¶ 805.3*a*. The agencies shall consider, but not be limited to, names forwarded to them by the jurisdictions as having been nominated by the Annual and Missionary Conferences but not elected by the Jurisdictional Conferences to general agency membership.

4. The membership of boards, committees, and agencies of The United Methodist Church, at the level of General and Jurisdictional Conferences and insofar as possible at the level of Annual and Missionary Conferences and local church, shall ensure adequate representation of racial and ethnic minority members; all such boards, committees, and agencies whose membership is set forth in the Discipline shall be authorized to elect as many additional members as necessary to meet this requirement. The provision is effectively immediately.

¶ **806.** *Committee to Nominate Additional Members.*—1. Each jurisdiction shall designate one clergy, one laywoman, and one layman whom it has elected to a general program agency or to the General Council on Ministries to nominate the additional members of that program agency or council (¶ 805.4). The fifteen members thus designated by the five jurisdictions in each general program agency and in the General Council on Ministries shall constitute a committee to nominate additional members for that agency and shall be convened as provided in ¶ 806.2.

2. An active bishop designated by the president of the Council of Bishops shall convene the committee as soon as practical after jurisdictional elections have been completed. The committee shall consider, but not be limited to, names forwarded to it by the jurisdictions as having been nominated by the Annual and Missionary Conferences but not elected by the Jurisdictional Conference to general program board membership, as well as names from caucuses and other appropriate groups.

3. The committee shall complete its work prior to the first meeting of the new program agency or the General Council on Ministries and report by mail to the previously elected members of the agency or the General Council on Ministries. All members shall be elected and seated before the program agency or council proceeds to the election of officers or any other business.

These nominating procedures shall go into effect immediately following the 1980 General Conference.

¶ **807.** *Organizational Meetings.*—1. In those years in which the General Conference holds its regular session, all general program agencies shall meet, organize, and conduct such business as may properly come before the agency not later than ninety (90) days after the close of the Jurisdictional Conferences. Each organizational meeting shall be convened by an active bishop designated by the president of the Council of Bishops.

2. All councils, boards, commissions, and committees established by a General, Jurisdictional, Central, Annual, or other Conference shall meet and organize as promptly as feasible following the selection of their members.

3. Unless otherwise specified in the Discipline or by the establishing conference, every council, board, commission, and committee shall continue in responsibility until its successor council, board, commission, or committee is organized.

¶ **808.** *Board Organization.*—1. Each program board shall elect a president and one or more vice-presidents from the voting membership of the board, and a secretary, treasurer, and such other officers as it deems appropriate.

2. Each program board shall elect chairpersons for its divisions from the voting membership of the board. The divisions shall elect a vice-chairperson, a secretary, and such other officers as it deems appropriate.

3. Terms of officers of boards and divisions shall be for the quadrennium or until their successors are elected.

4. No person shall serve as president or chairperson of more than one general agency or division thereof.

¶ **809.** *Membership.*—The membership of each program board shall be divided among the divisions or other subunits of the board in such number as the board determines. The board may add to the membership of each division such additional division members as it deems appropriate, *provided* that the total number of additional division members not exceed 25 percent of the voting membership of the general board. Additional members of a division are not members of the general board.

371

¶ 810. *Provisions Pertaining to General Agency Membership.*—
1. Members of all general agencies shall be members of The
United Methodist Church.[5]

2. Members of all general agencies and commissions shall be
persons of genuine Christian character who love the Church, are
morally disciplined and loyal to the ethical standards of The
United Methodist Church as set forth in the Social Principles, and
are otherwise competent to serve as members of general agencies
and commissions.

3. A voting member of a general agency shall be eligible for
membership on that agency for no more than two consecutive
four-year terms. The four-year term shall begin at the first
organizational meeting of that agency following General Conference. Service of more than one year in fulfilling an unexpired or
vacated position shall be considered as a full four-year term. To
provide a continuing membership on these agencies, it is
recommended that each nominating and electing body give
special attention to continuing and effective membership on
these agencies. If a general agency is merged with another
agency, the years served by members prior to the merger shall be
counted as part of the maximum specified above.

4. No person shall serve at the same time on more than one
general agency or any part thereof, except where the Discipline
specifically provides for such interagency representation; *provided,* however, that if this limitation would deprive a jurisdiction of
its full episcopal representation on an agency, it may be
suspended to the extent necessary to permit such representation.[6]
(*See* ¶ 1007.1*b.*)

5. A voting member of a general agency, by virtue of such
membership, shall become a voting member of the corresponding agency of the Annual Conference, unless such membership
would conflict with ¶ 723.1. This provision shall not apply to
episcopal members of general agencies nor to salaried Annual
Conference staff who are members of a general agency, unless
such voting membership is specifically provided by another
provision of the Discipline or by action of the Annual Conference.

[5]*See* Judicial Council Decision 426.
[6]*See* Judicial Council Decision 224.

6. No person who receives compensation for services rendered or commissions of any kind from an agency shall be eligible for voting membership on that agency.[7]

7. No elected member, officer, or other employee shall vote on or take part in deliberations on significant matters directly or indirectly affecting his or her business, income, or employment, or the business, income, or employment of a member of his or her immediate family.

8. When an ordained minister who has been elected as a representative of a jurisdiction to a general agency is transferred to an Annual Conference in another jurisdiction, or a lay person who has been so elected changes legal residence to another jurisdiction, that person shall cease to be a member of that agency at the time of the transfer or removal. The vacancy shall be filled in accordance with the appropriate provisions of the Discipline. If any member of a general or jurisdictional agency who was chosen to represent a certain Annual Conference shall remove residence permanently from such Annual Conference, that member's place shall automatically become vacant.

9. If a member of a general agency is absent from two consecutive regular meetings without a reason acceptable to the agency, that person shall cease to be a member thereof. In that case the person shall be so notified, and that place shall be filled in accordance with the appropriate provisions of the Discipline.

10. When a bishop is unable to attend a meeting of an agency of which that bishop is a member, that bishop may name another bishop to attend that meeting with the privilege of vote.

¶ 811. The councils, boards, committees, or commissions elected, authorized, or provided for by the General Conference shall have full power and authority to remove and dismiss at their discretion any member, officer, or employee thereof:

1. Who has become incapacitated so as to be unable to perform official duties.

2. Who is guilty of immoral conduct or breach of trust.

3. Who for any reason is unable to, or who fails to, perform the duties of the office, or for other misconduct which any

---

[7]*See* Judicial Council Decision 139.

council, board, committee, or commission may deem sufficient to warrant such dismissal and removal.

In the event that any member, officer, or employee of such council, board, committee, or commission, elected, authorized, or provided for by the General Conference, is found guilty of any crime involving moral turpitude by any federal, state, or county court or pleads guilty thereto, then and in that event, the council, board, committee, or commission of which that person is a member, officer, or employee shall be and is hereby authorized to remove such member, officer, or employee so convicted; and the place so vacated shall be filled as provided in the Discipline.

¶ **812.** *Vacancies.*—Unless otherwise specified, vacancies on general agencies occurring during the quadrennium shall be filled as follows: an episcopal vacancy shall be filled by the Council of Bishops; a vacancy in the basic membership shall be filled by the College of Bishops of that jurisdiction with notice of the vacancy sent by the agency to the secretary of the Council of Bishops; a vacancy in the additional membership shall be filled by the agency itself.

¶ **813.** The general secretary of each general program agency that is accountable to the General Council on Ministries shall be elected annually by ballot of the General Council on Ministries upon the nomination of the agency involved. Any general secretary of a general program agency who has not been elected by the General Council on Ministries shall not serve in such capacity beyond the end of that calendar year. Each program board shall elect annually by ballot its associate general secretary(ies) and may elect or appoint such other staff as may be necessary.

¶ **814.** *Provisions Pertaining to Staff.*—1. No elected clergy staff shall hold the same position more than twelve years. Years of service prior to January 1, 1973, are not counted. The agency responsible for the election of such staff may annually suspend this provision by a two-thirds ballot vote.

2. Official travel of the staffs of agencies shall be interpreted to include all travel which is necessary in the performance of official duties directly related to the agency functions. No staff person shall accept honoraria for such official duties. A staff member may accept an engagement not related to the functions

of the employing agency when such an engagement does not interfere with official duties; the staff member may accept an honorarium for services rendered in connection with such engagements.

3. Effective May 1, 1980, normal retirement with full pension benefit for all general agency staff personnel shall be at age sixty-five or the completion of forty years of service to The United Methodist Church in an elective, appointive, or employed capacity. Mandatory retirement shall be at age seventy. An employee may elect to retire at any time after attaining age sixty-two or completing thirty-seven years of service. Employees electing to retire early shall have their pension benefit reduced actuarially.

4. The general secretary of the General Council on Ministries and/or the general secretary of the General Council on Finance and Administration may convene the general secretaries of the general agencies as necessary for the purpose of obtaining opinion and recommendations to assist the councils in discharging their functions.

5. Applicants for executive staff positions shall be considered on the basis of their qualifications and in keeping with the nondiscriminatory policies of The United Methodist Church.

6. The general secretary, associate general secretaries, and assistant general secretaries of all general agencies shall be members of The United Methodist Church. This provision shall not apply to persons employed prior to the 1976 General Conference.

7. No member of the staff of a general agency shall be eligible for voting membership on any general or jurisdictional agency of The United Methodist Church except where the Discipline specifically provides for such interagency representation.

8. Elected staff shall be allowed voice but not vote in the agency and its subunits.

9. All management staff persons of general agencies and commissions shall be persons of genuine Christian character who love the Church, are morally disciplined and loyal to the ethical standards of The United Methodist Church as set forth in the Social Principles, and are competent to administer the affairs of a general agency.

¶ **815.** *Policies Relative to Nondiscrimination.*—It shall be the policy of The United Methodist Church that all administrative agencies and institutions, including hospitals, homes, and educational institutions, shall: *(a)* recruit, employ, utilize, recompense, and promote their professional staff and other personnel in a manner consistent with the commitment of The United Methodist Church to ethnic, racial, and sexual inclusiveness; *(b)* fulfill their duties and responsibilities in a manner which does not involve segregation or discrimination on the basis of race, color, age, sex, or handicapping condition; and *(c)* provide for adequate representation by laity.

¶ **816.** Each general agency shall keep a continuous record of its advocacy roles, coalitions supported by membership or funds, and endorsement or opposition of federal or state legislation. Information concerning these activities shall be available to United Methodist churches upon written request.

¶ **817.** All general funds administered by any general agency of The United Methodist Church which are proposed to be used for funding a program within an Annual Conference shall be disbursed after consultation with the presiding bishop and the Council on Ministries of that Annual Conference.

¶ **818.** Central Conferences of The United Methodist Church may request program and other assistance through direct relationships with the program agencies of The United Methodist Church.

¶ **819.** *Church Year and Quadrennium.*—1. The program and fiscal year for The United Methodist Church shall be the calendar year.

2. Unless otherwise specified in the Discipline for a specific purpose, the term "quadrennium" shall be deemed to be the four-year period beginning January 1 following the adjournment of the regular session of the General Conference.

¶ **820.** *Evangelical United Brethren Council of Administration.*— The General Council on Finance and Administration shall preserve the corporate existence of the Evangelical United Brethren Council of Administration until such time as attorneys shall advise its dissolution. The General Council on Finance and Administration shall nominate for election the Board of Trustees of the Evangelical United Brethren Council of Administration.

¶ **821.** *Church Name Outside the United States of America.*—The name of The United Methodist Church may be translated by any Central Conference into languages other than English. The United Methodist Church in the Central and Southern Europe Central Conference and the Central Conference in the German Democratic Republic and the Central Conference in the Federal Republic of Germany and West Berlin may use the name *Evangelisch-methodistische Kirche.*

¶ **822.** *Church Founding Date.*—The United Methodist Church has become the legal and ecclesiastical successor to all property, property rights, powers, and privileges of The Evangelical United Brethren Church and The Methodist Church; the two churches, from their beginnings, have had a close relationship.

The Methodist Church, the first of the two churches to organize, dates from the Christmas Conference of 1784. Therefore, The United Methodist Church recognizes as its founding date the year 1784.

All General Conferences shall be designated not in numerical sequence from any particular date, but merely by the calendar years in which they are respectively held. An Annual Conference, local church, or other body within The United Methodist Church which is composed of uniting units with differing dates of origin shall use as the date of its founding the date of founding of the older or oldest of the uniting units, or it may use such other founding-date formula as it may determine.

Section II. General Council on Finance and Administration.

¶ **901.** *General Statement on Church Finance.*—The work of the Church requires the support of our people, and participation therein through service and gifts is a Christian duty and a means of grace. In order that all members of The United Methodist Church may share in its manifold ministries at home and abroad and that the work committed to us may prosper, the following financial plan has been duly approved and adopted.

¶ **902.** *Name.*—There shall be a **General Council on Finance and Administration** of The United Methodist Church, herein-after called the council.

¶ **903.** *Incorporation.*—The council shall be incorporated in such state or states as the council shall determine. This corporation shall be the successor corporation and organization to the Council on World Service and Finance (including the Council on World Service and Finance of The United Methodist Church, an Illinois corporation; the World Service Commission of the Methodist Episcopal Church, an Illinois corporation; the General Council of Administration of The Evangelical United Brethren Church, an Ohio corporation; the Board of Administration, Church of the United Brethren in Christ, an Ohio corporation) and the Board of Trustees.

This corporation shall receive and administer new trusts and funds, and so far as may be legal be the successor in trust of: The Board of Trustees of The United Methodist Church; The Board of Trustees of The Evangelical United Brethren Church, incorporated under the laws of Ohio; The Board of Trustees of the Church of the United Brethren in Christ, incorporated under the laws of Ohio; The Board of Trustees of the Evangelical Church, an unincorporated body; The Board of Trustees of The Methodist Church, incorporated under the laws of Ohio; The Trustees of the Methodist Episcopal Church, incorporated under the laws of Ohio; The Board of Trustees of the Methodist Episcopal Church, South, incorporated under the laws of Tennessee; and The Board of Trustees of the Methodist Protestant Church, incorporated under the laws of Maryland; and so far as may be legal, as such successor in trust, it is authorized to receive from any of its said predecessor corporations all trust funds and assets of every kind and character, real, personal, or mixed, held by them or any one of them, or to merge into itself any one or more of its said predecessor corporations. Any such trusts and funds coming to it as successor corporation, either by transfer or by merger, shall be administered in accordance with the conditions under which they have been previously received and administered by said predecessor corporations or unincorporated body.

¶ **904.** *Amenability.*—The council shall report to and be amenable to the General Conference, and it shall cooperate with the Council on Ministries in the compilation of budgets for program agencies participating in World Service Funds, as defined in ¶ 906.1.

¶ **905.** *Organization.*—1. *Membership.*—The members of the council shall be elected quadrennially by the General Conference as follows: three bishops, nominated by the Council of Bishops; two clergy in full connection, two laymen, and two laywomen from each jurisdiction, nominated by the bishops of that jurisdiction; nine members at large, one-third laymen, one-third laywomen, and one-third clergy, at least one of whom shall not be over twenty-one years of age at the time of election, and at least two of whom shall represent racial and ethnic minorities, and most of whom shall be elected for special skills, nominated by the Council of Bishops without reference to jurisdictions. The general secretaries who serve as the chief executive officers of the general agencies and the publisher of The United Methodist Church shall be members of the council but without vote. The voting members, including bishops, shall not be eligible for membership on, or employment by, any other agency receiving funds administered by the council where the Discipline specifically provides for such interagency representation. They shall serve until their successors are elected and qualified. Vacancies occurring between sessions of the General Conference shall be filled by the council on nomination of the College of Bishops of the jurisdiction concerned (*see* ¶ 812) or, in the event of a vacancy among the episcopal members or members at large, on nomination of the Council of Bishops.

2. *Meetings.*—The council shall meet annually and at such other times as are necessary on call of the president or on written request of one fifth of the members. Twenty-two voting members shall constitute a quorum.

3. *Officers.*—The officers of the council shall be a president, a vice-president, a recording secretary, and a general secretary, who shall also be the treasurer of the council, all of whom shall be elected by the council (*see* §5). They shall serve until the adjournment of the next succeeding quadrennial session of the General Conference after their election and until their successors are duly elected and qualified. The president, vice-president, and recording secretary shall be elected from the membership of the council. The general secretary shall sit with the council and its executive committee at all sessions and shall have right to the floor without the privilege of voting.

379

4. *Committees.—a) Executive Committee.*—There shall be an **executive committee** of the council consisting of the episcopal members, the officers of the council, chairpersons of the committees on services, as defined in the council bylaws, the chairperson of the Committee on Council Operations, and up to three members at large to assure that, in addition to the episcopal members, there is at least one member from each jurisdiction and there is racial and ethnic minority participation. The executive committee shall be elected annually by the council. The executive committee shall meet on call of the president or of a majority of the membership and shall act for the council and exercise its powers in the interim between the meetings of the council, but it shall not take any action contrary to or in conflict with any action or policy of the council. A copy of the minutes of each meeting of the executive committee shall be sent from the central office to each member of the council as soon after the meeting as practicable.

b) Committee on Audit and Review.—The executive committee of the council shall appoint a **Committee on Audit and Review,** no members of which shall be officers or members of the executive committee of the council, and at least half of whom shall not be members of the council, whose duty it shall be to review financial reports and audits of all treasuries receiving general church funds, including the funds of the council. The committee shall report its findings to the annual meeting of the council.

c) Committee on Official Forms and Records.—The council shall maintain and supervise under the direction of its general secretary a **Committee on Official Forms and Records,** which shall have the duty of preparing and editing all official statistical forms, record forms, and record books for use in the Church. The committee shall consist of one bishop elected by the Council of Bishops and nine persons elected by the General Council on Finance and Administration, as follows: one member of the council from each jurisdiction and one conference secretary, one conference treasurer, one conference statistician, and one district superintendent. The following persons shall be consultants to this committee ex officio without vote: a staff representative of the council, the director of the Department of Statistics, a staff representative of the General Council on Ministries, a representative of The United Methodist Publishing House, and representatives of other general agencies when their programs are directly involved. All official statistical forms, record forms, and record books required for use in The United Methodist Church shall be printed and published by The United Methodist Publishing House.

d) Committee on Personnel Policies and Practices.—The council shall organize a committee consisting of four representatives from the General Council on Finance and Administration, one of whom shall serve as chairperson, two representatives from the General Council on Ministries, two representatives from the General Board of Pensions, one representative of each of the program boards, and one representative from each of the standing general commissions. Each of the aforementioned representatives shall be selected by the council, board, or commission represented from its membership. The committee shall have duties and responsibilities as defined in ¶ 907.7.

e) Committee on Legal Responsibilities.—The council shall organize a committee composed of six persons, three of whom shall be members of the council. The committee shall be amenable to the council and shall make recommendations to the council regarding the fulfillment of the responsibilities defined in ¶ 907.4.

f) Other Committees.—The council shall elect or appoint such other committees and task forces as needed for the performance of its duties.

5. *Staff.*—The council shall elect a general secretary as provided in § 3 above. On nomination of the general secretary, the council may elect associate general secretaries, who shall work under the direction of the general secretary. All employed personnel of the council shall be selected by and shall be amenable to the general secretary.

¶ **906.** *Fiscal Responsibilities.*—The council shall be accountable to The United Methodist Church through the General Conference in all matters relating to the receiving, disbursing, and reporting of general church funds, and agencies receiving general church funds shall be fiscally accountable to the council. In the exercise of its fiscal accountability role the council shall have the authority and responsibility to perform the following functions:

1. It shall submit to each quadrennial session of the General Conference, for its action and determination, budgets of expense for its own operation, the World Service Fund, the General Administration Fund, the Episcopal Fund, the Interdenominational Cooperation Fund, the Ministerial Education Fund, the World Communion Offering, the One Great Hour of Sharing Fund, the Temporary General Aid Fund, the Black College Fund, the Human Relations Day Fund, the United Methodist Student Day Fund, and such other general funds as the General Conference may establish. It shall also make recommendations regarding all other funding considerations to come before General Conference.

a) The council shall make recommendations to the General Conference as to the amount and distribution of all funds provided for in §1 above.

b) In the case of the World Service Fund, the General Council on Finance and Administration and the General Council on Ministries shall proceed in the following manner in developing budget recommendations as they relate to allocations to the general program agencies of the Church:

(1) The General Council on Ministries shall, in consultation with the General Council on Finance and Administration and the general program agencies, develop recommendations regarding the program and missional priorities of the Church and shall recommend to the General Council on Finance and Administration programs which will contribute to the implementation of those priorities.

(2) The General Council on Finance and Administration shall establish the total sum to be recommended to the General Conference for the annual budget of the World Service Fund. It shall likewise establish and communicate to the General Council on Ministries the total sum proposed for distribution among the general program agencies.

(3) The General Council on Ministries, taking into consideration program priorities and the total funds available to the general program agencies, shall recommend to the General Council on Finance and Administration the amount of the annual World Service allocation to each of those agencies, within the total

sum proposed by the General Council on Finance and Administration for distribution among such agencies.

(4) Only when the General Council on Finance and Administration and the General Council on Ministries agree on the allocations to the several general program agencies shall these allocations be included in the World Service budget to be recommended to the General Conference by the General Council on Finance and Administration.

(5) Before the beginning of each year the General Council on Finance and Administration shall determine and communicate to the General Council on Ministries the sum available at that time from World Service contingency funds to meet requests for additional funding from the general program agencies. The General Council on Ministries shall be authorized to approve allocations to the general program agencies for additional program funding up to the limit so established. No money shall be allocated by the General Council on Ministries from this source for general administrative costs, fixed charges, or capital outlay without approval by the General Council on Finance and Administration.

(6) The General Council on Ministries shall receive from the General Council on Finance and Administration copies of the proposed annual budgets of the general program agencies, in order that it may review such budgets in relation to the program proposals made by those agencies in their quadrennial budget requests.

c) It shall recommend the formulas by which all apportionments to the Annual Conferences shall be determined, subject to the approval of the General Conference.

d) The expenses of the council, including the cost of all its operations, shall be a first claim against all general funds received and disbursed by the council. The charges against the several funds or beneficiary agencies shall be in proportion to the funds' receipts.

2. It shall receive and disburse in accordance with budgets approved by the General Conference all funds raised throughout the Church for:

a) The World Service Fund, including World Service special gifts and Advance special gifts, *b)* The General Administration Fund,

c) The Episcopal Fund,

d) The Interdenominational Cooperation Fund,

e) The Ministerial Education Fund,

f) The Black College Fund,

g) The Missional Priority Fund,

h) The Temporary General Aid Fund,

i) The World Communion Fund,

j) The Human Relations Day Fund,

k) The United Methodist Student Day Fund,

l) The One Great Hour of Sharing Fund,

m) The Youth Service Fund, and

n) any other fund or funds as directed by the proper authority.

3. To perform the accounting and reporting functions for the General Council on Ministries and the agencies accountable to it. In the interest of sound fiscal management, the council will ensure that expenditures of agencies receiving general church funds do not exceed receipts and available reserves, and this within an approved budget. If necessary for the efficient performance of the accounting and reporting function, the council may establish branch offices.

4. It shall require all agencies receiving general church funds to follow uniform accounting classifications and procedures for reporting. It shall require an annual audit of all treasuries receiving general church funds, following such auditing procedures as it may specify. It shall have authority to pass on the acceptability of any auditing firm proposed by an agency. It shall also require annually one month in advance of its annual meeting, or as is deemed necessary, and in such form as the council may require, statements of proposed budgets of all treasuries or agencies receiving general church funds. It shall review the budget of each agency receiving general church funds in accordance with guidelines which it shall establish and communicate to the agencies, including the relationship between administration, service, and promotion. It shall include in its quadrennial report to the General Conference a fiscal report for each of the general agencies, including councils, boards, commissions, and committees of The United Methodist Church

that have been constituted by the General Conference. Such report shall be available upon request.

5. To establish policy governing the functions of banking, payroll, purchasing, accounting, and budget control for all agencies receiving general church funds. The council may upon mutual consent of the agencies involved, perform the functions of banking, check preparation, payroll, and purchasing on behalf of an agency in order to maximize efficiency of operation. All boards and agencies shall observe the uniform fiscal year (¶ 818).

6. To develop investment policies for, suggest investment counselors for, and review on at least a quarterly basis the performance of all invested funds of all agencies receiving general church funds. The council shall have complete authority to manage any portfolio of less than $1,500,000. The council is encouraged to invest in institutions, companies, corporations, or funds which make a positive contribution toward the realization of the goals outlined in the Social Principles of The United Methodist Church (¶¶ 70-76).

7. To receive, collect, and hold in trust for the benefit of The United Methodist Church, its general funds, or its general agencies, any and all donations, bequests, and devises of any kind, real or personal, that may be given, devised, bequeathed, or conveyed to The United Methodist Church as such or to any general fund or agency of The United Methodist Church for any benevolent, charitable, or religious purposes, and to administer the same and the income therefrom in accordance with the directions of the donor, trustor, or testator; and, in cooperation with the Board of Discipleship, to take such action as is necessary to encourage United Methodists to provide for their continued participation in World Service, in one or more of the World Service agencies, or in other general church benevolence funds or interests, through wills and special gifts (*see* ¶ 1315.7).

8. To establish standardized gift annuity rates and formulate policies for the writing of annuities by institutions and agencies operating under the auspices of The United Methodist Church.

9. Where Annual Conferences, individually or in groups, have established foundations, the council may provide staff leadership on request to advise in matters of financial manage-

ment, to the end that foundation assets shall be wisely managed on behalf of the Church.

10. To approve plans for financing all national conferences and convocations to be held under the auspices or sponsorship of any general agency of the Church.

11. To make recommendations to the General Conference, in consultation with the General Council on Ministries and the Council of Bishops, regarding any offerings to be received in connection with special days observed on a churchwide basis. These recommendations shall include the number and timing of such special days with offerings, the amount, if any, to be established as a goal for each such offering, the causes to be benefited by each, the method by which the receipts on each such offering shall be distributed among the causes benefiting from it, and the method by which such receipts shall be remitted and reported by local churches. All such recommendations are subject to the approval of the General Conference.

12. The council shall recommend to each conference Council on Finance and Administration a uniform procedure for presenting its report to the Annual Conference and shall prepare a form for the guidance of the conference treasurer in making his or her annual statement in the conference journal.

13. The council shall be responsible for ensuring that no board, agency, committee, commission, or council shall give United Methodist funds to any "gay" caucus or group, or otherwise use such funds to promote the acceptance of homosexuality. The council shall have the right to stop such expenditures.

¶ **907.** *Other Administrative Responsibilities.*—The council shall have the authority and responsibility to perform the following functions:

1. To establish general policy governing the leasing, sale, rental, renovation, or purchase of property by a general agency. The council shall consider the plans of any general agency proposing to acquire or sell real estate or erect a building or enter into a lease in the continental United States and determine whether the proposed action is in the best interest of The United Methodist Church. On the basis of that determination it shall approve or disapprove all such proposed actions. In the case of

such proposed action by a general program agency, it shall solicit and consider the recommendation of the Council on Ministries. If either council disapproves, the agency shall delay the project until it can be considered by the next General Conference. Nothing in the foregoing shall include the operational requirements of the Board of Publication.

2. The General Council on Finance and Administration and the General Council on Ministries, acting in concert, shall establish a procedure for a quadrennial review with the general agencies regarding the location of their headquarters and staff.

3. To exercise on behalf of General Conference a property reporting function by receiving reports annually from general agencies of the church concerning property titles, values, debts, general maintenance, lease or rental costs, space usage, and such other information as the council may deem relevant. The council may consult and advise with the general agencies concerning any property problems that may arise. A summary of the property data shall be reported to each quadrennial General Conference. This provision shall apply to headquarters buildings but not to properties which are part of the program responsibilities of the General Board of Global Ministries or to any of the properties of the General Board of Publication. Titles to historical shrines, landmarks, and such historical properties as may be acquired in the future shall be held by the General Council on Finance and Administration.

4. To take all necessary legal steps to safeguard and protect the interests and rights of The United Methodist Church; to maintain a file of legal briefs related to cases involving The United Methodist Church, and to make provisions for legal counsel where necessary in order to protect the interests of the Church at the request of a general agency or a bishop, as the council deems advisable. The council shall recommend to each general agency and unit thereof and to each Annual Conference Council on Finance and Administration a uniform procedure to be followed by the aforesaid agencies and, where applicable, local churches, relative to the certification and payment of ordained ministers' housing allowances in accordance with provisions of the Internal Revenue Code of the United States. The council shall have the authority to pursue policies and procedures necessary to

preserve the tax-exempt status of the denomination and its affiliated organizations.[8]

5. To provide direction and coordination in the design and implementation of operating systems in order to maximize the efficiency of operating personnel, equipment, and resources between and within agencies. During the quadrennium these agencies shall study their respective responsibilities, programs, and internal operations and institute such improvements and economies in their work as they find to be feasible and practicable. They shall cooperate with the council in working out, in advance of these studies, the general areas to be included and methods of carrying out this objective. They shall report their accomplishments in improvements and economies at the close of each fiscal year to the council, which shall prepare from this information a combined report for the General Conference.

6. To determine policy for ownership, lease, and use of computers by the general church agencies and to formulate policy governing the data-processing function carried out by general church agencies. Data processing shall include data gathering, storage, and retrieval.

7. *a)* The council shall require each general agency, including itself, to follow uniform policies and practices in the employment and remuneration of personnel, recognizing differences in local employment conditions.

b) The Committee on Personnel Policies and Practices (¶ 905.4*d*) shall prepare quadrennially, review annually, and recommend to the council an appropriate salary schedule, based upon responsibilities, for executive staff personnel of the councils, boards, and commissions represented on the committee. The committee shall develop and recommend to the council a schedule of benefits for an employee benefit program for general agency personnel and any changes required thereto from time to time, which program shall be administered by the General Board of Pensions under arrangements approved by the committee and the council.

c) The committee shall receive from agencies and institutions receiving general church funds statements regarding their

---

[8]*See* Judicial Council Decision 458.

compliance with the policy stated in ¶ 910.1. Based on these statements, and in consultation with and upon the advice of the Standing General Commission on Religion and Race and the Standing General Commission on the Status and Role of Women, the committee shall prepare for the Council on Finance and Administration reports and recommendations deemed appropriate by the committee.

d) In the event it is determined by the council that an agency or institution receiving general church funds is not in compliance with the equal employment opportunity policies and the salary and employee benefit schedules established by the committee, the council shall notify in writing the agency so named and suspend, after a three-month period of grace, an appropriate amount of future funding until the agency or institution complies.

8. To maintain a consultative service to assist general agencies in planning and making arrangements for national meetings, conferences, and convocations.

9. To maintain an accurate record of the mail addresses of all bishops; ministers in effective relation; local pastors, including retired ministers serving charges; and such lists of general, jurisdictional, conference, and district boards, commissions, and committees, and officers of same, and of local church commission chairpersons, as may be deemed necessary. No one other than authorized bodies or officers of the Church shall be permitted to use these records.

10. To prepare the important statistics relating to The United Methodist Church for the General Minutes, the Fact Book, or such other publications and releases as may be approved by the council. It shall provide for the distribution of statistical information to Annual Conferences, the general planning and research agencies of the Church, and other interested parties. The council may establish an appropriate schedule of fees and charges to defray the cost of such information distribution services.

11. To assist and advise the jurisdictions, Annual Conferences, districts, and local churches in all matters relating to the work of the council. These matters shall include, but shall not be limited to, business administration, investment and property management, data processing, and auditing. Matters related to

resourcing the development and implementation of financial programs within the local church Committee on Finance shall be the responsibility of the Board of Discipleship. The council may perform certain functions for the jurisdictions, Annual Conferences, districts, or local churches if the particular organization so elects and a suitable plan of operation can be determined.

12. To provide guidance and consultation in the area of local church business administration, including establishment of professional standards, a training program, certification of church business administrators, and associate church business administrators, sponsorship of an association of United Methodist church business administrators, and placement services.

13. To institute, manage, and maintain a churchwide insurance program for the protection of United Methodist Church property and persons, covering all areas involving the interest of The United Methodist Church and available to all churches, agencies, institutions, and persons within The United Methodist Church. An insurance trust shall be an integral part of the program.

14. To designate one of its staff members as the **business manager of the General Conference;** when acting in this capacity, this staff person shall be related operationally to the Commission on the General Conference.

¶ **908.** The treasurer of the General Council on Finance and Administration shall, not less than ninety days prior to the session of each Annual Conference or as soon thereafter as practical, transmit to the presiding bishop thereof, to the president of the conference Council on Finance and Administration, and to the conference treasurer a statement of the apportionments to the conference for the World Service Fund, the General Administration Fund, the Episcopal Fund, the Interdenominational Cooperation Fund, the Ministerial Education Fund, the Temporary General Aid Fund, the Black College Fund, the Missional Priority Fund, and such other funds as may have been apportioned by the General Conference. The treasurer shall keep an account of all amounts remitted by the conference treasurers and from other sources intended for the funds listed in ¶ 906.2. and any other fund so directed by the proper authority, and shall disburse the same as authorized by the General

Conference and directed by the council. A separate account shall be kept of each such fund, and none of them shall be drawn on for the benefit of another fund.

¶ **909.** The treasurer shall report annually to the council and to the respective conference councils as to all amounts received and disbursed during the year. The treasurer shall also make to each quadrennial session of the General Conference a full report of the financial transactions of the council for the preceding quadrennium. The treasurer shall be bonded for such an amount as may be determined by the council. The books of the treasurer shall be audited annually by a certified public accountant approved by the Committee on Audit and Review (¶ 905.4*b*).

GENERAL FUNDS

¶ **910.** *General Policies.*—1. The General Council on Finance and Administration shall withhold approval of the entire budget of any agency or any church-related institution receiving general church funds until such agency or church-related institution certifies to the council in writing that it has established and has complied with a policy of (*a*) recruiting, employing, utilizing, recompensing, and promoting professional staff and other personnel without regard to race, color, or sex, (*b*) fulfilling its duties and responsibilities in a manner which does not involve segregation or discrimination on the basis of race or sex, and (*c*) insofar as possible, purchasing goods and services from vendors who are in compliance with such policies as are described in sections (*a*) and (*b*) of this paragraph. In the fulfillment of this directive the council shall take the following steps to ensure that concerns of the Standing General Commission on Religion and Race and the Standing General Commission on the Status and Role of Women are represented: (1) consult with the two commissions in the development of a certification form to be submitted to the council by agencies and institutions receiving general church funds; (2) share copies of such certifications with the two commissions; (3) receive and consider recommendations from either of the two commissions regarding possible noncompliance with these policies by agencies and institutions receiving general church funds.

391

2. It shall withhold approval of any item or items in the budget or budgets receiving general church funds which in its judgment represent unnecessary duplication of administrative function; in cooperation with and on recommendation of the Council on Ministries, it shall withhold approval of any such item which represents unnecessary duplication of program within an agency or between two or more agencies. If the council finds that there is such duplication in existing activities, it shall promptly direct the attention of the agencies involved to the situation and shall cooperate with them in correcting the same, and may decline to supply from general fund receipts money to continue activities which have been held to duplicate each other unnecessarily or plainly violate the principle of correlation as applied to the total benevolence program of the Church.

3. An agency of The United Methodist Church proposing to borrow funds for a period in excess of twelve months or in an amount in excess of 25 percent of its annual budget or one hundred thousand dollars, whichever amount is smaller, whether for building or current expense purposes, shall submit such proposal, accompanied by a plan for amortization, to the council for approval. If the council disapproves, the agency shall delay such borrowing until it can be considered by the next General Conference.

4. Any general board, cause, agency, or institution or any organization, group, officer, or individual of The United Methodist Church or to which The United Methodist Church contributes financial support desiring or proposing to make a special churchwide financial appeal during the quadrennium shall present a request for authorization to make such appeal to the General Council on Finance and Administration at the time budgets for the ensuing quadrennium are being considered. All such appeals shall be reviewed by the General Council on Ministries and its actions shall be reported to the General Council on Finance and Administration. The council shall then report such request to the General Conference with a recommendation for its action thereon. "Special appeal" shall be understood to mean any appeal other than the general appeal for support of the World Service program as represented in the World Service budget. "Churchwide appeal" shall be understood to mean any

appeal to the Church at large except appeals to such special groups as alumni of an educational institution. In the interim between the quadrennial sessions of the General Conference such proposed churchwide financial appeal shall require the approval of the General Council on Finance and Administration and the Council of Bishops. In case of emergency the executive committee of either of these bodies may act in such matter for the body itself, but only by a three-fourths vote. The General Council on Finance and Administration shall withhold payment of the allocation from any general fund to any agency or institution which it finds to be in violation of the provisions of this paragraph.

¶ **911.** *The World Service Fund.*—**The World Service Fund** is basic in the financial program of The United Methodist Church. World Service on apportionment represents the minimum needs of the general agencies of the Church. Payment in full of these apportionments by local churches and Annual Conferences is the first benevolent responsibility of the Church.

1. The council shall recommend to each quadrennial session of the General Conference the amount of the annual World Service budget for the ensuing quadrennium and the method by which it shall be apportioned to the annual conferences. In cooperation with the General Council on Ministries it shall prepare and recommend a plan of distribution of World Service receipts among the World Service agencies, in accordance with the procedures described in ¶ 906.1*b*. In the planning of the World Service budget it shall be the role of the General Council on Finance and Administration to facilitate sound fiscal and administrative policies and practices within and among the general agencies of the Church. It shall be the role of the General Council on Ministries to relate the budget askings of the program agencies to one another in such a way as to implement the program and missional priorities of the Church.

2. The general secretary or other duly authorized representative of each agency of The United Methodist Church requesting support from the World Service Fund and the authorized representative of any other agency for which askings are authorized by the General Conference shall have the right to appear before the council at a designated time and place to

represent the cause for which each is responsible, provided that such representation has been previously made to the Council on Ministries.

3. The World Service agencies shall not solicit additional or special gifts from individual donors or special groups, other than foundations, unless approval for such solicitation is first secured from the council.

¶ **912.** *World Service Special Gifts.*—Individual donors or local churches may make special gifts to the support of any cause or project which is a part of the work of any one of the World Service agencies. Such gifts shall be sent to the Central Treasury of the Council on Finance and Administration. Bequests, gifts on the annuity plan, gifts to permanent funds, and gifts of property shall be classified as special gifts.

1. All special gifts made to or administered by a general agency, except as provided in § 4 below, shall be acknowledged by special-gift vouchers.

2. The vouchers acknowledging such gifts to World Service agencies shall be entitled "World Service Special-gift Vouchers"; *provided*, however, that vouchers for such gifts designated for approved general Advance projects of the World and National Divisions and the United Methodist Committee on Relief of the Board of Global Ministries shall be entitled "Advance Special-gift Vouchers"; and *provided* further, that gifts to any other cause or project which is a part of the work of those agencies shall be acknowledged as "Miscellaneous Gifts."

3. A World Service agency or any individual or agency authorized to make a churchwide appeal for funds shall channel all special gifts through the Central Treasury. Individuals soliciting such funds shall channel the money received through the Central Treasury, which shall issue the proper vouchers.

4. Bequests, gifts on the annuity plan at maturity, and gifts of real property shall be reported to the Central Treasury as supplemental contributions and shall not be subject to prorated service charges.

¶ **913.** *The Advance.*—1. The Advance is the official program within The United Methodist Church (except for World Service special gifts and programs of United Methodist Women) through which support may be designated for projects approved by the Advance Committee.

2. A general Advance special gift is a designated financial contribution made by an individual, local church, organization, district, or conference to a project authorized for this purpose by the Advance Committee.

a) Gifts as Advance specials may be made for specific projects or purposes authorized by the Advance Committee.

b) Gifts as Advance specials may be made for broadly designated causes (such as a type of work, a country, or a region), or for use as block grants to a certain country or administrative unit, provided such causes are authorized by the Advance Committee. In such case the administering agency shall provide the donor with information about the area to which the funds have been given and, where practicable, establish communication with a person or group representative of that type of work.

c) An Advance special gift may be given to an authorized agency (¶ 1007.5) rather than to a specific project, in which case the agency shall determine the Advance special project or projects to which such a gift shall be allocated, shall inform the donor where the gift has been invested, and as far as practicable shall establish communication between donor and recipient.

3. Funds given and received as a part of the general Advance shall be subject to the following conditions:

a) Churches and individuals shall give priority to the support of the World Service and Conference Benevolences and other apportioned funds. Advance giving shall be voluntary and in addition to the support of apportioned funds.

b) Funds shall be solicited or received only for authorized projects. Programs and institutions having general Advance special projects shall promote only for the projects approved and shall ask that gifts be remitted in the manner described in ¶ 913.4 below.

c) Funds received through the Advance shall be used solely for project support and are not to be used for administration or promotional costs.

d) Advance special gifts shall not be raised as a part of a fund apportioned by an Annual Conference. (For conference Advance special gifts *see* ¶¶ 718.1-.5.)

e) Upon receipt of funds for a general Advance special each administering agency shall communicate promptly with the donor, acknowledging receipt of the gift and suggesting avenues for communication, if communication has not already been established.

4. Receipts for general Advance specials shall be remitted by the local church treasurer to the conference treasurer, who shall make remittance each month to the participating agencies in a manner determined by the treasurer of the General Council on Finance and Administration. Individuals may remit directly to respective agencies in a manner determined by the treasurer of the General Council on Finance and Administration, with these remittances reported to the Annual Conference treasurer by the respective agencies.

¶ **914.** The following general directives shall be observed in the promotion and administration of the Advance and One Great Hour of Sharing:

1. In the appeal and promotion of Advance specials and One Great Hour of Sharing offerings there shall be no goals or quotas except as they may be set by the Annual Conferences for themselves.

2. The treasurer of the Council on Finance and Administration shall be treasurer of the Advance and One Great Hour of Sharing.

3. The expense of promotion for Advance specials shall be borne by the respective participating agencies in proportion to the amount received by each in Advance specials. The causes of the Advance shall be coordinated with other financial appeals and shall be promoted by the central promotional office of the section on interpretation of the Standing General Commission on Communication.

4. The appeal for Advance specials shall be channeled through bishops, district superintendents, and pastors, the details of the procedure to be determined by the section on interpretation of the General Commission on Communication in consultation with the Education and Cultivation Division of the Board of Global Ministries and the Advance Committee.

5. In each Annual Conference the conference Board of Global Ministries (if any; *see* ¶ 721), in cooperation with the

General Board of Global Ministries, shall promote Advance specials and One Great Hour of Sharing offerings through district missionary secretaries, conference and district missionary institutes, and other effective means as it may determine.

6. Should a clear emergency arise, any feature of the structure and administration of the Advance may be altered on the approval of a majority of the Council of Bishops and of the Council on Finance and Administration.

¶ **915.** *General Church Special-Day Offerings.*—The following are the special days with offerings to be used in support of general church causes:

1. *Human Relations Day.*—A **Human Relations Day** shall be observed on the last Sunday in Epiphany with an offering goal recommended by the General Council on Finance and Administration and adopted by the General Conference. The purpose of the goal is to further the development of better human relations through funding programs determined by the General Conference upon recommendation of the General Council on Finance and Administration after consultation with the General Council on Ministries. Net receipts from this observance shall be allocated as predetermined on ratio, with the funds being administered by the general boards under which approved programs are lodged.

2. *One Great Hour of Sharing.*—There shall be an annual observance of the **One Great Hour of Sharing** as a special offering for relief. The observance shall be under the general supervision of the Standing General Commission on Communication (¶ 1106.12) in accordance with the following directives:

   a) The One Great Hour of Sharing shall be observed annually on or about the fourth Sunday in Lent. All local churches shall be fully informed and encouraged to receive a freewill offering in behalf of the relief program.

   b) Insofar as possible, the planning and promotion of the One Great Hour of Sharing shall be done cooperatively with other denominations through the National Council of Churches, it being understood, however, that receipts of the offerings shall be administered by The United Methodist Church.

   c) Receipts from the offering, after payment of the expenses of promotion, shall be remitted by the treasurer of the General

Council on Finance and Administration to the United Methodist Committee on Relief (¶¶ 1537-1546) to be administered by that committee.

3. *United Methodist Student Day.*—The **United Methodist Student Day** offering, taken annually, the Sunday after Thanksgiving, shall be received for the support of the United Methodist Scholarships and the United Methodist Student Loan Fund. Receipts from the offering, after payment of the expenses of promotion, shall be remitted by the treasurer of the General Council on Finance and Administration to the General Board of Higher Education and Ministry to be administered by that board.

4. *World Communion Offering.*—In connection with **World Communion Sunday** there shall be a churchwide appeal conducted by the General Commission on Communication in accord with the following directives:

a) Each local church shall be requested to remit as provided in ¶ 915.6 all the Communion offering received on World Communion Sunday (on or about the first Sunday in October) and such portion of the Communion offering received at other observances of the Sacrament of the Lord's Supper as the local church may designate.

b) The net receipts, after payment of promotional costs, shall be divided as follows: 50 percent to the Crusade Scholarship Committee, 35 percent to the Ethnic Minority Scholarship Program, and 15 percent to the Ethnic Minority In-Service Training Program, the last two administered by the General Board of Higher Education and Ministry in consultation with the various minority groups.

5. Promotion of all authorized general church special Sunday offerings shall be by the General Commission on Communication in consultation with the participating agencies. Expenses of promotion for each offering shall be a prior claim against the receipts of the offering promoted. In each case such expenses shall be within a budget approved by the General Council on Finance and Administration upon recommendation of the General Commission on Communication after consultation with the participating agencies. In the promotion of these offerings there shall be an emphasis on the spiritual implications of Christian stewardship.

6. Receipts from all authorized general church special Sunday offerings shall be remitted promptly by the local church treasurer to the Annual Conference treasurer, who shall remit monthly to the treasurer of the General Council on Finance and Administration. A special-gift voucher for contributions to the offerings will be issued when appropriate. Local churches shall report the amount of the offerings in the manner indicated on the Annual Conference report form.

¶ **916.** *The General Administration Fund.*—1. **The General Administration Fund** shall provide for the expenses of the sessions of the General Conference, the Judicial Council, such special commissions and committees as may be constituted by the General Conference, and such other administrative agencies and activities as may be recommended for inclusion in the general administration budget by the Council on Finance and Administration and approved by the General Conference. Any agency or institution requiring or desiring support from the General Administration Fund shall present its case for the same to the council at a time and place which shall be indicated by the officers of the council. The council, having heard such requests, shall report the same to the General Conference with recommendations for its action and determination.

2. The apportionments for the general administration budget shall not be subject to change or revision either by the Annual Conference or by the charge or local church.

3. The treasurer of the council shall disburse the funds received for the General Administration Fund as authorized by the General Conference and as directed by the council. Where the General Conference has not allocated definite sums to agencies receiving money from the General Administration Fund, the council or its executive committee shall have authority to determine the amount to be allocated to each.

4. The expenses of the Judicial Council shall be paid from the General Administration Fund and within a budget submitted annually by the Judicial Council to the General Council on Finance and Administration for its approval.

¶ **917.** *The Interdenominational Cooperation Fund.*—1. The council shall recommend to the General Conference the sum which the Church shall undertake to provide as its share of the budget of the National Council of Churches, the World Council of Churches, and such other interdenominational causes as may be recommended by the council and approved by the General Conference for inclusion in the interdenominational cooperation budget.

2. As a service to the council, the Standing General Commission on Christian Unity and Interreligious Concerns shall provide recommendations for action on the Interdenominational Cooperation Fund.

3. United Methodist general agencies whose activities are primarily in the area of interdenominational and ecumenical relationships may also be included in this budget. The council shall also recommend to the General Conference for its action and determination the sum and conditions under which the expense of delegates of The United Methodist Church to official meetings of the National Council of Churches and the World Council of Churches may be paid. The sum approved by the General Conference for these purposes shall be the interdenominational cooperation budget. The money contributed by the local churches, boards, or other agencies for these purposes shall be known as the **Interdenominational Cooperation Fund** and shall be received and held by the treasurer of the council and disbursed as the General Conference shall direct.

¶ **918.** *Black College Fund.*—The council shall recommend to the General Conference the sum which the Church shall undertake for the black colleges and the method by which it shall be apportioned to the Annual Conferences. The purpose of the fund is to provide financial support for current operating budgets and capital improvements of the black colleges related administratively to the Church. The Division of Higher Education of the General Board of Higher Education and Ministry shall administer the fund according to the guidelines for support and a formula approved by the General Conference.

In the interim between sessions of the General Conference, these guidelines for support and this formula may be changed as necessary upon recommendation of the Council of Presidents of the Black Colleges and the General Board of Higher Education and Ministry and with the consent of the Council on Finance and Administration.

Promotion of the **Black College Fund** shall be by the Division of Higher Education and in consultation with the Council of Presidents of the Black Colleges, in cooperation with and with the assistance of the General Commission on Communication, the cost being a prior claim against the Black College Fund receipts and within a budget approved by the Division of Higher Education and the General Council on Finance and Administration.

¶ **919.** *The Temporary General Aid Fund.*—The council shall recommend to the General Conference the sum which the Church shall undertake for the purpose of providing grants-in-aid for pensions and minimum salaries to those Annual and Missionary Conferences that qualify under a formula adopted by the General Conference. The purpose of this fund is to raise the level of pensions and minimum salaries of the former Central Jurisdiction conferences and such ethnic minority conferences as the General Conference may determine and their successors, and conferences merging with such conferences. The pension portion of this fund is to be administered by the General Board of Pensions, and the minimum salary portion by the council. The apportionment and distribution are to be made by the council in accordance with formulas approved by the General Conference.

¶ **920.** *The Ministerial Education Fund.*—The council shall recommend to the General Conference the sum which the Church shall undertake for the **Ministerial Education Fund** and the method by which it shall be apportioned to the Annual Conferences, in accordance with the provisions adopted by the 1968 General Conference in establishing the Ministerial Education Fund. The purpose of the fund is to enable the Church to unify and expand its program of financial support for the recruitment and education of ordained ministers and to equip the Annual Conferences to meet increased demands in this area. The maximum amount possible from this fund shall go directly for programs and services in theological education, the enlistment and continuing education of ordained ministers, and the courses of study.

1. Of the total money raised in each Annual Conference for the Ministerial Education Fund, 25 percent shall be retained by

the Annual Conference which raised it, to be used in its program of ministerial education as approved by the Annual Conference and administered through its Board of Ordained Ministry. An Annual Conference may decide to use Ministerial Education Funds for those in diaconal ministry with the administration remaining with the Board of Ordained Ministry. No Annual Conference which had been participating in a 1 percent plan or other conference program of ministerial student scholarships and loan grants prior to the establishment of this fund shall receive less for this purpose than it received in the last year of the quadrennium preceding the establishment of the fund, provided the giving from that conference for ministerial education does not fall below the level achieved in the quadrennium preceding the establishment of the fund.

2. Of the total money raised in each Annual Conference for the Ministerial Education Fund, 75 percent shall be remitted by the conference treasurer to the treasurer of the council for distribution to the Division of Ordained Ministry of the Board of Higher Education and Ministry for distribution as follows:

a) At least 75 percent of the amount received by the division shall be distributed on formula established by the division after consultation with the Jurisdictional Committees on Ordained Ministry. All money allocated to the theological schools shall be used for current operations, not for physical expansion.

b) The remaining portion of the amount received by the division shall be administered by it, in order of priority, for distribution to the seminaries of The United Methodist Church to correct inequities in appropriations to the seminaries and for divisional use in its program in ministerial enlistment and development.

3. This fund shall be regarded by Annual Conferences as a priority to be met before any additional benevolences, grants, or funds are allocated to a theological school or school of religion.

¶ **921.** *Missional Priority Fund.*—There may be a **Missional Priority Fund,** established by the General Conference as a part of its action in the adoption of a missional priority (¶ 803.8). The council, following consultation with the General Council on Ministries and the Council of Bishops, shall recommend to the General Conference the sum which the Church shall undertake for this purpose and the method by which it shall be apportioned to the Annual Conferences. Receipts shall be administered by an agency or agencies designated by the General Conference upon recommendation of the General Council on Ministries and the General Council on Finance and Administration.

THE EPISCOPAL FUND

¶ **922.** The **Episcopal Fund,** raised in accordance with ¶ 924, shall provide for the salary and expenses of effective bishops and for the support of retired bishops and surviving spouses and minor children of deceased bishops. Subject to the approval of the Council on Finance and Administration, the treasurer shall have authority to borrow for the benefit of the Episcopal Fund such amounts as may be necessary for the proper execution of the orders of the General Conference.[9]

¶ **923.** The council shall recommend to each quadrennial session of the General Conference for its action and determination: (1) the amounts to be fixed as salaries of the effective bishops; (2) a schedule of such amounts as may be judged adequate to provide for their expense of house, office, and travel; (3) an annual operating budget for the Council of Bishops, including the office of the secretary of the Council of Bishops, and all travel authorized by the Council of Bishops, including "travel through the connection at large" (¶ 512.2); (4) the amounts to be fixed as annual pensions for the support of retired bishops; and (5) a schedule for allowance for the surviving spouses and for the support of minor children of deceased bishops. From the facts in hand the council shall estimate the approximate total amount required annually during the ensuing quadrennium to provide for the items of episcopal support above mentioned and shall report the same to the General Conference. This amount as finally determined shall be the estimated episcopal budget. The administration of the Episcopal Fund budget as determined by the General Conference shall be under the direction and authority of the General Council on Finance and Administration. Nothing in this paragraph shall preclude the

---

[9]*See* Judicial Council Decision 365.

Annual Conference or conferences of an episcopal area from including in their budgets amounts for an area expense fund.[10]

¶ **924.** The council shall estimate what percentage of the total salaries paid pastors and associate pastors by the entire Church will yield an amount equal to the estimated episcopal budget and shall make recommendations to the General Conference concerning the same for its action and determination. When such percentage has been approved by the General Conference, it shall be the basis of the annual apportionment to each Annual Conference for the Episcopal Fund. The apportionment to each Annual Conference shall be an amount equal to the approved percentage of the total cash salaries paid to the pastors and associate pastors serving charges under episcopal appointment or as local pastors in the most recent complete year as reported to the Annual Conference. This apportionment shall be distributed to the pastoral charges as the conference may determine. In every case the amount apportioned to a charge for the Episcopal Fund shall be paid in the same proportion as the charge pays its pastor.

¶ **925.** The treasurer of the General Council on Finance and Administration shall remit monthly to each effective bishop one twelfth of the annual salary and also one twelfth of the housing allowance as determined by the General Conference, and office expenses as approved by the council, less such deductions or reductions from the salary or office expense allowance as each bishop may authorize. Allowances for retired bishops and for the surviving spouses and minor children of deceased bishops shall be paid in equal monthly installments.

¶ **926.** The treasurer of the council shall pay monthly the claim for the official travel of each bishop upon presentation of an itemized voucher with such supporting data as may be required by the General Council on Finance and Administration. "Official travel" of an effective bishop shall be interpreted to include: (1) all visitations to local churches and to institutions or enterprises of The United Methodist Church within the area, (2) such travel outside the area, but within the jurisdiction, as is approved by the College of Bishops, and (3) such other travel as may be consistent

---

[10]*See* Judicial Council Decision 365.

with guidelines approved by the General Conference as being within the meaning of "official travel." No part of the expense and no honoraria for any such visitations shall be accepted from local churches or enterprises or institutions of The United Methodist Church, such expense being a proper claim against the Episcopal Fund. Nothing in this interpretation is intended to preclude special or nonofficial engagements of a bishop, other than the oversight of the temporal and spiritual affairs of the Church, such as series of lectures in educational institutions, baccalaureate addresses, and preaching missions for several days' duration when such engagements do not interfere with official duties, nor does it preclude the acceptance of honoraria for such services.

¶ **927.** *Pensions.*—1. The pensions for the support of retired bishops elected by General, Jurisdictional, or Central Conferences and the surviving spouses and minor dependent children of such deceased bishops shall be administered by the General Council on Finance and Administration in consultation with the General Board of Pensions and in accordance with such program and procedures as may from time to time be determined by the General Council on Finance and Administration with the approval of the General Conference.

2. The pensions payable to such persons shall be determined by the General Conference on recommendation of the council.

3. A bishop in active service may contribute to individual tax-sheltered annuity plans or other savings plans approved by the Council. The treasurer of the Episcopal Fund shall be authorized to withhold from such bishop's salary the amount so designated by the bishop for this purpose and make payments to the selected plan(s).

¶ **928.** Should any effective bishop in the interim of the quadrennial sessions of the Jurisdictional Conference be relieved by the College of Bishops of the jurisdiction from the performance of regular episcopal duties on account of ill health or for any other reason, the president of the said College of Bishops shall so notify the treasurer of the Episcopal Fund. Beginning ninety days after such notification, the said bishop shall receive the regular pension allowance of a retired bishop, and such pension allowance shall continue until the regular duties of an effective bishop are resumed or until the bishop's status shall have been determined by the Jurisdictional Conference. Assignment of another bishop or bishops to perform the regular episcopal duties of a bishop so disabled or otherwise incapacitated, for a period of sixty days or more, shall be interpreted as a release of the said bishop from the performance of regular episcopal duties.

¶ **929.** Should any retired bishop, in the interim of the quadrennial sessions of the Jurisdictional Conference, be called into active service and assigned to active episcopal duty (¶ 507.3), that bishop shall be entitled to remuneration for such service. The Episcopal Fund shall be responsible for the difference between the pension and housing allowance of a retired bishop and the remuneration of an active bishop as set by General Conference. In the event of such assignment of a retired bishop to active episcopal duty, the president of the Council of Bishops shall notify the treasurer of the Episcopal Fund. The treasurer of the Episcopal Fund shall make remittance accordingly.

MINISTERIAL SUPPORT

¶ **930.** Assumption of the obligations of the itineracy, required to be made at the time of admission into the traveling connection, puts upon the Church the counterobligation of providing support for the entire ministry of the Church. In view of this the claim for ministerial support in each pastoral charge shall include provisions for the support of pastors, district superintendents, bishops, and conference claimants.[11]

¶ **931.** Each Annual Conference shall determine what plan and method shall be used in distributing the apportionments to its several districts and charges for the Episcopal Fund (¶ 922), for the support of district superintendents and conference claimants, and for the Equitable Salary Fund (¶ 935), whether by percentages based on the current cash salary paid to the ministers serving pastoral charges under episcopal appointment and to local pastors or by some other method.[12]

---

[11]*See* Judicial Council Decisions 306, 455.
[12]*See* Judicial Council Decisions 208, 455.

¶ **932.** When the apportionments for bishops, district superintendents, conference claimants, and the Equitable Salary Fund for the several districts and charges have been determined, payments made to the same in each pastoral charge shall be exactly proportional to the amount paid on the ministerial salary or salaries (¶ 924). The treasurer or treasurers of each pastoral charge shall accordingly make proportional distribution of the funds raised in that charge for the support of the ministry and shall remit, monthly if practicable and quarterly at the latest, the items for bishops, district superintendents, conference claimants, and the Equitable Salary Fund to the proper treasurer or treasurers.[13]

¶ **933.** The several Charge Conferences shall determine the pastors' salaries according to the provisions of ¶ 249.10.

¶ **934.** No pastor shall be entitled to any claim for unpaid salary against any church or charge served after pastoral connection with the church or charge has ceased.

¶ **935.** *Equitable Salaries.*—1. There shall be in each Annual Conference a Commission on Equitable Salaries composed of an equal number of lay and clergy persons—including at least one lay and one clergy from churches of fewer than two hundred members—who are nominated by the conference Nominating Committee and elected by and amenable to the Annual Conference.

2. It is the purpose of the Commission on Equitable Salaries to support ministry in the charges of the Annual Conference by (1) recommending conference standards for ministerial compensation; (2) administering funds to be used in salary supplementation; and (3) providing counsel and advisory material on ministerial compensation to district superintendents and Pastor-Parish Relations Committees.

3. The commission shall carefully study the needs for additional ministerial support within the conference and the sources of income, and shall recommend annually to the conference for its action a schedule of minimum salaries for all full-time pastors, subject to such rules and regulations as the conference may adopt.[14]

---

[13]*See* Judicial Council Decisions 320, 401.
[14]*See* Judicial Council Decision 383.

4. Insofar as practicable this schedule of minimum salaries shall be observed by the bishops and district superintendents in arranging charges and making appointments.

5. On recommendation of the Commission on Equitable Salaries, the Annual Conference may authorize the utilization of the Equitable Salary Fund to provide for supplementing salaries beyond the minimum salary schedule.

6. In consultation with the Commission on Equitable Salaries, the Council on Finance and Administration shall recommend to the conference its estimate of the amount required to support the schedule of minimum salaries and salary supplements for the pastors, as adopted by the conference. The conference Council on Finance and Administration shall apportion the amount approved by the conference as an item of ministerial support to the districts or the charges as the conference may direct.[15]

7. The **Equitable Salary Fund,** secured as described above in ¶ 935.6, shall be disbursed under the direction of the Commission on Equitable Salaries.

8. Clergy couples, both husband and wife as separate individuals as members of the Annual Conference, have the right to full claim on the minimum salary fund when they accept a full-time appointment, either as pastors of adjoining churches or charges, or as co-pastors of a church or charge. At their joint initiative and after consultation with the district superintendent and/or bishop, they may jointly waive any portion or all of her/his share of the minimum salary fund. Such a request of waiver shall be presented, in writing, to the district superintendent and the Annual Conference Commission on Equitable Salaries. Such a waiver shall be received and established annually, as long as this appointment continues to have a claim on the minimum salary fund.[16]

9. Consistent with the provisions of this paragraph, the primary responsibility for the payment of pastoral salaries remains with individual pastoral charges.[17]

---

[15]*See* Judicial Council Decisions 90, 179.
[16]*See* Judicial Council Decision 433.
[17]*See* Judicial Council Decision 461.

COUNCIL ON FINANCE AND ADMINISTRATION ¶ 938

10. The Equitable Salary Fund, secured as described in §6, shall be used to provide each pastor who receives less than the minimum salary with an additional amount sufficient to make the salary approved by the pastoral charge plus the supplemental aid or income from other sources equal to the minimum salary approved by the conference; *provided* that nothing in this paragraph shall be construed as limiting the right of an Annual Conference to set a maximum amount to be used in attaining such minimum salary in any given case.[18]

11. The commission may suggest to the Annual Conference for its consideration equitable salary ranges for the pastors and/or charges, and the Annual Conference may suggest such equitable salary ranges to the charges for their consideration.

12. The commission may assemble and distribute to the charges and the district superintendents advisory material for use in the process of negotiating salary and benefit packages, the schedule of minimum salaries, and other information relevant to the establishment of more equitable salaries by the charges of the conference.

¶ **936.** *Sustentation Fund.*—An Annual Conference may establish a **Sustentation Fund,** which shall be administered by the conference Council on Finance and Administration or some other agency created or designed for the purpose of providing emergency aid to the ministers of the conference who may be in special need. On recommendation of the council, the amount needed for this purpose may be apportioned to the pastoral charges as the conference may determine.

¶ **937.** The total of all travel, automobile, and other expenses allowed and paid to a pastor in addition to his salary shall be reported for insertion in the journal of the Annual Conference, in a separate column from that of pastor's salary and adjacent thereto. These expenses shall be distinguished from the moving expenses of a new appointee to a pastoral charge.

¶ **938.** Every ministerial member of an Annual Conference appointed to any other field than the pastorate or district superintendency shall furnish annually to the conference secretary, at the time of the conference session, a statement of his

---

[18]*See* Judicial Council Decision 456.

remuneration, and the salaries or remuneration of all ministers in special service shall be published in the journal of the Annual Conference.[19]

Section III. The General Council on Ministries.

¶ **1001.** *Name.*—There shall be a **General Council on Ministries** of The United Methodist Church, hereinafter called the council.

¶ **1002.** *Incorporation.*—The council shall be incorporated in such state or states as the General Council on Ministries shall determine. This corporation shall be the successor corporation and organization to the Program Council of The United Methodist Church.

¶ **1003.** *Amenability.*—The council shall report to and be amenable to the General Conference.

¶ **1004.** *Purpose.*—The General Council on Ministries exists to facilitate the fulfillment of the objectives of mission and the program-related policies of the General Conference.

¶ **1005.** *Objectives.*—The objectives of the General Council on Ministries are:

1. To study missional needs, determine priorities, and adjust emphases between sessions of the General Conference.

2. To establish the processes and relationships that will ensure the coordination of the ministries and program emphases of The United Methodist Church through its general agencies and to minimize unnecessary overlapping or conflicting approaches to the local church and the Annual Conferences.

3. To enhance the effectiveness of our total ministries by reviewing the performance of the general program agencies and their responsiveness to the needs of the local churches and Annual Conferences.

4. To facilitate informed decision making at all levels of the church by engaging in research and planning in cooperation with the general agencies and the Annual Conferences.

¶ **1006.** *Responsibilities.*—The responsibilities of the council shall include, but not be limited to, the following:

---

[19]*See* Judicial Council Decisions 345, 465.

1. Upon a two-thirds vote of the members of the General Council on Ministries present and voting, and upon a two-thirds vote of the Council of Bishops present and voting, to make changes in missional priorities or special programs necessitated by emergencies or by other significant developments between General Conferences which substantially affect the life of the Church, and to make adjustments in program budget allocations accordingly; *provided* that such adjustments are made within the total budget set by the previous General Conference; and *provided*, further, that such adjustments are made after consultation with the affected boards and agencies and approval by a two-thirds vote of the General Council on Finance and Administration.

2. To take the following actions, in sequence, with respect to recommendations to the General Council on Finance and Administration for the allocation of World Service funds to general program agencies:

a) The General Council on Ministries shall, in consultation with the General Council on Finance and Administration and the general program agencies, develop recommendations to the General Council on Finance and Administration on needs of the general program agencies for the programs, missional priorities, and special programs.

b) The General Council on Ministries shall receive the recommendation the General Council on Finance and Administration proposes to make to the General Conference as to that portion of the total World Service budget to be available for distribution among the general program agencies.

c) The General Council on Ministries, taking into consideration program priorities and the total funds available to the general program agencies, shall recommend to the General Council on Finance and Administration the amount of the annual World Service allocation to each of those agencies, within the total sum proposed by the General Council on Finance and Administration for distribution among such agencies.

d) Only when the General Council on Ministries and the General Council on Finance and Administration agree on the allocations to several general agencies shall these allocations be included in the World Service budget to be recommended to the

411

General Conference by the General Council on Finance and Administration.

e) Before the beginning of each year the General Council on Finance and Administration shall determine and communicate to the General Council on Ministries the sum available at that time from World Service contingency funds to meet requests for additional funding from the general program agencies. The General Council on Ministries shall be authorized to approve allocations to the general program agencies for such additional program funding up to the limit so established. No money shall be allocated by the General Council on Ministries from this source for general administrative costs, fixed charges, or capital outlay without approval by the General Council on Finance and Administration.

f) The General Council on Ministries shall receive from the General Council on Finance and Administration copies of the proposed annual budgets of the general program agencies, in order that it may review such budgets in relation to the program proposals made by those agencies in their quadrennial budget requests.

3. To designate, in cooperation with the General Council on Finance and Administration, the general agency to undertake a special study ordered by the General Conference when the conference fails to make such a designation.

4. To assign responsibilities for implementation of missional priorities and/or special programs initiated between sessions of the General Conference to the general program agencies or to special task forces created by the General Council on Ministries.

5. To assure the development of a unified and coordinated program for promoting of the connectional ministries of the Church by:

a) Approving the scheduling and timing of all national conferences, convocations, and/or major consultations, subject to the approval of the General Council on Finance and Administration of plans for financing such meetings;

b) Maintaining a calendar of meetings on behalf of all agencies of The United Methodist Church as an aid to the agencies in regulating the number and the timing of such meetings;

c) Reviewing all plans of the general program agencies for the production, distribution, and timing of the release of free literature and promotional resource materials (except church school literature), avoiding duplication of both materials and activities.

6. To recommend to the General Conference, after consultation with the Council of Bishops, the number and timing of special days which are to be observed on a churchwide basis; *provided* that the General Council on Finance and Administration shall make recommendations to the General Conference as set forth in ¶ 906.11 regarding the special days to be observed with offering; and *provided* further, that the Council of Bishops and the General Council on Finance and Administration may authorize a special financial appeal in an emergency.

7. To relate to Annual Conferences, their Councils on Ministries, or other corresponding structures:

a) To provide resources for them related to their basic tasks;

b) To enhance two-way communication with them; and

c) To assist the conference councils in developing comprehensive approaches to planning, research, evaluation, and coordination.

8. To consider the plans of any general program agency to publish a new periodical (except church school literature). Any general program agency proposing to publish such a new periodical shall submit its request to the council. If the council disapproves, the agency shall delay such publication until the proposal can be submitted to the General Conference for determination.

9. To consult with the general program agencies, Standing General Commission on Communication, and the president and publisher of The United Methodist Publishing House with regard to their publishing and communication policies in order to avoid unnecessary overlapping and duplication.

10. To resolve any overlapping in structure or functions or lack of cooperation among the general program agencies by:

a) Coordination of any interagency program where two or more general program agencies are involved, unless otherwise specified by the General Conference; and

b) Approving the creation of any ongoing interagency

committee or task force. The council shall receive reports and recommendations from them and shall have the privilege of appointing observers to attend the meetings of any interagency group, including those that are part of the structure of program agencies.

11. To study the connectional structures of The United Methodist Church and, after consultation with the general agencies, recommend to the General Conference such legislative changes as may be appropriate to effect desirable modifications of existing connectional structures. Any such proposed legislative changes that would affect general fund budget allocations shall be studied in connection with the General Council on Finance and Administration and shall be recommended to the General Conference by these two councils acting in concert.

12. To provide for the training of the Annual Conference Council on Ministries directors and to cooperate with the Council of Bishops in providing training for the district superintendents.

13. To review and evaluate the effectiveness of the general program agencies in performing the ministries assigned to them (*see* ¶ 802).

14. To keep under review the concurrence of general program agencies with the Social Principles of The United Methodist Church.

15. The general secretary of each general program agency that is accountable to the General Council on Ministries shall be elected annually by ballot of the General Council on Ministries upon the nomination of the agency involved. Any general secretary of a general program agency who has not been elected by the General Council on Ministries shall not serve in such capacity beyond the end of that calendar year. Each program board shall elect annually by ballot its associate general secretary(ies) and may elect or appoint such other staff as may be necessary.

16. To give leadership to and participate in planning and research for The United Methodist Church, thereby helping all levels of the Church to evaluate needs, set goals, and plan strategy; to coordinate planning and research for the denomination in cooperation with the general program agencies of The United Methodist Church; and maintain a depository for

research and planning documents received from the general program agencies and the Annual Conferences.

17. To determine the need and develop plans for missional priorities and/or special programs for the ministry of the Church for any particular quadrennium and, after consultation with the Council of Bishops, to recommend them to the General Conference for consideration.

18. To devise and implement measures to assure full, effective representation and participation of Central Conference members in the work of The United Methodist Church.

19. To report to the General Conference for its approval a summary of all decisions and recommendations made dealing with program changes and structure overlap.

20. To receive reports from and refer matters to the Standing General Commission on Christian Unity and Interreligious Concerns on the participation of The United Methodist Church in the various aspects of ecumenism.

21. To organize the Advance Committee which shall have general oversight of the Advance program.

22. To relate to and cooperate with the National Association of Conference Council Directors.

¶ **1007.** *Organization.*—1. *Membership.*—*a)* The membership of the council shall consist of:

(1) One member from each Annual Conference and Missionary Conference within the United States and Puerto Rico elected by the Jurisdictional Conference from a list of nominees submitted by each Annual Conference and each Missionary Conference which shall include at least one laywoman, one layman, and one from the clergy, with special attention to the inclusion of clergywomen. The nominations from the Annual Conference shall be made from the General Conference delegates. If there is not an adequate number of persons from the nominees, additional nominees may be selected from the jurisdictional delegates, and if additional nominees are further required, they may be selected from the membership of the Annual Conference. The above members shall consist, so far as possible, of one-third laywomen, one-third laymen, and one-third clergy.

(2) A bishop from each jurisdiction and one bishop from the Central Conferences selected by the Council of Bishops;

(3) One youth from each jurisdiction under the age of eighteen at the time of their election nominated by the Jurisdictional Youth Caucus and elected by the Jurisdictional Conference;

(4) One young adult under age thirty at the time of their election from each jurisdiction elected by the Jurisdictional Conference;

(5) One non-staff representative or alternate selected by each of the general program agencies;

(6) Fifteen members at large to be elected by the council;

(7) Three persons from Central Conferences and one alternate for each (who may attend if the elected member for whom he/she is the alternate cannot attend) nominated by the Council of Bishops and elected by the General Council on Ministries;

(8) The secretary of the Council of Bishops; the general secretaries who serve as the chief executive officers of the general program agencies; the publisher and a representative selected by the General Board of Publication; the general secretary of the General Commission on Communication; and the director of the Advance shall be members with voice but without vote.[20]

b) Members of the council representing Annual Conferences, members at large, and bishops, except the bishop from the Western Jurisdiction, shall not serve on any boards or commissions or the divisions thereof having representation on the General Council on Ministries.

c) Of the members at large, elected by the council, in order to ensure that one fourth of the council's membership may represent racial and ethnic minorities, it is recommended that there shall be not less than two representatives from each of the following groups: Asian Americans, Black Americans, Hispanic Americans, and Native Americans. (The council shall receive nominations from the racial and ethnic caucuses and ethnic Annual Conferences of these respective groups prior to the report of their nominating committee.) Insofar as possible, these

---

[20]*See* Judicial Council Decision 423.

members at large should be one-third laywomen, one-third laymen, and one-third clergy, with special attention to the inclusion of at least one clergywoman from each jurisdiction.

d) It is recommended that each Jurisdictional Conference give consideration to electing to membership on the council at least one third of the same persons elected to the council by the preceding Jurisdictional Conference.

e) When the committee selected to nominate the at-large members of the General Council on Ministries meets prior to the organizational meeting, it shall determine the number of persons nominated by the Annual Conference and elected by the Jurisdictional Conference who were members of the council the previous quadrennium. If the number is less than twenty, the Nominating Committee shall nominate enough persons from the eligible membership of the council in the previous quadrennium to bring this number to twenty. These persons shall be in addition to the fifteen members at large.

f) The members of the council shall serve for four years or until the convening of the organizational meeting. No voting member shall be eligible to serve for more than two consecutive four-year terms.

g) If a bishop is unable to attend a meeting of the council, that bishop may designate an alternate bishop from the same jurisdiction.

2. *Meetings.*—Before the end of the calendar year in which regular sessions of the Jurisdictional Conferences are held, all persons who have been elected to membership on the council shall be convened by an active bishop designated by the president of the Council of Bishops for the purpose of organizing.

The council shall meet at least once during each calendar year. It may meet in special session or at other times upon the call of the president or upon the written request of one fifth of its members.

3. *Officers.*—The council shall have a president, one or more vice-presidents, a recording secretary, and a treasurer elected from the membership of the council. The president of the council shall be its presiding officer. Officers shall be elected for terms of four years and shall continue until their successors are duly elected.

417

4. *Internal Structure.*—The council shall determine its internal structure as it deems necessary for the performance of its duties.

5. *Advance Committee.*—There shall be an **Advance Committee,** which shall have general oversight of the Advance program. It shall be organized under the authority and direction of the General Council on Ministries. It shall consist of twenty members of the General Council on Ministries.

a) Director of Advance.—(1) There shall be a **Director of the Advance,** nominated by the Advance Committee from the staff of one of the participating agencies and elected by the General Council on Ministries. The participating agencies are National, World, United Methodist Committee on Relief, and Education and Cultivation Divisions of the General Board of Global Ministries; Division of Promotion and Benevolence Interpretation of the Standing General Commission on Communication; General Council on Ministries; and the General Council on Finance and Administration.

(2) The salary and related benefits of the director shall be paid by the participating agency. Other administrative costs of the Advance shall be borne by the General Council on Ministries.

(3) While continuing as a staff member of the participating agency, the director shall be a staff member of the General Council on Ministries related to the Advance Committee.

b) Responsibilities of Director.—The responsibilities of the Director of the Advance shall be:

(1) To coordinate the total program of the Advance, including its promotion, cultivation, and administration.

(2) To coordinate the staff work required of the participating agencies within the Advance.

(3) To report directly to the Advance Committee concerning the program and progress of the Advance.

(4) To keep a record of all general Advance special projects.

c) General Advance Special Projects.—It shall be the responsibility of the Advance Committee to determine which projects are approved to receive general Advance special gifts (¶ 913.2). The Advance fosters partnership between those who give and those who receive and affirms the right of persons to determine the priority of their own needs. Projects shall therefore be proposed by authorized persons closely related to the project and shall be recommended to the Advance Committee by the administering agency. The Advance Committee may consider and approve proposals for either specific projects or broadly designated causes, such as a type of work, a country, a region, or an administrative unit.

d) Administering Agencies.—Agencies authorized to recommend projects and receive and administer funds for general Advance special projects shall be the World, National, and United Methodist Committee on Relief Divisions of the General Board of Global Ministries, and such other agencies as are designated by the General Council on Ministries. The administering agencies shall report annually to the Advance Committee on the financial progress of projects and assist in providing programmatic information as requested.

No project within the boundaries of an Annual Conference shall be approved by the Advance Committee for promotion, cultivation, and administration as an Advance mission special without consultation with the Annual Conference board or agency delegated responsibility for missions by the Annual Conference.

6. *Staff.*—The council shall elect annually a general secretary and associate general secretaries as needed. The elected staff shall sit with the council with voice but without vote.

Section IV. Standing General Commission on Communication.

¶ **1101.** *Preamble.*—As United Methodists, our theological understanding obligates us, as members of the Body of Christ, to communicate our faith by speaking and listening to persons both within and outside the Church throughout the world, and to utilize all appropriate means of communication.

The responsibility to communicate is laid upon every church member, every pastor, every congregation, every Annual Conference, every institution, and every agency of the Church. Within this total responsibility, there are certain functions that The United Methodist Church has assigned to the General Commission on Communication, to be performed in behalf of all through the talents and resources at its command.

419

¶ **1102.** *Name.*—There shall be a Standing General Commission on Communication of The United Methodist Church which for communication and public relations purposes may be designated as **United Methodist Communications (UMCom).**

¶ **1103.** *Incorporation.*—The **Standing General Commission on Communication** is successor to the Joint Committee on Communications, incorporated in the State of Ohio, and shall be authorized to do business as United Methodist Communications (UMCom). It is authorized to create such other corporate substructures as the commission deems appropriate to carry out its functions.

¶ **1104.** *Amenability and Accountability.*—The Standing General Commission on Communication shall be amenable to the General Conference. As an administrative general agency which carries significant program functions in addition to its many service and support responsibilities, the commission shall be accountable to, report to, and be evaluated by the General Council on Ministries in program matters and shall be accountable to and report to the General Council on Finance and Administration for matters of finance.

¶ **1105.** *Purpose.*—The Standing General Commission on Communication shall give leadership to the Church in the field of communication in a holistic way. It shall serve in meeting the communication, public relations, and promotional needs of the entire church. It shall be responsible for providing resources and services to local churches and Annual Conferences in the field of communication. It shall have a consultative relationship to all general agencies of the Church and to any structures for communication and public relations at the jurisdictional, episcopal area, Annual Conference, district, or local church level.

¶ **1106.** *Responsibilities.*—Specific responsibilities and functions of the Standing General Commission on Communication and its staff are as follows:

1. It shall be the official news-gathering and distributing agency for The United Methodist Church and its general agencies. In discharging its responsibilities, in keeping with the historic freedom of the press, it shall operate with editorial freedom as an independent news bureau serving all segments of

church life and society, making available to both religious and public news media information concerning the Church at large.

2. It shall have major responsibility on behalf of The United Methodist Church in the United States to relate to the public media in presenting the Christian faith and work of the Church to the general public through broadcast, the press, and audio-visual media. It may develop such structures for broadcast and audio-visual communication purposes as are deemed helpful to the Church in its witness through the media. It shall serve in unifying and coordinating public media messages and programs of United Methodist general agencies.

3. It shall give special attention to television, including broadcast television, cable, videotape, videodisc, and satellite. It shall provide counsel and resources to Annual Conferences—and through conferences to districts and local churches—to develop and strengthen their television ministries. Responsibilities of the commission shall include program production and placement, and relationships to commercial broadcasters at the national level in the U.S.A.

4. It shall represent The United Methodist Church in the Communication Commission of the National Council of Churches, and in other national and international interdenominational agencies working in the area of mass communications. Budget allocations and other funds granted to these ecumenical agencies shall be administered in accordance with ¶ 917.3.

5. It shall have responsibility to work toward promotion and protection of the historic freedoms of religion and the press, and shall seek to increase the ethical, moral, and human values of media structures and programs.

6. It shall have general supervision over the conduct of public relations activities for The United Methodist Church in the United States, planning and carrying out public relations work at the denomination-wide level and giving counsel to the various units of the Church in regard to their public relations needs. It shall interpret to the constituency of the Church the significance of the denomination and its various programs.

7. It shall develop and oversee a unified and comprehensive program of audio-visuals for the Church. It shall plan, create, produce or cause to be produced, and distribute or cause to be

distributed, audio-visual materials that are informative and vital to the religious life of all United Methodists. It shall unify and coordinate the audio-visual programs of all United Methodist agencies dealing with projected pictures, recordings, videotape and other audio-visual or electronic materials.

8. It shall give oversight to a comprehensive communications system for the church, providing a total view of communication structure and practices. It shall create networks of communicators at all levels, including local church, district, conference, and general. These networks may include periodic consultations for such purposes as idea exchange, information sharing, joint planning, and monitoring and evaluating the total communication enterprise of The United Methodist Church.

9. It shall provide guidance, resources, and training for the local church coordinator of communications (¶ 261.5), provided that training at the local level shall be through and in cooperation with Annual Conferences.

10. It shall be responsible for education and training in the principles and skills of communication, including the following: *(a)* national workshops and training experiences in communication skills related to the various media; *(b)* consultation with and assistance to Annual Conferences, districts, racial and ethnic minority groups, in the training of local church persons, especially the local church coordinator of communications; *(c)* training experiences for bishops, personnel of general church agencies, and other groups on request; *(d)* providing and facilitating apprenticeship, internship, and scholarship programs for church communicators; *(e)* counseling schools of theology and other institutions of higher education about the training of faculty, ministerial students, and lay persons in the principles and skills of communication, media resource development, and media evaluation.

11. It shall determine and implement, after consultation with the Council on Finance and Administration, policy for the interpretation, promotion, and cultivation of all financial causes demanding churchwide promotion or publicity. The General Commission on Communication shall assist episcopal areas, Annual Conferences, and districts by means of a field service program providing counsel and resources in communication,

program interpretation, and the promotion of benevolence and administrative funds.

12. It shall be the central promotional agency for the purpose of promoting throughout the Church the following general church funds: World Service Fund (¶ 911.1), World Service Specials (¶ 912), Advance Specials (¶ 913), One Great Hour of Sharing (¶ 915.2 and ¶ 271.3b), The World Communion Offering (¶ 915.4 and ¶ 271.3f), Missional Priority Fund (¶ 921), General Administration Fund (¶ 916), Interdenominational Cooperation Fund (¶ 917), Temporary General Aid Fund (¶ 919), Ministerial Education Fund (¶ 920), Episcopal Fund (¶ 922), Human Relations Day (¶ 915.1 and ¶ 271.3a), Black College Fund (¶ 918), United Methodist Student Day (¶ 915.3 and ¶ 271.3h), Christian Education Sunday (¶ 271.3e), Golden Cross Sunday (¶ 272), and Youth Service Fund (¶ 1404), and all other general church funds approved by the General Conference, as well as any emergency appeals that may be authorized by the Council of Bishops and the Council on Finance and Administration (¶ 910.4). In the interpretation, promotion, and cultivation of these causes, this agency shall consult with the agency responsible for administration of the funds. Budgets for the above promoted funds shall be developed in cooperation with the General Council on Finance and Administration. In cases where the General Conference assigns a portion of the promotional responsibility to some other agency, such promotional work shall be subject to coordination by the General Commission on Communication. The cost of promotion of the funds shall be a prior claim against receipts, except that the cost of promotion for general Advance specials shall be billed to the recipient agencies in proportion to the amount of general Advance special funds received by each. The administration of the money thus set aside for promotion shall be the responsibility of the General Commission on Communication.

13. It shall undertake the promotion of any cause or undertaking, financial or otherwise, not herein mentioned, demanding churchwide promotion or publicity; *provided* that such action shall have been previously approved by the Council of Bishops and the General Council on Finance and Administration, or their respective executive committees. The General Council on

Finance and Administration shall determine the source of the funding for any such authorized promotions.

14. Appeals for giving that are made to United Methodists shall be consistent with the aims of Christian stewardship. There shall be cooperation between this agency and the General Board of Discipleship in order that programs and resource materials of the two agencies may be in harmony in their presentation of Christian stewardship.

15. It shall publish a program journal for pastors and other church leaders that shall present the program and promotional materials of the general agencies in a coordinated manner and shall be in lieu of general agency promotional periodicals. This agency shall determine the manner of selecting the principal editors, who shall be responsible for the content of the journal. This agency shall obtain from the churches or district superintendents the names of church officials entitled to receive the journal so as to compile a subscription list compatible with regulations of the U.S. Postal Service.

16. It shall supervise the use of the official insignia of The United Methodist Church and preserve the integrity of its design. It shall maintain appropriate registration to protect the insignia in behalf of The United Methodist Church. The insignia may be used by any official agency of the Church, including local churches, to identify the work, program, and materials of The United Methodist Church. Any commercial use of the design must be explicitly authorized by an appropriate officer of this agency.

17. It shall give leadership in study and research in the field of communication, applying research findings from the professional and academic communities to the work of the church, and in evaluative research in the field of communication. It shall cooperate with other agencies and other levels of the Church in research and development work in the field of communication and share the findings of study and research.

18. It shall represent the interests of The United Methodist Church in new technological developments in the field of communication, including research, the evaluation of new devices and methods, and the application of technological developments to the communication services of the Church.

19. It may develop information services and other innovative services which provide channels of communication to and from all levels of the Church.

20. It shall provide resources, counsel, and staff training for area, conference, and district communication programs and develop guidelines in consultation with persons working in areas, conferences, and districts.

21. It shall produce materials for program interpretation in cooperation with the General Council on Ministries and the general program boards.

¶ **1107.** *Organization.*—1. *Membership.*—The affairs of the Standing General Commission on Communication shall be governed by thirty-eight persons selected as follows: three bishops selected by the Council of Bishops, four persons (two men and two women including at least one clergy, one laywoman, and one layman) elected by each Jurisdictional Conference, and fifteen additional members elected by the commission to ensure membership of persons with expertise in the field of communication. It is recommended that each of the following groups be represented in the commission: Asian Americans, Black Americans, Hispanic Americans, Native Americans, clergywomen, youth, and young adults. The additional members shall be nominated by a committee composed of one commission member designated from each jurisdiction and one of the member bishops.

2. *Meetings.*—The commission shall hold at least one meeting in each calendar year. Fifteen members shall constitute a quorum.

3. *Officers.*—The commission shall elect a president, at least one vice-president, a recording secretary, and such other officers as it determines.

There may be an **executive committee** comprised of not more than one-third of the total membership of the commission and elected by the commission. The membership of the executive committee shall be representative of the composition of the commission.

4. *Internal Organization.*—The General Commission on Communication is empowered to create internal structures as it deems appropriate for effective operation.

425

5. *Staff.*—The commission shall elect annually a general secretary upon nomination by the executive committee or a nominating committee and shall elect such associate general secretaries as needed and shall provide for election or appointment of other staff. The general secretary shall cooperate with the General Council on Ministries for program services and with the general secretary of the General Council on Finance and Administration for financial services.

¶ **1108.** *Finance.*—The General Conference shall provide for the financial needs of the Standing General Commission on Communication upon recommendation by the General Council on Finance and Administration. The commission shall consult with the General Council on Ministries in the area of program matters in development of an annual budget which shall be reported to the General Council on Finance and Administration for approval.

Section V. General Board of Church and Society.

¶ **1201.** *Name.*—In keeping with the historic concerns of The Evangelical United Brethren Church and The Methodist Church, there shall be a **General Board of Church and Society** in The United Methodist Church.

¶ **1202.** *Incorporation.*—The General Board of Church and Society shall be a corporation existing under the laws of the District of Columbia, and shall be the legal successor and successor in trust of the corporations, boards, departments or entities, known as the General Board of Christian Social Concerns of The United Methodist Church; the Department of Christian Social Action of The Evangelical United Brethren Church; the Board of Christian Social Concerns of The Methodist Church; the Division of General Welfare of the General Board of Church and Society of The United Methodist Church; the Division of General Welfare of the General Board of Christian Social Concerns of The United Methodist Church; the Division of Alcohol Problems and General Welfare of the Board of Christian Social Concerns of The Methodist Church; the Division of Temperance and General Welfare of the Board of Christian Social Concerns of The Methodist Church; the Board of Temperance of The Methodist Church; the Board of Temperance, Prohibition and Public Morals of The Methodist Episcopal Church; the Board of World Peace of the Methodist Church; the Commission on World Peace of The Methodist Church; the Commission on World Peace of The Methodist Episcopal Church; the Division of World Peace of the General Board of Church and Society of The United Methodist Church; the Board of Social and Economic Relations of The Methodist Church; the Division of Human Relations of the General Board of Church and Society of The United Methodist Church.

¶ **1203.** *Purpose.*—The purpose of the board shall be to relate the gospel of Jesus Christ to the members of the church and to the persons and structures of the communities and world in which they live. It shall seek to bring the whole life of man and woman, their activities, possessions, and community and world relationships, into conformity with the will of God. It shall show the members of the church and the society that the reconciliation which God effected through Christ involves personal, social and civic righteousness.[21]

¶ **1204.** *Objectives.*—To achieve its purpose, the board shall project plans and programs that challenge the members of The United Methodist Church to work through their own local church, through ecumenical channels, and through society toward personal, social, and civic righteousness; to assist the District and Annual Conferences with needed resources in areas of such concerns; to analyze the issues which confront the person, the local community, the nation, and the world, and to encourage Christian lines of action which assist humankind to move toward a world where peace and justice are achieved.

¶ **1205.** *Responsibilities.*—Prime responsibility of the board is to seek the implementation of the Social Principles and other policy statements of the General Conference on Christian social concerns. Furthermore, the board and its executives shall provide forthright witness and action on those social issues that call Christians to respond as forgiven people for whom Christ died. In particular, the board shall conduct a program of research, education, and action on the wide range of issues confronting the

---

[21]*See* Judicial Council Decision 387.

Church consistent with the Social Principles and the policies adopted by the General Conference.

The board shall analyze long-range social trends underlying ethical values, systemic alternatives, and strategies for social change and explore alternate futures.

The board shall develop, promote, and distribute resources and conduct programs to inform, motivate, train, organize, and build networks for action toward social justice throughout society, particularly on the specific social issues prioritized by the board. Special attention shall be given to nurturing the active constituency of the board by encouraging an exchange of ideas on strategy and methodology for social change and enabling church members through conferences, districts, coalitions, and networks to identify and respond to critical social issues at the community, state and regional level.

The board shall speak to the Church, and to the world, its convictions, interpretations, and concerns, recognizing the freedom and responsibility of all Christians to study, interpret, and act on any or all recommendations in keeping with their own Christian calling.[22]

¶ **1206.** *Organization.*—The Board of Church and Society shall be composed according to the instructions defined for all program boards in ¶¶ 802-804 of the General Provisions.

¶ **1207.** *Vacancies.*—Vacancies in the board membership shall be filled by the procedure defined in ¶ 812 of the general provisions.

¶ **1208.** *Officers.*—The board shall elect a president, a vice-president, a recording secretary, a treasurer who shall serve as chairperson of the Finance Committee, and such other officers as it may determine.

¶ **1209.** *Executive Committee.*—The executive committee shall be composed of the officers of the board and such other members as the board may designate. The committee shall include representatives of racial and ethnic minorities, women, age groups, and of each jurisdiction. The committee shall have the power ad interim to fill any vacancies occurring in the elected staff and to transact such business and adopt such resolutions and

---

[22]*See* Judicial Council Decision 387.

statements as are authorized between the meetings of the board. It shall report all of its actions to the board promptly after each of its meetings and again for confirmation at the next meeting of the board. It shall have special responsibility for long-range planning, for reviewing and recommending program priorities to the board, and for recommending allocations of staff, budget, and program resources in accordance with such priorities. This would include long-range planning that anticipates the future needs of the board, the Church, and the society.

¶ **1210.** *Nominating Committee.*—A nominating committee of six members shall be constituted. It shall be composed of one member, ministerial or lay, from each jurisdiction, chosen by board members from that jurisdiction, and one bishop chosen by the bishops who are board members. The bishop shall serve as convenor. This committee shall nominate the officers of the board.

¶ **1211.** *Meetings.*—The board shall hold an annual meeting, at a time and place to be determined by its executive committee, and such other meetings as its work may require, and shall enact suitable bylaws governing the activities of the board and its employees. A majority of the membership shall constitute a quorum.

¶ **1212.** *Financial Support.*—1. The work of the board shall be supported from the general benevolences of the Church, the amount to be determined by the General Conference following the budgeting procedures established in ¶ 906.

2. Either on behalf of its total work or on behalf of one of its programs, the board may solicit and create special funds, receive gifts and bequests, hold properties and securities in trust, and administer all its financial affairs in accordance with its own rules and provisions of the Discipline. Funds vested in any of the predecessor boards shall be conserved for the specific purposes for which such funds have been given.

¶ **1213.** *Internal Organization.*—The internal organization and the operation of the board shall be developed and conducted by the board in the manner it determines insofar as this does not conflict with other provisions of the Discipline.

¶ **1214.** *General, Associate, and Assistant General Secretaries.*— 1. The **general secretary** shall be the chief administrative officer of the board, responsible for the coordination of the total program of the board, the supervision of staff, and for the administration of the headquarters office. The general secretary shall be an ex officio member of the executive committee, without vote, and shall sit with the board when it is in session with voice, but without vote.

2. Under the supervision of the general secretary there shall be two **associate general secretaries,** responsible for program development and implementation and such other duties as may be assigned by the board.

3. Under the supervision of the general secretary there shall be an **assistant general secretary** responsible for fiscal management and such other duties as may be assigned by the board.

¶ **1215.** *Headquarters.*—The headquarters location shall be determined by the General Council on Ministries. A United Nations Office shall be conducted in cooperation with the Women's Division of the Board of Global Ministries.

¶ **1216.** *Bylaws.*—The Board of Church and Society shall provide its own bylaws, which shall not violate any provisions of the Constitution or the Discipline, and which may be amended by a two-thirds vote of the members present and voting thereon at a regular or special meeting; *provided* that notice of such amendment has previously been given to the members.

Section VI. General Board of Discipleship

¶ **1301.** *Purpose.*—There shall be a **General Board of Discipleship,** the purpose of which is found within the expression of the total mission of the Church outlined in the objectives of mission. Its primary purpose shall be to assist Annual Conferences, districts, and local churches in their efforts to win persons to Jesus Christ as his disciples and to help these persons to grow in their understanding of God that they may respond in faith and love, to the end that they may know who they are and what their human situation means, increasingly identifying themselves as children of God and members of the Christian community, to live in the Spirit of God in every relationship, to fulfill their common discipleship in the world, and to abide in the Christian hope.

The board shall use its resources to enhance the meaning of

membership as defined in ¶¶ 211-215 which emphasizes the importance of the identification of church membership with discipleship to Jesus Christ. The board shall work with persons and through structures, such as districts and Annual Conferences, to lead and assist local churches in becoming communities of growing Christians, celebrating and communicating the redeeming and reconciling love of God as revealed in Jesus Christ to persons of every age, racial and ethnic background, and social condition, and to advocate and encourage the development of new congregations.

The board members and staff shall seek to fulfill this purpose in theory and practice.

¶ **1302.** *Responsibilities.*—All the responsibilities assigned to the units within the board shall be considered to be the responsibilities of the board. In addition to these, the board shall have authority:

1. To coordinate and harmonize the work of its units so as to provide its services to the Church in a unified manner.

2. To review and act upon reports of the units, the committees, and their officers and staffs.

3. To assign to one or several of its units any programs adopted by the General Conference or the Council on Ministries and assigned to the board.

4. To provide for special publications directed toward the local church age-level and family ministry coordinators, the work area chairpersons, the pastor, and the other local church officers for whom the board has primary responsibility.

5. To manage and publish *The Upper Room, alive now!,* and other devotional life publications.

6. To provide resources, guidance, and training to related district and Annual Conference agencies and their committees; to local church administrative officers; Councils on Ministries; age-level and family ministry councils; work area chairpersons for evangelism, stewardship, worship, and local church education; and work area commissions and task groups.

7. To cooperate with the various agencies of the Church in the training and nurturing of pastors and lay persons for leadership in the areas of evangelism, stewardship, worship, and

local church education; in creating new congregations; and in initiating new forms of ministry.

8. To provide programs for the training of pastors, parents, teachers, officials, and others in the work of the local church and to promote these programs through various types of training events, correspondence work, and such other agencies as it may see fit to establish. It shall have authority also to promote and conduct conferences, consultations, assemblies, and other meetings to further the work assigned to the board.

9. To develop a unified and comprehensive program and resources for leadership training to serve all age groups in the home, Church, and community.

10. To enable and strengthen the ministry with and to youth at all levels of the Church, including the calling together of youth and adults.

11. To provide representation in ecumenical and interdenominational agencies as they relate to the work of the board.

12. To cooperate with the Board of Global Ministries in jointly developing and recommending architectural standards for facilities needed to house the Church's program of worship, education, and fellowship; and to cooperate in recommending training ventures to interpret these recommended standards.

13. To respond to requests and needs for ministries in other lands in consultation with the Board of Global Ministries and other agencies.

14. To engage in research, experimentation, innovation, and the testing and evaluation of programs, resources, and methods to discover more effective ways to help persons achieve the purpose set forth in ¶ 1301. This responsibility will include authority for experimentation and research in all areas of ministry assigned to the Board of Discipleship and will encourage cooperation with other agencies in the conduct of such research and experimentation. This research and experimentation may be assigned to appropriate units within the board.

¶ **1303.** *Incorporation.*—The General Board of Discipleship shall be a corporation existing under the laws of Tennessee, and shall be the legal successor and successor in trust of the corporations known as the General Board of Evangelism of The United Methodist Church and the General Board of Laity of The

United Methodist Church, and shall further be responsible for the performance of the functions previously conducted by the Commission on Worship of The United Methodist Church, the Division of the Local Church, and the Division of Curriculum Resources of the General Board of Education of The United Methodist Church.

The General Board of Discipleship is authorized to take such action as is appropriate under the corporation laws of Tennessee so as to accomplish the end result stated above, and under which the General Board of Discipleship shall be one legal entity.

The divisions of the General Board of Education were not incorporated separately; it is the intent, however, that responsibility for the functions delegated to the divisions by prior legislative action be transferred consistent with the separation of the divisions between the General Board of Discipleship and the General Board of Higher Education and Ministry. In the division of the assets of the General Board of Education, it is the intent that all assets be used in keeping with the original intent and purpose for which they were established or acquired, and so be assigned as appropriate to the Boards of Discipleship and Higher Education and Ministry respectively. It is further intended that the annuities, bequests, trusts, and estates formerly held by the General Board of Education be used for the benefit and use of the Boards of Discipleship and Higher Education and Ministry (in accord with their purposes as defined in the Discipline) respectively as their interests may appear, and that real estate titles be authorized to be conveyed as appropriate and apportioned where indicated.

In the event that the intent of the original donor of existing annuities, bequests, trusts, and estates cannot clearly determined in relation to the interests of the two boards, such assets shall be divided equally between the two boards.

It is further intended that should additional assets accrue to the former General Board of Education by reason of annuities, bequests, trusts, and estates not now known and where the intent of the donor can be clearly ascertained, the assets shall be used in keeping with the original intent and purpose for which they were established or acquired and so be assigned as appropriate to the

Boards of Discipleship and Higher Education and Ministry respectively.

It is further intended that should additional assets accrue to the former General Board of Education by reason of annuities, bequests, trusts, and estates not now known and where the intent of the original donor cannot be clearly determined in relation to the interests of the two boards, such assets shall be divided equally between the two boards.

The president of the board, the general secretary, and the treasurer shall have the power to execute on behalf of the board legal paper such as conveyances of real estate, releases on mortgages, transfer of securities, contracts, and all other legal documents.

¶ **1304.** *Organization.*—1. The board shall consist of the number of members as defined in ¶ 805 of the general provisions. It shall be organized to accomplish its work through elected officers as prescribed in ¶ 808. One of the episcopal members of the board shall be a Central Conference bishop. One of the laymen elected by each jurisdiction shall be the president, or someone designated by the president, of the Jurisdictional Committee of United Methodist Men (¶¶ 635 and 805).

2. The board may elect an executive committee and establish such rules as necessary for the carrying out of its duties.

3. The board shall determine and establish the appropriate organization of the board and its staff, and may create or discontinue as deemed necessary, divisions, sections, committees, task forces, and consultations to carry out the regular or special duties of the board.

4. The board shall provide such bylaws as necessary to facilitate the work of the board, which shall not violate any provisions of the Discipline and which may be amended by a two-thirds vote of the members present and voting thereon at a regular or special meeting; provided that written notice to such amendment has been given to the members and the vote thereon shall be delayed at least one day.

5. Adequate provisions shall be made in its organizational structure for all responsibilities assigned to the board. These organizational units shall be amenable to and report regularly to the board and its executive committee.

¶ **1305.** *Organizational Units.*—The organizational units shall be organized by the board so as to fulfill the objectives and the responsibilities assigned to them within the mandate of the board (*see* ¶ 1304.3). The basic organization of these units shall be as follows:

1. *Membership.*—The units shall be composed of board members as provided in ¶ 805. In order to provide for unit members with special knowledge and experience, the board shall have authority to elect members at large to the units on nomination of the units and in accord with ¶ 805.

2. *Meetings.*—The units shall meet in conjunction with the meetings of the board. Special meetings may be called in a manner prescribed by the board. Presence of one third of the members of a unit shall constitute a quorum.

3. *Officers.*—Each unit shall have a chairperson, elected by the board; such vice-chairpersons as necessary; and a recording secretary, elected by the unit.

4. *Executive Committee.*—Each unit may elect an executive committee and establish such rules as necessary for the carrying out of its duties.

5. *Unit Staff.*—The administrative officer of each unit shall be elected by the board and shall sit with the unit and all its regular committees. In all of these relationships he or she shall have the right of the floor without the power to vote. All other staff persons are to be elected or appointed in a manner prescribed by the board (¶ 814).

¶ **1306.** *Financial Support.*—1. The financial support of the board shall be determined as follows: the General Conference shall determine and provide the budget for the board in accord with procedures defined in ¶ 906.

2. The board shall have authority to receive and administer funds, gifts, or bequests that may be committed to it for any portion of its work and to solicit, establish, and administer any special funds that may be found necessary for the carrying out of its plans and policies in accordance with ¶ 911.3.

3. No funds, property, and other investments either now in hand or hereafter accumulated by *The Upper Room* or other devotional and related literature hereafter produced by The Upper Room shall be used for the support of other features of the

board's work, but all funds from the sale of such publications shall be conserved by the board for the purpose of preparing and circulating such literature and cultivating the devotional life; *provided,* however, that this shall not prevent the setting up of a reserve fund out of such income as a protection against unforeseen emergencies.

4. When special missions are conducted or special projects are undertaken by the board, offerings and contributions may be received toward defraying expenses.

5. In the discharge of its responsibility for Christian education in The United Methodist Church, the board may establish, and provide for participation by church school groups in a fund (or funds) for missions and Christian education in the United States and overseas. Plans for the allocation of, administration of, and education for this fund(s) shall be developed cooperatively by such means as the board shall determine in consultation with the Board of Global Ministries.

EDUCATION

¶ **1307.** 1. The board shall have general oversight of the educational interests of the Church as directed by the General Conference. The board shall be responsible for the development of a clear statement of the biblical and theological foundations of Christian education, consistent with the doctrines of The United Methodist Church and the purpose of the board. The board shall devote itself to studying, supervising, strengthening, researching, evaluating, and extending the educational ministry of the Church. The board shall be responsible for the educational program which is carried on through the structure adopted for the local church.

2. The total Christian educational program of The United Methodist Church for use in local churches shall be developed by the board. The educational program shall seek to encourage persons to commit themselves to Christ and membership in his Church; to learn about and participate in the Christian faith and life, including study of the Bible, and to develop skills which enable them to become effectively involved in the ministry of God's people in the world. It shall include the educational

emphases and activities of all the general departments and interests of the denomination, such as evangelism, stewardship, missions, Christian social action, and Bible instruction. It shall be developed as a comprehensive, unified, and coordinated Christian education program for children, youth, adults, and families in local churches. It shall be promoted and administered by the board in cooperation with those agencies responsible for Christian education in jurisdictions, Annual Conferences, districts, and local churches.

3. The educational ministry in local churches shall provide for study, worship, fellowship, and service, including social action, recreational, evangelistic, stewardship, and missionary activities as education in the Christian way of life.

¶ **1308.** *Education Responsibilities.*—The board shall organize as may be necessary for carrying on the educational ministry throughout the whole life-span of persons. The board shall be responsible for the following:

1. Formulating and interpreting the educational philosophy and approach which shall undergird and give coherence to all the educational work of the Church; the church school and related activities; individual or group study; fellowship and action groups for children, youth, and adults; related educational programs provided by civic youth-serving agencies; week-day nurseries and kindergartens; day care centers; choirs, drama groups, mission studies; preparation for confirmation; education for leisure; outdoor education; camping; education of the mentally retarded and others of special need; special Bible study groups; human relations workshops; training in church membership responsibilities; continuing education for adults and educational ministries with older adults.

2. Developing, resourcing, and supporting flexible systems of organization and administration to provide for the Church's educational ministries with children, youth, adults, and families at the local, district, and conference levels with the cooperation of other agencies.

Developing educational approaches in a variety of settings which appeal to persons with different life styles and theological perspectives and which will enable persons of different racial, ethnic, and cultural groups to appropriate the gospel for their own life situations.

Providing guidance for local churches to promote participation through membership and attendance among children, youth, and adults in a wide variety of settings.

Providing guidance for local churches in organizing church schools for the study of the Bible and Christian tradition, beliefs, and values (*see* ¶ 262.1).

Developing the education ministries of the Church in keeping with the levels of faith development, learning capacities, and needs of persons and providing field and support services for leaders, teachers, and others responsible for the education of persons across the life-span.

3. Initiating programs of teacher recruitment, development, training, and retraining in biblical, theological, and ethical thinking, as well as in procedures and methods.

Providing guidance and training for volunteer workers recruited for Christian service.

Offering training courses and other aids needed for vocational guidance.

Providing programs for the training of pastors, parents, teachers, education work area chairpersons, superintendents of the church school, division superintendents, officials, and others in educational ministries of the local church and promoting these programs through various types of training schools, correspondence work, and such other agencies as it may see fit to establish.

Designing, guiding, resourcing, and conducting leadership development enterprises specifically for teachers and educational leaders at all levels including district and conference, and such other leaders as may be assigned.

Working with the colleges and seminaries of the Church wherever possible to forward the common interest in the training of professional Christian educators and the training of ministerial students in local church Christian education.

Providing programs of Christian education outdoors and camping through the training of Annual Conference camp directors, district camp directors, camp committee persons, director/managers and managers of sites. Provide national camp training events and assist jurisdictions and Annual Conferences in designing, guiding, and resourcing camp training programs.

4. Providing guidance resources and services related to the training and work of local church directors, ministers, and associates of Christian education and educational assistants.

5. Planning for and providing education in the processes and procedures by which teaching, learning, and educational communication occur; in the selection, development, and use of learning resources, media, and technology; and in the application of experimentation, innovation, and new approaches in education.

6. The board shall review and recommend for approval the curriculum plans developed in cooperation with the other boards and agencies in the Curriculum Resources Committee and shall interpret and support the curriculum developed by the committee.

7. The board shall be responsible for promoting the observance of Christian Education Week (¶ 271.3*e*).

8. Only those special funds which are approved by the Board of Discipleship may be promoted nationally in the church schools (¶ 1306.2).

¶ **1309.** *Educational Standards.*—The board shall establish and maintain standards and shall give direction to the program of Christian education in local churches, in districts, in conferences, and elsewhere as will nurture growth toward these standards.

1. The board shall set standards and provide guidance concerning programming, leadership, grouping, and grading procedures for the various educational settings of the Church.

2. The board shall establish standards for the church school, for programs of Christian education, for the functioning of educational leaders, for church school membership, for the organization and administration of the church school and for recording and reporting membership and attendance of the church school.

3. The board in cooperation with the General Board of Higher Education and Ministry, shall develop performance standards that encourage the continuing growth of local church directors, ministers, and associates of Christian education; educational assistants; and director/managers of church camping.

4. The board shall cooperate with the General Board of Higher Education and Ministry in developing standards for certifying local church directors, ministers, and associates of Christian education as provided in ¶ 1625.2.

5. The board shall develop standards governing all types of camping in regard to physical facilities, program, and leadership. All camps shall be available to persons without regard to race or national origin.

6. The board shall develop educational standards and provide guidance for local churches in equipment, arrangement, and design for church school buildings and rooms.

¶ **1310.** The board shall cooperate with other boards and agencies as follows:

1. The board shall cooperate with other general boards and agencies in the promotion of stewardship, evangelism, worship, mission education, and social action, and in the evaluation of these ministries from the perspective of sound educational procedure.

2. The board shall, in cooperation with the General Board of Higher Education and Ministry, give guidance to training which encourages the continued growth of local church directors, ministers, and associates of Christian education; educational assistants; director/managers of camping; and directors and ministers of music.

3. The board shall be responsible for developing a unified program of mission education for all age groups in the local church and for developing aids for use in colleges, universities, and schools of theology. The board shall cooperate with the General Board of Global Ministries in the interest of effective mission education. The mission education program shall include provisions for the following:

a) Linking emerging philosophies of mission and of education through information flow and cooperative work of the respective staffs and boards;

b) Developing and interpreting varied styles of mission education appropriate to different groups, including age groupings;

c) Curriculum planning for education in mission, providing mission information about projects supported by The United

Methodist Church (including ecumenical projects) through the church school resources, and preparing curricular and other materials for mission education;

d) Participating with various agencies in the design, development, and promotion of ecumenical mission education resources;

e) Developing and interpreting educational approaches and channels for mission giving of children, youth, and adults, such as the Children's Fund for Christian Mission;

f) Developing and interpreting models for new approaches to mission study and educational participation in mission, including travel and study seminars;

g) Certifying leaders for schools of mission through developing educational criteria;

h) Disseminating a comprehensive listing of mission resources for leaders.

4. The board shall have authority to cooperate with the jurisdictional, Annual Conference, district, and local church agencies responsible for education, with other agencies of the Church, and with ecumenical agencies in cooperative enterprises to further the cause of Christian education.

5. The board is authorized to cooperate with the Christian Educators Fellowship of The United Methodist Church in such ways as will develop and strengthen the educational ministries of the Church.

6. The board is authorized to cooperate with the General Board of Global Ministries in the planning and execution of programs for the strengthening and development of the town and country, urban, and ethnic minority local church ministries of The United Methodist Church and of interdenominational cooperation in these fields.

¶ **1311.** *Church School Extension.*—1. The board shall be authorized to project and promote plans for church school extension throughout the Church and to cooperate in the strengthening of Christian education.

2. The board shall have the responsibility to develop, in cooperation with jurisdictional agencies responsible for education, a general program and plan to further within the Annual Conferences all the interests of the Christian education within the purview of the board.

EVANGELISM, WORSHIP, AND STEWARDSHIP

¶ **1312.** The board shall share the blessing of the gospel of the Lord Jesus Christ with all persons by the development, promotion, and support of all forms and phases of evangelism, worship, stewardship, and devotional life throughout the membership of The United Methodist Church; promote evangelistic understanding, interest, and zeal; public, individual, and family worship and celebration; the practice of prayer; the use of hymns and music in praise of God; the reading of the Bible in public and private; prepare and encourage the use of ritual and approved orders of worship of The United Methodist Church on all occasions appropriate to the same; and bring United Methodists to an understanding of the theological meaning of Christian stewardship and its application to the entire life of the Christian, including the use of time, influence, personal abilities, and material resources.

¶ **1313.** *Evangelism Responsibilities.*—1. To set forth an adequate biblical and theological basis and understanding for the personal, corporate, and social aspects of evangelism, consistent with the doctrine of The United Methodist Church, and to communicate and interpret the same to the membership of the Church.

2. To give particular emphasis to the promotion of comprehensive and practical programs of evangelism at the conference, district, and local church levels, so that persons without a church affiliation will be included within the responsibility of some local church.

3. To give guidance to the Church in using leisure time and the appropriate days and seasons of the Christian calendar for special evangelistic emphasis.

4. To provide resources for programs in evangelism, including resources for the local church work area on evangelism (¶ 260.4) and related committees and task forces.

5. To cooperate with other program agencies of the Church in supporting and equipping both clergy and laity for involvement in evangelism ministries.

6. To foster experimentation and demonstration of addi-

tional evangelistic approaches, consistent with the nature of the Christian gospel and the Church, at all levels of the Church's life including new congregations and all racial and cultural groups.

7. To cooperate with the General Board of Higher Education and Ministry in developing standards governing the work of those persons seeking to be certified as local church ministers and directors of evangelism, and associate and assistant ministers and directors of evangelism. Such standards of certification shall be designed to acquaint persons with viable understandings of evangelism for the contemporary Church that will enable them to create and discover ways by which the gospel can be made real in the lives of persons and events.

8. To provide resources and services for those certified as local church ministers and directors of evangelism, and associate and assistant ministers and directors of evangelism.

9. To cooperate with the General Board of Higher Education and Ministry (¶ 1625.2) to set minimal standards for elders desiring to serve as conference-approved evangelists. The board shall send copies of these standards quadrennially to the bishops, district superintendents, conference Boards of Discipleship and conference evangelists. An elder who feels called of God to be a conference-approved evangelist should prepare definitely for such service under the guidance of the Annual Conference to which the person belongs.

10. To maintain and service the General Military Roll for The United Methodist Church and to work in cooperation with the General Board of Higher Education and Ministry so that United Methodist chaplains may be aware of and informed concerning all forms and phases of evangelism.

11. To relate and provide liaison services to denominational associations and fellowships of evangelism.

12. To seek mutual cooperation among and with the seminaries of the Church and the General Board of Higher Education and Ministry in the training and nurturing of persons for ministry and in continuing education where the responsibilities intersect.

13. To communicate with other agencies in whose programs the subject matter of evangelism would be included, and to

provide counsel, guidance, and resources for the implementation of such programs.

14. To participate in and cooperate with the work of the Curriculum Resources Committee of the board for the inclusion of evangelism concepts and resources in local church study curriculum.

¶ **1314.** *Worship Responsibilities.*—1. To cultivate the fullest possible meaning in the corporate worship celebrations of the Church, including liturgy, preaching, the Sacraments, music, and related arts.

2. To develop standards and resources for the conduct of public worship in the churches, including liturgy, preaching, the Sacraments, music, and related arts.

3. To make recommendations to the General Conference regarding future editions of the book of worship and the hymnal and, as ordered, to provide editorial supervision of the contents of these publications, which shall be published by The United Methodist Publishing House. The hymnals of The United Methodist Church are the hymnals of The Evangelical United Brethren Church and The Book of Hymns; the Ritual of the Church is that contained in the Book of Ritual of The Evangelical United Brethren Church, 1959, "The General Services of the Church" in The Book of Worship for Church and Home of The Methodist Church, and The Ordinal 1980.

4. To prepare revisions of the Ritual of the Church for recommendation to the General Conference for adoption.

5. To prepare and sponsor the publication of supplemental orders and texts of worship.[23]

6. To maintain a cooperative but not exclusive relationship with The United Methodist Publishing House in the preparation and publication of worship resources.

7. To advise the general agencies of the Church in the preparation, publication, and circulation of orders of service and other liturgical materials bearing the imprint of The United Methodist Church, including ethnic and minority worship resources and other language publications.

---

[23]*See* Judicial Council Decision 445.

8. To counsel with the editors of the periodicals and publications of The United Methodist Church concerning material offered in the fields of worship and the liturgical arts.

9. To participate in and cooperate with the Curriculum Resources Committee of the board for the inclusion of worship concepts and resources in local church study curriculum.

10. To encourage in the seminaries, and pastors' schools and other settings, the offering of instruction in the meaning and conduct of worship.

11. To counsel with those responsible for planning and conducting the worship services of the General Conference and other general assemblies of the Church.

12. To develop, in cooperation with the General Board of Higher Education and Ministry, performance standards that encourage the continuing growth of local church directors, ministers, and associates of music; music assistants; and others in the local church related to music and the other arts.

13. To cooperate with the General Board of Higher Education and Ministry in developing standards for certifying local church directors, ministers, and associates of music as provided in ¶ 1625.2.

14. To cooperate with the Fellowship of United Methodists in Worship, Music, and Other Arts in affirming the sacramental life embracing liturgy, preaching, music, and other arts appropriate for the inclusive worship life of the Church.

15. To give guidance to, and develop performance standards for, directors and ministers of music, in cooperation with the General Board of Higher Education and Ministry, and to cooperate with the General Board of Higher Education and Ministry in their certification of directors and ministers of music as provided in ¶ 1625.2.

¶ **1315.** *Stewardship Responsibilities.*—1. To interpret the biblical and theological basis for stewardship consistent with the doctrines of The United Methodist Church and inform the Church of the same through educational channels and study materials.

2. To develop and promote programs, resources, and training materials in such basic subject areas of stewardship as stewardship education, proportionate giving and tithing, fund-

ing, planned giving, financial planning, time and ability, economics and management, and life style.

3. To communicate and work cooperatively with other agencies in whose programs the subject matter of stewardship should be included.

4. To participate in and cooperate with the work of the Curriculum Resources Committee of the board for inclusion of stewardship concepts and resources in local church school curriculum.

5. To provide education, counsel, resourcing, and training for the local church stewardship work area chairperson, Commission on Stewardship, Committee on Finance, Committee on Finance chairperson, financial secretaries, and treasurers and to develop program resources and training materials for use with and by the above-named persons and/or groups (*see* ¶ 907.11). Matters relating to procedures involving official records, forms, and reporting of finances shall be the responsibility of the General Council on Finance and Administration.

6. To develop strategies and provide resources which will lead to a continuing improvement in the level of giving of United Methodists in providing adequate support for the mission of the Church.

7. To encourage United Methodists to provide for their continued participation in World Service, or in one or more of the World Service agencies, in Annual Conference, district, and local church programs, and in other humanitarian causes, through estate planning, wills, special gifts, and foundations.

8. To furnish counsel and guidance to associations such as the Association of United Methodist Foundations and the Association of Stewardship Leaders.

9. To counsel in the area of stewardship with jurisdictional and Annual Conference program agencies relative to their organizational structure and program responsibilities and assist them in their interpretation of program and resources.

10. To develop and promote sound methods to aid local churches, districts, Annual Conferences, areas, and their related institutions to raise funds for benevolent causes, current expenses, and capital needs. When projects of this nature are extended a fee may be negotiated.

11. To develop programs and materials to assist in securing adequate financial support for all United Methodist ministers and church-related employees.

12. To create within The United Methodist Church a renewal of personal and corporate Christian stewardship which includes the use and sharing of wealth, resources, and the practice of a Christian life style.

13. To cooperate with the National Division of the General Board of Global Ministries in the development, planning, and utilization of stewardship principles, guidelines, strategies, and resources for fundraising programs to assist local churches, Annual Conferences, and denominational institutions to obtain funds necessary for their continuing viability in mission. (*See* ¶ 1529.16c.)

¶ **1316.** *Devotional Life Responsibilities.*—1. To interpret and communicate the biblical and theological basis for the devotional life which takes seriously both personal and corporate worship and Christian involvement in the world.

2. To develop literature and programs for the cultivation of the devotional life.

3. To maintain and extend the worldwide ministry of *The Upper Room* and other publications, including other language editions, with continuing focus upon our ecumenical stance.

4. To cooperate with all other units within the board and other groups within United Methodism, as well as other denominations whose programs are related to the devotional life.

Lay Life and Work

¶ **1317.** The board shall interpret and spread through the Church all the rich meanings of the universal priesthood of believers, of Christian vocation, and of the ministry of the laity.

The United Methodist Church has the responsibility of training and enabling the *laos*—the whole body of its membership—to enter into mission and to minister and witness in the name of Jesus Christ, the Head of the Church. Although all units of the Church have some responsibility for this imperative, the Board of Discipleship has a preeminent responsibility in that it is charged with developing discipleship.

¶ 1318. 1. There shall be a **Committee on Family Life** which shall be related administratively to the Board of Discipleship.

The committee shall serve as an advocate for family life within the Church and in the larger society.

The responsibilities of the committee shall include the following:

a) To identify the needs and concerns of families in our rapidly changing society and the various societal factors which impact families.

b) To survey the Church's ministry with families and to identify and disseminate information on those models of experience that enhance Christian family life.

c) To sponsor explorations of theological and philosophical meanings of Christian family living and the Church's ministry to Christian families and to disseminate to the church appropriate reports of these explorations.

d) To recommend programs and emphases to agencies of The United Methodist Church for development and implementation, either separately or cooperatively.

e) To elect the representatives of The United Methodist Church to the North American Section of the World Methodist Committee on Family Life, and to nominate the United Methodist members of the World Methodist Committee on Family Life.

f) To advocate policies, activities, and services that would strengthen and enrich family life.

2. The committee shall consist of thirty-three members chosen to represent adequately the age, sex, and ethnic diversity within the Church, who shall be selected quadrennially as follows: eight members from the General Board of Discipleship, two of whom shall be bishops, to be elected by the board and representing the concerns of lay life and work, education, the Curriculum Resources Committee, evangelism, worship, and stewardship; seven staff persons to be named by the staff administrators of the Board of Discipleship; eight persons, one board member and one staff person to be named by each of the following: General Board of Global Ministries, General Board of Church and Society, General Board of Higher Education and Ministry, and the Standing General Commission on the Status

and Role of Women; and ten additional members, one of whom shall be a United Methodist member of the North American Section of the World Methodist Committee on Family Life, and at least one of whom shall be a youth, to be nominated by the eight board members and seven staff persons of the Board of Discipleship named above. Consultants as needed may be named by the committee.

The director of services to coordinators of family ministries shall be the executive secretary of the committee.

¶ **1319.** *Leadership Development and Training Possibilities.*— 1. To help develop an adequate understanding of the theological and biblical basis for lay life and work.

2. *a)* To develop and interpret an active lay ministry through lay careers, both within and without the institutional Church, and through volunteer service.

b) To develop professional standards and to cooperate with the General Board of Higher Education and Ministry in certification procedures for lay persons called to full-time professional church leadership in order that they may qualify for consideration for the diaconal minister relationship as provided in ¶ 1625.2; except where provision has already been made for such standards and procedures to be developed with another United Methodist board, agency, unit, or professional organization.

3. To provide resources, support services, and designs for the development and improvement of leaders in the local church, except as specifically delegated to other agencies, and especially those who serve as members of Charge Conferences, Administrative Boards, Councils on Ministries, Committees on Pastor-Parish Relations, Personnel Committees, Committees on Nominations and Personnel, Boards of Trustees, and those who serve as lay leaders and lay members of Annual Conferences.

4. To provide consultative services in organizational development and management skills for leadership development committees and other organizations in jurisdictions, conferences, and districts.

5. To provide resources and suggested plans for the observance of Laity Day in the local church.

6. To provide resources and support services for the certified lay speaker program, including standards for the certification of lay speakers and designs and resources for use by Annual Conferences and districts in the training of lay speakers.

7. To provide support services to conference and district lay leaders and conference and district Committees on Lay Life and Work and to other appropriate conference and district officers and agencies.

8. To initiate a process of coordination and collaboration in developing a comprehensive approach to leadership development and training within all program areas for which the General Board of Discipleship has responsibility.

¶ **1320.** *Age-Level and Family Ministries Responsibilities.*—1. To cooperate with other units of the board in the coordination of age-level and family ministries so that services of the board may be offered to the Church in a unified manner. Initiation of this responsibility lies within the area of age-level and family ministries.

2. To provide interpretation, resources, consultative and support services to age-level and family ministry coordinators as they carry out their responsibilities:

a) To facilitate the local churches' age-level and family ministries based on concerns and needs of persons as adults, as youth, as children, and as families.

b) To coordinate efforts of persons as they create and implement age-level and family ministries.

3. To provide in collaboration with other appropriate agencies resources, training, consultative and administrative services and support for specialized programs in age-level and family ministries. This includes but is not limited to marital growth and enrichment programs; human sexuality training for children, youth, adults, and families; and ministries with children, youth, adults, and families in informal and leisure settings.

4. To represent the General Board of Discipleship in specialized interdenominational and cooperative programs in age-level and family ministries. This includes the International Christian Youth Exchange and Christian Youth Publications in cooperation with other units of the board as appropriate.

GENERAL BOARD OF DISCIPLESHIP ¶ 1322

5. To provide administrative and program liaison relationships with the United Methodist Youth Ministry Organization.

¶ **1321.** *Men's Work Responsibilities.*—1. To provide resources and support services to foster the development of United Methodist Men's fellowships.

a) Provide specific and optional models for these organizations.

b) Receive recommendations from the National Association of Conference Presidents of United Methodist Men.

c) Promote the chartering and affiliation of local church men's fellowships with the General Board of Discipleship.

d) Establish models for jurisdictional, Annual Conference, and district level organizations for the purpose of carrying out the objectives as set out in ¶ 262.6.

e) Recognize officers of the National Association of Conference Presidents as the national officers of United Methodist Men.

2. To seek methods for involving men in a growing relationship to the Lord Jesus Christ and his Church.

a) Provide resources and support for programs of evangelism in cooperation with the area of evangelism which are geared to men's needs.

b) Provide resources and support for programs of stewardship in cooperation with the area of stewardship which will lead men to an understanding of their responsibility for stewardship, including time, talent, money, and prayer.

c) Seek resources and support for men as husbands and fathers in a rapidly changing society.

d) Continue in a constant search for new and better ways for The United Methodist Church to minister to and through men.

CURRICULUM RESOURCES COMMITTEE

¶ **1322.** There shall be a **Curriculum Resources Committee,** organized and administered by the General Board of Discipleship, which shall be responsible for constructing plans for curriculum and curriculum resources to be used in the church school. (*See* ¶ 262.1.) The plans for curriculum and curriculum resources shall be designed to help local churches carry out the Church's educational ministry with children, youth, adults, and

451

families, and to meet the needs of various racial, ethnic, age, cultural, and language constituencies, as well as the needs of persons of various learning capacities, backgrounds, levels of psychological development, and Christian maturity. They shall be for use in a variety of settings, both formal and informal, including outdoor experiences, family life, leadership education, campus ministries, and confirmation classes. The plans for curriculum and curriculum resources shall be consistent with the educational philosophy and approach formulated for the educational ministry of the Church by the General Board of Discipleship and shall reflect a unity of purpose and a planned comprehensiveness of scope. They shall be designed to support the total life and work of the Church and shall reflect the official positions of The United Methodist Church as authorized by the General Conference.

¶ **1323.** When the plans for curriculum and curriculum resources have been approved by the General Board of Discipleship, the editorial staff shall be responsible for the development of curriculum resources based on the approved plans. The curriculum resources shall be based on the Bible, shall reflect the universal gospel of the living Christ, and shall be designed for use in the various settings which are defined by the board.

¶ **1324.** The Curriculum Resources Committee shall review and may approve and recommend existing or projected resources from other agencies. All curriculum resources that are approved by the General Board of Discipleship shall be authorized for use in the church school.

¶ **1325.** *Relationships.*—1. The Curriculum Resources Committee shall be related to the General Board of Discipleship as follows:

a) The committee shall be responsible to the board with respect to educational philosophy and approaches and shall seek to maintain the standards set by the board.

b) The committee shall work with the General Board of Discipleship in setting policies for interpreting and promoting the use of approved curriculum resources.

c) The chairperson of the Curriculum Resources Committee shall serve as a member of the executive committee of the General Board of Discipleship.

d) When General Board of Discipleship meetings are held and staff are present, the editorial staff may sit with the board with the privilege of the floor without vote.

e) In preparation of the budget for presentation to the General Board of Publication, the editor of church school publications shall consult with the general secretary of the General Board of Discipleship (¶ 1836).

2. The Curriculum Resources Committee shall be related to The United Methodist Publishing House and the General Board of Publication as follows:

a) The publisher or chairperson of the General Board of Publication may sit with the General Board of Discipleship for consideration of matters pertaining to joint interests of the Curriculum Resources Committee and the Board of Publication and shall have the privilege of the floor without vote.

b) The General Board of Publication shall publish, manufacture, and distribute, through the facilities of The United Methodist Publishing House, the curriculum resources prepared by the editorial staff. The United Methodist Publishing House and the General Board of Discipleship shall be responsible jointly for interpretation and support of these resources.

c) The United Methodist Publishing House shall cooperate with the editor of church school publications in developing formats and types of curriculum resources, such as periodicals, books, booklets, graphics, recordings, and other audio-visuals. The publishing house shall have final responsibility in relation to publishing and financial matters, and in these matters the editor of church school publications shall recommend changes in formats of publications to be produced and shall work cooperatively with the publisher in the design and layout and in handling of proofs and equivalent steps in the case of nonprinted resources.

d) The work of the Curriculum Resources Committee shall be financed by the General Board of Publication.

3. The committee shall exercise these additional relationships:

a) The committee shall cooperate with other agencies of The United Methodist Church so that their assigned concerns are reflected in and supported by the church school resources.

b) The committee may explore and implement opportunities at home and overseas for cooperative planning and publishing wherever such cooperation seems best for all concerned and when it is found to be practicable and in harmony with editorial and publishing policies.

c) The committee may cooperate with The United Methodist Publishing House and the General Board of Discipleship in educational research, in the development of experimental resources, and in the evaluation of resources that are provided for the church school.

¶ **1326.** *The Editor of Church School Publications.*—1. The **editor of church school publications** shall be responsible for the administration of the work of the Curriculum Resources Committee and the editorial staff, the general editorial policy, and shall be responsible for final determination of editorial content of the church school publications.

2. The editor shall be elected by the General Board of Discipleship upon nomination by a joint committee composed of the president of the General Board of Discipleship, the chairperson of the Curriculum Resources Committee, one other member of the General Board of Discipleship representing educational concerns, the chairperson and two other members of the General Board of Publication. The election of the editor shall be subject to confirmation by the General Board of Publication.

3. The editor shall be responsible to the General Board of Discipleship for seeing that the content of church school publications is consistent with the educational philosophy formulated by the board.

¶ **1327.** *Membership.*—1. The Curriculum Resources Committee shall consist of forty-one voting members elected quadrennially by the General Board of Discipleship as follows:

a) A bishop who is a voting member of the General Board of Discipleship, to be nominated by the executive committee of the Board.

b) Twenty members, nominated by the executive committee of the board, of whom at least seven shall be pastors, at least three of whom shall be voting members of the board; and at least seven shall be lay persons actively participating as member/leader/teacher in the educational ministry in the local church, at least three of whom shall be voting members of the board; six members at large shall be nominated, three of whom shall be members of the board, with due consideration to the diversity in theological perspectives, educational attainments, sex, age, racial and ethnic differences, and sizes of local churches, and in consultation with the directors of Councils on Ministries or Boards of Discipleship in each of the Annual Conferences.

c) Twenty members from the program boards as follows: the general secretary of the General Board of Discipleship and the three general secretaries of the other program boards or someone designated by them; the editor of church school publications and five staff members of the Curriculum Resources Committee; six staff members representing educational concerns; one staff person representing lay life and work concerns; one staff person representing the concerns of evangelism, worship, and stewardship; the president and publisher of The United Methodist Publishing House and the vice-president in charge of publishing.

d) The chairperson of the committee shall be a member of the Board of Discipleship.

2. The Curriculum Resources Committee may select other persons to assist in its work as follows:

a) Consultants.—The committee may invite persons, upon nomination of the boards and agencies of the Church, to serve as consulting members of the committee. They shall have full privileges of membership in the sections of the committee and task forces to which they are assigned.

b) Specialists.—The committee may designate other persons of special interest or technical competence to aid the committee in its work.

The committee may prepare such bylaws and operating guidelines as are necessary to facilitate the work of the committee.

Section VII. United Methodist National Youth Ministry Organization.

¶ **1401.** There shall be a **National Youth Ministry Organization** accountable to the General Board of Discipleship whose purposes shall be: (1) to promote and administer the Youth Service Fund; (2) to encourage and enable youth and adults to recognize and respond to the needs and concerns of youth; and (3) to encourage the inclusion of youth as full members and participants in United Methodist ministries and structures. The organization shall provide a setting in which youth can speak their concerns to the Church. The organization shall be composed of two basic units: (1) a National Youth Ministry Organization Convocation, and (2) a National Youth Ministry Organization Steering Committee, which carries out the directives of the Convocation.[24]

1. The responsibilities of the **National Youth Ministry Organization Convocation** shall be as follows:

a) To provide for spiritual growth for the participants.

b) To provide training experiences for designated conference youth leaders in attendance.

c) To strengthen the connectional ties of youth ministry in The United Methodist Church.

d) To set national Youth Service Fund monetary goals.

e) To set the policy and criteria for selection of projects and distribution of the national portion of the Youth Service Fund.

f) To elect the National Youth Ministry Organization Steering Committee (in accordance with ¶ 1402.2).

g) To initiate and support special projects which are of particular interest to youth.

h) To be a forum for the free expression of the convictions of youth on issues vital to them, and to direct the advocacy of these convictions.

i) To make recommendations to and cooperate with other appropriate boards and agencies of the United Methodist Church on ways to strengthen youth ministry in areas of vital concern.

j) To empower youth throughout the Church, through the support of and communication with Annual Conference and jurisdictional youth ministry structures.

k) To support and facilitate renewal in the Church.

l) To support and facilitate the formation of racial/ethnic minority youth caucuses on the Annual Conference, jurisdictional, and general levels of the Church.

---

[24]*See* Judicial Council Decision 425.

m) To communicate its actions to the Board of Discipleship for information and response.

n) To promote an evangelistic outreach by and with youth.

o) To provide guidance to the National Youth Ministry Organization Steering Committee for programmatic concerns.

2. The membership of the National Youth Ministry Organization Convocation shall be:

a) Voting Members.—Three representatives from each Annual Conference selected by the conference Council on Youth Ministry. Of those selected, two are to be youth (one of which is the conference youth president or designate), and one adult (the conference youth coordinator or designate). It is strongly recommended that at least one of the conference representatives be from a racial/ethnic minority. An Annual Conference must have a youth present in order to exercise voting privileges.

b) Associate Members.—(1) Youth members of the general boards and agencies. (2) The National Youth Ministry Organization Steering Committee. Associate members shall have the right to participate in the convocation, with voice but without vote.

3. *Meetings.*—The National Youth Ministry Organization Convocation shall be held biennially, preferably during the summer months, at a location designated by the National Youth Ministry Organization Steering Committee. The expenses of the conference representatives shall be paid by the conference they represent. (A travel fund shall be established in order to equalize the expenses of each conference.) The expenses of the National Youth Ministry Organization Steering Committee, with the exception of general board and agency representatives, shall be paid from National Youth Ministry Organization funds. The general boards and agencies shall be responsible for the expenses of their youth members and representatives.

¶ **1402.** *National Youth Ministry Organization Steering Committee.*—1. *Membership.*—The **National Youth Ministry Organization Steering Committee** shall consist of twenty-four youth (it is strongly recommended that at least one half of these youth shall be from racial/ethnic minorities, so elected that each minority is represented); one Annual Conference coordinator of youth ministry from each jurisdiction; a bishop chosen by the Council of Bishops; and one board or staff member from each of the following agencies, to be selected at a regular meeting of the agency: the Board of Church and Society, the Education and Cultivation Division of the Board of Global Ministries; the Board of Higher Education and Ministry; the Standing General Commission on Religion and Race; and the Standing General Commission on the Status and Role of Women; the Curriculum Resources Committee of the Board of Discipleship; and three staff members of the Board of Discipleship representing the concerns of education, lay life and work, and evangelism, worship, and stewardship. A staff member related to youth ministry of the Board of Discipleship shall serve as liaison to the National Youth Ministry Organization Steering Committee. All youth elected to the Steering Committee shall be entering into the eleventh grade or younger; if not in school, their age shall be sixteen or under at the time of their election.

2. *Election.*—*a)* Fourteen youth and five adults shall be elected at the National Youth Ministry Organization Convocation in the following manner: Each jurisdictional caucus shall elect two youth and one adult; four youth shall be elected as additional members by the total voting membership of the convocation. Ten youth (two from each jurisdiction) shall be elected in the alternate years at the jurisdictional youth ministry convocations.

b) Any vacancy that occurs due to an unfulfilled term shall be filled by the jurisdiction in which the vacancy occurs according to the following criteria: (1) the jurisdictional convocation shall determine the definition of vacancy and the process for filling vacancies; (2) youth shall be elected to fill vacancies in youth positions and adults shall be elected to fill vacancies in adult positions.

3. *Term.*—The term for Steering Committee members (with the exception of board and agency representative) shall be two years. Members cannot serve two consecutive terms. Members shall begin their term immediately upon the adjournment of the convocation at which they were elected, either national or jurisdictional, and shall conclude upon the adjournment of the next respective convocation.

4. *Responsibilities.*—The National Youth Ministry Organization Steering Committee shall be responsible for:

a) Administering the national portion of the Youth Service

Fund, including the selecting of the national projects. They shall fulfill this responsibility according to the criteria set by the National Youth Ministry Organization Convocation.

b) Promoting Youth Service Fund education throughout The United Methodist Church in cooperation with the Annual Conference Councils on Youth Ministry (¶ 732.3*h*).

c) Planning and supervising the National Youth Ministry Organization Convocation.

d) Implementing the decisions of the National Youth Ministry Organization Convocation.

e) Recommending action goals and issues to the National Youth Ministry Organization Convocation.

f) Advocating youth concerns and participation in the Church: general, jurisdictional, conference, district, and local.

g) Calling together, when necessary, groups of concerned youth to study and recommend action on vital issues.

h) Effecting participation of youth in appropriate denominational and interreligious enterprises and deliberation.

i) Recommending youth to nominating committees of general boards and agencies, considering suggestions from Annual Conference Councils on Youth Ministry (¶ 732) and other youth organizations.

j) Communicating the actions of the National Youth Ministry Organization to the Board of Discipleship for its information and response.

5. *Staff.*—The National Youth Ministry Organization Steering Committee shall determine its need for staff. Staff of the National Youth Ministry Organization shall be nominated by the steering committee and elected by the Board of Discipleship. The staff shall be responsible to the steering committee for carrying out decisions of the National Youth Ministry Organization and for interpreting its actions. The Board of Discipleship shall provide access to office space and support services to the staff of the National Youth Ministry Organization. The staff shall be governed by the personnel policies and guidelines of the Board of Discipleship.

¶ **1403.** *National Youth Ministry Organization Funding.*—The National Youth Ministry Organization shall be responsible for administering its own budget.

The operating funds shall be derived from two main sources: General Church Funds and the national portion of the Youth Service Fund. General Church Funds will be used for the administrative expenses of the National Youth Ministry Organization (including office expenses, staff, and meetings of the Steering Committee). Youth Service Fund shall be used for projects and programs of the National Youth Ministry Organization. A minimum of 70 percent shall be used for projects. The projects shall be chosen according to the policies and criteria established by the Convocation. The National Youth Ministry Organization Steering Committee shall constitute a Project Review Committee to advise the steering committee in the selection of projects. The Project Review Committee shall be composed of four youth from the National Youth Ministry Organization Steering Committee and three adults who are members of The United Methodist Church but not members of the National Youth Ministry Organization Steering Committee or related to any general agency.

¶ **1404.** *Youth Service Fund.*—There shall be a **Youth Service Fund** which shall be a means of stewardship education and mission support of youth within The United Methodist Church. As a part of its cultivation the youth shall have been challenged to assume their financial responsibilities in connection with the total program and budget of the local church of which they are members. Local church treasurers shall send the full amount of Youth Service Fund offerings to the treasurer of the Annual Conference, who shall retain 70 percent of the amount for the Annual Conference Council on Youth Ministry and send monthly the remaining 30 percent to the treasurer of the General Council on Finance and Administration to be forwarded to the National Youth Ministry Organization.

Section VIII. General Board of Global Ministries.

¶ **1501.** There shall be a **General Board of Global Ministries,** the purpose of which is found within the expression of the total mission of the Church. It is a missional instrument of The United Methodist Church, its Annual Conferences, and local congregations in the context of a global setting.

¶ **1502.** *Responsibilities.*—1. To discern those places throughout the world where the Word has not been heard or heeded and to witness to its meaning on all six continents through a program of global ministries.

2. To encourage and support the development of leadership in mission for both the Church and society.

3. To challenge all United Methodists with the New Testament imperative to proclaim the gospel to the ends of the earth, expressing the mission of the Church, to recruit, send, and receive missionaries; enabling them to dedicate all or a portion of their lives in service across racial, cultural, national, and political boundaries.

4. To plan with others and to establish and strengthen Christian congregations where opportunities and needs are found, so that these congregations may be units of mission in their places and partners with others in the worldwide mission of the Christian church.

5. To advocate the work for the unity of Christ's Church through witness and service with other Christian churches and through ecumenical councils.

6. To engage in dialogue with persons of other faiths and with persons of differing colors, custom, and culture, and to join with them where possible in action on common concerns.

7. To assist local congregations and Annual Conferences in mission both in their own communities and across the globe by raising awareness of the claims of global mission and by providing channels for participation.

8. To express the concerns of women organized for mission and to help equip women for full participation both locally and globally in Church and world.

9. To engage in direct ministries to human need, both emergency and continuing, institutional and noninstitutional, however caused.

10. To engage in building societies and systems where full human potential is liberated and to work toward the transformation of demonic forces which distort life.

11. To identify with all who are alienated and dispossessed and to assist them in achieving their full human development—body, mind, and spirit.

12. To envision and engage in imaginative new forms of mission appropriate to changing human needs and to share the results of experimentation with the entire Church.

13. To affirm the concept of volunteers-in-mission (short-term) as an authentic form of personal missionary involvement and devise appropriate structure to interpret and implement such opportunities for short-term volunteers in the global community.

¶ **1503.** *Objectives.*—1. The objectives of the General Board of Global Ministries shall be:

a) To establish and review the objectives of the General Board of Global Ministries and the work in mission of The United Methodist Church.

b) To establish appropriate organization of board and staff to accomplish its program and achieve established objectives, including writing bylaws, electing officers, establishing committees for its work, and filling vacancies in accord with ¶ 812.

c) To determine, in cooperation with the divisions and agencies, the areas to be served and the nature of the work to be undertaken.

d) To determine policy and program, to establish goals and priorities, to project long-range plans, to evaluate the program and services of the General Board of Global Ministries and its divisions as to the progress made in fulfilling its purpose, and to seek to achieve its objectives through the programs of the divisions and agencies of the General Board of Global Ministries.

e) To coordinate and harmonize the work of the various units.

f) To elect or appoint, on nomination of the divisions, work units, and agencies, the staff of the respective divisions, work units, and agencies, to evaluate staff performance, to remove staff for cause, and to fill vacancies. (*See* ¶ 811.)

g) To give direction to the General Board of Global Ministries staff and its work through the assignment of responsibility and the delegation of authority to the executives and through general oversight of the administration.

h) To receive and properly administer all properties and trust funds, permanent funds, annuity funds, and other special funds coming into the possession of the board as a board for missionary and other purposes in accordance with ¶¶ 906.6, .8, 907.3.

i) To secure, appropriate, and spend money to underwrite its program and achieve its objectives.

j) To receive and act upon the reports of the divisions and work units and their staff, the treasurers, the official reports from all its committees, and all other reports related to its program.

k) To make a report of its activities during the quadrennium to the General Conference and the Jurisdictional Conferences.

l) To assist the organization and maintenance of cooperative relations with boards, committees, and other agencies of the General Conference, and with the Jurisdictional, Central, and Annual Conference boards and committees.

m) To be responsible for implementing a policy stating that The United Methodist Church is not a party to any interdenominational agreement that limits the ability of any Annual Conference in any jurisdiction to develop and resource programs of ministry of any kind among Native Americans, including the organization of local churches where necessary.

2. The board shall develop and maintain cooperative working relationships between its divisions and work units; with other general boards, commissions, and agencies of The United Methodist Church; and with colleague churches and ecumenical agencies on matters of mutual concern in the implementation of Disciplinary responsibilities.

3. The General Board of Global Ministries, through its World Division, shall facilitate and coordinate the program relationships of other program agencies of The United Methodist Church to colleague churches and agencies outside the United States.

¶ **1504.** *Authority of the Board.*—The General Board of Global Ministries shall have authority to make bylaws and regulate its proceedings in harmony with the Discipline of The United Methodist Church. Bylaws may be amended by a two-thirds vote of the members present and voting thereon at a regular or special meeting, *provided* that notice of such amendment has previously been given to the members. The board shall have the power and right to do any and all things which shall be authorized by its charter. It shall have authority to develop and carry out its functions as described in ¶ 1502; to buy, acquire, or receive by gift, devise, or bequest property, real, personal, and mixed; to hold, mortgage, sell, and dispose of property; to sue and be sued; to borrow money in case of necessity in a manner harmonious with ¶¶ 906-907; to develop and maintain ecumenical relations to carry out its responsibilities; and to administer its affairs through its respective divisions and joint agencies.

¶ **1505.** *Authority of the Divisions.*—The divisions shall have authority to make bylaws and to regulate their proceedings in harmony with the charter of the board and, with its approval, to develop and carry out the functions of the divisions; to buy and sell property; to solicit and accept contributions subject to annuity under the board's regulations and ¶¶ 906-907; and to recommend the appropriation of their funds for the work of the joint agencies of the board.

¶ **1506.** *Incorporation.*—1. The General Board of Global Ministries shall be incorporated and shall function through its divisions and/or work units. Within the board there shall be six divisions—namely: the Education and Cultivation Division, the National Division, the United Methodist Committee on Relief Division, the Women's Division, the World Division, the Health and Welfare Ministries Division; and two work units—namely: the Crusade Scholarship Committee and the Committee on Personnel in Mission. The divisions may each also be incorporated if required. These divisions shall be the corporate successors, respectively, of the Joint Commission on Education and Cultivation, the National Division, the United Methodist Committee on Relief, the Women's Division, the World Division of the Board of Missions of The Methodist Church, and the corporate successor of the Board of Missions of the Evangelical United Brethren Church, the Board of Missions of The United Methodist Church, the General Board of Health and Welfare Ministries of The United Methodist Church and the Commission on Ecumenical Affairs. The board and its divisions shall be incorporated in such state or states as the board may elect.

2. The Board of Global Ministries of The United Methodist Church shall be the successor to the following corporations: the Board of Missions of the Evangelical United Brethren Church,

the Home Missions and Church Erection Society of the Church of the United Brethren in Christ, the Foreign Missionary Society of the United Brethren in Christ, the Women's Missionary Association of the Church of the United Brethren in Christ, the Missionary Society of the Evangelical Church, and the Board of Church Extension of the Evangelical Church, and as such successor it shall be and is authorized and empowered to receive from its said predecessor corporations all trust funds and assets of every kind and character, real, personal, or mixed, held by them, and it shall and hereby is authorized to administer such trusts and funds in accordance with the conditions under which they have been previously received and administered by the said predecessor corporations.

3. It shall have control of all the work formerly controlled and administered by the following: the Board of Health and Welfare Ministries; the Board of Missions of The United Methodist Church; the Board of Missions and Church Extension of The Methodist Church; the Missionary Society, the Board of Foreign Missions, the Board of Home Missions and Church Extension, the Woman's Foreign Missionary Society, the Woman's Home Missionary Society, the Wesleyan Service Guild, and the Ladies' Aid Societies of the Methodist Episcopal Church; the Board of Missions, including the Woman's Missionary Society, the Woman's Board of Foreign Missions, the Woman's Board of Home Missions, the Woman's Missionary Council, and the Board of Church Extension of the Methodist Episcopal Church, South; the Board of Missions of the Methodist Protestant Church; and such other corporations or agencies of the General Conference as do similar work; but this list shall not be construed as exclusive.

4. Subject to the limitations hereinafter specified, each of the incorporated divisions shall be subject to the supervision and control of the General Conference of The United Methodist Church in all things not inconsistent with the Constitution and laws of the United States and of the states of incorporation.

5. The board and its divisions shall have the power to create those subsidiary units, sections, or departments needed in the fulfillment of designated functions, upon approval of the board.

¶ **1507.** *General Executive Committee.*—There shall be a

general executive committee whose membership and powers shall be determined by the board.

¶ **1508.** *Corporate Officers.*—1. *Board Officers.*—The board shall elect as its corporate officers a president, six vice-presidents who shall be the chairpersons of the divisions, a treasurer, a recording secretary, and such other officers as it shall deem necessary.

The Women's Division shall elect its chairperson, who shall be one of the six vice-presidents of the board. The board shall determine the powers and duties of its officers.

2. *Division and Work Unit Officers.*—Each division and work unit shall elect one or more vice-presidents, a treasurer, a recording secretary, and such other officers as it shall deem necessary.

Vacancies shall be filled by the divisions and work units or their executive committees. The divisions and work units shall determine the power and duties of their officers.

¶ **1509.** *Elected Staff.*—1. *Board Staff.*—*a)* The board, through a personnel committee, shall make nominations to the General Council on Ministries for the office of general secretary.

b) The board shall elect an associate general secretary for administration whose responsibilities shall include the administrative supervision of the staff of the work units.

c) The board shall elect additional staff as needed.

2. *Division and Work Unit Staff.*—*a)* The divisions shall each nominate, in consultation with the general secretary of the board, an associate general secretary for election by the board. The Women's Division shall nominate its associate general secretary for election by the division and the board after consultation with the president and general secretary of the board.

The associate general secretaries shall have administrative responsibility for the divisions and shall be responsible to the divisions and to the general secretary.

b) The divisions and work units shall nominate for election by the board such other staff persons as are deemed necessary to carry out the work assigned.

3. The president, general secretary, and treasurer of the board are ex officio members of the divisions and work units and their executive committees, without vote.

The board shall elect, on nomination of each division and in consultation with the general secretary, an associate treasurer of the General Board of Global Ministries, who shall have fiscal responsibility for the division. He or she shall be responsible to the treasurer of the General Board of Global Ministries for fiscal procedures and to the associate general secretary for all administrative procedures (¶ 803.7*b*).

¶ **1510.** *Personnel.*—1. *Selection.*—The board and its divisions and work units shall engage and elect and appoint staff on the basis of competency and with representation of ethnic and racial minorities, youth, young adults, and women.

2. *Staff Participation of Women.*—*a)* Of the following staff positions within the board—namely, the general secretary, the treasurer of the board, and the associate general secretaries, and of the total elected and appointed staff positions of the board—a minimum of 40 percent shall be occupied by women.

b) Of the following staff positions of each division within the board—namely, the associate general secretary, assistant general secretaries, and associate treasurers—a minimum of one third of the total of each division shall be women.

¶ **1511.** 1. All properties, trust funds, annuity funds, permanent funds, and endowments now held and administered by the Board of Missions, the Board of Health and Welfare Ministries, and the United Methodist Committee on Relief of The United Methodist Church; the Board of Missions of The Methodist Church; the Board of Missions of the Evangelical United Brethren Church; and their respective divisions shall be carefully safeguarded. The General Board of Global Ministries of The United Methodist Church and its divisions shall endeavor to invest in institutions, companies, corporations, or funds which make a positive contribution toward the realization of the goals outlined in the Social Principles of The United Methodist Church and to administer such investments in the interest of those persons and causes for which said funds were established. Such properties, trust funds, annuity funds, permanent funds, and endowments shall be transferred to the General Board of Global Ministries of The United Methodist Church or its respective divisions from merged boards and societies only when such transfers can be made in accordance with the laws of the states where the several boards and societies are chartered and on the recommendation of the respective divisions and the approval of such boards and societies. Funds of the administrative divisions and their preceding corporations and societies which are subject to appropriation shall be appropriated only on recommendation of the respective divisions (¶¶ 906.6, .8).

2. The financial affairs of the board shall be as follows:

a) The income of the divisions of the board, exclusive of the Women's Division, shall be derived from apportionments, assessments, or askings distributed to jurisdictions, Annual Conferences, and pastoral charges by the budget-making process of the General Conference in such manner as the General Conference may prescribe, and from church schools, gifts, donations, freewill offerings, annuities, bequests, specials, and other sources from which missionary and benevolence funds are usually derived, in harmony with the Discipline of The United Methodist Church and actions of the General Conference. Funds for the fulfillment of the responsibilities of the Women's Division shall be derived from annual voluntary pledges, offerings, gifts, devises, bequests, annuities, or money received through special emphases and from meetings held in the interest of the division.

b) Cultivation for Advance specials shall be through channels of the Church other than United Methodist Women.

c) All contributions to and income on all funds of the General Board of Global Ministries or its respective divisions should be used for current expenses and annual appropriations unless otherwise designated by the donor.

3. Askings shall be received from the fields, and budgets shall be prepared by the divisions in such manner as the board may prescribe, consistent with its constitution and charter, and this combined budget shall be presented to the General Council on Ministries in accord with ¶ 906.

4. The board shall not appropriate for the regular maintenance of its work in any one year more money than was received by it for appropriation the previous fiscal year, except as provided in consultation with the General Council on Ministries.

¶ **1512.** *Membership.*—The policies, plans of work, management, business, and all affairs of the General Board of Global Ministries of The United Methodist Church shall be governed and administered by the board, which shall be composed according to the conditions defined in ¶¶ 805, 809 of the General Provisions, with the following conditions:

1. The basic members (clergy, laymen, and laywomen) are elected by the jurisdiction upon the nomination of the Annual Conferences in accord with ¶ 805.1. The additional members of the board are nominated by a committee composed of three persons from each jurisdiction—a clergy member, a layman, and a laywoman—elected within each jurisdiction. The committee is to be convened by the president of the board, or if there be none, the secretary of the Council of Bishops.

2. The Women's Division membership procedures are an exception to those described in ¶¶ 805, 809 of the general provisions. This formula is defined in ¶ 1554. These persons may also serve on the membership of other divisions of the board.

3. The composition of the board and its divisions and units should reflect the major recognized categories of church members. One half of the nonepiscopal membership should be women; not less than one quarter should be clergy; and not less than one quarter should be laymen. One fifth should be under thirty-five years of age (of whom one half should be under twenty-five divided equally between those over eighteen and under at the time of election); membership among all age categories to be balanced between men and women and among racial and ethnic groups. One fifth should represent minority interests and one tenth youth and young adult interests. Any overseas representatives should also be selected through the additional member nomination process. These are not mutually exclusive or exhaustive categories.

4. Members of the board shall be distributed across the component divisions of the board in accord with ¶ 809.

5. The term of office of all members whose election is provided for in this paragraph shall begin and the board shall organize at a meeting to be held within ninety days after the adjournment of the last meeting of the several Jurisdictional Conferences held after the adjournment of the General Conference.

6. In addition to the episcopal members provided for by ¶ 805, the Council of Bishops shall elect three bishops and three

lay persons from Central Conferences who shall be members of the board and at least one of whom shall be a woman.

7. The general secretary and treasurer of the board and the associate general secretaries shall be members without vote.

8. Salaried members of a staff of any agency receiving appropriation funds from any division of the General Board of Global Ministries shall not be eligible to serve as voting members of said board, except in order to fulfill the provisions of ¶ 805.

EDUCATION AND CULTIVATION DIVISION

¶ 1513. *Purpose.*—1. The **Education and Cultivation Division** exists:

a) To undergird the total program of the General Board of Global Ministries affirming that relating persons to mission through communication, education, and cultivation is itself mission.

b) To initiate and develop programs and resources through which individuals and groups may understand the biblical background and theological basis of the Christian world mission, the involvement of The United Methodist Church in global ministries, the special concerns of women in mission, and the possibilities for personal and corporate witness involvement in and support of those ministries.

2. *Objectives.*—The objectives of the Education and Cultivation Division shall be:

a) To strengthen local congregations in global outreach and to enable persons to participate more actively in the mission of the church.

b) To promote understanding, participation in, and support of the global ministries of The United Methodist Church through study and use of resources.

c) To cultivate through appropriate channels of the Church, financial support for global ministries including Advance specials.

¶ 1514. *Responsibilities.*—The responsibilities of the Education and Cultivation Division shall be:

1. To interpret to the Church the programs, plans, and policies of the board and to plan and promote emphases on global ministries.

2. To initiate and develop in consultation with appropriate divisions/work units programs and resources through which individuals and groups may understand and participate in the global ministries of the Church and to make known channels through which these ministries may be supported.

3. To prepare, sell, and distribute printed and audio-visual resources and periodicals for the General Board of Global Ministries.

4. To cultivate, through channels of the Church other than United Methodist Women, the Advance special gifts for national and overseas ministries administered by the National, World, and United Methodist Committee on Relief divisions, in accordance with the General Council on Finance and Administration, assuming responsibility for providing information to the donors (¶ 913).

5. To develop and coordinate the plans for cultivating mission giving in consultation with the other divisions of the General Board of Global Ministries, the General Board of Discipleship, the General Council on Finance and Administration, and the Standing General Commission on Communication, subject to and in harmony with the general financial system of The United Methodist Church as adopted by the General Conference.

6. To cooperate with the Curriculum Resources Committee of the General Board of Discipleship, in providing opportunities for missional involvement and understanding at all age levels (¶ 1325).

7. To cooperate with the Standing General Commission on Communication in all ways as mutually agreed upon, including communications, training, audio-visual production, benevolence interpretation, and other areas of common concern.

8. To cooperate with other divisions, Jurisdictional and Annual Conferences, district superintendents, pastors, local churches, United Methodist Women, men's groups, and other groups within the Church in fulfilling these functions.

¶ **1515.** *Authority.*—The Education and Cultivation Division shall have authority to make bylaws and to regulate its proceedings in harmony with the charter of the board, and with the approval of the board to develop and carry out the responsibilities described in ¶ 1514; to recommend to the board and the Women's Division appropriations for its work, and to receive and administer funds allocated to it by the board and its divisions; and to solicit Advance special funds for the work of the World, National, and United Methodist Committee on Relief divisions, in cooperation with the General Council on Finance and Administration.

¶ **1516.** *Executive Committee.*—There shall be an **executive committee** whose powers shall be determined by the division. It shall be composed of the president, vice-president, and secretary of the division and seven members of the division; the associate general secretary and the treasurer of the division, ex officio without vote. One half of the members shall be women elected in accordance with ¶¶ 1512.3 and 1550.

¶ **1517.** *Membership.*—The Education and Cultivation Division shall be composed of twenty members, consistent with ¶ 1512.3: eight persons; one bishop; and ten persons, two each who are members of each of the other five divisions. One of the twelve must be a bishop. In addition, eight members at large of the division shall be elected in such manner as the division shall determine for their special competencies.

HEALTH AND WELFARE MINISTRIES DIVISION

¶ **1518.** *Purpose.*—The purpose of the **Health and Welfare Ministries Division** shall be to assist units of the Church and its people to become involved in direct service to persons in need through both residential and nonresidential ministries, especially in areas of child care, aging, health care, and handicapping conditions. The division shall provide services to assist agencies and programs related to units of The United Methodist Church to be professionally competent and Christian in their work. The division shall make its services available to other units and related agencies and programs of the General Board of Global Ministries to further the global mission of the Church.

¶ **1519.** *Responsibilities.*—1. To provide upon request consultation services to existing and emerging health and welfare agencies and direct service programs, and to jurisdictional, Annual Conference, and local church units.

a) Consultation services shall include assistance in: organization and administration, financial management and support, securing management level personnel, evaluation of current services, planning for new services and methods, and the development of affirmative action programs. (*See* ¶ 815.)

b) Upon request of the Annual Conference unit responsible for health and welfare ministries or other appropriate church unit, the division shall assist in evaluating plans for new or expanded residential and nonresidential ministries seeking approval from the Annual Conference or other church unit (*see* ¶ 721.4*a* (24)).

2. To formulate standards to implement the aims and ideals of The United Methodist Church and to encourage and assist institutions, agencies, and programs of service in attaining these standards.

3. To provide a program of leadership development for agencies, Annual Conferences, districts, and local churches to improve the quality of professional and volunteer leadership in health and welfare ministries; and, to promote the most effective relationship between these ministries and United Methodism.

4. To foster **Golden Cross** and other offerings within each Annual Conference to collect moneys and provide other material assistance in providing care for the sick, older persons, children and youth, and persons with handicapping conditions with special emphasis given to supporting those ministries which provide direct financial assistance to persons unable to pay for the cost of care.

5. To participate through educational and legislative efforts in policy-making, advocacy, and social change on behalf of the health and welfare rights and needs of all persons.

6. To support and interpret the work of the Church in health and welfare ministries, and to provide information and guidance in specific areas, through the development of printed, audio-visual, and other resources.

¶ **1520.** *Certification Council.*—The division shall maintain a **Certification Council** which shall develop criteria and procedures to implement a program of affiliation and certification of health and welfare institutions, agencies, and other programs of service related to a unit of The United Methodist Church providing health care services; services with the aged; services with children, youth, and families; and services with persons with handicapping conditions. Any such agency or program of service in the United States that is related to a unit of The United Methodist Church or looks to the United Methodist constituency for support, or uses the United Methodist name, shall be urged to have its affiliate relationship with a unit of the church verified by the Certification Council and shall be urged to attain and maintain certification under the rules established by the council. However, neither the Health and Welfare Ministries Division nor the Certification Council shall have the duty or authority to take any legal action against an agency which looks to the United Methodist constituency for support or which uses the United Methodist name and which does not have its affiliate relationship verified (*see* ¶ 721.4*a* (24)).

¶ **1521.** *National Association of Health and Welfare Ministries.*— The division shall cooperate with the National Association of Health and Welfare Ministries of The United Methodist Church (¶ 1527) in leadership development and shall make available staff and support services.

¶ **1522.** *Meetings.*—The division shall meet annually at the time of the meeting of the board and at such other times as it shall deem necessary. Written notice stating the place and purpose of all meetings must be given all members at least ten days prior to the meeting. A majority of the members of the division shall constitute a quorum.

¶ **1523.** *Executive Committee.*—There shall be an **executive committee** of the division, whose powers shall be determined by the division subject to approval of the board. It shall be composed of nine persons: the president, vice-president, recording secretary, and six other persons elected by the division, one of whom shall be a member of the Women's Division Executive Committee serving on the Health and Welfare Ministries Division.

The executive committee shall include at least two persons from racial and ethnic minority groups. The associate general secretary and treasurer of the division shall be members of the executive committee, ex officio and without vote.

¶ **1524.** *Financial Support.*—The division shall derive its financial support from World Service and other funds designated for the program of the Health and Welfare Ministries Division of the General Board of Global Ministries, including such proportion of undesignated gifts as may be determined by the board, and from gifts, devises, wills, and trust funds given specifically to the Health and Welfare Ministries Division. The division shall properly administer special gifts for approved work related to the Health and Welfare Ministries Division and cultivated through the Education and Cultivation Division. The division is authorized to receive financial grants and trusts from private foundations and funds from public agencies and is empowered to act as trustee for the administration of bequests.

¶ **1525.** *Membership.*—The Division of Health and Welfare Ministries shall be composed of thirty-five board members as follows:

1. At least two bishops, two laymen, two laywomen, and two clergy in full connection assigned by the general board, at least two of which must be minority persons;

2. Three persons elected to serve on both the general board and the division by each jurisdiction from nominations provided by Annual Conferences. Of this number there shall be one layman, one laywoman, and one clergy in full connection, at least one of whom, and not more than one, is the administrator of a United Methodist–related health and welfare agency;

3. Twelve persons at large elected by the division to serve on the division for the purpose of perfecting the representation of youth, young adults, retired persons, women, men, racial and ethnic minorities, and to provide special expertise in related fields.

The officers of the board, as specified in ¶ 1508, and the associate general secretary and treasurer of the division shall be eligible to attend all meetings of the division and its committees, ex officio and without vote.

¶ **1526.** *Limitation of Responsibility.*—The division shall not be responsible, legally or morally, for the debts, contracts, or obligations or for any other financial commitments of any character or description created, undertaken, or assumed by any institution, agency, or interest related to a unit of The United Methodist Church, whether or not such institution, agency, or interest shall be approved, accepted, or recognized by the division, or shall be affiliated with the division, or whether or not the promotion or establishment of the same shall be approved by the constitution of the division. No such institution, agency, or interest related to a unit of The United Methodist Church and no officer or member of this division shall have any authority whatsoever to take any action directly or by implication at variance with, or deviating from, the limitation contained in the preceding sentence hereof, except as the division may directly own and manage an institution in its own name.

NATIONAL ASSOCIATION OF HEALTH AND WELFARE MINISTRIES

¶ **1527.** *National Association of Health and Welfare Ministries.*— There may be organized a **National Association of Health and Welfare Ministries of The United Methodist Church** which shall be incorporated and have its own constitution and bylaws. The association shall foster a program of leadership development for agency administrators, key staff, and board members; for Annual Conference health and welfare unit leaders; and for volunteers and other designated leaders in the Church's health and welfare ministries. It shall cooperate with the Health and Welfare Ministries Division of the General Board of Global Ministries in fulfilling this function. The association may establish its own membership requirements and shall be supported primarily through its dues structure and income from its national convention, workshops, and seminars.

NATIONAL DIVISION

¶ **1528.** *Purpose.*—Within the expression of the total mission of the Church outlined in the objectives of mission and the purposes of the General Board of Global Ministries, the **National Division** exists to proclaim and witness to the saving grace of Jesus Christ through mission in the United States, Puerto Rico, and the Virgin Islands.

The National Division is committed to an expression of faith which understands that God, through Jesus Christ, is active in all of life and works in church and secular society for dignity and justice among persons and communities. This faith directs the development of national mission strategies and program. These require the development and strengthening of congregations as centers of Christian mission and the creation of ministries of compassion to persons and groups who suffer in body and spirit and to affect social patterns which continue such suffering.

¶ **1529.** *Responsibilities.*—The responsibilities of the National Division shall be:

1. To formulate the objectives and strategies for the national mission of The United Methodist Church; to determine fields of service and nature of the work by consulting with constituents to be served and the church in the vicinity, and to establish governing policies and evaluative procedures for measuring effectiveness.

2. To study and establish division strategies for the implementation of new forms of mission which deal with national mission concerns.

3. To develop, administer, and supervise the national mission program within the context of the objectives and functions of the General Board of Global Ministries, providing overall coordination for programs in areas within the United States, Puerto Rico, and the Virgin Islands.

4. To enable, encourage, and support the development of new and existing congregations, cooperative parishes, community centers, health, educational, and social welfare ministries in urban, suburban, and rural settings; to develop strategies in response to critical community issues with special attention to the needs of ethnic and language minorities, people in transitional relationships and those living under repressive systems.

5. To develop, administer, and supervise in cooperation with Annual Conferences a program of church and community ministry for assignment to local churches, cooperative parishes, and other units of mission in rural and urban settings; to cooperate with UMCOR in Disaster Response Coordination and deployment of personnel.

6. To consult with congregations, cooperative parishes, districts, and conferences of The United Methodist Church and to prepare self-study and guidance materials to assist in identifying the needs of community and congregations.

7. To conduct research to aid congregations, cooperative parishes, districts, conferences, and other units of The United Methodist Church in the identification of needs of mission opportunities and the structures needed to meet these needs.

8. To develop task forces on training opportunities and joint planning committees with congregations, cooperative parishes, districts, conferences, areas, jurisdictions, and other units of The United Methodist Church for studying, planning, and setting goals.

9. To cooperate with other national church agencies, United Methodist agencies, and secular agencies, in developing programs and strategic plans which impact national issues.

10. To encourage and participate in the development of regional structures, urban and rural, for cooperative mission strategy and program, with special reference to secular geographic planning units which may be multicounty and may cross district, conference, or jurisdiction boundaries. These may be United Methodist or ecumenical.

11. To cooperate with church leaders at all levels in strategic planning, developing program, and advocating legislation which impacts community issues.

12. To provide guidelines for conference church and community committees and regional, metropolitan, and district mission structures.

13. To work with appropriate United Methodist agencies for the extension of the Church, through consultation, joint planning, loans, and grants. There shall be a Joint Committee on Congregational Development with equal representation of members from the National Division and the General Board of Discipleship which shall meet at least annually to expedite cooperation between these two boards in the field of congregational development of both new congregations as well as the redevelopment of existing congregations.

14. To provide a housing consultative service, giving guidance and assistance to local churches, conferences, and general church agencies concerning housing for low and middle income persons, and to coordinate United Methodist participation in ecumenical and interfaith organizations focusing on such housing needs.

15. To promote and support the mission of the Church through the United Methodist Development Fund by maintaining an investment fund for the purpose of making first mortgage loans to United Methodist churches, including loans for the construction and major improvement of churches, parsonages, and mission buildings in accordance with policies adopted by the National Division; to incorporate and have direction over and administrative supervision of the United Methodist Development Fund; to elect the directors of the United Methodist Development Fund upon nomination of the United Methodist Development Fund; to approve and to elect the general secretary, who shall be nominated by the United Methodist Development Fund; to approve the officers of the United Methodist Development Fund who shall continue to serve with such approval; and to provide such staff as may be necessary.

16. To further national mission strategy and to equip local churches, districts, and Annual Conferences to be in mission, the division shall:

a) Assist and guide in mission fulfillment through effective fund raising by:

(1) raising funds for building and program needs of local churches to enable them to be in mission;

(2) raising funds for the retirement of church and other institutional obligations;

(3) providing consultation with district, conference, and missionary fund-raising personnel;

(4) raising funds for district, conference, and institutional needs, both capital and program, including conference pensions.

b) Correlate capital fund-raising with all other areas of mission strategy within the division, such as urban and rural work, church extension, new church development, educational institutions, hospitals, homes, community centers, and other agencies or ministries.

c) Cooperate with the General Board of Discipleship in the development, planning, and utilization of stewardship principles, guidelines, strategies, and resources for fund-raising programs to assist local churches, Annual Conferences, and denominational institutions to obtain funds necessary for their continuing viability in mission.

d) Charge a nominal fee for fund-raising services, with special consideration being given to new churches, minority and mission churches, other churches facing critical financial needs, and to Missionary and Provisional Annual Conferences.

e) Maintain a fund secured from gifts and legacies, the income of which shall be used for the support of the above functions.

17. To facilitate the development of ethnic and language ministries in accordance with national mission strategy.

18. To maintain relationship with Missions, Missionary Conferences, and Provisional Annual Conferences in accordance with ¶¶ 654, 657, 661.

19. To encourage and participate in ecumenical planning and program for church life and mission wherever opportunities and needs exist.

20. To develop and participate in joint efforts with other divisions and boards and ecumenical and secular coalitions, as the National Division carries out its responsibilities in mission.

21. To recommend for assignment in various fields of service deaconesses and home missionaries and other workers who have been approved by the General Board of Global Ministries.

22. To cooperate with the World Division, the Committee on Personnel in Mission, and other related agencies in recommending and facilitating the placement of deaconesses, missionaries, church and community workers, and others.

23. To recommend an annual budget and to make annual reports to the General Board of Global Ministries.

24. To provide counsel and coordination for local and national mission strategy of agencies related to the National Division, including community centers, residences, health care agencies, child care agencies, schools, and other educational agencies.

25. To cooperate with the General Board of Discipleship in jointly developing and recommending architectural standards for facilities needed to house the Church's program of worship, education, and fellowship, and for parsonages, and to cooperate in recommending training ventures to interpret those recommended standards.

26. To communicate to the bishops available information concerning deaconesses, missionaries, and the appointment of workers in their respective areas.

27. To relate to Goodwill Industries.

28. To sustain and undergird the mission of the entire United Methodist Church in Appalachia by working with the Appalachian Development Committee as the regional agency through which The United Methodist Church coordinates the activities of national, jurisdictional, and Annual Conference boards, agencies, and concerns.

¶ **1530.** *Authority and Organization.*—The National Division shall have the authority and power to:

1. Receive and properly administer funds assigned to the National Division, including:

a) World Service and other funds designated for the program of the National Division;

b) the Advance special gifts for work related to the National Division which are cultivated through the Education and Cultivation Division;

c) all donation aid, loan funds, and endowments contributed and established for the work of church extension, except such as may be administered by the Jurisdictional and Annual Conferences;

d) funds allocated by the Women's Division, keeping in mind the special concerns of women;

e) bequests, earnings on investments, and other income in accordance with the provisions by which they are given and available for work related to the National Division;

f) funds appropriated by the United Methodist Committee on Relief for coordination of disaster response ministries and church property damage caused by disasters.

2. Receive and properly administer all properties and funds, including:

a) all properties and trust funds, permanent funds, annuity funds, and other special funds coming into the possession of the National Division as part of a board for missionary and other purposes, in accordance with ¶ 1505;

b) all trust funds and assets of every kind and character, real, personal, or mixed, held by predecessor corporations, in accordance with the conditions under which such trusts and funds have been previously received and administered by the said predecessor corporations (¶ 1506.2).

3. Assign staff to develop programs, administer such appropriations as are committed to them, and cooperate with other divisions within the board, other boards, and agencies, as their work may affect the group itself.

4. Receive from Health and Welfare Ministries Division counsel and field consultation related to health care and services to the aging and children and youth.

5. Encourage rural, town, city, metropolitan, or district mission structures according to the following:

a) Such structures may be organized, under such names as may be determined, wherever, in the judgment of the bishop or bishops and district superintendents concerned, it is deemed advisable. When two or more districts, conferences, episcopal areas, or jurisdictions have churches in the same area, it is recommended that the structure be so organized as to include all United Methodist churches. "Metropolitan" or "rural" shall be defined with sufficient flexibility to include separate communities which are economically or socially related.

b) It is recommended that a majority of the governing body be from the laity, men and women, young adults and youth. All bishops, district superintendents, and superintendents of ethnic and minority ministries having jurisdiction within the geographic territory served by the structure may be ex officio members of the organization. Membership may also include representation from conference Boards of Global Ministries, conference or district United Methodist Women, community-based young adult ministries (¶ 262.3), rural, city and suburban parish churches, community centers, and other nonparish rural and urban ministries, poverty communities, youth, and racial and ethnic minorities.

c) The purpose of such a structure shall be to promote and coordinate the work of the Church in town and country or metropolitan areas. It may:

(1) Develop special ministries and new forms of mission appropriate to new metropolitan or town and country needs, including recruitment, training, involvement of clergy and laity, and cooperative models of ministry.

(2) Promote long-term regional planning and provide coordinating framework for town and country and metropolitan mission strategy for United Methodism, especially with small congregations and ethnic and language minorities.

(3) Enable and support rural, central city, and suburban church extension, including research, organization (but not the constituting) of churches, acquisition of real estate, and the erection and maintenance of buildings (having first secured the approval of the district Board of Church Location and Building). Wherever possible, consideration should be given to new concepts of church extension, such as leased space, shared facilities, revitalized small congregations, and other experimental styles.

(4) Help to initiate and participate in rural and urban coalitions and other associations with leaders in business, finance, industry, agriculture, labor, education, welfare, etc., to work cooperatively for mutually desired social change.

(5) Encourage and support the development of effective community organizations in rural, inner-city, and suburban communities, to the end that people may share in the decision-making processes, and open more effective channels of communication between all people's.

(6) Participate with federal, state, and local governments in programs of rural and urban renewal and development, with special reference to protection and enhancement of human values, families, and family farms and businesses.

(7) Cooperate with representatives of other churches and faiths in developing, implementing, and funding new patterns of joint mission.

(8) Raise funds for the support of its work in cooperation with the Annual Conference Council on Finance and Administration, including the securing and holding of endowments for general purposes and for designated churches, institutions, or types of mission. Consideration shall be given to the use of an area or conference United Methodist foundation for the investment management of bequests, endowments, trusts, and special gifts.

d) In order to receive financial assistance from the division the structure shall meet the following conditions:

(1) It shall be organized according to the Discipline.

(2) It shall have a governing board or executive committee meeting at least once each quarter.

(3) It shall be actively at work.

(4) It shall have made a report to the division in the prescribed form provided for that purpose.

e) Each Annual Conference shall promote the work of such mission structures within its boundaries and receive annual reports through the Annual Conference Board of Global Ministries. All moneys received shall be reported in the conference journal.

f) If a full-time executive officer is employed, it is recommended that he or she be invited into consultation with the bishop and district superintendents in the consideration of the appointments that affect missions or churches administered or aided by the organization which he or she represents.

g) Each such mission organization shall, in cooperation with the Annual Conference Board of Global Ministries, annually present its financial needs to the Annual Conference Council on Finance and Administration of the conference to which it is related, to determine how the needs shall be met, including possible apportionments to the churches in its geographic area.

h) All pastors whose charges lie within the territory of the mission organization shall each year present the interests of the organization to their congregations, taking an offering or otherwise promoting support of its work.

i) Any local church expecting to receive aid from the mission organization for building or improvement shall be required, as a condition of receiving such aid, to secure its approval with respect to location, plans, and methods of financing.

j) In a metropolitan area the National Division may cooperate, with the approval of the bishops and the conferences, in the organization of a **Metropolitan Commission,** which may be composed of bishops and district superintendents involved and a selected group of ministers, laymen, and laywomen, representing Annual Conference Boards of Global Ministries, Committees on Urban Ministries, Annual Conference United Methodist Women, community-based young adult ministries (¶ 262.3), city missionary societies, local churches, representatives of other boards and agencies, and others who have skills and experience enabling them to fulfill creative planning and strategy functions for United Methodism in the metropolitan area.

The purpose of such a commission is to promote long-term planning and to provide a coordinating framework for United Methodism's metropolitan mission strategy. These functions may be fulfilled by other city, metropolitan, or district mission structures as deemed appropriate.

¶ **1531.** There shall be an **executive committee** of the division whose powers shall be determined by the division, subject to the approval of the board. It shall be composed of fifteen persons including the chairperson of the division, one clergy in full connection, two laymen, two from ethnic and minority groups, and one from youth or young adult. One half of the nonepiscopal members shall be women, elected by the Women's Division in accordance with ¶ 1550.

¶ **1532.** *Membership.*—The National Division shall be composed of thirty members as follows: twenty-seven persons named in a manner consistent with ¶ 1512.3 and three bishops. In addition, fifteen members at large of the division shall be elected in such manner as the division may determine. These should include men, women, clergy in full connection, youth (under nineteen years of age), young adults (nineteen to thirty-one years of age), racial and ethnic minority representatives, all of whom are to be selected so as to maintain the ratio distribution of membership as adopted by the General Board of Global Ministries in accord with ¶ 1512.3. The division may have members at large to bring into the division special knowledge or background in accord with ¶ 805.2, officers of the board in accord with ¶ 1509.3, and the associate general secretary and treasurer of the division. The division shall meet annually at the time of the meeting of the board and at such other times as it shall deem necessary.

OFFICE OF DEACONESS AND OFFICE OF HOME MISSIONARY

¶ **1533.** *Office of Deaconess and Office of Home Missionary.*— 1. There shall be in The United Methodist Church the **office of deaconess and office of home missionary.** The purpose of these offices shall be to express representatively the love and concern of

the believing community for the needs in the world, and through
education and involvement to enable the full ministry and
mission of the people of God. Deaconesses and home missionaries
function through diverse forms of service directed toward the
world to make Jesus Christ known in the fullness of his ministry
and mission which mandate that his followers:

a) Alleviate suffering.

b) Eradicate causes of injustice and all that robs life of dignity
and worth.

c) Facilitate the development of full human potential.

d) Share in building global community through the Church
Universal.

2. Deaconesses and home missionaries are persons who have
been led by the Holy Spirit to devote their lives to Christlike
service under the authority of the Church. They are approved by
the General Board of Global Ministries upon recommendation of
the Committee on Personnel in Mission and the National
Division. They are commissioned by a bishop at a session of the
General Board of Global Ministries or at another location
mutually agreed upon. They shall have a continuing relationship
with the National Division of the board through the Committee
on Deaconess and Home Missionary Service. Home missionaries
may serve in any agencies or programs of the United Methodist
Church in the United States, Puerto Rico, and the Virgin Islands.
Deaconesses are available for service with any agency or program
of The United Methodist Church. Deaconesses may be appointed
outside the United States through the World Division. Both
deaconesses and home missionaries may also serve in other than
United Methodist Church agencies or programs provided that
approval be given by the National Division upon recommendation of the Committee on Deaconess and Home Missionary
Service in consultation with the bishop of the receiving area.

3. The appointment of deaconesses and home missionaries
shall be made as follows:

a) Worker and agency participate in the statement of
preference.

b) Recommendation to an appointment by the Committee
on Deaconess and Home Missionary Service after consultation
with the bishop of the area.

c) Confirmation of the appointment by the National Division.

d) The appointment shall be reviewed by the Cabinet, fixed by the bishop at the Annual Conference and printed in the list of appointments in the Annual Conference journal.

4. Deaconesses and home missionaries shall hold church membership in a local church within the conference where her or his appointment is located, and shall be voting members of the Charge Conference of that church. Those holding staff positions with a general board or a connectional agency of The United Methodist Church may hold church membership in an Annual Conference within reasonable distance of the headquarters of the board or agency served.

5. Deaconesses and lay home missionaries shall be seated at the sessions of the Annual Conference with voice; shall be eligible to serve on boards, commissions, or committees of the Annual Conference and hold office on the same; shall be eligible for election as delegates to the General and Jurisdictional Conferences as lay delegates.

6. Deaconesses and home missionaries shall be subject to the administrative authority of the program or agency to which they are appointed. In matters of appointment they shall be finally subject to the authority of the General Board of Global Ministries through the Committee on Deaconess and Home Missionary Service of the National Division and shall, therefore, enter into no contract for service which would nullify this authority.

7. Each deaconess and home missionary shall enroll in a pension plan. The rights of any deaconess or home missionary in any prior or existing agreement or pension plan shall be fully protected.

8. Deaconesses and home missionaries shall surrender their credentials when they are no longer available for appointment by The United Methodist Church. Persons may be reinstated on recommendation of the Committee on Deaconess and Home Missionary Service and with approval of the National Division of the General Board of Global Ministries.

¶ **1534.** *Committee on Deaconess and Home Missionary Service.*— 1. There shall be a **Committee on Deaconess and Home Missionary Service,** which shall be advisory to the General Board of Global Ministries and shall make recommendations to it.

2. The Committee on Deaconess and Home Missionary Service shall be composed of one bishop who is a member of the General Board of Global Ministries: two members who are deaconesses or home missionaries chosen by each Jurisdiction Association of Deaconesses and Home Missionaries; two ordained ministers selected by the executive committee from a slate composed of one nominee chosen by each jurisdiction association and elected by the full committee; the president of each jurisdictional United Methodist Women; two Directors of the National Division chosen by the National Division and one Director of the Women's Division chosen by the Women's Division, these to be selected in consultation with the Committee on Deaconess and Home Missionary Service; one staff representative of the Office of Missionary Personnel; and the associate general secretary of the National Division. The committee may co-opt others as needed; nomination of co-opted members to be by the executive committee. The secretary of the program office of Deaconess and Home Missionary Service (¶ 1536) shall be a member without vote.

3. There shall be an executive committee and other committees as necessary for carrying out the duties of the Committee on Deaconess and Home Missionary Service.

4. The work of the committee shall be carried out in accordance with the bylaws as approved by the National Division of the General Board of Global Ministries.

¶ **1535.** *Responsibilities of the Committee on Deaconess and Home Missionary Service.*—1. To provide the Church with a corps of committed and professionally competent persons who choose to serve under the authority of the Church as deaconesses and home missionaries.

2. To recommend new channels and fields of service for deaconesses and home missionaries.

3. To recommend to the General Board of Global Ministries through its National Division, policies, procedures, standards, and relationship to Church and society for the office of deaconess and the office of home missionary.

4. To facilitate the placement of deaconesses and home missionaries following the procedures described in ¶ 1535.3.

5. To initiate and recommend programs of continuing education and pastoral care for deaconesses and home missionaries that will contribute to their spiritual, professional, and emotional growth and to their corporate participation in mission.

6. To initiate, recommend, and cooperate with agencies and boards in interpreting the office of deaconess and the office of home missionary.

7. To establish and maintain international and ecumenical relationships in the diaconate.

8. To cooperate with the Women's Division and other agencies in administering properties, trust funds, permanent funds, other special funds, pension programs, and employment benefits and endowments now held and administered by and for the several forms of administration related to the deaconesses and home missionaries.

9. To cooperate with the Division of Diaconal Ministry of the General Board of Higher Education and Ministry and with other agencies in areas of mutual concern.

10. To cooperate with the Annual Conference Boards of Diaconal Ministry in matters related to deaconesses and home missionaries and with the Annual Conference Committees on Deaconess and Home Missionary Service where organized.

11. To initiate and recommend programs for the orientation of new deaconesses and home missionaries.

¶ **1536.** 1. The responsibilities of the Committee on Deaconess and Home Missionary Service shall be carried out through the program office of Deaconess and Home Missionary Service, which shall be related administratively to the General Board of Global Ministries through the National Division.

2. The General Board of Global Ministries shall appoint an assistant general secretary of the program office of Deaconess and Home Missionary Service who shall be a deaconess or home missionary. Nomination shall be by the National Division in consultation with the executive committee of the Committee on Deaconess and Home Missionary Service.

3. In each jurisdiction there shall be a Jurisdiction Association of Deaconesses and Home Missionaries as described in the bylaws of the Committee on Deaconess and Home Missionary Service.

UNITED METHODIST COMMITTEE ON RELIEF

¶ 1537. *Purpose.*—The **United Methodist Committee on Relief** shall have as its purpose assisting churches in direct ministry to persons in need. These ministries shall be administered in the spirit of Jesus Christ through programs of relief, rehabilitation, and service: to refugees, to those suffering from root causes of hunger and their consequences, and to those caught in other distress situations. These programs shall advance the dignity of persons without regard to religion, race, nationality, or sex and shall seek to enhance the quality of life in the human community.

¶ 1538. *Objectives and Responsibilities.*—The objectives and responsibilities of the United Methodist Committee on Relief shall be:

1. To provide immediate relief of acute human need.

2. To respond to the suffering of persons in the United States caused by natural and civil disaster.

3. To work for the rehabilitation of persons outside the United States caught in distress situations caused by natural disaster, political turmoil, persecution from any cause, or endemic factors.

4. To assist in rehabilitation and resettlement of refugees, and to work cooperatively with each Annual Conference's Refugee Resettlement Committee, if organized.

5. To attack root causes of hunger and their consequences through programs of economic and social development.

6. To communicate with the churches concerning appeals for help.

¶ 1539. *Finances.*—Sources of funds for the division shall include: voluntary gifts, One Great Hour of Sharing offering, Advance special gifts, supplementary gifts of United Methodist Women, churchwide appeals made by authority of the Council of Bishops and the General Council on Finance and Administration, and designated benevolence funds. Financial responsibility for administrative functions of the General Board of Global Ministries shall not be a claim against funds designated for the United Methodist Committee on Relief. Financial promotion shall be by the Education and Cultivation Division and the

Standing General Commission on Communication, in consultation with the associate general secretary of the division.

¶ **1540.** The United Methodist Committee on Relief is authorized to provide for its necessary expense of administration and promotion out of undesignated receipts.

¶ **1541.** The United Methodist Committee on Relief shall receive and allocate funds contributed by churches, groups, or individuals for the purposes designated.

¶ **1542.** Churchwide appeals for funds shall be made only with the approval of the Council of Bishops and the General Council on Finance and Administration.

¶ **1543.** The response of the United Methodist Committee on Relief in the United States shall include only the meeting of human needs growing out of natural or civil disaster. This response shall be made at the request of the appropriate body of The United Methodist Church.

Repair and reconstruction of churches and other church property shall be included in the funding response of the United Methodist Committee on Relief only when such response has been included in the appeal made for funds or the Advance special gifts made for this purpose.

In response to United States natural or civil disasters, the United Methodist Committee on Relief shall coordinate Annual Conference appeals.

¶ **1544.** *Organization.*—In fulfilling its purpose of assisting churches in direct ministry to persons in need, the United Methodist Committee on Relief shall:

1. Relate to other divisions and work units of the Board of Global Ministries in carrying out assigned functions and responsibilities by:

a) Consulting/cooperating with the National Division in domestic natural or civil disaster response.

b) Consulting/cooperating with the World Division in relationship to colleague churches in meeting emergency needs, development programs, rehabilitation and refugee concerns.

c) Consulting/cooperating with the Committee on Personnel in Mission in regard to short-term volunteers in meeting emergency needs.

2. Work in partnership with colleague churches, ecumenical bodies and with interdenominational agencies.

3. Cooperate with colleague churches and ecumenical bodies in responding to their requests for short-term volunteers in meeting emergency needs.

¶ **1545.** The United Methodist Committee on Relief shall elect an **executive committee** which shall have the powers granted to it by the division. It shall be composed of five members, including the president, vice-president, and secretary of the division. The associate general secretary and the treasurer of the division and the officers of the board as defined in ¶ 1509.3 shall be members ex officio. At least one half of the nonepiscopal members shall be women. The executive committee shall meet as determined by the division or on call of the president.

¶ **1546.** *Membership.*—The United Methodist Committee on Relief shall be composed of twenty-one board members as follows: nineteen persons named in a manner consistent with ¶ 1512.3 and two bishops. In addition, seven members at large of the division shall be elected in such manner as the division may determine, whose special knowledge or experience would increase the competence of the division. The associate general secretary and treasurer of the division and the officers of the board as defined in ¶ 1509.3 shall be members ex officio.

Women's Division

¶ **1547.** *Purpose.*—The **Women's Division** shall be actively engaged in fulfilling the mission of Christ and the Church and shall interpret the purpose of United Methodist Women. With continuing awareness of the concerns and responsibilities of the Church in today's world, the Women's Division shall be an advocate for the oppressed and dispossessed with special attention to the needs of women and children; shall work to build a supportive community among women; and shall engage in activities which foster growth in the Christian faith, mission education, and Christian social involvement throughout the organization.

¶ **1548.** *Responsibilities.*—The responsibilities of the Women's Division shall be:

1. To recommend program and policies to United Methodist Women.

2. To interpret the role and responsibility of the division in fulfilling the mission of Christ and the Church.

3. To provide resources and opportunities for women that enrich their spiritual life and increase their knowledge and understanding of the needs of the world and their responsibility in meeting those needs.

4. To secure funds through the channels of United Methodist Women for the support of the program of the Church through the General Board of Global Ministries, with special concern for the needs and responsibilities of women.

5. To project plans specially directed toward leadership development of women through appropriate planning with the other divisions and agencies of the board.

6. To strengthen the Church's challenge to women to enlist in the diaconate as missionaries and deaconesses.

7. To enlist women in activities that have a moral and religious significance for the public welfare and that contribute to the establishment of a just global society.

8. To work with the other agencies of the Church and community in areas of common concern and responsibility. A United Nations Office shall be conducted in cooperation with the General Board of Church and Society.

9. To give visible evidence of oneness in Christ by uniting in fellowship and service with other Christians, including the World Federation of Methodist Women, Church Women United, and other similar groups, thereby strengthening the ecumenical witness and program of the Church.

10. To formulate concepts of contemporary mission.

¶ **1549.** *Authority.*—1. The Women's Division shall have the authority to make its bylaws and to regulate its proceedings in harmony with the charter of the board, and with its approval, to develop and carry out the functions of the board as described in ¶ 1502; to buy and sell property; to solicit and accept contributions, subject to annuity under the board's regulations; and to appropriate its funds.

2. The division shall meet annually at the time of the meeting of the board, and at such other times as it shall deem necessary.

3. The Women's Division shall include in its responsibilities:

a) Those formerly carried by the Woman's Society of Christian Service of The Methodist Church and the Women's Society of World Service of the Evangelical United Brethren Church, the Women's Society of Christian Service of The United Methodist Church, and those other organizations of women of similar purposes which have operated in the churches forming the United Methodist tradition; including the Women's Missionary Association of the Church of the United Brethren in Christ; the Woman's Missionary Society of the Evangelical Church; the Woman's Foreign Missionary Society, the Woman's Home Missionary Society, the Wesleyan Service Guild, and the Ladies' Aid Societies of the Methodist Episcopal Church; the Woman's Missionary Society, the Woman's Board of Foreign Missions, the Woman's Board of Home Missions, the Woman's Missionary Council of the Methodist Episcopal Church, South; and the Woman's Convention of the Board of Missions of the Methodist Protestant Church. This list shall not be construed as exclusive.

b) All policy matters pertaining to the homes for retired workers owned by the Women's Division.

4. The Women's Division shall have the authority:

a) To organize jurisdictional, conference, district, and local church organizations of United Methodist Women, which shall be auxiliary to the General Board of Global Ministries, through the Women's Division, of The United Methodist Church.

b) To recommend constitutions and make bylaws for United Methodist Women.

c) To appropriate funds received through United Methodist Women.

d) To serve as the national official policy-making body of United Methodist Women, with the officers of the Women's Division designated as the national officers.

¶ **1550.** *Organization.*—The Women's Division shall elect an **executive committee** which shall exercise the powers of the division ad interim. It shall be composed of nineteen members, of whom the division shall elect six to serve on the executive committee of the World Division, six to serve on the executive committee of the National Division, two to serve on the executive committee of the Education and Cultivation Division. Members of the executive committee may also be named by the division to serve on other divisional executive committees. The associate general secretary and treasurer of the division and the officers of the board as defined in ¶ 1509.3 shall be members ex officio.

¶ **1551.** The Women's Division shall be organized into such sections as the division shall determine.

¶ **1552.** *Assembly.*—There may be an assembly of United Methodist Women, including a delegated body termed the Assembly. The division shall determine the time and place of meeting and the purpose, composition, functions, and powers of the Assembly.

¶ **1553.** *Finances.*—The funds for the fulfillment of the responsibilities of the Women's Division shall be derived from annual voluntary pledges, offerings, gifts, devises, bequests, annuities, or money received through special emphases and meetings held in the interest of the division. All funds, except those designated for local purposes, shall be forwarded through the channels of finance of United Methodist Women to the treasurer of the division. Undesignated funds received by the Women's Division shall be allocated by the division, on recommendation of the appropriate section or committee, for the work of the several sections of the Women's Division and to such other divisions and agencies of the General Board of Global Ministries as the division shall determine for the fulfillment of the responsibilities of the division. Funds appropriated for the work of the other divisions and agencies of the board may be given with specific designations and time limits, after which unspent funds are to be returned to the division.

¶ **1554.** *Membership.*—The Women's Division shall be composed of board members as follows: one of the episcopal members of the board, with residence in the United States; six basic members of the board; two clergy in full connection, two laymen and two laywomen; and fifty-eight women, forty of whom shall be nominated by the jurisdictional organizations of United Methodist Women and elected by the Jurisdictional Conferences (¶ 634.4); five shall be the jurisdiction presidents of United Methodist Women, and thirteen shall be elected by the division to board membership. In addition, ten members at large of the division only may be elected in such manner as the division shall determine. Officers of the board (¶ 1509.3), the associate general secretary, and treasurer of the division shall be members ex officio.

¶ **1555.** *Constitution of United Methodist Women.*—For the Constitution of United Methodist Women in the jurisdiction, *see* ¶ 634; for the Constitution of United Methodist Women in the conference, *see* ¶ 731; for the Constitution of United Methodist Women in the district, *see* ¶ 741; for the Constitution of United Methodist Women in the local church, *see* ¶ 262.5.

World Division

¶ **1556.** *Purpose.*—The **World Division** exists to confess Jesus Christ as divine Lord and Savior to all people in every place, testifying to his redemptive and liberating power in every sphere of human existence and activity, and calling all people to Christian obedience and discipleship.

The World Division, through responsibilities delegated to it by the General Board of Global Ministries and on behalf of The United Methodist Church, seeks to fulfill the purpose by:

1. Coordination of relationships and administration of program of The United Methodist Church as it relates to areas outside the United States.

2. Engaging mutually in mission with colleague churches and other bodies outside the United States, and facilitating their interaction with the Church and society in the United States so that all become more effective in Christian mission.

¶ **1557.** *Responsibilities.*—The responsibilities of the World Division, in order to fulfill its purpose, shall be:

1. To develop and administer the missional relationships of The United Methodist Church with Central Conferences, autonomous Methodist and United Churches and ecumenical bodies outside the United States.

2. To formulate the objectives and strategies for the world mission of The United Methodist Church, within the context of the cultural and historical understandings out of which relationships have developed with the Christian communities in other nations.

3. To foster the interaction of churches and ecumenical groups in other countries with the Church and society in the United States with the purpose of mutuality in the definition and implementation of Christian mission and of international concerns.

4. To administer programs of support for churches and ecumenical bodies outside the United States through the provision of financial resources and the training and support of persons in mission, including missionaries assigned by the division and national persons in service in their own or in other countries.

5. To provide services and information which facilitate the advocacy of public policies which support justice according to the Social Principles of The United Methodist Church and are relevant to the mission concerns and objectives of the World Division and of the General Board of Global Ministries.

¶ **1558.** *Authority.*—The World Division shall assist the General Board of Global Ministries to facilitate and coordinate the relationships of other units of the Board of Global Ministries and of other program agencies of The United Methodist Church to churches and agencies outside the United States by providing linkages and participating in the negotiation of such programmatic relationships.

The World Division shall prohibit the use of its personnel as paid or unpaid informer to any official or unofficial intelligence agency of any government.

¶ **1559.** The division shall meet annually at the time of the meeting of the board and at such other times as it shall deem necessary.

¶ **1560.** *Executive Committee.*—There shall be an **executive committee,** whose powers shall be determined by the division with the approval of the board. It shall be composed of fifteen members, including at least one bishop. The associate general secretary and treasurer of the division and the officers of the board as defined in ¶ 1509.3 shall be members ex officio. At least one half of the nonepiscopal members shall be women (*see* ¶ 1550).

¶ **1561.** *Liaison Committee.*—1. The General Board of Global Ministries, through its World Division, shall request each Central

Conference and its conferences, both Annual and Provisional, each affiliated autonomous Methodist church or United Church, where applicable, to make provision for liaison functions with the board through a committee which is representative of all phases of the world mission, particularly of the needs and responsibilities of women.

2. There may be a subcommittee on women's work of the committee, which shall deal with all the concerns of women in the Church appropriate to the committee. This subcommittee may be composed of all women members of the committee and additional co-opted members as desired.

¶ **1562.** *Administration of New Commitments.*—Where the World Division, with the approval of the General Board of Global Ministries, plans to develop mission relationships in countries where it presently has no commitments, the division shall do so through a working agreement negotiated either with the church or churches already in the area or with a united mission organization or with ecumenical bodies related to the area. Only where none of these approaches is possible should the World Division participate in the formation of a new United Methodist denominational structure, in which case it may request the Council of Bishops to provide any necessary episcopal oversight.

¶ **1563.** *Membership.*—The World Division shall be composed of thirty board members as follows: twenty-seven persons named in a manner consistent with ¶ 1512.3 and three bishops. In addition, fifteen members at large of the division only shall be elected in such manner as the division shall determine. The associate general secretary and treasurer of the division and the officers of the board as defined in ¶ 1509.3 shall be members ex officio.

CRUSADE SCHOLARSHIP COMMITTEE

¶ **1564.** There shall be a program of scholarships to provide assistance for the training of leaders for mission, enabling persons from churches abroad and from ethnic and language minorities in the United States to obtain preparation in their respective fields for service to the Church and society.

¶ **1565.** *Responsibilities.*—The responsibilities of the **Crusade Scholarship Committee** shall be to grant scholarships.

¶ **1566.** *Authority.*—The Crusade Scholarship Committee shall:

1. Set broad policies and establish criteria for the awarding of scholarships provided through the World Communion Offering and through other funds received for the program.

2. Plan for the promotion and cultivation of the Crusade Scholarship Program through the Education and Cultivation Division, the Advance Committee, and the Standing General Commission on Communication.

3. Receive report of and monitor the administration of funds for scholarships.

4. Receive reports on the progress of students under its administration.

5. Elect an executive committee which shall have its membership and powers specified in the bylaws of the Crusade Scholarship Committee.

¶ **1567.** *Membership.*—The Crusade Scholarship Committee shall be composed of fifteen members elected quadrennially as follows: eleven from the General Board of Global Ministries, three of whom shall be elected by the World Division, including at least one member from a Central Conference; three of whom shall be elected by the Women's Division, three of whom shall be elected by the National Division, one of whom shall be elected by the Education and Cultivation Division, and one of whom shall be elected by the Health and Welfare Ministries Division; one from the Standing General Commission on Christian Unity and Interreligious Concerns; three additional members, one of whom shall be elected by the General Board of Higher Education and Ministry, one of whom shall be elected by the Standing General Commission on Communication, and one of whom shall be elected by the General Council on Finance and Administration. The member elected by the General Council on Finance and Administration shall serve with voice but no vote. Vacancies shall be filled as early as possible by the agency in which they occur.

COMMITTEE ON PERSONNEL IN MISSION

¶ **1568.** *Purpose.*—The purpose of the **Committee on Personnel in Mission** is to facilitate the involvement of qualified people in mission service and to maintain mission personnel issues before the board.

¶ **1569.** *Responsibilities.*—The responsibilities of the committee are to:

1. Promote the opportunities for mission service related to the General Board of Global Ministries throughout the constituencies of the Church.

2. Recruit and select persons for missionary and deaconess service, and to assist the personnel-deploying divisions in training and evaluating personnel and in staffing mission agencies.

3. Assist persons, including missionaries and deaconesses, in discovering ways of fulfilling their missional vocation, through interpretation, referrals, transfer procedures, and career counseling.

¶ **1570.** *Authority.*—It shall have authority to set standards and qualifications of missionary candidates, including deaconesses, for service in the United States and overseas; and to constitute the relationship of deaconess and missionary through the act of commissioning.

¶ **1571.** *Membership.*—The Committee on Personnel in Mission shall be constituted by sixteen members of the Board of Directors, including representatives from the personnel-deploying units of the board. One half of the board members of the committee shall be women. Three additional members at large may be selected for their professional competence. The associate general secretary for administration shall be an ex officio member without vote. The treasurer of the board shall serve as treasurer of the Committee on Personnel in Mission.

¶ **1572.** The staff shall have functional relationship with the personnel-deploying units of the board, including those related to missionaries, deaconesses, voluntary service, and emergency relief; it shall serve as liaison with the Office of Vocation and Career/Life Planning of the General Board of Higher Education and Ministry.

Section IX. General Board of Higher Education and Ministry

¶ **1601.** *Name.* There shall be a **General Board of Higher Education and Ministry,** hereinafter referred to as the board.

¶ **1602.** *Incorporation.*—The General Board of Higher Education and Ministry shall be a corporation under the laws of Tennessee and shall be responsible for the functions previously conducted by the Division of Higher Education of the General Board of Education and the Commission on Chaplains and Related Ministries of The United Methodist Church.

The Board of Higher Education and Ministry is authorized to take such action as is appropriate under the corporation laws of Tennessee so as to accomplish the end result stated above, and under which the Board of Higher Education and Ministry shall be one legal entity.

The divisions of the General Board of Education were not incorporated separately; it is the intent, however, that responsibility for the functions delegated to the divisions by prior legislative action be transferred consistent with the separation of the divisions between the Board of Discipleship and the Board of Higher Education and Ministry. In the division of the assets of the General Board of Education, it is the intent that all assets be used in keeping with the original intent and purpose for which they were established or acquired, and so be assigned as appropriate to the Boards of Discipleship and Higher Education and Ministry respectively. It is further intended that the annuities, bequests, trusts and estates formerly held by the General Board of Education be used for the benefit and use of the Boards of Discipleship and Higher Education and Ministry (in accord with their purposes as defined in the Discipline) respectively as their interests may appear, and that real estate titles be authorized to be conveyed as appropriate and apportioned where indicated.

In the event that the intent of the original donor of existing annuities, bequests, trusts, and estates cannot be clearly determined in relation to the interests of the two boards, such assets shall be divided equally between the two boards.

It is further intended that should additional assets accrue to the former General Board of Education by reason of annuities, bequests, trusts, and estates not now known and where the intent of the donor can be clearly ascertained, the assets shall be used in keeping with the original intent and purpose for which they were established or acquired and so be assigned as appropriate to the

Boards of Discipleship and Higher Education and Ministry respectively.

It is further intended that should additional assets accrue to the former General Board of Education by reason of annuities, bequests, trusts, and estates not now known and where the intent of the original donor cannot be clearly determined in relation to the interests of the two boards, such assets shall be divided equally between the two boards.

¶ **1603.** *Amenability and Accountability.*—The board shall be amenable to the General Conference and between sessions of the General Conference it shall be accountable to the General Council on Ministries.

¶ **1604.** *Purpose.*—The board exists, within the expression of the total mission of the Church, for the specific purpose of preparing and assisting persons to fulfill their ministry in Christ in the several special ministries, ordained and diaconal; and to provide general oversight and care for institutions of higher education, including schools, colleges, universities, and theological seminaries.

¶ **1605.** *Objectives.*—All the objectives assigned to the divisions shall be considered to be the objectives of the board. In summary, the board shall have authority:

1. To maintain the historic mission of The United Methodist Church in higher education and to serve as advocate for the intellectual life of the Church.

2. To seek to understand and communicate the significance of the Christian mission in higher education and ministry throughout the world as the context in which values and Christian life style are shaped.

3. To provide counsel, guidance, and assistance to Annual Conferences through Boards of Ordained Ministry, Boards of Diaconal Ministry, Committees on Higher Education and Campus Ministry, and other such program units as may be organized in the Annual Conferences.

4. To study needs and resources for representative ministries, ordained and diaconal, including identification of new and valid types of ministry.

5. To develop and maintain standards and procedures for

certification in ministry careers, for consecration into the diaconal ministry and for ordination into the ordained ministry.

6. To promote and give direction to work among racial and ethnic groups for enlistment, training, and placement of persons in the ministries of the Church.

7. To coordinate and make visible information about career assessment opportunities and continuing education that will assist persons in professional growth and career planning.

8. To recruit, endorse, and provide general oversight of United Methodist ministers who desire to serve as civilian and federal chaplains.

9. To provide liaison with United Methodist ministers certified by such agencies as the American Association of Pastoral Counselors (AAPC) and the Association for Clinical Pastoral Education (ACPE).

10. To conduct research on human needs to be met by the Church through its resources in higher education.

11. To provide for the allocation of funds to institutions and to programs related to the board.

12. To maintain adequate fiduciary/legal relationships with institutions and ministries and to assist Annual Conferences and other judicatories in their responsibilities in these matters.

13. To provide counsel, guidance, and assistance to institutions of higher education in their relationships to governmental agencies.

14. To guard property and endowments entrusted to the institutions and to maintain and enforce adequate trust and reversionary clauses.

15. To monitor and interact with public education in terms of its reflection of the wholeness of persons and the meaning of life.

16. To promote, in cooperation with the Standing General Commission on Communication, special days and funds: Black College Fund, Ministerial Education Fund, United Methodist Student Day, World Communion Sunday, and other funds and special days ordered by the General Conference.

17. To evaluate United Methodist higher education and professional ministries with concern for the quality of their performance and the integrity of their mission.

18. To provide standards and support for and interpretation of the work of United Methodist theological schools.

19. To analyze needs for continuing education, including assessment of effectiveness, career planning, and funding.

20. To provide ministerial courses of study for orderly entrance into ministry.

21. To provide for a continuing discussion of the theological bases for professional ministries and higher education.

22. To provide such services as will create a climate of acceptance and empowerment for women and racial and ethnic minority persons in higher education and the professional ministries, and to be alert to the necessity of advocacy in behalf of professional ministries in questions of equity and justice.

23. To provide counsel, guidance, and assistance to professional associations and fellowships related to diaconal and other special ministries.

24. To plan and implement a continuing ministry to United Methodist laity in institutions and armed forces who are separated from their local churches.

25. To interpret, promote, and administer the loan and scholarship programs of the board.

26. To develop and provide services directed to enlistment for specialized ministries, career planning, and counseling.

27. To offer personnel and placement assistance for persons involved in professional ministries.

28. To engage in research related to personnel needs and interpretation of occupational opportunities in the Church.

29. To provide such support agencies as are deemed necessary to carry out the functions of the board.

30. To give priority to the planning and policy development functions of the board on behalf of the Church.

¶ **1606.** *Responsibilities.*—The responsibilities of the Board of Higher Education and Ministry shall be:

1. To establish and review the objectives of the Board of Higher Education and Ministry within the wider mission of The United Methodist Church.

2. To establish appropriate organizational structures within the board and staff to achieve established objectives, including

writing bylaws, electing officers, establishing committees, electing staff, and filling vacancies in accord with ¶ 812.

3. To determine policy and program, establish goals and priorities, project long-range plans, and to evaluate program and services of the board.

4. To give direction to the staff and to delegate authority to board executives through general oversight of the administration.

5. To report the activities of the board to The United Methodist Church through appropriate agencies of the General and Jurisdictional Conferences.

6. To develop and maintain cooperative relationships with ecumenical agencies and other denominations for the full discharge of the objectives of the board.

7. To cooperate with other agencies in The United Methodist Church in the fulfillment of the programs of the General Conference.

¶ 1607. *Organization.*—The membership of this board shall be constituted in accordance with ¶ 805 of the general provisions. If a vacancy occurs in the board, it shall be filled in accordance with ¶ 812.

¶ 1608. 1. *Divisions.*—The board shall be organized into four divisions: the Division of Chaplains and Related Ministries, the Division of Higher Education, the Division of Diaconal Ministry, and the Division of Ordained Ministry.

2. *Offices.*—The board, in implementing the objectives (¶¶ 1603, 1605), shall have authority to establish and maintain the following offices: *(a)* Vocation and Career/Life Planning, *(b)* Interpretation, and *(c)* Loans and Scholarships.

DIVISION OF CHAPLAINS AND RELATED MINISTRIES

¶ 1609. There shall be a **Division of Chaplains and Related Ministries** of the Board of Higher Education and Ministry.

¶ 1610. The division shall represent The United Methodist Church.

1. All persons have the right to receive the full ministry of the gospel of Jesus Christ. The Church is aware of its

responsibility to provide adequate professional ministry to persons in special situations beyond the local church. In order to assure high standards of competency, the Division of Chaplains and Related Ministries shall have responsibility for clergy in extension ministries (¶ 439.1*b*), such as: chaplaincy in the armed forces, Veterans Administration, industry, correctional, health care fields, and those other related ministries which conference Boards of Ordained Ministry and bishops may designate. Clergy to be appointed to any of the above extension ministries shall receive ecclesiastical endorsement through the Division of Chaplains and Related Ministries.

2. *Duties.*—*a) Recruitment.*—The division, in cooperation with other units of the General Board of Higher Education and Ministry and other agencies of the Church, shall recruit persons for ministry in the above categories through contacts in college, seminary, post graduate, national professional societies and also within the structures of the local church and boards and agencies of the Annual Conferences.

b) Interpretation.—The division is charged with the responsibility to interpret to the Church at large the need to have adequately trained clergy to staff hospitals, homes, corrections, industry, the armed forces, and counseling centers.

c) Endorsement.—In order to assure high standards of competency for ministers serving in extension ministries, all United Methodist ministers appointed in the above categories shall receive endorsement from the division prior to such appointment. However, provisional endorsement can be granted for appointment purposes to institutions related to an Annual Conference. Specific requirements of various ministries, requiring professional certification, where applicable, shall be met prior to endorsement and appointment. The division, through the evaluation of readiness of the candidate for endorsement, shall facilitate the entry of clergy into these ministries.

d) General Oversight.—The division shall provide general oversight for all those under endorsement, particularly for those serving outside the bounds of their Annual Conferences. The division shall assure conference Boards of Ordained Ministry of the validity of ministry and quality of performance of clergy serving under its endorsement.

e) Annual Recommendation.—The division shall verify annually to bishops and conference Boards of Ordained Ministry those clergy under its endorsement and request their reappointment.

f) Advocacy.—The division shall serve as an advocate for persons serving in extension ministries under its endorsement. Such advocacy may include: representing their interests within the nonchurch institutional systems where they serve; representing their interests within the connectional system of The United Methodist Church in conferences and boards and agencies; being in dialogue with the various professional and certifying agencies; helping to facilitate, as an agent on their behalf, the transition into or out of extension ministries; and giving attention to the needs for continuing education for those under endorsement.

3. *Overseas Laity.*—The division shall assist in providing a ministry to United Methodist laity in or associated with the armed forces stationed in overseas locations. The General Board of Higher Education and Ministry through the division shall cooperate with the General Board of Discipleship, General Board of Global Ministries, and other agencies of the Church in preparing materials, planning programs, and providing a continuing ministry, such as: retreats, confirmation classes, and other pastoral functions.

¶ **1611.** The division is authorized to receive such share of the World Communion offering as may be determined by the General Conference and such World Service funds as may be allocated by the board. Also, the division shall receive and distribute other funds and special gifts as have been or shall be given specifically to the division.

DIVISION OF HIGHER EDUCATION

¶ **1612.** *General Responsibilities.*—1. Higher education is a significant part of our Wesleyan heritage, our present task, and our future responsibility. The Church continues its historic mission of uniting knowledge and vital piety by maintaining educational institutions and a campus ministry, and through them an intellectual, spiritual, and material ministry to all persons within the academic community without respect to sex, race, creed, or national origin.

2. There shall be a **Division of Higher Education** representing The United Methodist Church in its relationships with educational institutions and the campus ministry. The division shall have an advisory relationship to all United Methodist–affiliated institutions, including universities, colleges, secondary and special schools, Wesley Foundations, and similar organizations as well as ecumenical campus ministry groups. The division will, on request, serve in an advisory and consultative capacity to all agencies of the Church owning or administering educational institutions and campus ministry units.

3. The nominating committee of the board shall, insofar as possible, provide representation for nomination as members of the Division of Higher Education an equitable number of persons directly related to the areas of concern of the division.

4. Principal objectives of the division are:

a) To determine the nature of the United Methodist mission in and for higher education.

b) To develop policy that enables The United Methodist Church to engage effectively in higher education.

c) To encourage the Church in programs designed to nurture and sustain educational institutions and campus ministry units as invaluable assets in the ongoing life of the Church.

d) To promote a campus Christian movement and a concerned Christian ministry of the educational community; to witness in the campus community to the mission, message, and life of Jesus Christ; to deepen, enrich, and mature the Christian faith of college and university men and women through commitment to Jesus Christ and the Church and to assist them in their service and leadership to the world, in and through the Church.

e) To interpret both the Church and its educational institutions and campus ministry to each other; to help the agencies of the Church and higher education participate in the greater realization of a fully humane society committed to freedom and truth, love, justice, peace, and personal integrity.

f) To foster within educational institutions the highest educational standards, the soundest business practices, the finest ethical and moral principles, and especially Christian ideals; to help people experience release from enslavement, fear, and violence; and to help people live in love.

g) To preserve and protect resources, property, and investments of The United Methodist Church or any conference, agency, or institution thereof, in any educational institution, Wesley Foundation, or other campus ministry unit founded, organized, developed, or assisted under the direction or with the cooperation of The United Methodist Church.

5. The division shall appoint personnel, including an assistant general secretary for campus ministry and an assistant general secretary for schools, colleges, and universities, and shall establish such committees and commissions as may be necessary for effective fulfillment of its objectives. It may adopt such rules and regulations as may be required for the conduct of its business.

¶ **1613.** *Responsibilities to General and Annual Conferences.*— The Division of Higher Education will cooperate with and assist the General and Annual Conferences and their respective commissions, committees, or other agencies organized in behalf of educational institutions and the campus ministry. (For Annual Conference committees *see* ¶ 721.2.)

1. The division shall:

a) Provide for the cooperative study of plans for maximum coordination of the work of United Methodist higher education with the Church's mission in Christian education.

b) Direct attention of church members to the contribution of United Methodist educational institutions and campus ministry units to the life and character of students and to the place the institutions and campus ministry have in the preservation and propagation of the Christian faith for our time.

2. The division shall assess institutional and campus ministry relationships with and responsibilities to the Church, and shall aid in the determination of the degree of active accord between institutional and campus ministry policies and practices and the policies of the church as expressed in the Discipline and in General Conference enactments.

3. The division shall assist educational societies and foundations related to the Annual Conferences for the promotion of Christian higher education and the campus ministry and shall

recognize such societies and foundations as auxiliaries of the division when their objectives and purposes, articles of incorporation, and administrative policies shall have been approved by the Annual Conference within whose boundaries they have been incorporated.

4. The division shall direct attention to the work and needs of those educational institutions which stand in special relationship to The United Methodist Church and shall request support for them. Due recognition shall be given to the needs of the black colleges historically related to The United Methodist Church. (*See* ¶¶ 918, 1620.)

¶ **1614.** *Responsibilities to Institutions.*—The Division of Higher Education shall establish policy and practice providing for consultation with and support of United Methodist educational institutions and campus ministry units in matters of institutional study and evaluation, promotion, interpretation, management, program, and finance.

1. The division shall, in cooperation with the University Senate:

a) Study trends in higher education, the needs of the Church, and public and private educational opportunities and requirements and make recommendations to the educational institutions, and to state commissions or other bodies or publics concerned with higher education.

b) Recommend and approve plans for institutional cooperation, consolidation, or merger between or among United Methodist–related colleges and/or between them and institutions of other denominations which ensure that the interests of The United Methodist Church are adequately protected.

c) Investigate, at its discretion, the objectives, academic programs, educational standards, personnel policies, plant and equipment, business and management practices, financial program, public relations, student personnel services, student development programs, religious life, and church relations of any educational institution claiming or adjudged to be related to The United Methodist Church.

d) Evaluate and classify institutions in order to authenticate relatedness to the Church; determine eligibility for church financial support in accord with the objectives of the Division of Higher Education.

e) Approve changes in institutional sponsorship, relationships to the General or Annual Conferences, including separation from United Methodist program boards, from the General or one or more Annual Conferences or from the University Senate as the certifying agency of The United Methodist Church.

2. The division shall, in regard to campus ministry, Wesley Foundations, and ecumenical campus ministry groups, provide a structure within the division in order to:

a) Assist in development of plans for the systematic evaluation of these units in cooperation with their regularly constituted boards of directors or trustees and with conference, area, or regional committees or commissions on Christian higher education and campus ministry or appropriate ecumenical agencies.

b) Study the reports of program and financial status required of each campus ministry unit receiving financial support from The United Methodist Church and interpret the same to the constituency as appropriate.

c) Affirm its commitment to an ecumenical approach to campus ministry; encourage local, campus, state, and regional units of that ministry to work toward ecumenical programming and structures where appropriate.

d) Recognize and cooperate with agencies with whom relationships may serve to further the objectives of the division.

e) Provide for representation and participation, as deemed necessary, in such agencies as the National United Ministries in Higher Education Policy Board and the National Staff of United Ministries in Higher Education.

f) Provide services to meet specific denominational needs.

3. The division shall, as it seeks to interpret higher education:

a) Promote the Church's mission in higher education, including the special missions and educational ministries to ethnic minorities, persons with handicapping conditions, and other peoples disadvantaged by world conditions.

b) Promote Christian instruction and provide opportunity for Christian service.

c) Encourage educational institutions and campus ministry units to inculcate human and humane values consistent with the gospel and the public good.

d) Foster the development of Christian community within the life of educational institutions and campus ministry units.

e) Make use of the existing church organization and publications for interpreting the mission of higher education.

f) Participate in the Crusade Scholarship program.

g) Design and organize Student Recognition Day to recognize United Methodist students in higher education.

¶ **1615.** *Financing Higher Education.*—1. In recognition of its heritage and the mandate to maintain its mission in higher education and in light of emergent fiscal concerns, The United Methodist Church affirms its commitment to higher education and to the means by which it can be continuously supported, renewed, and recycled.

2. The Division of Higher Education shall be empowered to take such action as may be necessary to:

a) Promote the financial support of Christian higher education within the Church.

b) Create arrangements which shall provide for the flow of supporting funds from the whole Church to the institutions affiliated with the Church as affirmed by the University Senate (¶ 1618).

c) Develop corporations, or other fiscal or fiduciary agencies, for the purpose of financing, creating, recycling, managing, or otherwise caring for institutions and campus ministry units or their assets and liabilities.

d) In cooperation with the General Council on Finance and Administration, develop long-range investments and fund-raising projects within the Church which shall guarantee, insofar as possible, the continuous flow of resources for United Methodist higher education for the decades and the centuries to come.

3. The division, in regard to fiscal matters, shall:

a) Study the financial status of United Methodist educational institutions and campus ministry units, encourage the Church to give them continuous support, and provide consultative services in fiscal affairs and other aspects of institutional management. The division shall study all appropriate related data and recommend to each conference or agency the support levels appropriate for each related institution or institutions.

b) Appropriate such funds as are available for the support of educational institutions, Wesley Foundations, or other campus ministry units related to The United Methodist Church under such rules as the board may adopt.

c) Take such action as is necessary to protect or recover resources, property, and investments of The United Methodist Church, or any conference, agency, or institution thereof, in capital or endowment funds of any educational institution, Wesley Foundation, or other campus ministry unit founded, organized, developed, or assisted under the direction or with the cooperation of The United Methodist Church should any such institution discontinue operation or move to sever or modify its connection with the Church or violate the terms of any rules adopted by the board or the terms of any such grant of new capital or endowment funds made by The United Methodist Church or any conference, agency, or institution thereof. In order to carry out its duties under this paragraph, the division shall at its discretion investigate, audit, and review all necessary records and documents of any educational institution claiming or adjudged by the division to be related to The United Methodist Church. In the event any such educational institution, Wesley Foundation, or other campus ministry unit shall endeavor to discontinue operation or move to sever or modify its connection with the Church or violate the rules adopted by the division in accordance with ¶ 1615.3*b*, it shall be the duty of the trustees and the administrators of such institutions and the conference agency on higher education in which such institution is located to confer at the earliest possible opportunity with appropriate representatives of the division to determine what resources and aid the division may be able to provide and to permit the division to carry out its responsibilities under this paragraph.

d) (1) Foster and aid through a special apportionment the United Methodist institutions historically related to education for black people. It shall have authority to institute plans by which colleges sponsored by the division may cooperate with or may unite with colleges of other denominations or under independent control; *provided* that the interests of The United Methodist Church are adequately protected. (2) Encourage such black colleges to secure adequate endowments for their support and maintenance. Whenever the division is assured that their support will be adequate and the property will be conserved and perpetuated for Christian education under the auspices and control of The United Methodist Church, it may transfer the colleges to boards of trustees under such conditions as the Board of Higher Education and Ministry may prescribe, which shall include the right of reversion to the board under conditions prescribed by the board.

University Senate

¶ **1616.** *Membership and Organization.*—1. The **University Senate** shall be the professional educational advisory agency for The United Methodist Church and all educational institutions related to it.

2. The senate shall be composed of twenty-one voting members who are actively engaged in the work of education and are fitted by training and experience for the technical work of evaluating educational institutions (*see* ¶ 810 for additional general agency stipulations). Nine of these members shall be elected quadrennially by the National Association of Schools and Colleges of The United Methodist Church, four by the Board of Higher Education and Ministry, four by the General Conference, and four shall be appointed by the Council of Bishops. In addition, the senate itself may elect up to four nonvoting members at large. Members elected by the General Conference shall be nominated and elected by the following procedure: Twelve persons shall be nominated by the Council of Bishops. At the same daily session at which the above nominations are announced, additional nominations may be made from the floor but at no other time. From these nominations, the General Conference shall elect without discussion, by ballot and by plurality vote, the four persons to serve on the senate. Should a vacancy occur in the members elected by General Conference in the interim prior to the next General Conference, the Council of Bishops shall appoint a replacement taken from the remaining

nominees. The election process shall be repeated at each succeeding General Conference. Care should be taken that women, minorities, and representatives from the United Methodist-related black colleges and graduate theological seminaries shall be members of the senate. If a member (other than the four elected by the General Conference) retires from educational work, or for any other cause a vacancy occurs during the quadrennium, it shall be filled by the agency by which the retiring member was elected at its next meeting. The general secretary of the Board of Higher Education and Ministry and the associate general secretaries of the Divisions of Higher Education and of Ordained Ministry of that board shall serve as ex officio members of the senate. There shall be one staff representative, without vote, from the Board of Global Ministries on the Senate named by the general secretary of the Board of Global Ministries.

3. The associate general secretary of the Division of Higher Education shall be the executive secretary of the senate. The general secretary of the board shall convene it for organization at the beginning of each quadrennium. The senate shall elect its own officers, including a president, a vice-president, and a recording secretary, and may appoint such committees and delegate to them such powers as are incident to its work. Thereafter, it shall meet semiannually at such time and place as it may determine. Special meetings may be called on the written request of five members or at the discretion of the president and the executive secretary.

4. After consultation with the officers of the senate, the Division of Higher Education shall provide in its annual budget for the expense of the senate as it may deem sufficient, except that expenses incurred by the senate on behalf of any other board of the Church shall be borne by that board.

¶ 1617. *Purposes and Objectives.*—1. To be the professional educational agency representing the common interests of The United Methodist Church and its affiliated schools, colleges, universities, and graduate theological seminaries.

2. To support the development of institutions whose aims are to address and whose programs reflect significant educational, cultural, social, and human issues in a manner reflecting the values held in common by the institutions and the Church.

3. To provide an effective review process so that institutions that qualify for University Senate affiliation and church support will be recognized as having well-structured programs, sound management, and clearly defined church relationships.

4. To establish effective annual reporting procedures that will provide the senate with the data necessary to complete its review of the institutional viability and program integrity of member institutions.

¶ **1618.** *Institutional Affiliation.*—1. Approval by the senate is prerequisite to institutional claim of affiliation with The United Methodist Church.

2. Every effort shall be made by both the Annual Conferences and institutions to sustain and support each other, but identification of an institution with The United Methodist Church shall depend upon its approval by the senate. The senate shall provide adequate guidelines and counsel to assist institutions seeking initial or renewed affiliation.

3. Only institutions affiliated with The United Methodist Church through approval by the senate shall be eligible for funding by Annual Conferences, General Conference, general boards, or other agencies of The United Methodist Church.

4. To qualify for affiliation with The United Methodist Church, institutions must maintain appropriate academic accreditation.

5. Assessment of church relationships shall be a part of the process for those institutions seeking approval of the senate for affiliation with The United Methodist Church. Inasmuch as declarations of church relationships are expected to differ one from the other, and because of the diversity in heritage and other aspects of institutional life, declarations of church relationship will necessarily be of institutional design.

¶ **1619.** *Responsibilities.*—1. Each year the senate shall publish a list classifying United Methodist–affiliated institutions. These institutions shall include secondary schools, colleges, universities, graduate theological seminaries, and special schools.

2. The senate shall also prepare annually a list of approved schools, colleges, universities, and graduate theological seminaries for use by Annual Conference Boards of Ordained Ministry in determining candidate educational eligibility for admission into full connection.

¶ **1620.** *Consultative Relationship with Institutions.*—1. Support for approved institutions shall include, through the appropriate divisions of the General Board of Higher Education and Ministry, consulting teams with skills in comprehensive institutional design, management, governance, and program.

2. Support for approved institutions shall include an interpretation of and consultation on data in the annual institutional reports.

3. The Division of Higher Education shall report annually to the senate on the level and types of institutional support rendered by related conferences and agencies and shall evaluate such support, including specific responses of conferences and agencies to recommended levels.

NATIONAL METHODIST FOUNDATION FOR CHRISTIAN HIGHER EDUCATION

¶ **1621.** The **National Methodist Foundation for Christian Higher Education** is incorporated in the state of Tennessee as a nonprofit, charitable organization with permanent ties to the Division of Higher Education, which elects its Board of Trustees. The general purpose of the foundation is to foster the growth and development of institutions of higher education by encouraging persons and corporations to provide financial support and by acting as a foundation for such support. The foundation is also authorized to serve as a trustee and administrator of gifts and bequests designated by donors to specific institutions.

COUNCIL OF PRESIDENTS OF THE BLACK COLLEGES

¶ **1622.** 1. There shall be an organization known as the **Council of Presidents of the Black Colleges.** It shall be composed of all the presidents of the United Methodist institutions historically related to the education of black people and with a current relationship to The United Methodist Church.

2. *Purposes and Objectives.*—The purpose of the council shall be to:

a) Help identify and clarify the roles of these colleges in higher education and The United Methodist Church.

b) Promote fund-raising efforts through the Church.

c) Study, review, and discuss programs of member institutions.

The council shall have a minimum of two regular meetings in each calendar year, and shall be amenable to the Division of Higher Education in the implementation of its responsibilities.

DIVISION OF DIACONAL MINISTRY

¶ **1623.** The Division of Diaconal Ministry shall be responsible for the work of the General Board of Higher Education and Ministry that relates to (1) persons preparing for the **office of diaconal minister,** (2) persons currently consecrated to the office of diaconal minister, (3) persons certified in various specialized ministries for which an agency of the church has set professional standards and (4) persons currently serving in professional ministry careers.

¶ **1624.** *Purpose.*—The purpose of the Division of Diaconal Ministry shall be:

1. To cooperate in the study of the needs of the United Methodist ministry, especially in regard to diaconal ministry, and to make recommendations accordingly.

2. To cooperate with other units of the board and other denominational agencies in interpreting the diaconal ministry as vocation and the educational preparation for such ministry.

3. To provide guidance and standards for the academic preparation for diaconal ministry.

4. To develop personal, church, and professional standards for persons in the diaconal ministry of The United Methodist Church and to provide guidance relating to the ethical and moral problems in specialized ministry.

5. To participate in the continuing study of the ministry so as to include matters of importance to the diaconal ministry in its reports to the General Board of Higher Education and Ministry and to the General Conference.

6. To study needs and develop standards and procedures for certification in professional ministry careers of The United Methodist Church.

7. To provide guidance and standards for the academic preparation for professional ministry careers.

8. To develop guidelines and resources for continuing education of persons subsequent to their consecration and/or certification, and to develop means of in-service training and continuing education to strengthen their ministry.

9. To develop guidelines and resources for the work of the conference Board of Diaconal Ministry.

10. To provide resources and training to the conference Board of Diaconal Ministry concerning counseling and examination of candidates for consecration to the office of diaconal minister and for certification in professional ministry careers.

¶ **1625.** *Responsibilities.*—The Division of Diaconal Ministry shall:

1. Develop and recommend to the General Board of Higher Education and Ministry and to the General Conference the requirements and standards that shall be minimal for consecration to the office of diaconal minister in The United Methodist Church.

2. Develop and recommend to the Board of Higher Education and Ministry and to the General Conference the requirements and standards that shall be minimal for certification in professional ministry careers of The United Methodist Church, after consultation with the agencies responsible for programs and areas of work related to the careers.

3. Work with the graduate theological seminaries, other graduate schools, colleges, and universities in development of curricula for the academic preparation of diaconal ministers and others in professional ministry careers, including the Foundational Studies for Diaconal Ministers and the Certification Studies in Ministry Careers.

4. Develop and recommend programs of continuing education for diaconal ministers and others in professional ministry careers.

5. Participate in the study and interpretation of career opportunities in the diaconal ministry.

6. Work with conference Boards of Diaconal Ministry in their responsibility to enlist women and men of all races and ethnic origins for diaconal ministry.

7. Work with conference Boards of Diaconal Ministry in their responsibility for administering the standards and requirements for the office of diaconal minister.

8. Work with conference Boards of Diaconal Ministry in their responsibility for administering the standards and requirements for certification in professional ministry careers.

9. Work with the Annual Conference Boards of Diaconal Ministry to encourage the recognition of persons at the time of their entrance into a career in the diaconal ministry, and at the time of the completion of their service in that career.

10. Work with conference Boards of Diaconal Ministry to assure for the diaconal minister conditions of employment, support, and benefits commensurate with the diaconal minister's training, ability, and experience.

11. Work with conference Boards of Diaconal Ministry and other United Methodist agencies to foster cooperative relationships among persons in the diaconal ministry of The United Methodist Church, and with their colleagues in other denominations and faiths.

12. Cooperate with the Christian Educators Fellowship of The United Methodist Church; the Fellowship of United Methodists in Worship, Music, and Other Arts; the United Methodist Association of Church Business Administrators; the United Methodist Association of Communicators; the United Methodist Association of Professors of Christian Education; the Associations of Deaconesses/Home Missionaries; and other professional associations and fellowships, in ways that will be supportive of their professional ministry careers.

13. Cooperate with other United Methodist agencies and general boards in their resourcing of members in the professional associations and fellowships.

14. Cooperate with the Division of Ordained Ministry and the Division of Chaplains and Related Ministries in the continuing study of the ministry and in other areas of mutual concern.

Division of Ordained Ministry

¶ **1626.** 1. The **Division of Ordained Ministry** shall be responsible for the work of the General Board of Higher Education and Ministry that relates to persons preparing for the ordained ministry and those currently serving under the appointment of a bishop. This responsibility shall be discharged in active relation with schools of theology, jurisdictional Boards or Committees on Ordained Ministry, Annual Conference Boards of Ordained Ministry, and appropriate departments of interdenominational bodies. This division shall be responsible for the promotion of theological education and its support for the whole Church.

2. Areas of concern shall include enlistment, preparation, continuing education, and career development of women and men of all races and ethnic origins in and for the ordained ministry of the Church.

¶ 1627. The Nominating Committee of the General Board of Higher Education and Ministry, in carrying out its responsibilities, shall provide an equitable number of persons directly related to areas of concern for the division.

¶ 1628. 1. The work and program of the Division of Ordained Ministry shall be supported from the general benevolences of the Church and the Ministerial Education Fund. Funds received by the board for the division from the Ministerial Education Fund shall be restricted to the support of theological schools and the Division of Ordained Ministry in the development of its program of enlistment, basic professional degree programs, and continuing education.

2. Administration and other programs of the division shall be supported solely from World Service moneys. The associate general secretary shall recommend through the general secretary of the board to the General Council on Finance and Administration the amount of financial support which should be allocated for the division.

¶ 1629. The specific responsibilities of the Division of Ordained Ministry shall be:

1. To study ministerial needs and resources in The United Methodist Church and to cooperate with appropriate groups in the interpretation of ministry as a vocation, in an effort to enlist suitable persons for ministry.

2. To prescribe the ministerial course of study, which shall include studies required for license to preach and the basic five-year course of study. It also shall provide advanced course of

study for preachers who have finished the above courses and meet the requirements of ¶ 424(3). All work in the ministerial course of study for candidates for elder in full connection (¶¶ 422-427), renewal of licenses (¶ 405), associate member (¶ 420), probationary member (¶ 415), and local pastors qualifying for appointment (¶¶ 408-409), shall be taken under the direction of the Division of Ordained Ministry in an approved course of study school. The division shall cooperate with the Boards of Ordained Ministry and other conference boards in organizing, financing, and conducting course of study schools. (For exceptional provisions for taking the ministerial course of study by correspondence, *see* ¶ 409.1.)

3. To cooperate with the Boards of Ordained Ministry in Annual Conferences by (*a*) providing guidance in counseling and examination of ministerial students, and (*b*) assisting in interpretation of current legislation concerning ordained ministry.

4. To recommend and help organize, finance, and conduct continuing education for all ministers subsequent to ordination and to advise means of in-service training and evaluation.

5. To lead in churchwide interpretation and promotion of the Ministerial Education Fund.

6. To maintain the educational standards of the ministry of The United Methodist Church and to study problems relating to ministerial status, morale, and support.

7. To study and support coordination and mutual ministry among the theological schools of The United Methodist Church, including possibilities for merger of schools.

8. To certify the course offerings in non–United Methodist seminaries for meeting the requirements in United Methodist history, doctrine, and polity specified in ¶ 424(3) and provide Boards of Ordained Ministry with a list of the courses approved.

9. To provide for recruiting and preparation of persons for ministry among minority groups, including the black community, Hispanic Americans, Native Americans, Asian Americans, and those of other national and ethnic origin. Provision for special resources in pretheological and theological education shall be undertaken as training for these distinctive minority ministries.

10. To participate in the Crusade Scholarship program.

¶ **1630.** 1. The schools of theology of The United Methodist Church are established and maintained for the education of ministers and the clarification of the Church's faith through research and prophetic inquiry on behalf of the whole Church. They exist for the benefit of the whole Church, and support shall be provided by the Church. They shall receive financial support for the current operating expenses from the Ministerial Education Fund, administered by the Division of Ordained Ministry. (*See* ¶ 920.)

2. The Ministerial Education Fund shall be regarded by Annual Conferences as a priority to be met before any additional benevolences, grants, or funds are allocated to a theological school or schools of religion in the conference's region.

3. No school of theology seeking affiliation and support from The United Methodist Church shall be established without first submitting its proposed organization to the Division of Ordained Ministry for prior approval.

¶ **1631.** United Methodist schools of theology, in addition to preparing their students for effective service for Christ and the Church, shall acquaint them with the current programs of The United Methodist Church, such as its educational, missional, social, and other service programs, and with the polity, organization, and terminology of the Church. Each school of theology, in consultation with the Division of Ordained Ministry, shall provide in its curriculum the courses in United Methodist history, doctrine, and polity specified in ¶ 424(3). (*See also* ¶ 1629.8.)

¶ **1632.** The United Methodist schools of theology share with the Boards of Ordained Ministry the responsibility for the selection and education of candidates for admission to the Annual Conferences.

Section X. General Board of Pensions.

GENERAL ADMINISTRATION

¶ **1701.** *Name, Corporations, and Locations of Offices.*— 1. There shall be a **Board of Pensions** of The United Methodist

Church, hereinafter called the board, having the general supervision and administration of the support, relief, and assistance and pensioning of ministers and their families, other church workers, and lay employees of The United Methodist Church, hereinafter referred to as beneficiaries, in succession to the Board of Pensions of The Evangelical United Brethren Church and in succession to the General Board of Pensions of The Methodist Church. The Board of Pensions of The Evangelical United Brethren Church, which is incorporated under the laws of the State of Ohio in that name, and the Board of Pensions of The Methodist Church, which is incorporated under the laws of the State of Illinois in that name, and the Board of Pensions of The Methodist Church, which is incorporated under the laws of the State of Maryland in that name, and the Board of Pensions of The Methodist Church, which is incorporated under the laws of the State of Missouri in that name, shall be continued, subject to the direction, supervision, and control of the General Board of Pensions of The United Methodist Church, but with their corporate names changed to and to be known as The Board of Pensions of The United Methodist Church, Incorporated in Ohio, and The Board of Pensions of The United Methodist Church, Incorporated in Illinois, and The Board of Pensions of The United Methodist Church, Incorporated in Maryland, and The Board of Pensions of The United Methodist Church, Incorporated in Missouri, respectively.

2. The general supervision and administration of the pension and benefit funds, plans, and programs of The United Methodist Church, subject to the direction, supervision, and control of the board, shall be conducted by and through the headquarters office.

3. The board shall have authority to establish, maintain, and discontinue from time to time such auxiliary offices as it shall deem proper and advisable.

¶ **1702.** 1. *Membership.—a)* The board shall be composed of one bishop, elected by the Council of Bishops; one minister, one layman, and one laywoman from each jurisdiction, elected by the respective Jurisdictional Conferences; two clergywomen in full connection, two laymen, and two laywomen, with not more than two from the same jurisdiction, elected by the General

Conference on nomination of the Council of Bishops; and eight additional members for the purpose of bringing to the board special knowledge or background, with consideration given to representation by women and racial and ethnic minority groups, not more than two from the same jurisdiction, nominated and elected by the board in such manner as it shall provide in its bylaws.

b) The ministerial membership of the board shall be limited to ministerial members of an Annual Conference in full connection and in the effective relation.

c) The general secretary of the board shall be an ex officio member thereof, without vote.

d) The terms of all members so elected shall be four years, to take effect at the annual meeting of the board following the General Conference. Members shall serve during the terms for which they are elected and until their successors shall have been elected and qualified.

e) A vacancy in the membership shall be filled for the unexpired term by the board.

f) The members of the board shall constitute the membership of the respective Boards of Directors of the aforesaid four constituent corporations. The general secretary shall be an ex officio member of each, without vote.

2. *Meetings.*—The annual meetings of the board and of the Boards of Directors of the constituent corporations shall be held at the same date and place, at which time the board shall review and consider responsibilities committed to its care and take such action as it deems advisable in the furtherance of the best interest of the funds, plans, and programs administered by the board. Special meetings of the board may be called by any two of the officers hereinafter named in ¶ 1703.

3. *Quorum.*—A majority of the members of the board shall constitute a quorum.

¶ **1703.** 1. *Officers.*—The board shall elect at its annual meeting next following the General Conference a president, a vice-president, and a recording secretary, all of whom shall be members of the board, and shall also elect a general secretary and a treasurer, all for four-year terms. The officers so elected shall serve during the terms for which they were elected and until their successors shall have been elected and qualified. The officers of the board shall also be elected by, and serve as the officers of, each of the four constituent corporations of the board. A vacancy in any of these offices may be filled by the board for the remainder of the unexpired term. Other offices that are deemed desirable and to the best interest of the board for carrying out its purposes may be created by the board, and persons may be elected or appointed to fill such offices.

2. *Executive Committee.*—An **executive committee** shall be elected by the board. The same committee shall also respectively be elected by, and serve as the executive committee of, each of the four constituent corporations unless otherwise required by applicable laws of the respective states of incorporations, in which case the board shall recognize such laws, and the board and the corporations shall have power to comply therewith.

3. *Committee on Rules and Regulations.*—The board shall elect quadrennially from its membership a **Committee on Rules and Regulations,** which shall consist of the bishop, one minister, and one lay person from each jurisdiction and two ministers and two lay persons from the membership of the board at large, whose responsibility it shall be to study the operation of the several pension and benefit funds, plans, and programs administered by the board, to present its recommendations for revision of the rules and regulations of the said pension and benefit funds, plans, and programs for consideration and action by the board, under authority granted to the board by the General Conference, and to present to the General Conference such proposed revisions of the Discipline as may be recommended by the board.

¶ **1704.** *General Authorizations.*—1. The General Board of Pensions is authorized to adopt and further any and all plans, to undertake any and all activities, and to create, obtain, accept, receive, manage, and administer any and all assets or property, absolute or in trust for specified purposes, for the purpose of increasing the revenues and of providing for, aiding in, and contributing to the support, relief, and assistance and pensioning of ministers and their families and other church workers and lay employees in The United Methodist Church and its constituent boards, organizations, and institutions; to do any and all acts and things deemed by the board to be necessary and convenient in connection therewith or incident thereto; and to perform any and all other duties and functions from time to time imposed, authorized, or directed by the General Conference of The United Methodist Church. No proposal shall be made to the General Conference which changes a benefit presently in effect without first securing through the General Board of Pensions an actuarial opinion concerning the cost and other related aspects of the proposed change.

2. The board is authorized to manage and administer pension and benefit funds, plans, and programs in such manner as may be deemed by the board to be reasonably necessary to achieve an efficient, equitable, and adequate operation; and to receive, hold, manage, and disburse the moneys related thereto in accordance with the provisions of the respective funds, plans, and programs.

3. The board is authorized to receive, hold, manage, merge, consolidate, administer, and invest and reinvest, by and through its constituent corporations, all connectional pension and benefit funds. The board is encouraged to invest in institutions, companies, corporations, or funds which make a positive contribution toward the realization of the goals outlined in the Social Principles of our Church, subject to other provisions of the Discipline, and with due regard to any and all special contracts, agreements, and laws applicable thereto.

4. The board is authorized to receive, hold, manage, adminster, and invest and reinvest, by and through its constitutent corporations, endowment funds belonging to Annual Conferences or other funds for pension and benefit purposes to be administered for such Annual Conferences. The board is encouraged to invest in institutions, companies, corporations, or funds which make a positive contribution toward the realization of the goals outlined in the Social Principles of our Church; *provided,* however, that at no time shall any part of the principal of the endowment funds be appropriated by the board for any other purpose. The net income of such funds shall be accounted for annually by the board and paid over to the Annual Conferences concerned.

5. The board is authorized, on request of an Annual Conference or conference organization or agency of The United

Methodist Church, to receive therefrom distributable and reserve pension funds and to make the periodic pension payments to the beneficiaries of such Annual Conference, conference organization, board, or agency, in accordance with a schedule of distribution which shall be provided for the guidance of the board in making such payments. The board shall report annually the details of transactions under this provision. The board shall be entitled to recover the cost of performing such services.

6. The board, by and through its constituent corporations, is authorized and empowered to receive any gift, devise, or bequest made or intended for beneficiaries of The United Methodist Church, being the legal successor to and vested with the legal title to any and all such gifts, devises, and bequests. If the language or terms of any gift, devise, or bequest are inexact or ambiguous, the board shall dispose of or administer the same in the manner deemed most equitable according to the apparent intent of the donor as determined by the board after careful inquiry into the circumstances in connection with the making of such gift, devise, or bequest, and after granting full opportunity to all interested parties to be heard, after due and timely written notice of the time and place of hearing. Such notice shall be mailed to each and all interested parties through their respectively known representatives, at their last known addresses.

7. The four constituent corporations shall, until otherwise determined by the board, continue to collect, receive, and administer such gifts, devises, and bequests, and other funds as may be specifically designated to them by donors, subject to the rules, regulations, and policies of the board with respect thereto. All undesignated gifts, devises, bequests, and donations shall be collected, received, and administered under the direction of the board.

8. The board shall share in the funds raised for the World Service budget of The United Methodist Church as provided for in ¶ 911 of the Discipline and in enabling acts.

9. The appropriations from the net earnings of the publishing interests which are contributed to the pension programs of The United Methodist Church, and of the several Annual Conferences, shall be distributed on the basis determined by the board.

10. The board shall compile and maintain complete service records of ministerial members in full connection, associate members, and probationary members of the Annual Conferences of The United Methodist Church and of local pastors whose service may be related to potential annuity claims. Such service records shall be based on answers to the Business of the Annual Conference questions as published in the journals of the several Annual Conferences and in the General Minutes of The United Methodist Church, or in comparable publications of either or both of the uniting churches, and from information provided by Annual Conference Boards of Pensions. The conference Boards of Pensions shall be responsible for providing census data when requested by the board on participants and their families including, but not limited to, such data as birthdates, marriage dates, and dates of death.[25]

11. The board shall administer a clearinghouse for the allocation of pension responsibility among the several Annual Conferences, in accordance with the principle of divided annuity responsibility, and for the collection and distribution of pension funds related to such responsibility.

a) For each beneficiary involved in the operation of the clearinghouse the board shall determine the division of responsibility on account of approved service rendered.

b) The board shall have authority to determine the pension responsibility of each Annual Conference, in accordance with the principle of divided annuity responsibility, and to collect from each Annual Conference, as determined on the basis of their respective pension programs, the amount required by the clearinghouse to provide the pension benefits related thereto. Each Annual Conference shall provide funds to meet its annuity responsibility to beneficiaries of other Annual Conferences on the same basis as it provides pension payments for beneficiaries related directly to itself.[26]

c) The board is authorized and empowered to make all the rules concerning details that may be necessary to the operation of the clearinghouse.

---

[25]*See* Judicial Council Decision 165.
[26]*See* Judicial Council Decision 360.

12. The board is authorized and empowered to continue the operation, management, and administration of the following pension and benefit funds, plans, and programs, not to be restricted to: The Ministerial Pension Plan; The Comprehensive Protection Plan; The Lay Pension Plan; The Basic Protection Plan; The Senior Plan; Ministers Reserve Pension Fund; The Minister's Reserve Pension Plan; The Current Income Distribution Pension Plan; Joint Contributory Annuity Fund; Staff Pension Fund; The Pension Plan for Lay Employees; Lay Employees Pension Fund; Cumulative Pension and Benefit Fund; Tax-Deferred Annuity Contributions Program; Hospitalization and Medical Expense Program; Death Benefit Program; Bishops Reserve Pension and Benefit Fund, in consultation with the General Council on Finance and Administration; The Printing Establishment of The United Brethren in Christ Fund; The Home Office Pension Fund of the Board of Global Ministries, in consultation with the Board of Global Ministries; Chaplains Pension Fund, in consultation with the Division of Chaplains and Related Ministries; Retirement Allowance for Bishops, General Church Officers, and Staff Personnel Plan of the former Evangelical United Brethren Church, with funds to be provided by the General Council on Finance and Administration; Temporary General Aid Fund, in consultation with the Standing General Commission on Religion and Race, as determined by the General Conference, with funds to be provided by the General Council on Finance and Administration. Effective immediately, the General Board of Pensions shall report to the General Conference, pension and benefit funds, plans, and programs to be proposed for the General Conference to receive, review, adopt, approve, or otherwise act upon this report.

13. The board is authorized to prepare and publish a pension manual related to the funds, plans, and programs administered by the General Board of Pensions, and such other materials not inconsistent with the Discipline as may be deemed reasonably necessary by the board to its efficient operation.

14. In all matters not specifically covered by General Conference legislation or by reasonable implication, the board shall have authority to adopt rules, regulations, and policies for

the administration of the support of beneficiaries of The United Methodist Church.

15. Pension for service approved for pension credit by an agency of The United Methodist Church receiving financial support from the World Service Fund, the General Administration Fund, the Episcopal Fund, or any authorized general benevolent or administrative fund shall be provided by the employing agency in uniformity with that provided by other agencies under one of the pension funds, plans, or programs administered by the Board of Pensions of The United Methodist Church; *provided,* however, that where service has been rendered in two or more agencies, the total pension benefit shall be calculated as if all such service had been with one agency and the final agency shall provide any additional pension benefits necessary to accomplish this; furthermore, such agency may not make any arrangement with a life insurance company or any other entity for the purchase of annuities for the benefit of individual effective or retired employees or take any steps to nullify, in whole or in part, the pension plans or program of The United Methodist Church by making contracts with outside parties.

¶ **1705.** *Permanent Funds.*—1. The **Chartered Fund** shall be administered by the General Board of Pensions for the benefit of all the Annual and Provisional Annual Conferences in The United Methodist Church, the boundaries of which are within the United States, its territorial and insular possessions, and Cuba, unless the General Conference shall order otherwise. Once a year the net earnings of the fund, after provision for depreciation, shall be divided equally among such Annual and Provisional Annual Conferences in accordance with the restrictive rule contained in ¶ 20.

2. The General Board of Pensions shall order and direct that the income from the **General Endowment Fund for Conference Claimants** (formerly known as the General Endowment Fund for Superannuates of The Methodist Episcopal Church, South) held by The Board of Pensions of The United Methodist Church, Incorporated in Missouri, shall be distributed on account of service of conference claimants rendered in an Annual Conference of The United Methodist Church; *provided,* however, that

such distribution shall be restricted to Annual Conferences which, directly or through their predecessor Annual Conferences, participated in raising this fund, in proportion to the number of approved years of annuity responsibility of each Annual Conference as shall be determined by the General Board of Pensions.

ANNUAL CONFERENCE ADMINISTRATION

¶ **1706.** *Powers, Duties, and Responsibilities.*—1. The Annual Conference, on recommendation of the conference Board of Pensions, shall determine the admissibility and validity of service approved for pension credit and the payments, disallowances, and deductions thereunder, subject to the provisions of the Discipline and the rules and regulations of the pension funds, plans, and programs of The United Methodist Church.[27]

2. *a)* Service rendered prior to January 1, 1982, by a minister or local pastor in The United Methodist Church, including service rendered in either or both of the uniting churches, prior to church union shall be approved for pension credit in accordance with provisions of the Discipline in effect and applicable thereto at the time such service was rendered. Pension for such service shall be provided in accordance with the past service provisions of the Ministerial Pension Plan.

b) Pension for full-time service rendered by a minister or local pastor in The United Methodist Church prior to January 1, 1982, shall be not less than an amount based upon pension credit for service prior to January 1, 1982, and the benefit levels in effect on December 31, 1981; *provided,* however, that the pension of a ministerial member whose membership was terminated prior to January 1, 1982, shall be determined in accordance with the provisions of the Discipline, pension funds, plans, and programs in effect at the time of such termination.

c) Pensions earned by bishops (elected by a Jurisdictional Conference), ministers, and local pastors, and protection benefits for such bishops, ministers, and eligible local pastors in The United Methodist Church after December 31, 1981, shall be

---

[27]*See* Judicial Council Decisions 81, 360, 379.

provided in accordance with the provisions of the Ministerial Pension Plan and the Comprehensive Protection Plan.

3. For service rendered prior to January 1, 1982, the following years of approved service in an Annual Conference of The United Methodist Church shall be counted for pension credit subject to the conditions stated in this paragraph:

a) By a minister who is a probationary member or who is in the effective relation as an associate member or a member in full connection in the Annual Conference: (1) as pastor, associate or assistant pastor, or other minister in a pastoral charge; (2) as district superintendent, presiding elder, conference president, conference superintendent, or other full-time salaried official of the conference; (3) under appointment beyond the local church to an institution, organization, or agency which in the judgment of the Annual Conference rendered to it some form of service, direct or indirect, sufficient to warrant pension credit, or to a community church, or as a conference-approved evangelist; *provided,* however, that such institution, organization, agency, community church, or evangelist accepts and pays such apportionments as the conference may require, with the recommendation that this apportionment shall be not less than twelve times the annuity rate of the conference; and *provided* further, that pension related to such service may be arranged through one of the pension funds or plans administered by the General Board of Pensions; (4) as a student appointed to attend school, but only if the minister serves subsequently with pension credit in an Annual Conference or conferences for three or more years under appointment other than to attend school, such credit as a student not to exceed three years; *provided,* however, that all years for which pension credit was given under legislation in effect prior to the 1972 General Conference, on account of appointment to attend school, shall be counted in determining the pension claim thereon; and *provided* further, that, if a ministerial member is again appointed to attend school after having served under appointment for six consecutive years as a minister in full connection with pension credit in an Annual Conference or conferences other than under appointment to attend school, pension credit shall be given for up to but not more than three additional years under appointment to attend school if the minister serves subsequently with pension credit in an Annual Conference or conferences for three or more additional years under appointment other than to attend school; (5) as a minister on sabbatical leave, *provided* that not less than five of the ten years just preceding the granting of such leave were served with pension credit in the Annual Conference which grants the sabbatical leave; and (6) as a minister on disability leave subsequent to the 1968 Uniting Conference, not to exceed fifteen years.[28]

b) By a person classified by the Board of Ordained Ministry as eligible to be appointed as a full-time local pastor, and by an approved supply pastor prior to Church union in 1968, as a pastor or assistant pastor of a pastoral charge in full-time service under appointment; *provided,* however, that such credit shall be conditional and subject to provisions hereinafter stated in this paragraph.[29]

c) By a minister from another Christian denomination who has not attained the age of mandatory retirement for a conference ministerial member, who has not retired from the denomination, and who is approved by the Annual Conference on recommendation of the Board of Ordained Ministry as provided · in ¶ 419.1, who renders full-time service under appointment as a pastor or assistant pastor subject to provisions hereinafter stated in this paragraph.

d) In calculating fractions of years of service for pension credit earned prior to January 1, 1982, the following formula shall be used:

(1) Any period of up to and including forty-five days shall not be counted.

(2) Forty-six days up to and including one hundred thirty-six days shall be counted as one quarter of a year.

(3) One hundred thirty-seven days up to and including two hundred twenty-eight days shall be counted as one half of a year.

(4) Two hundred twenty-nine days up to and including three hundred nineteen days shall be counted as three quarters of a year.

---

[28]*See* Judicial Council Decisions 180, 219.
[29]*See* ·Judicial Council Decisions 73, 206.

(5) Three hundred twenty days up to and including three hundred sixty-five days shall be counted as one year.

4. Concerning the normal conditions for pension credit and pro rata pension credit, the following provisions shall apply for service rendered prior to January 1, 1982, in determining approval for pension credit, eligibility for pension, and allocation of responsibility:

a) Normal Conditions.—The normal conditions required of a ministerial member or a local pastor for full pension credit shall be:

(1) That full-time service is rendered by a person appointed to a field of labor under provisions of ¶ 437.1;

(2) That this person not be attending school as a regular student except as provided in ¶ 1706.3*a*(4);

(3) That this person not be substantially employed in work other than that to which he or she is appointed by the bishop;

(4) That this person receive not less cash support per annum from all church and/or conference-related sources than that provided in the schedule of equitable salaries adopted by the Annual Conference for those in this person's classification.

b) Proportional Pension Credit.—Effective as of the closing day of the 1980 Annual Conference session, pro rata pension credit may be granted to persons appointed to less than full-time service under the provisions of ¶ 437.2 by a three-fourths vote of those present and voting in the Annual Conference session on recommendation of the conference Board of Pensions. Such pension credit shall be in one-quarter year increments; *provided,* however, that no one individual receives in excess of one year of pension credit per annum.

c) Full Pension Credit.—Full pension credit may be granted for persons not meeting some or all of the above conditions by a three-fourths vote of those present and voting in the Annual Conference on recommendation of the conference Board of Pensions.[30]

d) Service as a chaplain on full-time duty prior to December 31, 1946, which previous legislation includes as eligible to be

---

[30]*See* Judicial Council Decision 386.

counted in determining the annuity claim on an Annual Conference, shall be so recognized.

e) Pension responsibility on account of the appointment of a ministerial member of an Annual Conference to attend school shall be allocated to the conference or conferences in which the minister shall first thereafter render six years of service under appointment with pension credit other than to attend school; *provided* that if the minister does not thereafter render as much as six years of approved service other than to attend school, the responsibility for periods under appointment to attend school shall be allocated on a pro rata basis to the conference or conferences in which the minister rendered approved service subsequent to the period of appointment to attend school. This provision shall apply irrespective of whether such periods under appointment were before or after its enactment; *provided,* however, that such allocation shall not apply in cases where pension payments were in effect prior to January 1, 1973, on the basis of the allocation of responsibility under previous legislation.

f) Service of a local pastor may be approved for pension credit only by vote of the Annual Conference, on recommendation of the conference Board of Pensions, after consultation with the district superintendents. Such approval of service rendered in the year next preceding the session of the conference shall be recorded under the following Business of the Annual Conference question, which shall be included in the business of the conference: "What local pastors are granted pension credit on account of approved full-time service during the past year?" If at any session the conference does not grant credit for such service, it may do so later under the Disciplinary question, "What other personal notation should be made?"

g) Upon recommendation of the conference Board of Pensions and by a three-fourths vote of those present and voting in the Annual Conference, pension credit may be granted to a ministerial member of the conference on account of full-time service previously rendered as an approved local pastor or approved supply pastor to an institution, organization, or agency, which in the judgment of the Annual Conference rendered to it some form of service sufficient to warrant pension credit; *provided,* however, that such institution, organization, or agency shall accept and pay such apportionment as the conference may require.

h) On recommendation of the conference Board of Pensions and approval by the Annual Conference, appointments beyond the local church shall be listed in the conference journal as follows: (1) with pension credit by the Annual Conference or (2) with pension responsibility on the institution or agency served. If at any session the conference fails to make such listing, it may be done subsequently, whenever desirable, under the Business of the Annual Conference question, "What other personal notation should be made?"[31]

i) In the event of retirement under ¶ 447.2*b*, the actuarially reduced pension or subsequent pension resulting from annuity rate increases for service rendered prior to January 1, 1982, shall be determined by multiplying the pension (years times rate) by a percentage factor; such percentage factor shall be the greater of 100 percent minus one-half percent per month or fraction of a month of age less than sixty-five years attained on the date the actuarially reduced pension is to commence (or the date of such annuity rate increase), or 100 percent minus one-half percent per month for each month of difference between the assumed date at which pension payments would have been permitted by retirement under ¶ 447.2*c* by completion of forty years of service under appointment and the actual date the actuarially reduced pension or annuity rate increase is to commence under ¶ 447.2*b*. Such actuarially reduced pension shall be calculated by the General Board of Pensions and allocated pro rata to the Annual Conference or conferences which are charged with the pension responsibility.[32]

5. *a)* A pension shall be payable on account of pension credit as a full-time local pastor or supply pastor if (1) the local pastor shall have been admitted as a ministerial associate or probationary member or member in full connection in an Annual Conference and has subsequently been placed in the retired relation by the conference, or (2) the local pastor shall have rendered no less than four consecutive years of full-time service with pension credit in

---

[31]*See* Judicial Council Decision 95.
[32]*See* Judicial Decision 428.

one Annual Conference and has been recognized by an Annual Conference as a retired local pastor.

b) On recommendation of the conference Board of Pensions, a pension shall be payable on account of pension credit for a minister from another Christian denomination who shall have rendered not less than four consecutive years of full-time service with pension credit in one Annual Conference while qualified under ¶ 419.1, who has attained the age of voluntary retirement for a conference ministerial member and who has been retired by the denomination, providing the minister is not receiving a pension for the same period of service from another denomination. (*See also* §3c above.)

6. The Annual Conference, on recommendation of the conference Board of Pensions, shall have the power to revise, correct, or adjust a minister's record of pension credit as set forth in the minister's service record. Prior to the revision of such record, the General Board of Pensions may be requested to review relevant data and report its findings thereon. Such revisions, corrections, and adjustments shall be published in the journal of the Annual Conference in answer to Business of the Annual Conference questions and shall be reported to the General Board of Pensions by the conference Board of Pensions.[33]

7. The Annual Conference shall review annually the annuity rate for service rendered in the Annual Conference prior to January 1, 1982, for the purpose of adjusting the rate as appropriate, taking into account changes in economic conditions. Such annuity rate shall be determined each year without restriction, other than that contained in ¶ 1706.2b, but it is recommended that the rate reflect changes in pastors' salaries of the conferences. The annuity rate for approved service of local pastors shall also be determined by the conference each year and may be the same as the rate for service of conference members, but it shall be no less than 75 percent of that rate. A successor conference resulting from a merger involving a former Central Jurisdictional Conference shall establish for all for whom it has pension responsibility the same rate for past service of conference

---

[33]*See* Judicial Council Decision 386.

members in the Central Jurisdiction as for service in a geographic former Methodist jurisdiction and the same rate for past service of local pastors regardless of the jurisdiction in which the service was rendered.[34]

8. The Division of Chaplains and Related Ministries may provide a pension through the Chaplains Pension Fund, if not otherwise provided, on account of service rendered by a chaplain on full-time duty with the armed forces of the United States or to an institution, organization, or agency, in accordance with rules and regulations determined jointly by the General Board of Pensions and the Division of Chaplains and Related Ministries.

9. The responsibility for pension for service approved for pension credit shall rest with the Annual Conference in which the service was rendered; *provided*, however, that in the event of mergers, unions, boundary changes, or transfers of churches, such responsibility shall rest with the successor Annual Conference within whose geographical boundaries the charge is located.[35]

10. Pension for service approved for pension credit by an Annual Conference shall be provided by the Annual Conference under one of the pension funds, plans, or programs administered by the General Board of Pensions of The United Methodist Church.

11. An Annual Conference may not make any arrangement with a life insurance company for the purchase of annuities for the benefit of individual effective or retired ministers or take any steps to nullify, in whole or in part, the pension plans and programs of The United Methodist Church by making contracts with outside parties.

12. *Other Annual Conference Organizations.—a*) Annual Conferences, hereinafter called conferences, are authorized to establish, incorporate, and maintain investment funds, preachers aid societies, and organizations and funds of similar character, under such names, plans, rules, and regulations as they may determine, the directors of which shall be elected or otherwise designated by the conference, where permissible under the laws

---

[34]*See* Judicial Council Decisions 360, 389.
[35]*See* Judicial Council Decisions 203, 389.

of the state of incorporation, and the income from which shall be applied to the support of the pension program through the conference Board of Pensions.[36]

b) Distributable pension funds from all sources shall be disbursed by or under the direction of the conference Board of Pensions, excepting only such funds as are otherwise restricted by specific provisions or limitations in gifts, devises, bequests, trusts, pledges, deeds, or other similar instruments, which restrictions and limitations shall be observed.

c) It shall not be permissible for any conference or permanent fund organization thereof to deprive its beneficiaries who are beneficiaries in other conferences of the privilege of sharing in the distribution of the earned income of such funds through the clearinghouse administered by the General Board of Pensions.

d) (1) Prior to January 1, 1982, a conference subject to the laws of the state in which it is incorporated shall have power to require from its ministerial members and local pastors who are serving with pension credit from the conference an annual contribution to either its permanent or reserve fund or for current distribution or to a preachers aid society for the benefit of its beneficiaries, subject to the following provisions:[37]

(a) The annual payment may be made in installments as provided by the conference.

(b) The making of such payment shall not be used as the ground of contractual obligations upon the part of the conference or as the ground of any special or additional annuity claim of a member against the conference; neither shall it prevent disallowance of a member's annuity claim by conference action.

(c) The conference may fix a financial penalty for failure of the member to pay.

(d) In case membership in the conference is terminated under the provisions of the Discipline, the conference may refund the amount so paid, in whole or in part, after hearing has been given to the member, in case such hearing is requested.

---

[36]*See* Judicial Council Decision 218.
[37]*See* Judicial Council Decision 181.

(e) Ministers entering a conference shall not be charged an initial entry fee by any organization mentioned in §*a* above; furthermore, the annual contribution required from a ministerial member of the conference or a local pastor shall not exceed an amount equal to 3 percent of the minister's or local pastor's support.

(2) If a minister is participating in one of the pension funds, plans, or programs administered by the General Board of Pensions, the minister shall not be required by the conference or by an organization thereof related to the support of beneficiaries to make any other contribution for pension purposes.

e) Each conference, on recommendation of its conference Board of Pensions or one of the organizations mentioned in §*a* above, may select a Sunday in each year to be observed in the churches as Retired Ministers Day, in honor of the retired ministers, their spouses, and the surviving spouses of ministers in recognition of the Church's responsibility for their support. The bishop may request each conference in the area to insert a Retired Ministers Day in its calendar.

13. A conference Board of Pensions may make special grants to ministerial members or former ministerial members and to local pastors or former local pastors of an Annual Conference who have served under appointment in that conference; or to their spouses, former spouses, surviving former spouses, or surviving dependent children (including adult dependent children). A report of such special grants shall be made annually to the Annual Conference.

14. *a)* A former ministerial member of an Annual Conference whose membership was terminated on or after January 1, 1973, and prior to January 1, 1982, after the completion of ten or more years of service with pension credit in an Annual Conference or conferences, shall retain the right to receive a pension, subsequent to the close of the Annual Conference session in which the former minister last held membership which occurs in the year in which the former minister attains age sixty-two on or before July 1, based on the years of service approved for pension credit. Such former minister's pension shall be based on all years of service with pension credit if the former minister had twenty or more such years. If less than

twenty such years but at least ten years, the years used in the calculation of the benefit shall be a percentage of the approved service years; such percentage shall be determined by multiplying the credited whole years by 5 percent, resulting in 50 percent of such years for ten years of credited service and 100 percent for twenty years of such service. If pension begins prior to the age at which retirement under ¶ 447.2*c* could have occurred, then the provisions of ¶ 1706.4*i* shall apply.

b) A former ministerial member of an Annual Conference whose membership was terminated on or after January 1, 1982, after the completion of ten or more years of service under appointment in an Annual Conference or conferences, shall retain the right to receive a pension subsequent to the close of the Annual Conference session in which the former minister last held membership which occurs in the year in which the former minister attains age sixty-two on or before July 1 based on the years of service prior to January 1, 1982, approved for pension credit. If pension begins prior to the age at which retirement under ¶ 447.2*c* could have occurred, then the provisions of ¶ 1706.4*i* shall apply.

c) Effective at the close of the 1976 General Conference, former ministerial members of the Annual Conference whose membership was terminated on or after such date shall have any vested pension benefits calculated at the annuity rate in effect on the date such person's membership is terminated.

d) Ministerial members in an Annual Conference who voluntarily withdraw from the ministry of The United Methodist Church to enter the ministry of another Church or denomination, on the attainment of age sixty-two and retirement from the ministry of such other Church or denomination, on recommendation of the conference Board of Pensions and a three-fourths vote of those present and voting in any Annual Conference in which approved service was rendered prior to January 1, 1982, or the legal successor, may be recognized and granted pensions on account of approved service rendered in that conference. If pension begins prior to the age at which retirement under ¶ 447.2*c* could have occurred, then the provisions of ¶ 1706.4*i* shall apply.

15. The responsibility for providing pension on account of

service rendered prior to January 1, 1982, in a Missionary Conference, Provisional Annual Conference, or former Mission within the United States or Puerto Rico, which has been approved for pension credit, shall rest jointly with (a) the Missionary Conference, Provisional Annual Conference, or former Mission concerned, (b) the General Board of Pensions with funds provided by the General Council on Finance and Administration, and (c) the National Division of the General Board of Global Ministries. The revenue for pension purposes covering such service shall be provided by the aforesaid parties in accordance with such plan or plans as may be mutually agreed to by them.

16. A minister who has been granted the retired relation in a Central Conference or an affiliated autonomous church, shall be entitled to a pension from a conference or conferences in the United States or Puerto Rico for the years of approved service rendered therein upon attainment of the required age or the completion of the required years of approved service. Such minister shall notify the General Board of Pensions upon his or her retirement. The General Board of Pensions shall certify the years of approved service to each Annual Conference concerned. Payments due thereunder shall be collected from the conference concerned and forwarded to the claimant by the General Board of Pensions in such manner as it may deem most expedient and economical.

17. Pension and benefit contributions are the responsibility of the salary-paying unit of a participant in the Ministerial Pension Plan and the Comprehensive Protection Plan. Unless otherwise determined by vote of the Annual, Missionary, or Provisional Conference, the treasurer of a local church or pastoral charge shall remit such contributions to the General Board of Pensions related to the participant's compensation which is provided from local church funds. If compensation from the local church or pastoral charge is supplemented from other church sources, pension and benefit contributions related to such supplements shall be paid from that same source. If the entire compensation for a participant is from a salary-paying unit other than a local church or a pastoral charge, the unit responsible for compensation shall remit the pension and benefit contributions to the General Board of Pensions. Nothing in this paragraph shall

be understood as preventing an Annual, Missionary, or Provisional Conference from raising part or all of the annual contributions for the pension program of its pastors by an apportionment to the churches of the conference, remitting payments to the General Board of Pensions on behalf of all the pastors covered; there is no time limit on this provision.

18. Actual compensation, limited by the denominational average compensation, is the basic contribution base of the Ministerial Pension Plan and Comprehensive Protection Plan. Other options setting the contribution base as actual compensation limited by 150 percent of the denominational average compensation, or actual compensation, may be elected by the Annual Conference or other participating groups as they may determine. The above limits do not apply to personal contributions or tax-deferred annuity contributions.

19. An Annual Conference may establish a Pension Support Fund to be administered by the conference Board of Pensions. Local churches may request pension assistance from this fund when special circumstances arise which result in nonpayment of pension contributions and/or apportionments for pension and benefit purposes. The board shall present its estimate of the amount required to the conference Council on Finance and Administration which shall include it in its recommendation to the conference. If the amount is approved by the conference, it shall be apportioned as an item of ministerial support.

20. The Annual Conference Board of Pensions in consultation with the General Board of Pensions shall have the responsibility to enroll ministers and local pastors of the Annual Conference in the Ministerial Pension Plan and the Comprehensive Protection Plan in accordance with the provisions of such plans (*see* ¶ 408.9).

21. Optional provisions contained in the Ministerial Pension Plan and Comprehensive Protection Plan may be adopted by vote of the Annual Conference subsequent to the receipt of a recommendation from the conference Board of Pensions.

However, for service rendered after December 31, 1985, the percentage of the Contribution Base that may be paid to fund the Ministerial Pension Plan in any one year will be limited to:

a) Twelve percent, if the then current annuity rate is at least nine tenths of 1 percent of the Conference Average Salary, as computed by the General Board of Pensions.

b) Not more than 11 percent, if the then current annuity rate is at least eight tenths of 1 percent, but less than nine tenths of 1 percent of the conference average salary as computed by the General Board of Pensions.

c) Not more than 10 percent, if the then current annuity rate is less than eight tenths of 1 per cent of the conference average salary as computed by the General Board of Pensions.

¶ **1707.** *Financing Pension and Benefit Programs.*—The Annual Conference shall be responsible for annually providing moneys in the amount necessary to meet the requirements of the pension and benefit funds, plans, and programs of the conference.

1. The board shall compute the amount to be apportioned annually to meet the requirements of the pension and benefit programs of the conference.

2. After consultation with the board, the conference Council on Finance and Administration shall report to the Annual Conference the amounts computed by the board which are required to meet the needs of the pension, benefit, and relief programs of the conference.

3. Distributable pension funds from all sources, unless restricted by specific provisions or limitations, shall be disbursed by, or under the direction of, the conference Board of Pensions.

4. The board may accumulate a fund from the income for pension purposes, in order to stabilize the pension program of the conference.[38]

¶ **1708.** *Financial Policy.*—The following rules shall apply to the financial administration of Annual Conference pension and pension-related funds:

1. A member of the board connected or interested in any way with the securities, real estate, or other forms of investment sold to or purchased from such funds, or with an insurance program or a contract under consideration by the board, shall be

---

[38]*See* Judicial Council Decision 50.

ineligible to participate in the deliberation of the investment committee or of the board or to vote in connection therewith.

2. No officer or member of a conference agency handling such funds shall receive a personal commission, bonus, or remuneration, direct or indirect, in connection with the purchase or sale of any property, the loan of any money, the letting of any annuity or insurance contract, the making or acceptance of any assignment, pledge, or mortgage to secure the payment of any loan, or for the purchase or sale of any securities or other properties from or to that agency, or be eligible to obtain a loan in any amount from funds committed to the care of that agency. No investment shall be purchased from or sold to any member of the board or any member of the family of a member of the board.

3. To prevent development of any conflict of interest or preferential treatment and to preserve good will and confidence throughout the Church, no local church, church-related institution, or organization thereof shall be eligible to obtain a loan in any amount from such funds.[39]

4. The principle of diversification of investments shall be observed, with the agency encouraged to invest in institutions, companies, corporations, or funds which make a positive contribution toward the realization of the goals outlined in the Social Principles of our Church, however with primary consideration given to the soundness and safety of such investments.

5. Real property may hereafter be accepted as consideration for gift annuity agreements only with the stipulation that the annuity shall not exceed the net income from the property until such property shall have been liquidated. Upon liquidation, the annuity shall be paid upon the net proceeds at the established annuity rate.

6. An Annual Conference agency handling such funds shall not offer higher rates of annuity than those listed in the annuity schedule approved by the General Council on Finance and Administration.

7. *a*) There shall be printed in the Annual Conference journal a list of the investments held by each agency handling such funds directly or indirectly under the control of the Annual

_____

[39]*See* Judicial Council Decision 145.

Conference, or such list may be distributed directly to the members of the Annual Conference at their request. A copy of all such lists of investments shall be filed annually with the General Board of Pensions.

b) The conference Board of Pensions shall require an annual audit of pension and pension-related funds setting forth the total asset value of such funds and the distribution of income from such funds from persons and organizations appointed or employed for the management of these funds.

8. The borrowing of money in any conference year by a conference corporation or organization to enable the conference Board of Pensions to meet the requirements of the pension and benefit programs shall be done only on authority of the conference granted by three-fourths vote of the members present and voting.

9. *Depositories and Bonding.—a)* The conference Board of Pensions shall designate a bank or banks or other depository or depositories for deposit of the funds held by the board and may require a depository bond from such depository or depositories.

b) The board, through the conference Council on Finance and Administration, shall provide a fidelity bond in suitable amount for all persons handling its funds.

¶ **1709.** *Joint Distributing Committees.—1. Authorizations.—* Whenever two or more Annual or Provisional Annual Conferences are to be merged, in whole or in part, there shall be elected by each conference affected a Distributing Committee of three members and three alternates, which shall act jointly with similar committees from the other conference or conferences. The **Joint Distributing Committee** thus formed shall have power and authority: *(a)* to allocate the pension responsibility involved; *(b)* to distribute equitably the permanent funds and other pension assets of the conference or conferences affected, taking into consideration the pension responsibility involved; *(c)* to the extent not otherwise previously provided for by the conference or conferences involved, to apportion or distribute equitably any other assets or property and any other liabilities or obligations. It shall be governed by the legal restrictions or limitations of any contract, trust agreement, pledge, deed, will, or other legal instrument.

2. *Organization.*—The committee shall be convened by the general secretary of the General Board of Pensions, or by some other officer of that board designated by the general secretary in writing, and shall elect from its membership a chairperson, a vice-chairperson, and a secretary.

3. *Powers, Duties, and Responsibilities.*—*a)* The committee shall determine the number of years of service approved for pension credit rendered in the conferences which will lose their identity in the merging of conference territories, and the findings of the committee shall be final unless substantial evidence to the contrary is presented, and the annuity payments by the continuing conference or conferences shall be made accordingly. The determination of pension benefits in The United Methodist Church shall recognize all pension rights to which ministers are entitled under the pension plans in existence at the time of church union and shall recognize all approved service which has been rendered in the Evangelical United Brethren Church and The Methodist Church prior to the date of church union.

b) The committee shall keep complete minutes of its transactions, and a copy thereof shall be filed with the secretary of each Annual Conference involved and with the General Board of Pensions.

c) Until the committee's work shall have been completed, the corporate organization of each conference in the process of merger shall be maintained. After the committee shall have completed its work, the officers of such corporation, subject to the completion of its business, shall dissolve or merge it, in accordance with the laws governing the incorporation thereof, after being authorized to do so by the conference involved.

d) The committee, having completed its work in connection with the merger or mergers for which it was organized and having filed copies of its findings and actions with the secretaries of the conferences involved for publication in the respective conference journals, and with the General Board of Pensions, shall be dissolved; subject, however, to recall by the general secretary of the General Board of Pensions in the event of the discovery and presentation to the general board of data substantially at variance with those previously submitted, for the purpose of reviewing such data and possible revision of its previous actions.

Section XI. General Board of Publication.

¶ **1801.** *Publishing Interests.*—The General Board of Publication comprises the publishing interests of The United Methodist Church and shall hereafter be designated as The United Methodist Publishing House. It shall have responsibility for and supervision of the publishing and printing for The United Methodist Church. The General Board of Publication shall through agencies or instrumentalities it deems necessary achieve the objectives set forth in ¶ 1813. The General Board of Publication shall provide publishing and printing services for other agencies of The United Methodist Church and shall share with other agencies of The United Methodist Church in the total program of The United Methodist Church, as well as share in the total ecumenical program in the area of printing and publishing for the advancement of the cause of Christ and his Kingdom as the General Board of Publication shall determine to be appropriate.

¶ **1802.** *Organization.*—The **General Board of Publication,** hereinafter called the board, constituted coincident with or next following the Declaration of Union of The Evangelical United Brethren Church and The Methodist Church, shall consist of forty-five members, including two bishops selected by the Council of Bishops. Five members shall be members at large elected by the board. The remaining members shall be elected by the Jurisdictional Conferences on a ratio which will provide for an equitable distribution among the various jurisdictions, based on the memberships thereof; *provided* that no jurisdiction shall be represented by fewer than two members. Membership on the board shall be equally divided, as far as practicable, between ordained ministers and lay persons. Other paragraphs of the Discipline notwithstanding, membership shall also be by classes based on term of office for one, two, or three quadrenniums, attention being given to the principle of rotation so that, as far as practicable, one half of the membership shall be elected each quadrennium. At least two young adults, at the time of their election, shall be elected each quadrennium. It shall be the duty of the secretary of the General Conference to inform the various jurisdictional secretaries of the number of members to be elected from their jurisdictions, the ratio of such representation being computed on the basis of the latest official membership statistics available. In case a vacancy occurs between sessions of the Jurisdictional Conferences for any cause, the board shall fill the vacancy for the unexpired term from that jurisdiction in the representation of which the vacancy occurs, except in the case of additional members where such vacancies would be filled by the board in the prescribed manner without regard to geographic or jurisdictional relationship. The publisher of The United Methodist Church (¶ 1814) shall be an ex officio member of the board without vote. The provisions of this paragraph are effective immediately upon adjournment of the 1980 General Conference.

¶ **1803.** The board shall hold at least one meeting in each calendar year. The place and time of all meetings shall be designated by the board, but if it fails to do so, then the time and place shall be designated by the chairperson. It shall convene at such other times on call of the chairperson or by the board or by the executive committee. At all meetings of the board a majority of the members shall constitute a quorum.

¶ **1804.** The board shall keep a correct record of its proceedings and make written report thereof to the Church through the General Conference.

¶ **1805.** The members of the board and all officers of the board elected by it shall hold office until their successors are chosen and the new board is duly organized.

¶ **1806.** The board is authorized to perfect its organization from its membership, including the offices of chairperson, vice-chairperson, and secretary. The board shall elect from its membership an **executive committee** of sixteen members, including the chairperson, vice-chairperson and secretary of the board, who shall serve respectively as chairperson, vice-chairperson, and secretary of the committee. Not more than four members of the executive committee shall be from any one jurisdiction, and for the first three quadrenniums following the Declaration of Union two members shall be from the former Evangelical United Brethren Church. The bishops serving on the board shall be ex officio members, and the publisher of The United Methodist Church (¶ 1814) shall be an ex officio member without vote. Any vacancy occurring in the membership of the executive committee shall be filled by it, subject to confirmation by the board at its next meeting.

¶ **1807.** The executive committee shall have and may exercise all the powers of the board except those expressly reserved by the board and/or by the Discipline for board action. It shall meet quarterly to examine the affairs under its charge and shall keep and submit to the board correct records of its proceedings. Special meetings may be called by the chairperson on his or her own initiative and shall be called on the written request of five members of the executive committee. A majority of the members shall constitute a quorum.

¶ **1808.** The board shall be the successor in interest to and carry on the work of the Board of Publication of The Evangelical United Brethren Church and the Board of Publication of The Methodist Church.

¶ **1809.** *The United Methodist Publishing House.*—1. The board is empowered and authorized in its discretion to cause the general operations, if any, of the five existing corporations to be conducted under the name of **The United Methodist Publishing House.** The corporations are: The Methodist Book Concern, a corporation existing under the laws of the State of New York; The Methodist Book Concern, a corporation existing under the laws of the State of Ohio; The Board of Publication of the Methodist Protestant Church, a corporation existing under the laws of the State of Pennsylvania; Book Agents of the Methodist Episcopal Church, South, a corporation existing under the laws of the State of Tennessee; and the Board of Publication of The Methodist Church, a corporation existing under the laws of the State of Illinois.

2. The board is authorized and empowered at any time it may deem such action to be desirable or convenient to take corporate action in the name of said corporations to surrender the charter or charters of one or several or all of said corporations or to merge, consolidate, or affiliate such corporations, or any of them, in compliance with appropriate state corporation laws.

¶ **1810.** The members of the board shall serve and act as directors or trustees of the corporations named in ¶ 1809.

¶ **1811.** The corporations named in ¶ 1809 are agencies or instrumentalities through which The United Methodist Church conducts its publishing, printing, and distribution in the name of The United Methodist Publishing House in accordance with the objectives set forth in ¶ 1813. Each of these corporations shall comply with the policies set forth in ¶ 815.

¶ **1812.** The board shall examine carefully the affairs of The United Methodist Publishing House and make written report thereof to the Church through the General Conference.

¶ **1813.** *Objectives.*—The objectives of The United Methodist Publishing House shall be: the advancement of the cause of Christianity throughout the world by disseminating religious knowledge and useful literary, scientific, and educational information in the form of books, tracts, multimedia, and periodicals; the promotion of Christian education; the implementation of any and all activities properly connected with the publishing, manufacturing in a variety of media, and distribution of books, tracts, periodicals, materials, and supplies for churches and church schools, including the ecumenical outreach of Christianity, and such other activities as the General Conference may direct.

¶ **1814.** *Direction and Control.*—The United Methodist Publishing House shall be under the direction and control of the board, acting through an executive officer elected quadrennially by the board, who shall be the **publisher** of The United Methodist Church, and such other officers as the board may determine.

¶ **1815.** The net income from the operations of The United Methodist Publishing House, after providing adequate reserves for its efficient operation and allowing for reasonable growth and expansion, shall be appropriated by the board and distributed annually on the basis of an equitable plan provided by the General Board of Pensions to the several Annual Conferences for the persons who are and shall be conference claimants.

¶ **1816.** The net income from the operations of The United Methodist Publishing House shall be appropriated to no other purpose than its own operating requirements and for persons who are or shall be conference claimants as provided in ¶¶ 20 and 1815.[40]

---

[40]*See* Judicial Council Decisions 322, 330.

¶ **1817.** The members of the board and their successors in office are declared to be the successors of the incorporators named in the charters of The Methodist Book Concern issued by the States of New York and Ohio and in the charter of The Board of Publication of the Methodist Protestant Church issued by the State of Pennsylvania. The executive officer of the board, elected from time to time under this or any subsequent Discipline, is declared to be the successor in office of the Book Agents of the Methodist Episcopal Church, South, named in the charter issued to the corporation of that name by the State of Tennessee.

¶ **1818.** Subject to the provisions of ¶ 1814 and to the continuing control and direction of the General Conference of The United Methodist Church as set forth from time to time in the Discipline, the board is authorized and empowered to cause the operations of The United Methodist Publishing House to be carried on and the objectives defined in ¶ 1813 to be achieved in such manner, through or by means of such agencies or instrumentalities, and by use of such procedures as the board may from time to time determine to be necessary, advisable, or appropriate, with full power and authority in the premises to take all such action and to do all such other acts and things as may be required or found to be advisable. In particular, and without limiting the generality of the foregoing, the board is authorized and empowered, for the purposes of this section:

1. To use, manage, operate, and otherwise utilize all property and assets of every kind, character, and description of four corporations—namely, The Methodist Book Concern, a corporation existing under the laws of the State of New York; The Methodist Book Concern, a corporation existing under the laws of the State of Ohio; The Board of Publication of the Methodist Protestant Church, a corporation existing under the laws of the State of Pennsylvania; and Book Agents of the Methodist Episcopal Church, South, a corporation existing under the laws of the State of Tennessee—as well as all income from such property and assets and the avails thereof, all with liability or obligation to account for such property and assets, the use thereof, the income therefrom, and avails thereof, only to the General Conference of The United Methodist Church or as it shall direct.

2. To cause each of the said corporations to take all such action and to do all such things as the board may deem necessary or advisable to carry out the intent and purposes of this paragraph. The governing body of each of the said corporations from time to time shall take all action which the board deems necessary or advisable to carry out the intent and purposes of this paragraph. The board shall cause all legal obligations of said four corporations, now existing or hereafter incurred, to be met, fulfilled, and performed.

3. To continue to exercise the powers and administer the duties and responsibilities conferred on it as an agency of The United Methodist Church through the corporation named Board of Publication of The Methodist Church, incorporated under the laws of the State of Illinois in accord with authority delegated to it by the General Conference of 1952, or through such other means and agencies as it may from time to time determine to be expedient and necessary in order to give full effect to the purposes expressed in this section.[41]

¶ **1819.** 1. The property, assets, and income of the Illinois corporation shall be held by it, under the direction of the board, as an agency of The United Methodist Church and shall at all times be subject to the control and direction of the General Conference of The United Methodist Church as set forth from time to time in the Discipline.

2. In carrying out and executing its operations and functions, the Illinois corporation shall be entitled to hold, use, manage, operate, and otherwise utilize all property and assets of every kind, character, and description of each of the four corporations identified in ¶ 1818.1 (other than its corporate powers and franchises) and all income therefrom and avails thereof for the purposes and objectives defined in this section.

3. The governing body of each of the five existing corporations under the direction of the board shall from time to time take all such action as the board deems necessary or advisable to carry out the intent and purposes of this paragraph and section.

---

[41]*See* Judicial Council Decision 330.

4. The Illinois corporation shall be liable for and shall execute and satisfy all legal obligations of each of the four corporations named in ¶ 1818.1, but neither it nor the board shall have or be under any obligation to account for principal and income to any such other corporation or to otherwise report to any of them.

¶ **1820.** Pursuant to the Declaration of Union of The Evangelical United Brethren Church and The Methodist Church and under the authority of ¶¶ 939, 950-954 of the Book of Discipline of The United Methodist Church, 1968, The Otterbein Press, an Ohio corporation, and The Evangelical Press, a Pennsylvania corporation, have been legally dissolved and their charters have been surrendered. The proceeds of their corporate assets have been and are being administered pursuant to said Disciplinary provisions.

¶ **1821.** *Officers of the Corporations.*—The officers of each corporation under the direction of the board shall be elected annually in accordance with its charter and bylaws.

¶ **1822.** The executive officer (publisher) elected pursuant to ¶ 1814 shall also be elected the president of each corporation under the direction of the board.

¶ **1823.** The board shall fix the salaries of the officers of the corporations and shall report the same quadrennially to the General Conference.

¶ **1824.** The board shall require the president to submit quarterly to the executive committee and annually to the board written reports of the financial condition and operating results of The United Methodist Publishing House.

¶ **1825.** The president (publisher) and the board shall have authority to extend the activities of The United Methodist Publishing House in such manner as they may judge to be for the best interests of the Church.

¶ **1826.** The board shall require the president and other corporate officers to give bond conditioned on the faithful discharge of their respective duties. It also shall authorize the execution of a blanket bond covering all staff personnel whose responsibilities justify such coverage. The amount of the bonds shall be fixed by the board, and the bonds shall be subject to the approval of the board. The premiums shall be paid by The

United Methodist Publishing House, and the chairperson of the board shall be the custodian of the bonds.

¶ **1827.** The board shall have power to suspend, after hearing, and to remove, after hearing, the president or any of the officers for misconduct or failure to perform the duties of their offices.

¶ **1828.** *Book Editor.*—The board shall elect annually a **book editor** who shall be designated editorial director of general publishing. The book editor shall have joint responsibility with the publisher for approving manuscripts considered for publication. The book editor shall edit or supervise the editing of all books and materials of our publication. In the case of church school publications and official forms and records, the book editor shall collaborate with the editor of church school publications and the Committee on Official Forms and Records whenever such collaboration is mutually desirable and beneficial. The book editor shall perform such other editorial duties as may be required by the board.

¶ **1829.** The board, at its discretion, may continue the publication of the periodical *Religion in Life,* with the book editor responsible for its editorial content.

¶ **1830.** The board shall fix the salary of the book editor.

¶ **1831.** The board shall have power to suspend or remove, after hearing, the book editor for misconduct or failure to perform the duties of the office.

¶ **1832.** *Church School Publications.*—There shall be an **editor of church school publications,** elected as set forth in ¶ 1326.

¶ **1833.** The editor of church school publications shall be responsible for the preparation of all curriculum materials as set forth in ¶ 1323.

¶ **1834.** The curriculum of the church school shall be determined by the Curriculum Resources Committee, which shall include in its membership the vice-president in charge of publishing, and the publisher, as set forth in ¶ 1330.

¶ **1835.** The board shall fix the salary of the editor of church school publications and shall have full financial responsibility for all expenses connected with this work.

¶ **1836.** The publications of the Curriculum Resources Committee shall be manufactured, published, and distributed through The United Methodist Publishing House. In matters involving financial responsibility the final determination in every case shall lie with the board. After consultation with the publisher, the editor of church school publications shall prepare a complete budget for this work, including salaries of assistants and office secretaries and travel, etc., to be effective when approved by the board, and shall direct its operation from year to year.

¶ **1837.** There shall be one complete, coordinated system of literature published by the board for the entire United Methodist Church. This literature is to be of such type and variety as to meet the needs of all groups of our people.

¶ **1838.** The board and the publisher shall have authority to decline to publish any item of literature when in their judgment the cost would be greater than should be borne by The United Methodist Publishing House.

¶ **1839.** The editor of church school publications (¶ 1326) and a member of the General Board of Discipleship designated by the president shall have the right to sit with the board and shall have the privilege of the floor without vote for the consideration of matters pertaining to their joint interests.

¶ **1840.** The United Methodist Publishing House shall explore and engage in cooperative publication of United Methodist church school curriculum resources wherever both The United Methodist Publishing House and the Curriculum Resources Committee of the General Board of Discipleship find this to be practicable and in harmony with related editorial and publishing policies.

¶ **1841.** *Printing for Church Agencies.*—It is recommended that the general agencies and institutions of The United Methodist Church have all their printing done by The United Methodist Publishing House (¶¶ 626, 905.4c).

¶ **1842.** *Distributing for Church Agencies.*—It is recommended that all general agencies of The United Methodist Church use the distribution system of The United Methodist Publishing House for distribution of resources, materials, and supplies needed for use in the local church.

¶ **1843.** *Real Estate and Buildings.*—The United Methodist Publishing House shall not buy, sell, or exchange any real estate except by order of the General Conference or, between sessions of the General Conference, by a two-thirds vote of all the members of the board; nor shall the board authorize any new buildings or make any improvements, alterations, or repairs to existing buildings to cost in excess of $500,000 except by order of the General Conference or, between sessions of the General Conference, by a two-thirds vote of all members of the board. In either case such vote shall be taken at a regular or called meeting of the board, and if at a called meeting, the purpose of this meeting shall have been stated in the call.

¶ **1844.** The erection of a new building or the improvement, alteration, or repair of an existing building involving an expenditure of not more than $500,000 may be authorized by the vote of a majority of the executive committee. These provisions shall not prevent the making of investments on mortgage security or the protection of the same or the collection of claims and adjustments. (*See* ¶ 1843 above, for additional requirements and restrictions.)

Section XII. Standing General Commission on Archives and History.

¶ **1901.** *Name.*—The name of the official historical agency of The United Methodist Church shall be the **Standing General Commission on Archives and History.**

¶ **1902.** *Incorporation.*—The Standing General Commission on Archives and History shall be incorporated under the laws of whatever state the commission may determine.

¶ **1903.** *Purpose.*—1. The purpose of the commission shall be to gather, preserve, hold title to, and disseminate materials on the history of The United Methodist Church and its antecedents. It shall cooperate with other bodies, especially the World Methodist Historical Society and the World Methodist Council. It shall do any and all things necessary to promote and care for the historical interest of The United Methodist Church. It shall maintain archives and libraries in which shall be preserved historical records and materials of every kind relating to The United Methodist Church. It shall provide guidance for the creation and preservation of archives and records at all levels of The United Methodist Church.

2. The commission shall be accountable to the General Council on Ministries for all programmatic assignments.

3. The commission shall have responsibility for and supervision of its archives and historical libraries and other depositories of similar character, if any, established by The United Methodist Church.

¶ **1904.** *Membership of the Standing General Commission.*— 1. The commission shall be constituted quadrennially, and its members and all officers elected by it shall hold office until their successors have been chosen. The commission may fill interim vacancies during a quadrennium where not otherwise provided by the Discipline.

2. The commission shall be composed of thirty members in the following manner: thirteen members shall be elected by the General Conference on nomination of the Council of Bishops, which number would include at least two women, one young adult, one youth, and two persons from racial and ethnic minorities; two bishops, one of whom shall be the secretary of the Council of Bishops; the secretary of the General Conference; five presidents of the Jurisdictional Commissions on Archives and History or a person designated by the jurisdictional College of Bishops where no commission exists; and nine additional members elected by the general commission. Not less than ten of the total shall be women; not less than four of the members should be racial and ethnic minorities including one each of the following: Pacific and Asian American, Black American, Hispanic American, and Native American.

¶ **1905.** *Meetings.*—The commission shall meet annually at such time and place as it may determine, subject to the provisions of the act of incorporation. The commission may hold special meetings on the call of the president. A majority of the members of the commission shall constitute a quorum.

¶ **1906.** *Officers.*—The commission shall elect from its membership a president, vice-president, secretary, and such other officers as may be needed. The president shall be a bishop. The officers shall perform the duties usually incident to their positions.

¶ **1907.** *Staff.*—The commission shall elect a **general secretary** and such other staff officers as may be needed. The executive secretary shall be the executive and administrative officer and shall carry on the work of the commission, keep the records and minutes, serve as editor of official publications of the commission, supervise the depositories, make an annual report to the commission, and furnish such reports as are required to the General Conference and General Conference agencies. The general secretary shall attend meetings of the commission and the executive committee and have the privilege of the floor without vote. Archivists, curators, and librarians employed by the commission shall be responsible to the general secretary. They shall attend meetings of the commission and the executive committee when it is deemed necessary by the general secretary. When in attendance, they shall have the privilege of the floor without vote.

¶ **1908.** *Executive Committee.*—There shall be an **executive committee,** composed of the president, vice-president, secretary, and three other members of the commission elected by it. The executive committee shall perform the duties and exercise the authority of the commission between meetings. Its minutes shall be submitted to the commission for approval. The executive committee and the commission may vote on any matter by mail. Mail polls shall be directed by the general secretary, who shall state clearly the propositions to be voted on and announce the results to all the members.

¶ **1909.** *Finances.*—The commission shall be financed by appropriations of the General Conference, the sale of literature and historical materials, subscriptions to the commission's official publications, dues from associate members, and gifts, grants, and bequests of interested individuals and organizations.

¶ **1910.** *Historical Society.*—1. The standing general commission may organize a **Historical Society** of The United Methodist Church and encourage individuals to become members of it for the purpose of promoting interest in the study and preservation of the history of The United Methodist Church and its antecedents. They shall be encouraged to cooperate with the Annual Conference, Jurisdictional Conference, and General Commissions on Archives and History in the promotion of the historical interests of the Church. The officers of the commission shall be the officers of the Historical Society.

2. Individuals may become members of the Historical Society by paying such dues as the commission may direct, in return for which they shall receive such commission publications as are deemed suitable.

3. Once each quadrennium the commission may hold a **Historical Convocation,** to which may be invited members of the Historical Society, members of Jurisdictional and Annual Conference historical organizations, heads of departments of history in the universities, colleges, and seminaries of The United Methodist Church, and such other persons as may be interested.

¶ **1911.** 1. *Archival Definitions.—a)* **Archives,** as distinguished from libraries, house not primarily books, but documentary record material.

b) **Documentary record material** shall mean all documents, minutes, journals, diaries, reports, pamphlets, letters, papers, manuscripts, maps, photographs, books, audio-visuals, sound recordings, magnetic or other tapes, electronic data processing records, artifacts, or any other documentary material, regardless of physical form or characteristics, made or received pursuant to any provisions of the Discipline in connection with the transaction of church business by any general agency of The United Methodist Church or of any of its constituent predecessors.

c) **General agency** of The United Methodist Church or of its constituent predecessors shall, in turn, mean and include every church office, church officer or official (elected or appointed), including bishop, institution, board, commission, bureau, council, or conference at the national level.

2. *Custodianship of records.—*The church official in charge of an office having documentary record material shall be the custodian thereof, unless otherwise provided.

3. *Procedures.—a)* The standing general commission shall establish a central archives of The United Methodist Church and such regional archives and record centers as in its judgment may be needed.

b) The bishops, General Conference officers, general boards, commissions, committees, and agencies of The United Methodist Church shall deposit official minutes or journals, or copies of the same, in the archives quadrennially and shall transfer correspondence, records, papers, and other archival materials described above from their offices when they no longer have operational usefulness. No records shall be destroyed until a disposal schedule has been agreed upon by the General Commission on Archives and History and the agency. When the custodian of any official documentary record material of a general agency certifies to the Standing General Commission on Archives and History that such records have no further use or value for official and administrative purposes and when the commission certifies that such records appear to have no further use or value for research or reference, then such records may be destroyed or otherwise disposed of by the agency or official having custody of them. A record of such certification and authorization shall be entered in the minutes or records of both the commission and the agency. The Standing General Commission on Archives and History is hereby authorized and empowered to make such provisions as may be necessary and proper to carry this paragraph into effect.

c) The commission shall have the right to examine the condition of documentary record material and shall, subject to the availability of staff and funds, give advice and assistance to church officials and agencies in regard to preserving and disposing of documentary record material in their custody. Officials of general agencies shall assist the commission in the preparation of an inventory of records in their custody. To this inventory shall be attached a schedule, approved by the head of the agency having custody of the records and the commission, establishing a time period for the retention and disposal of each series of records. So long as such approved schedule remains in effect, destruction or disposal of documentary record material in accordance with its provisions shall be deemed to have met the requirements of ¶ 1911.3*b*.

d) The commission is authorized and directed to conduct a program of inventorying, repairing, and microfilming among all general agencies of The United Methodist Church for security purposes that documentary record material which the commission determines has permanent value and of providing safe storage for microfilm copies of such material. Subject to the availability of funds, such program may be extended to material of permanent value of all agencies of The United Methodist Church.

historic shrines and landmarks, according to the criteria which it shall prepare and which shall be compatible with the Discipline of The United Methodist Church. The commission shall further be responsible for recommending to the General Conference the redesignation or reclassification of the designated national historic shrines and national historic landmarks as such action may be appropriate in keeping with such criteria.

2. *a) National Historic Shrines.*—To qualify for designation as a **national historic shrine** of The United Methodist Church, a building must have been linked with significant events and outstanding personalities in the origin and development of The United Methodist Church or its antecedents so as to have distinctive historic interest and value for the denomination as a whole, as contrasted with local or regional historic significance.

b) Present National Historic Shrines.—The national historic shrines of The United Methodist Church are: Acuff's Chapel, state highway 126 between Blountsville and Kingsport, TN; Albright Memorial Chapel, Kleinfeltersville, PA; Barratt's Chapel, near Frederica, DE; Edward Cox House near Bluff City, TN; Green Hill House, Louisburg, NC; John Street Church, New York City; Old McKendree Chapel, Jackson, MO; Old Otterbein Church, Baltimore, MD; Rehobeth Church, near Union, WV; St. George's Church, Philadelphia; St. Simon's Island, Brunswick, GA; Cemetery and Site of Old Stone Church, Leesburg, VA; Robert Strawbridge's Log House, near New Windsor, MD; Wyandot Indian Mission, Upper Sandusky, OH; Whitaker's Chapel, near Enfield, Halifax County, NC; the town of Oxford, GA; and Peter Cartwright United Methodist Church, Pleasant Plains, IL.

3. *a) National Historic Landmarks.*—Locations which have little remaining in the way of structure or monuments but which otherwise qualify as national historic shrines may be designated as **national historic landmarks.**

b) Present National Historic Landmarks.—The national historic landmarks of The United Methodist Church are: the sites of the Lovely Lane Chapel, Baltimore, MD; Brooklyn Methodist Hospital, Brooklyn, NY; McMahan's Chapel, Bronson, TX; and John Wesley's American Parish, Savannah, GA.

4. *Sites.*—Jurisdictional and Annual Conferences may des-

ignate as **historic sites** buildings and locations within their regions which have been related to significant events and important personalities in the origin and development of The United Methodist Church or its antecedents. The president of the Commission on Archives and History of the conference making such a designation shall advise the general commission, which shall in turn keep a register of all historic sites.

Section XIII. Standing General Commission on Christian Unity and Interreligious Concerns.

¶ **2001.** *Name.*—The name of this agency shall be the **Standing General Commission on Christian Unity and Interreligious Concerns.**

¶ **2002.** *Purpose.*—The purpose of the Standing General Commission on Christian Unity and Interreligious Concerns shall be to fulfill two major responsibilities.

1. To advocate and work toward the full reception of the gift of Christian unity in every aspect of the church's life and to foster approaches to ministry and mission which more fully reflect the oneness of Christ's Church in the human community.

2. To advocate and work for the establishment and strengthening of relationships with other living faith communities, to further dialogue with persons of other faiths, cultures, and ideologies, and to work toward the unity of humankind.

¶ **2003.** *Responsibilities.*—The responsibilities of the Standing General Commission on Christian Unity and Interreligious Concerns shall be:

1. To enable ecumenical and interreligious understanding and experience among all United Methodists, including assistance to all United Methodist agencies.

2. To provide resources and counsel to conference Commissions or Committees on Christian Unity and Interreligious Concerns and to local church leadership.

3. To develop or assist in the development of resources and other educational materials which will stimulate understanding and experience in ecumenical and interreligious relationships.

4. To develop and interpret the primary relationships of The United Methodist Church to ecumenical and interreligious organizations (such as the World Council of Churches, regional

councils of churches, the National Council of Churches of Christ in the U.S.A., the World Methodist Council, and the Consultation on Church Union), to United Churches which include a former United Methodist–related church in the U.S.A., to churches with which a concordat of exchange of voting delegates has been established by General Conference.

5. To pursue or initiate relationships and conversations with other Christian churches on possible church unions and in general bilateral or multilateral dialogues.

6. To develop and engage in dialogue, cooperation, and unity discussions with the historic members of the Methodist denominational family in the United States; namely, the African Methodist Episcopal, the African Methodist Episcopal Zion, and the Christian Methodist Episcopal churches, and all those Wesleyan bodies in the United States related to the World Methodist Council.

7. To report to General Conference on Christian unity and interreligious developments and to make recommendations on any specific proposals for church union.

8. To pursue or initiate relationships and conversations with the Jewish and other religious and ideological communities in dialogue and in cooperative efforts.

9. To consider resolutions, pronouncements, and actions of ecumenical and interreligious councils and agencies, to be responsible for appropriate United Methodist responses, and to initiate or to channel counsel to ecumenical and interreligious bodies.

10. To receive, monitor, and coordinate all requests for funds from ecumenical and interreligious bodies to all United Methodist agencies and to act on requests for funding from its own cognate units in ecumenical bodies.

11. To advocate for adequate funding for the core budgets of the major ecumenical and interreligious agencies.

12. To provide from own budget where possible supplementary funding for cognate units in ecumenical agencies and ad hoc ecumenical and interreligious enterprises.

13. To recommend to the General Council on Finance and Administration the total goal and constituent allocations of the Interdenominational Cooperation Fund for its review and

recommendation for action by General Conference and to recommend to the General Council on Finance and Administration annual adjustments in payments from the fund to specific recipients from the fund.

14. To receive and administer funds allocated to it through the General Conference or the General Council on Finance and Administration and other sources.

15. To review the ecumenical and interreligious funding and commitments of all United Methodist boards and agencies; to report findings and to make recommendations to those boards and agencies and to the General Council on Ministries.

16. To report annually to the Council of Bishops on aspects of Christian units and interreligious developments, issues, and trends.

17. To channel and recommend to the Council of Bishops qualified United Methodists for service as representatives on ecumenical councils or agencies and to special meeting or assemblies, and to name such representatives to councils, agencies, or assemblies not named by the Council of Bishops.

18. To work as partners with agencies of The United Methodist Church on matters of mutual concern.

19. To care for other matters as may be deemed necessary by the commission or requested by the General Conference, the Council of Bishops (*see* ¶ 2407), or the General Council on Ministries.

¶ **2004.** *Authorities and Powers.*—The Standing General Commission on Christian Unity and Interreligious Concerns shall have the authority and power to fulfill all the responsibilities noted in ¶ 2003 and to fulfill other functions that may be requested of it by the Council of Bishops, the General Council on Ministries, or the General Council on Finance and Administration and General Conference. (*See* ¶ 2407 on relationships with the Council of Bishops.)

¶ **2005.** *Organization.*—The Standing General Commission on Christian Unity and Interreligious Concerns shall be organized quadrennially in conformity with ¶¶ 805-810. In addition:

1. The commission shall elect from its membership a chairperson and other officers as it may determine.

2. There shall be an executive committee of the commission with powers as determined by the commission. It shall be composed of the chairperson of the commission, other officers of the commission, and additional elected directors for a total voting membership of not less than eight or more than ten persons.

3. The general secretary shall be a member of the commission executive committee without vote.

4. The general secretary, in relationships with other churches, shall be referred to as the Ecumenical Staff Officer for The United Methodist Church, in conformity with common practice in other churches.

5. The commission shall meet annually and at such other times as it shall deem necessary. A majority of the members of the commission shall constitute a quorum.

6. The commission shall elect a general secretary and such other staff as may be required and for which budget is ensured.

7. Additional staff required and for which budget is ensured shall be nominated by the general secretary for confirmation by the commission.

8. The responsibilities of the general secretary are to be defined by the commission.

¶ 2006. 1. The Standing General Commission on Christian Unity and Interreligious Concerns shall be composed of thirty directors as follows: three bishops appointed by the Council of Bishops; three persons from each jurisdiction, elected by the Jurisdictional Conferences; twelve other directors selected by the elected commission at the organizational meeting.

2. All directors shall be selected with a view to balances envisioned in ¶ 805 and may well include persons from administration or faculty of United Methodist seminaries and undergraduate colleges, campus ministers, seminarians, conference Commissions on Christian Unity and Interreligious Concerns chairpersons, delegates to the World and National Councils of Churches and the Consultation on Church Union, and staff of regional and local cooperative agencies who are United Methodists.

3. The standing general commission shall be authorized to fill vacancies in its membership during the quadrennium according to the three categories of membership: (a) by

requesting appointment by the Council of Bishops; *(b)* by requesting replacement appointment by the appropriate Jurisdictional College of Bishops (*see* ¶ 812); and *(c)* by its own nomination and election process for the other directors.

4. All directors shall be chosen with a view to any stipulation of balances adopted by the 1980 General Conference.

¶ **2007.** *Joint Commission on Cooperation and Counsel.*—In continuation of the historical relationship between The United Methodist Church and the Christian Methodist Episcopal Church, there shall be a Joint Commission on Cooperation and Counsel. Its purpose shall be to foster cooperation at all levels and in all places between these two churches and to recommend and encourage those plans and services which may be undertaken better together than separately. It shall promote joint plans with and through established agencies of the two cooperating churches.

The commission shall be composed of an agreed upon number of members, such appointments to take account of the total life of the Church but giving major emphasis to those agencies which provide a channel of common concern and cooperative endeavor. The members from The United Methodist Church shall be named by the Standing General Commission on Christian Unity and Interreligious Concerns and shall include representatives from other United Methodist agencies as appropriate.

The commission shall elect such officers as it deems necessary and shall meet on call of its officers. The expenses shall be borne by the agencies designated by each denomination.

Section XIV. Standing General Commission on Religion and Race.

¶ **2101.** *Name.*—There shall be a **Standing General Commission on Religion and Race.**

1. *Amenability and Accountability.*—The standing general commission shall be amenable to the General Conference of the United Methodist Church. Between sessions of the General Conference, the commission shall be accountable to the General Council on Ministries by reporting and interpreting activities designed to fulfill the purpose of the commission and by

cooperating with the Council in the fulfillment of its legislated responsibilities.

¶ **2102.** *Purpose.*—The primary purpose of the Standing General Commission on Religion and Race shall be to challenge The United Methodist Church, including its general agencies, its institutions, and its connectional structures, to a full and equal participation of the racial and ethnic minority constituency in the total life and mission of the Church through advocacy and by reviewing and monitoring the practices of the entire church so as to further ensure racial inclusiveness.

¶ **2103.** *Membership.*—The total membership of the commission shall be forty-eight, composed of two bishops appointed by the Council of Bishops, six persons elected by each jurisdiction from the Annual Conference nominations, and sixteen additional members to be elected by the commission. It is recommended that at least two of the six persons elected by each Jurisdictional Conference be Black, at least two of other racial or ethnic minority groups, at least two women, and at least one under the age of thirty. Further, it is recommended that of the members at large, four members shall be elected from each of the four racial and ethnic minority groups (Asian American, Black American, Hispanic American, and Native American). Of the sixteen additional members there shall be two young adults between the ages of nineteen and thirty-one and two youth under nineteen.[42]

¶ **2104.** *Vacancies.*—Vacancies in the commission membership shall be filled by the procedure defined in ¶ 812 of the General Provisions.

¶ **2105.** *Officers.*—The Standing General Commission on Religion and Race shall elect as its officers a president, vice-president, a secretary, and such other officers as it shall deem necessary.

¶ **2106.** *Staff.*—The Standing General Commission on Religion and Race shall nominate a general secretary for election by the General Council on Ministries. The commission shall select by whatever process it chooses the additional staff needed to assist the general secretary in carrying out the commission's responsibilities.

---

[42]*See* Decision 5, Interim Judicial Council.

¶ **2107.** *Finances.*—The Council on Finance and Administration shall make provision for the support of the work of the commission, including provision for a general secretary and associated staff and an office for the commission.

¶ **2108.** *Responsibilities.*—The standing general commission will assume general church responsibility for such matters as:

1. Coordinating the denominational concern and providing a channel of assistance to ensure that ethnic and racial minority group members of The United Methodist Church will have equal opportunities for service, representation, and voice on every level of the Church's life and ministry.

2. Reviewing, evaluating, and assisting agencies of the Church as they seek to develop programs and policies of racial inclusiveness.

3. Reviewing, evaluating, and assisting Annual Conferences and their appointive Cabinets as they seek to develop appointments, programs, and policies for racial and ethnic minority inclusiveness.

4. Providing a channel of assistance to racial and ethnic minority groups as they seek to develop programs of empowerment and ministry to their communities.

5. Relating to and coordinating the concerns of the racial and ethnic minority groups as they relate to minority group empowerment and ministry within the Church.

6. Reviewing, investigating, and conducting hearings where necessary in responding to charges of alleged violation of the Church's policy of racial and ethnic inclusiveness which have not been satisfactorily resolved in the Annual Conference or general agency. All involved parties shall meet with the Standing General Commission on Religion and Race, or its designated representatives, presenting their briefs, arguments, and evidence related to said charges. The commission will submit its findings and recommendations to the appropriate parties, conferences, and the general agencies.

7. Administering the Minority Group Self-Determination Fund.

8. Providing resources for the local church work area on religion and race.

9. Counseling local churches that are seeking to establish

multiracial fellowships and encouraging and supporting local churches in maintaining a Christian ministry in racially changing neighborhoods.

10. Coordinating the denominational support and cooperation with various movements for racial and social justice, in consultation with the General Board of Church and Society, as appropriate.

11. Providing opportunities for multiracial and interethnic dialogue and meetings throughout the Church.

12. Working directly with the Council of Bishops and the related Annual Conferences to plan workshops, seminars, and consultations on racism.

13. Providing programs of sensitization and education at every level of the Church's life, on the nature and meaning of racism—attitudinal, behavioral, and institutional.

14. Relating to and assisting the Annual Conference Commission on Religion and Race.

15. Supervising the administration of the Temporary General Aid Fund, recommending such adjustments from time to time as may be necessary under legislation to achieve the intended purpose.

16. Developing leadership among racial and ethnic minority groups for the total ministry in the life of the Church.

17. Facilitating the delivery of program services and information to racial and ethnic minority local churches.

18. Reporting to the General Conference on the role of racial and ethnic minority groups in The United Methodist Church and on the progress toward racial inclusiveness.

Section XV. Standing General Commission on the Status and Role of Women.

¶ 2201. *Name.*—There shall be a **Standing General Commission on the Status and Role of Women** in The United Methodist Church.

¶ 2202. *Purpose.*—The primary purpose of the Standing General Commission on the Status and Role of Women shall be to challenge The United Methodist Church, including its general agencies, institutions, and connectional structures, to a continuing commitment to the full and equal responsibility and participation of women in the total life and mission of the Church, sharing fully in the power and in the policy making at all levels of the Church's life.

Such commitment will confirm anew recognition of the fact that The United Methodist Church is part of the Universal Church, rooted in the liberating message of Jesus Christ, that recognizes every person, woman or man, as a full and equal part of God's human family.

The standing general commission shall function as an advocate with and on behalf of women individually and collectively within The United Methodist Church; as a catalyst for the initiation of creative methods to redress inequities of the past and to prevent further inequities against women within The United Methodist Church; and as a monitor to ensure inclusiveness in the programmatic and administrative functioning of The United Methodist Church.

¶ **2203.** *Responsibility.*—The standing general commission shall be charged with the responsibility of fostering an awareness of issues, problems, and concerns related to the status and role of women, with special reference to their full participation in the total life of the Church at least commensurate with the total membership of women in The United Methodist Church.

1. In the fulfillment of its mandate, this commission shall have the authority to initiate and utilize such channels, develop such plans and strategies, and assign staff as may be required in the implementation of the following primary needs across The United Methodist Church: leadership enablement, resources and communication, affirmative action and advocacy roles, and interagency coordination.

Such plans and strategies related to these needs shall be directed toward the elimination of sexism in all its manifestations from the total life of The United Methodist Church, including general agencies as well as the various connectional channels and structures that reach the local church. The commission shall work with the respective agencies as needs may determine in achieving and safeguarding representation and participation of women, including racial and ethnic minorities.

2. The commission through its various research and monitoring processes shall continue to gather data, make

recommendations, and suggest guidelines for action as appropriate to eradicate discriminatory policies and practices in any form or discriminatory language and images wherever found in documents, pronouncements, publications, and general resources.

3. The commission shall stimulate ongoing evaluation procedures and receive progress reports toward the end of effecting the guidelines in §2 above in all responsible bodies of the Church.

4. The commission shall establish and maintain a working relationship with Annual Conference commissions, taking into account the objectives/guidelines for conferences in ¶ 730, and seeking to develop and strengthen the leadership of the conference for the realization of these objectives within the general context of the responsibilities of the general commission (¶ 2203.1).

5. The commission shall recommend plans and curricula for new understanding of theology and biblical history affecting the status of women.

6. The commission shall create needed policies and recommendations and program for immediate and long-range implementation related to the enhancement of the role of women in professional and voluntary leadership in the Church.

7. The commission shall serve in an advocacy role to ensure openness and receptivity in matters related to women's role in the Church's life, with particular attention to the contributions of clergy and lay professional women, racial and ethnic minority women, and those experiencing changing life styles.

8. The commission shall generate active concern and give full support toward immediate efforts in the fulfillment of the following directive: Councils, boards, commissions, committees, personnel recruitment agencies, seminaries, and other related institutions are directed to establish guidelines and policies for specific recruitment, training, and full utilization of women in total employment, which includes but is not limited to pastoral and related ministries, health and welfare ministries, and faculties and staffs of seminaries and other educational institutions.

¶ **2204.** *Membership.*—The policies, plans, and administration of the work of the standing general commission shall be determined by its membership which shall be composed in accord with the following guidelines:

1. The basic membership shall be nominated and elected by the Jurisdictional Conferences, assuring that the pluralism and diversity of the Church's membership is reflected in the representation of racial and ethnic minorities and various age categories. Each jurisdiction shall elect six persons for membership: two laywomen, two laymen, one clergywoman, and one clergyman. Of the persons elected by each Jurisdictional Conference, at least one should be from a racial and ethnic minority group and at least one shall be under thirty-one years of age at the time of election.

2. There shall be thirteen additional members elected by the standing general commission, in accord with the provisions of ¶ 805. The election of the additional members shall take into account the need to provide adequate representation of racial and ethnic minority groups and of the various age categories, and to include persons of special competence. The additional membership shall assure that the total membership shall maintain the one-third laymen, one-third laywomen, one-third clergy balance as well as majority membership of women.

3. There shall be two laywomen and one clergywoman named by the Women's Division from its members or staff to serve as ex officio members with vote.

4. There shall be two bishops named by the Council of Bishops.

5. In the total membership:

a) Persons over sixty-five years of age shall be included.

b) There should be no less than four persons (two women and two men) from each of these four racial and ethnic minority groups: Pacific and Asian Americans, Black Americans, Hispanic Americans, and Native Americans.

c) It is recommended that there be at least one member who is a diaconal minister.

6. The standing general commission shall be authorized to fill vacancies in its membership during the quadrennium.

¶ **2205.** *Officers.*—The president of the standing general commission shall be a woman elected by the total commission from its membership. Other officers shall be elected as the commission determines.

¶ **2206.** *Meetings.*—The standing general commission shall meet annually with such additional meetings as needs demand.

¶ **2207.** *Funding.*—The funds for carrying out the standing general commission's purpose shall be authorized by the General Conference.

¶ **2208.** *Staff.*—The standing general commission shall nominate for election by the General Council on Ministries **general secretariat** or **general secretary** who shall provide executive, administrative, and program staff leadership. The commission shall elect such other staff members as needs require within the General Conference mandates and the authority vested in the commission to develop policies and programs directed toward the realization of its purpose.

¶ **2209.** *Relationships.*—In order to fulfill its responsibilities and the directives of the General Conference, the standing general commission shall work with the Council of Bishops, the general agencies, institutions, and other appropriate structures and channels at all levels of the Church.

Section XVI. Commission on Central Conference Affairs.

¶ **2301.** *Commission on Central Conference Affairs.*—Recognizing the difference in conditions that exist in various areas of the world and the changes taking place in those areas, there shall be a **Commission on Central Conference Affairs** to study the structure and supervision of The United Methodist Church in its work outside the United States and its territories and its relationships to other church bodies. The commission shall prepare such recommendations as it considers necessary for presentation directly to the General Conference. All resolutions and petitions related to Central Conferences presented to the General Conference shall be referred to the commission for consideration and the commission shall report its recommendations directly to the General Conference.

The commission shall be composed of one bishop, one ordained minister, and one lay person from each jurisdiction who are delegates to the General Conference and named by the Council of Bishops; one bishop, one minister, and one lay person from each Central Conference who are delegates to the General Conference and named by the Council of Bishops; one bishop, one ordained minister, and one lay person who are elected members of the World Division of the Board of Global Ministries and named by the Council of Bishops. Special attention shall be given to the inclusion of women, clergy and lay.

The chairperson of the commission shall be a bishop.

The commission shall meet at the seat of the General Conference.

The episcopal members of the commission shall act as the executive committee between sessions of the General Conference.

Section XVII. Interdenominational Agencies.

¶ **2401.** The United Methodist Church is a member of the **World Methodist Council,** its predecessor Methodist and Evangelical United Brethren churches having been charter members of such body. The members of the section representing The United Methodist Church shall be nominated by the Council of Bishops, due regard being given to geographical representation. Financial support of the World Methodist Council shall be channeled through the Central Treasury, and shall be directed by the Council on Finance and Administration.

2. Each affiliated autonomous church and each affiliated united church which is a member of the World Methodist Council shall be entitled to send delegates as proposed in ¶ 650.3, respectively, to the World Methodist Council and to receive from the General Administration Fund the expense of travel and per diem allowances; *provided* that they shall elect to receive travel and per diem allowances for the meetings of the World Methodist Council instead of the General Conference of The United Methodist Church. No affiliated autonomous church or affiliated united church shall be entitled to send delegations at the expense of the General Administration Fund to both the World Methodist Council and the General Conference.

¶ **2402.** 1. The United Methodist Church is a member of the **National Council of the Churches of Christ in the United States of America,** its predecessor Methodist and Evangelical United Brethren churches having been charter members of such body. It has borne its proportionate share of financial support, and through the Interdenominational Cooperation Fund is authorized and directed to continue its support. (*See* ¶ 917.)

2. The United Methodist representatives and proxies to the National Council of Church of Christ in the U.S.A. Governing Board shall be selected by the Council of Bishops from nominations reviewed by the Standing General Commission on Christian Unity and Interreligious Concerns. Recommendations of names for consideration may be sent by Annual Conferences to the Jurisdictional Conferences. Each Jurisdictional Conference shall provide to the Standing General Commission on Christian Unity and Interreligious Concerns a panel of twelve names with biographical data from which four persons will be chosen by the Council of Bishops as voting delegates. Persons named to the panel shall represent consideration of quotas and balances required both by The United Methodist Church and the National Council of Churches. The Jurisdictional Conference may report order of selection or priority, if it desires. Delegates and proxies are to be selected from the panel in any subsequent replacements during the quadrennium.

In addition to the delegates representing the jurisdictions, the Council of Bishops shall name five of their number, one of whom is to be the secretary of the Council of Bishops, as part of the clergy quota. Also, the Council of Bishops shall, from the nominations by the Standing General Commission on Christian Unity and Interreligious Concerns name as delegates the appropriate number of staff persons to complete the current complement of delegates allowed from The United Methodist Church.

The Council of Bishops shall approve a list of proxies for the jurisdictional representatives, drawing wherever possible on the original panel of names provided. The Council of Bishops shall provide proxies for any of their own representatives who are unable to attend a particular session of the Governing Board. The Standing General Commission on Christian Unity and Interreligious Concerns shall choose proxies for a particular session for the designated staff delegates on recommendations from the chief executive of the agency from which the official delegate comes.

Representatives from The United Methodist Church to various unit committees and working groups of the National Council of Churches, normally nominated by the National Council of Churches' units, shall be cleared and affirmed or substitutions made by the standing general commission, in consultation with the Council of Bishops wherever necessary or desired by either the council or the commission.

3. United Methodist support of the National Council of Churches shall be channeled through the Central Treasury, as shall be directed by the General Council on Finance and Administration, which shall give due credit for United Methodist gifts and contributions to this cause and shall include them in its annual financial report to the Church. The sources of income shall include: (*a*) the National Council of Churches' share of the Interdenominational Cooperation Fund, as determined by the General Conference, and (*b*) such payments by the general agencies of the Church as each agency may deem its responsibility and proportionate share in the cooperative program of the council. Personal, group, or local church gifts shall be included as a part of the ratio distribution of the Interdenominational Cooperation Fund.

¶ **2403.** 1. The United Methodist Church is a member of the **World Council of Churches,** its predecessor Methodist and Evangelical United Brethren churches having been charter members of such body. It should bear its proportionate share of financial support, and through the Interdenominational Cooperation Fund is authorized and directed to continue its support.

2. The representatives of The United Methodist Church to the Assembly and other agencies of the World Council of Churches shall be nominated by the Council of Bishops and elected by the General Conference, due regard being given to geographical representation. When representatives must be chosen or vacancies must be filled between sessions of the General Conference, the Council of Bishops is authorized and instructed to do so.

3. United Methodist support of the World Council of Churches shall be channeled through the Central Treasury, and shall be directed by the Council on Finance and Administration, which shall give due credit for United Methodist gifts and

contributions received by the World Council of Churches and shall include them in its annual financial report to the Church.

¶ **2404.** The United Methodist Church is a member of the Consultation on Church Union, its predecessor Methodist and Evangelical United Brethren Churches having been involved in its very beginnings and in all its committees and plenary consultations. It has borne its appropriate share of financial support, and through the Interdenominational Cooperation Fund is authorized and directed to continue its support.

¶ **2405.** To encourage the wider circulation of the Holy Scriptures throughout the world and to provide for the translation, printing, and distribution essential thereto, the **American Bible Society** shall be recognized as one of the general missionary agencies of The United Methodist Church, and the General Council on Finance and Administration shall make appropriate provisions for participating in its support.

¶ **2406. Religion in American Life, Incorporated,** is recognized as an interdenominational and interfaith agency through which The United Methodist Church may work to direct attention to church attendance and loyalty to the Christian faith. In endorsing this program the Council of Bishops shall nominate three members, to be elected by the Religion in American Life Board of Directors. Further, the General Council on Finance and Administration shall recommend to the General Conference for its action and determination the amount to be included as the United Methodist share in this participation.

¶ **2407.** In formal relations with other churches and/or ecclesial bodies, the Council of Bishops shall be the primary liaison for The United Methodist Church. The secretary of the Council of Bishops shall be responsible for these relationships and shall work in cooperation with the Standing General Commission on Christian Unity and Interreligious Concerns in the fulfillment of these functions.

Chapter Eight
CHURCH PROPERTY

Section I. All Titles—in Trust.

¶ **2501.** The United Methodist Church is organized as a **connectional structure,** and titles to all properties held at General, Jurisdictional, Annual, or District Conference levels, or by a local church or charge, or by an agency or institution of the Church, shall be held in trust for The United Methodist Church and subject to the provisions of its Discipline.

¶ **2502.** The word "Methodist" is not by our approval or consent to be used as, or as a part of, a trade name or trademark or as a part of the name of any business firm or organization, except by corporations or other business units created for the administration of work undertaken directly by The United Methodist Church.

¶ **2503.** *Trust Clauses in Deeds.*—1. Except in conveyances which require that the real property so conveyed shall revert to the grantor if and when its use as a place of divine worship has been terminated, all written instruments of conveyance by which premises are held or hereafter acquired for use as a place of divine worship for members of The United Methodist Church or for other church activities shall contain the following trust clause:

In trust, that said premises shall be used, kept, and maintained as a place of divine worship of the United Methodist ministry and members of The United Methodist Church; subject to the Discipline, usage, and ministerial appointments of said church as from time to time authorized and declared by the General Conference and by the Annual Conference within whose bounds the said premises are situated. This provision is solely for the benefit of the grantee, and the grantor reserves no right or interest in said premises.

2. All written instruments by which premises are held or hereafter acquired as a parsonage for the use and occupancy of the ministers of The United Methodist Church shall contain the following trust clause:

In trust, that such premises shall be held, kept, and maintained as a place of residence for the use and occupancy of the ministers of The United

Methodist Church who may from time to time be entitled to occupy the same by appointment; subject to the Discipline and usage of said church, as from time to time authorized and declared by the General Conference and by the Annual Conference within whose bounds the said premises are situated. This provision is solely for the benefit of the grantee, and the grantor reserves no right or interest in said premises.

3. In case the property so acquired is to be used for both a house of worship and a parsonage, the provisions of both trust clauses specified in §§1 and 2 above shall be inserted in the conveyance.

4. In case the property so acquired is not to be used exclusively for a place of worship, or a parsonage, or both, all written instruments by which such premises are held or hereafter acquired shall contain the following trust clause:

In trust, that said premises shall be kept, maintained, and disposed of for the benefit of The United Methodist Church and subject to the usages and the Discipline of The United Methodist Church. This provision is solely for the benefit of the grantee, and the grantor reserves no right or interest in said premises.

5. However, the absence of a trust clause stipulated in §§ 1, 2, 3, or 4 above in deeds and conveyances previously executed shall in no way exclude a local church or church agency from or relieve it of its connectional responsibilities to The United Methodist Church. Nor shall it absolve a local congregation or church agency or Board of Trustees of its responsibility and accountability to The United Methodist Church; *provided* that the intent and desires of the founders and/or the later congregations or Boards of Trustees are shown by any or all of the following indications: (*a*) the conveyance of the property to the trustees of a local church or agency or any predecessor to The United Methodist Church; (*b*) the use of the name, customs, and polity of any predecessor to The United Methodist Church in such a way as to be thus known to the community as a part of such denomination; (*c*) the acceptance of the pastorate of ministers appointed by a bishop or employed by the superintendent of the District or Annual Conference of any predecessor to The United Methodist Church.

¶ **2504.** Nothing in the Plan of Union at any time after the union is to be construed so as to require any existing local church of any predecessor denomination to The United Methodist Church to alienate or in any way to change the title to property contained in its deed or deeds at the time of union, and lapse of time or usage shall not affect said title or control. Title to all property of a local church, or charge, or agency of the Church shall be held subject to the provisions of the Discipline, whether title to the same is taken in the name of the local church trustees, or charge trustees, or in the name of a corporation organized for the purpose, or otherwise.

¶ **2505.** Subject to and in accordance with the laws of the state, province, or country, the governing body of any church unit or agency owning land in trust for The United Methodist Church as provided in this Discipline may lease said land for the production of oil, gas, coal, and other minerals, upon such terms as it may deem best; *provided,* however, that such production shall not interfere with the purpose for which said land is held. The moneys received from such leases as rentals, royalties, or otherwise, shall be used so far as practicable for the benefit of the church unit and for the promotion of the interests of The United Methodist Church. The lessee shall have no control over or responsibility for the payments made under such lease.

Section II. Compliance with Law.

¶ **2506.** All provisions of the Discipline relating to property, both real and personal, and relating to the formation and operation of any corporation, and relating to mergers, are conditioned upon their being in conformity with the local laws, and in the event of conflict therewith the local laws shall prevail; *provided,* however, that this requirement shall not be construed to give the consent of The United Methodist Church to deprivation of its property without due process of law or to the regulation of its affairs by state statute where such regulation violates the constitutional guarantee of freedom of religion and separation of Church and state or violates the right of the Church to maintain connectional structure; and *provided* further, that the services of worship of every local church of The United Methodist Church shall be open to all persons without regard to race, color, or national origin. "Local laws" shall be construed to mean the laws of the country, state, or other like political unit within the geographical bounds of which the church property is located.[1]

¶ **2507.** In order to secure the right of property, with the appurtenances thereof, of the churches and parsonages of The United Methodist Church, care shall be taken that all conveyances and deeds be drawn and executed in due conformity to the laws of the respective states, provinces, and countries in which the property is situated and also in due conformity to the laws of The United Methodist Church. Deeds shall be registered or recorded directly upon their execution.

Section III. Audits and Bonding of Church Officers.

¶ **2508.** All persons holding trust funds, securities, or moneys of any kind belonging to the General, Jurisdictional, Annual, or Provisional Annual Conferences or to organizations under the control of the General, Jurisdictional, Annual, or Provisional Annual Conferences shall be bonded by a reliable company in such good and sufficient sum as the conference may direct. The accounts of such persons shall be audited at least annually by a recognized public or certified public accountant. A report to an Annual Conference containing a financial statement which the Discipline requires to be audited shall not be approved until the audit is made and the financial statement is shown to be correct. Other parts of the report may be approved pending such audit.

Section IV. The Methodist Corporation.

¶ **2509.** 1. The Methodist Corporation as constituted at the present time shall be continued through December 31, 1976.

2. Beginning January 1, 1977, the General Council on Finance and Administration shall be the successor to all right, title, and interest in and to all assets of The Methodist Corporation for the following purposes: to hold, to manage and/or to liquidate such assets if and when it concludes that it is not in the best interest of The United Methodist Church to undertake a development of or further holding of the property.

---

[1]*See* Judicial Council Decisions 11, 315.

3. The members of the General Council on Finance and Administration shall constitute the Board of Directors of The Methodist Corporation, which shall be continued as a legal entity until such time as said board shall deem it desirable and convenient to liquidate the corporation, at which time it is empowered and authorized to take the necessary corporate action to effect the surrender of its charter or to merge, consolidate, or affiliate it into or with the General Council on Finance and Administration, a corporation.

4. Upon the liquidation of the assets of The Methodist Corporation, the resulting fund, after the payment and satisfaction of all debts, shall be conveyed, assigned, and transferred by the General Council on Finance and Administration to such religious, charitable, scientific, literary, or educational organization or organizations as the General Conference of The United Methodist Church shall direct. No funds or property shall be distributed among or inure to the benefit of any private shareholder or individual.

Section V. Annual Conference Property.[2]

¶ **2510.** 1. Each Annual Conference shall have a **Board of Trustees,** which shall be incorporated unless the conference is incorporated in its own name. In either case the board shall consist of twelve persons, who must be at least thirty years of age and of whom six shall be ministers in the effective relation in the conference and six shall be lay members in good standing of local churches within the bounds of the conference, and such persons shall be the directors of the corporation. They shall be elected by the conference for a term of three years, except as to the first board, one third of whom shall be elected for a term of one year, one third for a term of two years, and one third for a term of three years, and shall serve until their successors have been elected and qualified; *provided,* however, that existing incorporated trustees of any Annual Conference may continue unaffected by this subsection unless and until such charter is amended.

---

[2]For authority regarding property held by general agencies of the Church, *see* ¶¶ 907.1, .3.

2. The said corporation shall receive, collect, and hold in trust for the benefit of the Annual Conference any and all donations, bequests, and devises of any kind or character, real or personal, that may be given, devised, bequeathed, or conveyed to the said board or to the Annual Conference as such for any benevolent, charitable, or religious purpose, and shall administer the same and the income therefrom in accordance with the directions of the donor, trustor, or testator, and in the interest of the church, society, institution, or agency contemplated by such donor, trustor, or testator, under the direction of the Annual Conference. The board shall have the power to invest, reinvest, buy, sell, transfer, and convey any and all funds and properties which it may hold in trust, subject always to the terms of the legacy, devise, or donation; *provided,* however, that the foregoing shall not apply to churches, colleges, camps, conference grounds, orphanages, or incorporated boards. The conference Board of Trustees is encouraged to invest in institutions, companies, corporations, or funds that make a positive contribution toward the realization of the goals of the Social Principles of our Church. When the use to be made of any such donation, bequest, or devise is not otherwise designated, the same shall be used as directed by the Annual Conference. Funds committed to this board may be invested by it only in collateral that is amply secured and after such investments have been approved by the said board or its agency or committee charged with such investment, unless otherwise directed by the Annual Conference.[5]

3. The board may intervene and take all necessary legal steps to safeguard and protect the interests and rights of the Annual Conference anywhere and in all matters relating to property and rights to property whether arising by gift, devise, or otherwise, or where held in trust or established for the benefit of the Annual Conference or its membership.

4. It shall be the duty of the pastor within the bounds of whose charge any such gift, bequest, or devise is made to give prompt notice thereof to said board, which shall proceed to take such steps as are necessary and proper to conserve, protect, and administer the same; *provided,* however, that the board may

---

[5]*See* Judicial Council Decisions 135, 160, 190.

decline to receive or administer any such gift, devise, or bequest for any reason satisfactory to the board. It shall also be the duty of the pastor to report annually to the Board of Trustees of the Annual Conference a list of all property, including real, personal, or mixed, within the charge belonging to or which should be under the control or jurisdiction of the said board.

5. The board shall make to each session of the Annual Conference a full, true, and faithful report of its doings, of all funds, moneys, securities, and property held in trust by it, and of its receipts and disbursements during the conference year. The beneficiary of a fund held in trust by the board shall also be entitled to a report at least annually on the condition of such fund and on the transactions affecting it.

¶ **2511.** When authorized by two thirds of the Annual Conferences comprising an episcopal area, an **episcopal residence** for the resident bishop may be acquired, which shall be under the management and control of, and the title to which shall be held in trust by, the trustees of the Annual Conference within which the residence is located; and the purchase price and maintenance cost thereof shall be equitably distributed by the trustees among the several conferences in the area. Any such property so acquired and held shall not be sold or disposed of except with the consent of a majority of the conferences that participate in the ownership. Should an Annual Conference contribute to the purchase of an episcopal residence and later be transferred to an area not owning one, if it shall ask payment for its equity, such claim shall not be denied.[4]

¶ **2512.** The Board of Trustees shall meet at least annually and organize by electing a president, vice-president, secretary, and treasurer, whose duties shall be those usually pertaining to such offices. They shall be amenable to the Annual Conference. Vacancies shall be filled by the Annual Conference for the unexpired term.

Section VI. District Property.

¶ **2513.** 1. A **district parsonage** for the district superintendent may be acquired, when authorized by the Charge

---

[4]*See* Judicial Council Decision 194.

Conferences of two thirds of the charges in the district or when authorized by a two-thirds vote of the District Conference, subject to the advice and approval of the district Board of Church Location and Building as provided in ¶¶ 2514-2518.

2. The title of district property may be held in trust by a **district Board of Trustees,** of not fewer than three nor more than nine members having the same qualifications provided for trustees of local churches (¶ 2519), who shall be nominated by the district superintendent in consultation with the district nominating committee, if one exists, and elected by the District Conference. Where there is no District Conference, they may be elected by the district Board of Stewards or by the Annual Conference on nomination of the district superintendent. They shall be elected for a term of one year and serve until their successors shall have been elected, and shall report annually to the District Conference or Annual Conference. If the title to the district parsonage is not held by a district Board of Trustees, the same shall be held in trust by the trustees of the Annual Conference of which such district is a part, and such trustees shall report annually to the Annual Conference. Except as the laws of the state, territory, or country prescribe otherwise, district property held in trust by a district Board of Trustees may be mortgaged or sold and conveyed by them only by authority of the District Conference or Annual Conference, or if such property is held in trust by the trustees of the Annual Conference, it may be mortgaged or sold and conveyed by such trustees only by authority of the Annual Conference. The purchase price and maintenance cost of a district parsonage shall be equitably distributed among the charges of the district by the district Board of Stewards.

3. When district boundaries are changed by division, rearrangement, or consolidation so that a district parsonage purchased, owned, and maintained by one district is included within the bounds of another district, each such district shall be entitled to receive its just share of the then reasonable value of the parsonage in which it has invested funds; and the amount of such value and just share shall be determined by a committee of three persons, appointed by the bishop of the area, who shall not be residents of any of the said districts. The committee shall hear

589

claims of each district regarding its interest therein before making decision. From any such determination there is reserved unto each of the interested districts the right of appeal to the next succeeding Annual Conference. Any sum received as or from such share shall be used for no other purpose than purchase or building of a parsonage in the district. The same procedure shall be followed in determining equities of a district in any other property which may be included in another district by changes in district boundaries.

¶ **2514.** There shall be in each district of an Annual Conference a **district Board of Church Location and Building,** consisting of the district superintendent, three ministers, and three lay persons nominated by the district superintendent in consultation with the district nominating committee, if one exists, and elected annually by the Annual Conference; *provided* that in a district of great geographical extent an additional board may be so elected. The board shall file a report of any actions taken with the Charge Conference of each local church involved, and the report so filed shall become a part of the minutes of the said conference or conferences. The board shall also make a written report to the District Conference (or if there is no District Conference, to the district superintendent), and this report shall become a part of the records of that conference.

¶ **2515.** 1. The Board of Church Location and Building shall investigate all proposed local church building sites, ascertaining that such sites are properly located for the community to be served and adequate in size to provide space for future expansion and parking facilities. (*See* ¶¶ 267.1, 2536.2.)

2. If there is a Metropolitan Commission (¶ 1533.5*j*) in the district, the board shall consider its recommendations in planning a strategy for continuing the service of The United Methodist Church in changing neighborhoods. If not, the board shall study the duties assigned to such a commission and seek ways to provide continuity of service in parishes where there is a change in the racial, ethnic, or cultural character of the residents, to the end that the resolutions of the General Conference involving such neighborhoods be given careful consideration.

¶ **2516.** 1. The board shall require any local church in its district, before beginning or contracting for construction or purchase of a new church or educational building or a parsonage, or remodeling of such a building if the cost will exceed 10 percent of its value, to submit for consideration and approval a statement of the need for the proposed facilities, preliminary architectural plans, an estimate of the cost, and a financial plan for defraying such costs, as provided in ¶¶ 2536.4-.5. Before finally approving the building project, the board shall ascertain whether the preliminary architectural design and financial programs have been reviewed, evaluated, and approved by proper authorities (¶ 2536.5).

2. When the local church has secured final architectural plans and specifications and a reliable and detailed estimate of the cost of the proposed undertaking as provided in ¶ 2536.8, the board shall require their submission for consideration and approval. The board shall study carefully the feasibility and financial soundness of the undertaking and ascertain whether the financial plan will provide funds necessary to assure prompt payment of all proposed contractual obligations, and it shall report its conclusions to the church in writing.

3. A final decision of the board approving purchase, building, or remodeling shall automatically terminate after a period of one year, where no action has been taken by the local church to carry out such decision.

¶ 2517. A decision of the board disapproving such purchase, building, or remodeling shall be final unless overruled by the Annual Conference, to which there is reserved unto the local church the right of appeal.

¶ 2518. The above provisions shall apply to the acquisition of a district parsonage.

Section VII. Local Church Property.

¶ 2519. In each pastoral charge consisting of one local church there shall be a **Board of Trustees,** consisting of not fewer than three nor more than nine persons, each of whom shall be of legal age as determined by law and at least two thirds of whom shall be members of The United Methodist Church. By action of the Charge Conference the local church may limit the age of trustees to a maximum of seventy-two years of age.

¶ **2520.** The members of the Board of Trustees shall be divided into three classes, and each class shall as nearly as possible consist of an equal number of members. At the Charge Conference, on nomination by the Committee on Nominations, of which the pastor shall be chairperson (or if the committee fails to nominate, on nomination of the pastor), or from the floor, it shall elect, to take office at the beginning of the ensuing conference year, to serve for a term of three years or until their successors have been duly elected and qualified, the required number of trustees to succeed those of the class whose terms then expire; *provided,* however, that nothing herein shall be construed to prevent the election of a trustee to self-succession.[5] The Charge Conference may assign the responsibility for electing trustees to a Church Conference.

¶ **2521.** 1. In a pastoral charge consisting of two or more local churches, a **Church Local Conference,** constituted and organized under the Discipline of The United Methodist Church in each local church therein, shall be vested with authority and power in matters relating to the real and personal property of the local church concerned. Such Church Local Conference shall elect the Board of Trustees of such local church in number and manner described in ¶ 2520, and the duties of such trustees, duly elected, shall be the same as and identical with the duties described in ¶ 2523. The duties, authority, and power vested in the Church Local Conference, insofar as they relate to the property, real and personal, of the local church concerned, are the same as and identical with the authority and power vested in the Charge Conference of a pastoral charge of one local church (¶ 2523); and the authority, power, and limitations therein set forth shall be applicable to the Church Local Conference as fully and to the same extent as if incorporated herein. The effect of the provisions for a Church Local Conference is to give to each local church in a charge of two or more churches, rather than to the pastoral Charge Conference, supervision over and control of its own property, subject to the limitations prescribed in the Discipline with regard to local church property.

---

[5]*See* Judicial Council Decision 130.

2. Whenever required under the Discipline of The United Methodist Church for matters relating to real or personal property of the local church or to mergers of churches, a local church in a pastoral charge consisting of two or more local churches shall organize a Church Local Conference. The membership of the Church Local Conference shall consist of the persons specified for membership of the Charge Conference (¶ 248.2) so far as the officers and relationships exist within the local church, except that the pastor shall be a member of each Church Local Conference. The provisions of ¶¶ 248.2-.8 relating to membership qualification and procedures of a Charge Conference shall be applicable to membership qualifications and procedures of a Church Local Conference.

¶ **2522.** 1. A pastoral charge composed of two or more churches, each having a local Board of Trustees, may have in addition a **Board of Trustees for the charge as a whole.** This board shall hold title to and manage the property belonging to the entire charge, such as parsonage, campground, burial ground, and such other property as may be committed to it. It shall receive and administer funds for the charge in conformity with the laws of the state, province, or country in which the property is located. This board shall consist of not less than three persons, at least two thirds of whom shall be members of The United Methodist Church and of legal age as determined by law. These trustees shall be elected by the Charge Conference for three years or until their successors are elected. By action of the Charge Conference the local church may limit the age of trustees to a maximum of seventy-two.

2. A cooperative parish composed of two or more charges may have, in addition to its charge trustees and local church trustees, a Board of Trustees for the cooperative parish as a whole. This board shall hold title to and manage the property belonging to the cooperative parish in accordance with ¶¶ 2503, 2521, 2522. These trustees shall be elected by the Charge Conference and/or Church Conference related to the cooperative parish.

3. The Board of Trustees of a charge shall provide for the security of its funds, keep an accurate record of its proceedings, and report to the Charge Conference to which it is amenable.

4. When two or more local churches compose a single pastoral charge having a parsonage and one or more thereof is separated from such charge and established as a pastoral charge or united with another pastoral charge, each such local church shall be entitled to receive its just share of the then reasonable value of the parsonage in which it has invested funds, and the amount of such value and just share shall be determined by a committee of three persons, appointed by the district superintendent, who shall be members of The United Methodist Church but not of any of the interested local churches. Such committee shall hear all interested parties and shall take into account the investment of any church in any such property before arriving at a final determination. From any such determination there is reserved to each of the interested churches the right of appeal to the next succeeding Annual Conference, the decision of which shall be final and binding. Any sum received as or from such share shall not be applied to current expense or current budget.

¶ **2523.** In a pastoral charge consisting of one local church, the Charge Conference, constituted as set forth in this Discipline, (¶ 248), shall be vested with power and authority as hereinafter set forth in connection with the property, both real and personal, of the said local church, namely:

1. If it so elects, to direct the Board of Trustees to incorporate the local church, expressly subject, however, to the Discipline of The United Methodist Church and in accordance with the pertinent local laws and in such manner as will fully protect and exempt from any and all legal liability the individual officials and members, jointly and severally, of the local church, and the Charge, Annual, Jurisdictional, and General Conferences of The United Methodist Church, and each of them, for and on account of the debts and other obligations of every kind and description, of the local church.

2. To direct the Board of Trustees with respect to the purchase, sale, mortgage, encumbrance, construction, repairing, remodeling, and maintenance of any and all property of the local church.

3. To direct the Board of Trustees with respect to the acceptance or rejection of any and all conveyances, grants, gifts, donations, legacies, bequests, or devises, absolute or in trust, for

the use and benefit of the local church, and to require the administration of any such trust in accordance with the terms and provisions thereof and of the local laws appertaining thereto. (*See* ¶ 2527.)

4. To do any and all things necessary to exercise such other powers and duties relating to the property, real and personal, of the local church concerned as may be committed to it by the Discipline.

¶ **2524.** The Board of Trustees shall organize as follows:

1. Within thirty days after the beginning of the ensuing conference year each Board of Trustees shall convene at a time and place designated by the chairperson, or by the vice-chairperson in the event that the chairperson is not reelected a trustee or because of absence or disability is unable to act, for the purpose of electing officers of the said board for the ensuing year and transacting any other business properly brought before it.

2. The Board of Trustees shall elect from the membership thereof, to hold office for a term of one year or until their successors shall be elected, a chairperson, vice-chairperson, secretary, and if need requires, treasurer; *provided,* however, that the chairperson and vice-chairperson shall not be members of the same class; and *provided* further that the offices of secretary and treasurer may be held by the same person; and *provided* further that the chairperson shall be a member of the local church. The duties of each officer shall be the same as generally connected with the office held and which are usually and commonly discharged by the holder thereof. The Church Local Conference may, if it is necessary to conform to the local laws, substitute the designations "president" and "vice-president" for and in place of "chairperson" and "vice-chairperson."

3. Where necessity requires, as a result of the incorporation of a local church, the corporation directors, in addition to electing officers as provided in §2 above, shall ratify and confirm, by appropriate action, and if necessary elect, as officers of the corporation, the treasurer or treasurers, as the case may be, elected by the Charge Conference in accordance with the provisions of the Discipline, whose duties and responsibilities shall be as therein set forth. If more than one account is maintained in the name of the corporation in any financial

institution or institutions, each such account and the treasurer thereof shall be appropriately designated.

4. "Trustee," "trustees," and "Board of Trustees," as used herein or elsewhere in the Discipline, may be construed to be synonymous with "director," "directors," and "Board of Directors" applied to corporations, when required to comply with law.

¶ **2525.** 1. Should a trustee withdraw from the membership of The United Methodist Church or be excluded therefrom, trusteeship therein shall automatically cease from the date of such withdrawal or exclusion.

2. Should a trustee of a local church or a director of an incorporated local church refuse to execute properly a legal instrument relating to any property of the church when directed so to do by the Charge Conference and when all legal requirements have been satisfied with reference to such execution, the said Charge Conference may by majority vote declare the trustee's or director's membership on the Board of Trustees or Board of Directors vacated.

3. Vacancies occurring in a Board of Trustees shall be filled by election for the unexpired term. Such election shall be held in the same manner as for trustees.

¶ **2526.** The Board of Trustees shall meet at the call of the pastor or of its president at least annually at such times and places as shall be designated in a notice to each trustee at a reasonable time prior to the appointed time of the meeting. Waiver of notice may be used as a means to validate meetings legally where the usual notice is impracticable. A majority of the members of the Board of Trustees shall constitute a quorum.

¶ **2527.** Subject to the direction of the Charge Conference as hereinbefore provided, the Board of Trustees shall receive and administer all bequests made to the local church; shall receive and administer all trusts; shall invest all trust funds of the local church in conformity with laws of the country, state, or like political unit in which the local church is located. The Board of Trustees is encouraged to invest in institutions, companies, corporations, or funds which make a positive contribution toward the realization of the goals outlined in the Social Principles of our Church. The Board of Trustees shall have the supervision, oversight, and care of all real property owned by the local church and of all property and equipment acquired directly by the local church or by any society, board, class, commission, or similar organization connected therewith; *provided* that the Board of Trustees shall not violate the rights of any local church organization elsewhere granted in the Discipline; *provided* further, that the Board of Trustees shall not prevent or interfere with the pastor in the use of any of the said property for religious services or other proper meetings or purposes recognized by the law, usages, and customs of The United Methodist Church, or permit the use of said property for religious or other meetings without the consent of the pastor, or in the pastor's absence the consent of the district superintendent; and *provided* further, that pews in The United Methodist Church shall always be free; and *provided* further, that the Church Local Conference may assign certain of these duties to a building committee as set forth in ¶ 2536.

¶ **2528.** If the local laws do not prescribe that title to property, both real and personal, shall be otherwise taken and held, in which event the provisions thereof shall take precedence and shall be observed and the provisions hereof subordinated thereto, the title to all real property now owned or hereafter acquired by an **unincorporated local church,** and any organization, board, commission, society, or similar body connected therewith, shall be held by and/or conveyed and transferred to its duly elected trustees, who shall be named in the written instrument conveying or transferring title, and their successors in office and their assigns, as the Board of Trustees of such local church (naming it and the individual trustees), in trust, nevertheless, for the use and benefit of such local church and of The United Methodist Church. Every instrument of conveyance of real estate shall contain the appropriate trust clause as set forth in the Discipline (¶ 2503).

¶ **2529.** Prior to the purchase by an unincorporated local church of any real estate, a resolution authorizing such action shall be passed at a meeting of the Charge Conference by a majority vote of its members present and voting at a regular meeting or a special meeting of the Charge Conference called for that purpose; *provided,* however, that not less than ten days' notice of such meeting and the proposed action shall have been given from the pulpit or in the weekly bulletin of the church; and *provided* further, that written consent to such action shall be given by the pastor and the district superintendent. (*See* ¶ 2536.)

¶ **2530.** If the local laws do not prescribe that title to real property of an **incorporated local church** shall be otherwise taken and held, in which event the provisions thereof shall take precedence and shall be observed and the provisions hereof subordinated thereto, the title to all property, both real and personal, now owned or hereafter acquired by an incorporated local church, and any organization, board, commission, society, or similar body connected therewith, shall be held by and/or conveyed to the corporate body in its corporate name, in trust, nevertheless, for the use and benefit of such local church and of The United Methodist Church. Every instrument of conveyance of real estate shall contain the appropriate trust clause as set forth in the Discipline (¶ 2503).

¶ **2531.** Prior to the purchase by a local church corporation of any real estate, a resolution authorizing such action shall be passed by the Charge Conference in corporate session, or such other corporate body as the local laws may require, with the members thereof acting in their capacity as members of the corporate body, by a majority vote of those present and voting at any regular or special meeting called for that purpose; *provided* that not less than ten days' notice of such meeting and the proposed action shall have been given from the pulpit or in the weekly bulletin of the local church; and *provided* further, that written consent to such action shall be given by the pastor and the district superintendent; and *provided* further, that all such transactions shall have the approval of the Charge Conference.

¶ **2532.** Any real property owned by, or in which an unincorporated local church has any interest, may be sold, transferred, or mortgaged subject to the following procedure and conditions:

1. Notice of the proposed action and the date and time of the regular or special meeting of the Charge Conference at which it is to be considered shall be given at least ten days prior thereto (except as local laws may otherwise provide) from the pulpit of the church or in its weekly bulletin.

2. A resolution authorizing the proposed action shall be passed by a majority vote of the Charge Conference members

present and voting and by a majority vote of the members of said church present and voting at a special meeting called to consider such action.

3. The written consent of the pastor of the local church and the district superintendent to the proposed action shall be necessary and shall be affixed to the instrument of sale, transfer, or mortgage. Prior to consenting to the proposed action to sell or transfer any United Methodist Church property they are to insure that a full investigation be made and an appropriate plan of action be developed for the future missional needs of the community by The United Methodist Church. The requirements of investigation and the development of a plan of action, however, shall not affect the merchantibility of the title to the real estate or the legal effect of the instruments of sale or transfer.

4. The resolution authorizing such proposed action shall direct that any contract, deed, bill of sale, mortgage, or other necessary written instrument be executed by and on behalf of the local church by any two of the officers of its Board of Trustees, who thereupon shall be duly authorized to carry out the direction of the Charge Conference; and any written instrument so executed shall be binding and effective as the action of the local church.

¶ **2533.** Any real property owned by, or in which an incorporated local church has any interest, may be sold, transferred, or mortgaged subject to the following procedure and conditions:

1. Notice of the proposed action and the date and time of the regular or special meeting of the members of the corporate body, i.e., members of the Charge Conference at which it is to be considered, shall be given at least ten days prior thereto (except as local laws may otherwise provide) from the pulpit of the church or in its weekly bulletin.

2. A resolution authorizing the proposed action shall be passed by a majority vote of the members of the corporate body present and voting at any regular or special meeting thereof called to consider such action and by a majority vote of the members of said church present and voting at a special meeting called to consider such action; *provided* that for the sale of property which was conveyed to the church to be sold and its

proceeds used for a specific purpose a vote of the members of said church shall not be required.

3. The written consent of the pastor of the local church and the district superintendent to the proposed action shall be necessary and shall be affixed to the instrument of sale, conveyance, transfer, or mortgage.

4. The resolution authorizing such proposed action shall direct and authorize the corporation's Board of Directors to take all necessary steps to carry out the action so authorized and to cause to be executed, as hereinafter provided, any necessary contract, deed, bill of sale, mortgage, or other written instrument.

5. The Board of Directors at any regular or special meeting shall take such action and adopt such resolutions as may be necessary or required by the local laws.

6. Any required contract, deed, bill of sale, mortgage, or other written instrument necessary to carry out the action so authorized shall be executed in the name of the corporation by any two of its officers, and any written instrument so executed shall be binding and effective as the action of the corporation.

¶ **2534.** Real property acquired by a conveyance containing trust clauses may be sold in conformity with the provisions of the Discipline of The United Methodist Church when its use as a church building or parsonage, as the case may be, has been, or is intended to be, terminated; and when such real estate is sold or mortgaged in accordance with the provisions of the Discipline of The United Methodist Church, the written acknowledged consent of the proper district superintendent representing The United Methodist Church to the action taken shall constitute a release and discharge of the real property so sold and conveyed from the trust clause or clauses; or in the event of the execution of a mortgage, such consent of the district superintendent shall constitute a formal recognition of the priority of such mortgage lien and the subordination of the foregoing trust provisions thereof; and no bona fide purchaser or mortgagee relying upon the foregoing record shall be charged with any responsibility with respect to the disposition by such local church of the proceeds of any such sale or mortgage; but the Board of Trustees receiving such proceeds shall manage, control, disburse, and expend the same in conformity to the order and direction of the Church

Local Conference, subject to the provisions of the Discipline of The United Methodist Church with respect thereto.

¶ **2535.** 1. No real property on which a church building or parsonage is located shall be mortgaged to provide for the current (or budget) expense of a local church, nor shall the principal proceeds of a sale of any such property be so used. This provision shall apply alike to unincorporated and incorporated local churches.[6]

2. A local church, whether or not incorporated, on complying with the provisions of the Discipline, may mortgage its unencumbered real property as security for a loan to be made to a conference Board of Global Ministries or a city or district missionary society; *provided* that the proceeds of such loan shall be used only for aiding in the construction of a new church.

¶ **2536.** Any local church planning to build or purchase a new church or educational building or a parsonage, or to remodel such a building if the cost will exceed 10 percent of its value, shall first establish a study committee to analyze the needs of the church and community, project the potential membership with average attendance, and write up its program of ministry. This information will form the basis of a report to be presented to the Charge Conference and to be used by the building committee (¶¶ 2536.3-.4). The study committee's findings become a part of the report to the district Board of Church Location and Building (¶¶ 2536.5, 2516.1).

1. It shall secure the written consent of the pastor and the district superintendent.

2. It shall secure approval of the proposed site by the district Board of Church Location and Building as provided in the Discipline (¶ 2515.1).

3. Its Charge Conference shall authorize the project at a regular or called meeting, not less than ten days' notice (except as local laws may otherwise provide) of such meeting and the proposed action having been given from the pulpit or in the weekly bulletin, and shall appoint a **building committee** of not fewer than three members of the local church to serve in the development of the project as hereinafter set forth; *provided* that

---

[6]*See* Judicial Council Decision 399.

the Charge Conference may commit to its Board of Trustees the duties of a building committee as here described.

4. The building committee shall:

a) Estimate carefully the building facilities needed to house the church's program of worship, education, and fellowship and/or to provide a residence for present and future pastors and their families.

b) Ascertain the cost of property to be purchased.

c) Develop preliminary architectural plans, complying with local building and fire codes, which shall clearly outline the location on the site of all proposed present and future construction. In all new church building plans and in all major remodeling plans, adequate provisions shall be made to facilitate entrance, seating, exit, parking, and otherwise make accessible facilities for persons with handicapping conditions.

d) Secure an estimate of the cost of the proposed construction.

e) Develop a financial plan for defraying the total cost, including an estimate of the amount the membership can contribute in cash and pledges and the amount the local church can borrow if necessary.

5. The building committee shall submit to the district Board of Church Location and Building, for its consideration and approval, a statement of the need for the proposed facilities, and the architectural plans and financial estimates and plans.

6. The building committee shall ensure that adequate steps are taken to obtain the services of minority (nonwhite) and female skilled persons in the construction of any United Methodist church, parsonage, institution, or agency facility in proportion to the racial/ethnic balance of the metropolitan area in which construction occurs. In nonmetropolitan areas racial and ethnic minorities are to be employed in construction where available and in relation to the available work force.

7. The pastor, with the written consent of the district superintendent, shall call a Church Conference, giving not less than ten days' notice (except as local laws may otherwise provide) of the meeting and the proposed action from the pulpit or in the weekly bulletin. At this conference the building committee shall submit, for approval by the membership, its recommendations

for the proposed building project, including the data specified herein.

8. After approval of the preliminary plans and estimates the building committee shall develop detailed plans and specifications and secure a reliable and detailed estimate of cost and shall present these for approval to the Charge Conference and to the district Board of Church Location and Building, which shall study the data and report its conclusions.

9. The local church shall acquire a fee simple title to the lot or lots on which the building is to be erected, by deed or conveyance, executed as provided in this chapter, and shall pay the purchase price thereof in full before beginning construction.

10. If a loan is needed, the local church shall comply with the provisions of ¶¶ 2532-2533.

11. The local church shall not enter into a building contract or, if using a plan for volunteer labor, incur obligations for materials until it has cash on hand, pledges payable during the construction period, and (if needed) a loan or written commitment therefor which will assure prompt payment of all contractual obligations and other accounts when due.

12. Trustees or other members of a local church shall not be required to guarantee personally any loan made to the church by any board created by or under the authority of the General Conference.

¶ **2537.** On acquisition or completion of any church building, parsonage, or other church unit, a service of consecration may be held. Before any church building, parsonage, or other church unit is formally dedicated, all indebtedness against the same shall be discharged.

¶ **2538.** Two or more local churches may merge and become a single church by pursuing the following procedure:

1. The merger must be proposed by the Charge Conference of each of the merging churches by a resolution stating the terms and conditions of the proposed merger.

2. The plan of the merger as proposed by the Charge Conference of each of the merging churches must in addition, if a Charge Conference includes two or more local churches, be approved by the Church Local Conference of each local church in accordance with the requirements of ¶ 2521.

3. The merger must be approved by the superintendent or superintendents of the district or districts in which the merging churches are located.

4. The requirements of any and all laws of the state or states in which the merging churches are located affecting or relating to the merger of such churches must be complied with, and in any case where there is a conflict between such laws and the procedure outlined in the Discipline, said laws shall prevail and the procedure outlined in the Discipline shall be modified to the extent necessary to eliminate such conflict.

5. All archives and records of a merged or closed church shall become the responsibility of the successor church or the conference Commission on Archives and History.

¶ **2539.** One or more local United Methodist churches may merge with one or more churches of other denominations and become a single church by pursuing the following procedure:

1. Following appropriate dialogue, which shall include discussions with the United Methodist district superintendent of the district in which the merging churches are located and the corresponding officials of the other judicatories involved, a plan of merger shall be submitted to the Charge Conference of the local United Methodist church and must be approved by a resolution stating the terms and conditions of the proposed merger, including the denominational connection of the merger church.

2. The plan of merger as approved by the Charge Conference of the United Methodist church, in a Charge Conference including two or more local churches, must be approved by the Church Local Conference of each local church in accordance with the requirements of ¶ 2521.

3. The merger must be approved in writing by the superintendent of the district, a majority of the district superintendents, and the bishop of the area in which the merging churches are located.

4. The provisions of ¶ 2503 shall be included in the plan of merger where applicable.

5. The requirements of any and all laws of the state or states in which the merging churches are located affecting or relating to the merger of such churches must be complied with, and in any

case where there is a conflict between such laws and the procedure outlined in the Discipline, said laws shall prevail and the procedure outlined in the Discipline shall be modified to the extent necessary to eliminate such conflict.

6. Where property is involved, the provisions of ¶ 2540 obtain.

¶ **2540.** 1. With the consent of the presiding bishop and of a majority of the district superintendents and of the district Board of Church Location and Building, and at the request of the Charge Conference or of a meeting of the membership of the church, where required by local law, and in accordance with the said law, the Annual Conference may instruct and direct the Board of Trustees of a local church to deed church property to a federated church.

2. With the consent of the presiding bishop and of a majority of the district superintendents and of the district Board of Church Location and Building and at the request of the Charge Conference or of a meeting of the membership of the local church, where required by local law, and in accordance with said law, the Annual Conference may instruct and direct the Board of Trustees of a local church to deed church property to another evangelical denomination under an allocation, exchange of property, or comity agreement; *provided* that such agreement shall have been committed to writing and signed and approved by the duly qualified and authorized representatives of both parties concerned.

¶ **2541.** 1. With the consent of the presiding bishop and of a majority of the district superintendents and of the district Board of Church Location and Building of the district in which the action is contemplated, the Annual Conference may declare any local church within its bounds discontinued or abandoned. It shall be the duty of its Board of Trustees to make such disposition of the property thereof as the Annual Conference shall direct; and if no such lawful trustees remain or if for any reason said trustees fail to make such disposition, then it shall be the duty of the trustees of the Annual Conference to sell or dispose of said property in accordance with the direction of the Annual Conference, *provided* that a public notice be given in the local newspaper at least thirty days before the property is announced for sale. It shall be the duty of the trustees thus effecting sale to remove, insofar as reasonably possible, all Christian and church insignia and symbols from such property. In the event of loss, damage to, or destruction of such local church property, the trustees of the Annual Conference are authorized to collect and receipt for any insurance payable on account thereof, as the duly and legally authorized representative of such local church.[7]

2. All the deeds, records, and other official and legal papers, including the contents of the cornerstone, of a church that is so declared to be abandoned or otherwise discontinued shall be collected by the district superintendent in whose district said church was located and shall be deposited for permanent safekeeping with the secretary of the Annual Conference. The conference may subsequently authorize that such documentary record material and historic memorabilia be deposited for safekeeping with its Commission on Archives and History.

3. Any gift, legacy, devise, annuity, or other benefit to a pastoral charge or local church that accrues or becomes available after said charge or church has been discontinued or abandoned shall become the property of the trustees of the Annual Conference within whose jurisdiction the said discontinued or abandoned church was located.

4. When a church property has been abandoned by its membership and no abandonment action has been taken by the Annual Conference and circumstances make immediate action necessary, the Annual Conference trustees may take control of the property, with the consent of the presiding bishop and the district Board of Church Location and Building of the district in which the property is located. And in the event of the sale or lease of said property the trustees of the Annual Conference shall recommend to the Annual Conference at its next session the disposition of the proceeds derived from such sale or lease.

¶ **2542.** The Board of Trustees shall annually make a written report to the Charge Conference, in which shall be included the following:

1. The legal description and the reasonable valuation of each parcel of real estate owned by the church.

---

[7]*See* Judicial Council Decisions 119, 138, 143.

2. The specific name of the grantee in each deed of conveyance of real estate to the local church.

3. An inventory and the reasonable valuation of all personal property owned by the local church.

4. The amount of income received from any income-producing property and a detailed list of expenditures in connection therewith.

5. The amount received during the year for building, rebuilding, remodeling, and improving real estate, and an itemized statement of expenditures.

6. Outstanding capital debts and how contracted.

7. A detailed statement of the insurance carried on each parcel of real estate, indicating whether restricted by co-insurance or other limiting conditions and whether adequate insurance is carried.

8. The name of the custodian of all legal papers of the local church, and where they are kept.

9. A detailed list of all trusts in which the local church is the beneficiary, specifying where and how the funds are invested, clarifying the manner in which these investments made a positive contribution toward the realization of the goals outlined in the Social Principles of the Church, and in what manner the income therefrom is expended or applied.[8]

¶ **2543.** In static and declining population areas, churches of fifty members or less shall study, under the leadership of the district superintendent, the District Board of Church Location and Building, and the appropriate conference agency, their potential in the area to determine how they shall continue to develop programs as organized churches, develop cooperative patterns with other congregations, or give special attention to relocation.

¶ **2544.** The provisions herein written concerning the organization and administration of the local church, including the procedure for acquiring, holding, and transferring real property, shall not be mandatory in Central Conferences, Provisional Central Conferences, Provisional Annual Conferences, or Missions; and in such instances the legislation in ¶¶ 636-646 and 653-662 shall apply.

---

[8]*See* Judicial Council Decision 420.

Section VIII. Requirements—Trustees of Church Institutions.

¶ **2545.** Trustees of schools, colleges, universities, hospitals, homes, orphanages, institutes, and other institutions owned or controlled by The United Methodist Church shall be at least twenty-one years of age. At all times not less than three fifths of them shall be members of The United Methodist Church, and all must be nominated, confirmed, or elected by some governing body of the Church or by some body or officer thereof to which or to whom this power has been delegated by the governing body of the Church; *provided* that the number of trustees of any such institution owned or controlled by any Annual Conference or Conferences required to be members of The United Methodist Church may be reduced to not less than the majority by a three-fourths vote of such Annual Conference or Conferences; and *provided* further, that when an institution is owned and operated jointly with some other denomination or organization, said requirement that three fifths of the trustees shall be members of The United Methodist Church shall apply only to the portion of the trustees representing The United Methodist Church.

Chapter Nine
JUDICIAL ADMINISTRATION

Section I. The Judicial Council.

¶ 2601. *Members.*—The **Judicial Council** shall be composed of nine members. In the year 1984 and each sixteen years thereafter there shall be elected three lay persons and two ministers other than bishops. In 1992 and each sixteen years thereafter there shall be elected three ministers other than bishops and two lay persons. In 1988 and each eight years thereafter there shall be elected two ministers other than bishops and two lay persons. They shall be members of The United Methodist Church. Elections shall be held at each session of the General Conference for only the number of members whose terms expire at such session. A member's term of office shall be eight years; *provided,* however, that a member of the council whose seventieth birthday precedes the first day of the regular session of a General Conference shall be released at the close of that General Conference from membership or responsibility in the council, regardless of the date of expiration of office.

Members of the council shall be nominated and elected in the manner following: At each quadrennial session of the General Conference the Council of Bishops shall nominate by majority vote three times the number of ministers and lay persons to be elected at such session of the General Conference. The number to be elected shall correspond to the number of members whose terms expire at the conclusion of such session. Each of the jurisdictions and the Central Conferences as a group shall be represented by at least one nominee, but it shall not be a requirement that each of the jurisdictions be represented by an elected member. One member shall be elected from the Central Conferences. At the same daily session at which the above nominations are announced, nominations of both ministers and lay persons may be made from the floor, but at no other time. The names of all nominees, identified with the conference to which each belongs and a biographical sketch which does not exceed one hundred words, shall be published by the *Daily Christian Advocate* immediately prior to the day of election, which shall be set by action of the General Conference at the session at which the nominations are made; and from these nominations the General Conference shall elect without discussion, by ballot and by majority vote, the necessary number of ministerial and lay members.

¶ **2602.** *Alternates.*—There shall be six alternates for the ministerial members and six alternates for the lay members, and their qualifications shall be the same as for membership on the Judicial Council. The term of the alternates shall be for eight years; *provided*, however, that an alternate whose seventieth birthday precedes the first day of the regular session of a General Conference shall be released at the close of that General Conference from membership or responsibility in the council regardless of the date of expiration of office.

The alternates shall be elected in the manner following: from the ministerial and lay nominees remaining on the ballot after the election of the necessary number of members of the Judicial Council to be elected at sessions of the General Conference, the General Conference shall by separate ballot, without discussion and by majority vote, elect the number of ministerial and lay alternates to be chosen at such session of the General Conference. An election shall be held at each session of the General Conference for only the number of ministerial and lay alternates whose terms expire at such session of the General Conference, or to fill vacancies.

¶ **2603.** *Vacancies.*—1. If a vacancy in the membership of the Judicial Council occurs at the conclusion of a General Conference because of a required retirement of a member because of age, such vacancy shall be filled by General Conference election of a minister to fill a ministerial vacancy and a lay person to fill a lay vacancy, such election to be held in the manner hereinbefore provided in this section, and the person so elected shall hold office during the unexpired term of the member whom the newly elected person succeeds.

2. If a vacancy in the membership of the council occurs during the interim between sessions of the General Conference, a ministerial vacancy shall be filled by the first-elected ministerial alternate and a lay vacancy by the first-elected lay alternate. The alternate filling such vacancy shall hold office as a member of the

Judicial Council for the unexpired term of the member whom the alternate succeeds. In the event of any vacancy, it shall be the duty of the president and secretary of the council to notify the alternate entitled to fill it.

3. In the event of a forced absence of one or more members of the council during a session of the Judicial Council, such temporary vacancy among the ministerial members may be filled for that session or the remainder thereof by the first-elected ministerial alternate who can be present, and such temporary vacancy among the lay members by the first-elected lay alternate who can be present, but inability or failure to fill a vacancy does not affect the validity of any action of the council so long as a quorum is present.

4. Any permanent vacancy among the alternates shall be filled by election at the next quadrennial session of the General Conference of a minister to fill a ministerial vacancy and a lay person to fill a lay vacancy, and the person or persons so elected shall hold office during the unexpired term of the alternate whom each respectively succeeds.

5. If vacancies in the membership of the Judicial Council occur after exhaustion of the list of alternates, the council is authorized to fill such vacancies for the remainder of the quadrennium.

¶ **2604.** The term of office of the members of the council and of the alternates shall expire upon the adjournment of the General Conference at which their successors are elected.

¶ **2605.** Members of the council shall be ineligible for membership in the General Conference or Jurisdictional Conference or in any general or jurisdictional board or for administrative service in any connectional office.[1]

¶ **2606.** The Judicial Council shall provide its own method of organization and procedure, both with respect to hearings on appeals and petitions for declaratory decisions. All parties shall have the privilege of filing briefs and arguments and presenting evidence, under such rules as the council may adopt from time to time. The council shall meet at the time and place of the meeting of the General Conference and shall continue in session until the adjournment of that body, and at least one other time in each

---

[1]*See* Judicial Council Decision 196, and Decision 3, Interim Judicial Council.

calendar year and at such other times as it may deem appropriate, at such places as it may select from time to time. Seven members shall constitute a quorum. An affirmative vote of at least six members of the council shall be necessary to declare any act of the General Conference unconstitutional. On other matters a majority vote of the entire council shall be sufficient. The council may decline to entertain an appeal or a petition for a declaratory decision in any instance in which it determines that it does not have jurisdiction to decide the matter.

¶ **2607.** 1. The Judicial Council shall determine the constitutionality of any act of the General Conference upon an appeal by a majority of the Council of Bishops or one fifth of the members of the General Conference.

2. The Judicial Council shall have jurisdiction to determine the constitutionality of any proposed legislation when such declaratory decision is requested by the General Conference or by the Council of Bishops.

¶ **2608.** The Judicial Council shall determine the constitutionality of any act of a Jurisdictional or a Central Conference upon an appeal by a majority of the bishops of that Jurisdictional or Central Conference or upon an appeal by one fifth of the members of that Jurisdictional or Central Conference.[2]

¶ **2609.** The Judicial Council shall hear and determine the legality of any action taken by any General Conference board or body, or Jurisdictional or Central Conference board or body, upon appeal by one third of the members thereof, or upon request of the Council of Bishops or a majority of the bishops of the Jurisdictional or Central Conference wherein the action was taken.

¶ **2610.** The Judicial Council shall hear and determine the legality of any action taken by a General Conference board or body, or Jurisdictional or Central Conference board or body, on a matter affecting an Annual or a Provisional Annual Conference, upon appeal by two thirds of the members of the Annual or Provisional Annual Conference present and voting.[3]

¶ **2611.** The Judicial Council shall hear and determine any appeal from a bishop's decision on a question of law made in a

---

[2]*See* Judicial Council Decision 338.
[3]*See* Judicial Council Decision 463.

Central, District, Annual, or Jurisdictional Conference when said appeal has been made by one fifth of that conference present and voting.[4]

¶ **2612.** The Judicial Council shall pass upon and affirm, modify, or reverse the decisions of law made by bishops in Central, District, Annual, or Jurisdictional Conferences upon questions of law submitted to them in writing in the regular business of a session; and in order to facilitate such review, each bishop shall report annually in writing to the Judicial Council, on forms provided by the council, all the bishop's decisions of law, with a syllabus of the same. No such episcopal decision shall be authoritative, except in the case pending, until it has been passed upon by the Judicial Council, but thereafter it shall become the law of the Church to the extent that it is affirmed by the council.

¶ **2613.** The Judicial Council shall hear and determine an appeal of a bishop when taken from the decision of the Trial Court in the bishop's case.

¶ **2614.** The Judicial Council shall have power to review an opinion or decision of a Committee on Appeals of a Jurisdictional Conference if it should appear that such opinion or decision is at variance with an opinion or decision of a Committee on Appeals of another Jurisdictional Conference on a question of law. Under such circumstances:

1. Any person, conference, or organization interested therein may appeal the case to the Judicial Council on the ground of such conflict of decisions; or

2. The Committee on Appeals rendering the last of such opinions or decisions may certify the case to, and file it with, the Judicial Council on the ground of such conflict of decisions; or

3. The attention of the president of the Judicial Council being directed to such conflict or alleged conflict of decisions, the president may issue an order, in the nature of a writ of certiorari, directing the secretaries of the Committees on Appeals involved to certify a copy of a sufficient portion of the record to disclose the nature of the case, and the entire opinion and decision of the Committee on Appeals in each case, to the Judicial Council for its consideration at its next meeting.

---

[4]*See* Judicial Council Decision 153.

The Judicial Council shall hear and determine the question of law involved but shall not pass upon the facts in either case further than is necessary to decide the question of law involved. After deciding the question of law, the Judicial Council shall cause its decision to be certified to each of the Committees on Appeals involved, and such Committees on Appeals shall take such action, if any, as may be necessary under the law as determined by the Judicial Council.

¶ **2615.** *Declaratory Decisions.*—1. The Judicial Council, on petition as hereinafter provided, shall have jurisdiction to make a ruling in the nature of a **declaratory decision** as to the constitutionality, meaning, application, or effect of the Discipline or any portion thereof or of any act or legislation of a General Conference; and the decision of the Judicial Council thereon shall be as binding and effectual as a decision made by it on appeal under the law relating to appeals to the Judicial Council.[5]

2. The following bodies in The United Methodist Church are hereby authorized to make such petitions to the Judicial Council for declaratory decisions: (*a*) the General Conference; (*b*) the Council of Bishops; (*c*) any General Conference board or body, on matters relating to or affecting the work of such board or body; (*d*) a majority of the bishops assigned to any jurisdiction, on matters relating to or affecting jurisdictions or the work therein; (*e*) any Jurisdictional Conference, on matters relating to or affecting jurisdictions or Jurisdictional Conferences or the work therein; (*f*) any Jurisdictional Conference board or body, on matters relating to or affecting the work of such board or body; (*g*) any Central Conference, on matters relating to or affecting Central Conferences, or the work therein; (*h*) any Central Conference board or body, on matters relating to or affecting the work of such board or body; and (*i*) any Annual Conference, on matters relating to Annual Conferences or the work therein.[6]

3. When a declaratory decision is sought, all persons or bodies who have or claim any interest which would be affected by the declaration shall be parties to the proceeding, and the petition shall name such parties. Except for requests filed during the

---

[5]*See* Judicial Council Decisions 106, 172, 301, 434, 443, 454, 463, 474.
[6]*See* Judicial Council Decisions 29, 212, 255, 301, 309, 382, 452.

General Conference, any party requesting a declaratory decision shall immediately upon filing such request submit for publication in *The Interpreter* or its successor—which shall in its next edition publish the same without cost—a brief statement of the question involved. The Judicial Council shall not hear and determine any such matter until thirty days after such publication. If the president of the council determines that other parties not named by the petition would be affected by such a decision, such additional parties shall also be added, and the petitioner or petitioners, upon direction of the secretary of the Judicial Council, shall then be required to serve all parties so joined with a copy of the petition within fifteen days after such direction by the secretary of the Judicial Council. In like manner any interested party may, on the party's own motion, intervene and answer, plead, or interplead.[7]

¶ **2616.** The decisions of the Judicial Council of The Methodist Church, heretofore issued, shall have the same authority in The United Methodist Church as they had in The Methodist Church, persuasive as precedents except where their basis has been changed by the terms of the Plan of Union or other revisions of Church law.

¶ **2617.** The Judicial Council shall have other duties and powers as may be conferred upon it by the General Conference.

¶ **2618.** All decisions of the Judicial Council shall be final. However, when the Judicial Council shall declare any act of the General Conference unconstitutional, that decision shall be reported back to that General Conference immediately.

¶ **2619.** The decisions of the Judicial Council on questions of law, with a summary of the facts of the opinion, shall be filed with the secretary of the General Conference and shall be published in the following manner:

1. Within ninety days following each session of the Judicial Council, the digest of decisions of the Judicial Council shall be published in *The Interpreter* or its successor publication.

2. The decisions of the Judicial Council rendered during each year shall be published in the General Minutes.

---

[7]*See* Judicial Council Decision 437.

Section II. Investigations, Trials, and Appeals.

¶ **2620.** *Preliminary Assumptions.*—The following procedures are presented as much for the protection of the rights of individuals guaranteed under Section III, Article IV, of our Constitution as they are for the protection of the Church. The innocence of the accused is assumed unless and until the facts of the case prove otherwise.

¶ **2621.** *Chargeable Offenses.*—1. A bishop, ministerial member of an Annual Conference (¶ 412), local pastor, or diaconal minister may choose a trial when charged with one or more of the following offenses: *(a)* immorality; *(b)* practices declared by The United Methodist Church to be incompatible with Christian teachings; *(c)* crime; *(d)* failure to perform the work of the ministry; (1) indifference, (2) incompetence, (3) inefficiency; *(e)* disobedience to the Order and Discipline of The United Methodist Church; *(f)* dissemination of doctrines contrary to the established standards of doctrine of the Church; *(g)* relationships and/or behavior which undermines the ministry of another pastor.

2. A lay member may choose a trial when charged with the following offenses: *(a)* immorality; *(b)* crime; *(c)* disobedience to the Order and Discipline of The United Methodist Church; *(d)* dissemination of doctrines contrary to the established standards of doctrine of the Church.

¶ **2622.** *Charges.*—Charges against bishops, ministerial members, local pastors, diaconal ministers, and lay members shall be subject to the following guidelines:

1. A charge shall not allege more than one offense; several charges against the same person, however, with the specifications under each one of them, may be presented at one and the same time and tried together. When several charges are tried at the same time, a vote on each specification and charge must be taken separately.

2. Amendments may be made to a bill of charges at the discretion of the presiding officer; provided that they relate to the form of statement only and do not change the nature of the alleged offense and do not introduce new matter of which the accused has not had due notice.

3. Charges and specifications for all trials shall define the offense in keeping with the provisions of ¶ 2621 and shall state in substance the facts upon which said charges are based.

¶ 2623. *Investigation Procedures.*—1. *General.*—*a)* All accusations shall be submitted in writing and signed by the accuser.

b) No charge shall be considered for any alleged offense which shall not have been committed within two years immediately preceding the filing of the complaint.

c) If possible, the accused and accuser shall be brought face to face, but the inability to do this shall not invalidate an investigation. Other supporting witnesses shall not be permitted at the investigation.

d) The parties may be represented by counsel at an investigation.

e) Proceedings in the investigation shall be informal. No oaths shall be taken. All procedural decisions shall be made by the chairperson and shall be final.

f) The appropriate **Committee on Investigation** (¶¶ 2623.2, .3, .4) shall conduct the investigation, and if in the judgment of a majority of the committee there is reasonable ground for such accusation, they shall prepare and sign accusation, they shall prepare and sign the proper charges (the general offense or offenses under ¶ 2621) and the specifications (the time, place, and specifics of events alleged to have taken place). They shall then forward a copy to the accused and to appropriate church officials (¶¶ 2623.2*d*, .3*d*, and .4*b*).

2. *Investigation of a Bishop.*—*a)* There shall be a Committee on Investigation consisting of seven elders in full connection elected by each Jurisdictional or Central Conference, with not more than one elder from each Annual Conference, if possible. Three reserves shall also be elected. The committee and its chairperson shall be elected on nomination of the College of Bishops.

b) If a bishop shall be accused in writing of any of the offenses in ¶ 2621, the president of the College of Bishops (or, if the accused is the president, the secretary) shall convene the Committee on Investigation within sixty days of receiving such accusation.

c) In the best interests of the bishop and the episcopal area, in exceptional circumstances the College of Bishops may suspend the bishop pending investigation.

d) Any charges and specifications adopted shall be sent to the accused, to the secretary of the Jurisdictional or Central Conference, and to the President and Secretary of the College of Bishops.

e) If five or more of the committee so recommend, the College of Bishops may suspend the bishop pending trial.

3. *Investigation of a Ministerial Member of an Annual Conference, Local Pastor, or Diaconal Minister.—a)* There shall be a Committee on Investigation consisting of seven elders in full connection nominated by the presiding bishop and elected by the Annual Conference. Three reserve members shall also be elected.

b) If a ministerial member of an Annual Conference, local pastor, or diaconal minister shall be accused in writing of any of the offenses in ¶ 2621, the accused person's district superintendent shall within sixty days of receiving such accusation convene the Committee on Investigation. (If the accused is a district superintendent, the bishop shall appoint another district superintendent as convener.)

c) In the best interests of the ministerial member or local pastor, in exceptional circumstances, the presiding bishop may, with the unanimous concurrence of the district superintendents, suspend the accused from all ministerial responsibilities pending investigation.[8]

d) Any charges and specifications adopted (¶ 2622.1*f)* shall be sent to the accused, the secretary of the Annual Conference, the accused person's district superintendent, and the presiding bishop.

e) If five or more of the Committee on Investigation so recommend, the bishop may suspend the accused from all ministerial responsibilities pending trial.

4. *Investigation of a Lay Member.—a)* If charges of offenses under ¶ 2621 are made in writing to the pastor in charge against a member of the Church, the pastor in charge shall appoint a Committee on Investigation, consisting of seven lay members of the church in good standing. The pastor shall preside at the investigation, and the district superintendent shall be informed of the investigation and have the right to be present.

---

[8]*See* Judicial Council Decision 89.

b) Any charges and specifications adopted shall be sent to the accused, to the recording secretary of the Charge Conference, the pastor, and the district superintendent.

c) If five or more of the committee so recommend, the pastor may suspend the accused lay person from exercising any church office pending trial.

¶ **2624.** *Trial Procedures.*—1. *General.*—*a)* Church trials are to be regarded as an expedient of last resort. Only after every reasonable effort has been made to correct any wrong and adjust any existing difficulty should steps be taken to institute a trial. No such trial as herein provided shall be construed to deprive the accused of legal civil rights. All trials shall be conducted in a consistent Christian manner by a properly constituted court, after due investigation. The administration of oaths shall not be required.

b) Officers of the Trial Court.—Officers shall consist of a presiding officer (¶¶ 2624.2, .3, .4) and a secretary appointed by the presiding officer.

c) Convening of the Court.—The official charged with convening the court (*see* ¶¶ 2624.2*a*, .3*a*, and .4*a*) shall, within twenty days after receiving a copy of the charges and specifications, appoint counsel for the Church and notify the accused in writing to appear at a fixed time and place no less than ten days after service of such notice and within a reasonable time thereafter to select the members of the Trial Court. At the appointed time in the presence of the accused, counsel for the accused, counsel for the Church, and the presiding officer, thirteen persons shall be selected as a Trial Court out of a pool of twenty-one persons selected according to ¶¶ 2624.2*c*, 2624.3*c*, and 2624.4*c*. The counsel for the Church and the accused shall each have up to four peremptory challenges and challenges for cause without limit. If by reason of challenges for cause being sustained the number is reduced to below thirteen, additional appropriate persons shall be nominated, in like manner as was the original panel to take the places of the numbers challenged, who likewise shall be subject to challenge for cause. This method of procedure shall be followed until a Trial Court of thirteen members has been selected.

d) Time and Place of Trial.—The official charged with

convening the Trial Court (¶¶ 2624.2*a*, .3*a*, and .4*a*) shall also fix the time and place for the trial, which may immediately follow the convening of the Trial Court, if notice of the convening is so specified. If such notice was not provided, then the presiding officer shall fix the time and place for the trial not less than ten days following the convening of the Trial Court, unless all parties consent to an earlier trial. Announcement of this trial date may be made at the time of the original convening of the Trial Court.

e) Notice.—(1) All notices required or provided for in the chapter shall be in writing, signed by or on behalf of the person or body giving or required to give such notice, and shall be addressed to the person or body to whom it is required to be given. Such notices shall be served by delivering a copy thereof to the party or chief officer of the body to whom it is addressed in person or by registered mail addressed to the last-known residence or address of such party. The fact of the giving of the notice shall affirmatively appear over the signature of the party required to give such notice and becomes a part of the record of the case.

(2) In all cases wherein it is provided that notice shall be given to a bishop or district superintendent and the charges are against that particular person, then such notice (in addition to being given to the accused) shall be given, in the case of a bishop, to another bishop within the same jurisdiction and, in the case of a district superintendent, to the bishop in charge.

f) Counsel.—In all cases an accused person shall be entitled to appear and be represented by counsel, a ministerial member of The United Methodist Church if the accused is a bishop, a ministerial member, a local pastor, or a diaconal minister, and a lay member of the said Church if the accused is a lay member. An accused person shall be entitled to have counsel heard in oral or written argument or both. The interest of the Church shall be represented by a ministerial member selected by the bishop. In all cases of trial where counsel has not been provided, such counsel shall be appointed by the presiding officer. The counsel for the Church and for the accused each shall be entitled to choose one assistant counsel who may be an attorney.

g) Witnesses.—Notice to appear shall be given to such witnesses as either party may name and shall be issued in the name of the Church and be signed by the presiding officer of the Trial Court. It shall be the duty of a minister or a member of the Church to appear and testify when summoned.

h) Power of the Trial Court.—The court thus constituted shall have full power to try the accused and upon conviction by a vote of nine or more thereof shall have power to suspend the accused from the exercise of the functions of office, to remove the accused from office or the ministry or both, to expel the accused from the Church, or in case of conviction of minor offenses to fix a lesser penalty. Its findings shall be final, subject to appeal to the Court of Appeals of the Jurisdictional Conference or the Central Conference, as the case may be.

i) Trial Guidelines.—(1) As soon as the trial has convened, the accused shall be called upon by the presiding officer to plead to the charge, and the pleas shall be recorded. If the accused pleads "guilty" to the charges preferred, no trial shall be necessary, but evidence may be taken with respect to the appropriate penalty, which shall thereupon be imposed. If the accused pleads "not guilty" or if the accused should neglect or refuse to plead, the plea of "not guilty" shall be entered, and the trial shall proceed. The court may adjourn from time to time as convenience or necessity may require. The accused shall, at all times during the trial except as hereinafter mentioned, have the right to produce testimony and that of witnesses and to make defense.

(2) If in any case the accused person, after due notice (ten days) has been given, shall refuse or neglect to appear at the time and place set forth for the hearing, the trial may proceed in the accused's absence. However, if, in the judgment of the presiding officer, there is good and sufficient reason for the absence of the accused, the presiding officer may reschedule the trial to a later date.

(3) In all cases sufficient time shall be allowed for the person to appear at the given place and time and for the accused to prepare for the trial. The presiding officer shall decide what constitutes "sufficient time."

(4) The court shall be a continuing body until the final disposition of the charge. If any member of the court shall be unable to attend all the sessions, that person shall not vote upon the final determination of the case, but the rest of the court may

proceed to judgment. It shall require a vote of at least nine members of the court to sustain the charges.

(5) All objections to the regularity of the proceedings and the form and substance of charges and specifications shall be made at the first session of the trial. The presiding officer, upon the filing of such objections, shall, or by motion may, determine all such preliminary objections and may dismiss the case or in furtherance of truth and justice permit amendments to the specifications or charges not changing the general nature of the same. But after the Trial Court is selected as provided for in ¶ 2624.1*d* and convened for the trial, the authority of the presiding officer shall be limited to ruling upon proper representation of the Church and the accused, admissibility of evidence, recessing, adjourning, and reconvening sessions of the trial, and such other authority as is normally vested in a civil court judge sitting with a jury, but he/she shall not have authority to pronounce any judgment in favor of or against the accused other than such verdict as may be returned by the Trial Court, which body shall have the exclusive right to determine the innocence or guilt of the accused.

(6) Objections of any part to the proceedings shall be entered on the record.

(7) No witness afterward to be examined shall be present during the examination of another witness if the opposing party objects. Witnesses shall be examined first by the party producing them, then cross-examined by the opposite party, after which any member of the court or either party may put additional questions. The presiding officer of the court shall determine all questions of relevancy and competency of evidence.

(8) The presiding officer shall not deliver a charge reviewing or explaining the evidence or setting forth the merits of the case. The presiding officer shall express no opinion on the law or the facts while the court is deliberating unless the parties in interest be present. The presiding officer shall remain and preside until the decision is rendered and the findings are completed and shall thereupon sign and certify them.

(9) The testimony shall be taken by a stenographer, if convenient, or recorded by other appropriate means and reduced to writing and certified by the presiding officer and

secretary. The record, including all exhibits, papers, and evidence in the case, shall be the basis of any appeal which may be taken.

(10) A witness to be qualified need not be a member of The United Methodist Church.

(11) The presiding officer of any court before which a case may be pending shall have power, whenever the necessity of the parties or of witnesses shall require, to appoint, on the application of either party, a commissioner or commissioners, either a minister or a lay person or both, to examine the witnesses; *provided* that three days notice of the time and place of taking such testimony shall have been given to the adverse party. Counsel for both parties shall be permitted to examine and cross-examine the witness or witnesses whose testimony is thus taken. The commissioners so appointed shall take such testimony in writing as may be offered by either party. The testimony properly certified by the signature of the commissioner or commissioners shall be transmitted to the presiding officer of the court before which the case is pending.

2. *Trial of a Bishop.—a)* The president of the College of Bishops of the Jurisdictional or Central Conference, or in case the accused is the president, the secretary of the college, shall proceed to convene the court under the provisions of ¶ 2624.1*d*.

b) The president of the College of Bishops (or in the case the accused is the president, the secretary) may preside or designate another bishop to serve as presiding officer.

c) The Trial Court shall be convened as provided in ¶ 2624.1*c*, with the twenty-one member pool to consist of twenty-one elders in full connection, named by the College of Bishops in approximately equal numbers from each episcopal area within the Jurisdictional or Central Conference.

d) Counsel for the Church shall be a bishop or another elder in full connection.

e) The Trial Court shall, at the conclusion of the proceedings, send all trial documents to the secretary of the Jurisdictional or Central Conference who shall keep them in custody. If an appeal is taken, the secretary shall forward the materials forthwith to the secretary of the Judicial Council. After the appeal has been heard, the records shall be returned to the secretary of the Jurisdictional or Central Conference.

f) A bishop suspended or removed from office shall have no claim upon the Episcopal Fund or salary, dwelling, or any other expenses from the date of such suspension or removal, but in case this bishop is thereafter found not guilty of the charge or charges for which suspended or removed, the bishop's claim upon the Episcopal Fund for the period during which deprived of the function of office shall be paid.

3. *Trial of a Ministerial Member of an Annual Conference, Local Pastor, or Diaconal Minister.—a)* The bishop of the accused shall proceed to convene the court under the provisions of ¶ 2624.1*d.*

b) The bishop may preside or may designate another bishop, a district superintendent, or elder in full connection to be presiding officer.

c) (1) The Trial Court for a ministerial member shall be convened as provided in ¶ 2624.1*c,* with the twenty-one member pool to consist of elders in full connection. If there are not enough persons in appropriate categories in an Annual Conference to complete the pool, additional persons may be appointed from other Annual Conferences. All appointments to the pool shall be made by the district superintendents.

(2) The Trial Court for a local pastor shall be convened as provided in ¶ 2624.1*c* and shall consist of a twenty-one member pool who shall be local pastors or, when necessary, members of the church.

(3) The Trial Court for a diaconal minister shall be convened as provided in ¶ 2624.1*c* and shall consist of a twenty-one member pool who shall be diaconal ministers or, when necessary, members of the church.

d) Counsel for the Church shall be an elder in full connection.

e) The Trial Court shall, at the conclusion of the proceedings, send all trial documents to the secretary of the Annual Conference who shall keep them in custody. Such documents are to be held in a confidential file and shall not be released for other than appeal purposes without a signed release from both the accused minister and the presiding officer of the Trial Court which tried the case. If an appeal is taken, the secretary shall forward the materials forthwith to the president of the Court of

Appeals of the Jurisdictional or Central Conference. If a president has not been elected, the secretary shall send the materials to such members of the Court of Appeals as the president of the College of Bishops shall designate. After the appeal has been heard, the records shall be returned to the secretary of the Annual Conference, unless a further appeal on a question of law has been made to the Judicial Council, in which case the relevant documents shall be forwarded to the president of that body.

4. *Trial of Lay Member.*—*a)* The district superintendent of the accused shall proceed to convene the court under the provisions of ¶ 2624.1*c.*

b) The district superintendent may be the presiding officer or may designate another elder in full connection to preside.

c) The Trial Court shall be convened as provided in ¶ 2624.1*c,* with the twenty-one member pool to consist of lay members in good standing of the accused's local church.

d) Counsel for the Church shall be a lay person who is a member in good standing.

e) The Trial Court shall, at the conclusion of the proceeding, deposit all trial documents with the secretary of the Charge Conference. If an appeal is taken, the secretary shall deliver all documents to the district superintendent. After the appeal has been heard, the records shall be returned to the custody of the secretary of the Charge Conference.

¶ **2625.** *Appeal Procedures.*—1. *General.*—*a)* In all cases of appeal the appellant shall within thirty days give written notice of appeal and at the same time shall furnish to the officer receiving such notice, and to the counsel for the Church, a written statement of the grounds of the appeal, and the hearing in the appellate court shall be limited to the grounds set forth in such statement.

b) When any appellate court shall reverse, in whole or in part, the findings of a Committee on Investigation or a Trial Court or remand the case for a new hearing or trial or change the penalty imposed by that committee or court, it shall return to the convening officer of the Committee on Investigation or Trial Court a statement of the grounds of its action.

c) An appeal shall not be allowed in any case in which the accused has failed or refused to be present in person or by counsel at the investigation and the trial. Appeals, regularly taken, shall be heard by the proper appellate court, unless it shall appear to the said court that the appellant has forfeited the right to appeal by misconduct, such as refusal to abide by the findings of the Committee on Investigation or Trial Court; or by withdrawal from the Church; or by failure to appear in person or by counsel to prosecute the appeal; or prior to the final decision on appeal from conviction, by resorting to suit in the civil courts against the complainant or any of the parties connected with the ecclesiastical court in which the appellant was tried.[9]

d) The right of appeal, when once forfeited by neglect or otherwise, cannot be revived by any subsequent appellate court.

e) The right to take and to prosecute an appeal shall not be affected by the death of the person entitled to such right. Heirs or legal representatives may prosecute such appeal as the appellant would be entitled to do if living.

f) The records and documents of the trial, including the evidence, and these only, shall be used in the hearing of any appeal.

g) In no case shall an appeal operate as suspension of sentence. The findings of the Committee on Investigation or the Trial Court must stand until they are modified or reversed by the proper appellate court.

h) The appellate court shall determine two questions only: (1) Does the weight of the evidence sustain the charge or charges? (2) Were there such errors of law as to vitiate the verdict? These questions shall be determined by the records of the trial and the argument of counsel for the Church and for the accused. The court shall in no case hear witnesses.

i) In all cases where an appeal is made and admitted by the appellate court, after the charges, findings, and evidence have been read and the arguments conclude, the parties shall withdraw, and the appellate court shall consider and decide the case. It may reverse, in whole or in part, the findings of the Committee on Investigation or the Trial Court, or it may remand

---

[9]*See* Judicial Council Decision 3.

the case for a new trial. It may determine what penalty, not higher than that affixed at the hearing or trial, may be imposed. If it neither reverses, in whole or in part, the judgment of the Trial Court, nor remands the case for a new trial, nor modifies the penalty, that judgment shall stand. The appellate court shall not reverse the judgment nor remand the case for a new hearing or trial on account of errors plainly not affecting the result. All decisions of the appellate court shall require a majority vote.

j) In all cases the right to present evidence shall be exhausted when the case has been heard once on its merits in the proper court, but questions of law may be carried on appeal, step by step, to the Judicial Council.

k) Errors of defects in judicial proceedings shall be duly considered when present on appeal. (1) In regard to cases where there is an investigation under ¶ 2621 but no trial is held as a result thereof, errors of law or administration committed by those in charge of the investigation are to be corrected by the presiding officer of the next conference on request in open session, and in such event the conference may also order just and suitable remedies if injury resulted from such errors. (2) Errors of law or defects in judicial proceedings which are discovered on appeal are to be corrected by the presiding officer or the next conference upon request in open session, and in such event the conference may also order just and suitable remedies if injury has resulted from such errors.

2. *Appeal of a Bishop.—a)* A bishop shall have the right of appeal to the Judicial Council in case of an adverse decision by the Trial Court; *provided* that within thirty days after the conviction the bishop notify the secretary of the Jurisdictional or Central Conference in writing of intention to appeal.

b) It shall be the duty of the secretary of the Jurisdictional or Central Conference, on receiving notice of such appeal, to notify the secretary of the Judicial Council, and the council shall fix the time and place for the hearing of the appeal and shall give due notice of the same to the appellant and to the secretary of the Jurisdictional or Central Conference, who in turn shall notify the counsel for the Church.

3. *Appeal of a Ministerial Member of an Annual Conference, Local Pastor, or Diaconal Minister.—a)* Each Jurisdictional and Central

Conference, upon nomination of the College of Bishops, shall elect a Court of Appeals, composed of nine itinerant elders, who have been at least six years successively members of The United Methodist Church, and an equal number of alternates. In addition, two local pastors and two alternates shall be elected in the same manner, to serve as members of the Court of Appeals in the event, and only in the event, that the appellant is a local pastor. In addition, the Court of Appeals shall have two diaconal ministers and two reserves elected in the same manner who will serve in the event, and only in the event, that the appellant is a diaconal minister. This court shall serve until its successors have been confirmed. This court shall have full power to hear and determine appeals of ministerial members taken from any Annual Conference within the jurisdiction. The court shall elect its own president and secretary and shall adopt its own rules of procedure, and its decisions shall be final, except that an appeal may be taken to the Judicial Council upon questions of law.

b) In case of conviction in a Trial Court a ministerial member, local pastor, or diaconal minister shall have the right of appeal to the Jurisdictional or Central Conference Court of Appeals above constituted; provided that within thirty days after the conviction the appellant shall notify the president of the conference and the president of the Trial Court in writing of the intention to appeal.

c) When notice of an appeal has been given to the president of the Trial Court, the president shall give notice of the same to the secretary of the Court of Appeals of the Jurisdictional or Central Conference and submit the documents in the case, or in case the documents have been sent to the secretary of the Annual Conference, instruct the secretary to send the documents to the president of the Court of Appeals. The Jurisdictional or Central Conference Court of Appeals shall give notice to the president of the conference from which the appeal is taken and to the appellant of the time and place where the appeal will be heard. Both the Annual Conference and the appellant may be represented by counsel. The president of the conference shall appoint counsel for the Church.

d) All necessary traveling and sustenance expense incurred by the Court of Appeals, the counsel for the Church, and the counsel for the defendant, in the hearing of an appeal case coming from an Annual Conference and appearing before any Jurisdictional or Central Conference Court of Appeals, shall be paid out of the administration fund of the Central or Jurisdictional Conference in which the proceedings arise.

4. *Appeal of a Lay Member.*—*a)* A lay member convicted in a Trial Court shall have the right of appeal and shall serve written notice of appeal with the pastor and the district superintendent within thirty days of conviction.

b) The district superintendent shall, on receipt of notice of appeal, give written notice to all concerned of the time and place of the convening of a Court of Appeals, not less than ten or more than thirty days after such notice has been delivered.

c) The Court of Appeals shall be constituted in the following manner: the district superintendent shall appoint eleven lay persons who are members of local United Methodist Churches other than the appellant's, and who hold office either as lay leader or lay member of the Annual Conference. At the convening of the Court of Appeals, from seven to eleven of these shall be selected to serve on the Court. The counsel for appellant and the counsel for the Church shall have the right to challenge for cause, and the decisions on the validity of such challenges shall be made by the presiding officer, who shall be the district superintendent.

d) The findings of the Court of Appeals shall be certified by the district superintendent, to the pastor of the church of which the accused is a member.

5. *Other Appeals.*—*a)* The order of appeals on questions of law shall be as follows: from the decision of the district superintendent presiding in the Charge or District Conference to the bishop presiding in the Annual Conference, and from the decision of the bishop presiding in the Annual Conference to the Judicial Council, and from a Central Conference to the Judicial Council.

b) When an appeal is taken on a question of law, written notice of the same shall be served on the secretary of the body in which the decision has been rendered. It shall be the secretary's duty to see that an exact statement of the question submitted and the ruling of the chair thereon shall be entered on the journal. The secretary shall then make and certify a copy of the question and ruling and transmit the same to the secretary of the body to which the appeal is taken. The secretary who thus receives said certified copy shall present the same in open conference and as soon as practicable lay it before the presiding officer for a ruling hereon, which ruling must be rendered before the final adjournment of that body, that said ruling together with the original question and ruling may be entered on the journal of that conference. The same course shall be followed in all subsequent appeals.

¶ 2626. *Miscellaneous Provisions.*—1. Any ministerial members residing beyond the bounds of the conference in which membership is held shall be subject to the procedures of ¶¶ 2620-2625 exercised by the appropriate officers of the conference in which he/she resides.

2. When a bishop, ministerial member, local pastor, or diaconal minister is accused of an offense under ¶ 2621 and desires to withdraw from the Church, the Jurisdictional or Central Conference in the case of a bishop, the Annual Conference in the case of a ministerial member, or the District Conference (where there is no District Conference, the Charge Conference) in the case of a local pastor or diaconal minister, may permit withdrawal, in which case the record shall be "Withdrawn under charges," and that person's status shall be the same as if expelled.

3. If a deaconess or home missionary is accused of an offense and desires to withdraw from the office, the Committee on Deaconess and Home Missionary Service or, if this committee does not exist, then the Board of Diaconal Ministry, may recommend to the National Division that the person be permitted to withdraw, in which case the record shall be "Withdrawn under complaints." If formal charges have been presented, such person may be permitted to withdraw; in which case the record shall be "Withdrawn under charges." In either case the status shall be the same as if the deaconess or home missionary had been expelled from the office.

4. When a member of the Church is accused of an offense and desires to withdraw from the Church, the Charge Conference may permit such member to withdraw, in which case the record shall be "Withdrawn under complaints." If formal charges have been presented, such member may be permitted to

withdraw, in which case the record shall be "Withdrawn under charges." In either case the status shall be the same as if the member had been expelled.

5. In all matters of judicial administration the rights, duties, and responsibilities of ministerial members of Missions, Missionary Conferences, and Provisional Annual Conferences are the same as those in Annual Conferences, and the procedure is the same.

6. Any ministerial member or local pastor who shall hold a religious service within the bounds of a pastoral charge other than that to which appointed when requested by the preacher in charge or the district superintendent not to hold such service shall be subject to charges of disobedience to the order and Discipline of the Church and/or relationships and/or behavior which undermines the ministry of another pastor, and if that minister shall not refrain from such conduct, he/she shall then be liable to the provisions of ¶ 2623.

GLOSSARY

This glossary, like the index, is not part of the law of the Church but rather a guide to that law, arranged in alphabetical order for the convenience of readers. So far as possible, the definitions are based on the Constitution and legislation and use the Disciplinary language. Where there is no specific legislation, they are based on historical usage and accepted practice. For terms not defined here, see the index, where paragraphs containing definitions or definitive information are indicated by boldface type.

Accountability. The requirement upon an organized structural unit in The United Methodist Church to report, explain, or justify its action(s) to another unit in the church structure. It also implies willingness to receive from and give careful consideration to references and recommendations made to it by the unit to which it is accountable. *See* Amenability. (¶ 802.)

Administrative Board. The primary administrative body of the local church to which the members, organizations, and agencies of the local church are amenable. The board functions under and is amenable to the Charge Conference. (¶¶ 252-255.)

Advance, Advance Specials. The program for promoting special gifts to missionary causes over and above apportioned World Service and other general funds and conference benevolences. Moneys given through this program are known as Advance special gifts. (¶¶ 913-914.)

Advanced Study. A four-year course of study prescribed by the Division of Ordained Ministry for associate membership with exceptional promise meeting in part education qualifications for probationary and full conference membership.

GLOSSARY

Affiliate Member. A lay person residing away from home for an extended period who is enrolled in a nearby church for fellowship, pastoral care, and participation in activities, but is still counted as a member of the home church. (¶ 227.)

Affiliated Autonomous Church. A self-governing church in whose establishment The United Methodist Church or one of its constituent members (The Evangelical United Brethren Church and The Methodist Church) has assisted and which by mutual agreement has entered into a covenant of relationship with The United Methodist Church.

Affiliated United Church. A self-governing church which is the result of a union of several churches (at least one of which has had historical roots in The United Methodist Church) and in whose establishment The United Methodist Church has assisted and which by mutual agreement has entered into a covenant of relationship with The United Methodist Church.

Affiliation. A designation that a health and welfare agency has had its relationship with one or more connectional unit of the Church verified by the Certification Council and conforms to the provisions of ¶¶ 721.4*b* (10), (11), (24), (25), and 815 where applicable.

Agency. A term used generically to include any council, board, division, commission, committee, or other body established to carry out the work of the Church. General agencies are constituted by the General Conference and defined in ¶ 802.

Amenability. The requirement upon an organized unit in The United Methodist Church to answer to, act under instruction of, agree with, yield to, or submit to another unit in the church structure. It connotes legal responsibility. *See* Accountability. (¶ 802.)

Appointment. All ministerial members who are in good standing in an Annual Conference shall receive annually appointment by the bishop unless they are granted a sabbatical leave, a disability leave, or are on leave of absence or retire. The appointment may be to a pastoral charge or to special appointments beyond the local church. The term is also often applied to the position to which the minister is assigned by the bishop. (¶¶ 436-440, 527-531.)

634

Appointment Beyond the Local Church. Ministers may be appointed to serve in ministries beyond the local church which extend the witness and service of Christ's Church. Such appointments include the connectional structures of the denomination, including theological school faculties; missionaries and various types of chaplaincies; and certain types of outreach activities. Such appointments remain within the itinerancy and such ministers are accountable to the Annual Conference. (¶ 439.)

Appointment, Ministerial. All ordained ministerial members who are in good standing in an Annual Conference shall receive annually appointment by the bishop unless they are granted a sabbatical leave, a disability leave, or are on leave of absence or retire. The appointment may be to a pastoral charge or to special appointments beyond the local church. The term is also often applied to the position to which the ordained minister is assigned by the bishop.

Appointment, Service. All diaconal ministers who are in good standing in an Annual Conference shall receive annually a service appointment, negotiated by the employing agency and the diaconal minister, recommended by the conference Board of Diaconal Ministry, reviewed by the Cabinet, and approved by the bishop unless they are granted a sabbatical, disability leave, leave of absence, or retirement. The term may also be applied to the position held by the diaconal minister.

Appointment to a Pastoral Charge. A pastor is an ordained or licensed person approved by vote of the ministerial members in full connection, appointed by the bishop to be in charge of a station, circuit, larger parish, or on the staff of one such appointment. (¶ 438.)

Apportionment. An amount assigned to a local church or other United Methodist body by proper church authority to be raised by that body as its share of some church fund.

Area, Episcopal. The Annual Conference or Conferences assigned to a bishop for residential and presidential supervision. In a less technical sense, the geographical region covered by such conference or conferences. (¶¶ 53-54, 622.3, 638.6.)

Articles of Religion. A series of thirty-nine doctrinal definitions first adopted by the Church of England in 1563. In 1784, John Wesley abridged this list to twenty-four (filtering out their original Calvinist emphasis) and sent them to America as an appendix in his proposed prayerbook for the American Methodists. Later, they were moved to the front of the Discipline and were understood by many as the statement of orthodox Methodist doctrine.

Associate Member, Lay. A lay member of another denomination, residing away from home for an extended period, who is enrolled in a nearby United Methodist church for fellowship, pastoral care, and participation in activities, but who is still counted as a member of the home church. (¶ 227.)

Associate Member, Ministerial. These ministers are in the itinerant ministry of the Church. They have not met all the requirements of full ministerial membership in their Annual Conference. They are eligible for ordination as deacons and may vote on matters coming before the Annual Conference, with the exception of three matters reserved to the full members, and they may serve as member of conference boards and agencies. (¶¶ 419-421.)

Autonomous Church. A self-governing church. More specifically, a self-governing church in whose establishment The United Methodist Church or one of its constituent bodies (Evangelical United Brethren and Methodist Churches) has assisted.

Bar of the Conference. The spatial area within which the business of the Annual Conference is transacted. Usually the floor of the auditorium extending far enough to include the seating of all members.

Benevolences. A term used to describe monetary gifts to causes which are carrying out the mission of the Church, as distinguished from moneys given to provide for the administration of the church organization, such as current expenses and salaries in the local church and administrative activities on the conference and general levels.

Bishop. A general superintendent of The United Methodist Church. An elder who has been elected to the office of bishop by a Jurisdictional or Central Conference and duly consecrated by other bishops. (¶¶ 50-59, 503-514.)

Board. A continuing body of the Church created by the General Conference to carry out certain functions of mission. Four of the boards are related to program: Church and Society, Discipleship, Global Ministries, and Higher Education and Ministry. Two boards perform service functions: Pensions and Publication. The chief staff officer of a general board is a general secretary. (¶ 803.7.)

Cabinet. The resident bishop and the district superintendents of an Annual Conference acting together as a body.

Candidacy for Ministry. Steps required of every person seeking to become part of the ordained or diaconal ministry of The United Methodist Church. These steps involve inquiry into potentials of personal, spiritual, academic, and professional aspects of ministry.

Certification. A designation that a health and welfare agency is affiliated with a connectional unit of the Church and that it has met certain professional, scientific, and Church standards acknowledged by the Health and Welfare Ministries Division or other accrediting association approved by the division to reflect a high level of professional care and competence.

Certification Council. That unit of Health and Welfare Ministries Division which: (*a*) establishes Church and professional standards for health and welfare agencies related to one or more connectional units of the Church so as to assist an institution which desires to provide care with a high level of professional competence; (*b*) recognizes bona fide relationships between health and welfare agencies and connectional units of the Church; and (*c*) recognizes those institutions which have attained standards acknowledged by the Certification Council to reflect a high level of professional care and competence.

Certification, Leadership. A procedure of The United Methodist Church whereby persons meet specific standards for designated leadership roles such as laboratory leader, seminar teacher, lay speaker, etc.

Certification, Professional. A procedure of The United Methodist Church whereby persons employed by the Church may meet personal, Church, academic, and service standards set through the Board of Higher Education and Ministry and receive authorization by the Church as ministers, directors, and associates in fields such as education, music, evangelism, church business administration, communication, etc.

Certification Studies. Alternate to graduate degree studies for certification as an associate in education, evangelism, or music.

Charge, Pastoral. One or more local churches which are organized under and subject to the Book of Discipline, governed by a single Charge Conference and to which a minister or local pastor is appointed as pastor in charge. (¶ 205.1)

Church and Community Ministry. A program of the National Division of the Board of Global Ministries which places church and community workers in settings to assist in church leadership and community development in organizing for ministry. The National Division and the Annual Conference share in the assignment and funding of these workers.

Church and Community Workers. Professional personnel assigned by the National Division of the Board of Global Ministries to projects within Annual Conferences upon request to serve in church leadership and community development in organizing to augment and strengthen the leadership within the area.

Church, Local. A connectional society of persons who have professed their faith in Christ, have been baptized, have assumed the vows of membership in The United Methodist Church, and are associated in fellowship as a local United Methodist church in order that they may hear the Word of God, receive the Sacraments, and carry forward the work which Christ has committed to his Church. Such a society of believers being within The United Methodist Church and subject to its Discipline is also an inherent part of the Church Universal, which is composed of all who accept Jesus Christ as Lord and Savior, and which in the Apostles' Creed we declare to be the holy catholic Church. (¶ 203.)

Church School. The program of the local church for instructing and guiding its entire constituency in Christian faith and living. Church school settings include the Sunday church school and all other ongoing and short-term classes and learning groups for persons of all ages. (¶ 262.1.)

Circuit. Two or more local churches which are joined together for pastoral supervision, constituting one pastoral charge. (¶ 205.2.)

Cluster Group. A group of churches located in the same geographical area with a loosely knit organization which allows the participating congregations and pastoral charges to engage in cooperative programs in varying degree. A district may be divided into cluster groups for administrative purposes. (¶ 206.3.)

College of Bishops. All the bishops assigned to or elected by a Jurisdictional or Central Conference. This group, which annually elects a president and secretary from among its membership, carries out various responsibilities assigned it by the Book of Discipline or by the Council of Bishops. (¶ 53.)

Commission. At the general level, an organization established by the General Conference for the fulfillment of a specific function for either an indefinite or a limited period of time. The standing commissions are Archives and History, Christian Unity and Interreligious Concerns, Communication, Religion and Race, and Status and Role of Women. (¶ 803.3.) At the Annual Conference level, there shall be counterpart commissions to the standing commissions.

Committee. At every level of the Church, a body, either temporary or permanent, created to carry out certain functions of mission, study, oversight, or review. It is amenable to its parent body. (¶ 803.4.)

Conciliar, Conciliar Principle. Terms referring to the pattern of church governance in doctrine as well as practical affairs by councils or synods at various levels. Councils, though bound to the Scriptures as their norm, have authority in the development of doctrine in their churches.

Concordat. A formal agreement between General Conference of The United Methodist Church and a similar body of an autonomous or United Church that provides for reciprocal membership in the highest legislative body of each. Existing concordats provide for vote exchange with The Methodist Church of Great Britain, The Methodist Church in the

Caribbean and the Americas, and The Methodist Church of Mexico. Implicit in such concordats is commitment to mutual cooperation.

Conference, Annual. The basic administrative body in The United Methodist Church, bearing responsibility for the work of the Church in a specific territory as established by the Jurisdictional or Central Conference. (¶¶ 36-41, 701-733.) Also, the term is commonly used to indicate the territory administered by such a body.

Conference Benevolences. The various causes and missional budgets of The United Methodist Church are known as benevolences. Conference benevolences are causes approved by the Annual Conference and included in the conference budget. (¶ 710.3.)

Conference Budget. The total amount to be apportioned for conference causes including conference benevolences, service causes, administration, and the work of all agencies receiving financial support from the Annual Conference.

Conference, Central. A body representing one or more Annual Conferences located outside the United States, comparable in function to a Jurisdictional Conference within the United States, developing their own Disciplines within the context of their cultures. (¶¶ 27-30, 636-638.)

Conference, Charge. The governing body of the pastoral charge. (¶¶ 48-49, 248-249.) A Church Local Conference is a body similarly constituted in each local church of a circuit, with its authority limited to certain property concerns of that local church. (¶ 2521.)

Conference, Church. An assembly open to all the members of a charge after having been authorized by the district superintendent on request of the Administrative Board, 10 percent of the church membership, or at the superintendent's discretion. When so authorized, it can assume all the functions of the Charge Conference. (¶ 251.)

Conference, Church Local. If a pastoral charge consists of two or more churches, those members of its Charge Conference who are members of each local church will meet separately as a Church Local Conference for the purpose of electing officers of that local church. They may also meet to act in regard to property matters or any other concerns which are properly those of a single local church rather than of the entire charge. (¶ 2521.)

Conference Claimants. Retired ministers, the surviving spouses of deceased ministers, and the dependent children of deceased ministers are claimants upon the conference retirement funds.

Conference, District. An assembly held annually in each district where so directed by the Annual Conference. It includes lay and ministerial representatives from each local church and performs the duties assigned to it. (¶¶ 734-741.)

Conference, General. The legislative body for the entire Church, meeting every four years and having full legislative power over all connectional matters (other than constitutional amendments, which also require a vote of all the members of all the Annual Conferences). It is composed of elected lay and ministerial members, in equal numbers, from all the Annual Conferences. (¶¶ 12-21, 601-610.)

Conference, Jurisdictional. The representative regional body, of which there are five in the United States, composed of an equal number of lay and ministerial delegates from the several Annual Conferences located within the jurisdictional boundaries and meeting every four years. It elects the bishops to serve in that jurisdiction and certain members of the general boards and agencies of the Church. Further structure varies from jurisdiction to jurisdiction. (¶¶ 22-26, 611-638.)

Conference, Missionary. A body similar to an Annual Conference, but with limited powers, which because of its limited membership, ministry, financial strength, and property requires administrative guidance and large financial aid from the General Board of Global Ministries. (¶¶ 657-660.)

Conference, Provisional Annual. A body similar to an Annual Conference which, because of small membership, has limited powers. It receives special administrative consultation and financial aid from the General Board of Global Ministries.

Connectional, Connectional Principle. The principle that all United Methodists and United Methodist congregations are connected in a network of conciliar and legal relationships. This and the appointive system, in which the bishop has final authority, constitute two of the most distinctive features of United Methodist polity.

Consecration. The act of conferring a ministerial office or function as for a bishop or diaconal minister.

Consultation. A basic part of the itinerant system wherein the district superintendent confers with pastors and Pastor-Parish Relations Committees. It is a continuing process with more intense involvement during the period of change of appointment. Consultation gives careful consideration to the criteria developed for the parish, performance evaluation of the pastor, and the mission of the Church.

Cooperative Parish or Ministry. Two or more pastoral charges or local churches which, because of geographic location or particular needs, coordinate program and organization to fulfill a ministry directed to all the people in the general geographic area. (¶ 206.)

Council. On the general level, a continuing body of the Church created by the General Conference or established in its Constitution. Examples of the former are the General Council on Finance and Administration and the General Council on Ministries. Examples of the constitutional councils are the Council of Bishops and the Judicial Council. (All these councils are described elsewhere in the glossary.) Each of these councils has been charged with review and/or oversight authority over some aspect of the organizational life and work of the denomination.

Councils on the conference, district, and local church levels are governing bodies for these powers and functions are ascribed to them by the Book of Discipline or by the proper authorizing bodies.

Council of Bishops. The body consisting of all the bishops of all the Jurisdictional and Central Conferences of the Church. (¶ 52.)

Council on Finance and Administration, Annual Conference. Each Annual Conference shall have a Council on Finance and

Administration, whose purpose is to develop, maintain, and administer a comprehensive plan of fiscal and administrative policies, procedures, and management services for the Annual Conference. (¶¶ 707-716.)

Council on Finance and Administration, General. It is accountable to the General Conference for matters relating to the receiving, disbursing, and reporting on general church funds, and it provides property, investment, and management functions for the general Church. (¶¶ 906-907.)

Council on Ministries, Annual Conference. The primary program planning and correlating agency of the Annual Conference, with which Annual Conference agencies are to cooperate; amenable to the Annual Conference (¶ 717.)

Council on Ministries, District. It has within the district responsibilities and functions similar to those of the conference Council on Ministries. (¶ 737.)

Council on Ministries, General. A representative body of The United Methodist Church to which general program boards and agencies are accountable in the carrying out of program and which has authority to set new priorities of program for the denomination within policy guidelines set down by the General Conference, reporting all such actions to the next session of the General Conference, to which it is amenable. Each Annual Conference is represented, with the basic membership one-third laymen, one-third laywomen, and one-third clergy. (¶¶ 1001-1007.)

Council on Ministries, Local Church. The primary planning and programming group in each local church, made up of the pastor and elected officials and amenable to the Administrative Board. (¶¶ 256-257.)

Covenant of Relationship. An agreement between The United Methodist Church and an autonomous church, covering such items as transfer of ministers, transfer of church members, and mutual representation in legislative bodies. An autonomous church which has entered into such a covenant is known as an affiliated autonomous church.

Credentials. The official documents certifying to ministerial ordination or consecration.

Deacon. A person who has progressed sufficiently in preparation for the ministry to be received by an Annual Conference as either a probationary member or an associate member and who has been ordained deacon in accordance with the Order and Discipline of The United Methodist Church.

Deaconess. A woman who, in response to God's call and on recommendation of the Committee on Personnel in Mission of the General Board of Global Ministries, has been commissioned by a bishop to share faith in Jesus Christ and to minister to persons in need. Deaconesses serve the Church in any capacity not requiring full clergy rights. They are related to the General Board of Global Ministries through the National Division. A lifetime commitment to mission is presumed.

Diaconal Minister. A person who in response to God's call has committed his/her life to professional or full-time ministry in The United Methodist Church, and who has met standards set by the General Conference, the Division of Diaconal Ministry, and the conference Board of Diaconal Ministry and has been consecrated in accordance with the Discipline of The United Methodist Church by the laying on of hands of a bishop at a session of the Annual Conference.

Diaconal Ministry. Serving ministries in The United Methodist Church, often Christian education, evangelism, music, church business administration, communication, health and welfare, church and community work, etc.

Diaconate. The office to which diaconal ministers are consecrated.

Diakonate. The root of the words *deacon, deaconess, diaconate,* and *diaconal* is the Greek word *diakonia,* meaning service.

Director. In a local church, a lay person or specialized minister certified as having full qualifications to lead the program of Christian education, music, or evangelism; at the Annual Conference level, the executive office of the conference Council on Ministries sometimes called the conference council director.

Disciplinary. In accordance with the Constitution and laws of The United Methodist Church, as set forth in the Book of Discipline.

Discipline. A shorthand phrase for the Book of Discipline of The United Methodist Church, which is the official published statement (revised quadrennially to reflect actions of the General Conference) of the Constitution and laws of The United Methodist Church, its rules of organization and procedure, and a description of administrative agencies and their functions.

District. The major administrative subdivision of an Annual Conference, the number of which is established by the Annual Conference and the boundaries of which are set by the bishop after consultation with the district superintendents. It comprises all the pastoral charges in the prescribed territory and is under the supervision of a district superintendent. (¶ 517.)

District Superintendent. A minister appointed by the bishop to administer the work of the Church within a district. (¶¶ 501-502, 517-522.)

Division. A major component within a board or council along functional lines for the purpose of accomplishing a part of the total work of the board or council. The chief staff officer of a division is an associate general secretary. (¶ 803.7*b*.)

Ecumenical. From *oikumene*, meaning the whole inhabited earth. Ecumenical thought and action pertains to the given oneness and wholeness of the Christian church, the body of Christ. It involves dialogue and joint action among various sectors of the Christian community; the healing of divisions and elimination of divisiveness among Christian churches; efforts toward unification of membership and ministries for worship and witness in a more truly inclusive fellowship.

Elder, Counseling. A ministerial member in full connection assigned by the Cabinet to provide counsel to a local pastor in fulfilling his or her requirements. The elder would ordinarily live near the local pastor to whom assigned. (¶ 411.)

Elders. Elders are ministers who have completed their formal preparation for the ministry of Word, Sacrament, and Order; have been elected itinerant ministers in full connection with an Annual Conference; and have been ordained elders in accordance with the Order and Discipline of The United Methodist Church by the laying on of hands of a bishop and other elders. (¶¶ 432, 435.) This is the higher ministerial order in the denomination.

Episcopacy. The system of church polity whereby bishops serve as general superintendents and exercise certain authority within the denomination. In The United Methodist Church this authority is constitutional, but subject to some definition by the General Conference. (¶¶ 50-59, 501-514.)

Evaluation. A process recommended by the Discipline in many areas of the Church's life wherein a person, program, or agency is evaluated against measurable goals, the evaluation done either by peers or a consultant. The local congregation is to be evaluated by the Administrative Board, and the general boards are evaluated by the General Council on Ministries. Performance evaluation for ministry is done by the Pastor-Parish Relations Committee; the appraisal of district superintendents by the Committee on District Superintendency; and the bishop by the conference Committee on Episcopacy.

Foundation Studies. The basic academic studies required by the Church for consecration as a diaconal minister—Bible, Old and New Testament, theology, church history (including United Methodist history), United Methodist doctrine and polity, mission of the Church in the contemporary world.

General Rules. A set of directions first drawn up by John Wesley in 1748 to demonstrate the connection between saving faith and Christian behavior. The three basic rules for all those whose desire for salvation is genuine and sincere are (1) to refrain from evil, (2) to be active in good works, and (3) to avail oneself of all "the means of grace."

Group Ministry. A loosely organized group of two or more pastoral charges in which ministers are appointed to charges. The ministers and/or lay council, representing all churches, may designate a coordinator. (¶ 206.3.)

Handicapping Conditions, Persons with. Persons whose disability or difference in appearance or behavior creates a problem of mobility, communication, intellectual comprehension, or personal relationships and which interferes with their participation or that of their families in the life of the Church.

Home Missionary. A person of the laity or clergy who in response to God's call and on recommendation of the Committee on Personnel in Mission of the General Board of Global Ministries, has been commissioned by a bishop to share faith in Jesus Christ and to minister to persons in need. Home missionaries are related to the General Board of Global Ministries through the National Division. A lifetime commitment is presumed.

Interreligious. Pertaining to relations between different religions; specifically, relations between Christians and persons of other living faiths.

Itinerary. The system of The United Methodist Church by which ministers are appointed to their charges by the bishop and are under discipline to accept such appointment.

Judicial Council. The highest judicial body of The United Methodist Church, elected by the General Conference. It determines, either on appeal or through declaratory decisions, the constitutionality of acts or proposed acts of the General, Jurisdictional, Annual, or Central Conferences, as well as whether other acts of official bodies of the Church conform to the Book of Discipline, all according to procedures set forth in said Discipline. (¶¶ 60-63, 2601-2619.)

Jurisdiction. A major regional division of The United Methodist Church within the United States, composed of several Annual Conferences (*see* Conference, Jurisdictional). (¶¶ 22-26.)

Laity. From *laos,* meaning people of God. More specifically, lay persons are those who are not of the ordained ministry.

Larger Parish. A number of congregations working together, using a parish-wide Administrative Board, Council on Ministries, and other committees and work groups as the parish may determine; providing representation on boards and committees from all churches; guided by a constitution or covenant; and served by a staff appointed to the parish and involving a director. (¶ 206.3.)

Lay Person. A member of a local church.

Lay Speaker. A member of a local church who has been certified by a district or conference Committee on Lay Speaking as qualified to conduct or assist in services of worship and to carry out a witness of the spoken word. (¶¶ 273-275.)

Leave of Absence, Ministerial. This relation is granted because of impaired health or for other equally sufficient reason when a minister is temporarily unwilling or unable to perform the full work of an appointment. The relationship is voted by the Annual Conference and it is reviewed annually. (¶ 444.)

License as a Local Pastor. License given by a district committee upon receipt of certificate of candidacy and completion of the requirements for the license, by which an unordained person may serve as a pastor with all rights and responsibilities. (¶¶ 406-407.)

Local Pastor. A lay person approved by the ministerial members in full connection in an Annual Conference who is authorized to perform all the duties of a pastor, including the Sacraments, while assigned to a particular charge under the specific supervision of a counseling elder, subject to annual renewal. (¶¶ 408-410.)

Location, Honorable. The voluntary termination of ordained minister's membership in an Annual Conference. Such action carries no moral stigma; the located person retains ministerial rights in the Charge Conference in which membership is held. (¶ 448.2.)

Member, Annual Conference. The membership of an Annual Conference is composed of an equal number of lay and ministerial members. The vast majority of the lay members are elected annually by their Charge Conference to serve as members of the Annual Conference. A few persons are members of the Annual Conference by virtue of elected office which they hold in the Annual Conference.

Diaconal ministers, by virtue of having completed educational and other requirements, may be elected annually as lay members of the conference in order to equalize the numbers of ordained ministers and laity.

Ordained ministers are members of the Annual Conference by virtue of having completed educational and other requirements and having been elected to membership by the ordained members of the Annual Conference. Ordained ministerial members hold their membership only in the

Annual Conference and are not members of a local church. Local pastors are also considered ministerial members of the Annual Conference.

Member, Church. A person who has been baptized and confirmed, entering into solemn covenant with the members of the Church as provided in the Ritual.

Minister, Diaconal. See Diaconal minister.

Minister in Effective Relation. A ministerial member of an Annual Conference who is not on leave of absence or retired.

Minister in Full Connection. A person who has satisfactorily completed all of the Disciplinary requirements for ministers in full connection and has been elected to this status by the ministers in full connection in an Annual Conference. The term "full member" is used synonymously with "member in full connection." (¶¶ 422-428.)

Minister, Retired. A minister who because of age, years of service, or other reason has been placed in the retired relation by action of the Annual Conference. This relation is granted automatically at the conference session following the ministers' seventieth birthday. A retired minister is eligible to be appointed but regardless may exercise ministerial rights, including voting membership in the Annual Conference. In past years, the term "superannuated" also referred to retired ministers. (¶ 447.)

Ministerial Course of Study. A four-year course of study prescribed by the Division of Ordained Ministry for associate membership with exceptional promise meeting in part education qualifications for probationary and full conference membership.

Ministerial Support. A primary fiscal concept of The United Methodist Church whereby each local church assumes responsibility for undergirding the entire ministry of the denomination. This includes support of its own appointed pastor, providing minimum salaries for all pastors, and support of district superintendents, bishops, and retired ministers and their spouses.

Ministry, General. The ministry of Christ belongs to all Christians by their Baptism. It is a ministry of witness and nurture as well as service.

Ministry, Ordained and/or Representative. Out of the general ministry some are called to be representative of the entire ministry of Christ in the Church and of the ministry required of the entire Church to the world. By training and vocation they are to enable the general ministry in their task.

Mission. a) The total outreach of the Church in witness, service, and community formation

b) More specifically, the administrative body of a field of work outside any Annual Conference, Provisional Annual Conference, or Missionary Conference, which is under the care of the General Board of Global Ministries and exercises in a general way the functions of a District Conference.

Missionary. a) A lay person or clergy who, upon offer of service in response to a commitment to mission and on recommendation of the Office of Personnel in Mission, has been commissioned by the General Board of Global Ministries and assigned to fulfill a task with colleagues in the Church or related institutions in the United States or in other parts of the world.

b) A minister or lay person from the Christian community outside the United States, resident and participating in the mission of an Annual Conference by invitation of that conference in consultation with the General Board of Global Ministries.

Multiple-Charge Parish. A number of congregations maintaining clear local identity on the organizational level but meeting parish-wide for Charge Conference; served by ministers appointed to charges and to the parish; and governed by a parish council. (¶ 206.3.)

Office. A support service unit within a board or council. (¶ 803.2*d*.)

Order (Person). The groupings of persons in various specialized and/or representative ministries (in The United Methodist Church there are two ministerial Orders: deacon and elder).

Order (Structure). The process by which the Church organizes and diversifies its life together and its mission in the world.

Ordination. The act of conferring ministerial orders, presided over by a bishop. (¶¶ 429-432.)

Parish. An area of service ministered to by one or more churches. These churches may be of different denominations. (¶ 206.3.)

Pastor. See Appointment to a Pastoral Charge.

Person in Mission. a) In general, any person involved in the mission of the Church.

b) More specifically, a term used by the General Board of Global Ministries for a person whose involvement in mission is in some way specifically facilitated by that board. The person may be a missionary of the General Board of Global Ministries or a person of another country responsible to the Church in that country.

Pluralism, Doctrinal. Expounded thoroughly in Wesley's famous sermon "Catholic Spirit," an attitude toward Christian truth that, recognizing the limitations of language, allows for more than one verbal statement of truth, each statement pointing to the truth but not exhausting truth nor excluding all other expressions of truth. This principle maintains the continuity and identity of the Christian message but assumes that this may find legitimate expression in various theological "systems" or in special-interest theologies. Differences may be argued fruitfully in terms of evidence and cogency.

Probationary Member. A person who, after meeting the conditions set forth in the Book of Discipline, has been received by vote of the ministers in full connection of an Annual Conference as a probationary ministerial member of that body. (¶¶ 413-418.)

Program Agency. A general board or commission which is responsible for implementing a specific sector of the program of The United Methodist Church and/or for the exercise of advocacy functions on behalf of the Church. The program agencies are the boards of Church and Society, Discipleship, Global Ministries, Higher Education and Ministry, and the standing general commissions on Christian Unity and Interreligious Concerns, Religion and Race, and the Status and Role of Women. The General Council on Ministries is responsible for the review of performance and the evaluation of the program agencies.

Reception on Credentials. The process by which a minister from some denomination is received into conference membership (full, probationary, or associate) on presentation of ministerial credentials from the other denomination. (¶ 428.)

Registrar for the Board of Ordained Ministry. One or more persons on a board responsible for keeping records and/or files on every candidate, local pastor, and probationary member of an Annual Conference.

Ritual. The rites and ceremonies which have been authorized for use in the administration of the Sacraments of the Lord's Supper and Baptism, in marriage, in the burial of the dead, ordination, and other offices for the conduct of private and public worship.

Sabbatical Leave. An appointment granted by the bishop upon approval of the Annual Conference to a ministerial member who has served an appointment full-time for six (for full members) or eight (for associate members) years. It is granted for an approved program of study or travel. (¶ 425.)

Secretary, Assistant General. On the general church level, the assistant staff officer of a council or board, or the chief staff officer of a section. (¶ 803.7c.)

Secretary, Associate General. On the general church level, the associate staff officer of a board or a council, or the chief staff officer of a division of a board or a council. (¶ 803.7b.)

Secretary, General. On the general church level, the chief staff officer of a council, board, or commission.

Section. A functional subunit of a division of a board or council, whose chief officer is an assistant general secretary. (¶ 803.2b.)

Speaking for the Church. No person, no paper, no organization, has the authority to speak officially for The United Methodist Church, this right having been reserved exclusively to the General Conference. (¶ 610.)

Special, Advance. A special gift to a specific benevolent cause, pledged and paid by a local church in addition to its apportioned benevolences. Such gifts may also be made by individuals or various church groups. (¶ 913.)

Special Appointment. See Appointment Beyond the Local Church.

Special Day. A day designated to emphasize certain needs or a specific program. The designated day may be observed with or without an offering. (¶¶ 270-272.)

Specialized Ministries. See Ministry, Ordained and Diaconal.

Town and Country, Urban. For United Methodist use, "country" refers to rural countryside, villages and towns of less than 2,500 population; "town" refers to larger towns and small cities of under 50,000 population; and "urban" refers to metropolitan areas of 50,000 and more, including suburbia, residential areas, and areas of the inner city. The terms are used for assigning responsibilities within boards, agencies, jurisdictions, Annual Conferences, and districts.

Trustees. The official body with the responsibility of acquisition, sale, maintenance, and management of church property. (¶¶ 2510, 2513, 2519.)

World Service. The basic general benevolences of The United Methodist Church, approved by the General Conference and apportioned through the Annual Conferences to the local churches. (¶ 911.)

World Service Special. Special gifts to the support of any cause or project which is a part of the work of any one of the World Service agencies. (¶ 912.)

INDEX

The numbers refer to paragraphs (¶¶) and to subparagraphs. Subparagraphs are indicated by the figures following the decimal points. Numbers in **bold-face type** indicate main references. For definitions of other Methodist terms *see* the Glossary.

A

Abandoned church, 2541
  records of, 521.5*a, d, e*

Abortion, 71G

Absence, leaves of
  bishop, 510
  diaconal minister, 313.1
  minister, 444, 449.1*f*

Abstinence, 72I, *footnote, pages 181-85*

Accountability of general agencies, 802

"Acknowledgement of transfer of membership," 240

Administrative Board, 252-55
  administrative officer, pastor as, 253, 255
  administrative responsibilities, 255.1
  amenability to Charge Conference, 249.1, 255.6
  appointment of optional committees, 266.4
  apportionment promotion, 255.4, .5

Administrative Board, *cont'd:*
  at-large members, 247.2, 249.4
  audit of membership rolls, 233
  benevolence promotion, 255.4
  budget establishment, 255.3*d*
  chairperson, 246.1, 257, 266.3
  character of members, 253
  as Charge Conference members, 248.2
  in cooperative parish, 206.3
  Council on Ministries recommendations to, 250.1*a*, .3*b*
  depositories for church funds, 266.3*d*
  ecumenical responsibilities, 255.8
  financial responsiblities, 255.3*d, e*, .4, .5
  honorary members, 250.10
  lay speaker, recommendation of, 274.1*b*, 275. 1*c*
  meetings, 252.2
  membership, 253, 266.1
  membership review, 230.5, 255.3*b*
  membership secretary reports to, 235
  new churches, encouragement of, 255.7
  Nominations and Personnel Committee, work with, 266.1
  officers, 254
  organization, 254

Affiliated United Church, *cont'd:*
and World Methodist Council,
2401.2

Affiliate member
of local church, 227
as delegates to General and Jurisdictional Conferences, 658.4*b*
of Missionary Conference, 658.4*b*

Affiliate Membership Roll, 227,
232.5

Affiliate relationship
of appointee beyond the local
church, 439.3*b*, .4

**Age-level and family coordinators,
258,** 262

Age-level and family councils, 263,
717.6

Age-level and family ministries,
720.6*c*, 1320

Age-level coordinators, 258, 262,
263
combination of, in small churches,
245.1*d*
on Council on Ministries, 257
election of chairperson, 247.1, 253

Age-level councils
Adult Council, 263.3
Adult/Older Adult Council, 262.4
Adult/Young Adult Council, 262.3
Children's Council, 263.1
Older Adult Council, 263.3
Young Adult Council, 263.3
Youth Council, 263.2

**Agencies, Annual Conference, 706-
33.** For detailed listing *see* Annual
Conference agencies

Agencies, general church, 801-22.
For detailed listing *see* General
agencies

Agencies, Jurisdictional, 627-35.
For detailed listing *see* Jurisdictional agencies

Age of retirement, 313.2*b*, 447.1, .2*b*,
508.1

Aging
ministry to, 261.3
rights of the, 72E

Air, use of, 70A

Alcohol, 72I, *footnote, pages 181–85*

alive now!, 1302.3

Amenability
of Administrative Board to Charge
Conference, 255.6
of bishops, 620
of conference program agencies,
717.9*a*
of Council on Ministries, local
church, 256
of Finance and Administration,
Conference Council on, 708.5
of general agencies, 802
of local church administrative
body, 244.1
of local pastor, 408.8
of minister, 412.1
of minister on honorable location,
448.2*b*
of minister under appointment
beyond the local church, 439.2*a*

Amendment to the Constitution,
64-66, 608

**American Association of Pastoral
Counselors,** 1605

Amercian Bible Society, 2405

Animal life, 70C

Annual Conference, 10, **36-40, 701-
42**
abandoned church, 2541

659

Annual Conference, *cont'd:*
voting rights in, 37, 413.2, 419.1,
.4, 423, 439.4, 701.1*a-d*, .2, .4
World Service budget, 710.3
worship responsibility, 720.4
youth ministry, coordinator, 732.3*j*
Youth Ministry, Council on, 732

Annual Conference agencies, 706-
33
additional committees, 706.2
Archives and History, Commission
on, 727
Christian Unity and Interreligious
Concerns, 728
Church and Society, Board of,
719.2-.4
Council on Ministries, 717-18
Deaconess and Home Missionary
Service, Committee on, 721.6
Diaconal Minstry, Board of, 724
Disability, Joint Committee on, 733
Discipleship, Board of, 720
Episcopacy, Committee on, 725
establishment of new agency,
721.4*a* (25)
Finance and Administration,
Council on, 707-16
general agency members as ex
officio members, 706.5
Global Ministries, Board of, 721
Higher Education and Campus
Ministry, Board of, 722
Laity, Board of the, 720.8
membership, 706.4
Ordained Ministry, Board of, 723
Parish and Community Develop-
ment, Committee on, 721.5
Pensions, Board of, 726
program agencies defined, 710.3*c*
program boards, 706.1
Religion and Race, Commission
on, 729
Status and Role of Women, Com-
mission on, 730
treasurer of, 715.3
United Methodist Women, 731
Youth Ministry, Council on, 732.
For detailed listing *see* each indi-
vidual agency

**Annual Conference journal, 705.2-
.6.** For detailed listing *see* Journal,
Annual Conference

**Annual Conference program agen-
cies and institutions defined,**
710.3*c*

Annual Conference property, 2510-
12

Annual Conference secretary. *See*
Secretary, Annual Conference

Annual Conference statistician,
702.6

Annual Conference treasurer,
708.2*a*, .3, 709.8, 714.1, **715**, 716

**Appalachian Development Com-
mittee,** 1529.28

Appeal
appellate court role in, 2625
of bishop, 621, 2625.2
in Central Conference, 638.17
counsel in, 2625.1*h*, .3*c*, .4*c*
Court of Appeals, Jurisdictional
and Central Conferences,
2625.3
death of appellant, 2625.1*e*
errors, decision in light of reversal
of, 2625.1*i*
errors of law, correction of,
2625.1*k*
evidence used in, 2625.1*f*
expenses from, 2625.3*d*
of lay member, 2625.4
of ministerial member, local pastor, diaconal minister, 2625.3
penalty determination, 2625.1*i*
questions determined by, 2625.1*h*
on questions of law, 2625.5
questions of law affecting outcome,
2625.1
presence of accused at trial,
2625.1*c*
restrictions disallowing, 2625.1*c*
reversal of findings, 2625.1*b, i*
right of, 18, 2625.1*c-e*

INDEX

Apportionments, *cont'd:*
District Board of Stewards responsibility, 711.3
to districts, 711.3
for district superintendent support, 710.1*a*
for Episcopal Fund, 710.1*b*, 924
formulas, 709.3, 906.1*b*
handling of by conference treasurer, 715.2
local church promotion, 255.4-.5
for ministerial support, 931-32
notice of:
to Annual Conferences, 908
to local churches, 249.11
for other causes, 710.4
for pension needs, 710.1*e*
proportionate payment of, 726.4
for World Service and conference benevolences, 710.3*d*, 711.4

Approved supply, pension credit for, 1706.3*b*, .4*g*, .5*a*

Architectural standards, church facilities, 1302.12, 1529.25

Archives, 1911.1, .2

Archives and History, Annual Conference Commission on, 727
records of merged or closed churches, 2441.2, 2538.4.

Archives and History, Jurisdictional Commission on, 630, 1904

Archives and History, Standing General Commission on, 1901-12
accountability, 1903-12
as administering agency, 803.6
archives:
central and regional, 1911.2*a*
definition of, 1911.1
and libraries, maintenance of, 1903.1, .3
bishop as president, 1906
central archivist, 1911.2*i*
custodianship of records, 1911.2*b*
depositing procedures, 1911.2*b*

Archives and History, Standing General Commission on, *cont'd:*
designation of shrines and landmarks, 1912.1
disposal of records, 1911.2*b*, *c*
executive committee, 1908
financial support, 1909
general agencies:
official documents of, 1911.2*g*
publications of, 1911.2*f*
records of, 1911.2*d*, *e*
general secretary, **1907,** 1908
Historical Convocation, 1910.3
Historical Society, 1910
historic sites, 1912.4
incorporation, 1902
meetings, 1905
membership, 805-806, 1904
name, 1901
national historic landmarks, 1912.3
national historic shrines, 1912.2
officers, 1906
personal papers deposited with, 1911.2*l*
purpose, 1903
quorum, 1903
records and documents to be deposited with, 1911.2
review and reclassification of landmarks, shrines, 1912.1*b*
voting procedure, 1908

Area expense fund, 710.2*b*, 923

Area superintendent, 717.2, 721.5*a*

Armaments, 75C

Articles of Religion, *pages 55-63,* 16, 306.3*f*, 414.7*c*

Assistant general secretary, 803.7*c*

Associate general secretary, 803.7*b*

Associate member, Annual Conference, 419-21
amenability, 412.1
appointment, 419

663

Associate member, Annual Conference, *cont'd:*
in Central Conference, 638.9
continuing education for, 441
course of study, 1629.2
as deacon, 419.3, 433.1, 1629.2
as delegate to General and Jurisdictional Conferences, 419.5
disability leave, 446
doctrinal examination, 420
educational requirements, 420
as elder, 419.3
eligibility, 419
honorable location, 448.2
involuntary termination, 449.1
leaves, 419.7, 444
as local pastor, 408.2
location, 419.7
maternity leave, 445
minimum salary for, 419.7
missionaries as, 419.6
ordination eligibility, 419.3
from other denominations, 419.1
pension credit for, 419.7, 1706.3a
psychological testing, 420
requirements for election, 420
requirement of, 447
rights, 419
sabbatical leave for, 444
service on annual boards, committees, 419.5
voluntary termination, 448.2
voting rights, 419.1, .4, 701.1c

Associate member, local church, 227
World Division overseas personnel as, 238

Associate Membership Roll, 227, 232.6

Associate of Christian Education, 253

Association, defined, 803.11

Association for Clinical Pastoral Education (ACPE), 1605

Association of Deaconesses/Home Missionaries, 1625.12

Association of Stewardship Leaders, 1315.8

Association of United Methodist Foundations, 1315.8

Audio-visuals, 1106.7

Audit
Audit and Review, Committee on, 905.4b
of church records and financial officers, 266.3c
of general church funds, 906.4
of General Council on Finance and Administration, 909
of membership rolls, 233

Audit and Review, Committee on, 905.4b

Autonomous church, 647
becoming part of The United Methodist Church, 651
World Division relationship to, 1556.1

Autonomy, proceedings for, 649

B

Baptism
appointees beyond the local church administering, 439.3a
certificate of, 222
of children, 221-23
of children of military personnel, 218
local pastor's right to administer, 408
pastor's right to administer, 438.2b
as prerequisite for church membership, 216.1
register of baptized children, 223

Birth control, 72H

Board of Stewards, district, 711.3, 2513.2

Board of the Laity, Annual Conference, 720.8

Board of Trustees, 903

Board of Trustees, Annual Conferences, 2510-12
abandoned church property, 2541
amenability, 2512
episcopal residence, 2511
incorporation, 2510.1
investment policy, 2510.2
meetings, 2512
membership, 2510.1
officers, 2512

Board of Trustees, district, 2513.2

Board of Trustees, local church, 245, **2519-22**
abandoned church property, 2541
Administrative Board, relation to, 255.1
age of, 2519
as building committee, 2536.3
chairperson, 253
Charge Conference authority over, 2523
in cooperative parish, 2522.2
district superintendent cooperation with, 521.2
duties of, 2527
election of, 246.5, 2520, 2522.1
on Finance Committee, 266.3
as guarantor of loans, 2536.12
meeting of, 2526
membership of, in United Methodist Church, 2525.1
in multiple church charges, 2521-22
officers of, 2524.2-.3
organization of, 2524-26
removal of member, 2525.2
report to Charge Conference, 2542
sale of real property with trust clauses, proceeds from, 2534

Board of Trustees, local church, *cont'd:*
as titleholders in unincorporated local church, 2528
training for, 1319.3
vacancy on, 2525.3

Bonding
of church officers, 2508
of conference and conference agency officers, 714
of treasurer of General Council on Finance and Administration, 909
of United Methodist Publishing House officers, 1826

Book editor, 1828-31

Book of Hymns, The, 1314.3

Book of Ritual of the Evangelical United Brethren Church, 1959, 1314.3

Book of Resolutions, 610.2*a, c*

Book of Worship, 720.4*b*, 1314.3

Boundaries
Annual Conference, 26.4, 30.4, 45
Central Conference, 43
authority to fix, 638.10
changes in, 44
episcopal areas, 622.3*b*
Jurisdictional Conference, 42
Provisional Central Conference, 642

Brooklyn Methodist Hospital, 1912.3*b*

Budget, Annual Conference, 710, 717.10*l*

Budget, local church, 250.3*e*, 266.3

Buildings
architectural standards for, 1302.12, 1529.25

Buildings, *cont'd:*
Building Committee, local church, 2536.6-.8
programs, 2536

Burial, authority to perform, 408.1, 434

Burial ground, title to, 2522.1

Business administrator, local church, 266.3

Business manager
General Conference, 907.14
local church, 253

C

Cabinet
administrative location, role of in granting, 449.2*b, c*
appointment beyond the local church, annual meeting with those holding, 439.2*b*
appointment of deaconess and home missionary, 1533.3*d*
appointment to extension ministries, 439.1*d*
appointment to less than full-time service, 437.2
consultation in appointment-making, 515, 529.2, .4
as corporate expression of superintendency, 526.2
council director's relation to, 717.7*a*
counseling elder, appointment of, 411
diaconal minister:
appointment of, 310.3*d*
change in conference relationship, 313
district superintendent's relation to, 526
evaluation training for Pastor-Parish Relations Committees, 427
frequency of appointments, 531
ministerial supply and demand report to, 527.2

Cabinet, *cont'd:*
new local church, consent needed for, 267.1
probationary member, recommendation of under special circumstances, 416.2
readmission role, 450-52
reinstatement of local pastor, 410.4
retired minister's return to effective relationship, 447.7
representation on Board of Ordained Ministry, 723.1*b*

Camping and outdoor ministry
acquisition and disposition of properties for, 720.1*d*
title to campground, 2522.1*d*

Campus minstry, 1612.2, .3*c, d, e, g,* .5, 1613.1*b,* .2, .3, 1614.2
funding of, 1615.3*b, c*
Higher Education and Campus Ministry, Annual Conference Board of, 722
local church work area on higher education and, 260.5
pastor in, 218

Campus pastor, 218

Candidacy registrar, 404

Candidate
for diaconal ministry, 303-06
Diaconal Ministry, Annual Conference Board of, responsibility for, 724.3*d-j, l, u*
for ordained ministry, 404-05
certification of, 735.3, 739.6-.8
Ordained Ministry, Annual Conference Board of responsibility toward, 723.2
Ordained Ministry, District Committee on, responsibility toward, 739.3-.8
records of, 723.3

Capital punishment, 74F

Career/Life Planning, Office of Vocation and, 1572

Certification Council, 721.4*a*(27), 1520

Certification Studies in Ministry Careers, 1625.3

Certified lay speaker, 249.9, 440
certification of, 274
renewal of, 275
consecration of, 274.2
functions, 273.2, .3
qualifications, 273.1, 274.1
report to Charge Conference, 275.1*c*
training course for, 274.1*a*, 275.1*c*

Certified lay worker, 724.4, 1319.2*b*

Chancellor, Annual Conference, 702.7

Changes in Annual Conference relationships, 443-47, 723.2*f*, 724.3 *m-n*

Chaplains
appointments to extension ministries, 439.1*b*
authority to adminster church membership vows, 217
Baptism of children of military personnel, 218
evangelism awareness, 1313.10
fields of service, 1610.1
membership for military personnel, process to be used, 218
pension credit, 1706.4*d*, .8
responsibility for, 1610

Chaplains and Related Ministries, Commission on, 1602

Chaplains and Related Ministries, Division of, 1608.1, **1609-11**
advocacy role, 1610.2*f*
annual required recommendation, 1610.2*e*
duties, 1610.2
extension ministries included in, 1610.1

Chaplains and Related Ministries, Division of, *cont'd:*
overseas laity, ministry to, 1610.3
pension consultation, 1704.12
pension fund provision, 1706.8
records of membership and Baptism of military personnel, 218
World Communion Offering, 1611
World Service Funds, 1611

Chaplains Pension Fund, 1704.12, 1706.8

Chargeable offenses, 2621, 2626.6

Charge Conference, 248-52
Administrative Board as members of, 248.2
administrative body amenable to, 244.1, 249.1, 255.6
appointee beyond local church as affiliate member, 439.3*b*, 514.4
apportionments and conference benevolences, reports to concerning, 249.11
audit of funds report to, 266.3*c*
Board of Trustees:
age of, 2519
election of, 2520, 2522.1
report from, 2542
candidates for church-related vocations, examination of, 249.7
candidates for ministry:
examination of, 249.5
recommendation of, 404-05
renewal of candidacy, 249.6
chargewide structures, right to provide, 249.13
as Church Conference, 242.6, 251
church historian, 250.4
Church Location and Building, reports from district Board of, 2514
church membership reports to, 233, 236, 249.12
continuing education for pastor outlined, 441.3
date of, 242.1, .3, .6, .7
definition of, 242.9

**Church and Society, General Board
of,** 1201-16
accountability, 802, 803.5
amenability, 802
assistant general secretary, 1214.3
associate general secretaries,
1214.2
bylaws, 1216
executive committee, 1209, 1211,
1216.1
Finance Committee, 1208
financial support, 1212
fiscal management, 1214.3
funds from predecessor boards,
1212
general secretary, 1214.1
headquarters, 1215
incorporation, 1202
internal organization, 1213
meetings, 1211
membership, 805-06
name, 1201
Nominating Committee, 1210
nominations to, 805.1
objectives, 1204
officers, 1208
organization, 1206
Police Community Relations Program, 271.3a(3)
predecessor boards, corporations,
departments, 1202
program development and implementation, 1216.2
as program-related agency, 803.5
purpose, 1203
quorum, 1211
representation on:
Family Life, Committee on,
1318.2
National Youth Ministry Organization, 1402.1
responsibilities, 1205
United Nations Office, 1217,
1547.8
vacancies, 1207

**Church and society, local church
work area on, 260.2**
chairperson, 259
representation on:

**Church and society, local church
work area on,** *cont'd:*
Adult Council, 263.3
Children's Council, 263.1
Youth Council, 263.2
responsibilities, 260.2
in small churches, 245.1c

Church Conference, 251
Board of Trustees election, 2520
in building program, 2536.7
election of church officers, 246
conference-wide special appeal
for, 718.3
district appeal for, 718.4
in metropolitan areas, 1530.5c
National Division responsibility
for, 1529.13, 1530.5
special session of Charge Conference, 242.6

Church founding date, 822

Church historian, 247.1, 250.4

Church Local Conference
Board of Trustees election, 2521.1
merger of two churches, role in,
2538.2, 2539.2

**Church Location and Building, dis-
trict Board (Committee) on,** 255.7
1530.5, 2513.1
abandoned church, 2541.1
building and remodeling plans,
2515-17
building sites, 2515
in church building program,
2536.1, .5, .8
district parsonage, 2518
district superintendent, cooperation with, 521.2
fifty-member-or-less churches,
2543
sale of church property:
to another denomination,
2540.2
to federated church, 2540.1

Church membership, 208-43

Church membership, *cont'd:*
restoration of, 230.4, 243
Social Principles, member's responsibility regarding, 214
temporary, of persons of another denomination, 227
terminated membership roll, 230.4, .5
of terminated minister, 447.2a, .5
termination of, 236
transfer of, **237-41**
  from another denomination, 220
  to another denomination, 241, 242
  to another United Methodist church, 240
of transient persons, 227
youth, rights of, as full members, 226, 262.2
youth classes in, 226
vows, 211, 230.1
withdrawal from, 230.1, .2, 242, 243
of World Division overseas personnel, 238

Church name, outside U.S., 821

Church property, 2501-45. For detailed listing *see* Property; Property, local church

Church School
Administration, 262.1c
Children's Fund for Christian Mission, 262.1f
curriculum, 262.1b. *See also* Church school publications; Curriculum; Curriculum Resources Committee
Discipleship, General Board of:
  resourcing of and guidance for, 262.1a
  role of in organizing, 1308.2
divisions, 262.1d
Education, Commission on, 262.1c
election of teachers, counselors, officers, 256

Church School, *cont'd:*
equipping, designing, arranging, 1309.8
extension promotion, 720.1e, 1313
Fourth Sunday offering, 262.1e
mission education, 262.1f
officers, 262.1d
organization, 262.1d
purpose, 262.1a
settings, 262.1d
special fund promotion, 1308.8
standards, 262.1a, 1309.2
superintendent, 247.1, 253, 256, 257, **261.2,** 262.1c
teacher recruitment and training, 720.1f

Church school publications, 1828, 1832-40
coordinated system of, 1837
editor of, 1832, 1835-36, 1839
see also Curriculum; Curriculum Resources Committee

Church School superintendent, 247.1, 253, 256, 257, **261.2,** 262.1c

Church-State separation, 74B

Church treasurer, 246.3, 253, 266.3, **.3b**

Churchwide appeals, 910.4, 912.3, 1539, 1542

Churchwide offerings, 270, 271.1, .3
see also Special days

Church Women United, 1547

Church year, 819.1

Circuit, 205.2

Civil authority, *pages 63, 68*

Civil disobedience, 74F

Clergy couples, 658.6, 935.8

Cluster groups, 206.3

Communications, director of, 717.5*a*

Communication, district Committee and/or coordinator of, 737.5

Communication, Standing General Commission on, 1101-08
accountability, 802, 1104
as administrative and program agency, 803.6
Advance promotion, 914.3
amenability, 802, 1104
audio-visual responsibility, 1106.7
Black College Fund promotion, 918
Book of Resolutions, editing, 610.2*c*
Comprehensive Communication System, 1106.8
Crusade Scholarship promotion, 1566.2
executive committee, 1107.3
field service program, 1106.11
financing, 1108
fund promotion and interpretation, 1106.11-.13
General Councils on Finance and Administration and Ministries, cooperation with, 1107.5, 1108
general secretary, 1007.1
incorporation, 1103
local church coordinator of communications, 1106.9, .10
meetings, 1107.2
membership, 805-06, 1107.1
name, 1102-03
National Council of Churches, cooperation with, 1106.4
nomination to, 805.1
officers, 1107.3
One Great Hour of Sharing, role in, 271.3*b*, 915.2
organization, 1107.1, .4
program journal, 1106.15
Promotion and Benevolence, Division of, 1007.5*b*
promotion and interpretation funding, 1106.12
public relations function, 1105,

Communication, Standing General Commission on, *cont'd:*
1106.2, .6
purpose, 1105
quorum, 1107.2
relationship to other church bodies, 1105
representation on:
Crusade Scholarship Committee, 1567
Personnel Policies and Practices, Committee on, 905.4*d*
special day offerings promotion, 271.1, 915.5, 1106.12
staff, 1107.5
stewardship cooperation with Board of Discipleship, 1106.14
television ministry, 1106.3
training responsibilities, 1106.10
UMCOR promotion, 1539
World Communion offering, role in, 271.3*f*, 915.4

Communities, alternative, 71B

Communities in transition, 207

Community, Nurturing (Social Principles), 71-75

Community Developers Program, 271.3*a*(1)

Complaints, formal, 449.1. *See also* Charges

Comprehensive communications system, 1106.8

Comprehensive Protection Plan, 1704.12, 1706.2*c*
disability leave policy, 446.4, 1706, 1706.17, .19, .20
for local pastors, 408.9

Concordat agreements, 647.5, 651, 654

Concordat churches, 351, 2003.4

Council on Ministries, district,
cont'd:
financing, 735.6
program plans approved by conference Council on Ministries, 735.5*m*

Council on Ministries, General, 1001-07
Advance, participating agency in, 1007.5*b, d*
Advance Committee organization, 1006.21
amenability, 1003
Annual Conference Councils on Ministries, relationship with, 1006.7
Annual Conference records sent to, 705.2
Archives and History accountability to, 1903.2
bishop's presence at meetings, 1007.1*g*
calendar maintenance, 1006.5*b*
Central Conference, assuring full participation of, 1006.18
Christian Unity and Interreligious Concerns:
reports to, 2003.14
responsive to, 2004
churchwide offerings, consultation on, 271.1
Church and Society, Board of, headquarters location, 1215
Communication, Commission on, relationship with, 1104, 1107.5, 1108
connectional structure study, 2006.11
depository for planning and research documents, 1006.16
duplication and overlapping in agency structure and function, 2006.10
ecumenical responsibility, 1006.20
evaluation of general agencies, 802, 1006.13
General Conference legislation review, 610.2*b*
General Council on Finance and

Council on Ministries, General,
cont'd:
Administration, cooperation with in World Service Fund budgeting, 1006.2
general agencies accountability to, 802
general agency budgets, 906.1*b*(6), 1006.1
general agency studies assignment, 1006.3
general secretaries of program agencies election, 813, 1006.15
general secretary, 814.4, 1007.6
incorporation, 1002
jurisdictional youth member of, 632.8
meetings, 1007.2
membership, 805-06
makeup, 1007.1*a*
restrictions on, 1007.1*b*
racial and ethnic, 1007.1*c*
missional priorities:
changes in, 1006.1
determination of need, 1006.17
implementation, 1006.4
Missional Priority Fund consultation, 921
name, 1001
National Association of conference council directors, 1006.22
nominations to, 805.1
objectives, 1005
officers, 1007.3
organization, 1007
periodical, general agency, approval of, 1006.8
program budget changes, 1006.1
publishing duplication and overlapping, 1006.9
purpose, 1004
representation on:
Official Forms and Records, Committee on, 905.4*c*
Personnel Policies and Practices, Committee on, 905.4*d*
resource, promotional literature review, 1006.5*c*
responsibilities, 1006
special days recommendations,

Council on Ministries, General, *cont'd:*
271.2*d*, 906.11, 1006.6
staff, 1007.6
structure, internal, 1007.4
term of office, 1007.1*f*
training responsibilities, 1006.12
World Service Fund budgeting and allocation, 906.1*b*, 911, 1006.2

Council on Ministries, Jurisdictional, 628

Council on Ministries, local church, 256-65
Administrative Board, relationship to, 255.1
Adult Council, 263.3
Adult/Older Adult Council, 262.4
Adult/Young Adult Council, 262.3
age-level councils, 263
age-level and family coordinators, 258
amenability, 256
chairperson, 246.1, 253, 266.3
Charge Conference election of members to, 257
Children's Council, 263.1
church school, 262.1,
officers, election of, 262.1*d*, 256
in cooperative parish, 206.3
Education, Commission on, 262.1*b*
expansion of, 256
family councils, 263.4
Finance, Committee on, work with, 256
inactive members, role regarding, 230
members, care of, 228, 229
membership, 257
Nominations and Personnel, work with Committee on, 266.1
officers, 257
Older Adult Council, 263.3
older adult ministry, 262.4
organization, 256
Pastor-Parish Relations Committee, work with, 256
responsibilities, 256

Council on Ministries, local church, *cont'd:*
in small churches, 245.1*a*
structure, 256
task groups, 265
training for, 1319.3
United Methodist Men, 262.6
United Methodist Women, 262.5
work areas, 259-60
Young Adult Council, 263.3
young adult ministry, 262.3
Youth Council, 262.2, 263.2

Council on Youth Ministry, Annual Conference, 732

Course of study
advanced studies in, 416.2
for associate members, 420
in Central Conference for all workers, 638.20
for local pastor, 409.1, .2
for nonstudents, 405.2
Ordained Ministry:
Annual Conference Board of, responsibility for, 723.2*c*
General Board, responsibility for, 1629.2

Counseling elder, 407, **411,** 518.4

Court of Appeals, 2624.1*h*, 2625.3, 2625.4*b-d*

Credentials
from another denomination, admission of, 428
for diaconal minister, 307
of member in full connection, 435.4
restoration of, to probationary member, 450
return of, to minister uniting with another denomination, 448.3
surrender of:
local pastor, 410.1
ministerial office, 448.4
probationary member, 448.1
under complaints or charges, 448.4

Crime, 74F

Crusade Scholarship Committee, 271.3*f,* 915.4*b,* 1506.1, **1564-67**

Crusade Scholarships, 721.3*f,* 1564-67, 1614.3*f,* 1629.10

Curriculum, church school
approval of, 1308.6, 1323-24
biblical basis, 1323
contents, 261.1*b*
coordinated system, 1837
editor of church school publications, 1832-33, 1835-36, 1839
evangelism concepts in, 1313.4
general description, 1322
stewardship concepts, 1315.4
worship concepts, 1314.9
see also Curriculum Resources Committee

Curriculum Resources Committee, 1308.6, 1313.14, 1314.9, 1315.4, **1322-27**
budget, 1325.1*e*
bylaws, 1327.2*b*
chairperson, 1325.1*e,* 1326.1, 1327.1*d*
cooperative publication, 1325.3*b*
curriculum plans, general, 1322
development of curriculum, 1323
Discipleship, relationship with Board of, 1325.1
editorial staff, 1323, 1325.1*d*
editor of church school publications, 1325.1*e,* .2*c,* 1326, 1327.1*c*
financing, 1325.2*d,* 1836
format, curriculum, 1325.2*c*
membership, 1327
promotion and interpretation, curriculum, 1325.1*b,* .2*b*
representation on National Youth Ministry Organization Steering Committee, 1402.1
United Methodist Publishing House relationship to, 1325.2, 1834, 1836, 1840

Curriculum resources secretary, church school, 262.1*d*

D

Daily Christian Advocate, 2601

Date of founding, 821

Day care, 261.3, 263.1

Deacon
appointment, 515.3
associate member as, 419.4
authority, 434
definition, 433.1
order of, 434
ordination, 434.3, 513.4, *footnote, pages 181-85*
probationary members as, 413.1
qualification as elder, 435.1, .2

Deaconess
accountability, 1533.6
on Administrative Board, 253
Annual Conference seating, 1533.5
assignment, 1529.21, .22, .26, 1533.3, 1535.4
career fulfillment assistance, 1569.3
Charge Conference and Church membership, 1533.4
commissioning, 513.4, 1533.2
continuing education, 1535.11
Deaconess and Home Missionary Service, Annual Conference Committee on, 721.6
Deaconess and Home Missionary Service, Committee on, 1534-36
Deaconess/Home Missionaries, Jurisdictional Association on, 631
definition, 1533.2
as delegate to General and Jurisdictional Conferences, 1533.5
Diaconal Ministry, Annual Conference Board of, responsibility for, 724.5
listing in conference journal, 721.6*b*(8)
National Division relationship with office of, 1533

Deaconess, *cont'd:*
orientation, 1535.11
pension, 1533.7
recommendation, 1533.2
records of, 721.6*b*(7)
recruitment, 1569.2
service, 1533.2
standards for, 1570
surrender of credentials, 1533.8
withdrawal, 2626.3

**Deaconess and Home Missionary
Service, Annual Conference
Committee on,** 1535.10, **721.6**

**Deaconess and Home Missionary
Service, Committee on,** 1533.2,
.3*a*, .6, .8, **1534-36**

**Deaconesses and Home Mission-
aries, Jurisdictional Association
of, 631,** 1534.2, 1536.3

Death Benefit Program, 1704.12

Death with dignity, 71H

Delegates
to Central Conference:
election, 637.1
minimum number, 636.2
ratio of, 637.1
to General Conference:
affiliate members as, 439.4
from affiliated autonomous
churches, 648.3
certification of election, 601.1-.3
from concordat churches,
650.4*a, b*
election, 601.3
formula for Annual Conference
delegations, 601.1-.3
from Missionary Conference,
658.3
probationary member as, 413.3
from Provisional Annual Conference, 655.4
to Jurisdictional Conference:
affiliate members as, 439.4
election of, 614

Delegates, *cont'd:*
formula for number of, 613
minimum number, 613.1
from Missionary Conference,
658.3
probationary member as, 413.3
from Provisional Annual Conference, 655.4
for special session of, 619.3
voting rights in election of, 413.2,
419.1, .4, 423

Depositories, local church, 266.3*d*

Deserts, spread of, 70A

Developing nations, 75B

Diaconal minister, 301-11
on Administrative Board, 253
amenability, 308
Annual Conference approval of
candidates, 306
Annual Conference relationships,
308-09
changes in, 313, 724.3*m, n*
appeal, 2625.3
appointment, 310, 514.3
benefits, 724.3*r*
candidacy, 304-06
Charge Conference relationships,
314.1-.4
charges against, 2621-22
consecration, 307, 724.3*j*
continuing education, 313.1*c,*
315.3, 920.1, 1625.4
credentials, 307, 312
curricula, 1625.3
definition, 301-02
Diaconal Ministries, Annual Conference Board of, responsibility
toward, 724.3*d*
disability leave, 313.1*a*
educational requirements, 306.3
employing agency, relationship to,
315
evaluation of, 724.3*k*
examination and recommendation
of, 724.3*l*
investigation of, 2623

Director of evangelism, 1313.7

Director of parish development, 206.2, 717.2, 721.5*a*

Director of religion and race, district, 729.2

Disability, Joint Committee on, 446.4, **733**

Disability leave
for bishop, 510.3
for diaconal minister, 313.1*a*
for minister, 446
pension credit for, 1706.3*a*

Discipleship, Board of, Annual Conference, 720, 1313.9, 1327.1*b*
devotional life responsibility, 720.6
education responsibility, 720.2
evangelism responsibility, 720.3
lay life and work responsibility, 720.7
stewardship responsibility, 720.5
worship responsibility, 720.4

Discipleship, General Board of, 1301-27
accountability, 802, 803.5
alive now!, 1302.5
amenability, 802
architectural standards, setting of, 1302.12, 1529.15
bylaws, 1304.4
church schools resourcing and guidance, 261.1*a*
Congregational Development, Joint Committee on, 1529.13
Communication, cooperation with Commission on, 1106.14
cooperative publication of church school curriculum, 1840
curriculum plans approval, 1323-24
curriculum promotion and interpretation, 1325.2*b*
Curriculum Resources Committee, 1322-27. For detailed listing *see*

Discipleship, General Board of, *cont'd:*
Curriculum Resources Committee
Curriculum Resources Committee, election of, 1326.1
devotional life promotion, 1316
devotional publications, 1302.3
divisions, creation and discontinuance, 1304.3
ecumenical responsibility, 1302.11
editor of church school publications, 1326.1
education responsibility, 1307-11
camping and outdoor ministries, 1308.3, 1309.4
certification of personnel, 1309.4
Christian Education Week promotion, 1308.7
church school extension, 1311
church school organization, 1311
curriculum plans approval, 1308.6
educational program types, 1308.1
ethnic and cultural group involvement, 1302.2
leadership development, 1308.3
mission education, 1310.3
special funds promotion approval, 1308.8
standards of education, establishing, maintaining, 1309
teacher recruitment and training, 1308.3
town and country ministries, 1310.6
evangelism responsibility, 1312-13
conference-approved evangelist, 1313.9
curriculum, evangelism concepts in, 1313.14
General Military Roll, 1313.10
liaison services, 1313.11
local church evangelism personnel, 1313.7-.8
local church resources, 1313.4
special evangelistic emphasis,

Discipleship, General Board of, *cont'd:*

1313.3
executive committee, 1304.2, .5, 1325.1*c*, 1327.1*b*
Finance, local church Committee on, responsibility for, 907.11
financial support, 1306
funds for mission education, 1306.5
fund solicitation, 1306.2
general roll of military personnel and families, 218
general secretary, 1325.1*e*, 1327.1*c*,
legal power, 1303
Global Ministries, cooperation with, 1302.12-.13
Higher Education and Ministry, Division of, assets with, 1303
incorporation, 1303
lay life and work responsibility, 1317-21
age-level and family ministries, 1320
certification of lay persons, 1319.2*b*
Family Life, Committee on, 1318
Laity Day observance, 1319.5
lay speakers program, 1319.6
leadership development, 1319
local church training, 1319.3
men's work, 1321
National Youth Ministry Organization, 1320.5
leadership training, 1302.6-.9
National Youth Ministry Organization, relationship to, 1401-02
membership, 805-06
nominations to, 805.1
offerings, contributions to, 1306.4
organization, 1304-05
overseas laity, ministry to, 1610.3
president, 1303
as program agency, 803.5
publications for church officers, 1302.4
purpose, 1301
representation on:
National Youth Ministry Organization Steering Committee,

Discipleship, General Board of, *cont'd:*

1402.1
Publication, General Board of, 1839
research and evaluation, 1302.14
responsibilities, 1302
stewardship responsibility, 1315
Annual and Jurisdictional Conference assistance, 1315.9
bequests and other gifts, encouragement of, 1315.7
counsel for stewardship organizations, 1315.8
curriculum, stewardship concepts in, 1315.4
financial support for ministers and church-related employees, promotion of, 1315.11
fund-raising aid, 1315.10
life style awareness, 1315.2
local church training, 1315.5
mission fund-raising programs, 1315.3
treasurer, 1303
United Methodist Men, chartering, 262.6
units, 1305
Upper Room, The, 1302.5, 1306.3, 1316.3
Wills Task Force, local church, resourcing of, 260.8
worship responsibility, 1314
Book of Worship, 1314.5
certification of worship personnel, 1313.13, .15
curriculum, worship concepts in, 1314.9
General Conference worship services, 1314.11
hymnal, 1314.3
Ritual of the Church, 1314.1
standards for worship personnel, 1314.12, .15
supplemental worship materials, 1314.5
United Methodist Publishing House, cooperation with, 1314.6
youth, ministry to, 1302.10

Discipline
autonomous churches, 649.3
Central Conference, 638.21, .31

Discontinued local church, 231, 521.6, 2541

District Board on Church Location and Building. *See* Church Location and Building, district Board of

District Committee/coordinator on Communications, 737.5

District Committee on Ordained Ministry. *See* Ordained Ministry, district Committee on

District Conference, 47, **734-41**
appeal for church extension, 718.4
apportionments made to, 77.3
associate lay leader, 736.2
Board of Stewards, 711.3
Board of Trustees, 2513.2
certificates for ministry candidates, 735.3
Church Location and Building, reports from Committee on, 2514
Church and Society, Committee/director, 738
Communications, coordinator/Committee, 737.5
Council on Ministries, 737
District Superintendency, Committee on, 740
District Union, 735.4
incorporation, 735.4
Judicial Council, appeals to, 2611-12
lay leader, 736
membership, 735.1
Ordained Ministry, district Committee on, **739**
order of business, 735.2
property, 735.4, 2513-18
religion and race, director, 729.2
secretary, 735.2
United Methodist Women, 741

District lay leader, 720.8*b*, 736

District steward, 247.1, 711.3

District Superintendency, Committee on, 449.1, 515, 516, 517, **740**

District superintendent, 501-02, 515-22
abandoned churches, 2541.1
accountability to Cabinet, 526.3
administrative responsibilities, 518, 521
Annual Conference meeting place, right to change, 702.3
appeals of lay members, role in, 2625.4*b-d*
appointment-making responsibility, 59, 519.6, 528-30
appointment of, 513.2
Board of Trustees nominations by, 2513.2
Cabinet relationship, 526
candidacy role, 404, 519.3
as chairperson of district Board of Stewards, 711.3
Charge Conference duties, 248.3, .4, .6, 521
as chief executive officer of district Council on Ministries, 737.4
Church and Joint Church Conference, authority to call, 251
clergy supervision, evaluation, 518.2
cluster-building, 518.4
on conference Council on Ministries, 522.2, 717.2
in consultation process, 529
continuing education for clergy, responsibility for, 519.5
counseling elder reports to, 411
counseling with clergy, 520.2
criteria for appointment-making, 530
diaconal minister:
appointment of, 310.2, .3*d*
continuing education for, 313.1*c*
Disability, Joint Committee on, 733
disability leave approval, 446.2
District Superintendency, Com-

Ethnic Minority In-Service Training Program, 271.3*f*, 915.4*b*

Ethnic Minority Scholarship Program, 271.3*f*, 915.4*b*

Evaluation
of bishop, 725.3*f*
of diaconal minister, 724.3*j*
of district superintendent, 740.4*e*, .5
of general agencies, 802
of ordained minister, 723.2*k*
of pastoral effectiveness, 420.1*b*, 427
process, 266.2*f*(3)

Evangelism
conference-approved evangelist, 720.3*f*
director or associate of, 253, 1313.7, .8
Discipleship, Annual Conference Board of, responsible for, 720.3
Discipleship, General Board of, responsibility for, 1312-13
local church commission on, 230.3, .4, .5
local church work area on, 235, **260.4**
   chairperson, 230.3, .4, 259
   representation on age-level councils, 263
   in small churches, 245.1*b, c*

Evangelist
conference-approved, 440, 720.3*f*
pastor's hiring of outside denomination, 440.1
pension credit for, 1706.3*a*
standards for, 1313.9

Examination
of diaconal minister, 306.5
for full membership, 424
of ministerial candidates by conference Board of Ordained Ministry, 723.2*d*
of ministers at Annual Conference, 704.5-.6

Examination, *cont'd:*
for probationary members, 414.7
Wesley's questions for candidacy, 403

Executive secretary, 813

Extended ministry, 206.3

Extension ministries
appointments, 439.1*b*
Chaplains and Related Ministries responsible for, 1610
unusual ministries, appointment to, 439.1*d*
validation of, 723.2*l*

F

Fact Book, 907.10

Family, 71A

Family Council, 262, 263.4

Family Life, Committee on, 1318

Family ministry coordinator, 257, 258

Family ministries, Board of Discipleship responsibility for, 1320

Farming, 72K

Farm workers, 73F

Fellowship, defined, 803.11

Fellowship of United Methodists in Worship, Music, and Other Arts, 720.4*c*, 1314.14, 1625.2

Finance, local church Committee on, 266.3
Administrative Board, relationship to, 255.1
Council on Ministries, relationship to, 256
Discipleship, General Board of, responsibility for, 907.11

Finance and Administration, General Council on, *cont'd:*
apportionments to Annual Conference, notice of, 908
Audit and Review, Committee on, 905.4*b*
audit:
of general church funds, 906.4
of treasurer's books, 909
associate general secretaries, 905.5
banking responsibilities, 906.5
bequests and other gifts, 906.7
bishop, resigned, determination of compensation, 508.4
bishop under assignment after retirement, compensation for, 508.2*b*
Black College Fund, 917
bonding of treasurer, 909
business manager, General Conference, 907.14
borrowing of funds, approval for, 910.3
budgets submitted by, 906.1
churchwide appeals approval, 1542
churchwide funds disbursement, 906.2
churchwide offerings recommendations, 271.1
committees, 905.4
connectional structure study, 1006.11
Communication, Standing General Commission on:
accountability to, 1104
cooperation with, 1106.11, .12, 1107.5, 1108
Council Operations, Committee on, 905.4*a*
data processing responsibility, 907.6
duplication of program, preventing, 910.2
election of, 905.1
emergency financial appeal authorization, 1006.6
Episcopal Fund, 922-29. For detailed listing *see* Episcopal Fund
equal employment opportunity re-

Finance and Administration, General Council on, *cont'd:*
sponsibility, 907.7*d*
executive committee, 905.3, .4*a*, 916.3, 917.3
expenses, 906.1*d*
fiscal responsibilities, 906
forms for Annual Conference records, 705.7
foundation assets, management, 906.9
General Administration Fund, 916
general agency accounting to, 804
general agency budgets, 906.1*b*(6)
General Council on Ministries, cooperation with in World Service Fund budgeting, 904, 1006.2
general funds policies, 910
general secretary, 814.4, 905.3, .5
General Episcopal Fund determination, 638.4, .5
headquarters location, general agencies, 907.2
Higher Education Division investments and fund-raising, 1615.2*d*
homosexuals, prohibition of funds to, 906.13
housing allowance certification, 907.4
Human Relations Day, 915.1
incorporation, 903
insurance program, 907.13
Interdenominational Cooperation Fund, 917, 2003.12
investment responsibility, 906.6
Legal Responsibilities, Committee on, 905.4*e*
legal responsibility, 907.4
local church administration guidance, 907.12
local church training responsibility, 1315.5
mailing list maintenance, 907.9
meetings, 905.2
membership, 905.1
membership forms approval, 234.1, .2
Methodist Corporation, successor to, 2509.2-.4

Full connection, members in, *cont'd:*
from other denominations, 428
pension credit, 1706.3*a*
questions for examination of, 424
requirements for admission, 424
retirement, 447
rights, 423
sabbatical leave, 442
sole responsibility in matters, 701.1*a*
transfer, 514.5
voting rights, 423, 701.1*a see also* Minister; Pastor

Full Membership Roll, 208, 232.1

Full-time service, 437.1, 438.3*a*

G

Gambling, 73G

General Administration Fund, 916, 1704.12, 2401.2
budget, 906.1
disbursement, 906.2
notice of apportioned amount, 908
promotion, 1106.12

General agencies, 801-22
absence from meetings, 810.2
accountability, 802
additional members, 805.2*c*, .4, 806
administrative, 803.6
advocacy roles, records of, 816
amenability, 802
answering questions concerning actions, 802
assignment of members to divisions, 809
assistant general secretary, 803.7*c*
associate general secretary, 803.7*b*
association defined, 803.11
bishop's attendance, 810.10
board defined, 803.2
borrowing funds, 910.3
Church membership of members, 810.1
commission defined, 803.3*a, b*

General agencies, *cont'd:*
compensation for voting members, 810.6
constitutionality of acts, 2609-10
convening of general agency secretaries, 814.4
council defined, 803.1
definition, 801
division, defined, 803.2*a*
duplication of programs, 910.2
election to, 805
episcopal membership, 805.2*b*
evaluation of, 802, 1006.13
executive secretary, election of, 813
executive staff members of UMC, 814.6
executive staff titles, 803.7
ex officio representation on Annual Conference agencies, 706.5
fellowship defined, 803.11
financial accounting, 804
funds for Annual Conference projects, use of, 817
General Administration Fund, procedure for obtaining, 916.1
general secretaries, 803.7*a*
election of, 813, 1006.15
on General Council on Finance and Administration, 905
on General Council on Ministries, 1007.1
headquarters location, 907.2
honoraria for staff, 814.2
legal residence of members, 810.8
membership, 805, 809, 810
missional priority defined, 803.8
national conferences and convocations, 906.10, 907.8
nominations to, 805.1
nondiscriminatory employment, 814.5, 815
office defined, 803.2*c*
officers, 808.1
official documents filed with Archives, 1911.3*g*
organizational meetings, 807.1
overlapping of, 1006.10
pensions for staff, 814.3
personnel policies, 907.7

General Conference, *cont'd:*
church union in Central Conference, approval of, 638.26
Commission, 604, 907.14
composition, 12.1, 13, 14, 601
concordat agreement approval, 651.3*a, b*
constitutionality of acts, 61, 2606, 2607.1, 2618
date of, 13
delegates:
affiliate Annual Conference members as, 439.4
from affiliated autonomous church, 648.2
from Annual Conferences, 12.2, 13
associate members as, 419.5
from autonomous Methodist churches, 12.2
certification of, 601.3
from concordat churches, 651.4*a-b*
election of, 12.2, 38-40, 601.3
from Great Britain, 12.3
lay, 40
members in full connection, 423
ministerial, 39
from Missionary Conferences, 12.1, 13, 658.3
probationary members as, 413.3
from Provisional Annual Conference, 655.4
effective date of legislation, 609, 819.2
in non–English-speaking countries, 638.22
episcopal supervision of territory not in Central Conference, 645
expenses, 916
formula for number in Annual Conference delegation, 606.1-.3
granting power to conferences, 644
Interjurisdictional Committee on Episcopacy, election of, 611.1
Judicial Council:
duties of, 2617
election of, 2601-02, 2603.1, .4
member of, ineligible as delegate

General Conference, *cont'd:*
to conference, 2605
petitions to, 2615.2
jurisdictional boundaries, powers to set, 15.12
Jurisdictional Conference official record sent to, 626.1
legislative power, 15
meetings, 13
membership, 601
Methodist Corporation Fund distribution, 2509.4
Missionary Conference, approval of change in status of, 659
numerical designation of, 822
pension reports to, 1704.12
periodicals, general agency, approval of, 1006.8
petitions to, 607
place of, 13
Plan of Organization and Rules of Order, 605
presiding officer, 15.11, 602
Provisional Central Conference, granting power to, 641
quorum, 606
representation ratio, 14
restrictions, 16-21
review of legislation by general agencies, 610.2*b*
Rules of Order, 605
secretary of, 649.5, 638.7, 651.3*b*, 1904.2, 2619
election of, 603
adjusting delegate formula, 601.3. For detailed listing *see* Secretary, General Conference
secretary-designate, 603-04
speak for the Church, authority to, 610
special days approval, 271.1, .2*d*
special session, 13
testimony before legislative body, 610.3
translation of legislation, 638.22
United Methodist Publishing House real estate and buildings, authority over, 1843
University Senate members ap-

Home missionary, *cont'd:*
on Administrative Board, 253
Annual Conference seating, 1533.5
appointment, 514.3, 1533.3, 1535.4
assignment, 1529.21
Charge Conference and Church membership, 1533.4
commissioning of, 513.4, 1533.2
conference journal listing of, 721.6*b* (8)
continuing education, 1535.5
Deaconess and Home Missionary Service, Annual Conference Committee on, 721.6
definition, 1533.2
as delegates to General and Jurisdictional Conferences, 1533.5
Diaconal Ministry, Annual Conference Board of, responsibility for, 724.5
Jurisdictional Association of Deaconesses and Home Missionaries, 631
National Division relationship with, 1533.2
orientation, 1535.11
pension, 1533.7
record of, 721.6*b*(7)
service of, 1533.2
surrender of credentials, 1533.8
withdrawal under complaints, charges, 2626.3

Homosexuality, 71F, *footnote, pages 181-85*
prohibition of funding to, 906.13

Honorable location, 448.2
readmission following, 451
as remedial action for member facing complaints, 449.2*f*

Housing allowance, 266.2*f*(4), 907.4, 925

Humans Relations Day, 270, **271.3a,** 722.5*b*(4), **915.1,** 1605.16
budget, 906.1
disbursement, 906.2
promotion, 1106.12

Human rights, 72, 74A

Human sexuality, 71F, 1320.3

Hunger, UMCOR responsibility concerning, 1538.5

Hymnal, 15.6, 720.4*b*

I

Inclusiveness, 4, 729.3*b, c, m*
appraisal of, 725.3*e*
violation of, 2108.6

Information, freedom of, 74C

Institutions
affiliated relationship, church's legal authority in, 1520
change in relationships, 722.5*b*(6)
church's limitation of responsibility for, 1526
definition, Annual Conference, 710.3*c*
Higher Education and Campus Ministry, relationship with, 722
nondiscriminatory personnel policies, 815
student recruitment, 260.5*a*
trustees of, 2545
see also Higher Education, Division of

Insurance protection, Annual Conference, 709.13

Interdenominational agencies, 2401-07
American Bible Society, 2405
Consultation on Church Union, 2404
National Council of the Churches of Christ in the United States of America, 2402
Religion in American Life, Incorporated, 2406
responsibility for relationships with, 2407
World Council of Churches, 2403
World Methodist Council, 2401

INDEX

716

INDEX

Local pastor, *cont'd:*
withdrawal under charges, 410.2,
2626.2

Local pastor license, 405.2, 406-07,
409.1

Location
administrative, 449.2*a*, 451
Annual Conference right to place
on, 703.4
of associate member, 419.7
honorable, 449.2*f*, 451

Lord's Supper, *page 60*
right to administer:
appointee beyond the local
church, 439.3*a*
local pastor, 408
pastor, 438.2*a*

M

Mandatory retirement
bishop, 508.1
diaconal minister, 313.2*a-b*
of minister, 447.1

Marijuana, 72I

Marital growth and enrichment,
1320.3

Marriage, 71C
Central Conference conformation
of to laws of country, 638.19
local pastor's right to perform, 408
of ministers, *page 61*
pastor's performance of, 438.2*c*

Maternity leave, 445

Maternity/paternity leave, 313.1*b*

Medical experimentation, 72J

Membership, church, 208-43. For
detailed listing *see* Church membership

Membership secretary, 222, 230.2,
235, 236, 247.1, 253

Members in full connection, 422-27.
For detailed listing *see* Full connection, members in

**Members removed by Charge Con-
ference action,** 230.4, 232.3

Men
Jurisdictional Committee on United Methodist Men, 635
representation among local church
officers, 246.5, 247.4
United Methodist Men, 262.2

Men's work, 1321
see also United Methodist Men

Merger
of local churches, 2538
with another denomination,
2539
pensions in merged church, 1706.9
pensions in merged conference,
1709

Methodist Corporation, 2509

Methodist, use of, as trademark,
2502

**Metropolitan area mission develop-
ment** 721.5*g*

Metropolitan Commission, 1530.5*j*

Migrant workers, 73F

Military, 74G
baptism of children of military
families, 218
counseling concerning alternatives
to, 437.2*c*(8)
Higher Education and Ministry,
Board of responsibility for,
1605.24
receptions of military personnel
into the church, 218

717

718

Minister, *cont'd:*
    Annual Conferences and affiliated autonomous churches, 648.2
    to another conference, 703.6, .7
    from another denomination, 428
    from another Methodist denomination, 428.8
    between autonomous churches, 650.4*d*
    travel expense publication, 937
    trial, right to, 449.1*f*, 449.3, 2624.3
    vows of church membership, authority to administer, 217
    withdrawal under complaints or charges, 448.5, 2626.2
    see also Associate member; Full connection, member in; Local pastor; Ordained ministry; Pastor; Probationary member

Ministerial Education Fund, 722.5b(4), **920,** 1605.16
    Annual Conference share, 920.1
    budget, 906.1
    diaconal minister's use of, 724.3*u*
    disbursement, 906.2
    distribution, 920.2
    notice of apportioned amount, 908
    Ordained Ministry, Division of, funding of, 1628
    priority status, 920.3, 1630.2
    promotion, 266.2*f*(6), 1106.12, 1629.5
    theological schools support, 1630.1

Ministerial Pension Plan, 1704.12, 1706.2*c*, .18, .20, .21

Ministerial supply and demand report, 527.2

Ministerial support, 930-38
    Administrative Board responsibility for, 255.5
    apportionments for, 931-32
    of clergy couples, 935.8
    equitable salaries, 710.1*d*
    Equitable Salary, Commission on, 935

Ministerial support, *cont'd:*
    Equitable Salary Fund, 935.5, .7, .10
    Finance and Administration, conference Council on, responsibility for, 710.1
    housing allowance, 907.4
    minimum salary, 935.3-.6
    moving expense, 710.1*e*
    salary:
        determination, 243.9, 932
        unpaid, 934
    Sustentation Fund, 710.1*e*, 936

Minister's Reserve Pension Fund, 446.3

Minister's Reserve Pension Plan, 1704.12

Ministry
    diaconal, 107-08, 110
    general, 104-06
    nature of, 101, 104
    ordained, 107, 109-10
    representative, 107-08
    see also Diaconal Ministry; Ordained Ministry

Ministry Sunday, 722.5*b*(4), 1605.16

Minority groups. *See* Racial and ethnic minority

Minority Group Self-Determination Fund, 2108.7

Mission, 661-62
    administration of, 662.1
    composition, 662.2
    examination of local pastors and traveling preachers, 662.5
    judicial administration, 2626.5
    meeting, 661
    presiding officer, 661, 662.4
    property provisions, 2544
    as Provisional Annual conference, 654
    representatives to Central Conference, 637.1
    superintendent, 662.3

Mission

Children's Fund for Christian Mission, 262.1*f*

church school education in, 262.1*f*

education in, 1310.3

fund-raising for, 1315.13

Global Ministries, Annual Conference Board of, responsibility for, 721.4*a-b*

Global Ministries, General Board of, responsibility for, 1502

in metropolitan areas, 721.5*g*

Missional Priority Fund, 906.2, 921, 1006.1, .17, 1106.12

National Division responsibility for, 1529-30

Personnel in Mission, Committee on, 1568-72

rural areas, responsibility for development in, 721.5*f*

structures, 1530.5

traveling preachers, 662.2, .4, .5

World Division responsibility for, 1556-57

Missional priority

changes in, 1006.1

definition, 803.8

determination of need for, 1006.17

Fund, 906.2, **921,** 1106.12

implementation, 1006.4

Missional Priority Fund, 921

disbursement, 906.2

promotion, 1106.12

Missionary

assignment to mission, 662.2, .4

as associate members, 419.6

career fulfillment assistance, 1569.3

Personnel in Mission, Committee on, 1568-72

placement, 1529.22

recruitment and enlistment of, 1569.2

seating, Annual Conference, 701.2

standards for, 1570

Missionary Conference, 657-60

Advance projects, 658.2

affiliate relationship to, 658.4*b*

as Annual Conference, 22

budgets, 658.2

building projects, 658.2

change in status of, 659

clergy couples, 658.6

conference superintendent and/or district superintendent, 658.1

definition, 658

delegates to General and Jurisdictional Conferences, 14, 658.4

episcopal supervision, 658.1

full ministerial membership in, 658.4*c*

funding, 658.2

Global Ministries, General Board of, relationship to, 657

judicial administration, 2626.5

less than full-time appointment in, 658.7

mission agencies representation, 658.5

National Division relationship with, 1529.18

nominations to general agencies, 805.1

organization, 658

pension responsibility for, 1706.15

as Provisional Annual Conference, 654

representation on General Council on Ministries, 1007.1

representatives to Central Conference, 637.1

right to make changes and adaptations, 660

waiver of minimum salary claim, 658.4*d*

Mission (church), establishing, 267.1

Missions, local church work area on, 260.6

chairperson, 259

representation on age-level councils, 263

in small churches, 245.1*c*

Mission structures, 1530.5

Mission traveling preachers, 662.2, .4, .5

Monopolies, 73C

Moving expenses, 710.1*e*

Multiple-charge parish, 206.3

Multiple-church charge
chargewide organization, 249.13-.15
lay leaders in, 250.1
parsonages, 2522.4
Pastor-Parish Relations Committee in, 266.2*c, e*

Music personnel, 253, 260.9

N

Name, church, outside U.S., 2820

National Association of Conference Council Directors, 1006.22

National Association of Conference Presidents of United Methodist men, 1321.1

National Association of Health and Welfare Ministries of The United Methodist Church, 721.4*a*(29), 1521, 1527

National Association of Schools and Colleges of The United Methodist Church, 1616.2

National Council of Churches, 728.4*f*, 917.1, 2003.4, **2402**
Communication, Commission on, cooperation with, 1106.4
local church interpretation, 260.1
One Great Hour of Sharing, cooperation in, 271.3*b*, 915.2

National Division, Board of Global Ministries, 1528-36
Advance participation, 1007.5*b, d*
Appalachian Development Committee, 1529.28
architectural standards development, 1329.25
associate general secretary, 1532, 1534.2
authority, 1530
budget responsibility, 1529.23
church and community workers, 1529.12
church extension, 1529.13
Community Development Program, 271.3*a*(1)
conference relationships, 1529.18
Congregational Development, Joint Committee on, 1529.13
as corporate successor, 1506.1
Deaconess and Home Missionary Service, 1536
deaconess, assignment, appointment, confirmation, 1529.21, .22, 1533.3*c*
Disaster Response Coordination, 1529.5
Discipleship, General Board of, cooperation with, 1315.13, 1529.13, .16*c*
ecumenical activity, 1529.19-.20
ethnic and language ministries, 1529.17
executive committee, 1531
Finance and Administration, cooperation with Annual Conference Council on, 1530.5*c*
fund administration, 1530.1
fund-raising services, 1529.16
fee for, 1529.16*d*
Goodwill Industries, 1529.27
Health and Welfare Ministries Division, cooperation with, 1530.4
home missionary assignment, appointment, confirmation, 1529.21, 1533.3*c*
housing consultation service, 1529.14
inner city community organization, 1530.5*c*

Ordained ministry, *cont'd:*
of; Ordained Ministry, district
Committee on; Ordained Ministry, General Board of; Pastor

**Ordained Ministry, Annual Confer-
ence Board of, 723**
administrative location, 449.2
amenability, 723.1*a*
appointment beyond the local
church, annual meeting with,
439.2*b*
associate member from another
denomination, approval of,
419.1, .2
changes in conference relationships, 443-47, 723.2*f*
complaints against minister,
449.1*d. e, f*
confidentiality, ensuring, 723.2*h*
counseling retiring ministers,
447.4
course of study guidance, 723.2*c*
Diaconal Ministry, Annual Conference Board of, cooperation with,
723.2*p*, 724.2, .3*u*
Disability, Joint Committee on, 733
district superintendent as executive of, 519.3
duties, 723.2
enlistment responsibility, 723.2*a*
evaluation of minister's character,
723.2*k*
evaluation process materials,
266.2*f*(3)
evaluation training for Pastor-Parish Relations committees, 427
examination of ministerial candidates, 723.2*d*
extension ministries, designation
and verification of, 1610.1, .2*e*
financial aid promotion, 723.2*o*
guidance and counsel for retiring
minister, 447
interviewing and recommending
candidates, 722.2*f*
less than full-time service, approval
of, 437.2
local pastor, classification of, 409
local pastor from another denomi-

**Ordained Ministry, Annual Confer-
ence Board of,** *cont'd:*
nation, approval of, 408.7
meetings, 723.1*c*
membership, 723.1*a, b*
ministerial absence from Annual
Conference, 701.6
Ministerial Education Fund administration, 920.1, 923.2*m, n*
ministerial supply and demand
report to, 527.2
notification of, of extension of
education requirement, 408.2
officers, 723.1*c*
one-year candidacy requirement,
405.2
Ordained Ministry, Division of,
cooperation with, 723.2*h*,
1629.2, .3
probationary members:
annual review of, 413
extension of time limit for completion of studies, 417
recommendation of, 414, 416.2
psychological and health data,
right to require, 408.9
readmission role, 450-52
recommendation of:
associate member, 420
extension ministry appointments, 439.1*d*
full members, 424
probationary members, 414,
416.2
records:
of discontinued local pastor,
410.1
of ministerial candidates, 723.3
registrar, 723.3
reinstatement, local pastor, 410.1
retired minister's return to effective relationship, 447.5*d*
retirement, local pastor, 410.5
right to seek personal information
from school of theology, 418.3
sabbatical leave approval, 442
special ministries validation, 723.2*l*
support services for minister,
723.2*j*
transfer of minister:

INDEX

Pensions, General Board of, *cont'd:*
convenor of, 1709.2, .3*d*
gift and bequest management,
1704.6, .7
incorporation, 1701.1
investment policies, 1704.3-.4
location, 1701.1-.3
manual, 1704.13
meetings, 1702.2
membership, 805-06, 1702
Missionary Conference, responsibility for, 1706.15
names, 1701
nominations to, 805.1
officers, 1703.1
payment to conference beneficiaries, 1704.5
permanent funds, 1705
Provisional Annual Conference, responsibility for, 1706.15
publishing, net income from, 1704.9, 1815-16
quorum, 1702.3
reports from Annual Conference Board of Pensions, 726.5
reports to General Conference, 1704.12
representation on Committee on Personnel Policies and Practices, 905.4*d*
Rules and Regulations, Committee on, 1703.3
service records of ministers, 1704.10
support of beneficiaries, 1704.14
Temporary General Aid Fund, 919
term of office, 1702.1*d*
transfer of ministers, written notice of, 515.5
undesignated gifts and bequests, 1704.7
vacancies, 1702.1*e*
World Service Fund share, 1704.8
see also Pensions

Pension Support Fund, 1706.19

Pentecost Sunday, 728.4*f*

Periodical, General Council on Ministries approval of new, 1006.8

Permanent church register, 234.1

Personal leave, 313.1*d*

Personnel Committee, Annual Conference, 717.4

Personnel Committee, local church, 266.2*f*(9)

Personnel in Mission, Committee on, 1568-72
authority, 1506.1, 1570
Board of Directors, 1571
ecumenical responsibility, 1544.2, .3
liaison with Office of Vocation and Career/Life Planning, 1572
membership, 1571
purpose, 1568
responsibilities, 1569
short-term volunteer requests, 1544.3
staff relationships with Global Ministries divisions, 1572
treasurer, 1571
UMCOR, cooperation with, 1544.1*c*

Personnel policies, 907.7

Personnel Policies and Practices, Committee on, 905.4*d*, 907.7*b-c*

Persons with handicapping conditions
eligibility for ministry, 306.4
ministries concerning, 261.2
nondiscriminatory hiring, 815
representation on:
conference agencies, 706.4
district Council on Ministries, 737.2
general agencies, 805.1*b*, .2*a*
jurisdictional agencies, 627
local officers, 246.5, 247.4

Sabbatical leave, *cont'd:*
diaconal minister, 313.1c
minister, 442
pension credit for, 1706.3a
as remedial action for minister facing complaints, 449.2f
salary for, 442

Salary
Administrative Board recomendation, 255.3e
Charge Conference setting of, 249.10
of district superintendent, 710.1a
Finance and Administration, Conference Council on, responsibility for, 710.1
of local pastor, 409.1, .2
for maternity leave, 445.3
minimum, 935.3-.6, .8
of minister in pastoral charge, 438.3
Pastor-Parish Relations Committee role in setting, 266.2f(4)
of retired minister under appointment, 447.6
for sabbatical leave, 442
see also Equitable Salary; Equitable Salary Fund; Minimum salary; Ministerial support

Scholarships, 260.5a
Crusade, 271.3f
Ethnic Minority Scholarship Program, 271.3f
Hispanic, Asian, Native American Fund, 722.5b(4)
United Methodist, 271.3h, 915.3

Sea, use of, 70A

Secretary, Annual Conference
Annual Conference proceedings, 705.1
answers to question about conducting Annual Conference, 703.11
certificate of organization, 703.10
certification credentials for elders, 435.4

Secretary, Annual Conference, *cont'd:*
charges against ministers, 2623.3d
on Council on Ministries, 717.2
credentials for diaconal minister, 307
election of, 702.6
General Minutes listing of appointments beyond the local church, 439.5d
records, closed churches, 2541.2
reason for Annual Conference absence, 701.6
surrendered credentials, 410,1, 448.1, .4, .5
trial proceedings holder, 2624.3e, 2625.3c

Secretary, General Conference, 638.8
adjustment of delegate formula, 601.3
Archives and History, member of Commission on, 1904.2
autonomous status, signing of, 649.5
Board of Publication election, duty to inform jurisdictions of, 1802
concordat agreement, signing of, 651.3b
election of, 603
Judicial Council decisions, 2619
report to of Central Conference bishop assignment, 638.7
secretary-designate:
election of, 603
transfer of responsibility to, 604

Section, defined, 803.2b

Separation of Church and State, 74B

Sex education, 71F, 72C

Sexism, 2203.1

Sexuality, human, 71F

Shared ministry, 206.3

Sick leave, 510.3

INDEX

Treasurer, Annual Conference, *cont'd:*
as director of administrative services, 716
election, 715.1
Finance and Administration, member of conference Council on, 708.2a, .3, 715.1
handling of conference funds, 715.2
investment of funds, 715.5
removal of, 715.1
reports from, 715.4
term, 715.1
treasurer for other conference agencies, 715.3
vacancy of office, 715.1

Treasurer, local church, 246.3, 253, **266.3**

Trial, 2621, **2624**
amendments to charges, 2624.1i(5)
appeals, 2624.1h, .2e, .3e, 2625
For detailed listing *see* Appeals
of bishop, 2624.2
in Central Conference, ministers and lay, 638.17
chargeable offenses, 2621, 2626.6
charges, guidelines for filing, 2622
convening of the court, 2624.1c
counsel, 2624.1c, f, i(11)
dismissal of case, 2624.1i(5)
examining commissioners, 2624.1i(11)
guidelines, 2624.1i
investigation of procedures, 2623
of lay member, 2624.4
of local pastor, 410.3
of minister, local pastor, diaconal minister, 2624.3
of ministerial members of other conferences, 2626.1
minister's right to choose, 449.1g, .2
notice of, 2624.1e
objectives, 2624.1i(5) (6)
officers of Trial Court, 2624.1b
place of, 2624.1d
plea, 2624.1i(1), 2625.1c

Trial, *cont'd:*
presence of accused, 2624.1i(2)
presiding officers duties, 2624.1i(8) (11)
procedures, 2624
reversal of verdict, 2625.1b
right to, 18
"sufficient time," 2624.1i(2)
testimony, recording of, 2624.1i(9)
time of, 2624.1d
Trial Court, decision of in case of appeal, 2625.1g
Trial Court selection, 2624.1c
vote necessary to convict, 2624.1h, i(4)
witnesses, 2624.1g, i(7) (10) (11)

Trial Court. *See* Trial

Trustees, Board of. *See* Board of Trustees

Trustees, of church institutions, 2545

Truth in pricing, packaging, lending, advertising, 73D

U

Unemployment, 73

United Church, 525, 1557.1, 1561.1

United Methodist Association of Church Business Administrators, 1625.12

United Methodist Association of Communicators, 1625.12

United Methodist Association of Professors of Christian Education, 1625.12

United Methodist Committee on Relief, General Board of Global Ministries, 1537-46
administrative expenses, 1540
Advance, participating agency in, 1007.5b, d

Women
employment, 2203.8
inclusion in ministry, 412.2
representation on:
Archives and History, Standing
General Commission on,
1094.2
conference agencies, 706.4
Council on Ministries:
conference, 717
staff, 717.8
Episcopacy, Annual Conference
Committee on, 725.1
district, 737.2
general, 1007.1a(1)
Finance and Administration:
conference, 708.2
General, 905.1
general agencies, 805.1b, .2a
General Conference delegation
of affilated autonomous
church, 648.3
Health and Welfare Ministries
Division, 1525.2, .3
jurisdictional agencies, 627
Laity, conference Board of the,
720.8b
local church officers, 246.5,
247.4
National Division, 1531, 1532
Personnel in Mission, Committee on, 1571
Religion and Race:
conference, 729.2
general, 2103
Status and Role of Women:
conference, 730.2, .3
general, 2204.1, .2
University Senate, 1616.2
rights of, 72F
Status and Role of Women, Conference Commission on, 730
Status and Role of Women, Standing General Commission on,
2201-09
United Methodist Women:
Annual Conference, 731
district, 741
jurisdictional, 634
local church, 262.5

Women, *cont'd:*
Women's Work, Central Confer-
ence Committee on, 638.15, .16
World Division Subcommittee on
Women's Work, 1560.2
World Federation of Methodist
Women, 638.15
see also Status and Role of Women,
Standing General Commission
on; United Methodist Women;
Women's Division

**Women's Division, Board of Global
Ministries,** 1547-55
Assembly of United Methodist
Women, 1553
associate general secretary, 1550,
1554
authority, 1549
bylaws, 1549.1
as corporate successor, 1506.1
executive committee, 1550
funding, 1511.2a, 1553
meetings, 1549.2
membership, 1512.2, 1554
predecessor groups, 1549.3a
property rights, 1549.1
purpose, 1547
representation on:
Crusade Scholarship Committee, 1567
Deaconess and Home Missionary Service, Committee on,
1534.2
other Global Ministries divisions,
sections, 1550, 1551
Status and Role of Women,
Standing General Commis-
sion on, 2204.3
responsibilities, 1548, 1549.3
treasurer, 1550, 1554
United Methodist Women:
jurisdictional: 634
local church, 262.5
United Nations office, 1215,
1548.8

**Women's Work, Central Conference
Committee on,** 638.15, .16

Work, 73C

Youth, *cont'd*:
General Commission on,
1904.2
Communication, Standing General Commission on, 1107
conference agencies, 706.4
Council on Ministries:
conference, 717.2
district, 737.2
General, 1007.1
local church, 257
Episcopacy, Annual Conference Committee on, 725.1
Family Council, 263.4
Family Life, Committee on, 1318.2
Finance and Administration, Conference Council on, 708.2
general agencies, 805.1*b*, .2*a*
Global Ministries, Board of, 1512.3
Health and Welfare Ministries Division, 1525.3
jurisdictional agencies, 627
Laity, Conference Board of the, 720.8*b*
local church officers, 246.5, 247.4
National Division, 1531, 1532
Nominations and Personnel, Committee on, 266.1
Pastor-Parish Relations Committee, 266.2
Religion and Race:
conference Commission on, 728.2
Standing General Commission on, 2103
Status and Role of Women, conference Commission on 728.2
Youth Ministry, Council on,

Youth, *cont'd:*
732.2
rights of, 72D
United Methodist Youth Fellowship, 262.2
voting rights, 262.2
Youth Council, local church, 249.4, 262.2, 263.2, .4
Youth Ministry, Council on, Annual Conference, 732
Youth Service Fund, 732.3*g-i* 1401-04

Youth Council, local church, 249.4, 262.2, 263.2, .4

Youth Ministry, Conference Council on, 632, 720.8*b*, **732**
coordinator, 732.3*j*
National Youth Ministry Convocation representatives, 1401.2*a*
Youth Service Fund, 1402.4*b*, 1404

Youth ministry coordinator, Annual Conference, 732.3*j*

Youth ministry coordinator, local church, 249.4, 258

Youth Service Fund, 262.2, **1401-04**
administration, 1402.4*a*
allotment of, 1404
disbursement, 906.2
education about, 1402.4*b*
goal-setting, 1401.1*d*
handling of in Annual Conference, 732.3*g*
Project Review Committee, 732.3*i*
project selection, 1401.1*e*, 1403
promotion, 732.3*h*, 1106.12
use of by National Youth Ministry Organization, 1403

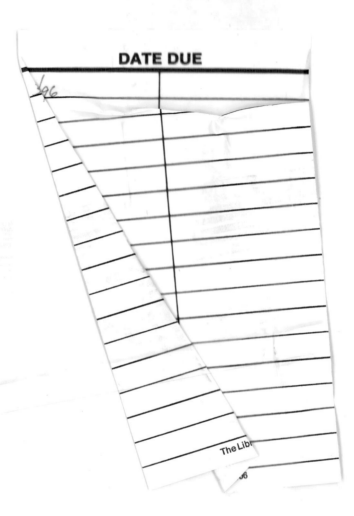

DATE DUE

The Lib